# Management History

*Management History* is not simply a book about the history of business or even the history of management. The goal of this book is to demonstrate that despite the relative newness of management science as an academic subject, management theory has been around since ancient times. Through understanding the history of management thought, one is able to approach the complex and challenging problems of modern management from a new perspective.

The book not only traces the development of management theory from history to the present day, but also examines the way this evolution impacts how management is practised today and how it may develop in the future. It incorporates case studies from around the world cutting across a range of time periods, from the Egyptian royal tomb builders of Deir el-Medina, to H.J. Heinz, Cadbury Brothers and J.R.D. Tata.

*Management History* is ideal for instructors wishing to incorporate historical content and analysis into management education courses, modules and training programme, particularly at the MBA level and higher.

**Morgen Witzel** is a writer and historian of management. He is an Honorary Senior Fellow at the University of Exeter Business School, UK and a senior consultant with the Winthrop Group of business historians. He is the author of more than a dozen books on management and management history.

# Management History

Text and cases

**Morgen Witzel**

Routledge
Taylor & Francis Group

LONDON AND NEW YORK

First published 2009 by Routledge
2 Park Square, Milton Park, Abingdon, Oxon OX14 4RN

Simultaneously published in the USA and Canada
by Routledge
270 Madison Ave, New York, NY 10016

*Routledge is an imprint of the Taylor & Francis Group, an informa business*

Typeset in Times New Roman by Taylor & Francis Books
Printed and bound in Great Britain by TJ International Ltd, Padstow

*British Library Cataloguing in Publication Data*
A catalogue record for this book is available from the British Library

*Library of Congress Cataloging-in-Publication Data*
Witzel, Morgen.
Management history : text and cases / Morgen Witzel.
p. cm.
Includes bibliographical references and index.
1. Management--History.   2. Management science--History.   I. Title.
HD30.5.W58 2009
658.009--dc22
2009017557

ISBN 10: 0-415-96334-6 (hbk)
ISBN 10: 0-415-96335-4 (pbk)
ISBN 10: 0-203-86686-x (ebk)

ISBN 13: 978-0-415-96334-3 (hbk)
ISBN 13: 978-0-415-96335-0 (pbk)
ISBN 13: 978-0-203-86686-3 (ebk)

# Contents

# Contents

# Preface

> We must study the present in the light of the past for the purposes of the future.
>
> –John Maynard Keynes, *Essays in Biography*

The oldest coherent theories of management are only about a hundred years old. Writers on operations, marketing and what we now call human resource management first began publishing in the late 1890s and early 1900s; the first writings on business strategy *per se* appeared in the early 1960s, and we have to wait until the 1980s and 1990s for the first theorists on the management of knowledge in a business context.

But what did managers do before management was invented? For the term 'manager' goes back to the Middle Ages, and we can find other people, with different titles but identifiably managers in terms of their duties and roles, right back to the ancient world. And there were many large business ventures – the banks and international trading houses of the classical world, the very large landed estates of the Middle Ages, the chartered companies of the seventeenth and eighteenth centuries that traded halfway around the world, the factories of the Industrial Revolution, the railways and shipbuilders, department stores and news agencies and mass tourism providers and all the other companies in the new industries that began to emerge in the nineteenth century – which needed to be managed.

Where did the managers of these firms, both the owners themselves and the salaried agents they employed to manage on their behalf, learn how to manage? From where did they get their ideas and their inspiration? Today, we have a large battery of theory and research and experience to draw upon when trying to solve the problems of management. Earlier managers did not have these resources. So, how did they do it?

The initial purpose of this book is to try to answer some of these questions. But there is more. Simply knowing how managers managed before our own time might be interesting, it might even be inspirational in the sense of throwing up some good ideas that have otherwise been forgotten. It might also help us not to reinvent the wheel, and avoid some of the pitfalls that managers have fallen into in the past.

The real purpose of this book is to use the past experience and past practices of management to help people think in new ways about management as it is done in the present, and even perhaps as it might be done in the future. In *Images of Organization* (1986), Gareth Morgan argued that organisations are best viewed from several different perspectives: no single perspective will ever allow for a complete picture. Organisations need to be viewed in the round in order to be fully understood. So it is, not just with organisations, but all of management. We need multiple perspectives in order to understand fully the complexity of the subject and the tasks of management. This book uses the past as a lens or a mirror in order to provide a new perspective and help people to look at management in new ways.

It is possible that nothing terribly radical will come from this; possible indeed that the perspective of the past will sometimes merely confirm what we already know. But that too can be helpful. If it turns out that at least some of the things successful managers do today are more or less similar to what successful managers did a thousand years ago, then that surely helps to confirm that we are on the right track. And when we look at things that have changed, things that are now being done differently from before, then we have another opportunity for learning. Why have things changed, what pressures have led to change? Answering these questions allows us an insight into the way we do things now. Experience shows that 'studying the present in light of the past' sometimes leads people to question the present and ask whether the way we do things now is necessarily the best way, and whether there might be further alternatives to be explored.

How has the material on past management practice been gathered? This book is based in part on a general study of the history of management practice and theory which has been conducted intermittently over the past fifteen years, and in part on a series of focused studies on the management practices of particular companies and organisations. Over 300 business organisations have been studied, along with a further 35 non-business organisations – governments, military organisations, civil service organisations, monastic institutions, charities and the like. Some of these focused studies are presented in condensed form as case studies in this book. Importantly, these studies go as far back in time as written records allow, and include examples from China, India, Japan and the Middle East as well as Europe and America. The aim has been to look for common examples of best practice, but also for examples of best practice that have developed out of particular cultures.

The companies studied were selected in part for their excellence. Either they enjoyed a very long period of high profitability and growth, or they pioneered new ways of managing, or they pioneered new industries or markets; or sometimes two or even all three of these things. (There are a few wild cards: the case studies on the Ming dynasty's navy and Sir Basil Zaharoff are intended to get readers thinking about the opposite of best practice.) There were indeed very many companies and institutions in the ancient world and the Middle Ages and Industrial Revolution that did not follow best practice – as indeed there are today – and this is acknowledged in the book. The point is that the best and most creative and most visionary managers were capable of imagining new markets and new methods of management and then implementing their ideas. That same level of vision and creativity, I would argue, is what we need to aim for today. It is my belief that these examples of best practice can help us to understand better our own tasks and the challenges that await us. Hence this book.

## Purpose of the book

This book was designed for two purposes. The first is as a resource for lecturers wishing to teach courses or modules on the history of management. The second is as a sourcebook for those teaching courses or modules on subjects such as strategy, OB, marketing, HRM, finance, innovation, knowledge management, leadership and so on. Individual chapters and case studies can be lifted out of the book and used as background reading or taken as the basis for one or more sessions within a larger course. In this way, lecturers can take advantage of the historical 'lens' to add a new dimension to existing courses and modules.

### Courses on management history

*Management History* is based in large part on the module 'From the Medici to Microsoft: The Making and Integration of Management', which has been taught as a core module on the MBA programme at the University of Exeter over the past five years. The experience of teaching this course has helped to refine this book to a great extent, and most particularly has helped to validate the view that business school students can use past experience as a way of learning more about the present and future. The introduction of this course was something of an experiment – and typical, in my experience, of Exeter's willingness to innovate in management education – and I am proud and pleased to say that the experiment has, so far at least, been a success. Students have enjoyed the module, not just for the novelty of its content, but because it enables them to think about problems in new ways.

This book could be used to run a similar module or course, and the chapter structure follows the outline of the module taught at Exeter, where we run ten sessions each devoted to a particular topic in management, with the final session devoted to the presentation of research projects undertaken by the students. The chapters can serve as the basis for lectures and/or discussion. The text in the chapters is sometimes more an outline than a detailed description, and readers might be surprised to find some apparently important topics given comparatively little space. But this book is not intended as a complete history of management. Each chapter is meant as a basis for discussion and further development of ideas; readers are strongly encouraged to do further research of their own after reading each chapter.

Also, although the chapters occasionally make reference to modern literature on subjects such as strategy, HR, marketing and so on, this has usually been done in order to draw comparisons. I have deliberately *not* explored modern literature and theory and how it compares to past theory and practice. That, I feel, is something best done in the classroom. Students and lecturers alike will have their own ideas drawn from modern literature, and I wanted to give as much room as possible for creative discussion and learning. It should be emphasised that this book does not give right and wrong answers to any questions. There is no attempt to formulate any all-embracing theories (in part, because I do not believe such theories exist). To restate, its purpose is to get people to think in new ways about management.

Each chapter also includes a selection of case studies. These are 'round' case studies in that they describe more than one facet of each organisation's activities. Thus the cases that accompany the strategy chapter have a primary focus on strategy, but some of the cases also include notes on the marketing and HR policies and ethical behaviour. People are free to use these cases in any way they see fit; cases are not tied to a particular chapter, and if anyone wants to read or teach a case from Chapter 2 in conjunction with Chapter 4 – or any other combination that appeals – then they are quite welcome to do so (indeed, I would be interested to hear of such experiments and how they work).

### Other courses

As noted above, lecturers on courses in other areas of management are free to plunder this book for resources. Some of the chapters are naturally focused on a particular subject area. Others are a little more diffused, but should still be useful resources for lecturers on business ethics or innovation, for example. Material from the book can be given to students to read and discuss, or incorporated into lecture notes: whatever works. In order to make the individual chapters as useful as possible, so that they can be lifted out of the book without people needing to read the entire text, I have tried to make sure that each chapter stands alone. I have kept cross-referencing between chapters to a minimum, and have sometimes repeated particularly relevant examples or ideas in more than one chapter (at risk of irritating those who are reading the entire book through). Again, I very much welcome comments on this, on how well the system works and what problems are encountered.

The case studies, again, can be used in any way that the reader desires. Although the case studies attached to each chapter are intended to highlight particular ideas in that chapter, depending on particular interests and focuses, other case studies may prove to be equally valuable. The strong hope is that this book is flexible enough for people to pull out the pieces that they find most useful and add them to existing teaching material and resources.

## Structure of the book

The book is divided into ten chapters, with all but the final chapter (Conclusion) including four or five short case studies.

Chapter 1 introduces the subject. It shows how managers and management have been perceived in the past, and argues that 'management' has been a constant theme throughout human civilisation. What management is and how it has changed over time are the main themes for discussion.

Chapter 2 is on organisation. There is a heavy emphasis on organisational form and structure, and how these have changed and evolved in response to various pressures and external forces. Areas such as organisational dynamics and organisational change are not discussed in detail here, and this may be seen as a weakness. We concentrate on form and structure because this is the subject on which there is the most direct evidence over a long period. Other aspects of organisation behaviour deserve to be discussed, but will require more extensive research.

Chapter 3 discusses strategy. The opening section of the chapter discusses the influences of military and political strategy on business thinking, and we then move on to discuss strategy as it can be observed in practice and isolate some of the strategic options used by businesses in the pre-modern era. Some of these are very similar to the options used by modern firms, others less so. We discuss the development of strategic principles and also the use of what we would now call 'emergent strategy'.

In Chapter 4 we move on to human resource management, as it is now known. Many of the problems faced by HR managers today have their roots in the distant past, and in social structures and organisations that are far beyond business. We discuss how society has influenced business practice, and how some of the practices which became ingrained in the past are proving slow to die out.

Chapter 5 looks at marketing and the evidence for past marketing practices. It concludes that although marketing has become more sophisticated in terms of research and the variety of concepts that are employed in theory, the basics of marketing practice have perhaps not changed as much as we might think. Establishing reputation and building customer relationships are common features of all successful marketing as far back as records go.

In Chapter 6 we turn to the world of financial management. This subject is now far more complex than it was a hundred – or fifty, or twenty – years ago. Yet it remains true that business success requires sound financial management. How financial management has changed and how the demands on finance managers have increased is one of the major topics for discussion in this chapter.

Chapter 7 examines the roles played by technology, innovation and knowledge in businesses in the past. Innovation has long played a key role in business success, and the importance of knowledge too has been clear for a long time, even if systems for managing both had not yet been developed. We look at some of the ways in which pre-modern firms leveraged technology and knowledge for business success, introducing disruptive technologies and creating new markets and new kinds of business.

In Chapter 8, business and society, we look at the subjects that we know today as business ethics and corporate social responsibility. These are today considered as separate academic subjects, but in former times they were closely linked; the notion of ethical business and the duties of business to society were two halves of the same coin. Considering how these issues were addressed may provide insights for our own troubled times.

In Chapter 9 we discuss leadership, which has to some extent been a running theme throughout the book. Modern theorists sometimes draw a distinction between leadership and management, but in earlier times the distinction between the two was distinctly fuzzy. Attitudes to leadership and expectations of leaders have also changed over time, in part due to societal pressures and in part due to new understanding of the relationship between leaders and those they lead.

Finally, the Conclusion sums up some of the issues that were discussed in earlier chapters and offers some overall thoughts on how the past affects the present in management. For those using this book as a textbook for a management history course, there are also some suggestions for student research projects. These have been part of the module at Exeter from the beginning, and have proved extremely useful in helping to shed light on some of the issues and problems discussed above.

Once again, I am very interested to hear from people who have used this textbook, either students or lecturers, and to gather feedback on its utility and any problems that have been encountered. Please don't hesitate to get in touch with me, and I am happy to answer any questions so far as I am able.

Morgen Witzel
April 2009

# Acknowledgements

This book has been many years in the making, and there are many people to whom I owe a debt of gratitude for making it happen. First and foremost I would like to thank Nancy Hale of Routledge for commissioning this book and for her support, and likewise Terry Clague and Sharon Golan who have seen the book through to publication. Routledge's enthusiasm for this project has been a constant source of support, both moral and practical. My thanks also to Sara Barnes for her excellent and precise copy-editing of a manuscript that, thanks to personal illness, was delivered very late indeed. I am indebted to her for spotting and correcting my faults. Any errors that do remain are, of course, entirely my responsbility.

To name all of the colleagues who have influenced my thinking and generously shared ideas would take many pages, but I must single out Malcolm Warner, Karl Moore, David Lewis, Peter Starbuck and the late Edward Brech for particular thanks; and also my colleagues at the Winthrop Group, George Smith and John Seaman, who have opened my eyes to some of the practical applications of history in the business world.

To Marilyn Livingstone go, as ever, my eternal thanks. As well as reading and commenting on drafts and preparing the index, she has been a constant source of strength through the writing process. Without her, I doubt very much if any of my various projects would ever see the light of day.

Several years ago the University of Exeter Business School took a chance on an innovative new module for its MBA programme. This book is one of the outcomes of that decision. To the School, and especially to Professors Ian Hipkin and Steve Brown, I offer my grateful thanks for their support. No praise is too high for Maureen Costelloe, who organises the programme (and me) and on whom I have relied utterly since the module's inception.

Finally, in the post of honour, I would like to thank the students at Exeter who have taken the module and worked with me. I don't know how much they learned from me. I do know that I learned a great deal from them. Their thoughts and comments and ideas have helped shape both the module itself and this book. To them all go my heartfelt thanks.

Morgen Witzel
Northlew, Devon
2009

# 1   Introduction to management history

---

**Learning objectives**

This chapter is intended to help readers do the following:

1 understand the evolution of management in its historical context;
2 understand the nature of managerial tasks and responsibilities, including both how they have changed and how they have remained constant;
3 see how the systematisation of management in the late nineteenth and early twentieth centuries impacted the profession;
4 compare and contrast how management was done in earlier times with how it is done now, or may be done in future.

> Industry is not a machine; it is a complex form of human association. The true reading of its past and present is in terms of human beings – their thoughts, aims and ideals – not in terms of systems or of machinery. The true understanding of industry is to understand the thoughts of those engaged in it.
>
> –Oliver Sheldon, *The Philosophy of Management*

> The enterprise can decide, act and behave only as its managers do – by itself the enterprise has no effective existence.
>
> –Peter Drucker, *The Practice of Management*

## 1.1 Introduction

Management is one of the essential features of civilisation. Throughout recorded history, wherever human beings have gathered together to undertake great works – build monuments, found cities, establish trade routes, create business and industrial concerns, establish hospitals or universities or religious foundations, publish books and music – there have been managers working on these projects. Indeed, we can go so far as to say that most of these projects could not have been completed without managers, who planned and guided the projects and saw them through to completion.

As the late Peter Drucker observed, businesses do not run themselves. A business enterprise cannot survive without good management, or at least not for long. That was as true four thousand years ago as it is today.

Why study the history of management? It is an interesting subject, full of surprising facts, and the careers of some managers in the past can provide us with useful ideas, even inspiration. Much more importantly, though, the study of management in the past can tell us a great deal about what management is, and how it evolves and changes. And understanding the nature of management is in turn important when we come to the search for best practice today.

The titles of the two works quoted above are as important as the quotes themselves. Oliver Sheldon, who at the time he wrote these words was a senior executive with the Rowntree company in Britain, argued that management is a mental activity. Management, he said, is not something that can be delegated to machines; it is something that must be done by people. How those people conceive of management, how they think about management and its tasks and responsibilities – in other words, their philosophy of management – has a direct impact on how well they carry out those tasks and shoulder those responsibilities. That argument continues to be made today, for example by Richardson (2008) who argues that managers need to spend more time thinking about philosophy and less about science.

Drucker, still the world's most popular and widely read management guru, would have agreed with Sheldon, but he believed that the managerial tasks and responsibilities themselves were of paramount importance. Ultimately, in

Drucker's view, management is about doing things. It is about making things happen, getting results, satisfying customers, generating profits, creating value. It follows that anything managers can do to improve their performance will result in more satisfactory outcomes: more satisfied customers, more profits, more value and so on.

A little reflection will show that both are right. Philosophy and practice are both essential; indeed, they complement each other. Management is an activity which is carried out by people (albeit with the assistance of various bits of technology, ranging in sophistication from the abacus to the Black-Berry). Any business is only as good as the people who are running it, and of all the parts of a business, it is management that in the end makes the greatest contribution to success – or failure. That means we must pay attention to both process – *what* managers do and *how* they do it – and purpose – *why* they do it.

Before these questions can be answered, however, there is another that should first be considered. What is *management*? How do we define the term, whether we are speaking philosophically or practically? All too often, this question is sidestepped. We assume that we already know what management is, and proceed blithely to talk about the management of technology, or innovation, or people, or finance, without really stopping to think what tasks and responsibilities are involved, or about what it really means to be a manager.

A second assumption is that management is relatively new. We are told repeatedly that management – sometimes the caveat 'professional management' is added – only began in the twentieth century. But consider the following:

- *The Duties of the Vizier*, the first text on management which set out the goals of management and the tasks of the manager, was written over 3,500 years ago during the 18th Dynasty of Ancient Egypt.
- in the mid-fifteenth century, one of the richest men in Europe, Giovanni d'Amerigo Benci, was a professional manager who had worked his way up from the bottom to become managing partner of Europe's largest business venture of the day, the Medici Bank.
- the first known brand, in the modern sense of using an identifying mark on a product to establish reputation and quality, was established by the Liu family in northern China in the 11th century AD.
- the first modern business school, established with the purpose of teaching managers the necessary skills to do their jobs more effectively, was founded by the East India Company at Hayleybury, Bedfordshire in 1805.

One way and another, management has been around for quite a long time. And yet when asked what the word means, many of us still hesitate. The first purpose of this chapter is therefore to answer the question: what is management? We shall then go on to consider two further questions: where does management come from? And, why do we manage businesses in the ways that we do? We begin this chapter by trying to define what the terms 'management' and 'manager' might mean, and in order to do so we shall go back and look at the origins of the words themselves.

## 1.2 Definitions

The English word 'manager' first appears in an official document of 1589, referring to someone who had been entrusted with responsibility for looking after a landed estate. The root word is the Latin *manus*, which means literally 'by hand', but also has connotations of power and jurisdiction. During the Roman Empire, if people were described as 'under the hand' of an official, it meant that this official had power over those people and could give them orders; but, significantly, it also meant that the official was responsible for those people, for both their safety and their conduct. The term lasted into the Middle Ages, and by the thirteenth century the Italian word *maneggiare* had appeared, used in a business context to refer to people who were in charge of production facilities such as cloth manufacturing workshops, or overseas trading offices. The French word *manegerie* (from which we also derive the word 'menage') had appeared by the fifteenth century with an approximately similar meaning, with the transition to English occurring in the century following. By 1700 the term 'manager' was in common currency, used to describe anyone whose function was to supervise the activities of others.

Between 1700 and 1850 the terms 'management' and 'manager' were widely employed. The catalogue of the British Library records over a hundred books on management published during this period – small compared to the thirty thousand-plus items currently available from online bookseller Amazon.com, but significant in terms of the overall volume of publication during that time. Most of these works are highly specialised, and refer to the management of particular industries or occupations. Agriculture predominates, but there are books on the management of forestry, shipping companies, schools, hospitals, religious institutions and charitable bodies, even the management of child care. Then, quite abruptly in the mid-nineteenth century the word fell out of fashion – very possibly because it had been overused. The term was revived in America at the beginning of the twentieth century with the advent of 'scientific management' (of which we shall hear much more anon).

---

### What is this 'management'?

Even though the word 'management' has been in circulation for centuries, until quite recently many people were not familiar with the concept. In 1945 Walter Puckey, chief executive of the British arm of vacuum cleaner makers Hoover, wrote a primer on the subject entitled *What Is This Management?* Aware that many of his audience would be unsure of the meaning of the term, he took a very basic approach. He defined 'the manager' as 'every single person to whom is delegated the control of some other person's activities'. In describing what made a good manager, Puckey gave a list of qualities which he grouped into three areas: (1) personal, including ability to listen, judgement and leadership, (2) organisational, including organisational skills, coordinating skills and analytical ability, and (3) technical, meaning an understanding of the technical basics of one's field of business. Of these, Puckey reckoned that personal qualities were by far the most important, followed by organisational qualities and then technical qualities last of all.

(Puckey 1945)

There were other words which denoted the same concept. Another term widely used in the Middle Ages was the Italian word *fattore*, which in English became 'factor'. A *fattore* or factor was originally an accountant, literally 'someone who counted' (the term is of course also used in mathematics). Over time, the term began to be applied to people in charge of particular branches of a business, especially remote locations such as overseas trading posts. The big English trading companies such as the Hudson's Bay Company and the East India Company continued to refer to the heads of their Canadian and Indian trading operations as factors until well into the nineteenth century, and other companies used the term as well (the trading posts themselves were known as 'factories', from which comes our modern word for an industrial plant). Factors were responsible not only for financial matters – though that remained an important part of their job – but also for the independent management of their business units, which were often out of contact with head office for months at a time. A considerable weight of responsibility rested on their shoulders.

Another important term is 'administrator', which came into vogue in the late nineteenth century. Again the original word is Latin, *administratio*, meaning 'to give direction', although interestingly there are also connotations of giving help or assistance to another person; by implication this means that administrators were originally assistants to the head of the organisation. The term was – and remains – most common in public sector management, but was popular in Britain during the 1920s and 1930s as a term for private sector management as well. And of course in 1908 Edwin Gay, dean of the newly established Harvard Business School, decided that the post-graduate degree in management offered by the school would be known as the Master of Business Administration, or MBA.

In general, though, 'administrator' was preferred by those who felt that the title 'manager' was lacking in status, with too many connotations of the shop floor. The same is true of 'executive', which emerged in America in the 1950s and originally referred to someone responsible for overseeing the execution of plans. By styling themselves administrators or executives, the holders of these posts sent a clear signal to the world that they were responsible for directing the manual labour of others, not for doing it themselves.

Thus we have four terms, whose original meanings we can sum up roughly as follows:

- Manager: one who has jurisdiction over others and supervises the activity of others, and is responsible for them.
- Factor: one responsible for money and accounts; someone to whom responsibility is devolved and can work independently of direct control from above.
- Administrator: one who gives direction and issues orders, assisting the owner or principal in the business.
- Executive: one who oversees the execution of a plan.

Taken together, these four definitions show something of the range of tasks and responsibilities expected of managers (and from this point on we will use the terms 'manager' and 'management' as synonymous with factors, administrators and executives).[1] When we find people in managerial roles in the past, whatever official names or titles they might have, we see several common distinguishing features. First, they do not work alone: they work with teams of people and are responsible for directing their efforts, but also very often are responsible for the welfare and well-being of the people who report to them. Second, they have fiscal responsibility: they must account for money they spend, and ensure that money received is remitted to the owners of the business, avoiding financial loss through carelessness or theft. Third, they are responsible to the owners of the business, in particular for the execution of plans passed down to them. The extent to which managers are themselves involved in planning depends on the organisation and their own level of seniority. Giovanni d'Amerigo Benci, managing partner of the Medici Bank, worked closely with the majority shareholder, Cosimo dei Medici, to formulate plans and strategies; his junior colleague Angelo Tani, the factor in Bruges (in modern-day Belgium) was much more likely to be tasked with receiving the plan and carrying out his part of it, although Benci and Cosimo would consider information received from Tani when making their plans (see Case Study 1A).

## 1.3 The origins of management

We noted above the prevalent view that management is something new. For many years the prevailing view was that before the nineteenth century, nearly all businesses were small family-run enterprises serving very localised markets. There was little economic growth, and most businesses existed in a steady state. The first large businesses, so the belief went, were created following the Industrial Revolution, and only then did the need for a formal discipline of management emerge. Professional managers then began taking over from family entrepreneurs.

This is only partly true. The discipline of management did indeed begin to emerge at the end of the nineteenth century, with the first business schools following soon after. But the early management thinkers themselves did not believe they were creating anything new. Paul Cherington, first professor of marketing at Harvard Business School, wrote that his work consisted of observing, defining and systematising practices that already existed (Cherington 1920). Lyndall Urwick, the leading British management thinker of the twentieth century, believed it possible to trace the elements of marketing practice back to the seventeenth century (Urwick 1933). As we shall see, it is possible to trace them back a good deal further than that.

The notion that there was little economic growth before the Industrial Revolution has now been widely disproved. For example, the economic historian Bruce Campbell has shown that in England between 1086 and 1300, GDP grew by an average of 5 per cent per annum – a very respectable figure (Campbell 2000). There were peaks and troughs, but there was certainly enough growth to allow room for businesses to grow. The fourteenth century was a time of economic downturn, but entrepreneurs like John Pulteney and William de la Pole were still able to build very large businesses dealing in the export and shipping of wool; like many modern business leaders in Britain, both men were knighted for their services to commerce.

Other parts of Europe exhibited still more rapid growth. In Germany in the year 1000, most of the land east of the river Elbe was lightly populated forest. By 1500, the country as far east as the Vistula river had been occupied by German settlers, the forests cleared and the swamps drained, towns and cities built and trade routes established. No figures exist to measure this growth, but one can see evidence everywhere in the built environment, not just the cathedrals and castles built by this newly generated wealth, but the stone houses and warehouses of merchants that line many streets in cities such as Lübeck, Danzig and Torún.

Nor is it fair to say that all or nearly all businesses served only local markets. Moore and Lewis (2000, 2009) have shown how, right from the dawn of civilisation, societies traded their surpluses with neighbours who needed resources. The rich river valleys of the Indus, the Tigris and Euphrates produced surpluses of food but lacked minerals; neighbouring states in the highlands of Persia and Iran had minerals but needed food. By 2500 BC, they say, 'Asia minor was now an integral part of a web of commerce stretching from the Hellespont to the Hindu Kush' (2000: 21). It is possible to know a fair amount about some of the businesspeople engaged in this trade. Interestingly, women often played leading roles as managers, working as full partners alongside their husband. One husband-and-wife team in the nineteenth century, Pusu-ken and his wife Lamassi, ran a business trading wheat, copper, cloth and other goods between Assyria and Anatolia; Lamassi managed the 'head office' in the Assyrian city of Ashur, while Pusu-ken himself managed the trading station at Kanesh in Anatolia.

With time, trade routes grew still more extensive. The long land trade route from China to Western Europe known to later writers as the Silk Road was up and running by the time of the Roman Empire, and Chinese silks were favoured by Roman senators and their wives. In the thirteenth century when the Italian friar Giovanni di Pian del Carpini reached the city of Karakorum in modern-day Mongolia, he found a thriving community of several hundred European merchants and craftsmen. Nor was the trade only one way. In 1289 the Chinese Christian priest Rabban Sauma visited Western Europe and called on King Edward I of England, and we know that other Chinese and Turkish traders travelled as far west as Constantinople. At the same time Arab businessmen had established trade routes from the Persian Gulf and Red Sea east to India and then the islands of modern-day Indonesia. By the fifteenth century, big Italian trading businesses like the Banco di San Giorgio of Genoa or the Medici Bank in Florence had agents as far east as Afghanistan and India.

From the fifteenth century the journeys of Portuguese traders, closely followed by those of Spain, the Netherlands, England and France, into south Asia, the Far East and North and South America created a new trading dynamic. The Arabs and Indians were displaced forcibly from the spice trade routes across the Indian Ocean, and two large and powerful globe-spanning businesses, the British East India Company and the Dutch East India Company, competed for dominance. The term globe-spanning is used deliberately here. The British East India Company, by the time of its demise in 1858–59, had operations on every continent except Antarctica. It was East India Company tea that was poured into Boston harbour in 1773 in an act of defiance that would lead to the American Revolution two years later.

Another big long-distance trading company, the Hudson's Bay Company, was founded in 1670 to exploit the global fur trade (see Case Study 1C). Other large firms existed too: the Tongrentang pharmacy business in China, which expanded from Beijing to operate in several Chinese cities; the Indian banking house of Jagat Seth, which in the eighteenth century was believed by the British to have more money than the Bank of England; the German House of Fugger, based in Augsburg but with branches all over Europe and diversified into everything from money to banking; and so on.

But were these firms managed professionally? In fact, many of them were. Family-owned businesses were most common, but were not universal; both East India Companies and the Hudson's Bay Company were owned by shareholders, some of whom were related to each other but many not. In other cases, businesses could keep ownership within the family: the Assyrian traders Pusu-ken and Lamassi used their four children as managers and agents. But not every entrepreneur had a large family. Some like the English wool dealer Sir John Pulteney had no family at all (he married late and had a single son who was still young when he died). In other cases the size of the business increased to the point where there were not enough available family members to fill the gaps. In all these businesses, the owners were forced to recruit managerial help from outside the family circle.

Prior to the mid-twentieth century (and later in some parts of the world), apprenticeship was the most common form of management training. Managers learned their tasks and responsibilities on the job. The system was formalised in many countries: British companies, for example, had a system of 'gentleman apprentices', where young men who were judged to have potential for high managerial posts were taken on and served in different positions around the firm, from the shop floor to the chairman's office, learning both the nature of the business itself and how to manage. Many of these gentleman apprentices rose to become chairmen in turn: William Pirrie of shipbuilders Harland & Wolff and the engineer Charles Parsons who developed the steam turbine are examples.

But professional training appears surprisingly early. We know of at least two places where there were schools teaching management skills by the end of the thirteenth century. The first of these was northern Italy. There were *scuole d'abaco* (literally, abacus schools) in Venice and Florence, two of the biggest commercial centres of the region, and probably in other cities as well. Here students were taught the use of the abacus and the fundamental principles of accounting; they also learned about currency exchange rates, trade routes, important fairs and markets, and the prices of goods at each of these. Learning was supported by lectures and textbooks, and a number of the latter still survive, showing the extent of the curriculum. Some graduates of these abacus schools went on to high managerial positions in banks and trading houses.

The second place was the University of Oxford. By 1300, the law school at Oxford was engaged in training young men for the profession of estate manager. Most medieval English knights and nobles were busy men. They were often summoned away from their homes for long periods of military service, but even in peacetime they were likely to be called upon to act as sheriffs or undertake other administrative duties which took them away from home. Many also owned lands scattered around the country; the Earls of Arundel, for example, owned lands in more than a dozen counties. As landlords could not be everywhere at once, there was a burgeoning market for capable professionals who could manage their landed estates – the primary source of their wealth – for them. Oxford's law school was a favoured training ground. Here again there were textbooks. A treatise on agricultural management written by a man named Walter of Henley – who was himself possibly an estate manager, though details are scarce – some time before 1300 describes not only farming methods and land management but, in its final section, looks at the financial side of land management, provides tips on buying and selling, and discusses forms of accounting for estate revenues.

---

### Hayleybury

The first 'business school' in the modern sense was probably the East India Staff College at Hayleybury in Bedfordshire, established in 1805. During the eighteenth century the East India Company transformed itself from a purely trading institution into a kind of private-sector military-industrial complex, raising its own army and engaging in wars with Indian potentates. By the end of the eighteenth century, large portions of the Indian sub-continent had come under the East India Company's direct rule, and the Company did not have enough trained administrators to run its newly 'acquired' lands. An early attempt at founding a staff college in India failed, but the governors of the Company (the equivalent of the board of directors) decided that the idea had merit and resolved to put it into practice in Britain and founded Hayleybury to train managers and administrators for the Company's service.

The first principal was an American, Dr Samuel Henley, who had previously taught at William and Mary College in Virginia. The economist Thomas Robert Malthus and distinguished historian and lawyer Sir James Mackintosh were founder members of the faculty. Trainee administrators undertook a two-year programme during which they were taught law, history, political economy, mathematics and accounting, natural sciences, literature and Oriental culture and languages. Among its many innovations, the college hired Oriental scholars to teach the latter subjects wherever possible: among the faculty at Hayleybury were Mirza Khalil and Abdul Ali, assistant teachers from 1809–12; Ghulam Hyder, Oriental writing master from 1809–22; and Mirza Mohammed Ibrahim, Professor of Persian and Arabic Literature from 1826–44. In 1858–9 the British government dissolved the East India Company and took over direct rule of India, and the staff college was closed.

---

Economic growth and the rise of large businesses saw increasing demand for professional managers, men – and very rarely, women – who were hired and paid a wage to discharge duties and responsibilities that we would call managerial. These were professional managers, who often spent their entire working lives in managerial posts. With the Industrial Revolution and the factory system there developed a new class of manager, the mill or factory superintendent who managed mills on behalf of the owner. Richard

Arkwright, who at one stage had investments in thirteen different textile mills, relied heavily on hired superintendents. Robert Owen (see case 1D), who went on to own his own mill, worked for several years as a paid professional manager in the employ of the Manchester mill-owner Peter Drinkwater.

Professional management evolved to fill a need.[2] Wherever people were unable to manage their own businesses or estates or public works projects, they hired salaried managers to do this for them. There were managers, or at least people doing tasks we would recognise as managerial, on the Great Pyramids and the Great Wall of China, and as Moore and Lewis have shown, there have been professional managers in businesses for millennia. There have even been managers who were slaves. The Athenian banker Pasion began his career as a slave in the service of the bankers Antisthenes and Archistratus. Being numerate, he was put to work as an accountant, and showing talent for his job, was given charge of the bank's branch at the port of Piraeus, near Athens. His competence earned him his freedom, and he later inherited the bank from his former masters. As well as building up the bank, Pasion also invested in shipping and died a very rich man. In turn he bequeathed a share in the bank to his own former slave and accountant, Phormio, who had enjoyed a rise similar to his own. Phormio then married Pasion's widow in order to keep the capital of the bank together (Moore and Lewis 2000: 69).

## 1.4 The qualities of the manager

At the end of section 1.1 we summarised the tasks and responsibilities of the manager as they have been observed in practice in the past:

- Managers are responsible for directing the efforts of people in order to achieve goals.
- Managers are responsible for the organisations they manage, for money of course, but also for the people who work for them.
- Managers are responsible to the owners of the businesses that employ them (or in the public sector, responsible to the government that employs them) and are tasked with the execution of plans passed down to them.

What sort of person was required to carry out these tasks and responsibilities? Let us look at the first person who set out to specifically define managerial competencies, the rather unlikely figure of the friar and saint Bernardino of Siena some time around 1440 (de Roover 1967; Origo 1962). Like some other medieval theologians, including St Thomas Aquinas, Bernardino was keenly interested in economic matters and did not share the view of more conservative colleagues that all merchants and traders were doomed to hellfire and damnation. Again, like Aquinas, he saw them as vital and necessary parts of society. In his sermon 33, he commented on the need for merchants to employ good managers who will run their businesses well, and also noted that managers of exceptional ability were rare. He then went on to define the factors that he believed made for a good manager. These were:

- The manager should be efficient.
- The manager should be hardworking.
- The manager should accept the responsibilities of his position.
- The manager should be willing to accept and assume risks.

Efficiency, or *industria*, Bernardino defined as meaning that managers should be well informed about market conditions and opportunities, and attentive to detail, 'which in the conduct of business is most necessary'.

The first three of these are unexceptionable, and are present in most lists of managerial competencies down to the present, although the exact terminology changes. The fourth is interesting. Most modern lists of managerial competencies do *not* list risk-taking among them. Indeed, managers are sometimes encouraged to avoid risk. Why did Bernardino think this important to mention? Quite simply, managers in the fifteenth century lived on a daily basis with very high levels of risk, far higher than most do in the present day. War, political instability, disease and, above all, weather impacted very strongly on people's lives. The Venetian merchant Marino Sanudo recorded in his diary that he calculated his costs and prices in such a way that if he sent out five ships and four of them were lost in storms or to pirates, the cargo of the fifth should still earn him enough money to recoup his costs. This same formula is used by other writers, suggesting it might have been a standard risk management metric of the time. Managing in pre-modern times took courage and steady nerves.

## 1.5 Evolution and complexity

Thus far the nature of management looks comparatively simple (although as Karl von Clausewitz the Prussian writer on strategy once said, we must always remember that things that are *simple* are not necessarily *easy*). However, several trends over the past thousand years or so have been combining to make management more complex. These are (1) the ability of firms to expand geographically, (2) the ability of firms to increase in size and scale, and (3) the ability of firms to absorb new technologies.

*Geographical scope*   As we saw above, firms have been extending themselves outside of their own local markets for several millennia. They did so for much the same reasons that firms do so today: to tap into new markets, to gain access to new sources of supply or raw material, to grow their businesses and so on. They also encountered many of the same problems encountered by firms expanding multinationally in our own time: cultural and linguistic differences, the challenge of operating under different legal frameworks, exchange rate risk, higher transaction costs in general and, above all, the difficulties of exercising oversight and control over subsidiary business units operating at a distance from the rest of the firm.

The last of these problems was often the most problematic thanks to the difficulty of communication. Until the middle of the nineteenth century, speeds of communication were measured in miles per hour. Over land most messages were carried by hand by couriers, either on foot or on horseback. Ships carried messages by sea, but were frequently delayed by weather and were sometimes lost altogether. Some national governments and large firms like the Medici Bank maintained post-houses with relays of couriers and horses, rather like the Pony Express in nineteenth-century America. Using this method, it was reckoned possible to get urgent messages from the Bank's *fondaco* in Bruges to head office in Florence in about two weeks. For the East India Company factors in India and Java, the delay between sending a message to London and its receipt by the court of directors could be anything up to six months.

There were experiments with other methods of communication. In the early nineteenth century the London banking firm of Rothschild used carrier pigeons to transmit information between branches. Famously, Rothschild agents on the continent informed head office of the Battle of Waterloo within a day of the event. The rest of the City of London only heard the news when despatches came by courier from the Duke of Wellington's headquarters several days later, by which point rumours had begun to spread that Wellington had in fact been defeated by Napoleon. By keeping this information to themselves, the Rothschilds gained a brief but valuable advantage, buying shares cheaply in a jittery stock market. Generally, however, it was not until the advent of the telegraph later in the nineteenth century that communications began to improve.

Given these primitive communications, managers in the field had to be responsible and capable of independent thought and action. And both field managers and managers at head office had to be capable of managing uncertainty. Without detailed and up-to-date knowledge of what was going on elsewhere in the firm, their ability to make precise plans was limited. Lack of knowledge also meant higher levels of risk. Flexibility and in particular the ability to respond quickly and adapt to suit changing circumstances became important virtues once a company increased its geographical scope.

### Growth and stability

Generally speaking, businesses tended to grow in geographical scope when there was political stability. The empires of Assyria and Rome and the Mongol Empire in Asia, once the first wave of conquest had passed, brought peace to their domains and encouraged the flow of goods and people. All three of these empires saw the growth of multi-site businesses dealing in luxury goods but also in staples such as corn, pottery and metal goods.

But political stability was not essential. The eastern Mediterranean and its littoral during the Middle Ages was a very violent place, racked by frequent wars, and yet the great merchant cities of Venice, Genoa and Pisa grew steadily and each developed large and prosperous trading houses with connections across the Mediterranean and far beyond. The merchant ships they used for their trade could be easily adapted for naval warfare, and were often pressed into service when these cities fought each other for control of vital ports and trade routes. And even in times of peace, rival merchants quite commonly launched piratical attacks on each others' ships; there are literally hundreds of cases of such incidents in the records of the law courts of the day. So difficult is it to distinguish between commerce, warfare and piracy that one modern historian, John Guilmartin, suggested that all three words should be scrapped and replaced with the single term 'armed violence at sea'.

Typical of the business leaders of the day was the Genoese Benedetto Zaccaria (1248–1307). In the late 1270s Zaccaria secured a licence to mine and export alum, a chemical agent used in fixing dyes in cloth and also in pharmaceuticals, from the Byzantine Empire to the West. He invested the profits of this in a cloth-manufacturing business, a bank and a fleet of trading ships. As well as running these businesses, with the aid of partners and hired managers, he served at various times as a diplomat and negotiator, admiral of the Genoese fleet in a victorious war with Pisa, the leader of anti-piracy operation in the Aegean sea, and also engaged in piracy himself against Pisan and Venetian ships during peacetime. The careers of men like Zaccaria show how the distinction between commerce and warfare, and between private and public sector, could become very blurred.

(Guilmartin 1976; Lopez 1933)

*Size and scale*   The earliest large-scale enterprises about which we have much detail were developed in the public sector. The great building projects of ancient Egypt required the efforts of thousands of people and often took years to complete. Contrary again to Hollywood films, projects like the Great Pyramids of Giza, near Cairo, were not built using slave labour. Workers were paid wages (in kind, not cash, as Egypt did not have a money economy) and were hired on contracts. Slave labour *was* widely used during the building of the Great Wall of China and the Grand Canal begun during the reign of Emperor Qin Shi Huangdi (221–210 BC) and in many – but not all – of the big Roman public works projects like the aqueducts and the Colosseum.

The first large-scale business enterprises whose management can be studied in detail are to be found in Europe during the Middle Ages. Foremost among them were the large cloth manufacturing businesses of Flanders and north Italy. The production of woollen cloth was a complex affair requiring sixteen separate steps in production, many of which were carried out by specialists. In most parts of Europe cloth production was on a craft basis with the various tasks 'put out' to workers who worked from home or in small workshops. In centres such as Florence and Ghent, however, workers were brought together in large workshops where most of the production process was carried out on site. These cloth-making businesses employed hundreds, sometimes thousands of people. Larger still were the big landed estates of Europe, particularly those owned by the monasteries.[3] The two largest monastic orders, the Benedictines and Cistercians, each owned estates of millions of acres across Europe, and employed thousands of labourers and craftsmen in addition to their tenant farmers (see Case Study 2B).

As the owners and controllers of these enterprises quickly discovered, the problems of managing these large concerns were rather different from running a small workshop. The Chinese and Egyptians solved the problem by inventing interlocking layers of management, what we now call bureaucracy. (The builders of the Great Pyramids worked with stone tools, bronze and iron not yet being in use, and did not have a money economy, but they had an administrative structure with fourteen separate layers of management.) The Europeans of the Middle Ages had bureaucracy too but they also experimented with other methods of control and coordination. But in every case, it was clear that one of the main requirements of a manager in a large business – or public works project – was the ability to organise. Given the difficulties of communication described above, only by means of extremely efficient organisation could such enterprises and projects be managed.

*Technology* The ability of businesses to expand in scale and scope, to borrow a phrase from the business historian and writer on strategy Alfred Chandler,[4] was greatly enhanced by the advent of new technologies. As we shall see in Chapter 7, the pace of technological advance and the pace of business growth have tended throughout history to track each other. The growth in overseas trading firms late in the Middle Ages, for example, was in part a result of advances in shipbuilding technology and also in navigation, with the compass, cross-staff and astrolabe all coming into common use. In the eighteenth century the development of the power loom, the spinning jenny and other devices revolutionised cloth manufacture in Europe and led to the beginning of the factory system. This system soon spread to other industries, notably steel. Advances in steel-making technology in turn led to advances in steam power, which in turn led to steamships and the railways.

While advances in *production* technology enabled businesses to increase in scale, at the same time advances in *communications* technology enabled them to increase in scope. One of the greatest revolutions in business was undoubtedly the introduction of the telegraph. The first working telegraph line was completed in 1844; by 1870 there were telegraph networks criss-crossing Europe and much of North America, and the first Atlantic cable linking the two had been laid in 1858. The telegraph cut communications times from weeks and months to minutes. Suddenly, managers could transmit up-to-date information between parts of geographical dispersed firms. This enabled better managerial control and coordination, and – in theory at least – reduced uncertainty and risk.

Increases in scale and scope and the impact of new technology demanded further competencies from managers. By the end of the nineteenth century, three more competencies in addition to the four given by St Bernardino had been identified:

- The manager should be knowledgeable.
- The manager should be able to organise.
- The manager should be capable of managing across distance.

> Labour is a process going on between man and nature, a process in which man [*sic*] through his own activity, initiates, regulates and controls the material reactions between himself and nature.
>
> –Karl Marx, *Das Kapital*

The role of knowledge in management had been alluded to by the likes of Walter of Henley, who believed that estate managers had to be knowledgeable about market conditions, prices, weather and seasonal conditions and the like. But by the nineteenth century we start to see emerging a more sophisticated view of the role played by knowledge in management. In his *Political Economy*, published in 1830, the economist Nassau Senior wrote that knowledge was an essential pre-requisite for controlling and coordinating the actions of others, while Karl Marx wrote in *Das Kapital* that knowledge plays an essential role in all work. Another leading economist, Alfred Marshall, thought that the relative importance of manual labour was declining, while that of mental labour was increasing.

The necessity of organisation in these large businesses will be at once apparent. Small-scale firms can operate with limited organisational structures but, as we shall see in Chapter 2, once firms begin to grow structure of some sort is essential. James Mooney, a senior executive with General Motors in the 1920s and 1930s, wrote that organisation is one of the essential management skills: no one can call themselves a manager, he said, if they do not know how to organise (Mooney and Reilley 1931).

Finally there was the need to manage across distance, which had already been present in large trading enterprises like the Medici Bank and the East India Company, but was now becoming increasingly important for many firms in industries old and new. No longer could the manager physically see and speak to the workers for whom he was responsible. The ability to manage people unseen, working at a distance, became a critically important skill.

### 1.5.1 New firms, new industries

The Scientific Revolution of the eighteenth and nineteenth centuries helped enable the Industrial Revolution that happened around the same time. In terms of scale and scope, the Scientific Revolution helped to push the development and growth of three types of business enterprise:

- large *concentrated* firms, in industries such as textiles and steel-making. New production technologies enabled the factory system, which led to the concentration of production in single sites. By the end of the nineteenth century a steel mill might employ thousands of people on one site; the Krupp steel mill at Essen in Germany, for example, employed 13,500 workers in 1884, and numbers rose still further in the next century.
- large *dispersed* firms, in industries such as railways and shipping. These employed large numbers of people, but relatively few of them were concentrated in one spot. Shipping lines like Peninsular & Orient (P&O) had by the 1880s ships operating right around the world. The big long-distance railway networks in the United States and Canada likewise had trains and staff operating over thousands of miles of distance, their movements and timings coordinated by means of the telegraph.
- large *hybrid* firms that were both dispersed and concentrated, operating several large production facilities spread over a wide distance. Examples might include Carnegie Steel, which operated more than one mill in America, or the early oil companies like Royal Dutch/Shell and Standard Oil with large extraction and refining facilities on several continents.

All three types of firm had existed before, but the scientific and industrial revolution meant that there were more of them, and that they were larger in scale and scope than before. Other factors were at work too. Improvements in public health, particularly the decline in infant mortality and the eradication of cholera and typhus from much of Western Europe and North America by the late nineteenth century, led to rising populations and increased demand for goods and services. The age of empire, however we might view the morality of the actions of the empire builders today, did increase global trade and offered opportunities for businesses to expand.

A further dimension to the increasing complexity of management was the emergence of entire new industries. We noted above the emergence of the railways and wire services, enabled by advances in technology. These in turn helped the growth of other sectors, such as mass tourism, pioneered by

Thomas Cook in the 1840s (see Case Study 5E). But the story of the nineteenth century is not just one of economic and business growth. It was also a time of extreme social unrest. Rising populations meant, paradoxically, that while there were more wealthy people around, the numbers of the poor were increasing also. Radical political and social philosophies such as communism, socialism, syndicalism and anarchism took root.

### 1.5.2 Turbulent times

The year 1848 saw violent revolutions in nearly every European country except Britain; the French monarchy was overthrown, and other governments clung to power only with difficulty. From the 1880s onwards, anarchism was a constant menace in both Europe and America. President McKinley of the USA, Empress Elizabeth of Austria, Tsar Alexander II of Russia, President Carnot of France, King Umberto I of Italy and scores of senior politicians – and many hundreds of innocent bystanders – died in anarchist bombings and shootings. Business leaders were often targeted too. The political left regarded the business elites as their enemies because they controlled the wealth that left-wing leaders believed should be shared equally by all people.

But many business leaders did not help themselves by running factories and mills where people worked long hours for low wages in very unsafe conditions. The 'business doctor' (today we would call him a turnaround specialist) Arthur Chamberlain found, upon taking over the Kynoch gunpowder works in 1889, that boys as young as fourteen working on the production lines were starting work so early that they had no time to eat breakfast at home. They brought food with them and heated it over candles placed next to open containers filled with gunpowder. The death and injury rate was, needless to say, high. Nor were such stories uncommon. Industrial deaths and injuries were commonplace in industries such as coal mining, vividly depicted in books such as Richard Llewellyn's novel *How Green Was My Valley*.

The disparities between wealth and poverty and the apparently callous attitude of many business leaders to the health and safety of their people led to violent clashes between workers and the authorities in America and Europe. A strike at Carnegie's steel works at Homestead, Pennsylvania in 1892 degenerated into a small war when workers barricaded the factory and refused to let anyone inside. Carnegie's general manager, Henry Clay Frick, brought in several hundred armed men from the Pinkerton agency (who specialised in strike-breaking) to reopen the plant. The strikers responded with gunfire of their own, even wheeling out a small cannon. The ensuing firefight killed seven people and left many others injured, and in the end it took 4,000 Pennsylvania state militia to reopen the works. In retaliation, a few days later the anarchist Alexander Berkman forced his way into Frick's office and shot him several times before attacking him with a knife. Despite being gravely injured, Frick managed to overpower his opponent. Other business leaders lived under constant threat. Jack Morgan, eldest son of the banker J.P. Morgan, was the target of several assassination attempts; on one occasion a clergyman standing near Morgan was shot dead, apparently the victim in a case of mistaken identity.

## 1.6 Towards a system of management

Thus far we have seen elements of the practice of management and definitions of the capabilities expected of the manager. But there had not, by the mid-nineteenth century, yet emerged any coherent *system* of management. And increasingly, the need for such a system was being felt. Thoughtful observers on both sides of the Atlantic recognised that the business world was playing a central role in the rising tide of social unrest, and could also play a role in helping to calm that unrest. There was increasing recognition, too, that many of the new companies and enterprises emerging in Europe and North America were highly inefficient. Not only were they dangerous places to work, they also sometimes made products that were dangerous to use. And even when not a threat to life and limb, they were often very poorly run. Herbert Casson, the Canadian-born management consultant and writer, later recalled what he first found when beginning his consulting career:

> Managers had never studied management. Employers had never studied employership. Sales managers had never studied the art of influencing public opinion. There were even financiers who had never studied finance. On all hands I found guess-work and muddling ... A mass of incorrect operations was standardized into a routine. Stokers did not know how to stoke. Factory workers did not know how to operate their machines. Foremen did not know how to handle their men. Managing directors did not know the principles of organization. Very few had LEARNED how to do what they were doing.
>
> (Casson 1931: 222–23)

The economic and social implications of this lack of systematic management were being discussed as early as the 1830s. In his *Philosophy of Manufactures* (1835), the chemist Andrew Ure called on British industry to invest more in knowledge and training, and to take steps to improve the welfare of workers. In *The Economy of Machinery and Manufactures* (1835), the mathematician and inventor of the computer Charles Babbage warned British business leaders that they would fall behind foreign competitors unless they were prepared to make their businesses more efficient and do more to engage with their employees. Babbage was one of the first to argue for profit-sharing schemes in business, whereby workers would share in the profits of the business rather than just collecting a wage. Such schemes would make people work harder, he said, and would also help them to earn more and lift themselves out of poverty.

---

**Benefits of profit sharing**

According to Babbage, the benefits of profit sharing were fourfold:

1. Every person engaged in the factory would have a *direct* interest in its prosperity.
2. Every person concerned in the factory would have an immediate interest in preventing any waste or mismanagement in all departments.
3. The talents of all connected with it would be strongly connected to its improvement in every department.
4. None but workmen of high character and qualifications could obtain admission into such establishments.

(Babbage 1835: 257)

---

By the early twentieth century hundreds of British and continental firms offered profit-sharing schemes, and while these did increase worker prosperity and reduce unrest – at least, at those particular firms – these were simply a solution to a particular problem. They were not a system of management *per se*.

In America, the first step towards such a system was taken in 1886 at a meeting of the American Society of Mechanical Engineers, one of whose members, Henry Robinson Towne, presented a paper criticising the current state of engineering shop management. He declared that 'the management of works is unorganized, is almost without literature, has no organ or medium for the interchange of experience, and is without association or organization of any kind' (quoted in Urwick 1956: 26), and called upon the Society to take steps to come up with a coherent set of management methods. One of those who read the paper and pondered on it was a young engineer named Frederick Winslow Taylor.

### 1.6.1 Scientific management

Taylor, like other working managers interested in innovation such as Towne, Henry Gantt and Frederick Halsey in America and James Rowan in Britain, concentrated first of all on the methods by which workers were paid, thinking that if workers felt they were being rewarded fairly for their efforts they would work harder and productivity and efficiency would increase. His first published papers reflect this view. However, he became convinced that motivation was only part of the answer. *How* people worked was as important as *why* they worked. As well as motivation, he also needed to understand method.

Working as a foreman in a steel mill, Taylor set out to study working practices using scientific methods. Taking as his watchword Lord Kelvin's dictum that 'science begins with measurement', Taylor broke down every activity carried on at the mill into its composite tasks, and then, using a stopwatch, measured how long it took each worker to perform each task. This enabled him to do two things. First, it enabled him to set a benchmark for performance, based on the mean performance times he had observed. Those who exceeded the benchmark would be rewarded with a bonus on top of their pay; those who fell below it would not.

Second, it enabled Taylor to 're-engineer' tasks in order to make them more efficient and save time. In this he was greatly assisted by the husband-and-wife consultancy team of Frank and Lillian Gilbreth, who independently had come up with the concept of motion study (which they used to do everything from redesign working methods in brickyards so as to reduce worker fatigue, to redesigning operating theatres in hospitals so that doctors could reach surgical instruments more easily). The aim of motion study was to eliminate unnecessary or wasteful movements which made work progress more slowly and increased fatigue. The resulting technique of 'time and motion study' became widely used in America, Europe and Japan, and is still used by consultants today.

From there, Taylor and his colleagues, including the Gilbreths, the engineer Henry Gantt and the mathematician Carl Barth, went on to develop an overall system which they called *scientific management*. The 'bible' of the movement was Taylor's book *The Principles of Scientific Management* (1911), published a few years before his own death. The basic assumption is that management, like work, can be broken down into sub-disciplines, procedures and tasks. By following these in methodical manner, managers can become more efficient and more effective. Scientific management also relied heavily on measuring and monitoring, setting targets for performance, checking to see that the targets were being met and, when they were not, analysing the reasons for failure and taking corrective action.

While Taylor and his associates in America concentrated on developing a system of what we might call 'micro-level management', breaking tasks down into their component parts and redesigning them, in Europe the approach was at a more macro level. British writers before the First World War, notably Joseph Slater Lewis and Edward Elbourne, concentrated on organisation and structure, with Lewis (1896) in particular also urging managers to take a more exact and scientific approach to issues such as estimating and costing. Elbourne (1914) and the accountant Lawrence Dicksee advocated professional training for managers, although there was resistance to this. It was felt that the present system of gentleman apprentices was sufficient, and there was also a widespread – though by no means universal – view that good managers were 'born, not made', that is, that the ability to manage was something innate and could not be imparted by training.

More important was the work of the French mining engineer Henri Fayol, who developed a 'theory of administration' which concentrated on the role of top management. Fayol did not publish his work until relatively late, 1917, but his ideas were known and in circulation for some years before the Second World War. His fourteen management principles (see display box) are still studied today. Mention should be made too of the Polish mining engineer

Karel Adamiecki who, quite independently, developed a system of scientific measurement and design of labour processes which looks very similar to that of Taylor. It was widely used in the Russian empire until 1917. After the Russian Revolution, the incoming communist government turned to the ideas of Frederick Taylor instead, Lenin going so far as to order Taylor's *The Principles of Scientific Management* to be serialised in the Soviet newspaper *Pravda*. Adamiecki's work was largely forgotten.

All these attempts at developing a system of management had several common purposes. First, they attempted to understand just what it was that people had to do in order to manage firms well. Second, and this was very much in the spirit of the Scientific Revolution, they believed that if the tasks of management could be analysed and its underlying principles discovered, then it would be possible to improve management so as to make it more efficient and more effective. In the first two decades of the twentieth century it was quite common for people to write or speak of the 'science of management' or the 'philosophy of management'. And third, the analysis of management and its reduction to a discipline was intended to make it easier to teach to inexperienced people.

Frederick Taylor himself was sceptical about the value of management education, believing that learning on the job was a superior method. But others in the scientific management movement were eager supporters of the first business schools, the Wharton School at the University of Pennsylvania, the Tuck School of Business Administration at Dartmouth College and Harvard Business School. Arch Shaw, publisher of the magazine *System*, effectively the house magazine of the scientific management movement in America, was a strong supporter of Harvard Business School and helped to develop the case study method still used by business schools around the world today (Cuff 1996). The basic premise of management education, then, was twofold: (1) what could be understood could also be improved, and (2) what could be understood could also be taught.

There is a final point on which the proponents of all theories of management were agreed, however, and this was that they alone were right and the proponents of all the other systems were wrong. In France there was open hostility between followers of Fayol's theory of administration and those who favoured scientific management. In America, theorists of the human relations school and of scientific management attacked each other in print. The scientific management movement itself was riven with dissension; Lillian Gilbreth and Frederick Taylor were no longer on speaking terms when the latter died in 1915. Each believed that there was one 'best' system of management – in Frank Gilbreth's words, the 'one best way' – and that they alone had the secret of it. (The legacy, the idea that there is a 'best' way of doing management and that other methods and techniques are necessarily inferior, has persisted to this day; pick up any recently published book by a consultant, and you will usually find it begins with an explanation as to why this book is superior to all others in publication.)

**Fayol's fourteen principles**

1. division of labour, so as to achieve the maximum efficiency from labour;
2. the establishment of authority;
3. the enforcement of discipline;
4. unified command, so that no employee reports to more than one supervisor;
5. unity of direction, with all control emanating from one source;
6. subordination of individual interests to the interest of the organisation;
7. fair remuneration for all (though Fayol was not in favour of profit sharing)
8. centralisation of control and authority;
9. a scalar hierarchy, in which each employee is aware of his or her place and duties;
10. a sense of order and purpose;
11. equity and fairness in dealings between staff and managers;
12. stability of jobs and positions, with a view to ensuring low turnover of staff and managers;
13. development of individual initiative on the part of managers;
14. *esprit de corps* and the maintenance of staff and management morale.

(Fayol 1917)

### 1.6.2 External influences on management

It is important to note that all of these theories about management did not come out of thin air. Early theorists on management created theories based on what they already knew. Taylor and Fayol were engineers, and they took engineering approaches to solving the problems of management, Taylor by breaking it down into its component parts and Fayol by taking almost a 'project management' approach and trying to determine what held management together (the fact that Taylor was a foreman and Fayol a company chairman might also explain the different approaches).

Other theorists on management used their own background in similar ways. Men who had seen military service drew on military science; those with training in biology or chemistry saw businesses as biological organisms or molecular structures. Academic figures did the same; Walter Dill Scott, who pioneered the study of marketing at Northwestern University, was interested in psychology and introduced psychological concepts to marketing, while at Harvard Business School there was a strong influence of business economics and law.

Others borrowed more widely still. An example is the American engineer Harrington Emerson, who developed his own system of management which he called the 'theory of efficiency'. Like scientific management, it concentrated on making tasks more efficient and easier to perform, but Emerson took a more holistic approach and looked at the entire business, not just the shop floor. He became a very successful consultant, and for a time was more popular than Taylor. Emerson argued that management is in effect a natural phenomenon, occurring in the natural world as well as human affairs, and its principles can be seen all around us if we know where and how to look. He cites examples from biology, chemistry, psychology, military science, art, music, politics and history (Emerson 1913). At one point he gives his readers the three most important influences on his own system of management: a railway surveyor, a conductor of classical music and a breeder of champion racehorses!

### 1.6.3 Management: art or science?

But scientific management had its critics. The Taylor system did undoubtedly make some businesses more efficient, but it failed in its secondary purpose of quelling social unrest. Many workers disliked the system and felt that managers would use it to try and squeeze more work out of them for less money – and some managers undoubtedly did just that. Both Taylor's original system and a later version called the Bedaux system, invented by the French consultant Charles Bedaux in the 1920s, met with widespread resistance when introduced into Britain, ranging from workers sabotaging time and motion studies by deliberately slowing up their work when they knew they were under observation, to outright strikes.

---

**The abuse of Taylor's system**

The most extreme example of the use of Taylor's system comes from the Soviet Union where, in 1935, a coal miner named Aleksei Stakhanov reported a production figure of 102 tons of coal in the course of a single six-hour shift, fourteen times the normal output. Stakhanov claimed to have achieved this figure through a mixture of motivation, a well-trained team and good equipment. News of this achievement was spread all over the Soviet Union and gave rise to the Stakhanovtsy movement, which claimed that if properly motivated and trained, all workers could increase production far beyond current levels. Stakhanovtsy spread throughout Soviet industry and became the dominant management phenomenon of the late 1930s and 1940s.

In fact, the movement became a cruel sham. Equipment and training were rarely forthcoming except at a few showpiece work sites, and workers were expected to achieve superhuman performance targets often with only the crudest tools; coal miners equipped only with picks and shovels were expected to achieve the same target as Stakhanov's original team. In most cases, though, Stakhanovtsy achieved its results through terror, with workers and their families threatened with the Gulag or worse if they failed. Many actually were sent to labour camps, and died there.

In 1988, investigation by Russian journalists revealed the fraud; Stakhanov and his colleagues had added together production figures from several teams to achieve their record-breaking figure. A perversion of management principles had claimed the lives of thousands of people.

(Vronskaya and Chuguev 1992)

But others questioned the principle of breaking down management – and indeed, all work – into individual tasks. Business organisations, it was argued, are not machines that can be analysed in terms of moving parts. Workers are human beings; they cannot be re-engineered or re-configured to fit a space. The counter-argument developed that rather than analysing businesses as mechanistic organisations, they should be seen as social organisms, as micro-societies.

The scientific management movement had been led by engineers. This new movement, which began around the end of the First World War and became known as the *human relations school*, was led by psychologists and political scientists, and included a number of people with strong religious principles. The most important figures of this movement were the Harvard psychologists Elton Mayo and Fritz Roethlisberger, the American labour management specialist Henry Metcalfe, and the political scientist Mary Parker Follett in America, and in Britain the Quaker businessman Benjamin Seebohm Rowntree and John Lee, a former senior manager with the Post Office in Britain.

The human relations school took the view that management was a matter of human interactions, and that it had to be recognised that workers and other managers had minds and wills of their own. Mary Parker Follett's *Creative Experience* (1924), read widely on both sides of the Atlantic, hammered home this point: people could be led, but they could not be driven. In business as in any other organisation, human nature was the essential driving force. In a later essay, published posthumously, Follett argued that the idea of *control* is an illusion. All organisations function through *coordination* of their parts, and the ideal type of organisation is one where as many people as possible are engaged in that coordination.

If you accept my definition of control as a self-generating process, as the interweaving experience of all those who are performing a functional part of the activity under consideration, does not that constitute an imperative? Are we not every one of us bound to take some part consciously in this process? Today we are slaves to the chaos in which we are living. To get our affairs in hand, to feel a grip on them, to become free, we must learn, and practice, I am sure, the methods of collective control. To this task we can all devote ourselves. At the same time that we are selling goods or making goods, or whatever we are doing, we can be working in harmony with this fundamental law of life. We can be assured that by this method, control is in our power.

(Follett 1937: 169)

This, it will be seen, is radically different from the Taylor system as a way of understanding management. Further support for the views of the human relations school came from a series of pioneering experiments conducted by Elton Mayo and Fritz Roethlisberger at the Western Electric plant at Hawthorne, Illinois, from 1928–33.[5] This was a large plant employing about ten thousand workers making telephone receivers and switches. Western Electric, following the principles of scientific management, had been experimenting with changes in the workplace environment in the hope of improving productivity. Its managers had stumbled across an anomaly. They found that when lighting levels in the workplace were increased, productivity rose. But when, as a control measure, they reduced lighting to below the previous level, productivity rose also.

The Hawthorne experiments went on to look at almost every other variable in the workplace including temperature, length of rest breaks and so on, and found that there were no discernable patterns to increases or decreases in productivity. Their conclusion was that productivity rose not because of improvements in the workplace, but because the workers themselves were interested in the experiments and felt stimulated by them. Quite subconsciously in most cases, they increased their work rates because they were happier and more interested in their work (for more on these experiments see Mayo 1933; Roethlisberger and Dickson 1939; Dickson and Roethlisberger 1966).

So, did Taylor get it wrong? Is motivation more important than method? Can managers improve performance simply by encouraging their employees and making them feel more involved? Or do tasks still need to be engineered?

## 1.7 Questions and discussion: the way we manage now

Management as it is practised today still shows strong influences of both the human relations school and scientific management. From Taylorism we have inherited the emphasis on measurement and quantitative analysis, not just on the shop floor but in all areas of work. Its influence can be seen strongly in such modern management techniques as the balanced scorecard (Kaplan and Norton 1996), and business process re-engineering, one of the most important management movements of the 1990s, was described by one critic as 'scientific management for the information age'. Scientific management has also been partly responsible for the greater specialisation of managers and development of sub-disciplines such as organisation behaviour, strategy, finance, marketing and so on.

The human relations school continues to exert an influence too. Decentralisation, participation, workplace democracy and employee involvement are all common themes in management theory and practice. When in the 1980s Ricardo Semler set out to radically transform the management of his Brazilian company, devolving responsibility to his staff and substituting coordination for control (Semler 1993), he was following – perhaps subconsciously – the ideas that Mary Parker Follett had elucidated in the 1920s.

One further inheritance of this time is the continuing emphasis on management training. It took some time for the idea to catch on around the world, but the last quarter of the twentieth century saw an explosive rise in the number of business schools all over the world. It is now generally accepted that management is something that *can* be learned as a skill and that managers must abide by professional standards. There is little doubt that on the level of individual skills and competencies, management has improved significantly since the mid-nineteenth century.

But, as this book goes to press, the business world is undergoing its second major crisis in less than ten years. Twice we have seen explosive growth followed by crashes, which have destroyed some companies and wiped billions off the value of others. Despite all the increases in competency and skill, there are questions as to whether professional management is delivering on its promises. In the USA in the first few months of 2009 there were a number of calls for a re-evaluation of the roles and capabilities of managers, especially top managers.

Is the way we manage now the best possible way of doing so? Management changes with time, but have we got the right management for the right times? Is the systematic approach to management, derived from scientific management, the right approach for the present day? Quantitative analytical tools and metrics are indeed very powerful, but critics believe that Western businesses rely on them too much. Chinese businesses, which rely more heavily on qualitative data, are widely seen as more flexible and better able to react to both crises and opportunities.

So does this mean we should turn towards a more human-centred approach, relying on motivation and coordination rather than measurement and control? This is clearly tempting, particularly to those of us educated in the liberal tradition of the West that values democracy and equality. But is motivating people in and of itself going to be enough to help the enterprise reach its goals?

And what have we inherited from the pre-modern period, before the rise of systematic theories of management? Let us look again at the seven competencies we identified earlier:

- The manager should be efficient.
- The manager should be hardworking.
- The manager should accept the responsibilities of his/her position.

- The manager should be willing to accept and assume risks.
- The manager should be knowledgeable.
- The manager should be able to organise.
- The manager should be capable of managing across distance.

Are these still valid today? If they are not, then we need to construct a new list to replace them. But if they are still valid, then we need to consider how to make certain that these really *are* part of the core competencies of the manager, not just things which are talked about and discussed in a classroom. One thing that the history of management teaches us is that any theory of management must be judged not by the neatness of the theory itself or the skill with which it is presented, but by the impact it makes on the real world.

---

**Takeaway exercise**

Ask a group of colleagues how they define 'management' and what they believe the core competencies of a manager are. How closely do their views identify with (a) scientific management, (b) the human relations approach, or (c) what we know of management in the period before 1900, before systematic theories were developed? Are their views roughly similar to each other, or are there divergences? If there are divergences, what does this tell us about the multiple perspectives that managers use in their work? This is an exercise that might also be worth repeating at intervals, to gauge how people's thinking – and your own – progresses under the influences of time and experience.

Although this can be a nice theoretical discussion, the exercise should have practical value too. Knowing how colleagues perceive their tasks and their competencies should help to understand their actions and behaviour, how and why they act and react to events and pressures as they do.

---

## Case Study 1A

### The Medici Bank

The origins of the Medici Bank are obscure. The Medici family had lived in the Italian city of Florence for centuries; according to their own traditions, the family was founded by a knight who had served the Emperor Charlemagne in the early ninth century. According to some traditions the family were physicians and pharmacists, according to others they made a living as pawnbrokers. By the late thirteenth century they had achieved some prominence in the city and had interests in banking and cloth manufacturing. During the fourteenth century Florence became the largest banking centre in

Europe; the Florentine banking houses of Bardi and Peruzzi acted as bankers to the government of England, and other houses had similar ties elsewhere. The fourteenth century was however a difficult time for banking: both the Bardi and the Peruzzi suffered heavy losses in the 1340s when debtors defaulted on their loans, and the Medici Bank also suffered losses around the same time and had to sell much of its property. The firm crashed again in 1370, and Giovanni de Bicci dei Medici, who took over as head of the family business, found it reduced to a house, two woollen cloth manufacturing workshops, and a small banking operation which, as well as the head office, had branches in Rome, Naples, Venice and Genoa, each managed by a member of the Medici family.

Giovanni had a stroke of luck when, in 1410, his friend Cardinal Baldassare Cossa was elected to the papacy, taking the name Pope John XXIII. The pope appointed the Medici to be his personal bankers. Although some Catholic theologians in the Middle Ages denounced merchants in general and bankers in particular, condemning the practice of usury (lending money at interest), this view was by no means universally held. The papacy itself was probably the largest borrower of money in medieval Europe. And while the profits made on this business were small – the papacy was chronically short of money, and could usually only make loan repayments by borrowing still further – the prestige associated with the post of papal banker could be turned to good advantage. In return for favourable credit terms, popes were willing to recommend their bankers to other clients. On the back of this appointment, Giovanni dei Medici quickly expanded the Medici banking business, establishing branches in Bruges, the main banking centre of northern Europe, and London. At the same time he also invested some of his banking profits in an expansion of the cloth-making side of the business, diversifying into silk as well as woollen cloth.

Giovanni's son Cosimo dei Medici was born in Florence on 27 September 1389. He was educated at the monastery school of Santa Maria degli Angeli, where as well as the basic curriculum he studied languages including German, French, Greek and Arabic. His education was strongly humanistic in nature, very typical of the Italian Renaissance, and Cosimo developed a lifelong interest in philosophy and the arts.

In 1414, aged twenty-five, Cosimo joined the family business on a full-time basis and was sent first to visit the various banking branch offices in Italy to learn the trade, and later to northern Europe to study the opportunities for business expansion there. After two years of a kind of informal apprenticeship, in 1416 he was appointed general manager of the Rome branch, taking personal responsibility for dealings with the pope and his court, the curia. In 1419 he was recalled to Florence and made a member of the *maggiori*, the group of senior partners who controlled the Medici Bank and its subsidiaries. In the early 1420s he was appointed as overall general manager. Giovanni dei Medici handed over many of his duties to his son and went into semi-retirement, dying in 1429.

Under Cosimo's management, the Medici Bank became a truly international business. As well as the headquarters in Florence, there were branches in all the main cities of Italy: Rome, Milan, Pisa, Genoa, Naples and Venice. Along with the already established branches in Bruges and London, new branches were opened in Geneva (later transferred to Lyons) and Avignon, and agency relationships were established using existing firms of merchants and bankers in Barcelona, Valencia and several ports in the Eastern Mediterranean, notably Alexandria, a major centre for the trade in pepper and other spices. Medici agents operated in Scandinavia and Iceland, purchasing furs, fish and tallow. Their network of client relationships was also very strong in the Middle East, expanding up the Silk Road to the Orient with agents in important markets such as Aleppo and Tabriz, and the name of Medici was known to bankers in India and China.

The woollen cloth and silk manufacturing arms of the business grew steadily, and the Medici Bank also integrated vertically by investing in the mining of alum, a scarce mineral which was used as a fixative in dyeing cloth and also formed an ingredient in many pharmaceuticals. By the mid-fifteenth century the Medici had organised a cartel which had a virtual monopoly on the mining and production of alum in Europe. They also diversified their banking operations to include not only foreign exchange but also investments and insurance. Their large geographical network allowed them to become involved in international trade, though usually as financiers of shipments rather than as actual transporters, and they were an important element in the growth of international trade between northern and southern Europe in the fifteenth century, particularly in the importation of high-quality English wool into Italy and the export of silks to the north.

In the early 1430s, as the business grew and became more complex, Cosimo restructured it into a form which the twentieth-century historian Raymond de Roover calls a prototypical holding company, but which also bears a strong resemblance to the multi-divisional form (M-form) adopted by early twentieth-century American corporations (compare with Case Study 2A). The main holding company was the Medici Bank, directed by Cosimo and his general managers. Below this came three semi-independent divisions. Silk manufacturing and woollen cloth manufacturing, which used different processes and had different structures, each had their own divisional structure with their own accountants, production facilities, distribution, and purchasers and sales agents based out of the Medici Bank's foreign branches. Banking and international trade formed the third division; this consisted of the Tavola, the banking head office in Florence, and the eight foreign branches and the various agencies. The divisions did interact to some degree (as noted, most foreign branches were used as bases by sales and purchasing agents for the manufacturing divisions) but were financially and structurally independent.

The primary device for controlling these various divisions and branches was the partnership. The use of partnerships as a device for managing and organising business ventures had a long history in medieval Italy. It is possible to know a great deal about how these partnerships worked thanks to the survival of many business records from the period, not only those of the Medici but also of many other firms. The most notable archive is that of Francesco Datini (*c.*1335–1410), a middle-ranking Florentine merchant whose records and accounts have survived almost intact (see Origo 1957). Typically, each new business venture was established as a separate partnership, a method which allowed for flexibility but also limited risk (if one partnership failed, other partnerships were less likely to be affected as there were no direct financial links). Often the same group of partners would found a number of partnerships together, occasionally taking in outsiders who had capital or skills to contribute. Partnerships were of short duration, usually only two years, at which point they were renewed, renegotiated or dissolved at the wish of the partners. Not all the partners contributed capital; each partnership usually had one or more men who were recruited for their technical skills or market knowledge, and received a share of the partnership in exchange for these skills and knowledge. Viewed from this angle, some of the large businesses of the Italian Middle Ages and Renaissance resembled not so much the heavily vertically structured corporations of the early twentieth century, but the more flexible network organisations and limited life consortia which had begun to appear at the end of the century.

In the middle of the fifteenth century, the Medici Bank was structured as a cascading series of partnerships. At the top were the *maggiori*, the partners in the 'holding company' who functioned as a kind of board of directors. Most were members of the Medici family. Below these was the central office, with Cosimo himself functioning as the equivalent to a modern chairman, and an experienced professional manager, first Antonio Salutati and later the talented Giovanni d'Amerigo Benci, as general manager overseeing all operations, the equivalent to the modern chief executive officer. Under his authority came the various operating divisions. These were governed by thirteen separate partnership agreements between the *maggiori* and their managers: one with the heads of the silk manufacturing division, Berlinghieri Berlinghieri and Jacopo Tanaglia; two separate partnerships with the joint heads of the woollen cloth division, Antonio di Taddeo and Andrea Giuntini; one with Giovanni Ingherhami, the head of the Tavola; one with each of the heads of the eight foreign branches; and finally one with Benci, the general manager at head office. Partnerships normally included only the senior partner or head of each division, though junior partners were sometimes invited in as well, especially in the important branch at Bruges where Angelo Tani and his deputy Tomasso Portinari both held partnerships. Partners normally received from one-eighth to one-sixth of the profits of their own business unit; the case of Benci was special, in that he received a one-eighth share of the profits of the entire Medici Bank. Below these, the operating units could form other partnerships, usually for limited life ventures to fulfil particular projects.

Partners were occasionally junior members of the Medici family or client families like the Portinari, but most were like Benci and Ingherami, men who had worked their way up from posts as office boy and clerk to salaried factor and finally to partner by dint of their own talents and hard work. Part of the strength of the Medici system, as directed by Cosimo, was its ability to spot and reward managerial talent. The career of Giovanni de Benci is a case in point. Five years younger than Cosimo, Benci was born into a middle-class Florentine family in 1394. In 1409, aged fifteen, he was taken on by the firm as an office boy and joined the Rome office. Proving adept at double entry bookkeeping, he had by 1420 risen to be the branch's chief accountant. In 1424, when the Medici made their first expansion north of the Alps, Benci was sent to Geneva to help establish the branch there, and for the first time was taken into a minor partnership. In 1433 he set up a temporary office in Basel, to provide financial services for the dignitaries gathered for the Council of Basel (an assemblage of senior Catholic church figures, most of whom like the pope were continually short of money), and the success of this venture brought him to the attention of top management. Cosimo dei Medici then brought Benci back to Florence and brought him into the central office, first as deputy to general manager Salutati and, after the latter's death in 1443, general manager in his turn. Described as 'a very efficient businessman with an orderly and systematic mind' (de Roover 1962: 57), he helped to engineer the bank's extraordinary expansion and growth across Europe and the Middle East, and was particularly instrumental in setting up agency relationships in Asia and expanding the diversified operations in cloth manufacturing and alum mining. He was eventually appointed one of the *maggiori* and at the time of his death in 1455 was one of the richest men in Florence.

Other professional managers could be found throughout the Bank. Tomasso Portinari at Bruges was unusual in that his family were closely related to the Medici; many other senior managers and partners were promoted on merit. The brothers Giovanni and Francesco Ingherami are another case in point. Born around 1412, Giovanni di Baldino Ingherami was trained at a *scuole d'abaco*, or bookkeeping school, and then joined the Medici Bank around 1430. By 1435 he had risen to head the Rome office and his salary had increased from the apprentice's starting rate of 5 ducats a year to 80 ducats a year. In 1440 he was called back to Florence and given the general management of the Tavola, the banking division. Highly trusted, Ingherami was given the power to make out bills of exchange in the name of the Tavola, a power held until then only by Cosimo and his general managers. Despite this, he was not made a partner until 1445. His younger brother Francesco joined the Tavola shortly after 1440 as a bookkeeper and was similarly trusted and promoted, taking over the management of the Tavola after Giovanni's death in 1454. The brothers are good examples of how educated men from the lower middle classes could rise through the organisation's professional ranks on merit alone.

Decentralising the business and handing over responsibility to his professional managers allowed Cosimo to concentrate on another vital task, the management of Florentine and Italian politics. The volatile political situation in fifteenth-century Italy meant that large businesses ignored politics at their peril. Only by helping to ensure political stability could they achieve the corresponding economic stability necessary for prosperity. In the early years Cosimo overplayed his hand, becoming highly visible and making a number of political enemies, with the result that he was briefly exiled from the city in 1433. Thereafter he made sure his influence was never overt, and in public at least, deferred to the city's republican institutions and supported democracy. Behind the scenes, though, he was the acknowledged ruler of Florence. His emphasis on stability and prosperity made him highly popular. He was also a patron of the arts, who founded Florence's Platonic Academy to give a home to refugee scholars from Constantinople (after its capture by the Ottoman Turks in 1453) and whose patronage was important to the careers of leading humanists such as Poggio Bracciolini and Leonardo Bruni. Likewise he supported artists such as Luca della Robbia, Donatello, Brunelleschi and Ghiberti, whose public works still adorn Florence to this day. When he died in 1464, the Florentine populace voted to give him the title *Pater Patriae* (Father of the Country).

His son Piero dei Medici managed the business effectively until his own death in 1469, but thereafter the Medici family were increasingly distant from the management of the company and control passed into the hands of inept general managers who were not closely supervised by the owners. The bank failed in 1494, prompting an urban revolt and the takeover of the city by a fundamentalist government led by the preacher Savonarola.

Cosimo dei Medici was not alone in creating a large multinational business. In the late thirteenth and early fourteenth centuries, the Florentine-based Society of the Bardi had banking and trading links across Western Europe, and in the thirteenth century the Genoese entrepreneur Benedetto Zaccaria had trading interests in Spain, France, Italy, Greece, the Byzantine Empire and the Middle East. But whereas these others were largely family-based organisations with tight personal control, Cosimo was able to use the partnership system and divisional structure to decentralise his business and make it more flexible. As a business model, this was to endure for centuries; Richard Arkwright's multiple partnerships in the Industrial Revolution were less sophisticated versions of the same principle (see Case Study 7B). Not until the coming of the joint stock corporation at the end of the nineteenth century did this model lose its appeal. Today, partnership networks between institutions and corporations are becoming an increasingly common way of doing business.

### Analysis

Questions you might wish to consider include:

- What were the strengths of the partnership system used by the Medici Bank? What were its weaknesses?

- Why did the Medici employ so many professional managers like Benci and the Ingherami brothers?
- How important were these professional managers in helping the Medici Bank to expand and grow?
- More generally, how important was *good* management in that expansion and growth?

## Sources

For further reading you might wish to consult:

de Roover, Raymond (1962) *The Rise and Decline of the Medici Bank*, Cambridge, MA: Harvard University Press.
Hale, J.R. (1977) *Florence and the Medici*, London: Thames and Hudson.
Hibbert, Christopher (1979) *The Rise and Fall of the House of Medici*, London: Penguin.
Origo, Iris (1957) *The Merchant of Prato*, London: Jonathan Cape.
Parks, Tim (2005) *Medici Money: Banking, Metaphysics and Art in Fifteenth-Century Florence*, New York: W.W. Norton.
Richards, G.R.B. (ed.) (1932) *Florentine Merchants in the Age of the Medici*, Oxford: Oxford University Press.
Schevill, Ferdinand (1961) *Medieval and Renaissance Florence*, vol. 2, *The Coming of Humanism and the Age of the Medici*, New York: Harper & Row.
Witzel, Morgen (2001) 'Benci, Giovanni d'Amerigo' and 'Ingherami, Giovanni di Baldino', in M. Witzel (ed.), *Biographical Dictionary of Management*, Bristol: Thoemmes Press, vol. 1, pp. 71–72 and 474–75.

## Case Study 1B

### The tomb workers of Deir al-Medina

The village of Deir el-Medina lies on the west side of the ancient Egyptian royal city of Thebes. In Egyptian times it was known as *Set Maat her imenty Waset*, meaning 'the place of truth'; its inhabitants sometimes called themselves the 'servants of the place of truth'. The village was home to the skilled workmen who built the great royal tombs in the Valley of the Kings outside Thebes. The village and community of workmen were first established in the reign of Pharaoh Amenhotep (1526–1506 BC), and was closed down during the reign of Ramesses XI (1107–1078 BC). The workmen of Deir el-Medina were responsible for some of the most spectacular monuments of ancient Egypt, including the tombs of Seti I and Ramesses II and the latter's wife, Queen Nefertari.

Thanks to archaeological excavations of the Deir el-Medina site in the early twentieth century, it is possible to know a great deal about the workers themselves, how they worked and even their personal lives. The workers included the excavators and stonemasons whose task was to dig into the hillsides in the Valley of Kings and shore up the interiors of the tombs, the plasterers and artists responsible for decorating the tombs with scenes from the afterlife and passages of hieroglyphic text, the foremen who directed their work and the scribes and accountants who recorded progress and kept track of tools and costs. These latter kept records on *ostraca*, shards of unglazed pottery on which notes and records were scratched with a sharp stylus, and it was the discovery of thousands of these at Deir el-Medina that has made it possible to reconstruct the work and management structure of the tomb builders.

Ancient Egypt operated on a ten-day week, and workers spent eight days on site, living in camps near the tomb currently under construction, then returning to their homes in the village for the remaining two days. Their wives and children remained in the village, in charge of food production and domestic chores. Despite its complex social organisation and bureaucracy, Egypt under the pharaohs did not have a money economy; coin only came into widespread circulation in the fourth century BC following the conquest by Alexander the Great. As well as receiving free food rations, the workers and their families were paid in goods, and bartered away surpluses in exchange for other goods they desired. They would appear to have been well paid, as their own tombs, close by the village, were small but lavishly decorated.

Working conditions seem to have been fairly relaxed much of the time, and men were allowed days off for family illnesses or celebrations or for religious observance. Notes of the reasons for absence were kept on ostraca; there survives one such note in which a worker asked for the day off so that he could embalm his mother. One area in which the foremen and scribes were quite strict was the care of the tools used by the tunnellers and masons and plasterers. These were government property and were valuable items, and men were expected to account for any that were damaged or went missing.

In terms of organisation, it was customary to divide the workers on a tomb project into two teams, each with its own foreman. Each was responsible for one side of the tomb, so that typically there would be a left-side team and a right-side team. Each team had its own specialist excavators, masons, plasterers and artists, and it was usual for them all to work at the same time: after the masons had shored up one chamber they would move on to the next, the plasterers coming to do their work and following on, and the artists moving in last of all to do their decorative work. Over the course of several centuries, a highly organised and systematic approach was developed, and teams would often compete to see who could finish their side of the tomb first. This competition was encouraged by the higher authorities, who liked to see tombs finished quickly; should a pharaoh or his queen die suddenly, it was essential that the tomb be ready to receive them so that they could cross over into the afterlife.

The two most important managerial posts were the scribe and the foreman. As noted, there were usually two foremen on each project, each in charge of a team. These were responsible for all the technical aspects of the project. They directed the excavators and masons, and made sure that only high-quality stone was used and that it was laid properly in order to prevent tunnel collapses. They checked on the work of the plasterers and artists too, making sure that the latter followed the designs and texts the pharaoh and his staff had specified. They were responsible for ordering supplies, including scaffolding and plaster. As most of the work was done far underground, lamp oil was a major expenditure as well. They were also responsible for what we would now call human resource management, for the recruitment of new workers when needed, for the writing of contracts and for any disciplinary problems that might occur. As wages and working conditions were good, there were always people wishing to join the tomb workers, and the foremen had to be able to select the best and most skilled applicants.

An example of such a foreman is Neferhotep the Elder, who around 1300 BC was promoted to the post of foreman of the right-side team working on the tomb of Seti I. He played a key role in the construction of this tomb, often described as the finest achievement of the tomb-builder's craft. He went on to oversee teams on the tombs of Ramesses II and his wife Nefertari, also superb pieces of building and design. It is thought that he was originally an artist, who was hired as a tomb decorator and rose to the rank of foreman by dint of his organisational abilities. He and his wife Iy-em-wau had several children, and one of their sons, Nebnefer, became a foreman in his turn.

Overseeing the entire operation as a kind of works manager or site manager was the scribe. His role was the supervision of the workers on the tomb sites: his duties included keeping records of work completed, collecting blunt tools for recasting and weighing, and distribution of supplies, pay and rations to the workers. In addition to his supervisory duties, he also reported to superiors further up the hierarchy. One of his tasks was to keep a running diary of events, making notes on ostraca and then drawing up formal reports on papyrus scrolls.

A contemporary of Neferhotep, Ramose son of Amenemheb was born in the Egyptian city of Thebes around 1325 BC. He trained as a scribe (or clerk), probably at one of the temples on the west bank of the Nile near Thebes. His competence at scribal work brought him to the attention of Paser, the vizier of Upper Egypt and head of the Egyptian civil service in the region (Paser was the same man who had spotted and promoted Neferhotep). During the reign of pharaoh Ramesses II, Ramose was appointed to take charge of the tomb workers and moved with his wife Mutemwia to Deir el-Medina. He spent the rest of his career at the necropolis. From both the records of his career and the quality of the work done under his direction, we can deduce that Ramose, a well-paid and high-skilled professional, was also a conscientious manager who looked after his employer's interests.

Things did not always run so smoothly. A few years after time of Neferhotep and Ramose, a man named Pa-ser bribed the local vizier and was given the post of foreman despite having no qualifications for the job. It is also alleged that he murdered the previous foreman in order to create a vacancy for which he could then apply. Other crimes laid at his door included stealing stone intended for a royal tomb to build his own tomb, theft of supplies and the rape of the wives of some of his workmen. The workers appealed to higher authority, and Pa-ser was brought to trial, dismissed from his post and sent to work as a labourer in a stone quarry.

More generally, the workers were not slow to protest at perceived infringements of their rights. During the reign of Ramesses III (1186–1155 BC), there was an interruption to food supplies and the workers had to barter for food themselves. After eighteen days they went on strike – possibly the earliest recorded strike in history – and informed the local vizier that they would not return to work until the deficit in rations was made up. Food supplies were found and the work continued. Although details are not clear, it would appear that the foremen and scribe supported the workers in this case. In succeeding years, however, as the economy declined and central control in Egypt began to fail, there were more interruptions to food supplies and more strikes. The workers also began robbing the tombs they themselves had built, stealing valuables interred with the dead pharaohs and selling these in order to make a living. Finally during the reign of Ramesses XI, a rebellion broke out in the city of Thebes and royal troops were sent to restore order. These discovered the tomb robberies, and the 'place of truth' was shut down and the work crews disbanded, a rather sorry end to an organisation that had been responsible for some magnificent architectural and artistic achievements.

## Analysis

Questions you might wish to consider include:

- What managerial competencies were required by the foremen and scribe at Deir el-Medina?
- Is it fair to describe these men as 'managers' in the modern sense? How did their function and responsibilities differ from that of a modern manager?
- Are there any lessons about management that we can learn from the case of Pa-ser and the strikes and more general decline of Deir el-Medina?

## Sources

For further reading you might wish to consult:

Bierbrier, M. (1982) *The Tomb-Builders of the Pharaohs*, London: British Museum.
Lesko, Leonard H. (ed.) (1994) *Pharaoh's Workers: The Villagers of Deir el Medina*, Ithaca, NY: Cornell University Press.
Yurko, Frank J. (1999) 'Deir el-Medina' in Kathryn A. Bard (ed.), *Encyclopedia of the Archaeology of Ancient Egypt*, London: Routledge, 247–50.

## Case Study 1C

### *Hudson's Bay Company*

The Company of Adventurers of England Trading into Hudson's Bay received its charter from King Charles II of England on 2 May 1670. Its first governor was Prince Rupert of the Rhine, the king's cousin, and there were seventeen other named investors. By the terms of the charter, the company was awarded a monopoly of all trade with the regions around the shores of Hudson's Bay and the drainage basin of all the rivers flowing into it, an area comprising about 1.5 million square miles. Later the lands between the Rocky Mountains and the Pacific Ocean were added to the monopoly. This area was formerly named Rupert's Land in honour of the prince.

Although fish and other goods were traded, the primary object of the Hudson's Bay Company, as it became known, was to establish a trade in furs. Beaver, used primarily for making hats, was the most important and valuable fur traded, but wolf, fox, marten and many other furs were traded too. The company's trading partners were the native American tribes who inhabited Rupert's Land. They did the actual trapping and harvesting of furs. Initially they brought their furs to the company's posts on the shores of Hudson's Bay, but by the mid-eighteenth century the company's agents were pushing into the interior and establishing trading posts along the network of rivers.

The Hudson's Bay Company was the latest in a series of chartered companies established in Britain to promote overseas trade. The first of these, the Muscovy Company, had been chartered in 1551 to develop trade with Russia through the so-called Northeast Passage around the northern coast of Scandinavia. Others included the East India Company, founded in 1600 to trade with India and the Far East. In each case merchants were given a monopoly, meaning that other English merchants were not allowed to compete with them, and help would also be given to prevent foreign merchants from interfering. These were in theory private sector businesses, but in practice the British government kept a close watch on their activities and often interfered. The equivalent of chairman of the Hudson's Bay Company was the governor, who was often an important figure in government, and the court of directors usually had connections at government or court too. In time, though they remained private sector companies, the East India Company and Hudson's Bay Company became instruments of British political control over the areas in which they traded.

While the governor and court of directors remained in London, the bulk of the company's staff were deployed in Rupert's Land. The company employed many boatmen and servants, including some native Americans and later many Métis, who had a mixed heritage of native American and French-Canadian ancestry. Most of the traders, however, were Scots, many recruited from very poor families who saw employment with the Hudson's Bay

Company as a chance to escape a life of poverty and perhaps make their fortune. At one point, nearly three-quarters of the Company's staff in Canada were recruited from the Orkneys, a group of islands off the northern coast of Scotland. The eastern county of Ross was also a favourite recruiting ground.

There were a few English in the Company's ranks, including Charles Bayly, the first superintendent of operations in Canada. A Quaker, Bayly had been several times arrested as part of a general religious persecution of the sect, and was actually in prison in the Tower of London when he was appointed to the post in 1670, probably thanks to the influence of a sympathetic director. Released, Bayly went to Rupert's Land in 1670 and spent ten years establishing the first posts on the shores of Hudson's Bay. He was charged with mismanagement and recalled in 1680. A later and more successful English recruit was Samuel Hearne, a former Royal Navy sailor recruited in 1763, who led expeditions into the Arctic in search of furs and copper and established one of the first inland posts, Cumberland House.

Posts like Cumberland House were even more isolated than those on the shores of Hudson's Bay. Hundreds of miles apart, each was staffed by a tiny group of traders who endured physical danger and the extreme hardship of northern Canadian winters. Communication was largely by river, on foot across the ice in winter and by fragile birchbark canoes in summer. Survival depended in part on the resourcefulness of the factors in charge of each post, but also on continuing good relations with their native American trading partners. Maintaining these good relations was a matter of strict company policy. Unlike other trading companies, the Hudson's Bay Company rarely traded alcohol to the native Americans, which would have had a terrible affect on their society and their individual welfare.[6] Instead the company traded its famous trade blankets and a variety of metal goods and glassware, both of which were in short supply among the native Americans.

Also, unlike the situation in other colonies, the Company sanctioned and even encouraged the marriage of its traders with native American women. One factor who married locally, James Douglas, later became governor of the colony of British Columbia when it was created in 1857; his native American wife became first lady of the colony, very much liked and respected by the British population. This was entirely in keeping with the meritocratic tradition of the company. People were promoted if they showed talent, regardless of their social status. Douglas, the son of a farmer, joined the Company at sixteen and ended his career as Sir James Douglas, one of the most respected men in Canada. George Simpson, the illegitimate son of a farmer from Ross, became superintendent of the company in Canada and was also knighted. Donald Smith, who began as a clerk at the age of eighteen, rose to become governor of the company and was ennobled as Lord Strathcona.

The company also had its own fleet of ships that carried supplies and trade goods to Canada, and brought the harvested furs home again. These ships and the trading posts themselves were armed. They had to be; at least for the first hundred years, the company operated beyond reach of British military protection. The vulnerability of its operations was demonstrated in 1686 during a larger war between Britain and France, when a raiding party from the French colony of Québec captured several Hudson's Bay Company trading posts. In 1697 the French-Canadian privateer Pierre d'Iberville destroyed the Company's fleet and burned its headquarters at York Factory on Hudson's Bay.

Commercial rivalries could turn violent too. In 1779 a rival group of Scottish merchants based in Montréal, the North West Company, began encroaching on the Hudson's Bay Company's monopoly.[7] When traders from the two companies met in the field, the result was often violence. In 1816 a pitched battle between Hudson's Bay Company and North West Company staff at Seven Oaks in Manitoba cost the lives of twenty-one men. Another dangerous rival was the American Fur Company, founded by the dynamic entrepreneur John Jacob Astor. The competition between these two companies usually stopped short of violence, but could be very ruthless. When American traders began entering Oregon territory the Hudson's Bay Company's local factor John McLoughlin ordered eastern Oregon to be 'trapped out', in other words for all fur-bearing mammals to be trapped and killed immediately to deny the Americans access to furs.

Violence between the Hudson's Bay Company and North West Company continued to escalate, and in 1820 the British government stepped in, ordering a ceasefire and forcing the two companies to merge. This was not an easy task; the traders of both companies had been embittered by past violence, and were in no mood to cooperate. The task of implementing the merger on the ground in Rupert's Land was given to George Simpson, the newly appointed governor of the Athabaska Department. Simpson had been with the company for less than a year; unusually, he had not risen through the ranks of the Company but had been hired in from outside on the recommendation of Andrew Colvile, one of the directors. He had never been to Canada before and had never worked in the fur trade.

A small man of boundless energy – he seems to have modelled himself on Napoleon – Simpson impressed everyone with his determination and drive. By proving to the former North West Company traders that they could trust him, he won their respect. They may still have hated their former rivals, but they were ready to acknowledge Simpson as their leader.

When the articles of amalgamation were finally signed and the two companies merged (under the name Hudson's Bay Company, to the disgust of many Nor' Westers), there was unanimous agreement that the new general superintendent of the company in North America should be George Simpson. Still only in his mid-thirties, Simpson now controlled a business across an area ranging from Montréal to the Pacific, and from Fort McPherson on the Beaufort Sea to Yerba Buena (now San Francisco) in California.

That was only the beginning. The company, now 150 years old, had become set in its ways. There were too many unprofitable trading posts and too many people not contributing to the bottom line. Over the course of the next two decades, Simpson revamped the organisation. He reviewed the accounts of each trading post in detail, and closed those that were not making sufficient profit and laid off excess staff. He phased out the old birchbark canoes, the primary mode of travel and transport to which many employees had a sentimental attachment, and replaced them with the York boat, a solid wooden craft that was easy to build and maintain and had far greater cargo capacity. He also began squeezing his main suppliers, the native American tribes who trapped furs and sold them to the Company, and drove fur prices down while pushing margins up.

In the early years, Simpson governed this highly geographically dispersed business through constant travel and inspection. He travelled for as many as forty weeks a year, even in winter, visiting every post in the Hudson's Bay Company empire, settling accounts, replacing incompetent factors and promoting reliable men into their places. His energy was legendary; he often travelled for sixteen hours a day, and once made the journey from York Factory on Hudson's Bay to Fort Langley on the Pacific, 3,200 miles across the Great Plains and over the Rocky Mountains, in sixty-five days by canoe and horseback, at an average speed of nearly fifty miles a day. This constant surveying and inspection of the Company's work, or 'management by canoeing around', eventually put Simpson into a position where he knew that the bulk of the company's posts and departments were reliably staffed and could be trusted to run their own affairs. Only then, after twenty years of effort, did he step back and hand over some of his responsibilities to others. He established his headquarters in Montréal, the commercial capital of the British colony of Canada, and became more involved in policy making and strategy. Not the least of his achievements was persuading the governor and court of directors to allow the general superintendent and his staff in Canada to take responsibility for strategy and overall direction.

Simpson's death in 1860 marked the end of an era. In 1859 the Company's monopoly over the fur trade in Rupert's Land was formally ended. In 1867 the Dominion of Canada was created, and in 1870 the Company sold its concession to Canada; henceforth, although the company continued to trade, its lands, now known as the North West Territories, were part of Canada.[8] Gradually as settlers from eastern Canada and Europe began to occupy much of this vast tract of land, the Company changed in character. It still traded in furs, but its trading posts also became shops, supplying a range of goods needed by the settlers. Across much of northern and western Canada, the Hudson's Bay trading posts were the only retail outlets in existence.

In the later twentieth century, the fur trade declined, in part due to changing fashions and in part to public revulsion against the trapping of fur-bearing animals. In 1987 the Company sold its fur trading business and formally ended its association with fur trading, 317 years after it had begun. But long before this the Company had re-invented itself. This re-invention was in part the work of Donald Smith, a farmer's son from Forres in Scotland who had joined the Company as a junior clerk at age 18. He had been promoted to high positions, and had played a key role in the sale of the concession to the Canadian government; he went on to become governor in 1889. Smith and his staff saw that the future of their trading company lay not in trading furs but selling goods to the growing towns and cities in western Canada. The Hudson's Bay Company opened its first department store in Winnipeg in 1881. More followed, and by the 1930s the Company had consolidated its position as the largest retail chain in Canada with hundreds of stores across the country. Today the Hudson's Bay Company remains Canada's largest chain retailer, a company very different in character and nature than that founded in 1670.

## Analysis

Questions you might wish to consider include:

- What are the most important management problems and challenges to be faced when managing a company over a large geographical space with poor communications?
- What are the primary risks involved in this kind of management? How can they be offset?
- What has changed about the management of these dispersed companies? Is their management easier/harder today than it was before?

## Sources

For further reading you might wish to consult:

Innes, Harold A. (1930) *The Fur Trade in Canada*, Toronto: University of Toronto Press.

MacKay, Douglas (1936) *The Honourable Company; A History of the Hudson's Bay Company*, Indianapolis: Bobbs-Merrill.

Newman, Peter C. (1987) *Company of Adventurers*, Markham, Ont.: Viking.

Willson, Beckles (1900) *The Great Company (1667–1871): A History of the Honourable Company of Merchants-adventurers Trading Into Hudson's Bay*, London: Smith, Elder and Co.

Woodcock, George (1970) *The Hudson's Bay Company*, Toronto: Collier.

## Case Study 1D

### Robert Owen

Robert Owen was born in Newtown, Montgomeryshire, Wales on 14 May 1771 into a fairly humble family; his father was an ironmonger and saddle maker. The youngest of seven children, he was largely self-educated. He later described as his two formative influences Defoe's novel *Robinson Crusoe*, which taught him self-reliance, and the Methodist tracts handed out by the local ladies, which he said turned him into an atheist by the age of ten. In 1781 he left home to live and work with his elder brother in London; a year later, aged eleven, he was apprenticed to a draper in Stamford, Lincolnshire. Here he learned how to gauge the quality of cloth, and he also continued his self-education, reading before and after work.

Owen completed his apprenticeship at age fifteen and moved back to London, taking a job as a shop assistant. Disliking the work, he moved instead to Manchester in 1787. This northern city was in the grip of the Industrial Revolution, and new textile factories were being built all around the city. Quickly seeing where the opportunities lay, Owen quit his job and set up a partnership with a mechanic named John Jones to make and sell spinning mules, a relatively new piece of technology designed by Samuel Crompton in 1779. Jones made the machines; Owen sold them, handled the finances and managed the firm's forty workmen. His almost total lack of technical knowledge at the outset of the venture never proved a hindrance, and the partnership prospered. Owen then sold his share and used the profits to buy three spinning mules. With these he set up a small workshop and began spinning and selling high-quality yarn. By 1790 he was earning profits of around £6 a week.

The next turning point in his career came when a local mill-owner, Peter Drinkwater, advertised for a mill manager. Owen applied for the post. When asked what salary he expected, he asked for £300 per year. When Drinkwater pointed out that this was double what any other candidate had asked, Owen responded saying that he was already earning this much in his own business and would not be interested in working for less. When he showed Drinkwater his books and his workshop, the latter was so impressed that he offered Owen the job of managing a modern factory employing over five hundred people.

Although still short on technical experience – and still only nineteen years old – Owen was emerging as a born manager of people. He introduced new working methods and found new sources of high-quality cotton from North America (it should be noted that unlike Indian cotton, American cotton was largely cultivated and harvested using slave labour). Under his management, product quality improved and productivity nearly trebled in the first two years. Drinkwater, who clearly believed in the separation of ownership and control – Owen says he visited his mill just three times in four years – rewarded Owen with a partnership and a free hand in managing the business. However, the partnership did not last for long. The ambitious young mill-owner Samuel Oldknow, Drinkwater's son-in-law, persuaded Drinkwater to dissolve the partnership and hand the mill over to himself. Owen was offered the job of mill manager at any wage he cared to name, but he disliked Oldknow and was not prepared to work with him. In any case, Owen was also now ready to strike out on his own.

In 1795, now aged twenty-four, he founded the Chorlton Twist Company in Manchester, overseeing the building of the new mill and then managing the business once it was in operation. He was now quite prosperous and a man of affairs in Manchester. He became a member of the Literary and Philosophical Society of Manchester and gave several papers before it, and numbered among his friends scholars and scientists such as Robert Fulton, to whose plans for canal-building Owen gave encouragement. Owen's new business took him frequently to Glasgow, where he met David Dale, owner of New Lanark, one of the largest and most prosperous mills in Scotland. He also met and fell in love with Dale's daughter Caroline. There was a major obstacle to their marrying: the Dales were devoutly religious, while Owen was an atheist. This obstacle vanished, however, when Owen offered to buy New Lanark for the colossal sum of £60,000, to be paid in instalments. Dale agreed, and the purchase and marriage both went ahead. Owen raised the money by forming a partnership with several other investors, including John Walker and William Allen. Owen himself was to be managing partner, responsible for the running of the mill.

Owen took over New Lanark in 1800, and managed it for the next twenty-eight years. The early years were difficult financially, largely because of the heavy debt encumbrance, but once this had been paid off New Lanark became hugely profitable. The patience, attention to detail and people management skills that Owen had developed in Manchester now came fully into their own. New Lanark was a much larger establishment than the Drinkwater mill or his own Chorlton Twist Company, with several thousand workers; in addition, it was located some way out of Glasgow, and most of the workers and their families lived on site. The problems of management were correspondingly more complex.

Some mill-owners during the Industrial Revolution made attempts to look after their employees both in and out of the workplace. Others did not, and many mills were dangerous, unsanitary places with illness and accidents taking a heavy toll among the workers, many of whom were women and children. Owen was from the beginning opposed to child labour, and later strongly supported legislation prohibiting the practice. In his own mill he immediately raised the minimum working age from ten to twelve, and later to fourteen. Instead of working, children were given an education free of charge at a school established by Owen. Owen also cut the working day from fourteen hours to ten and three-quarter hours – still long by our standards, but a radical step for the time – and provision was made for meals and adequate rest breaks. Owen ensured his mill was clean and as safe as possible given the technology he was using, and in particular made sure that there were adequate sanitary facilities.

Discipline and control were strong in New Lanark, and there was a hierarchy of supervision; drunkenness was not tolerated and those who behaved badly or did not work hard were liable to dismissal. One of the more interesting pieces of motivational psychology that Owen used was the so-called 'silent monitor', a coloured symbol which was placed over each worker's station to denote his or her conduct and performance at work the preceding day. If the worker's conduct had been poor, the symbol was black; if merely indifferent it was blue; good conduct was rewarded by a yellow symbol, and excellent conduct by a white one. Records were kept of what symbols had been awarded over time, in a manner similar, said Owen, to the recording angel marking down the good and bad deeds of the human character. Any worker who felt he or she had been unjustly treated and marked unfairly could appeal to Owen in person.

This right of appeal was in fact an important element in Owen's system of discipline. In particular, he kept a watchful eye on his managers and super-intendents, ensuring that these did not abuse their powers over the workers. He felt that the key to good discipline was equity and fairness. In a system where all were treated fairly and according to merit, no one could complain if they were punished for a genuine transgression (and even if they did, they would get little support from their co-workers).

Owen believed that by improving the quality of life and the physical con-ditions of work for his workmen and their families, not only would he be contributing to the good of society, but also happier, healthier workers would also be more efficient and productivity and quality would improve. He had already tried some limited experiments of this sort while in Manchester, and on coming to New Lanark resolved to attempt widespread reforms. As he later wrote:

> My intention was not to be a mere manager of cotton mills as such mills were at this time being managed – but to introduce principles in the conduct of the people which I had successfully commenced with the work-people at Mr Drinkwater's factory, and to change the conditions of the people who, I saw, were surrounded by circum-stances having an injurious influence upon the character of the entire population of New Lanark. I had now, by a course of events, got under control the groundwork on which to try the experiments long wished for, but little expected ever to be in my power to carry into execution.

The houses of the factory workers at New Lanark were cleaned and enlarged, and new accommodation was built, with good drainage and sanitation. Health care was provided free of charge. Private shops which had been overcharging workers had their leases terminated, and Owen established company-owned shops which offered good-quality food and other goods at fair prices. Many other model communities of the nineteenth century were strictly teetotal, but Owen's shops sold beer and spirits at cost price.

Another important aspect of the New Lanark model community was edu-cation. There had been education at New Lanark under Dale's ownership, but it had been mostly religious in nature. Owen abolished this and instituted a secular education programme, first for children and later for adults as well. There has been much debate as to whether Owen's reforms were motivated by genuine social concern or for the advancement of his enterprise's profit, but in fact at New Lanark it is difficult to disentangle the two motives. As the economist G.D.H. Cole later commented, 'first and foremost Owen believed in the power of education, rightly directed, to turn the world's affairs into a prosperous course' (Cole 1930: 126).

It should be added that Owen's actions were considered controversial by many, including some of his own partners. These objected to the spending of money on education, which they did not feel was their responsibility and which reduced their profits. Owen's atheism, which he tended to flaunt publicly, also upset some of his more religious partners. But there was no denying the success of his methods. New Lanark prospered and expanded, and Owen became a very rich man. By 1820, he was a hero to many in Britain, and his name was becoming known overseas as well. As many as two thousand visitors a year came to see the New Lanark mill and village; among them were the anti-slavery campaigner William Wilberforce, the future US president John Quincy Adams and the Russian Grand Duke Nikolai, afterwards Tsar Nicholas I. Economists and philosophers including Jeremy Bentham, James Mill and Thomas Robert Malthus were also among the visitors, and Bentham was so impressed that he bought a one-sixth partnership in the business.

Initially, Owen tried to persuade other industrialists to follow his lead, arguing that they needed to treat their human employees with at least as much care as their factory machines. A few followed his lead, but most turned a deaf ear. Owen became increasingly disillusioned with the system of which he himself was a part, and in his *Observations on the Effect of the Manufacturing System* (1815) stated his belief that managers who managed solely for pecuniary gain were destructive of the happiness of the nation and of society. He began considering how to propagate the New Lanark model more directly, and became involved with various other communities who attempted to work on his model, even giving financial support to some. Unfortunately, many of these communities were run by visionary utopians or downright cranks, and most failed. Most famously, Owen tried to establish a community of his own in the USA at New Harmony, Indiana, but gave up after finding it impossible to persuade the community to stick to his principles. The venture not only cost him a great deal of money, but also New Lanark itself; in 1825 during his absence in America, a cabal of his partners led by William Allen stripped him of his powers as managing partner. Owen later sold his shares and withdrew from the company altogether.

Retiring from business, Owen devoted himself to social causes. Realising that many mill-owners would never see that proper treatment of their workers was not only good for society but good for themselves, he decided that the workers would need to organise in order to press for their rights. In 1833–34 he helped to establish the Grand National Consolidated Trades Union, with half a million members. This organisation did not last long, but it did give rise to later organised labour bodies such as the Trades Union Congress in Britain. Owen also supported the cooperative movement, which he saw as embodying many of his principles of communal working, solidarity and improving prosperity and living conditions for all. Here, Owen the atheist found willing allies among the churches, particularly the dissenting faiths. By 1830 the cooperative movement numbered more than 300 societies throughout the UK and had spread to continental Europe. Owen was quick to perceive the opportunities the movement offered for worker management, which he believed would give workers still more control over their lives and greater prosperity.

Owen's influence has been widespread. In the UK, he became the archetypical social capitalist, a man who showed how a successful business could be an ethically sound one: Titus Salt, George and Edward Cadbury, Benjamin Seebohm Rowntree and William Lever all knew of his ideas, and the model villages at Saltaire, Bourneville and Port Sunlight owe a great deal to New Lanark. In the mid-twentieth century there was renewed interest in his personnel management methods, and the consultants and business historians Lyndall Urwick and Edward Brech described him as one of the founders of modern management.

Comparison is sometimes made between Owen and one of the founders of modern communism, Friedrich Engels. Inheriting ownership of a Manchester mill from his father, Engels was at one and the same time Karl Marx's chief collaborator in the development of a theory of communism, and a successful businessman with considerable personal wealth, two sisters as his mistresses and membership of the local fox hunt. Engels's argument, however, was a pragmatic one: the workers' revolution would one day overthrow the capitalist system, but that day had not yet come, and so in the meantime he had a responsibility to his employees and their families to run an efficient business and keep them in work (the mistresses and the fox-hunting presumably showing that even socialists were allowed personal recreation). Owen took a different view. To him, running a successful business and the egalitarian principles of socialism were not incompatible or mutually exclusive. Rather, business was necessary to create prosperity, while a socialist system was indispensable to its just distribution.

Donnachie (2000), author of the best recent biography of Owen, says that his thinking was often woolly at best; as an economist he was second rate, and he was so impressed by the potential shown in New Lanark and some of the other successful communities with which he was associated that he believed this potential stemmed entirely from the character of the people who lived and worked there. He failed to understand that a large portion of the success of these communities was due to himself, to his vision and leadership and, above all, to his ability to manage people.

## Analysis

Questions you might wish to consider include:

- Owen believed that socialism and business were not incompatible. Was he right?

- Why did not more business leaders follow Owen's methods of management and put them into practice?
- Would his methods work if put into practice today?

## Sources

Cole, G.D.H. (1930) *The Life of Robert Owen*, London: Macmillan.
Donkin, Richard (2001) *Blood, Sweat and Tears*, London: Texere.
Donnachie, Ian (2000) *Robert Owen*, East Linton: Tuckwell Press.
Owen, Robert (1812) *A Statement Regarding the New Lanark Establishment*, Edinburgh: n.p.
Owen, Robert (1815) *Observations on the Effect of the Manufacturing System*, London: n.p.
Pollard, Sidney (1965) *The Genesis of Modern Management*, London: Edward Arnold.
Urwick, Lyndall and Brech, E.F.L. (1949) *The Making of Scientific Management*, vol. 2, *Management in British Industry*, London: Management Publications Trust.

## Notes

1 This is not entirely uncontroversial. There is an ongoing debate, lasting from the 1920s to the present day, as to whether administrators and managers are the same thing, and in some American firms there remains a divide between executives and managers, with the latter term being used for lower-status line managers. However, it does not do to get hung up on semantics. From this point on, we are less concerned with what the person is called, and more with what they do. It seems clear that administrators and executives also manage, whatever else they might do.

2 This of course bypasses the point that owner-managers are themselves by definition managers, and much of what this book has to say describes their actions too. It has been theorised that owner-managers and professional managers have different behaviours and motivations, an issue we discuss in later chapters.

3 Today we are unaccustomed to thinking of landed estates as businesses, but they most certainly are. Agriculture accounted for about 70 per cent of GDP in most pre-modern societies, and the very large estates such as those of the monasteries were among the largest business enterprises of the time.

4 Alfred D. Chandler, Jr, *The Visible Hand: The Dynamics of Industrial Capitalism*, Cambridge, MA: Harvard University Press, 1977.

5 An earlier series of experiments had been carried out by Western Electric itself from 1924–28; the Harvard team only became involved in the latter year.

6 This remains a somewhat controversial subject, and the Hudson's Bay Company has frequently been accused of this practice. Some Company agents undoubtedly did give alcohol to the native Americans, but this was not company policy, and the practice was suppressed whenever it was discovered by senior managers.

7 Montréal, like the rest of French Canada, was now in British hands, having been conquered in 1761.

8 This territory included the modern North West Territories and Yukon Territory and the provinces of Manitoba, Saskatchewan and Alberta; British Columbia had become a crown colony in 1858, and part of Canada shortly after confederation in 1867.

# 2 Organisation

---

**Learning objectives**

This chapter is intended to help readers do the following:

1 understand how and why various forms of organisation have emerged;
2 understand some of the key drivers of organisational form and structure;
3 understand better why organisations evolve as they do.

Structure arises as soon as people begin to do something together.
    –Thomas North Whitehead, *Leadership in a Free Society*

Organization is older than history, for the earliest documents, such as the code of Hammurabi, show evidence of many generations of systematized social life. The real pioneers are the unknown pioneers of the stone age, and the system-makers of the bronze age. Long ago, almost every conceivable experiment with organization was made. The records of history tell us of large units and small ones, of great and slight differentiation of functions, of extreme divisions and extreme concentrations of authority, of mild and severe sanctions, of appeal to system and appeal to passion, of trust in numbers and trust in leadership. Of the vast variety of units of organization through which human intelligence has worked, and through human purpose has been achieved, or thwarted, the greater part has passed away.
    –Edward D. Jones, 'Military History and the
    Science of Administration'

## 2.1 Introduction

One of the things that fascinated early thinkers and writers on management was the human propensity to organise. This was, or seemed to be, a universal feature of human civilisation. Everywhere one looked, in business, government, the army, education, religion, science, art, one found organisations.

Over the years, scientists have proposed various reasons why we as a species are so dependent on organisation in order to get things done. Anthropologists remind us that we are descended from apes, which are themselves pack animals; on the plains of East Africa, our remotest ancestors banded together for safety and security and to hunt for food, and later in Egypt and Mesopotamia and the river valleys of ancient China and India they congregated in order to conduct agriculture and begin the working of tools. Sociologists and psychologists have suggested that we create and join organisations because we have a need to communicate and express ourselves, and a need also to validate ourselves by winning the respect of others, which in turn increases our own self-esteem. Some political scientists and historians have argued that organisations are created deliberately by some people who are in pursuit of power over others, and that they are a means of social dominance and control.

All of these ideas are summed up at least in part by the Egyptian philosopher and theologian Muhammad 'Abduh, who was active in the late nineteenth and early twentieth centuries. Noting that 'mankind has a natural propensity for community', 'Abduh remarked that what sets us apart from other community-building species like bees is our ability to think. Bees know instinctively how to build a hive and proceed to do so without questioning the reasons. People, on the other hand, tend to rationalise and look for other and different ways of doing things. People also face the struggle between the demands of the individual for freedom and the right to do things one's own way, and the demands of the community for conformity and the following of mutual rules. 'Abduh believed that those who can truly function without a community, such as hermits, are very rare. Most of us need community, and the path of wisdom consists in submitting ourselves to the community and following its rules. This, he said, is the true natural order of things.

---

### The importance of community

Man is of a species with natural common instincts, pursued within a society of many communities. Each individual, however, has something to do in maintaining the whole, while the community in turn has its role which none can dispense with for his growth and subsistence. There is in each person a feeling that he needs the other members of the community comprehensively as one whole – a fact which needs no lengthy argument, since the history of mankind attests it.

A sufficient proof that man always needs to live gregariously is the fact of speech. Only from the need for mutual understanding do we make sense of the tongue with its ready ability to put ideas into words and expressions. There would be no point in mutual comprehension between two or more people if they were free to dispense with one another.

There can, then, be no doubt of this need of the individual for the community. The more the demands of the individual's existence increase, the more his need grows for the contributions of others. This need intensifies and serves to explain the progression from family to tribe and on to nation and mankind as a whole. Our time gives unmistakable evidence of how this involvement through need can extend into the entire human race.

–Muhammad 'Abduh, *Risalat al-Tawhid*

---

So it seems fairly clear that, for whatever reason, there is a basic human need for organisation, and that extends of course to the business world. What is curious is that until very recently there was no concept of 'business organisation' *per se*. Businesses had organisations, of course, but they borrowed their organisational forms from other organisations existing elsewhere in society and adapted them for business purposes. Even the most recent and up-to-date organisational forms like networks, matrix organisations and virtual organisations often have their origins elsewhere. The influence of this borrowing and adaptation can still be seen in the organisational forms we use today.

### 2.2 Forms of organisation and their adaptation to business uses

Pre-modern society produced five basic forms or types of organisation: *familial organisations, bureaucracies, military organisations, religious organisations* and *communal organisations*, all of which were at some point adapted for business use. It should be noted that businessmen and businesswomen did not necessarily adapt from just one of these forms; there was a certain amount of cross-pollination, and it is not uncommon to find hybrids exhibiting features of two or more forms.

### 2.2.1 Family organisations

The oldest business organisations for which records exist were founded by families or family groups. In the majority of cases they also managed the business, as in the case of the Assyrian trader Pusu-ken, his wife Lamassi and their sons whom we saw in Chapter 1. In other cases, like the holders of great landed estates in medieval England, the owners exercised a broad managerial oversight but employed salaried managers to manage parts of their estate.

We are accustomed to think of 'family businesses' as being businesses owned and/or managed by people linked by ties of blood or marriage. But the Roman word *familia*, from which our word 'family' is derived, also had a broader meaning. It could also refer to a household, including the head of the family, his wife and children and other relations, and their dependents, including servants, employees and slaves. In ancient Greece and Rome, all members of such a household were linked by a common bond. In medieval England the word *famulus* again referred to a household of people, not specifically a family. The head of the household is responsible for the well-being of all those below him – or very rarely, her – in the household, while the other members owe the head of the household a duty of obedience.

A very similar description of family roles is found in the ancient Chinese writings of Confucius and his disciples. Confucius gave a pyramidal view of family/household hierarchy based on age and seniority. The head of the household was always the eldest male; the next generation owed him a duty of obedience, while the generation below owed obedience to the generation above, and so on down the line. But again, the notion of reciprocity was important. In exchange for obedience, the head of the household had what we would now call a duty of care to its junior members.

The first family businesses worked in just such a way. The head of the family was also the head of the business, and other members of the family occupied subordinate positions, often based on their own seniority and rank within the family rather than merit. When the organisation grew beyond the family, there was a tendency to ensure that family members occupied the most important positions where a high level of trust was required. Family businesses continue to be organied in much the same way today (see for example the description of Chinese family businesses in Chen 1995).

The study of family businesses in earlier times and modern-day analysis of them (Gersick *et al.* 1997; Fleming 2000; Ward 2004; Kets de Vries *et al.* 2007; Colli and Rose 2007) suggests that they had many of the same strengths and weaknesses then that they do now. Strengths include flexibility and adaptability, a reliance on trust rather than formally defined relationships, a strong sense of purpose as far as family unity is concerned, and a tendency to be more caring of members of the family and their interests (and if we use the concept of *familia*, this means all employees, not just those related to the owner). These strong traits are one reason why the family business model continues to be the most widely used business model in the world.

There are, however, also weaknesses, and these include first and foremost the tendency of members to put the interests of the family ahead of the interests of the business. Thus decisions are sometimes taken which, while maximising the wealth of family members, are not actually in the best interests of the business itself. This means family businesses can sometimes be conservative when it comes to investing in new things or ideas, as family members prefer to take out money for their own use. The second key weakness is succession. Lack of children and the ending of the genetic line often brings family businesses to an end; this happened to the English wool dealer Sir John Pulteney, whose very large business ended with his death; today, the Hilton hotel corporation faces a similar dilemma. An even more common problem occurs when children have no interest in taking on the burdens of the business and choose other careers, a problem which is particularly acute in British farming in the early twenty-first century, for example. In the case of the Medici Bank (see Case Study 1A), later generations of the family evinced little interest in the business and hired incompetent managers to run it for them, leading to the ultimate failure of the bank.

A third set of problems occurs when there are disputes between family members, either about the conduct of the business or other, personal matters. This destroys the unity of the business and can lead to factional infighting, loss of focus and even the collapse of the business itself. Disputes within the family often hampered the efficient management of the Du Pont company (see case study 2A). Finally, family businesses often do not keep detailed records – there are exceptions, but in general most of what we know about family businesses comes from what other people say about them, rather than what they say about themselves – and there is a tendency to rely on memory rather than written records. This is not necessarily a weakness in itself, but often leads family businesses to rely on tradition and a set way of doing things that impedes or even negates their inherent flexibility.

These and other problems mean that, both today and historically, few family businesses grow to achieve great size, and many close after just one or two generations of ownership (again there are exceptions, such as the Zildjian firm of musical instrument makers which has been owned and managed by the same family since 1623). Paradoxically, despite their being the most common business type, family businesses are one of the least studied and we know least about their internal workings and dynamics of any of the five types considered here. Their lack of record keeping means that most family businesses simply disappear off the radar screen when they are dissolved or go bankrupt. The family businesses about which we know most – the Medici Bank, the Fuggers of Augsburg, Arkwright, Wedgwood, Rothschild, J.P. Morgan, Mitsubishi, Toyota, Fiat, Hutchison Whampoa – are those that rose to considerable size, at which point they begin to lose some of the characteristics of family businesses and often pass out of family ownership altogether, as in the case of Wedgwood and Mitsubishi.

Despite its weaknesses, the family business model persists, and has influenced other models too. Among the influences of the family model which became more widespread we can include:

1    The notion that the head of the business is responsible for his or her employees.

2    The notion of reciprocal relationships, of obedience in exchange for a duty of care, became widespread in business philosophy in the nineteenth century. Business leaders like Robert Owen, George and Edward Cadbury of Cadbury Brothers, John Patterson of National Cash Register, the Yorkshire textiles manufacturer Titus Salt and others adopted a paternalistic approach, assuming responsibility for the welfare of their employees and their families to the extent of providing benefits such as health care, education and housing. Today 'paternalism' is something of a dirty word, but the notion that companies owe their employees something more than a wage or salary remains widespread. 'We treat our staff like family' remains a common mantra.

3    The sense of identification with the community within which the business operates. Families also have reciprocal relationships with other families, be they families within a tribe of aboriginal peoples or families of merchant bankers in medieval Florence. These relationships also entail a certain amount of social responsibility and require the family to cooperate as well as compete with others around it. This sense of identification with the community is not unique to the family – some religions organisations exhibit this also (see below). But the idea of businesses as micro-societies within a larger society is largely inherited from the family model.

### 2.2.2 Bureaucracies

The first bureaucracies appeared in what we would now call the public sector, and evolved in societies where there was (a) a large population generating economic surpluses and (b) a strong central government. These bureaucracies were the tools by which sovereigns managed their lands and peoples. The bureaucracies of Egypt and Assyria had begun to evolve by about 2000 BC, that of China perhaps a little later, while the northern Indian kingdom of Chandragupta in the fourth century BC had a bureaucracy that almost certainly evolved from earlier models; by the second century BC a bureaucracy was beginning to emerge in Rome.

---

### Duties of the Vizier

*Duties of the Vizier* was probably written during the second half of the reign of the Pharaoh Ahmose (*c.*1539-1514 BC). Four copies of the text have been discovered, all in the tombs of high officials, suggesting that it might have been required reading. The text sets out the duties of the important royal official known as the *t3ty*, a title usually translated as 'vizier'. It is divided into nineteen short sections, each of which defines some aspect of the vizier's managerial role. These in turn can be classed into three groups: (1) those relating to the management of the royal household itself, the *pr-nsw*; (2) those relating to the command and control of the centralized civil administration; and (3) a more general category concerning powers delegated to the vizier by the pharaoh. Procedures are laid down for internal communication (daily reports were required from key departments), security, the appointment and management of key subordinate personnel, and operational control over the key departments of the civil service. Mention is also made of the vizier's own department, the *h3 n t3ty*, consisting of support staff who helped him to carry out these functions. The overall picture describes an authoritarian, top-down but minutely detailed system of management and administration.

(van den Boorn 1988)

---

Quite when bureaucracy began to be adopted as a business model is not clear, but the most important influence seems to have been in companies which had strong connections to the state. The chartered companies founded by Britain and other European countries in the sixteenth and seventeenth centuries to engage in exploration and overseas trade are examples. The Hudson's Bay Company and British and Dutch East India Companies all replicated governmental organisations. For example, they had separate departments to deal with different functions, all reporting to 'head office', the governor and court of directors in London or Amsterdam. They had strongly defined managerial roles, and placed a great deal of importance on control. France, Prussia, Russia, Sweden and other countries also founded similar chartered companies, all with very similar forms of organisation. Earlier, the Medici Bank had instituted a divisional structure in order to organise its various business activities, and it is possible that this too was derived from the civil administration of Florence, in which the Medici played an important role.

'Bureaucracy' today has become something of a synonym for any large, cumbersome, overly complex and inefficient organisation. But not all bureaucracies were inefficient. Egypt's bureaucracy built the pyramids and monuments of the Valley of the Kings; it also maintained the complex irrigation system along the banks of the Nile river that ensured Egypt's population was fed. The bureaucracy of China during the reign of Emperor Qin Shi Huangdi in the third century BC built the Great Wall and the Grand Canal and brought harmony and efficiency to the administration of the country. In England in the late twelfth century, a series of administrative reforms led by the treasurer, Richard FitzNeal (or FitzNigel) gave the country a small but highly efficient bureaucracy which in turn reformed the finance and legal systems and made England one of the most efficiently administered countries in the world. England's bureaucracy and centralised administration meant that for several hundred years the country could 'punch above its weight' in military and diplomatic terms. FitzNeal's book the *Diologus de Scaccario* (Course of the Exchequer) was described by Livingstone (2001: 302) as 'a mixture of personnel manual, description of the jobs of each member of the Exchequer staff, and procedural guide' (see also Richardson and Sayles 1963; Clanchy 1993).

Corporate bureaucracies could be equally efficient. The Hudson's Bay Company ran a very large dispersed business with a small number of employees: around 300 traders in 1800, plus boatmen, servants and other support staff. The late Peter Drucker remarked admiringly that the British East India Company administered India with a staff of a few thousand while the modern-day Indian government requires a civil service of twenty million (Drucker 1989).[1]

The Bank of England, which likewise had strong government connections and was structured as a bureaucracy, helped to transform the state finances of England. The example of the Bank of England and the Bank of Scotland was later copied by other British banks such as Coutts, Gibbs, Barings and Martins in the nineteenth century as they began to move away from the family model (see for example Healey 1992; Mathew 1981). By the early twentieth century nearly all British and European banks had adopted bureaucratic structures and American banks were following their lead.

Bureaucracies had, and still have, a number of strengths. They are very good at focusing resources and efforts on defined tasks, which makes for efficiency. They offer people well-defined roles and procedures: everyone understands, or should understand, what is required of them and what their goals are. This can reduce personal uncertainty and provide reassurance that one is doing the right thing. Bureaucracies also offer a sense of permanence and stability. Successful bureaucracies can last for hundreds of years; the Chinese civil service lasted as an institution for more than two thousand years, surviving many changes of government and occupation by foreign powers. They are far less fragile than family businesses and less likely to be torn apart by internal feuds and pressures.

Against this are a number of weaknesses. Bureaucracies tend to emphasise control rather than coordination; even in well-run bureaucracies, management tends to be something that is done *to* people rather than *with* people. Internal communication is often poor, as the departmental structure of bureaucracies erects barriers and walls; people from different departments do not talk to each other, and often do not even know of each others' existence.

Unlike some other forms of organisation such as religious and military organisations, bureaucracies exist to carry out the will of someone else, the sovereign or chief executive, and this means they often lack a purpose of their own. For this reason bureaucracies are sometimes called 'soulless'. Lack of purpose can in turn lead to organisational drift, of the kind famously described by C. Northcote Parkinson (1958) who commented that the primary purpose of a bureaucracy is to replicate itself. His dictum known as Parkinson's Law, that in a bureaucracy, 'work expands to fill the time available', is often quoted. Lack of purpose can also lead to corruption, not just financial but moral corruption of the kind described with great wit and cynicism by the seventeenth-century French courtier Eustache de Refuge in his book *Treatise on the Court*. This is essentially a bureaucratic survival guide, telling people how to claw their way to the top of a bureaucracy and, once there, how to maintain their position against jealous rivals who will try to undermine their authority. Too often, the quest for personal power and position obscures the ends towards which the bureaucracy is supposed to be working.

---

**Treatise on the Court: the role of bad men**

As I have said, there are always many more bad men than good at court, and they are typically useful to bad princes in one of two ways. The first is that they flatter their princes and carry out their evil plans, their obedience enhanced by the approval and applause they receive for their behaviour. The second is that they enable princes to seem better than they are in contrast to the bad men who surround them, which makes some princes feel more secure in their company. It is customary for anyone who knows that he is prone to a particular vice to try to appear less bad by setting himself in company with others who are even worse. This is the origin of a common courtly trick: *choosing an unpromising successor so that one's own actions can appear better and more illustrious by comparison.*

(Refuge 2008: 57; italics added)

---

The final weakness of bureaucracy is that its vertical structure and emphasis on control can lead to a mechanistic organisation in which people slavishly follow orders from the top and do not exercise initiative. The principal early ideologue of Chinese bureaucracy, Han Feizi, believed this should be encouraged. In his philosophy, the sole purpose of bureaucrats was to obey orders relayed from the emperor and his ministers. Those who failed, those who deviated from those orders or in any way stepped outside the limits of their authority, should be punished by death. Han Feizi believed that this fear of punishment would compel people to be obedient. In fact, as we now know, it is more likely to demotivate them and render them less efficient. But the principle of ruling by fear and force continues to be found in some bureaucracies (Watson 1964).

The strengths and weaknesses of bureaucracy were highlighted when its modern version, the multi-divisional form or M-form corporation, was introduced in the early twentieth century. Developed by Pierre du Pont, first at gunpowder makers Du Pont and then at General Motors, the M-form consisted of a number of semi-independent operating divisions, all reporting directly to a small and streamlined firm headquarters (see Case Study 2A). As originally designed, the M-form had all the virtues of bureaucracy: it allowed for concentration of resources, established roles and responsibilities, and gave structure to businesses which had hitherto been rather chaotic in nature. The model was widely admired and adopted, first in the USA and later in Europe and Japan. Alfred Chandler (1962, 1977) assigns the M-form an important role in the growth and development of American big business in the twentieth century.

But as history also shows, not every company reaped the benefits of the M-form. By the end of the 1970s, as Peters and Waterman described in their book *In Search of Excellence* (1982), many of these big corporate bureaucracies had become moribund and top-heavy, with too many middle managers and too many specialists, none of whom were creating value. They had lost their purpose and lost their way. At large corporations like IBM, conformity was the norm and people were actively discouraged from using their initiative. IBM senior managers were largely unaware of this. Among other things, they cultivated the myth of 'wild geese', maverick individualists within the corporation who were not afraid to try new things and news ideas and infused the corporation with their dynamism and spirit. In fact those individuals had been squeezed out of IBM long ago. 'What happens to wild geese?' ran the bitter joke told by IBM managers. 'They get shot.'

### 2.2.3 Military organisations

Like bureaucracies, the first organised standing armies were developed in cultures with large populations generating economic surpluses that enabled soldiers to serve full time and be equipped and trained, and where there was a strong central control. Other countries had to be content with 'militias', ordinary citizens who could be conscripted for varying lengths of time to serve their city-state or country. Although these militias had an organisation of sorts, it was temporary and often rather loose in structure.

Standing armies, on the other hand, were structured into permanent units, the legions of the Roman army being a particularly important example. The legions were divided into subordinate units, cohorts and centuries, each composed of fighting soldiers. But they also had their own teams of support staff: armourers, cooks, transport drivers and porters, clerks and administrative staff, etc. A Roman legion was not just a fighting force, it was also an administrative unit (Vegetius 1993). What we know about the armies of ancient China suggests that they were organised in much the same way (Wee *et al.* 1991).

After the collapse of the Roman Empire, permanent standing armies largely disappeared from Europe and the Middle East.[2] Most countries relied on temporary levies of soldiers who were called up for short periods of time. By the seventeenth century, however, standing armies had begun to re-appear. During the Thirty Years War (1618–48), the Austrian commander Count Wallenstein raised his own army and also built a network of support services, including textile mills to make his soldiers' uniforms, gunpowder works, iron mines and smelters and armouries to make swords, muskets and cannon (Wedgwood 1938). National governments began following suit and by the eighteenth century standing armies – and navies – were the norm in Europe.

Military organisations still lagged behind bureaucracy, however, and it was not until the mid-nineteenth century that the increasingly complex nature of warfare began forcing armies and navies to adopt more sophisticated forms of organisation. The Royal Navy became the first organisation in the world to adopt a matrix organisation. The navy was divided into squadrons, each consisting of a number of ships (typically between four and twelve). Each ship contained a number of specialists such as gunners and engineers. At the same time, each squadron also had a chief gunnery officer and a chief engineering officer, who were responsible for all matters relating to gunnery and engineering in that squadron. The subordinate officers in these branches on each ship were responsible to both their own ship's captain and the squadron chief officer in charge of their specialist branch.

Ex-army and navy officers came to be seen as good candidates for business management posts. Thanks in part to the extensive use of railways made by the Union Army in the American Civil War (1861–65), many army officers were recruited by the railway companies in the expansion that followed the war. Their ability to manage complex systems and precise timetables was particularly valued.

But the event that really caused business thinkers and practitioners to examine military models of organisation more closely was the Franco-Prussian War (1870–71). When war broke out, pundits predicted a French victory. The French army was large, very well equipped and had recent combat experience.

The Dreyse needle-guns of the German infantry had only half the effective range of the French Chassepot rifles. The German army had almost no combat experience apart from a brief war with Austria a few years earlier. The German commander, Field-Marshal Helmuth von Moltke, had never led troops on a battlefield when he took over the top job in 1858. But events confounded the pundits. The German army swept into France, defeated two French armies and captured French emperor Napoleon III and then moved rapidly on to surround Paris. Within six weeks of war being declared, the Prussian cavalry were watering their horses in the fountains at the Palace of Versailles (Howard 1961; see also Moltke 1992).

Early management theorists, like the American engineer Harrington Emerson (who witnessed some of these events while a student in Munich), pored over accounts of the war trying to discover the secret of Moltke's success. The Prussians succeeded, Emerson and others declared, not because they were superior soldiers but because they had a superior system. Emerson referred to the Prussian military organisation as the 'line and staff' system. The army consisted of two parts. First there was the 'line', the infantry and cavalry and artillery, well drilled and trained to follow orders precisely. Second, there was the 'staff', small and flexible and highly competent, which issued the orders and guided the line so that its members were in the right place at the right time.

Emerson (1909, 1913) argued that this division of line and staff was in fact the hallmark of *every* successful organisation, and counselled businesses to adopt it. He insisted that this was a natural ordering of human affairs. The line he compared to a person's arms and feet, which make the body capable of locomotion, handle tools and carry out work; the staff he compared to the head, which provided guidance and direction to the rest of the human body. He also argued – there are overtones of Darwinian theory and eugenics in his thought here – that some people were naturally more intelligent and therefore better fit to be members of the staff, while others were better suited for manual labour and so should be part of the line.

---

### Emerson's Twelve Principles of Efficiency

1 clearly defined ideals: the organization must know what its goals are, what it stands for, and its relationship with society.
2 common sense: the organization must be practical in its methods and outlook.
3 competent counsel: the organization should seek wise advice, turning to external experts if it lacks the necessary staff expertise.
4 discipline: not so much top-down discipline as internal discipline and self-discipline, with workers conforming willingly and readily to the systems in place.

5 the fair deal: workers should be treated fairly at all times, to encourage their participation in the efficiency movement.
6 reliable, immediate and adequate records: measurement over time is important in determining if efficiency has been achieved.
7 despatching: workflow must be scheduled in such a way that processes move smoothly.
8 standards and schedules: the establishment of these is, as discussed above, fundamental to the achievement of efficiency.
9 standardized conditions: workplace conditions should be standardized according to natural scientific precepts, and should evolve as new knowledge becomes available.
10 standardized operations: likewise, operations should follow scientific principles, particularly in terms of planning and work methods.
11 written instructions: all standards should be recorded in the form of written instructions to workers and foremen, which detail not only the standards themselves but the methods of compliance.
12 efficiency reward: if workers achieve efficiency, then they should be duly rewarded.

(Emerson 1913)

This sounds like a fairly deadening sort of organisation to be part of, if you were a member of the line, but Emerson argued very strongly against coercion. Workers cannot be forced to work, he said; they had to be motivated and willing to work, and had to be fairly treated by their employers and by the staff. Again there is a sense of reciprocal obligations, which is also found in the military; in the best armies, at any rate, officers are responsible for their men and look after their welfare, and spend much of their time making sure that their men are motivated and prepared. Emerson's line and staff principle of organisation was taken up by other consultants and widely adopted in America, especially after the First World War. Luther Gulick, who founded the National Institute for Public Administration in New York in 1921 and was responsible for training several generations of public administrators and civil servants in America, was an admirer of the line and staff system and included it in NIPA's teaching curriculum (Fitch 1997; Gulick 1948).

Emerson also noted another reason why the Prussian army was victorious, namely that it had a strong sense of purpose and its soldiers were focused on their tasks. This notion of singleness of purpose also appears in many writings on military science, from the ancient Chinese works of Sunzi down to the present. Certainly the notion of purpose and focus on goals was and is one of the great strengths of a professional army (or navy or air force). Other strengths include discipline and training, meaning that armies are – or should be – constantly ready and prepared for the tasks that might lie ahead.

Well-managed armies also are very good at concentrating resources where and when they are needed. Finally, good armies and navies and air forces also have a strong sense of cohesion and identity, sometimes known by the French term *esprit de corps*.

This is something which is much prized by the military, and much time and effort is spent on building *esprit de corps*. This is why many army regiments, for example, have traditions which might seem arcane and absurd to outsiders, but are full of symbolic meaning and are taken very seriously by members of the regiment. Every year on 30 April, the officers of the French Foreign Legion gather to hold a formal dinner and celebrate the Battle of Camerone in 1863. This might seem odd, as the Foreign Legion company that fought the battle was annihilated by its Mexican opponents. But the Legion remembers not the defeat, but the courage and honour of the men who fought and upheld the traditions of their regiment.

Traditions and identity and unity of purpose can be powerful strengths for any organisation, but military organisations suffer from weaknesses too. The foremost of these is a tendency to rigidity and inflexibility. Armies can become very set in their ways, and find it hard to adapt to new thinking. Paradoxically, armies which have been successful are most likely to fall prey to this tendency; those that have suffered a setback or reverse are more likely to be open to new ideas. Secondly, the internal discipline that all armies have is not conducive to the questioning of authority. In his book *On the Psychology of Military Incompetence*, Norman Dixon notes that one of the purposes of military organisation is 'to control aggression so that it is projected only upon legitimate targets while keeping other outlets blocked' (1976: 174). Dixon also believes that this tight control over people also discourages imagination and creative thinking.[3]

Finally, and following on from the need for discipline and control, military organisations tend to subordinate the needs of the individual to those of the group. The Foreign Legion soldiers at Camerone were asked to sacrifice their own lives, rather as King Leonidas of Sparta and his hoplites did at Thermopylae two millennia earlier. Again, some business thinkers and business leaders thought this is also a laudable quality in the commercial world. Luther Gulick believed that workers in businesses should think like soldiers in this respect:

> The prestige of top management must be maintained even though this involves a certain shifting of responsibility for individual failures and successes to subordinate organizations and men. This is cruel to those organizations and men, but it preserves the integrity of total management in a world of trial and error. In administration, as in baseball, it is the batting average that counts, not the occasional strikeout. Top management must be held accountable for the total record, not each segment.
>
> (Gulick 1948: 32)

But unless business organisations have the same *esprit de corps* and traditions of self-sacrifice that military organisations do, employees and junior managers are unlikely to be happy about taking the blame in order to 'preserve the integrity of total management'.

It is relatively rare to find examples where the military model of organisation has been adopted wholesale. Some public services, like the police and fire services for example, do have organisations that strongly resemble military organisations, in part because they were often founded by and recruited from ex-military personnel. In general, however, other organisations borrowed elements from the military model rather than adopting it wholesale. The multi-divisional form or M-form corporation, while structured as a bureaucracy, also borrowed the line and staff principle. Again, with many ex-soldiers and sailors in high positions – Robert Wood, president of Sears Roebuck & Co., was formerly an army general; James Mooney, head of the international division of General Motors, had been an artillery officer – this influence is not surprising. This led in time to a strong hierarchical division between management and workers, the divide between so-called 'blue collar' and 'white collar' employees. The use of hierarchical ranks, whereby each person's title indicates their level of authority, is also a borrowing from the military. And when we look at organisation charts even today, we are looking at something descended from the organisation charts developed by the military in the nineteenth century.

And finally, many businesses have tried to emulate the military's sense of *esprit de corps* by encouraging employees to develop a stronger sense of identity. The uniforms worn by postal workers, railway and airline employees, tellers in some banks, hotel porters and employees in fast-food restaurants, for example, are a direct descendant of military uniforms; until the military model became influential, no one ever thought of putting employees into uniforms. The railways copied the military, and other firms copied the railways.[4]

Today, the study of military organisation by businesses and business academics has become somewhat unfashionable (and also, military organisations themselves have changed greatly since Moltke's time, and have become much more flexible and less hierarchical). Many people are uncomfortable with associating business, an essentially peaceful activity, with war and violence. This is understandable. But the influence of military science over business did happen, and affected things other than organisation (see Chapter 3 on strategy, for example). We cannot turn back the clock, and an understanding of the influence of military thinking is necessary if we are to understand business organisations more generally. It is worth noting too that the study of military organisations is not necessarily the same thing as the study of war. As Black (2007) points out, Japan's armed forces, among the largest in the world, have not fired a shot in anger since 1945. In sum, much as we might dislike war, it is impossible to avoid the influence that military thought and practice have had on modern business.

## Some strengths and weaknesses of organisational forms

This list is based on both studies of organisational forms in the past, and current literature; it is not intended to be exhaustive, but rather to serve as a basis for discussion.

### Family/household

*Strengths*

- flexibility and adaptability
- reliance on trust rather than formal relationships
- strong sense of purpose so long as family unity is preserved
- tendency to be caring and inclusive

*Weaknesses*

- tendency to conservatism
- uncertain succession
- tendency to fracture when family unity is lost
- reliance on memory rather than record

### Bureaucracy

*Strengths*

- focus resources and efforts on set tasks
- well-defined roles and procedures reduce uncertainty
- sense of permanence and stability

*Weaknesses*

- emphasis on control rather than coordination
- poor internal communication
- lack of purpose
- mechanistic and slavish to authority

### Military organisation

*Strengths*

- strong sense of purpose
- discipline and training
- concentration of resources
- sense of identity and *esprit de corps*

*Weaknesses*

- tendency to rigidity and inflexibility
- discourages the questioning of authority
- subordinates individuals to the group

### 2.2.4 Religious organisations

Like bureaucracy and the military, religious organisations appeared in societies with large populations generating economic surpluses and with relatively stable political organisations. Religious cults became established in certain places and as they grew popular, portions of the economic surplus could be diverted to the feeding of priests and priestesses, who in turn offered spiritual benefits to believers. Unlike military and bureaucratic organisations, however, many temples engaged in business and trade from a very early date. In some cases land or houses were donated to a temple, the rents from which went towards its upkeep. In another case the temple purchased land – or houses, or trading ships – and engaged in commerce as an additional way of generating revenue.

This latter practice was particularly common in the Ancient Near East, where in some cases the temples also controlled the civil government (theocracies) and had control over the army and bureaucracy. Moore and Lewis (2000) describe the activities of the temple of Melqart in the Phoenician port of Tyre (the modern Sur in southern Lebanon). Its high priest, Itobaal, ruled the city as well as the temple, and directed a network of commercial ventures stretching across Syria, Anatolia and the eastern Mediterranean. Tyrian merchants ventured further afield still; they are believed to have traded for tin (one the constituents of bronze) in England, and one Tyrian adventurer may even have circumnavigated Africa (see also Silver 1995).

The early Christian church had comparatively little in the way of organisation, but this began to change after the legitimation of Christianity by the Roman Emperor Constantine I in 313. As the church began to grow and acquire property and more followers, it found that a structure was necessary; not only to manage its growing portfolio of assets, but also to ensure unity of belief and counter the various heretical and dissenting movements which threatened that unity.

Lack of structure in the monastic movement in particular led one man to do something about it. A little after 500 AD, the monk Benedict of Nursia was invited to become abbot of a small community of monks to the east of Rome. The monks had taken vows of poverty, chastity and obedience, and Benedict understood the latter to mean that they would be obedient to his orders and direction. But when he tried to enforce his authority over the monks, some of the monks rebelled, even attempting to poison him. Abandoning this monastery, Benedict founded a new one at Monte Cassino to the southeast of Rome. As part of the foundation, he wrote a rule which all members of the monastery would be required to live by. In addition to their vows, the monks also had to accept Benedict's authority. In fact, this was an extremely popular move. Not only did many monks come to join Benedict, including some from other monasteries, but other institutions quickly began adopting the Rule of St Benedict, as it was later known. By 600 AD there were several hundred monasteries following the Rule, and more joined the movement in later centuries (Cary-Elwes 1988).

What Benedict had created was in effect an early form of procedures manual. The Rule is divided into 73 precepts, which lay out the duties of the monks. It begins with a statement of goals: monks are to dedicate their work to the glory of God. The remainder of the Rule specifies how those goals should be carried out, setting not only times of work, meals, prayer and rest but also the hierarchy and chain of command within each monastery. Supreme over all was the abbot, who directed the affairs of each monastery; below him were subordinate officers such as the treasurer, and then came the general body or 'chapter' of monks. The monks were to obey the orders of the abbot, but those orders had to be explained in chapter, and monks could voice their own views about the abbot's decisions. The Rule did what any good procedures manual should do: it began with purpose and goals, then set out the steps required to reach them and the duties of all involved.

So popular was the Rule that it was widely imitated by other organisations. Later monastic organisations such as the Cistercians (see Case Study 2B) developed their own Rules along the same model. So did military bodies like the Knights Templar, who drew their Rule almost word for word from the Cistercians. Civic bodies developed rules too: hospitals, universities, merchant guilds and parish confraternities all had Rules, sometimes greatly simplified but all following the same structure as the Rule of St Benedict, setting out purpose and goals, then duties and procedures and responsibilities of members. Even the articles of association of chartered companies, such as the Hudson's Bay Company, show the influence of the Rule of St Benedict, and modern articles of association are descended directly from this. The general influence of the Rule on modern management practice and thought has been alluded to by Kennedy (1999).

As well as influencing the organisational forms of many other institutions, businesses included, religious organisations continued to engage in business in their own right. The Cistercians, Benedictines and Knights Templar were all major landholders across Europe, and engaged in a number of commercial ventures. Many other smaller religious organisations engaged in agriculture and trade as well. Medieval monks were dedicated servants of God, but the more senior of them were also administrators and managers. Most seem to have seen little or no conflict between these roles.

Religious organisations have some of the same strengths as military organisations and bureaucracies (and, of course, share some features with both). A shared religious belief tends to result in both a strong sense of purpose and shared goals, and a strong common culture and identity shared by members of the organisation. This is true whether they identify themselves by faith (Christians, Muslims, Buddhists) or by group within a faith (Benedictines, Shaolin Buddhists, etc.). Most religious organisations – but not necessarily most religious faiths – also define roles for their members, sometimes reinforced by formal documents like the Benedictine Rule. Religious organisations also tend to be very long-lived, giving members a sense of permanence and stability.

Against this there are some weaknesses. Religious organisations can over time become rather exclusive and secretive, which leads to suspicion among outsiders and can also have a corrupting influence within the organisation itself; the Knights Templar and many monastic organisations suffered this fate. There is a tendency for members to be deferential to authority, and this may indeed be required by the organisation's rules; the Rule of St Benedict gives the abbot of each monastery complete authority over all its members, including the power to expel members for disobedience. And finally, although the sense of purpose is one of a religious organisation's greatest strengths, if that sense of purpose is lost then these organisations can be very vulnerable. Members who lack purpose may well leave in hopes of finding a new purpose elsewhere. This is what happened to the monastic orders, which declined drastically in numbers right across Europe from the fifteenth century onwards; most are now shadows of their former selves. In general, though there are exceptions, we can say that religious organisations, unlike bureaucracies, find it hard to perpetuate their own existence once their primary purpose has been lost.

### 2.2.5 Communal organisations

Truly communal organisations, in which all members share work and reward equally, are quite rare. They do exist, however – commonly cited examples in the literature include partnerships of lawyers and hippie communes – and there has been some influence on business organisations.

The reasons why such organisations have been rare are twofold. First, as we saw at the outset of this chapter, we all need some form of organisation, and most forms of organisation include structure and hierarchy. The need for these also seems to be innate in most of us. If we follow Emerson's – not uncontroversial – view that only about 20 per cent of us are capable of leading, then this presumes that the remaining 80 per cent are looking for a leader, if they have not already found one. These figures can be debated, but it is generally accepted (if sometimes rather reluctantly) in the leadership literature that not everyone has the potential to lead, at least not all the time. So, hierarchy is something we find it hard to do without, and on close examination even law firms and communes have a pecking order, even if only an informal one.

Partnerships have a long history in business, going right back to antiquity. Whether partnerships are truly a form of communal organisation is an open question. In cases where several people own shares in a business but none of them is involved in managing it, or where the partners appoint a managing partner and then step back, then the answer is probably no. In cases where a large number of partners are involved in the organisation, work for it and share in the rewards, then the answer is probably yes. There is of course a considerable grey area between the two.

Cooperatives are another form of community organisation. Cooperative businesses in which whole communities took a share have a long history in both Europe and Asia, but as with family businesses, few grew to a substantial size and few left much in the way of records, making it difficult to know much about them. From the nineteenth century, however, a number of cooperatives were developed, and some succeeded in growing to considerable size. By far the largest and most successful of these was the Mondragón cooperative established in the Basque region of Spain in 1956. Now the Mondragón Cooperatives Corporation, it is one of Spain's largest business entities and has operations in many countries (see Case Study 2D). As well as businesses founded on cooperative principles, some more conventional businesses turned to a model of worker ownership, the John Lewis retail group in Britain being an example. Apart from its ownership structure, however, John Lewis remains a fairly conventional corporation with a bureaucracy and hierarchy of management.

Truly communal businesses – managed and run jointly by the partners with all taking an equal share of the profits – have several strengths. They tend to be established by people with strong ideologies and beliefs, which permeate the organisation as a whole. This in turn leads to a strong set of shared values and a strong common identity and culture. The fact that all have a stake in the venture means that members are more likely to be willing to work for the common good. Finally, their guiding ideology is often shared by members of the society within which they are rooted, meaning that stakeholder relationships are often very strong. All these factors together have helped to make Mondragón a success.

Against this, communal businesses are even more vulnerable than family businesses to internal dissent. Lack of an acknowledged leader means that there is often no one to mediate in disputes. Disagreements, either personal or professional, can pull the organisation apart, and this indeed often happens in professional service firms that are structured as partnerships. Another problem is that lack of hierarchy can in turn lead to a lack of accountability and responsibility for the actions of either individuals or the group as a whole. There is no one who says, 'the buck stops here', which means that blame for mistakes gets passed while no one takes corrective action. Finally, the lack of hierarchy again means that communal organisations often find planning and control difficult to manage. There are steps that communal organisations can take to overcome these problems, but the fact remains that few manage to do so. In the case of Oneida (Case Study 2C), the strictly communal form of organisation was finally modified to include elements of conventional bureaucracy.

---

**Some strengths and weaknesses of organisational forms, cont'd**

**Religious organisation**

*Strengths*

- strong sense of purpose and shared goals
- strong common culture and identity
- clear role definition
- permanence and stability

*Weaknesses*

- exclusive membership, high barriers to entry
- excessively deferential to authority
- vulnerable if purpose is lost

**Communal**

*Strengths*

- strong sense of purpose and shared goals
- strong common culture and identity
- willingness of members to work for the common good
- often strongly rooted in society

*Weaknesses*

- vulnerable to internal dissent
- potential lack of accountability and responsibility
- difficulties with planning and control

---

Of course, along with all these organisational forms, there are also many other organisations that exhibit features of one or more forms. Examples of *hybrid* organisational forms might include hospitals, especially those run by religious or charitable foundations, which include elements of both religious organisation and bureaucracy; very large family-run businesses like those of East Asia, which combine elements of family business and bureaucracy; the Knights Templar, who combined religious and military organisation; and the later Oneida business which combined bureaucracy with communal organisation, as indeed Mondragón has come to do as well. These hybrids emerged for several reasons. Some were deliberately created in order to capitalise on the strengths of both types of organisation (and avoid the weaknesses). Others evolved over time, either changing organisational form as they grew and expanded, or as new generations of managers and staff introduced their own concepts of organisation (for example, former army officers introducing elements of military organisation into M-form bureaucracies).

## 2.3 Themes and influences

### 2.3.1 The pressures of size and scope

As we saw in Chapter 1, the increase in physical size of an organisation, and the increase in the geographical area across which it operates, both put pressures on the management of that organisation. They also put pressures on the structure of the organisation itself. A tight-knit family group or a community association may be the perfect form of organisation when the operation itself is small: a single workshop or retail outlet, a ship or other small transport business, etc. In the days when merchants carried their own goods and travelled from town to town looking for markets, it was possible for such organisations to exist in their pure forms.

But as soon as an economy grew to the point where large-scale and large-scope businesses could be supported, the inherent structural weaknesses of family organisations and community organisations began to make themselves felt. If the business was to grow, then its members had to adapt the features of other forms. It is no accident that the growth in influence of bureaucracy and religious organisations in the later Middle Ages took place just at a time when the business world was expanding rapidly and more large and medium-sized firms were emerging. The strong influence of military organisation in the late nineteenth and early twentieth century took place at another time of rapid growth in scale and scope.

In Chapter 1 we noted the emergence of two types of firm:

- large concentrated firms such as textile mills or steel mills, employing large numbers of people on a single site, and
- large dispersed firms employing people spread over a large geographical distance, such as long-distance trading companies or railways,

as well of course as firms which had features of both, such as the Carnegie Corporation with its multiple steel mills and mines at different sites, or the large oil companies with their oil wells, tanker routes and refineries. These businesses required increasingly complex forms to support them. Some firms adopted bureaucratic structures and strong central control and hierarchy, drawing inspiration from bureaucratic and military models, even if they remained family owned. Among these we can identify firms like the chartered companies, the Hudson's Bay Company, East India Companies and so on, and also the afore-mentioned steel and oil businesses, which were very tightly controlled from the top by men like Alfred Krupp, Andrew Carnegie and

John D. Rockefeller. Daniel Guggenheim's copper mining corporation ASARCO is another example, as is William Lever's Unilever (Case Study 3A) and the food producer H.J. Heinz (Case Study 5A). These firms are sometimes known as *unitary firms* because of their single point of authority and control.

The other solution, particularly popular with firms managing over distance was to disperse control to a greater or lesser extent. The Medici Bank used the common Italian system of interlocking partnerships, and in theory subordinate employees reported to all the partners of the governing group, the *maggiori*. Cosimo dei Medici was in practice the dominant partner, but we can safely assume that this was due to his own personality. In another, rather smaller Italian firm of the time, the cloth-making and trading business of Francesco Datini based in Prato, just outside Florence, a much more democratic system was in place. Datini and his partners took decisions collectively, and partners who did not like the direction the business was taking but had been outvoted by their colleagues could leave when the two- or three-year partnership agreement expired (Origo 1957). These types of firms are variously known as *confederacies*, *associations* or *networks*. In all three cases the meaning is much the same: the owners and senior managers, at least, were drawn together by common interests and the idea of mutual gain, and operated in a collaborative manner, and subordinates were allowed a greater degree of autonomy. Coordination, rather than control, was the guiding management principle.

Throughout recorded history, these organisations have always been in a minority. Centrally controlled unitary organisations have been the norm, in business as well as the rest of society. Why is this? Some, like Emerson, have hypothesised that the natural order of things is for some people to dominate and others to be dominated, and that provided relations between them are fair and equitable, both parties will be happy with the bargain. Others, like the French sociologist Michel Foucault, have seen organisations primarily as instruments of control. The foundation of any organisation is power, he said, and the nature of any organisation depends on who controls power and how they exercise it over others; indeed, the primary purpose of organisations is to do exactly that, exercise control over others. Foucault likened organisations – of all kinds, not just businesses – to prisons in the way that they define roles and set expectations, and ruthlessly weed out all that is perceived to be abnormal or deviant (Foucault 1966, 1975). Earlier we saw the example of IBM in the 1970s and 1980s where all the 'wild geese', the creative and original thinkers, had been driven out of the organisation because they refused to conform to its norms.

And therein lies the source of the first major problem for the organisers of business. Foucault is right to the extent that *all* forms of organisation tend to punish and exclude those who it is felt do not belong, and this again has been true since the beginnings. Soldiers who do not obey orders are court-martialled, even shot; and as we saw, Han Feizi believed that bureaucrats who did not obey orders to the letter should also be executed. Few bureaucracies go so far, but they punish deviation in other ways. Monks who failed to acknowledge the authority of the abbot were expelled from their monasteries. Family members who rebel against parental authority are often shunned. Communes, even those that claim to be free-thinking, also have a way of disposing of dissidents.

---

### The road to Damascus

In the 1890s Herbert Casson, a firebrand Methodist preacher turned socialist agitator in Boston, campaigned long and hard to keep the USA out of conflict with Spain. When the Spanish-American war broke out, Casson retreated to a socialist commune where he hoped to find spiritual peace among like-minded fellows. He lasted just six months; the commune was in chaos, no work was being done, members were fighting amongst themselves, and when Casson attempted to remonstrate with them they turned on him instead. Disillusioned, Casson went to Ohio and visited the National Cash Register factory run by John Patterson, an autocrat but one who treated his workers fairly and looked after their welfare. Finding more social harmony at NCR than he had at the commune, Casson became a convert to capitalism, going on to become a management consultant and widely published author.

(Casson 1931)

---

### 2.3.2  The search for an ideal form

The second major problem, which relates in part to the first, is that none of these organisational forms is perfectly suited to the needs of all businesses. Until about 1880, the idea of 'organisation science' had never been considered, except in a limited fashion by the military when trying to work out the ideal way of organising troops and ships for battle. *All* business organisations were based on the forms above, or hybrid versions of them. It was only in the twentieth century, after several thousand years of activity by businesses large and small, that theorists and practitioners began searching for an ideal type of organisation. The multi-divisional form, or M-form, discussed above was the first serious attempt at developing such a form. But as discussed, it is effectively another hybrid, a combination of the bureaucratic and military forms. It has the strengths of both, but it also has their weaknesses. It was not necessarily, as some of its proponents claimed, the best way of organising a business.

What of some of the other forms that have been developed for business use in recent years? Much attention has been paid to business networks, the technically enabled version of the old Italian system of interlocking partnerships. Business networks can be powerful, but they share some of the weaknesses of those other, less formally controlled organisational types, the family and the commune. The matrix organisation, pioneered by the Royal Navy, came into use in business in the 1950s, Polaroid being an early adopter. It too has met with mixed success; some organisations have been able to implement it and make it work well, others have failed – including Polaroid (see McElheny 1998). Or there is the virtual organisation, which also makes its appearance in prototype form in the nineteenth century; Reuter's was arguably the first virtual organisation (see Case Study 7A). As Warner and Witzel (2004) point out, the virtual form of organisation is potentially a very powerful one, but it is not suitable for all firms; it is hard to imagine a virtual steel mill or a virtual oil refinery, for instance.

The problem, as is now well recognised by theorists, is that there is no one ideal form of organisation, certainly not one that will stand the test of time. Chandler (1962), for all his admiration of the M-form, still argued that 'structure follows strategy', while Miles and Snow (1978) concluded that the guiding principle should be 'organizational fitness for purpose'. Organisations, they believed, varied in three key dimensions: goals, technology and structure. The first concerns the organisation's destination, the second two the means by which it gets there. They conclude that the variables are generated within organisations as part of an 'adaptive process' whereby each organisation struggles to come to terms with its environment in a unique way, and develops characteristics accordingly. The reason why such responses differ is in turn due to the complexities of the environment, which they see as 'not a homogeneous entity but rather … a complex combination of factors such as product and market conditions, industry conditions and practices, governmental regulations, and relations with financial and raw material suppliers. Each of these factors tends to influence the organization in its own unique way' (Miles and Snow 1978: 18) This is in effect a more sophisticated version of the Chandler argument which recognises that strategy and structure impact on each other; there is not a one-way relationship.

Others such as Schein (1985, 1999) and Argyris (1964, 2000; Argyris and Schön 1974) have focused less on organisational forms and more on the dynamic nature of organisation and more on the processes that go on inside them, taking a psychological rather than an organisational approach. Yet here too it is very difficult to make generalisations. Researchers on the role played by culture in organisations (Hofstede 1980, 1991; Hampden-Turner and Trompenaars 1993; Kluckhohn and Strodtbeck 1961; Child 1981; Adler 1997) make it clear that what is 'right' for one organisational culture can easily be 'wrong' for another.

And it is probably right that we stop looking for unitary answers. In his *Images of Organization* (1986), Gareth Morgan argues that no single way of looking at organisations can ever provide all the answers. Indeed, by taking just one perspective, we are in danger of oversimplifying organisations. We need to recognise, he says, that organisations are complex and paradoxical things. If we accept Miles and Snow's concept of organisational fitness for purpose, then the answer to any problem of organisation – or reorganisation – is to determine what qualities will be required to make an organisation fit for purpose. And that determination in turn requires that the organisation be viewed from many different angles and different perspectives, through different lenses.

---

**Complexity and paradox**

Organizations are complex and paradoxical phenomena that can be understood in many different ways. Many of our taken-for-granted ideas about organizations are metaphorical, even though we may not recognize them as such. For example, we frequently talk about organizations *as if* they were machines designed to achieve predetermined goals and objectives, and which should operate smoothly and efficiently. And as a result of this kind of thinking, we often attempt to organize and manage them in a mechanistic way, forcing their human qualities into a background role. By using different metaphors to understand the complex and paradoxical character of organizational life, we are able manage and design organizations in ways that we may not have thought possible before.

(Morgan 1986: 13)

---

### 2.3.3   Drivers of organisational form

In this context, the historical perspective may help us to understand organisations a little more clearly. It does not provide all the answers, not by any means, but it may provide some.

One thing which is suggested by the study of organisations and organisational forms as they have emerged – and disappeared – in the past is that organisational forms in business evolve out of need. That is, they are not simply 'dreamed up' as ideal types of organisation, but evolve under pressure. Family organisations were the first business organisational form, not only because the family was the earliest social unit, but because 'keeping it in the family' offered a number of benefits, including control and security. Familial bonds of trust were important in business environments with high levels of risk; they continue to be so today, as studies of business cultures in the developing world remind us. Likewise bureaucracies emerged as political and later business organisations grew too large for a single family or extended family to control. Bureaucracies loyal to the sovereign or business leader offered a way of extending personal control, at least so long as the bureaucrats remained loyal and motivated.

Military organisations are structured as they are because in order to be effective they need to be disciplined and purposeful and obedient to authority;

especially, they need to be trained not to take authority into their own hands (even if throughout history they quite frequently have done so). Religious organisations again took the form they did because of the need for obedience to higher authority and for greater focus on purpose and role. Both were designed to be 'efficient', each in their own way. Both were influential in business because they promised something that business leaders felt they lacked: discipline, control and a strong guiding purpose and identity. Discipline and control in turn promised security and efficiency, two things that every business needs. And finally, military and religious organisations offered real and obvious value to society in the form of physical security from attack and spiritual guidance.

Only communal organisations did not always evolve in response to external pressures. These, as noted, were often ideologically driven and evolved as a response to the desires of their members to propagate their own ideas and to put those ideas into practice. Yet even this is not universal. The Quakers, for example, who were heavily persecuted by the authorities in seventeenth-century Britain, tended to congregate amongst themselves. Out of their communities came notable businesses in later centuries, companies like Cadbury and Rowntree which, if not communal in structure nonetheless showed strong communal influences in the ways they were managed and in their guiding philosophies.

What drives organisational form and structure? What determines how a business will organise itself? Historical study of business organisations suggests that there are six key drivers, six things that businesses seek to have, or to do, that determine how they exist and function. These six are *security, governance, efficiency, flexibility*, a sense of *purpose* and the provision of *value*. These can be observed, to a greater or lesser extent, across every business organisation – certainly every successful business organisation that has ever been created throughout recorded history, no matter what organisational form it chose.

*Security*  When we speak of security we mean two things: (1) the physical security of the assets of the business, and their protection against theft, loss and harm; and (2) the security of the organisation itself. In order to achieve its purpose a business has to survive, and to do so, it needs a stable organisation that can withstand shocks. It must also be structured in such a way that dissent by some members of the organisation does not cause it to collapse. Members of the organisation, in order to be most effective, also need to feel secure in belonging to it and must know what their roles are. This may require rules and procedures manuals, strong bonds of trust, or more often a mixture of both. These also help to ensure the security of the business assets, for example by imposing sanctions for theft or pilfering.

*Governance*  Related to this, there is a need for the organisation to be governed. We are using this word rather than 'control' to account for Follett's (1924) view that true control is a myth and what we describe as control is actually a form of coordination. Whatever word or meaning we describe, the organisation must be capable of being managed. That is, the leaders of the business need to know what is going on around them, what other members of the organisation are doing, whether they are working to meet the organisation's goals and, if so, what progress they are making. Other managers and employees likewise need to know what is expected of them and what they are meant to do.

*Efficiency*   No organisation can be successful for long if it is not efficient, and most inefficient organisations do not survive, though some inefficient bureaucracies manage to perpetuate themselves and last longer than they theoretically ought. One of the decisions that senior managers must make, either when founding a new organisation or restructuring an old one, is what kind of organisation is best fit for purpose. Historical evidence supports Miles and Snow's (1978) contention that there is a balance to be struck between goals, technology and organisational structure. Further, as businesses grow and evolve and their purpose changes, their structure must change too. Hence successful family businesses often take on aspects of bureaucratic form once they reach a size where they are too large to be governed directly by the owning family. The purpose of this is to ensure the organisation remains efficient.

*Flexibility*   Similarly, organisations must be adaptable and able to change, and if necessary to re-configure themselves in order to adapt to the times. When the era of the fur trade came to an end, the Hudson's Bay Company moved to become a chain retailer, and designed a new business structure for itself to support this new purpose. It needs to be remembered that structure is the servant of organisation, not its master. There is no virtue in being a family business or an M-form or a virtual organisation just for its own sake. History suggests that all business organisations that are successful over the long term have a built-in capacity to adapt and change.

*Sense of purpose*   Successful organisations require not just goals, but a commitment by members to reaching those goals and an understanding not just of *what* they doing, but *why* they are doing it. This does not necessarily have to be any high or noble ideal, nor does it require the kind of self-sacrifice described by Gulick. If employees are able to match their own self-interest to the interests of the organisation, that is very often sufficient. But an organisation that has no purpose, whose members turn up to work only because they can think of nothing else to do, is vulnerable, particularly if it faces strong competition. Bureaucracies seem to be able to perpetuate themselves without a sense of purpose, at least for a time, but for family businesses and communal businesses especially, a sense of shared purpose is the vital element that keeps them together.

*Provision of value*   Finally, a successful business organisation must provide value, certainly to customers and shareholders, and we would argue to employees as well (this links to the sense of purpose described above). It could be argued that this is not something to do with organisation; provision of value to customers is a matter for marketing, while value to employees is a matter for human resources. This is in part true, and we will discuss this in more detail in later chapters. But the provision of value is also a function of organisation. It is something that the organisation must be capable of doing. How well it does so depends on how well it responds to the other five drivers.

We can see these drivers at work helping to shape the organisations discussed in the case studies at the end of this chapter, but let us summarise their impact briefly by looking at a business discussed in Chapter 1, the Medici Bank. How did the organisation respond to the six drivers:

- security: the Medici Bank used a system of interlocking partnerships each governed by contract at the top level, while lower level employees were engaged by their division managers or factors, also on contracts. The partnership system protected assets.
- governance: the partnership system was supplemented by the use of trained accountants who reported directly to the managing partner. These added a bureaucratic element to the system, but enabled the flow of vital financial information. Division managers and overseas factors also reported directly to the managing partner. The post of general manager was created to coordinate the various parts of the organisation.
- efficiency: the organisation was constantly restructured by dissolving some partnerships and adding new ones, expanding operations where opportunities arose. Non-performing or low-performing business activities could be easily terminated or sold.
- flexibility: the familial nature of ownership and top management ensured flexibility in terms of strategic thinking and response, while the partnership system ensured that new ventures could be established quickly.
- sense of purpose: the guiding ideology of the business was that of the family. Key members of staff were induced to share that ideology through partnerships.
- provision of value: that the banking, trading and manufacturing divisions were providing value could be measured by the balance sheets of each division. Success in this regard being configured to respond to the previous five drivers: in other words, security of assets, good management control and coordination, an efficient and flexible business and a strong sense of purpose combined to ensure that the Medici Bank could and did provide value to its customers.

The importance of these drivers is also demonstrated by what happens when the organisation fails to respond to them. In the case of the Medici Bank, the first failure was the loss of sense of purpose. The grandsons of Cosimo dei Medici retained ownership but did not get involved in management, and handed over responsibility to incompetent general managers. This in turn led to a loss of efficiency and failures of governance. The firm then failed to provide value and began to make financial losses, which endangered its security; it collapsed in 1494.

## 2.4 Questions and discussions: the best organisation, or the right organisation?

At the start of this chapter we quoted Thomas North Whitehead, who was one of the researches involved in the Hawthorne experiments (see Chapter 1) as saying that 'structure arises as soon as people begin to do something together'. If we accept this, then we accept that any business which employs more than one person requires a structure. The next decision is, what should that structure be?

As we have seen, through the course of history businesses have answered this question in different ways, choosing different organisational forms according to need and circumstance, but always in response to drivers such as the six mentioned above. It can be debated as to whether this is a full and complete list of organisational drivers: most probably it is not, but these are the six that study of past organisations suggests are in common with all successful businesses over time. Once again, history does not provide all the answers, just a few of them.

Historical analysis supports the current view that there is no 'one best way' of organising, but that each business must choose an organisational form that best suits its needs and the needs of its members. But historical analysis also suggests that no organisational form will last for long. Professor Edward Jones (1912) argued that organisational forms tend to disappear once the need for them is past, suggesting that organisations are engaged in a constant series of responses to pressures from outside, and sometimes from inside too. This brings up the tricky subject of organisational change, a subject on which much has been written, but with no definite conclusions reached as to the best way of changing an organisation.

We know, in fact, that organisational change is very difficult, one of the most difficult things a business does, and that very many organisations fail at the task of restructuring (see for example Jarrett 2009). Again there are many reasons for this, but we suggest that one reason is that newly restructured organisations often do not respond fully, or at all, to some of the six drivers. For example, in seeking to make themselves more efficient, companies might actually harm their existing sense of purpose, de-motivating employees and leading them to question their core assumptions about the company; this happened during the business process re-engineering movement in the 1990s, for example. The same thing happens sometimes when companies try to become more flexible. Changes to ensure better governance and control can hamper efficiency and flexibility, and so on.

What is the answer to the problem? It seems likely that, whether we see an organisation as a precision-engineered machine, a biological organism, or any of the other metaphors for organisation in use today, the answer depends on balance. An organisation must not just pick one of the six drivers and seek for excellence in that area. It needs to respond to all of them. This is what Handy (1976, 1994) refers to as the paradox of organisations: they need to be controlled *and* flexible, structured *and* purposeful, efficient *and* providers of value. And Handy, like many other writers before and since, argues that in the end whether an organisation can do these things depends on its members: who they are, their skills, how they relate to each other and how they interact.

Any successful organisation, business or otherwise, is always greater than the sum of its parts. And organisation itself is an inert concept, a chart on the wall or a PowerPoint slide on a screen. Nothing happens in an organisation but that which people make happen. People are the animating force, but even so, a group of people in an organisation are nothing more than a club – or a mob – unless they have something to guide them and direct their energies. That force is called strategy, and we will turn our attention to it in the next chapter.

---

### Takeaway exercise

Look at your own business or organisation, or any business or other organisation for which you have worked in the past. On a sheet of paper, describe briefly – 2 to 3 paragraphs at most – how it is structured and what you think the key features of its organisation are, using the themes and ideas discussed in this chapter. Next, write down in summary form what you think the organisation's purpose is. What are its goals? What is this organisation actually for? Finally, compare the two. Is the structure of the organisation suited to its purpose? Are there things about the structure that are perhaps hindering it from meeting its purpose? And how would you close the gap? What things would you change about the organisation in order to make it better fit for purpose?

This is an exercise which can be done more than once. If you are still working with the same organisation, consider repeating the exercise after six months or a year and seeing if anything has changed.

---

## Case Study 2A

### *Pierre du Pont and the M-form business*

Between 1902 and 1924, Pierre du Pont took over and restructured two failing companies, the gunpowder maker E.I. Du Pont de Nemours and the car maker General Motors. In each case, he put into place a management system and organisation that turned the firms into competitive giants that dominated their respective industries. He also played a leading role in the development of the multi-divisional form (M-form) of business organisation which became one of the most important organisational forms in twentieth-century America, and was also adopted in other parts of the world, notably Britain and continental Europe. The M-form is believed by some business historians to be a major factor in America's industrial domination during the twentieth century.

Du Pont was the great-grandson of the French chemist Eleuthére du Pont de Nemours, who emigrated from France to America in 1802 and founded a gunpowder works near Wilmington, Delaware. The firm was moderately prosperous, remaining in family hands through the nineteenth century; the owners, the du Pont family, also managed the business. Lammot du Pont, Pierre du Pont's father, became president of the firm in 1872, serving until his death in 1884. Other members of the family took over its management, but the company became increasingly less prosperous and lacked direction and focus. Its several gunpowder works in different parts of the eastern USA were each managed by a works manager who reported directly to the board; all cost and other decisions were made by the board and there was little if any attempt at innovation. By 1900 these older managers were seriously considering selling the company to one of its competitors.

Pierre du Pont studied chemistry at the Massachusetts Institute of Technology and then joined his cousin, Coleman du Pont, as an owner-manager at the Johnson and Lorain Steel Company, which had works in Pennsylvania and Ohio. The two younger du Ponts had progressive ideas, and were among the first American managers to adopt the methods of scientific management being pioneered by the engineer Frederick Winslow Taylor. They eventually sold their company to United States Steel at a considerable profit. Pierre du Pont then spent several years managing the street car system in Dallas, Texas.

In 1902, Pierre and Coleman du Pont with another cousin, Alfred, bought out the older generation of owner-managers and set about restructuring the firm. Pierre du Pont became treasurer, with specific responsibility for reorganising the company's finances. He also helped to establish an executive management committee, to which the board of directors agreed to devolve responsibility for the day-to-day running of the company. He himself was one of the leading members of that committee, and designed the subsequent reorganisation that transformed Du Pont from a moribund gunpowder maker to a world leader. By 1904, the Du Pont company controlled 70 per cent of the American gunpowder and explosives market, and was exporting aggressively.

One of the first elements of this reorganisation was the establishment of a professional management team, no longer relying on owner-managers as before. From Johnson and Lorain the du Ponts recruited several experienced managers, including Arthur Moxham and John J. Raskob. Other managers such as J. Amory Haskill came from companies which Du Pont acquired in the course of its expansion. One of the most important areas to be transformed was the treasury office, whose staff grew from twelve to over one hundred in the course of two years. Du Pont hired able accountants such as Russell Denham and Donaldson Brown, and encouraged them be innovative and find new and better ways of managing and measuring cash flow and costs.

Professional management and better control had enabled rapid expansion, mostly through acquisition. The much larger Du Pont company needed a new organisation to cope with that expansion. The old system of works managers all reporting directly to head office was confusing and chaotic, with too many people sending too many reports and too few people to read them. Du Pont's response was the divisional structure. He created three operating divisions, pulling together all the company's interests in black powder, smokeless powder and dynamite, respectively, combining all the plants and production facilities for each under a single management.

To support these came three further divisions: sales, purchasing and head-quarters. The sales division merged all the company's sales offices and brought them under central control, at the same time establishing a more professional sales organisation with full-time sales staff and regular training courses to help the staff learn more about the products they were selling. The company's product line required a broad range of raw material inputs, some-times of small or irregular quantities; the purchasing division was established to speed up and standardise raw material supplies. It accomplished this in the main through vertical integration up the supply chain, setting up its own transport and raw materials production facilities, notably its own nitrate mines in Chile.

Perhaps most radical of all was the establishment, as an adjunct to the headquarters, of a development department under the management of Arthur Moxham. This department had three operating units, which rather confusingly were also referred to as 'divisions'. The experimental division, based near Wilmington, supervised research laboratories, investigating in particular problems of process control. The raw materials division worked closely with purchasing, monitoring raw materials quality and investigating new sources. Finally, the competitive division worked with the sales depart-ment to provide information on competitors and customers. Moxham reported to and was a member of the executive committee, which also included the three du Ponts and the head of each operating division. This committee was the primary instrument through which the activities of the divisions were coordinated.

In his own financial office, Pierre du Pont concentrated initially on improving the quality of financial information. Scientific methods of cost analysis and control were introduced, and the company developed a sophisti-cated and highly accurate system of cost accounting. Turning his attention to accounting for profits, Pierre du Pont rejected the standard definition of earnings as a percentage of sales (or alternatively, of costs) and instead chose to focus on the rate of return on capital invested. By 1910 there was a further advance as Donaldson Brown worked out a method of relating turnover (the value of sales divided by total investment) and then relating this to earnings as a percentage of sales. These methods, pioneered at Du Pont, remain standard accounting tools in business today.

In 1909, Pierre du Pont took over as president of the company and guided its rapid expansion during the First World War. Production of smokeless powder rose from 8 million tons in 1913 to 455 million tons in 1917. Thanks to its efficient organisation and accounting systems, the company coped almost effortlessly with the rapid expansion. Only at the top was there trouble; a dispute developed between Coleman du Pont and the rest of the family over share dealings, and Pierre sided with Coleman. He resigned the presidency in 1919. By this time, however, he had a new interest. He had taken a substantial stake in the troubled car maker General Motors, and since 1915 had been a member of its board. In 1920, the affairs of GM reached a crisis.

General Motors had been founded in 1908 by William C. Durant, a former carriage and wagon maker, with the intention of challenging Henry Ford for leadership of the car market. General Motors became his vehicle for acquiring other small companies, initially Buick and later Cadillac, Oldsmobile and Chevrolet. Although GM made a profit of $10 million in 1909 and the Chevrolet in particular became a success, coming second only to the Model T Ford in terms of units sold, Durant made a series of bad investments and acquisitions. He lost control of the company from 1910–15, returning as president in 1916 with the financial backing of Pierre du Pont. Durant continued to expand and diversify, but his headstrong temperament and risky approach to management led to clashes with du Pont, who was much more methodical and systematic. By 1920, Buick and Chevrolet were making money but the rest of the group was not. Durant was removed from the board, and du Pont took over as president.

Du Pont's first task was to overhaul the management structure of General Motors and bring in the requisite talent at the top. He used his Du Pont corporate connections well in this regard, bringing Walter Carpenter, one of the star managers of the Du Pont development department, onto the board of directors; he also brought in a Briton, Harry McGowan, chairman of Nobel Explosives in the UK and a friend and long-time business associate of du Pont. John Raskob, Donaldson Brown and Amery Haskell came across from du Pont to strengthen the management team. He also headhunted talent from inside and outside the group, promoting promising managers. Alfred P. Sloan, president of United Motors, GM's wholly-owned parts supplier, knew the Du Pont system and had instituted similar systems of accounting and control at his own company. Sloan was now brought onto the board and made du Pont's *de facto* deputy. Plucked from near obscurity was James D. Mooney, then head of a small GM subsidiary called Remy Electrics, who by 1922 had been promoted to run all of GM's operations outside the USA.

Another important recruit was William Knudsen, Henry Ford's talented head of production who left in 1921 after a quarrel with his employer. Du Pont immediately hired him and put him in charge of production of the Chevrolet, where he worked closely with Sloan. The development and marketing of Chevrolet as a higher quality alternative to the Model T was a central feature of GM's competitive strategy over the next decade; in 1922 the Model T was outselling the Chevrolet by five to one, but by 1929 Chevrolet had overtaken its rival and forced the Model T off the market.

Stage two of the restructuring was to implement on a group-wide basis the kinds of accounting and control systems du Pont had developed and which Sloan had implemented. Stage three was an overhaul of the structure of the company. Pierre du Pont and Sloan felt that General Motors was too large for the kind of functional divisions that had worked so well at Du Pont. Instead, they opted for a 'business unit' approach with the core operating divisions defined by the markets they served. They developed what Sloan later called the price pyramid, with one division at the top, Cadillac, selling small numbers of highly priced cars, and another at the bottom, Chevrolet, selling a large volume of inexpensive cars; the other three divisions were positioned in between at various levels on the pyramid. Parts and accessories continued to function as autonomous divisions. Virtually all responsibility for day-to-day operations and line management was handed over to the divisions, and the enlarged and strengthened headquarters took over responsibility for planning, forecasting, assessments of quality and progress towards goals, measuring managerial effectiveness and a variety of other staff functions.

At the top of the organisation was a four-man executive committee consisting of du Pont himself, Sloan, Raskob and Haskell, who handled all major operating decisions that did not require board approval. By 1924 this committee had been expanded to ten, but it remained small enough and flexible enough to allow the corporation to respond quickly to events and sort out problems as they arose. Sloan would later add further interdepartmental and interdivisional committees to ensure better and more frequent communications between the line and staff and between the different operating units.

Du Pont stepped down as president of General Motors in 1924, feeling that the business would be better handled by Sloan, whose career and background were in the automobile business and who had a better feel for the market. He remained chairman of the board until 1929 and a director for many years thereafter. He died in 1954. Sloan went on to make General Motors into the world's largest corporation.

The multi-divisional form of business appeared in two somewhat different forms at Du Pont and General Motors. It was quickly copied by other companies and spread to other industries. By the middle of the twentieth century, probably the majority of American large corporations were structured in this way. During the post-war reconstruction of Europe and Japan, the M-form was one of a battery of American management methods exported overseas, where it quickly took hold, becoming the dominant form of large business organisation for most of the twentieth century.

## Analysis

Some of the questions you might want to consider in connection with this case include:

- Why did du Pont choose the divisional structure? What other options were open to him? Would they have worked?
- How important was the divisional structure in the success of Du Pont and General Motors? What other factors might have been at work?
- What are the strengths and weaknesses of the multi-divisional structure?
- How important was professional management in the success of both companies?
- Business historians think that the M-form contributed to America's global business dominance. Does this seem likely?

## Sources

Chandler, A.D.(1962) *Strategy and Structure: Chapters in the History of American Industrial Enterprise*, Cambridge, MA: MIT Press.

Chandler, A.D. (1977) *The Visible Hand: The Managerial Revolution in American Business*, Cambridge, MA: Harvard University Press.

Chandler, A.D. and Salsbury, S.(1971) *Pierre S. du Pont and the Making of the Modern Corporation*, New York: Harper & Row.

Drucker, P. (1946) *Concept of the Corporation*, New York: The John Day Company.

Langworth, R.M. and Norbye, J.P. (1986) *The Complete History of General Motors, 1908–1986*, New York: Beekman House.

Sloan, A.P. (1964) *My Years With General Motors*, New York: Doubleday.

## Case Study 2B

### *The Cistercian Order*

The Cistercian Order was founded in 1098 at the abbey of Cîteaux in Burgundy, in what is today eastern France. Its first members were a group of twenty-one Benedictine monks, who believed that the Benedictine Order had become too much focused on worldly matters and was in danger of losing its purpose as a religious order dedicated to contemplation and prayer.[5] They wished to return to the original principles set out by St Benedict, which they felt that the rest of the Benedictine Order was in danger of forgetting. Taking over a small tract of land, which had so far been unsettled as it was marshy and not suitable for agriculture, the monks built a monastery and then began draining the land and converting it into farmland. Attracted by the high ideals espoused by the monks of Cîteaux, more people came to join them, and in 1108 Cîteaux formally separated from the Benedictines and the Cistercian Order was founded as an independent religious organisation. A new rule was established, the *Carta Caritatis* (Charter of Charity) which defined the new Order's organisational structure.

By 1111 numbers at Cîteaux had grown to the point where a second monastery was established at La Ferté near Chalon-sur-Sâone in order to accommodate the increasing numbers. In 1113 a monk named Bernard from a minor noble family in Champagne arrived at Cîteaux and joined the monastery. Two years later he was sent to establish another monastery at Clairvaux with himself as abbot, and it is as Bernard of Clairvaux that he became known to history. In all, nine new monasteries were founded as 'daughter houses' of Cîteaux.

These daughter houses then went on to found monasteries of their own. Recruits flocked to join the new Order, some moving over from the Benedictines, others attracted by the piety and austerity of the Cistercians and seeking religious fulfilment. But although they accepted new members from the Benedictines, the Cistercians did not take over existing monasteries. All the houses they founded were new, and nearly all were on waste or unclaimed ground, usually heath land, forests or swamps. Here they would settle, build their monasteries and set about turning the ground into land that could be used for agriculture, and exploiting other resources as they found them too.

The movement quickly spread beyond France, with the first Cistercian monasteries established in England in 1128 and two large and famous foundations in Yorkshire, Rievaulx in 1131 and Fountains Abbey in 1132. By 1150 there were more than 300 Cistercian monasteries across Europe; by 1200, there were more than 500 establishments, and by 1400 there were over 750. Every country in Western Europe and most of Eastern Europe had large numbers of Cistercian houses; England alone had more than 80.

Together, these monasteries represented an immense enterprise. No one has yet taken a Europe-wide census of the Cistercian Order and its holdings, but the larger monasteries such as Fountains and Rievaulx in Yorkshire or Tintern on the Welsh borders could have as many as 500 monks and lay brothers (the latter were subordinate members of the organisation who did not take full monastic vows). Landholdings varied depending on the establishment and its location, but the largest houses in England owned as much as 40,000 acres each; and these were dwarfed by some of the huge Continental houses such as Leibus in eastern Germany, whose total landholdings were over 600,000 acres. The Order as a whole owned tens of millions of acres and at the height of its power in the fourteenth century included tens of thousands of monks and lay brothers.

The key to the rapid growth and success of the Cistercians lies in part in their organisation, at both macro and micro levels. As noted above, each of the original 'daughter houses' of Cîteaux founded new establishments and became in turn a 'founder house' with 'daughters' of its own. These 'daughters' in turn became 'founders', and so on. Each founder house remain responsible for its daughter houses after their foundation, effectively acting as a kind of parent and supervising their activities; each daughter house received a visit – usually quarterly or twice yearly, depending on distance between the two – from the abbot of the parent house to ensure that the rules of the Order were being kept and its affairs were in order. Because each founder house was also in its turn a daughter house, each supervising monastery was itself supervised, with reporting going on up through the organisation to the original four daughter houses and finally to Cîteaux.

This relationship was one of supervision and control only. The daughter houses paid no contributions to their founders; each was what we would now call a free-standing profit centre and could use its income as it liked, within the rules of the Order. This meant that daughter houses had a great deal of freedom. However, there was another device which ensured coordination across the Order. This was the General Chapter of the Order, a kind of annual general meeting held at Cîteaux every year. Every abbot in the Order was expected to attend the General Chapter, or to send a senior representative from his staff. In this way, the Abbot of Cîteaux was able to keep his finger on the pulse of the organisation.

In tandem with the *Carta Caritatis* was a second document, the *Institutiones*, or Rule of the Order. While the first set out the Order's structure, the second spelled out the duties and responsibilities of its members. The Rule combined the features of mission statement and procedures manual, explaining in exact detail not only what was to be done but why it was to be done. The daily lives of monks and lay brothers, business and commercial activities, styles of architecture to be used in monastery buildings, all were regulated and tied to the Order's primary purpose.

Organisation at the local level was treated just as carefully as the macro structure of the Order. As noted, Cistercian houses were always new foundations, usually on land which had not previously been cultivated or settled. Once land had been cleared or drained and put into production, each monastery established production units called 'granges'. Each grange was a self-contained unit, farming about 500–700 acres; if the monasteries were independent profit centres, then the granges can be regarded as production centres, each with its individual accounts and quotas. The Benedictines used a system of tenant farming, where land was parcelled into manors farmed by either free tenants or serfs, but the Cistercians preferred to work their landholdings directly, with monks and lay brothers supervising a paid labour force. On the larger monasteries, this paid labour force could run into the hundreds or even thousands of people, depending on the season and what large projects were under way.

The ideological leader of the early Cistercians was Bernard of Clairvaux, later St Bernard, who died in 1152 and is remembered as Europe's foremost theologian and preacher of his time. Among other things he wrote the rule for the newly founded Knights Templar, one of whose early leaders was a cousin of his. In the Cistercian Order, Bernard decided everything from the colour of the monks' and nuns' habits (white or grey, to distinguish them from the black-robed Benedictines) to the amount of sculpture and other decoration permitted in the Order's churches. The emphasis was on severity and austerity in the tradition of the founders at Cîteaux. Bernard ordained that all new monasteries were to be built on the exact pattern of Cîteaux, and it was said that a blind monk, if transported from one monastery to another, would be able to immediately find his way around, so similar were the layouts of each monastery.

In the early days of the Order, it was Bernard who had two critical insights which were instrumental in the Order's success. The first of these concerned the need for the Order to be independent. The Benedictine Order had operated under a system of patronage, whereby local lay landlords donated lands and money to the monasteries in exchange for a say in how they were run. Disagreements between abbot and patron could create difficulties in terms of administration and control. Bernard resolved that the Cistercians would not accept patronage. Each monastery would be responsible only to its founder house, and to no other authority. In other words, there was to be no divided command.

The second insight concerned the direction the Order should take. In the eleventh century in Western Europe there were still large tracts of unsettled land, usually covered in forest or swamp. Bernard reasoned that the Order could acquire these lands cheaply or as gifts from landowners only too happy to dispose of them, and could then improve these lands to the standards necessary for profitable farming. As noted above, this was the pattern of development which the Order followed over the succeeding centuries. Mountainous lands in eastern France, swamps in the Low Countries and Prussia, desolate moorlands in Yorkshire all became home to Cistercian abbeys. Their achievements were prodigious by any standard: at the monastery of Les Dunes in Flanders (modern Belgium) the monks and their hired workers drained and cleared 25,000 acres of land in a few years, turning a former swamp into one of the richest farms in the region.

Agriculture in the Middle Ages is often thought of as simple subsistence farming, with each household or monastery growing only what it needed for food. In fact by the year 1100, if not before, a sophisticated market economy was already operating all across Western Europe, with cash crops, wholesaling, long-distance trade, credit and most of the paraphernalia of a modern economy. The Cistercians, with their large landholdings and efficient organisation, became an important part of that economy. The grange system proved to be very well suited for this purpose. A monastery with 10,000 acres might have 20 granges, each of which could be set to producing a specific resource. Quotas were set to ensure not only subsistence for the monastery but also surpluses for revenue generation.

Nor was specialisation limited to the granges; in certain areas, entire monasteries turned to specialising in local produce. For example, some houses in Burgundy and the Mosel Valley of Germany specialised in wine production, and Cîteaux itself established the vineyard of Clos-Vougeot, which later became one of the most famous Burgundy vintages. Some monasteries in

Normandy specialised in fruit-growing. Other monasteries developed live-stock, with the large abbeys in Yorkshire rearing sheep and producing wool while some German houses specialised in horse-breeding. There were other, non-agricultural specialisms as well: fishing in Germany and at Tintern Abbey on the Welsh border, iron mining in Lancashire and eastern France, coal mining in Scotland and Bohemia, and banking at Savigny in France. There was considerable internal trade between these specialist houses within the Order.

All of this vast network of enterprises had to be managed, and Cistercian monks and nuns turned into managers. In monasteries with large populations and relatively small landholdings, junior monks and nuns might still labour in the fields; but there were not many of these. The monastery of Leibus, cited above, had 600,000 acres of lands and, at the very maximum, 500 monks and lay brothers. That would have meant each person being responsible for tilling 1,200 acres of land each year, a clear impossibility given the technology of the time. Instead, and much more commonly, monks and nuns became super-visors, assigned to a particular grange and overseeing the labour of hired workers. Above the level of the ordinary monks of the chapter, there were others such as the treasurer and his or her deputies, responsible for financial affairs. Cistercian nunneries had their own properties and granges, and though they sometimes used lay brothers or hired overseers to supervise work in the field, they still controlled their own financial affairs and managed the enterprise.

Contemporary recognition of the business and management skills of the Cistercians is easy to find. Abbots of Cistercian monasteries were widely known as able administrators, and were often seconded to national and local governments to head important commissions, oversee tax levies or special works projects, and so on. They also found broader employment within the Catholic Church; many served as bishops, and several were elected to the papacy, where they were usually known for their energy and ability. It is no exaggeration to say that the Cistercian Order profoundly influenced the development of modern state bureaucracy and, from thence, had an impact on the formation of business management techniques.

By now it will probably come as no surprise to find that the Cistercians were also at the forefront of technological innovation. Nearly every mon-astery had a watermill, and water power was used to power everything from grain mills and olive presses to trip-hammer forges for working iron. A group of monasteries in the Langres region of eastern France developed this last technology to a degree not seen before in Europe. Instead of a blacksmith forging hot iron by striking it manually with a hammer, a water wheel pro-pelled a system of gears which in turn controlled a mechanical trip hammer, or a whole series of them. In France and several parts of Eastern Europe, the Cistercians were the leading iron makers of the day. In areas where wool was produced, the Cistercians built water-powered fulling mills for making cloth. The historian of technology Jean Gimpel (1976: 47) describes the Cistercians as 'running the most modern factories in Europe', and assigns them a key role in the dissemination of new water-power technologies across Europe. In the eighteenth century when Richard Arkwright began the Industrial Revolution at Cromford in Derbyshire, his first mill used water power in very much the same way that the Cistercians had.

The Cistercian Order began to decline in the fifteenth century, as fewer people were inclined to join monastic orders and a general disillusionment with the Catholic Church began to set in. The English monasteries were closed by Henry VIII and their lands confiscated, and many of the German and Scandinavian monasteries closed after the Protestant reformation. More monasteries were destroyed during the French Revolution and the campaigns of Napoleon. Today there are around a hundred monasteries and nunneries of Cistercians and associated orders such as the Trappists scattered around the world, but landholdings are small and the Order has none of its old economic strength.

Bernard and his successors saw opportunities where others could see none. Pious and ascetic, he was not one of those who, like St Thomas Aquinas, believed that trade and commerce were natural and good. A theological conservative, Bernard looked down on merchants and traders, and would doubtless have been horrified at the extent to which the Order became involved in commerce after his death. But at the same time, he gave the Order a guiding vision and purpose that helped it to achieve astonishing things. He himself believed that a combination of imagination and action could achieve results beyond anything previously thought possible. 'You will find', he wrote to his brother monks, 'in the woods something you will never find in books. Stones and trees will teach you a lesson you never learned from your masters at school. Honey can be drawn from rock, and oil from the hardest stone.'

## Analysis

Some of the questions you might want to consider in connection with this case include:

- What were the key strengths of the Cistercian Order as described above? What weaknesses can be detected?
- What role did organisation and structure play in ensuring the success of the Cistercians?
- What role did vision and purpose play in that success? Might another organisational structure have been equally successful?

## Sources

Evans, G.R. (2000) *Bernard of Clairvaux*, Oxford: Oxford University Press.
Gimpel, Jean (1976) *The Medieval Machine: The Industrial Revolution in the Middle Ages*, London: Penguin.

Murphy, Sean (1998) 'Bernard of Clairvaux', in Edward Craig (ed.), *Routledge Ency-clopedia of Philosophy*, London: Routledge, vol. 1, 753–54.
Witzel, Morgen (1998) 'God's Entrepreneurs', *Financial Times Mastering Management Review* 18: 16–19.

## Case Study 2C

### Oneida Community Ltd

The Oneida Community was founded at Oneida, New York in 1848 as a utopian socialist commune. Its ideological leader and most important member was John Humphrey Noyes. Born into a deeply religious family in Vermont, Noyes studied at Yale University's divinity school with the aim of becoming a minister. During his time at Yale he formulated a heterodox religious doctrine which he called 'Perfectionism', believing that it was possible for people to reach a state of perfection, by which he meant complete absence from sin. This did not sit well with the church authorities, and Noyes was denied ordination as a minister. He seems to have suffered a mental breakdown not long after, and when he recovered he began writing a series of articles for radical magazines, denouncing marriage as an institution, arguing the case for free love and finally announcing that he was God's chosen agent to spread the new doctrine of perfectionism.

In 1836 Noyes returned to Vermont and settled in the small town of Putney where, changing his stance on marriage, he married Harriet Worden in 1838. By 1846 he had gathered a small group of followers in a commune at Putney, where among other radical social innovations they developed what Noyes called 'group marriage', where every man in the community was considered married to every woman there. This led to outrage and the state authorities charged Noyes with adultery. In 1848 the group moved to the town of Oneida in the state of New York, where they established the Oneida Community. More converts came to join them, and at its height the commune numbered about 300 people.

The Oneida Community practised self-sufficiency, and all its members were required to work. Although they had initially just forty acres, the 'communitarians', as they were known, worked hard and diligently and soon acquired more land. Even more successful was a range of craft industries. As well as bottling and preserving fruits and vegetables, communitarians started businesses making hats, furniture and silk thread, and then branched out into metalwork. They became specialists in the making of animal traps, and at one point were a major supplier of traps for the fur trade, the Hudson's Bay Company being an important customer. In the 1870s the Community also began making high quality silver-plate tableware, a venture which proved immediately successful as the American middle class was expanding rapidly and there was a strong market.

Initially all work was done by communitarians, but as time passed the Community began employing workers, especially in its craft industries; by 1870 Oneida was employing more than 200 people from outside the commune. Communitarians continued to do menial labour such as working on the land or doing chores in the communal house where all lived together. Senior members of the community were excused manual labour, performing administrative duties. There were a number of these. Despite being a utopian socialist commune, Oneida also exhibited many features of a bureaucracy. At one point there were twenty-one standing committees overseeing the work of forty-eight departments. These latter included not only the agricultural and craft workshops but also departments looking after the medical health and dentistry of the communitarians, and even a department of barbers.

There were, however, some unpleasant aspects to life at Oneida. Internal discipline took the form of 'mutual criticism', where those who were deemed to have transgressed against the rest of the community were paraded before either a committee or the full community and subjected to criticism; this often turned into bullying. Despite Noyes professing equality of the sexes, one of the standing committees was the committee of 'stirpiculture' which determined which women were permitted to have children. Only women who were considered to be of good health and high intelligence were so permitted, indicating that Oneida was practising an early form of eugenics. Unsurprisingly, Noyes's wife Harriet Worden was one of the women permitted, giving birth to two sons, Theodore and Pierrepont. As before in Vermont, the community practised 'group marriage', but with an unpleasant difference. Noyes instituted a hierarchy of communitarians ranging from senior to junior, and developed a doctrine stating that junior members – especially women – could gain merit and reach perfectionism by having sexual relations with senior members – especially men, like himself. This practice caused increasing unhappiness among communitarians, who in the 1870s rebelled and ended the practice of group marriage and contracted lawful marriages, or in some cases simply went back to their original spouses.

Noyes, aware that his authority was crumbling, then decided to hand over the leadership of the community to his elder son Theodore. The communitarians were unhappy about not having a say in the succession, and when they learned that Theodore Noyes was secretly an atheist, rebelled again and rejected him entirely. In 1879 the New York state authorities filed charges against John Noyes alleging sexual relations with a minor, and he fled to Canada, remaining in exile at Niagara Falls, Ontario until his death in 1886. The new leaders of the community decided to dissolve it, but there was a problem in that there were several successful small businesses operating from its premises, and no one could agree on who should own the property.

Eventually the leaders took the somewhat unusual step of converting the commune to a joint-stock company, giving shares to all adult members of the former community. Thus in 1880 the Oneida Community became Oneida Community Ltd. However, none of the leaders had much commercial experience or acumen, and prospects for Oneida looked bleak. In 1894 it was suggested that Noyes's second son Pierrepont should be invited to take over the business. He was twenty-four years old, with a degree from Colgate University and no business experience whatever, but unlike his brother and late father he was liked and trusted by the former communitarians.

Upon returning, Noyes saw at once that the only hope of saving Oneida Community Ltd was to restructure and modernise. The directors, who were former senior communitarians and strongly conservative in nature, resisted for some time, but in 1899 Noyes called a general meeting of the individual shareholders and won them over. He was appointed general manager in 1899 and president in 1910, serving in that role until he retired in 1950.

Pierrepont Noyes had seen what the directors could or would not see, that most of the small craft industries were never going to be sufficiently profitable to enable the business to grow and earn the owners a decent living. The one business that did have a future was silver-plate tableware. Noyes sold off the other businesses to raise capital and concentrated on tableware. The silver-plate business was dominated by the firm of Rogers based in Connecticut, and most competitors tried to undercut them on price. Noyes decided to attack on quality instead and launched the Community Plate range as a premium brand, priced slightly higher but of significantly better quality and design. At same time, he created a selling organisation to market the product.

The first pattern, Avalon, was marketed in 1902. Takeoff was slow at first, with some resistance by retailers, but Noyes responded with strong advertising and promotional campaigns aimed directly at the consumer to stimulate demand. In 1910 Oneida launched a ground-breaking series of advertisements built around illustrations of young, stylish women by the artist Coles Phillips, which associated the product with smart, attractive young people. Oneida also secured endorsements from leading socialites, which further enhanced the brand's appeal.

With no formal business education or training, Noyes had proved to be an adept commercial manager. He was equally adroit at labour relations. Determined not to sacrifice the original ideals of equality and democracy which had motivated the Oneida Community, he saw how these could be turned to the advantage of both the workers and the business as a whole. He saw employee welfare not in terms of philanthropy but as a duty. He once remarked that employers should 'make no welfare moves from fear, but always and only because you believe that company success should add to the comfort and happiness of every member of the working group', and that 'when your employees really believe that you take a practical interest in their welfare and that you mean what you say, you will have acquired an asset money alone could never buy' (Edmonds 1948: 8). He believed that the best form of welfare came through paying good wages.

For all his emphasis on equality, Noyes could be authoritarian when needed. In 1899 he broke a strike at the company's Niagara Falls workshop, not because he was opposed to unions – quite the contrary – but because he did not believe the Oneida ethic could work in a unionised shop. Fiercely loyal to his own workers, he asked for and usually got their strong loyalty in turn. Lowenthal (1927) reports that during the recession of 1921, Noyes called a meeting at the plant and asked the workers if they would take a pay cut in exchange for a greater share of profits should any be made; the proposal 'received the greatest handclap in the history of the company' (1927: 117).

When Rogers ran into financial trouble following the Wall Street crash of 1929, Noyes bought his rival and continued to expand the company even through the Depression. He also took on many civic roles, including serving after retirement as president of the Saratoga Springs Authority, overseeing the $5 million development which made Saratoga Springs into North America's leading spa resort. Oneida, now called simply Oneida Ltd, continued to expand after his retirement and then death in 1959, diversifying into the production of stainless steel tableware in the 1960s and later opening a chain of retail outlets. In the late 1990s Oneida became the last maker of tableware to continue production in the United States, a distinction it clung to proudly for some years. In 2006 the last American factory was closed and production was outsourced to China and Indonesia.

## Analysis

Some of the questions you might want to consider in connection with this case include:

- Could Oneida have expanded as it did under Pierrepont Noyes while retaining its original communal structure? If so, what adaptations might it have had to make?
- If not, what does this tell us about the relative strengths and weaknesses of bureaucratic and communal structures?
- What key features of the organisational forms discussed in the chapter did Noyes bring together in Oneida to achieve 'organisational fitness for purpose'?

## Sources

Edmonds, W.D. (1948) *The First Hundred Years, 1848–1948*, Oneida, NY: Oneida Ltd.

Klaw, Spencer (1993) *Without Sin: The Life and Death of the Oneida Community*, London: Penguin.

Lowenthal, E. (1927) 'The Labor Policy of the Oneida Community Ltd.', *Journal of Political Economy* 35(February): 114–26.

Noyes, Pierrepont (1937) *My Father's House: An Oneida Boyhood*, London: John Murray.

# Case Study 2D

*Mondragón Cooperatives Corporation*

The Mondragón Cooperatives Corporation was inspired by a Catholic priest, Father José Maria Arizmendiarrieta. A Basque (a minority linguistic and ethnic group in northern Spain) by birth, he attended theological college with the intention of becoming a priest. He was still in the midst of his training when the Spanish Civil War broke out in 1936. José Maria, like many of his fellow Basques, supported the Republican cause against General Franco. In 1937 when the Basque region was captured by forces loyal to Franco, José Maria and many of his fellow theology students were arrested, and sixteen were shot. It seems that José Maria was intended for execution also, but thanks to a bureaucratic error he was instead released without charge. He resumed his training as a priest, and in 1941 was sent to the town of Mondragón (whose previous priest had been one of those executed in 1937).[6]

General Franco won the civil war and established himself as dictator of Spain, and the Basque region suffered both economic deprivation and political persecution under his rule. Parish priests played an important role both in alleviating poverty and helping maintain social cohesion. Father José Maria's first attempts to help his new community were fairly traditional, including the organisation of social activities and a sports club. He was strongly aware, however, that the greatest need was for economic prosperity to combat the region's crippling poverty. In 1943 he established a small technical college in the town, supported by donations from local people. The college, which survives today as the Mondragón Eskola Politeknikoa, provided technical and engineering education and helped graduates find jobs in factories.

But Spain's economy remained weak in the 1950s and jobs were not easy to find; also, some Spanish employers discriminated against Basques. In 1956 five graduates, unable to find jobs, approached Father José Maria for help in setting up a business to make oil stoves and lamps. At the priest's suggestion they established the business as a cooperative, and thus Ulgor, the first worker cooperative in Mondragón, was born. Father José Maria helped the group find premises and recruit new members, and within a surprisingly short time Ulgor was making a modest profit. Seeing the potential, Father José Maria began encouraging other groups to found their own small manufacturing cooperatives.

A major turning point came in 1959 when Father José Maria, realising that lack of capital was holding back the growth of the cooperatives and establishment of new ones, persuaded Ulgor and the others to establish the Caja Laboral Popular, a kind of savings bank or credit union. The purpose of this was to fund cooperative ventures and help them raise capital. Almost at once, more manufacturing cooperatives were established.

Realising that some sort of structure was needed, in 1965 at Father José Maria's suggestion the cooperatives banded together to form Ularco, a cooperative group which provided administration, accounting and legal services for the cooperatives. In the 1980s Ularco changed its named to Fagor and went on to become Spain's leading producer of white goods (Whyte 1996).

There seemed no end to Father José Maria's ideas. Among the cooperatives established during the 1960s and early 1970s were:

- Eroski, a retail cooperative which went on to open stores right across the Basque region and now owns supermarkets in Spain and France and which includes both consumer and producer members.
- Alecop, a student cooperative initially set up to help polytechnic students gain work experience, run by the students themselves; it later expanded to design and produce technology for other cooperatives and for schools.
- Ikasbide, originally established as a cooperatively owned and managed training centre providing services to other cooperatives; later under the name Otalora it developed into a fully-fledged management training and research centre.
- Ikerlan, set up by the members of Ularco in 1975 with a capital of $2 million to provide research and development services for the cooperatives; today it continues in this role and also has an extensive range of R&D contracts with clients outside the cooperative group.

The key element in this early growth according to observers (Bradley and Gelb 1983; Whyte and Whyte 1989; Whyte 1996) was the Caja Laboral Popular, the credit union. 'By financing the building of educational, manufacturing and service co-operatives, an R&D co-operative and housing co-operatives as well as other types, the Caja has helped to provide an integrated financing and supporting system which is the basis of Mondragón's success' (Whyte 1996: 3520). But the Caja also played an important coordinating role. It was the one institution with links to all the other cooperatives, having contracts with all of them. These contracts stated that in exchange for investment funding, each cooperative was to set aside 30 per cent of its profits into a reserve fund. The Caja administered this fund and used it to fund investment and other activities such as R&D. Thus far, however, the venture was a fairly loose association, coordinated by the Caja and guided by the spirit and ideals of Father José Maria. He did not take a direct hand in managing the cooperatives, but his spirit was behind everything that they did; and to some extent still is to this day.

Father José Maria Arizmendiarrieta died in 1976, a year after General Franco. The economic climate in Spain began slowly to improve. And by this time the Mondragón movement was strong enough to keep on growing, and it duly did. In the 1980s a series of studies conducted by the Caja suggested that more structure and organisation were needed. Accordingly in 1989, after lengthy debate, the Mondragón Cooperatives Corporation was established. This corporation was established as a multi-divisional form (M-form) corporation. The cooperatives were organised into nine divisions (since expanded to sixteen divisions) on the model of the already established Ularco/Fagor, each headed by a vice-president with a seat on the board. The head of Fagor, Javier Mongelos, was elected the first president of the corporation. However, Mongelos was not a conventional CEO. He was responsible directly to the Cooperatives Congress, which included representatives from every cooperative and acted as a kind of permanent shareholders' council with the power to review and then ratify or reject every decision by the board.

In the 1990s, with Spain now part of the European Common Market (later European Union), Mondragón began developing its export markets. Growth continued and by 2000 there were more than 120 cooperatives. Today Mondragón has subsidiaries in eighteen countries outside Spain, including unsurprisingly extensive interests in Latin America but also a number of operations in China. It is one of the largest business entities in Spain, and has been widely imitated, for example by El Grup Cooperatiu de Valencia set up in the southern city of Valencia in the early 1970s. Modelled strongly on Mondragón, this group also includes a credit union and R&D cooperative. There has been interest in the Mondragón model in other parts of the world as well, but as yet no other cooperative has reached the same levels of growth. In 2007, Mondragón employed more than 103,000 people worldwide and had a turnover of €16.3 billion.

'There is general agreement', says Whyte (1996: 3521) 'that a single worker co-operative, surrounded by a sea of private enterprises, has very poor prospects for long-term survival.' The key to Mondragón's success, he believes, lies in the way in which it has developed a system for integrating member cooperatives for mutual support, leveraging their various strengths to build something greater than the sum of its parts. Despite growing to great size, Mondragón has adopted a governance structure which preserves many aspects of communal life and work. As well as the Cooperatives Congress, there are also two councils, the Governing Council which oversees management, and a Social Council which represents the interests of the workers. Both are elected by all workers, and the larger cooperatives like Eroski each have their own Governing Council and Social Council as well. The distinction between workers and management in Mondragón is a very fuzzy one; but it has been designed to appeal to the strengths of the organisation and to overcome its weaknesses.

But the other factor that helped and continues to help propel Mondragón to success is the philosophy of its founding father, José Maria Arizmendiarrieta. What he brought to Mondragón was a personal philosophy based on notions of democracy and empowerment, combined with a sound knowledge of sociology, economics and the factors of production. A highly educated and well-read man, his intellectual influences included Herbert Marcuse, Jacques Maritain, John Kenneth Galbraith and Karl Marx. He believed that given time, cooperation could become an effective alternative to capitalism. He was not an unthinking anti-capitalist, but rather a pluralist who believed that there were many approaches to the market. What he disliked and feared was the total dominance of capitalism to the exclusion of other forms. As he once wrote:

> In the mind of the co-operators is the idea that future society probably must be pluralist in its organisations, including the economic. There will be action and interaction of publicly owned firms and private firms, the market and planning, entities of paternalistic style, capitalistic or social. Every juncture, the nature of every activity, the level of education and the development of every community will require a special treatment ... not limited to one form of organization, if we believe in and love man, his liberty, and justice, and democracy.
>
> (quoted in Whyte and Whyte 1989: 253)

## Analysis

Some of the questions you might want to consider in connection with this case include:

- Is the cooperative structure itself solely responsible for the success of Mondragón? If not, then what other factors have contributed?
- How would you describe the purpose of this organisation?
- The modern Mondragón is a fusion of at least two different types of organisation as described in the chapter. Which types can you identify, and what are their key features as represented in Mondragón?

## Sources

Bradley, K. and Gelb, A. (1983) *Co-operation at Work: The Mondragón Experience*, London: Heinemann.

Ormachea, J.M. (1993) *The Mondragón Cooperative Experience*, Mondragón: Mondragón Cooperative Corporation.

Whyte, William Foote (1996) 'Mondragón' in Malcolm Warner (ed.) *International Encyclopedia of Business and Management*, London: Routledge, vol. 4, pp. 3518–22.

Whyte, W.F. and Whyte, K.K. (1989) *Making Mondragón: The Growth and Dynamics of the Worker Cooperative*, Ithaca, NY: ILR Press.

## Notes

1 This is not an entirely fair comparison, and also leaves out the East India Company's large standing army which at its peak numbered around 100,000 men.
2 Rome's successor, the Byzantine empire based in Constantinople, retained a permanent standing army until the eleventh century, but thereafter largely replaced it

with hired mercenary forces. Other powers maintained small permanent forces, usually acting in the role of bodyguard for the head of state; an example is the corps of *mameluks* who guarded the Caliph of Islam.

3 Dixon's views should be treated with respect; he was formerly an officer with the British army bomb squad, not merely an academic observer.

4 Not all uniforms were derived from the military. The uniforms and headgear still worn by nurses in hospitals in some parts of the world, especially those with religious affiliations, are derived from the habits of nursing sisters and nuns, who served as nurses in the hospitals of the Middle Ages.

5 Some sources refer to the founders as 'Cluniacs'. This refers to the reform movement within the Benedictine movement based at the French monastery of Cluny. 'Cluniacs' are sometimes discussed as if they were a separate monastic order, but this is misleading; they were Benedictine reformers who were attempting to restore cohesion and control to the Order along the lines advocated by the founder. In fact, there was little to separate them ideologically from the Cistercians.

6 Mondragón is the Spanish name; in the Basque language the town is known as Arrasate.

# 3   Strategy

---

**Learning objectives**

This chapter is intended to help readers do the following:

1  understand how business leaders conceived of and practised strategy in the days before formal theories of business strategy had been articulated;
2  understand some of the influences from the past that have helped to shape modern thinking about strategy;
3  examine some of the modern theoretical approaches to business strategy in the light of earlier practice.

> Everything in strategy is very simple, but that does not mean that everything in strategy is very easy.
>
> –Karl von Clausewitz, *Vom Kriege*

> You read a book from beginning to end. You run a business the opposite way. You start with the end, and then do everything you must to reach it.
>
> –Harold Geneen, *The Synergy Myth, and Other Ailments of Business Today*

## 3.1 Introduction

If organisation is as old as civilisation itself, then business strategy, at least in the sense of its being a formal discipline, is very new. The first two books to deal specifically with the concept of business strategy, Alfred Chandler's *Strategy and Structure* and Igor Ansoff's *Corporate Strategy*, appeared in 1962 and 1965 respectively, and 'business strategy' is held to have originated around this time.

This poses a question: if business strategy was only invented in the early 1960s, what did managers and businesses do before then? How did they plan and make decisions and choose which paths to take to reach their goals? One standard answer to this question is that people simply used their common sense. As Karl von Clausewitz pointed out in the early nineteenth century, the fundamentals of strategic thinking are actually fairly simple, and most intelligent people are capable of working out the best course of action in a given situation.

But as Clausewitz also said, just because strategy is simple does not mean it is easy, and implementing a very simple strategy can often be extremely difficult. The first people to begin working out what we would now call principles of strategy were military and political leaders. Sunzi's *The Art of War* was written over two thousand years ago, and there have been numerous other writings on military and political strategy since; and we know that business leaders were aware of these works, and borrowed concepts from them.

But did the principles of what we now call business strategy exist before they were first articulated by Chandler and Ansoff? The answer is that some of them did, though not all of them; some of the strategic options we take for granted today simply were not available to business leaders and managers of earlier generations. But other strategic options like specialisation, diversification, cost reduction and so on did exist, and it is comparatively easy to find examples of businesses practising these.

What is surprising is that it took people as long as it did to turn all this into a coherent body of thought. Scientific management and other theories of management that emerged in the late nineteenth and early twentieth centuries took little notice of strategy. The reason for this is not clear, but we can hypothesise that many of the early writers on scientific management in particular were familiar with the principles military strategy. They may have concluded that the works of Clausewitz and Helmuth von Moltke constituted the last word on the subject and that there was little they could add. By the early 1960s, however, people had begun to realise the very distinct limitations of military strategy when applied to business, and the search for a new discipline began.

## 3.2  Early theories of strategy

### 3.2.1  The ancient world

Had they been asked to do so, early business leaders would probably have struggled to distinguish between the concepts of military strategy, political strategy and business strategy. Strategy was strategy, no matter what field of human endeavour it was applied in. In part this is due to the nature of society; political leaders were often expected to be military leaders as well, and in many places such as the medieval Italian city-states, Florence and Venice and Genoa, merchants played leading roles in both business and war.

That said, we cannot really get away from the fact that the concept of strategy has its roots in the military. Cummings (1993) reminds us that the word 'strategy' comes from the Greek *strategos*, meaning a general. In Athens there were ten of these generals who formed a war council and were responsible for the conduct of all military affairs. The post was first created around 508 BC. The first writings on strategy began to appear in the fourth century BC; early writers include Ainias the Tactician and Xenophon, who was also a famous military commander in his own right. The biography of Alexander the Great by Arrian contains much musing on his strategy, and in the Roman world Frontinus and, especially, Vegetius produced notable textbooks on strategy. Both continued to be translated and read right through the Middle Ages in Europe, and the *Epitoma Rei Militaris* of Vegetius is sometimes quoted in the correspondence of Italian merchants and bankers.

The two books are different in nature. Frontinus, when discussing particular problems in strategy, draws together examples of different responses in different situations. For example, in a section on 'determining the character of the war', he offers different examples from history. Alexander the Great, knowing he had a strong army, often sought to force his enemies to fight in the open field. In an earlier war the Byzantines, knowing they had a weak army but a strong fortress, forced the enemy to besiege them. In yet another example, the Roman general Fabius Maximus knew he could not defeat Hannibal in open battle so retreated and forced the enemy to march after him.

What Frontinus is saying, to use modern language, is that strategy is *contingent* and *situational*. There is no one right or wrong method of making war, because what is right in one set of circumstances will be quite wrong in another. He invites readers to discuss the solutions that others have used in the past, and make their own judgements about the applicability of each (Cummings (1993) describes this as similar to the case study method used in business schools). A similar approach is used in an anonymous Chinese work from about the same time, the *Thirty-Six Stratagems*. This offers a series of stratagems which can be used in certain situations, and readers are invited again to consider which ones might be useful to them and in what situations, but there is no pretence of universal applicability.

An earlier writer who did try to draw some universal lessons was the general Sunzi (or Sun Tzu), who probably lived in the fourth century BC.[1] The text was heavily re-written by another general, Cao Cao, in the third century AD. He distributed copies to his officers and ordered them to read it. The book is still widely read today by both Japanese and Chinese business leaders as well as at least some in the West. Its influence is felt in some modern writings too, notably Kenichi Ohmae's *The Mind of the Strategist* (1982). In 2001 the coach of the Australian cricket team gave extracts to his players to read before beginning a series of matches against England. Part of this enduring appeal is derived from the fact that the book reduces strategy to a set of general principles which can be easily learned and followed. Sunzi believed there were fundamentals in strategy which had always to be observed. The foundation of all strategy, he said, consisted of five basic principles:

1 the *moral law*, which 'causes the people to be in complete accord with their ruler';
2 *heaven*, meaning literally the weather and the seasons, environmental factors which have an effect on how the strategy is carried out:
3 *earth*, the physical space in which military operations are conducted;
4 the *commander*, meaning the character and nature of the leader;
5 *method and discipline*, the organisation and structure of the army and how its soldiers are trained.

In a passage on planning, Sunzi said that there are again five 'working fundamentals', namely aims and goals, the environment, the physical terrain, leadership and doctrine or art. Ambler *et al.* (2008: 90) suggest that these translate easily into concepts in business planning:

1 aims and goals = what kind of business are we/should we be in?
2 environment = analysis of the competitive environment
3 physical terrain = competitive positioning
4 leadership = and motivational factors
5 doctrine or art = implementation.

It is notable, though, that Sunzi's precepts concern planning and preparation. He did not offer strategic options; he contented himself, like Frontinus, by observing a few examples of 'best practice', things that have worked well in the past. In Sunzi's view, the key to any successful strategy lay in knowledge and understanding of one's own abilities and those of the enemy. 'If you know the enemy and know yourself, you need not fear the result of a hundred battles', he wrote. 'If you know yourself but not the enemy, for every victory gained you will also suffer a defeat. If you know neither the enemy nor yourself, you will succumb in every battle' (Chapter 3, §17).

---

**The importance of planning**

Now the general who wins a battle makes many calculations in his temple ere the battle is fought. The general who loses a battle makes but few calculations beforehand. Thus do many calculations lead to victory, and few calculations to defeat: how much more no calculation at all! It is by attention to this point that I can foresee who is likely to win or lose.

(*The Art of War*, Chapter 1, §26)

---

Very similar points are made by the late Roman writer Vegetius, writing some time between 370 and 400 AD. Strategy and warfare, Vegetius said, should be conducted according to principles, not left to chance. But again, Vegetius does not offer prescriptive solutions, and he most definitely does not tell commanders in the field what they should do in each given situation. The principles Vegetius describes refer to matters such as training, discipline, military organisation, equipment and supplies. His argument is that a well-trained and well-equipped army that is organised for maximum effectiveness will, in the great majority of cases, defeat an army that is none of these things.

Another much admired figure from China's past was Zhuge Liang, prime minister of the kingdom of Shu and the principal opponent of Cao Cao, mentioned above. The long and dramatic struggle between the two is described in the Chinese epic *The Three Kingdoms*, by Luo Guanzhong. Wang (1995) has distilled sixteen strategic precepts from Zhuge Liang's words and actions, but again these do not have much to do with strategy in action. Indeed, many of these precepts are almost passive in nature: they include such things as 'observing and listening', 'being perceptive', 'looking ahead' and 'observation'. While Cao Cao conducted war and statecraft in a methodical fashion, Zhuge Liang was more inclined to watch and wait for opportunities and then strike quickly.

### 3.2.2 The Renaissance

As noted, Sunzi's *The Art of War* continued to be the leading influence on strategic thought in East Asia down to almost the present day. In the Western world, the precepts of Frontinus and Vegetius guided strategic thinking through the Middle Ages as far as the Renaissance. The humanists of the Renaissance, however, doubted the existence of strategic precepts. They saw each situation as unique, therefore requiring unique solutions. Precept is of little value and can even lead people astray.

The most important writer on strategy from this period is the Florentine civil servant Niccolò Machiavelli, who wrote in the early fifteenth century. His two most important books, *The Prince* and *The Discourses*, were on politics and political strategy. *The Prince* is a short book on statecraft and power, while *The Discourses* is a longer reflection on the workings of government and how best to ensure the security and safety of a state. Machiavelli became notorious for his suggestion that 'the ends justify the means', which led to accusations of immorality; his books were even banned in some places. In fact, most modern authorities now agree that Machiavelli was simply 'telling it like it is', describing the world he saw around him.

The two most important concepts in Machiavelli's writings on strategy are *virtú* (ability or capacity) and *fortuna* (serendipity or luck). *Virtú* Machiavelli believed to be the primary quality of a successful strategist. *Virtú* allows leaders to recognise and seize opportunities and to outthink and outfight their opponents. However, the strategist must always beware of *fortuna*, remembering that unexpected events can upset even the most carefully laid plans. Machiavelli maintains that a sufficiency of *virtú* allows people to recognise when chance has given them an opportunity, and to take advantage of *fortuna* by reacting quicker than competitors or opponents. In *The Discourses*, Machiavelli suggests further that *virtú* can be inherent in organisations, not just in individuals.

Rather than strategy by precept, then, the Renaissance view of strategy was that it was an *ad hoc* activity, the nature of which was in large part dictated by circumstances. Machiavelli remarks in *The Prince* that *fortuna* dictates half of human actions.

---

### The importance of timing

I think it may be true that fortune is the ruler of half our actions, but that she allows the other half or thereabouts to be governed by us. The prince who bases himself entirely on fortune is ruined when fortune changes. I also believe that he is happy whose mode of procedure accords with the needs of the times, and similarly he is unfortunate whose mode of procedure is opposed to the times. I conclude then that fortune varying and men remaining fixed in their ways, they are successful only so long as these ways conform to circumstances, but when they are opposed then they are unsuccessful.

Machiavelli, *The Prince* (1961: 91–94)

To manage strategy is not so much to promote change as to know *when* to do so. Advocates of strategic planning often urge managers to plan for perpetual instability in the environment. But this obsession with change is dysfunctional. Organisations that reassess their strategies continuously are like individuals who reassess their jobs or their marriages continuously – in both cases, they drive themselves crazy, or reduce themselves to inaction.

–Henry Mintzberg, *Mintzberg on Management* (1989: XX)

### 3.3.3 *The nineteenth century*

However, the belief that strategy could be guided by fundamentals or precepts did not entirely fade away, and by the early nineteenth century the search was on once more. In part this was due to the influence of the Scientific Revolution. It was believed that every human activity was capable of being systematised, and strategy was no exception. Further, in the aftermath of the cataclysm of the Napoleonic Wars, there was a great deal of interest in the methods of successful strategists like Napoleon and, a few generations earlier, King Friedrich Wilhelm II of Prussia, more generally known as Frederick the Great.

The best-known book to come out of this period was written by one of the men who helped to defeat Napoleon, the Prussian staff officer Karl von Clausewitz. His book *Vom Kriege* (On War), first published in 1819, was for many years required reading in military staff colleges around the world. It also exercised a good deal of influence over thinking about strategy in business, both through ex-military officers who went on to careers in management, and through others who were aware of Clausewitz's work. Field-Marshal von Moltke, the victorious commander in the Franco-Prussian War of 1870–71, was a disciple of Clausewitz, and Moltke's own approaches to strategy and organisation were studied by management theorists (see Chapter 2).

Much of *Vom Kriege* is about the conduct of war itself including matters such as supply and transport, and need not detain us here. There are two important concepts to come out of Clausewitz that have implications for business. First, there is his view that war is not an independent phenomenon. It is waged for a purpose, one that is determined by the will of the commander. There is a difference between the purpose of war and war itself; the latter is simply 'an act of violence meant to force the enemy to do our will' (1984: 90).

Second, it is easy to set a purpose for war, and easy too to make plans for the defeat of the enemy and set these plans in motion. However, it is another matter to carry out these plans as intended, and leaders are constantly beset with the problem of staying true to their own purposes. The key factor is 'friction': 'countless minor incidents – the kind you can never really foresee – combine to lower the general level of performance, so that one always falls far short of the intended goal' (1984: 119). Friction, says Clausewitz, is what distinguishes real war from plans made on paper. Strategic planning is based on statistical facts; but real war can never amount to more than probabilities. Many factors lead to friction, but the most important are the courage and ability of the leader, and the experience and spirit of the troops he commands. Should these fail at any point, previously determined plans will be jeopardised. Field-Marshal von Moltke famously said that 'no plan survives contact with the enemy'. From a business perspective we could amend this simply to 'no plan survives'. It is rare in the extreme for a plan to be implemented exactly as it is written; friction always makes its presence known at some point. Just as in war, while plans are based on statistical facts, our understanding of what will happen in business can only be based on probabilities.

These two basic concepts – that strategy is subordinate to purpose, and that the achievement of any given strategic goal is never certain – have influenced many later thinkers and writers on strategy.

---

**Approaches to strategy change over time**

The ancient world (Frontinus, Sunzi, Vegetius): strategy should be governed by fundamental precepts, but with an emphasis on planning and preparation.

The Renaissance (Machiavelli): strategy should be made when needed, an *ad hoc* response to events and pressures, with an emphasis on the strength and character of the strategy-maker.

The nineteenth century (Clausewitz): strategy must always be subordinated to the purpose of the organisation. Although plans are useful, friction means that they often must be modified or abandoned under pressure of events.

---

## 3.3  Strategy in practice

The previous section described briefly some of the main theoretical approaches to strategy. We know that they were influential and that business leaders knew about them, although their actual influence varied according to time and place.

But what impact did these theories have on business leaders? To return to our first question, what did business leaders do before strategy was invented? It will have been seen above that all the ideas of the military and political strategists would have needed some modification to fit into a business setting.

The problem is compounded by the fact that business leaders themselves tell us about their approaches to strategy only indirectly. There are no discussions of 'strategy' *per se* in their memoirs or correspondence. To understand their approaches to business strategy, then, we can do two things. The first is to look at such written evidence as exists and identify 'strategic' ideas, comments about plans and future intentions, discussions of goals and how to achieve them and resources required, and so on. Second, we can examine the actions of firms and look at what they actually did, and try to infer ideas from those actions. This last is somewhat risky, as we can never know for certain what those ideas were. But across the three hundred firms studied and analysed in preparation for writing this book, there are some detectable patterns of common behaviour.

The first comment to be made, and this will probably come as no surprise, is that in practice we find a mix of both strategic precept and *ad hoc* strategy-making. Business organisations before the present day were certainly not bound by plan. There is little or no evidence for formal planning of the kind undertaken by political and military organisations, and which had become commonplace in the latter by the nineteenth century. Occasionally, as in the case of the German steel-maker Alfred Krupp, there are references to memoranda or letters which set out the leader's view of where the business should go and the necessary steps to be taken, but in general these are more statements of intent than plans as such. The voluminous correspondence of the medieval Italian merchant Francesco Datini (see Case Study 3B) includes letters where he sometimes spelled out his ideas to his partners, but these again are more in the ways of suggestions or possibilities; there is no evidence of formal planning.

That there was a preference for *ad hoc* strategy-making is understandable when we consider that businesses in past times often operated under very high levels of risk, far higher than most businesses experience today. As discussed in Chapter 1, war, bad weather, bio plagues and other hazards were all common. The outbreak of war or rebellion could change the business environment very dramatically, and such things could happen at a moment's notice. Strategies for managing risk were an essential feature of all strategy-making up almost to the present day, and risk analysis was one of the key activities of a strategy-maker. These had not only to evaluate the likelihood that a particular threat might materialise, but also come up with ways of avoiding or mitigating the risk. Sometimes risks could be avoided; one could choose not to trade in places that were very risky, for example. Others could not; most bulk trade went by sea, and no one could prevent storms. So businessmen like Marino Sanudo of Venice made their calculation: if we send out five ships and four of them are lost in storms, we should still make enough profit from the fifth cargo to cover the losses of the other four.

That risks had to be covered and managed was one strategic precept that we can see from earliest times to the present. What others were there? It is tempting to apply modern strategic frameworks and see if business strategy in the past conforms to the same patterns. The answer is that it does and it doesn't. Some of the strategic options we have today were not always available in earlier times. For example, it was often not possible to compete on price, one of the favoured strategic options of modern consultants. Many early economic systems, right through to the Middle Ages and often beyond, had very strict price controls; all comparable goods had by law to be sold in the same market for the same price. A Roman corn merchant engaged in importing Egyptian corn in a highly regulated market had to sell at the same price as his rivals, and probably had little chance to compete on quality either.

---

**Strategic options for early businesses**

Choose to specialise or diversify
Product or market diversification
Cost reduction
Vertical integration
Innovation
Build networks to share/spread risk
Eliminate competition

---

The box accompanying the text lists some of the key strategic options open to businesses up to the end of the nineteenth century. Some of these options will look familiar to students of modern strategy, others not. Again, it is worth remembering that strategies are shaped and conditioned by the times and environment in which the business operates; we should not expect a list of strategic options for a business in the fourteenth century to be identical with one for the twenty-first. What is interesting, however, is that there are *some* common features.

One very common strategic consideration was the choice of whether to *specialise or diversify*. In general, we can observe that most firms chose to diversify, if they had the resources available to do so. Product and market diversification both were very important ways of spreading risk. This is particularly true of market diversification. Even relatively small firms would, as soon as they could raise the capital, diversify into different markets, like the Roman brick maker Decius Alpinus, who in the second century AD set up a subsidiary operation at the town of Vienne in eastern France to serve the fast-growing building trade in the Rhône valley. This not only opened up a new market, but would serve to keep the business going if the market in Rome were to suffer a downturn. Medieval merchants like Francesco Datini or the Adorno family of Genoa used diversification into new markets as a means of protecting their businesses at times when political conditions in the home market were particularly volatile and trade was threatened. The Adornos set up a branch in Bruges in Flanders (modern Belgium), and in the later fifteenth century went on to enter markets in Scotland and the Baltic.

Today, we often think of internationalisation as a highly risky strategy. In fact, early business leaders often used internationalisation as a way of laying off risk. Of course, internationalisation also exposed a company to new risks, such as the risk of bad weather or pirates destroying ships alluded to earlier. But it was often felt that these were acceptable risks to run, and preferable to putting all of one's eggs into one basket. One could recover from the loss of a ship, but not the loss of an entire core market.

Product diversification was fairly common too, and again we can observe that we are likely to see more product diversification in times of high risk. Many Roman merchants like the brick maker Decius Alpinus specialised in one product line, entering new markets when the opportunity arose. In China and in India during times of political stability, too, firms remained relatively focused in terms of the products they made and/or sold but opted to diversify into new markets. In Europe during the Middle Ages and the Renaissance, a time of political fragmentation and frequent conflict, it was much more common to find companies like the Medici Bank, the Adornos of Genoa, the German merchants of the Hanseatic League in the Baltic diversifying into a wide range of products. Although the evidence is less certain, it appears the same was also true in China and India. For example, the Arab merchants who controlled the Indian Ocean trade until the sixteenth century traded in a wide range of goods. Sometimes there was a distinct bias towards one product, as in the case of the Hudson's Bay Company (Case Study 1D) which specialised in furs but, initially at least, had sidelines in other trades such as fish and mineral extraction. In general, if we refer to Porter's (1980) matrix of generic strategies, the most common strategic option chosen was *focused differentiation*, as making and/or selling a range of products in several markets was perceived to be an efficient way of managing risk.

*Cost reduction* was another important strategic option, one sometimes linked to diversification. While wages and prices in individual markets were very often fixed, there was no uniformity between markets. The authority to set prices and wages rested in many cases with civic authorities, in the Middle Ages very often with the various merchant and craft guilds in each city or town. However, it was rare for any attempt to be made to coordinate wages and prices *between* cities, even in the same kingdom, so that silk cloth might sell for one price in Paris, but another and rather lower price in Lyons, which became a centre of silk production. Fish were sold at a cheaper price in Hull or Bristol than in London, and olive oil was far cheaper in Seville than in Rome. Cost reduction strategies, then, usually focused on trying to buy raw materials in other locations at cheaper prices, or in the case of finished goods, going closer to the source and buying more cheaply. It was just this that drew the Venetian merchants Niccolò and Maffeo Polo and their young kinsman Marco Polo to China in the late thirteenth century: they were not seeking to explore or have adventures, they were looking for a source of cheap goods that they could sell profitably at home. They were by no means the only ones.

*Vertical integration* could help to reduce costs. The Medici Bank's cloth business controlled manufacturing and wholesaling and had some involvement in retailing, and another branch of the firm controlled the mining of alum, an essential ingredient in dyeing (see Case Study 1A). In the nineteenth century we find the big emerging industrial combines practising vertical integration for similar reasons. Andrew Carnegie's steel company owned its own mines; Standard Oil under John D. Rockefeller controlled oil extraction, pipelines, transportation and refineries, in much the same way that many oil companies do today. As well as reducing costs, vertical integration could also be used as a means of ensuring product quality by controlling the quality of raw materials. It was for this reason that Lever Brothers integrated backwards to control most of the production of raw materials for its soap brands, for example (see Case Study 3A). However, vertical integration was not for everyone. Large amounts of capital were needed, and firms also had to have the requisite knowledge and experience in order to manage each stage of the value chain.

Managers before the twentieth century were aware of the value of *innovation* and knew – or rather, then as now the best of them knew – how to use innovation to differentiate themselves from competitors. In the Middle Ages in Europe, architects and builders like Villard d'Honnecourt in France or the Englishman James of St George became specialists in a particular kind of building (cathedrals in the case of Honnecourt, fortifications in the case of St George) and established lucrative careers; Honnecourt became a kind of international consultant, travelling all over Europe to advise on cathedral building. We do not know if Giovanni di Dondi, builder of the first weight-driven mechanical clock in the late fourteenth century, became rich off the back of his invention, but others who saw the potential of his invention and set up clock-making businesses of their own certainly did.[2] And while Johannes Gutenberg went bankrupt after inventing the printing press with movable type (demonstrating perhaps that first-mover status does not always provide an advantage), others who used his system like the Englishman William Caxton built very successful businesses.

Sometimes too, innovation would be carried out by group rather than an individual. At Toledo in Spain and Dalarna in Sweden, master steel-makers developed processes for making superior quality steel (the processes themselves remaining closely guarded secrets). Spanish and Swedish steel blades were sold all over Europe and the Middle East, commanding premium prices.

In the eighteenth and especially the nineteenth centuries there was a sudden rush of new scientific inventions, and with these came companies bent on exploiting those inventions. Sometimes the innovation was developed and taken to market by an entrepreneurial inventor, like the American Cyrus McCormick with his patented mechanical reaper, the ancestor of the combine harvester, or the Englishman Titus Salt who developed a method of weaving alpaca wool into cloth and founded a very successful company. In other cases, the technologies were borrowed from elsewhere. John Patterson did not invent the cash register, but he saw its commercial potential, purchased the patent from its bankrupt owner and went on to found a business. Still other businesses made the exploitation of new technologies an ongoing process. Both the Krupp steelworks in Germany and the Carnegie Company in America made a point of adopting new steel-making processes as they came out, and the Belfast shipbuilder Harland & Wolff led the way in pioneering new shipbuilding technologies for several decades (see Case Study 3D).

Another strategic option, again related to risk management, was the *building of networks* outside the firm. This option was particularly popular with, but not restricted to, smaller firms or those with less capital to invest in options such as vertical integration. Interfirm cooperation was extremely common, and the law, far from discouraging such cooperation, even provided coordinating mechanisms on occasion. At a small scale, all business leaders in a particular industry in the same location were members of the same guild; for example, the heads of Florentine woollen cloth weaving businesses, large and small, were members of the Arte del Lana, while all the bankers and moneychangers and pawnbrokers were members of the Arte del Cambio. These guild arrangements facilitated collaboration and allowed firms to work together on specific projects, even while competing against each other in other areas. For example, two or three cloth-making firms might join together to experiment with a new dye, or several banks might join forces to underwrite a large marine insurance policy for a convoy of ships sailing to the East.

More ambitious firms looked further afield and developed partnerships with other firms in other areas. In the nineteenth century the banking house of Rothschild, using in part its own extended family connections, developed a banking network that spread across Europe. Later, J.P. Morgan and his father Junius Morgan set up a trans-Atlantic banking network; each owned an independent firm, Junius in Britain and his son in America, but they collaborated on a number of loans and acquisitions. In the eighteenth century the Calcutta-based banking house of Jagath Seth established a network of relationships with other Indian banks right across the sub-continent, giving it perhaps the largest geographical reach of any bank of its day in the world.

In modern parlance we would call these firms with extensive external networks *low concentration, high coordination* firms. Building networks took time, but required relatively little in the way of capital and was a good way of extending reach. However, their success required managers who were good at coordination and who did not insist on control. Such managers were not always available. The medieval Italian entrepreneur Francesco Datini (see Case Study 3B) had a wide-ranging network that encompassed the Mediterranean, France and England, but he was not always an easy man to work with; something of a 'control freak' in modern parlance, he often insisted that he was right and in any dispute over strategy would demand he get his own way. As he often controlled most of the capital invested in his various ventures, he usually did, but he was not always an easy partner.

A final strategic option, often practised, was to *eliminate competition*. This could be done in various ways. Intermarriage was a common practice in both Europe and America up to the early twentieth century, and still remains popular in the East. Marriage of one's own son to the daughter of the owner of another firm (or vice versa) can turn a rival into an ally and ensure that the two firms merge when the next generation takes over management. Outright purchase of a rival, especially one that was struggling financially, was always an option too, again provided one had the capital; Du Pont consolidated its grip on the American gunpowder industry in the early years of the twentieth century by buying up many of its rivals. More aggressive methods included price wars designed to steal market share from weaker competitors, and even outright violence. In the 1870s and 1880s Standard Oil used tactics including intimidation and sabotage to force rival business owners to sell their firms. And in the early seventeenth century, the English and Dutch East India Companies fought an outright war for control of the spice trade from the East Indies, a war in which several hundred people were killed on both sides (see Case Study 3C). Even as late as the early nineteenth century the rival fur traders of the Hudson's Bay and North West Companies sometimes settled their differences with firearms.

Although they deplored violence – publicly at least – a good many economists and business leaders down through the centuries have argued that the elimination of competition was a good thing. The medieval Catholic theologian St Thomas Aquinas, who believed that competition helped to create a fair market and ensure that the consumer paid a 'just price', was in the minority. More took the view of General Francis Amasa Walker, first president of the American Economics Association in the late nineteenth century, that competition was inherently wasteful. Others, like the banker J.P. Morgan and the American entrepreneur Charles Flint, went still further and argued that competition should be abolished altogether. Flint in particular was a passionate advocate of monopoly, arguing that monopolies were more efficient than businesses that faced competition, as they did not incur costs of competition such as advertising and marketing (Flint *et al.* 1902). When questioned about the unethical methods used by Standard Oil to drive its rivals out of business, Standard Oil vice-president Henry Rogers defended these on the grounds that they had been necessary to create an oil monopoly, which was a good thing not just for Standard Oil but for the country as a whole (Tarbell 1904).

A less drastic and more peaceful solution to the 'problem' of competition than monopoly was cartels, in which firms agreed to fix prices and sometimes production quotas too, thus reducing competition to a minimum. Although Adam Smith in *The Wealth of Nations* (1776) had referred to cartels as 'conspiracies against the public', in the words of Fear (2008: 268), 'before 1945 most of the world thought that cartels brought widespread benefits'. Whether through cooperation or aggressive action, removing competitors or the threat of competition has been one of the most popular strategic options of all time.

---

### Competition and warfare

The question of attitudes to competition highlights once again the comparisons between business strategy and warfare. The comparison has often been made. The ancient Greek orator Demosthenes was perhaps the first to make it explicitly, describing warfare as akin to business with each party seeking victory over the other. Demosthenes was referring explicitly to the relationship between buyer and seller, each struggling to 'win' by getting the best deal, but others quickly began to use warfare as a metaphor for the struggle between competitors.

Is it entirely a fair comparison? It depends on the situation. In the struggle between the English and Dutch East India Companies, for example, competition did not just resemble warfare, it *was* warfare with all the features of warfare at the time including battles, sieges and the inhumane treatment of prisoners. But more generally, businesses have shown themselves as anxious to collaborate as to compete. Whereas countries can only be induced to collaborate with some difficulty and after long negotiations, many businesses are actively on the lookout for opportunities for collaboration. Modern-day gurus such as Gary Hamel (2001) believe that collaboration is a very important strategic option. Indeed, in most economies we require an array of legislation and rules to prevent excessive collaboration and to force companies to compete.

The other problem is that warfare is often rather simple when compared with business competition. In almost every war, there are two sides: two opposing armies or coalitions of armies engaging in direct competition with each other. This is actually fairly rare in business, where the number of competitors, each with their own goals and strategies, can number three, four, five, ten, twenty or more. A strategy aimed at defeating one competitor can sometimes leave the firm vulnerable to another. In this respect, business strategy needs to be much more complex than military strategy.

While observing that there are definite limits to the comparison between war and business, it is also worth noting that on one occasion the comparison was made in the other direction, with business used as a metaphor for war. In 1805 the Prussian officer Heinrich von Bülow wrote a tract on strategy in which he argued that war needed to be treated like business. The military force available to a nation was its 'capital', which needed to be kept in circulation. Concentration of capital and assets at the appropriate points would yield a return on investment, and capital had to be flexible so that it could be concentrated quickly where needed. His approach to strategy emphasised strategic goals over processes and methods. It should be added that the Prussian authorities were not much impressed with this idea, and Bülow was arrested and imprisoned on charges of insanity not long after (Palmer 1986).

## 3.4 Themes and influences

Setting aside for a moment the body of theoretical and practical knowledge about business strategy which has been built up since the early 1960s, let us review what we know about the way that business people practised strategy before that time. From both the literature on military and political strategy and the evidence we have from what we might call the 'strategic behaviour' of companies and leaders, we can see three different approaches. The first we shall call the *principles approach*, in which it is held that successful strategy depends on following certain basic principles, and that doing so is necessary – though not always sufficient – for success. The second we can name the *emergent approach*, which holds that principles are of limited use and that successful strategy-making and implementation depend on how flexible and adaptive a business is and how quickly it can respond to changing circumstances and take advantage of opportunities. The third we shall call simply the *imitative approach*, which holds that the best strategy is to imitate the actions of successful companies immediately around one and try to copy their recipe for success.

### 3.4.1   The principles approach

Probably more than anyone else before the 1960s, the Chinese warrior Sunzi exemplifies the principles approach. Sunzi gives us lists of explicit principles, very often in groups of five. His principles are things that must be considered and thought about and analysed before the strategy is implemented. They are essential prerequisites but of themselves they do not guarantee success (although Sunzi does come close to such a guarantee when he says that the commander who knows both the enemy and himself need not fear the result of a hundred battles). But he does provide lists of things that the strategist needs to do. It would be easy to organise *The Art of War* into a series of boxes that could be ticked.

This is by no means a criticism of the book. Strategy-makers are everywhere surrounded by uncertainty and the unknown, and any tools that help them to make sense of the world around them are understandably taken up with enthusiasm. Stacey (1993) famously referred to strategy as 'order emerging from chaos', and Sunzi certainly provides the tools to enable this to happen.

Yet few other writers on military and political strategy are as definite as Sunzi (which of course could account for Sunzi's enduring popularity). The Roman writers Vegetius and Frontinus agreed that there were some essential prerequisites to successful strategy: training, discipline, weapons, supplies, adequate knowledge of terrain and the enemy's capabilities, an assessment of the enemy's likely intentions and so on. These things are essential to do. But once the conflict actually begins, Vegetius and Frontinus tend to offer sets of options from which a choice can be made depending on circumstances, rather than hard recommendations for action.

In this, they are very little different from modern principles-based writers on strategy. Michael Porter's (1980, 1985) five forces model bears more than a passing resemblance to Sunzi's five fundamentals (there are even five factors in each case). And when it comes to the choice of strategy, Porter, like Sunzi, offers a range of options for discussion. Once again, there are no guarantees that any option, if chosen, will lead to success. Like Sunzi, despite his reservations about the role played by friction, Porter offers a way of distinguishing order from chaos. A more recent book, Jorge Vasconcellos e Sá's *Strategy Moves* (2005), echoes Sunzi in many ways and begins by quoting Clausewitz to the effect that 'war is the stage of uncertainty'. His book offers a range of strategic options and discusses each with examples of how they have been used successfully in the past, in a manner very reminiscent of both Clausewitz and Frontinus.

---

**Nothing is written**

Nothing is written. One can be small and win; equally, one can be large and lose. It all depends on how well one applies the rules of war. The leader who knows what strategies to carry out, when to perform them, and how to succeed in them, will win. The other leader loses.

(Vasconcellos e Sá 2005: ix)

---

To sum up the principles-based approach, then, there are certain things that a strategist must do. Doing them will not guarantee success, but *not* doing them greatly reduces the chance of failure. Most of these things that must be done concern preparation. The organisation must be prepared and ready to implement the chosen strategy and have the necessary capabilities to do so, it must have a clear sense of purpose and mission, and it must have adequate knowledge of the business environment and of competitors, customers and other players in the field. If it does all these things, it increases its chances of success, or at least reduces the chances of failure (not necessarily the same thing). Further, there are certain strategic options which have been used in the past and which *may* (depending on circumstances) be successful again. Stacey's idea of strategy as order emerging from chaos has considerable explanatory power here. As much as anything, following strategic principles gives people a sense that they are following tried and tested methods, not just going in blind, and that can help to focus and sharpen thinking.

Yet the curious fact emerges that until very recently, while thinkers on military and political strategy adduced various principles and wrote them down, thinkers on business did not. There is no adequate reason for this. We know from our observations of business behaviour and practice that there *were* certain commonly understood principles: the need for knowledge of the market and of competitors and the need to assemble adequate resources including capital were clearly understood. And managers also understood the idea of strategic options. Diversification to spread risk, vertical integration to cut costs and increase quality, innovation in order to develop new markets and distance oneself from competitors, eliminating competition: these were all options that were understood and put into practice. Why then did no one think to write them down? How did each new generation of strategists learn? Did they unpick the methods used by successful companies in the past, or did each generation re-invent the wheel? Unfortunately, one of the things about history is that it is not always possible to prove everything we would like to prove. In this case, we shall probably never know.

### 3.4.2 The 'emergent' approach

The title is of course an anachronism, borrowed from Henry Mintzberg's concept of emergent strategy, but the title is appropriate. The leading early theorist of this approach was Machiavelli with his emphasis on the role of *virtù* and *fortuna*, strength and resilience on the one hand and circumstance and change on the other. His view that 'half of our actions are guided by fortune' suggests that to some extent we are always going to be on the back foot, responding to change rather than being proactive. But that is too simplistic, for Machiavelli reminds us of *virtù* and argues that the strategist who can understand *fortuna* and master it can go on to compete and win against weaker rivals.

Forget strategic principles, says Machiavelli in effect, they do not win. There is no point in planning for the future because we cannot predict and we do not know what fortune will throw at us, good or bed. He argues that the strategist needs to cultivate the inner strength and discipline to be ready to take advantage of any opportunity that comes along. Clausewitz, for all that he felt the importance of strategic principles, was reluctantly impressed by this and reminded his readers repeatedly of the importance of 'friction' and that even the most carefully prepared plans were likely to be thrown off track.

In terms of business strategy, this would suggest that rather than having a fixed idea of how to get to a goal, firms are constantly scanning their environment and looking for opportunities. Once these are spotted, and if they have the resources to do so, firms then move quickly to take advantage of these opportunities. Looking at past practice, one can see plenty of evidence of this. Few strategists were quite as wide-ranging in their search for opportunities as the medieval merchant Francesco Datini (see Case Study 3B), who diversified into cloth manufacturing, banking and trade and had business ventures all over the western Mediterranean. But opportunistic approaches to strategy were very common. The banker Jakob Fugger, based in Augsburg in southern Germany but with financial interests all over Europe, once wrote that he spent every day looking for new opportunities to make money, and if he went to bed at night without having found one, he counted the day wasted. He may have been exaggerating for effect, but this is quite in keeping with the opportunistic way in which Fugger managed his business.

How does this compare with present-day thinking about strategy? The similarity with Mintzberg's emergent strategy has been noted. But there are echoes of this approach too in Kenichi Ohmae's *The Mind of the Strategist* (1982). Ohmae's belief that strategic success depends on how well one is able to think about strategy and respond to opportunities looks not dissimilar to Machiavelli's concept of *virtù*. We might also mention the strategic contingency theory of Ansoff (1988), who maintained that the environment is composed of four distinct, yet related factors: complexity, familiarity, rapidity of change and visibility of change. Ansoff also believed that companies had to adjust their strategies so that they reflected the degree of turbulence in the environment, 'turbulence' being defined here as the level of dynamism and volatility present in the business environment. High levels of turbulence call for different strategies than low levels. The concept of turbulence is very similar to Clausewitz's idea of friction, and both owe a debt to Machiavelli's *fortuna*. More recent books like Doz and Kosonen's *Fast Strategy* (2008) and Larreche's *The Momentum Effect* (2008) emphasise the need for preparedness, agility and toughness rather than trying to identify strategic options.

The ideas of another practitioner, a more recent one, might also be relevant here. In his book *Only the Paranoid Survive* (1996), former Intel CEO Andrew Grove reflects on the nature of change and how it affects managers. Rather than viewing change as a continuous process, Grove sees major changes as taking the form of a series of flashpoints, which he calls 'strategic inflection points'. These are events, he says, in which the fundamentals by which a business has existed and operated suddenly change, sometimes without apparent warning. The appearance of one of these points can mean new opportunities, or it can mean the beginning of the end. Formal strategic planning cannot anticipate these kinds of changes, and therefore managers have to be able to respond to the unanticipated. He cited an incident where a flaw in one of Intel's microprocessor chips, which had already been launched on the market and was installed in thousands of personal computers, could potentially have destroyed the company's reputation and even the company itself. Fast action by Intel in replacing the defective chips restored its reputation, and although the affair cost Intel around $1 billion, the company survived and remained the industry leader. But Grove acknowledged that things could easily have gone the other way.

---

**Only the paranoid survive**

I believe in the value of paranoia. Business success contains the seeds of its own destruction. The more successful you are, the more people want a chunk of your business and then another chunk and then another until there is nothing left. I believe that the prime responsibility of a manager is to guard constantly against other people's attacks and to inculcate this guardian attitude in the people under his or her management.

(Grove 1996: 3)

---

No matter how carefully prepared the strategy, every firm is vulnerable to such incidents. When the world's largest and most luxurious ocean liner, *Titanic*, sank on her first voyage with huge loss of life, the reputation of her builders, Harland & Wolff, was seriously threatened. Prompt action by the company's management restored that reputation. But no one had predicted this incident, and it tested Harland & Wolff's resilience to the utmost. When the first cannon sold by Alfred Krupp to the Prussian army exploded upon being fired, killing several of their gunners, Krupp himself had a nervous breakdown and only recovered with difficulty; more to the point, it was only because he had spent many years cultivating good relationships with the Prussian army's commanders that they were prepared to offer him a second chance. Less skilful or less fortunate were the managers of the powerful Standard Oil who, in 1906 as a result of a series of articles by a single journalist, Ida Tarbell, found themselves in court facing anti-trust charges; despite a vigorous legal defence, their company was broken up on the orders of the US government (see Case Study 8A). Similarly unfortunate or unskilful nearer our time was Gerald Ratner, who had built up the world's largest retail jewellery chain store and then in 1991 made a joke in front of the British press that some of the products sold in his stores were 'crap'. His company was nearly destroyed and Ratner himself was forced to resign as chairman (Ratner 2007).

The point is that no matter how carefully a company or a manager plans for the future, there is always the chance that the unexpected will not just threaten to derail the plan, but threaten the company itself. In these cases, how resilient the company is and how well it is able to change track and respond may determine not just the success of its strategy, but its survival.

### 3.4.3 *The imitative approach*

Strategists using the imitative approach look around to see what strategies other successful companies are using in similar circumstances and then try to adopt the same or similar strategy themselves, the reasoning being that 'if they can do it, then so can we'. The notion that the actions of successful strategists can be copied by others with equal success is found in some writings on military strategy: it is implicit in the work of Frontinus, for example when he talks of the Roman general Fabius Maximus retreating before the larger and superior army of Hannibal. Readers are invited to draw the conclusion that, in similar circumstances, they too should follow a strategy of retreat. Later European writers like Maurice of Nassau and the Italian general Montecuccoli recommended that commanders should study the campaigns of Alexander and Julius Caesar and draw lessons from them.

We have no evidence that business leaders looked back to the past to draw lessons from successful firms, and it seems unlikely that they did. But they certainly did look around in their own time and imitate those whom they considered to be successful. Firms learned by example. The strategy of product/market diversification was seen to work in the Middle Ages, and so firms adopted it. They were notably more likely to do so in places like Italy and Germany where there was a high degree of political fragmentation and higher levels of risk. In medieval England, which was normally more politically secure, there was a greater degree of product concentration; merchants like John Pulteney and William de la Pole, for example, built very large businesses based around a single commodity, wool (though both did deal in other goods as well).

The European chartered companies that went out to exploit the resources of Africa and Asia and the Americas used similar strategies to the first companies, the Muscovy Company and the East India Companies of England and the Netherlands. They integrated vertically where possible, cut costs and strove to eliminate competition. As late as the end of the nineteenth century we can see chartered companies like the African Lakes Company and the Royal Niger Company using almost exactly the same strategies as their predecessors (see Pakenham (1991) for a brief description of both these later companies).

In the late eighteenth century in England, Richard Arkwright's strategy of concentrating resources in a single location and leveraging technology in order to dominate a particular product market (see Case Study 7B) was also widely imitated as the Industrial Revolution began; we know that in some cases this strategy was disseminated to other firms by former Arkwright managers, such as Thomas Marshall, the former Arkwright mill manager who emigrated to the USA in 1791 and founded the first factory there. And in the late nineteenth century in both America and Europe, the elimination of competition by the formation of monopolies and cartels was a common and widely used strategic option, especially by large firms.

It is tempting to think that these are just fads and that the imitative strategists are merely copy-cats. But there may be more to it than that. Equally tempting is the hypothesis that some strategic options are better suited to a particular time and place than are others – this, of course, is the backbone of Ansoff's strategic contingency theory. Perhaps, rather than simply slavishly following in the footsteps of other companies, some at least of these imitative strategists are watching what others do and learning from their successes and their mistakes.

---

**The mind of the strategist**

There is no such thing as a line of ready-made packaged strategies waiting to be picked off the supermarket shelf. The drafting of a strategy is simply the logical extension of one's usual thinking processes. It is a matter of a long-term philosophy, not short-term thinking. In a very real sense, it represents an expression of an attitude to life. But like every creative activity, the art of strategic thinking is practiced most successfully when certain operating principles are kept in mind and when certain pitfalls are avoided.

(Ohmae 1982: 78–79)

---

## 3.5 Questions and discussion: thinking about strategy

What have we learned from this admittedly brief and rather patchy discussion of strategic thinking and practice before our own time? There is first the notion that firms and managers were aware of strategic principles and strategic options, even if they did not write them down in the same way that military and political strategists did. This is interesting, but it may be of limited value to the manager wrestling with strategic problems today. There is also the discovery that both formal and emergent strategy have long antecedents and are not entirely 'new' ideas. Again, this in and of itself is a historical curiosity of limited value.

Perhaps the most important thing to come out of this examination of strategy as it was conducted in the past is a strong validation of strategic contingency theory. What constitutes the 'right' strategy will always vary, depending both on the organisation itself, its resources and capabilities, and on the external environment, the degree of turbulence or friction to be found there or, if you like, the actions of Fortune.

Over the former – resources and capabilities – the strategist has some control. Firms can change and adapt in order to become better fit to carry out a chosen strategy. The Italian trading firms of the Middle Ages and Renaissance deliberately chose a form of organisation structure not found anywhere else, the system of interlocking partnerships, which enabled this adaptation to take place relatively quickly and easily (see Chapter 2).

Over the external environment, however, the firm has at best very limited control. Thus the importance of Clausewitz's dictum, quoted at the head of this chapter, that 'everything in strategy is very simple, but that does not mean that everything in strategy is very easy', and with it the notion that no plan, no matter how carefully laid, is ever executed exactly as it is laid down.

Given this, it is not surprising that when we come to look at how firms practised strategy, there is no clear-cut distinction between principles-based strategy and emergent strategy. Elements of both can be found in the conduct of successful businesses. Again, the mixture of elements depends on the time and place. Francesco Datini of Prato, trading in the very uncertain environment of Italy in the late fourteenth century, was more reactive and tended to wait for opportunities to appear, then move quickly to seize them. Other companies, facing lower levels of environmental turbulence, opted for a more principles-based approach, while remaining mindful of the need to react quickly. The case studies that accompany this chapter illustrate some of the different combinations and approaches to be found.

Management gurus for the last fifty years have argued strongly for the superiority of some forms of strategy-making over others. Some say that strategic planning is essential, others have proclaimed its death. Some say emergent strategy is the only pragmatic solution, others believe it a recipe for chaos. But as we have seen, both have their strong points. As Sunzi recognised two and a half thousand years ago, focusing on principles concentrates our thinking on things that matter: it helps bring order out of chaos. But if we follow plans slavishly without recognising the powerful role that turbulence or friction – or Fortune – plays, then we are almost certainly heading for trouble.

The lesson of the past would seem to be that we need to do both at once. Remember that Machiavelli, the forefather of emergent strategy, also argued that those who simply follow Fortune will be ruined when Fortune changes; in other words, one cannot simply be reactive all the time. Again, when we look at successful companies in the past, we see evidence of this. Planning and preparation, building of capabilities and resources, choosing to diversify or specialise, choosing to vertically integrate or build networks, setting out to eliminate competition: these were not things done on the spur of the moment. Yet these same successful companies were also highly adaptive and able to react quickly to threats and opportunities, if need be jettisoning their old strategies and inventing new ones almost overnight.

One final thing which we have not really touched upon above but which comes strongly out of the study of past business strategy – and indeed of military strategy too – is the importance of people. People make strategy, and people implement strategy. It follows that the more knowledgeable and committed and capable those people are, the better the chances that the strategy will succeed. Clever strategists knew this and factored it into their own thinking, and tried to avoid strategic options that were unlikely to be implemented successfully; that is why Sunzi argued that knowing oneself was as important as knowing the enemy. We will turn to the management of people in the next chapter.

---

**Takeaway exercise**

Taking either your own company or organisation at present, or a company or organisation you know well and perhaps have worked for in the past, analyse its strategy over the past few years in light of the discussion in this chapter. Would you say its strategy has been principles-based, emergent, or some mix of the two? Has the organisation been consistent in its strategy, or has it adapted; if the latter, what were the key pressures that forced it to adapt? And finally – and this is highly subjective – how successful has that strategy been? Has the organisation made significant progress towards its goals, or has it been held back in some areas?

These are not questions with right/wrong answers. Instead, the purpose of the exercise is to get you thinking not so much about the organisation's strategy as such, but how its members think about, make and implement strategy. In particular, you should ask yourself whether the organisation is addressing the key prerequisites for strategy. Has it the right resources, the right structure? Does it know its own capabilities and does it understand the business environment? Is it thoroughly assessing all strategic options, or is there something missing? Answering these questions can lead on to a more detailed critique of the organisation's approach to strategy.

## Case Study 3A

*Lever Brothers*

William Lever began his career as a grocer in a small town in Lancashire, and ended it as head of a global corporation that was also a world leader in domestic products, particularly soap. His rise is sometimes ascribed simply to superior marketing methods, and he is often described, rightly, as a marketing genius. But the growth of his company, Lever Brothers (now Unilever), is more correctly attributed to the working out of a clear strategy based on many elements: good marketing, sound products, vertical integration, consolidation, global expansion and enlightened self-interest.

Lever was born in Bolton, Lancashire in 1851, the son of a grocer. He joined his father in the family firm at age sixteen, and was made a partner at twenty-one. By the time he was in his late twenties he had effectively taken over the business. Lever's father had built up a moderately prosperous firm, but he was conservative in his instincts and did business by traditional methods. His shop in Bolton purchased goods from local producers and market gardens, and tended to offer for sale whatever was available at a given moment. Promotion was primarily by word of mouth. Lever, who was aware of new techniques of advertising and promotion being developed in Britain and in the USA, felt that there were opportunities for growth. He began studying his customers, mainly Lancashire housewives, observing their buying habits and spending power and especially looking at the products they needed and wanted most. Leaving the retail grocery in the hands of his father and brother, he began building up a wholesale grocery business based out of Bolton and reaching customers across the north-west of England. He began to use print advertising – mostly posters and newspaper advertisements – in an attempt to reach both his own retail customers and the end consumers.

Studying his customers, Lever was convinced that there was a major opportunity to develop the soap market. Rising working-class incomes and improved methods of production meant that soap, once a luxury, could now be offered for sale at a price that most of the population could afford. A few firms had already ventured into this market, and one in particular, Pears, had shown that advertising could be very effective. Pears's gifted young general manager, Andrew Barrett, had in the 1870s launched advertising campaigns in the London area that had made Pears a household word in the city: the strapline 'Good morning! Have you used Pears today?' entered popular culture for a time, and even featured in the libretto of a West End musical. In the north-west of England, however, the market was still wide open.

Even before beginning production, Lever's first step was to find a brand. As was common at the time, he sought advice from a Liverpool trademark agent. Officially, the main purpose of these agents was to register trademarks, but many also provided advice and suggestions for brand names and marks and acted at a very basic level as branding consultants. Among the names this agent suggested was Sunlight. Lever dismissed the idea; indeed, he was not at first happy with any of the names suggested. In later years he recalled that several days passed before he looked at the list of names again, and this time his reaction was entirely different. He chose Sunlight, a brand name which is still sold around the world today.

Lever's experience in the grocery trade had taught him that the two product features housewives prized most were reliability and cheapness. To be successful, the Sunlight brand had to deliver good quality at an affordable price. He tried for several years to find reliable suppliers but was never satisfied with the quality of the products, and finally decided to expand vertically and set up his own factory. In 1885 Lever purchased the soap works Winser & Co. in Warrington, Cheshire, and recruited several top technicians to run the factory. Lever himself knew nothing about making soap, but he knew how to manage the people who did. Sunlight quickly became known as a product of good quality and providing good value for money. Demand grew rapidly, and the Warrington plant could no longer handle the volume required, necessitating the building of a new facility. In 1889, the Lever Brothers factory at Port Sunlight on the Mersey opened, having been purpose-built on a greenfield site along with its surrounding village, shops and support services. Port Sunlight itself was later expanded several times, and by the early twentieth century more factories were opening on other sites.

Over the period 1900–14 Lever Brothers expanded overseas, acquiring production facilities for raw materials in Africa and the Pacific, and marketing its products in continental Europe, America and Australia. By the time the First World War began, the company had operations on six continents. Lever himself began to withdraw from the active management of Lever Brothers at about this time, handing over to his son. He went into politics, was knighted and then made a baron and finally a viscount. He set up several other ventures including the Mac Fisheries company in Scotland, and became interested in the development of the Congo. He died in 1925, probably of a tropical illness contracted while on a visit to the Congo.

It is for his marketing and advertising campaigns that Lever is most famous. Lever's advertising programmes went through two phases. The first phase, to use modern terminology, was aimed at creating *product awareness*, providing information to customers and alerting them to the potential of the product itself. Later, when soap became an accepted product and many rival brands were fighting for market share, Sunlight's advertising switched its emphasis to *brand awareness*, with the goals of retaining customers and distinguishing the brand from its rivals. In terms of actual advertisements, Lever was by no means the most innovative; other advertisers, such as Pears, put together better and more sophisticated campaigns. But Lever knew how to exploit advertising through scale. Between 1885 and 1905 he is estimated to have spent £2 million on advertising, a huge sum for the time and far more than any of his competitors. He also used other promotional tools in tandem with advertising, including product giveaways and, especially, contests with prizes. In these latter, in order to enter the contest, entrants had to send in a certain number of soap wrappers. These methods at first evoked derision from his rivals, but as they were shown to work, contempt was followed by alarm and then by imitation. Lever was also aggressive in terms of developing new products to follow Sunlight, and launched a major new brand every two years between 1885 and 1914. Each of these products had its own distinctive brand, marketed under the umbrella of the Lever Brothers corporate brand.

Lever is also known as an exemplary Victorian entrepreneur in terms of his views on social welfare. Port Sunlight was conceived of as a model community which would provide workers with a better standard of living. Poor housing and overcrowding were commonplace in the rapidly growing cities of the north-west of England, and Lever felt strongly that there was a need for housing reform. He himself designed and laid out the town of Port Sunlight, and for the workers' housing set out precise requirements for living space, size of gardens and other features which he considered essential to healthy living. Lever was a paternalist, who rejected profit-sharing on the grounds that the workers might spend their increased wages on things which were bad for them (such as drink), and instead set up a scheme which he described as 'prosperity sharing' in which the company's profits were ploughed back into inalienable benefits for the workforce such as housing, education and welfare. These benefits came with strict controls: Lever laid down detailed regulations for the inhabitants of Port Sunlight, which included a prohibition on the hanging of laundry in front gardens. His own office was a panopticon-like structure in the centre of the factory with walls made of glass, so that he could see every worker and note what was going on at all times.

Although 'prosperity sharing' was possible at Port Sunlight, it was not always possible at the other plants established by Lever Brothers as the firm grew. Also, many were in urban areas and it was not possible to provide purpose-built housing. In 1909 Lever abandoned his opposition to profit-sharing and introduced a system of co-partnership in which employees received preference shares in the company. Lever himself had controlled virtually all the ordinary shares since 1895, when his brother had retired on grounds of ill health, and thus there was no danger of his losing actual control; but the employees gained the further benefit of dividends. The scheme seems to have been popular, and Lever Brothers could always rely on a loyal and efficient workforce.

Like many of his contemporaries, notably the American banker J.P. Morgan, Lever was opposed to competition on principle. He believed that competition ultimately meant ruin for many businesses, and this was to the long-term disadvantage of the consumer. In 1899 he began a policy of amalgamation with other soap makers in both the UK and the USA, and seemed on the way to acquiring a monopoly. Unfortunately for him, his attempt came at a time when public sentiment, spurred in part by the anti-trust movement in the USA, was against monopolies. In 1906 the newspaper proprietor Lord Northcliffe launched a campaign against Lever on the grounds that his monopoly was against the public interest (although the fact that concentration in the soap industry would mean fewer advertisers and less revenue for Northcliffe newspapers may also have been a factor). Public pressure forced Lever to abandon his consolidation strategy, but Lever did have the satisfaction of suing Northcliffe and his papers for libel and winning over £140,000 in damages, a record sum for the time.

With the consolidation strategy abandoned, Lever now sought to protect his core business in other ways. As both wholesaler and retailer, he had been confronted by the problem of ensuring that the brand image he had created was backed up by product quality. His initial answer had been to take over the manufacturing process himself. However, soap quality depended to a great extent on the quality of the ingredients with which it was made. Concerned about securing adequate stocks of high-grade palm oil in particular, Lever then embarked on further vertical integration. His first plantations in the Solomon Islands in the South Pacific were established in 1905; by 1913 he had 300,000 acres under cultivation there. In 1902 he had begun to investigate supplies of palm oil in Nigeria, and followed this up in 1911 with the securing of a major concession in the Belgian Congo, the beginning of his interest in that region. By securing his own supply chain, Lever was able to keep prices low and to manage through the periodic fluctuations in the palm oil market, while his competitors who bought their supplies on the open market were less able to manage their risk effectively.

William Lever quite literally lived for business; it was his passion and his overriding interest. Even after he stepped back from the active management of Lever Brothers, handing over much responsibility to his son, he continued to set up business ventures in Scotland and Africa. He once summed up his own business and personal philosophy as follows:

> My happiness is my business. I can see finality for myself, an end, an absolute end; but none for my business. There one has room to breathe, to grow, to expand, and the possibilities are boundless. One can go to places like the Congo, and organize, organize, organize, well, very big things indeed. But I don't work at business only for the sake of money. I am not a lover of money as money and never have been. I work at business because business is life. It enables me to do things.

Lever pioneered the mass marketing and mass advertising of fast-moving consumer goods, and his methods were used by many who came after him, not least his younger contemporary William Procter of the American firm Procter & Gamble. Lever understood all the core concepts of marketing: consumer needs and perceptions of value, designing products that would provide maximum value, the importance of product quality, the importance of effective communication and branding, and how to distribute and sell products at a location and price that were suitable for the customer. All his other work – the vertical integration, the consolidation strategy, the overseas expansion, even the enlightened self-interest evident at Port Sunlight – was aimed at supporting and reinforcing the core proposition he offered to his customers.

## Analysis

Some of the questions you might want to consider in connection with this case include:

- How would you describe Lever's strategy? Do you think there was a coherent strategy, or was he just 'making it up as he went along'?
- Why do you think he chose the strategy he did? What options were open to him?
- Was vertical integration necessary to the extent that Lever practised it? What else might he have considered?
- Was his 'enlightened self-interest' at Port Sunlight and elsewhere linked to his business strategy, or was it something quite separate?

## Sources

Jolly, H.P. (1976) *Lord Leverhulme: A Biography*, London: Constable.

Reader, W.J. (1985) 'Lever, William Hesketh', in D.J. Jeremy (ed.), *Dictionary of Business Biography*, London: Butterworth, vol. 3, pp. 745–51.

Wilson, Charles (1954) *The History of Unilever: A Study in Economic Growth and Social Change*, London: Cassell, 2 vols.

## Case Study 3B

### Francesco Datini

Francesco di Marco Datini was born in the Italian town of Prato, north-west of Florence, in 1335.[3] He came from humble origins; his father was a tavern-keeper, and in 1348 when Datini was thirteen both his father and mother died of the Black Death. At age fourteen he went to work as an apprentice to a trader in nearby Florence, and at fifteen, using a small legacy left by his father, travelled to Avignon in France. A little over forty years earlier, the popes had transferred their residence and court from Rome to Avignon, and the city now was home to a thriving Italian financial and business community. Datini found work in this community, and by 1361 had accumulated enough capital to go into business on his own account. Trading first in arms and armour, by the middle 1360s he had branched out into areas as diverse as cloth, salt, home furnishings and works of art. Like many small businessmen of the time, he dealt in both the wholesale and retail trades. By 1378 he had accumulated enough capital to start his own bank. He married Margherita Bandini, the daughter of a fellow merchant, in Avignon in 1380; the couple had no children, but they later adopted Datini's illegitimate daughter by a slave girl who was a servant in their household.

In 1382 the papacy was restored to Rome and Avignon lost some – though not all – of its commercial importance. Datini returned to Prato after an absence of more than thirty years, and at once began a further diversification, this time into manufacturing. He invested in a small woollen cloth business owned by another Prato businessman, Niccolò di Giunta. The two men signed a partnership agreement, by the terms of which Datini was to provide capital in order to expand the business while Giunta provided no money but brought his specialist knowledge of cloth-making and its management. This sort of partnership, with one partner providing capital and the other providing knowledge and expertise, was common at the time.

In 1386, Datini began to expand outside of Prato. His first move was to nearby Florence, where he established a series of partnerships including a retail shop and wholesale/distribution ventures in bulk commodities and luxury goods. Iris Origo, author of the best English-language introduction to Datini, gives some idea of the breadth of goods in which he traded:

> English wool from London and Southampton and African or Spanish wool from Majorca and Spain, salt from Ibiza, silk from Venice, leather from Cordoba and Tunis, wheat from Sardinia and Sicily, oranges and dates and bark and wine from Catalonia ... Small wonder that Francesco's fellow-citizens gaped, as the great bales came pouring in, and whispered that he was the 'greatest merchant who ever came out of Prato!'
>
> (Origo 1957: 8)

It needs to be added that Datini continued to deal in arms and armour from time to time, and that like many international traders in the Mediterranean, he also bought and sold slaves on occasion. This was not seen as immoral by the standards of the time, when even popes often owned slaves. Some of these slaves were employed as domestic servants in large households, others were employed as translators or clerks, like the famous Leo Africanus who spent a number of years as a papal slave in the sixteenth century and was employed by the papacy as a confidential adviser on African affairs.

Following the success of his initial ventures, Datini expanded quickly. As well as maintaining his interests in Avignon, he established ventures in Pisa in 1382, Genoa in 1388 and Barcelona in 1392 (with branch offices in Valencia and Majorca). At one point, Datini was the controlling partner or *capo* in eight businesses in Italy, Spain and France. Typically for the time, each venture was established as a separate partnership (although in many cases the same partner was involved with Datini in more than one venture). Partnerships were of short duration, usually only two years, at which point they were renewed, renegotiated or dissolved at the wish of the partners.

Datini also understood fully the need for information, and spent much of his own time gathering and analysing information about markets around Europe. In addition to his own partners at home and abroad, he had agents and correspondents in many parts of Western Europe and around the Mediterranean, and he corresponded with these frequently; he seems to have been able to read and write at least eight languages. He organised his own correspondence; as he once wrote to a friend, 'I would look over each of my papers and set them in order and mark them, so that I may be clear about each man with whom I have to do' (Origo 1957: 105). He also kept centralised accounts for each partnership. In the wool-manufacturing business, his accounts showed both the cost of each stage of production and the consolidated final production cost, giving him exact information about the financial status of the business.

His management of information was an important factor in his success, but so too was his own ambition and vision. As Origo comments, 'the fundamental distinction between the international merchant and the "little man" did not consist in whether his trade was wholesale or retail, or even in the quantity of his merchandise, but rather in the outlook of the two different kinds of men' (1957: 89). The ability to 'think strategically', coupled with his skills at managing information, mark Datini out as an exemplary manager. His business, although it impressed the people of small-town Prato, was not large by comparison with the big international trading houses of Florence and Venice and Genoa. Although he was a rich man, his fortune was tiny compared to that of some of his rivals. But he was an agile and versatile businessman who could spot opportunities and move quickly to take advantage of them, and he used his limited capital to the best of his ability.

As his business interests expanded, Datini left the day-to-day management of the branches to his partners or to appointed general managers, or *fattori*, who were paid salaries rather than taken on as partners. He himself concentrated on the broader picture. In strategic terms, as noted above, he followed a steady policy of diversification, investing in manufacturing, banking and trading and expanding geographically as opportunities allowed. He also built networks and relationships with trusted merchants and partners, both at home and in other cities. Often, as in the cloth-manufacturing business in Prato, Datini provided the capital while others provided knowledge and expertise. In other cases, partners put up capital of their own; for example, Stoldo di Lorenzo, who was a partner in a number of Datini ventures over the course of twenty years, was another like Datini himself, a self-made man who was keen to invest and diversify. Not surprisingly, Datini and Lorenzo became good friends as well as business partners. However, not all partnerships were as amicable. Luca del Sera, his partner in Valencia, engaged in some rather shady foreign exchange dealings of which Datini did not approve, and after the latter's complaints failed to have effect, the partnership was dissolved. In general, it seems Datini could at times be a difficult man to work with; to his subordinates he was often a kindly man, sending gifts to those who were ill and paying pensions to the families of those who died. But to his equals he could be forceful and overbearing, insisting on getting his own way. As he was the major provider of capital in many of his ventures, this is perhaps understandable.

Datini's correspondence shows that he had two clear strategic priorities: to take advantage of opportunities as they emerged, and to reduce risk to manageable levels. Today, we might describe him as an 'emergent' strategic thinker. There is no evidence among his papers of a strategic plan, or any reference to one. His fundamental goal was the stability and perpetuity of the business: he had worked hard to build this business up, and he wanted to see it survive, at least through his own lifetime. In order to achieve this, he sought constantly for opportunities to develop new businesses and new markets, and urged his partners and subordinates to do the same. A letter to one of his *fattori* in Pisa around 1390 shows his mindset:

> See to doing whatever is needful, and think day and night about what you have to do. And do not put so many things into your head, that one makes you forget the other, and make a note of what you cannot keep in mind, for it is not possible to remember all that one has to do, but one should always keep one's eye on what is most needful.
>
> (quoted in Origo 1957: 119)

In other words, Datini wanted his staff to concentrate on the most important tasks they faced rather than getting bogged down in details, and keep their minds firmly fixed on their goals.

Diversification into new markets and new lines of business was also Datini's primary means of managing risk. Most of his trade was conducted by sea, and here he was exposed on several levels. As well as the cargoes he and his agents had purchased and which were sent by sea, Datini was also part owner of several ships. Through his bank he was also engaged in marine insurance: in exchange for a premium – often quite high – Datini would agree to compensate the owners of a ship and its cargo if they were lost. This happened commonly. In the uncertain political situation of the late fourteenth century, piracy was rife and Datini more than once lost ships and cargoes to pirates (with typical resourcefulness, he immediately broadcast the news of his losses in hopes that this would persuade the authorities to reduce his taxes). The Italian peninsula was also frequently torn by war, and even in times of peace the mercenary armies known as 'free companies' – the most famous being Sir John Hawkwood's White Company, based in Florence – would turn to banditry in order to make a living. Finally, there was the bubonic plague or Black Death, which had killed Datini's parents and continued to break out at intervals through his lifetime.

To conduct an international business under these conditions clearly took great nerve, and an acceptance that losses were inevitable. Diversification meant that losses in one area could be covered by money switched from other ventures. As the dominant partner and main provider of capital in most of his business ventures, he could transfer funds from one to the other without hindrance from his partners (they could and did object, but Datini had the power to override them). But there were finite limits to Datini's resources and he could not always cover every loss. His correspondence shows him to have been obsessed with financial details, and he examined personally the account books of every partnership and constantly tinkered with his costs and margins in order to try to ensure that, if the worst happened, each venture could survive with limited help from outside. It should be added that, although he owned a bank, Datini never used loans himself to raise capital; all his investments came from retained earnings. His correspondence shows him to be quite averse to borrowing money, and he often urged his partners to refrain from borrowing as well.

Even with constant scanning of the environment and careful calculation of risk and margins, however, Datini was still vulnerable. A serious outbreak of the Black Death in 1399–1400 killed many of his trusted partners in Florence, Prato and Genoa, and Datini himself was forced to move to Bologna for a time to escape the plague. In the aftermath of this disaster he closed several businesses and scaled back his activities, going into semi-retirement before his death in 1410. As he had no heirs, his businesses were liquidated upon his death and his wealth was distributed among a number of charities in Prato and Florence.

Remarkably, his business papers and correspondence have survived almost intact in Prato. The papers disappeared from view after his death, but were discovered once more in the nineteenth century, and continue to be analysed today. The collection includes an astonishing 130,000 business letters (plus another 11,000 items of personal correspondence), 500 account books, 300 deeds of partnership, 400 insurance policies and several thousand other documents including bills of lading, bills of exchange and cheques, enabling us to analyse in detail how Datini managed his business. The Datini archive remains a valuable resource for the study of medieval business practices.

## Analysis

Some of the questions you might want to consider in connection with this case include:

- What were the key strategic constraints under which Datini operated?
- Datini was in many ways a typical example of an emergent strategist. Might a more formal approach to planning have assisted him? If so, how?
- What were the strengths and weaknesses of Datini's diversification strategy?

## Sources

Bensa, E. (1928) *Francesco di Marco da Prato*, Milan: n.p.
Brun, R. (1930) 'A Fourteenth-Century Merchant of Italy: Francesco Datini of Prato', *Journal of Economic and Business History.*

Istituto Internazionale di Storia economica 'F. Datini' (2000) 'The Datini Company System', http://www.istitutodatini.it/schedule/datini/eng/sistema2.htm, 14 February 2001.

Origo, I. (1957) *The Merchant of Prato*, London: Jonathan Cape.

## Case Study 3C

### Jan Pieterszoon Coen

The Vereenigde Oost-Indische Compagnie, or United East India Company, more generally known in English as the Dutch East India Company (to distinguish it from the English and later British East India Company), was founded in 1602 with a charter from the States-General, the government of the Netherlands. Its purpose was to engage in trade in the Far East, and in particular to get involved in the trade in spices. Eastern spices such as cinnamon, cloves and nutmeg were valuable commodities in Western Europe, used not just in cooking but also in medicines and in perfumes and toiletries. Until the beginning of the sixteenth century, the trade in these spices had been in the hands of Arab middlemen, who transported them across the Indian ocean from Indonesia to ports in the Middle East, from which they were shipped over land to other ports on the Mediterranean and thence to Western Europe.

Following the arrival of the Portuguese navigator Vasco da Gama in India in 1500, this trade was soon taken over by Portuguese seamen and merchants, who quickly drove out the Arabs and established their own fortified posts in the Persian Gulf, the Indian sub-continent and South-east Asia, extending as far as China and Japan. But Portugal was a small company and the costs of establishing and defending these trade routes outweighed the gains from the trade itself. The Portuguese kingdom went bankrupt, and for a time the country was occupied by its neighbour Spain.

When the Portuguese empire collapsed, other countries moved in to fill the vacuum in the Eastern trade. The two principal contenders were England and the Netherlands. England was a maritime power, with many experienced sailors and captains. The Netherlands was much smaller and weaker. The country had only recently become independent after a long and costly rebellion against its Spanish overlords. The economy was weak, the country had no natural resources beyond fish, and the country was not even self-sufficient in terms of food, being forced to import grain in order to feed the population of its towns.

In chartering the East India Company, therefore, the States-General were taking a very considerable risk. Much of the country's capital, both privately held and from the public treasury, was invested in the new company. If it succeeded, the Netherlands would become an important entrepot for international trade and the country could grow rich by selling spices on to other parts of Europe, as Italian cities such as Venice had done during the Middle Ages. If it failed, the result could mean a state bankruptcy and loss of independence, just as had happened in Portugal.

Initial progress was slow. In 1603 the Dutch East India Company established its first trading post at Banten in Java, and in 1611 went on to found another at Jakarta on the same island. By 1604 the company had also established posts at Ambon and at Banda, two of the chief centres of spice production; Banda and its surrounding islands were the centres of the nutmeg trade. Almost at once the Dutch company was involved in violent clashes, first with the remaining Portuguese traders who were unwilling to surrender their own trading position, and then with the English traders of the 'other' East India Company, who had begun arriving in Eastern waters at about the same time.

Both the Dutch and English companies claimed to have a monopoly on the spice trade. Each had in fact been granted a monopoly by their respective governments. Each felt themselves justified in enforcing that monopoly and expelling the interlopers. And as each was operating thousands of miles beyond the political control of their governments, each had no hesitation in using force. The ships and men of both companies were heavily armed. The war they fought in the Indonesian archipelago was not just a trade war, but a shooting war as well.

Initially, things went in favour of the English. In 1604 English and Dutch ships fired cannon at each other off Ambon. By 1611 the English East India Company had established half a dozen posts across the region. The English had their own post at Jakarta near the Dutch one, and had fortified the islands of Pulau Ai and Pulau Run not far from Banda, with the clear intent of carving out their own share of the nutmeg trade. By 1617, although the Dutch East India Company was returning profits, there were fears that the English were set to dominate the trade and the Dutch would be marginalised. The board of directors in Amsterdam, known as the Seventeen, took the decision to recall the governor-general (the senior official in the Far East), Laurens Reael, and replace him with the man in charge of the Company's operations on Java, Jan Pieterszoon Coen.

Coen was then thirty years old. He had been apprenticed as an accountant, and joined the Dutch East India Company soon after it was founded. He had sailed to the East Indies for the first time as an 'under-merchant' (a kind of junior trader) and had done well, being quickly promoted to the more senior rank of 'upper-merchant'. Thereafter his rise was rapid. He returned to the East in 1612 and in 1613 was appointed a factor and put in charge of the post at Banten; soon after he was also appointed factor of Jakarta, the Company's largest and most important post. In 1614 he was made director general of all the Company's posts on the islands of Java. He at once distinguished himself by his vigour and his energy, and by the fact that he did not hesitate to use force when required. The English trading post at Jakarta was under the protection of the local sultan and could not be touched, but Coen made life as difficult as possible for its staff, interfering with their supplies of food and water and inciting locals to riot against the English. Elsewhere he used muskets and artillery to physically drive the English from their posts.

During his first term as governor-general, from 1617 to 1623, Coen devoted himself to driving the English out of the Indies. His reasoning was simple. England was larger, stronger and more powerful than the Netherlands, and the English East India Company could command more resources. So long as it had a single base in the East Indies, it posed a threat to the Dutch. To Coen, this was a matter of survival. There was no room for competition; one side or the other had to be driven out, and he was determined that it would not be the Dutch. And, significantly, once he had settled on that goal, Coen resolved that he would use every means at his disposal. There would be no gentlemanly competition here; this was a war to the death.

He had few resources at his disposal, a few dozen ships and never more than a thousand men, but he used them well. Disregarding the wishes of the sultan, he attacked the English trading post at Jakarta and drove the English traders out, killing several. In the course of the violence, much of the town of Jakarta was destroyed by fire; Coen rebuilt it and turned the town into the capital of the Dutch trading empire, dispossessing the Javanese sultan. At Banda he attacked the English on Pulau Ai and drove them out with heavy loss of life. A small English force under Captain Nathaniel Courthope held out on Pulau Run for several years, but after Courthope was killed in a skirmish, the remaining English surrendered. By 1623 Coen had driven the English East India Company out of every post it held save one tiny station in Aceh, in north-western Sumatra.

Modern accounts tend to focus on Coen's military exploits, but he was a highly efficient and imaginative commercial manager as well. He inspected the accounts from all posts in the East Indies and demanded to know the reasons for any delays or failures. He set targets for increasing the volume of spices traded, and ensured his factors met them. His relationship with the Seventeen was usually stormy, but the meteoric rise in trade and profits under Coen's governor-generalship attested to the success of his methods.

One of his most important contributions was to make the spice trade self-financing. At the outset, the Dutch traders had paid for the spices they bought with gold and silver coin brought from the West. This affected the Dutch balance of payments and caused a serious drain on money supply. Coen solved the problem by stimulating trade between the Indies and neighbouring countries, and established trading posts in Taiwan, Ceylon (modern Sri Lanka) and at Nagasaki in Japan. Profits gained from this regional trade were then used to purchase spices for shipment to Europe, stopping the outflow of gold and silver from the Netherlands.

Coen also forced the directors, the Seventeen, to devolve more control and decision-making to the Company's managers on the ground. Until his appointment as governor-general, the Seventeen had insisted on maintaining tight control and making all important decisions, even though they were on the far side of the world and it could take from six months to a year for messages to pass between Amsterdam and Jakarta. Coen argued that the Seventeen could not possibly run the Company efficiently in this manner. He believed that the Seventeen should set policy and then allow its managers to carry out the policy in ways they saw fit. He went so far as to deliberately mislead the Seventeen on some occasions; in 1619, he wrote to them in his usual direct style: 'I swear to you by the Almighty that the Company has no enemies who do so much to hurt and hinder it, as the ignorance and thoughtlessness (do not take ill of me) which obtain among Your Honours, and silence the voice of the reasonable' (Day 1904: 90). But he made his point, and the Seventeen handed over operational control to the governor-general and his staff from this point on.

In 1623 Coen was recalled to the Netherlands and given a hero's welcome. But in 1627, with the situation in the Indies deteriorating again, the Seventeen asked Coen to return as governor-general. He spent the next two years defending Jakarta and the other posts in Java, not from the British but from the local Javanese sultans who had finally realised that the Dutch presence threatened their own independence. He died in 1629.

Coen's achievements have been largely overlooked by English-language historians, who have been preoccupied with the affairs of the defeated British East India Company. In his colourful but not always especially accurate account, Milton (1999) blackens Coen's character without recognising his accomplishments. In fact, these were considerable. With slender resources, and in the face of strong opposition, Coen had maintained a string of trading stations spread across two thousand miles of the Indonesian archipelago, consolidated his position, and defeated a dangerous rival. By the time of his death the English East India Company had taken the decision to abandon the East Indies altogether and concentrate on India. Coen's strategy of eliminating competition had worked. The Dutch East India Company expanded and became highly profitable: annual dividends over the next hundred years were sometimes as high as 40 per cent. Eventually the Company became moribund, and was finally declared bankrupt and its assets were nationalised in 1796. Its territories in the East Indies passed under the control of the Dutch government, where they remained until Indonesia declared its independence in 1945.

Coen achieved his goals through a mixture of efficiency and ruthlessness. In terms of the latter he often went to extremes, even by the standards of the day. His insistence on the use of force to drive the English out of their posts worried many on the Seventeen; they eventually accepted his view that simple commercial competition would not achieve the required end and that force was the only answer, but their correspondence with Coen makes it clear that they had moral reservations about the rightness of what he was doing. The killing of Captain Courthope, allegedly shot in the back when he was not trying to resist or fight back, caused outcry, but that was nothing compared to the so-called Ambon Massacre in 1623 when ten English traders at Ambon were arrested on charges of spying and were subsequently tortured and executed. This incident nearly led to a war between England and the Netherlands. Coen was not present, having returned to the Netherlands, but he must bear part of the responsibility for the incident, having encouraged his subordinates to be as ruthless as he.

These incidents pale in comparison with Coen's treatment of the people of Banda. Not content with trading for nutmeg, he occupied the island by force and expelled the entire population, turning over the entire island to the production of nutmeg. Many of the islanders died of hunger or illness, and the remainder were forced to live in poverty on Java. Coen's remit was to build a trading business, but he often treated the people of the islands as if he were their conqueror.

Again, Coen himself regarded the seizure of political control as entirely justified. He believed that in the often chaotic political situation in the East Indies, the Company would have to achieve a measure of political control if it were to safeguard its commercial interests. Violence had to be used if trade were to prosper. As he told the Seventeen in 1614, 'trade with the Indies must be conducted and maintained under protection and the favour of your own weapons, and that the weapons must be supplied from the profits enjoyed by the trade, so that trade cannot be maintained without war or war without trade' (Day 1904: 46). This attitude is of course reprehensible by today's standards, but was a common one at the time. Coen differed from his colleagues and rivals only in that he had the willpower and the ruthlessness to carry his chosen strategy through to the end. A hundred and fifty years later, Robert Clive and Warren Hastings would choose the same strategic option for the British East India Company, taking a measure of political control in order to safeguard trade, and thus laying the foundations of empire in India.

Coen was by no means a pleasant nor an admirable man. But, at least in commercial terms, he was successful. As Colenbrander points out in his biography, Coen's efforts ensured that the Dutch East India Company would grow and prosper. For generations after, the name 'Coen' was synonymous with the company's success (Colenbrander 1934: 448).

### Analysis

Some of the questions you might want to consider in connection with this case include:

- Coen's chosen strategy was to eliminate his main competitor. What other strategic options were open to him?
- How important was the gaining of operational control to the success of Coen's strategy? What does this tell us about strategy and implementation?
- Coen clearly believed that the ends justify the means. Is this acceptable? Should Coen have used less violent and more ethically acceptable means, even if this increased the risk of failure?

## Sources

Colenbrander, H.T. (1934) *Jan Pieterszoon Coen*, s'Gravenhage: Martinus Nijhoff.
Day, Clive (1904) *The Policy and Administration of the Dutch in Java*, New York: Macmillan.
Hyma, A. (1942) *The Dutch in the Far East: A History of the Dutch Commercial and Colonial Empire*, Ann Arbor, MI: George Wahr.
Milton, Giles (1999) *Nathaniel's Nutmeg*, London: Sceptre.

## Case Study 3D

### *Harland & Wolff*

The shipbuilding firm Harland & Wolff was first established under that name in Belfast, Northern Ireland in 1861. Its founder was Edward Harland, the son of a doctor from Yorkshire who rejected the study of law in order to become an engineer. In 1846 at age fifteen he became an apprentice at Robert Stephenson and Company's shipyard at Newcastle on the river Tyne (Stephenson's father George Stephenson, pioneer of the steam locomotive, and Harland's father were old friends). Stephenson's shipyard was then pioneering the techniques of building iron-hulled ships for the first time, and Harland received his technical training in one of the most technologically advanced workshops in the world.

Another family friend, the Hamburg and Liverpool merchant Gustav Christian Schwabe, helped Harland get his first job as a journeyman, at the Clydebank engine-maker J. & G. Thomson, where he rose to the position of lead draughtsman. In 1853, he was offered a job as manager of Thomas Toward's shipyard in Newcastle. At twenty-two, Harland had already mastered the essentials of management, as he describes his work at Toward's:

> I found the work, as practised there, rough and ready; but by steady attention to all the details, and by careful inspection when passing the 'piece work' ... I contrived to raise the standard of excellence, without a corresponding increase in price ... I observed that quality was a very important element in all commercial success.
>
> (Moss and Hume 1986: 15)

After a year with Toward, Harland went to Belfast where he was appointed manager at Robert Hickson's yard. Again, his energy and drive made an impact. He instilled firm discipline among the workforce, who responded by striking. Partly as a result of the strike, the firm experienced severe financial difficulties, but Harland was nevertheless able to complete several major orders. In 1858 he bought out Hickson, taking over the yard. In 1861 Gustav Schwabe's nephew, Gustav Wolff, came on board as a partner, and so Harland & Wolff was born. Although Wolff played an important role in the firm until he retired, Harland was always the senior partner and most of the important strategic decisions were his alone.

Belfast was not then a major centre for shipbuilding; there were only a few small yards, no supporting infrastructure and no pool of expertise. Harland saw this as an advantage: to him, Belfast was a blank sheet on which he could write his own design for a modern, high-technology shipyard without having to adapt to or overcome previous traditions and working practices. Belfast also had an immense pool of cheap, if unskilled, labour, and he could recruit trained technicians and foremen from established shipbuilding centres on Tyneside and the Clyde.

Connections also helped. The Harland family's old friend Schwabe was a major shareholder in the Liverpool-based shipping line John Bibby & Sons, and soon after Harland took over the yard in 1858, Bibby placed an order for three iron-hulled steamships. A further order for six ships followed in 1860, and other clients began following Bibby's lead. During the period 1861–64, despite an economic downturn, Harland & Wolff launched sixteen ships.

The shipbuilding industry was very recession-prone, and overcapacity was a constant threat. Harland's strategic response to this problem was twofold. In terms of technology, he became a constant innovator, adopting new building technologies, new deck and hull structures, new engines and so on. There was a small but important pool of premium customers wanting these high-cost and high-priced ships. At the same time Harland continued to build wooden sailing vessels into the 1880s, knowing that these small, cheap ships always had a market, even if the profits were lower than for the big iron ships. Through this dual-marketing strategy, Harland & Wolff launched over 100 ships in its first twenty years.

In 1869, Schwabe brought Harland together with Thomas Ismay, then in the process of establishing the White Star passenger line on the trans-Atlantic routes. Ismay placed an order with Harland for five large passenger steamers. Harland agreed to build these on the basis of cost plus 4 per cent commission on the first cost of the ship; cost included materials and labour, but not overheads. This imaginative arrangement was repeated with other clients, and again allowed Harland & Wolff to attract premium business. Harland & Wolff continued to build ever larger and grander ships for White Star; other passenger lines, seeing the success of White Star, then came to Harland with orders for similar ships.

By the 1880s Harland was withdrawing from active management of the shipyard in favour of a career in politics. In 1887 he was elected as an MP in the British House of Commons and moved to London, handing over responsibility for management of the firm to his chosen successor William Pirrie. The son of a Belfast ship-owner, Pirrie had become a 'gentleman apprentice' at Harland &Wolff in 1862, at age fifteen. Gentlemen apprentices were moved around the firm, seeing everything from the shop floor to the chairman's office; those that showed potential were, when their apprenticeship ended after several years, offered managerial posts. Pirrie was one of these. Harland's partner Gustav Wolff spotted early on that the young man had great potential, and Pirrie rose rapidly through the firm, becoming a partner in 1874 when he was just twenty-seven.

Pirrie proved to be a talented marketing man, and took over much of the company's marketing efforts in the 1870s. Edward Harland's wife Rosa once commented that 'my husband builds the ships, but Mr Pirrie gets the orders for them'. Pirrie used a relational approach to marketing, learning as much as possible about his key customers and getting close to them personally. Moss and Hume (1986: 47) cite the story of a Liverpool shipbuilder who appeared in public 'looking very melancholy. "What is the matter?" asked a friend. "Pirrie", he replied, "has just persuaded me to order a ship and I don't know what the deuce I'll do with it."' Another observer noted that 'he was at his most dangerous when apparently most cordial' (Jefferson 1947: 287).

Pirrie took control of the management of the firm as both Edward Harland and Gustav Wolff went into semi-retirement, and after their deaths dominated it, acquiring a controlling interest. Under his management Harland & Wolff became the largest shipbuilder in the world. Pirrie concentrated on the high-technology, high-price sector first developed by Harland, and gradually stopped building the older and lower priced ships that had once been the company's mainstay. Harland & Wolff was the first shipbuilder in the world to build in steel on a large scale; in 1880–81, despite a severe recession, the company invested £15,000 in the latest steel-building technology, and was ideally placed when the market turned up again in 1882–84.

In 1889–90 Harland & Wolff launched the *Teutonic* and *Majestic*, the new flagships of White Star Line. With very strong hulls, they were the best-built ships of their day, and also the most sumptuous. The lavish interiors were largely designed by Pirrie himself, based on continental luxury hotels. The age of the great ocean liners had begun, as other shipbuilders saw White Star's liners and rushed to order their own. Every client wanted ships that were larger, faster and more luxurious than those of their rivals, and they flocked to Pirrie with their orders.

Another of Pirrie's marketing innovations was the customer club. In 1890, during another downturn, Pirrie offered to build on fixed commission for his major customers, meaning they could get their ships more cheaply. He also promised to always have shipbuilding berths ready for regular customers, so they could start building at once; in return, owners agreed to put their repair work to Harland & Wolff and to pay cash in advance rather than on delivery. Pirrie thus created a group of favoured clients who could be relied upon to put business his way even when the market was slow. Harland & Wolff sometimes also helped finance clients who were having cash flow problems, so that building could continue.

In Belfast's troubled political climate, Pirrie always stood for reconciliation between the Nationalist (in favour of Irish independence) and Unionist (in favour of uniting Britain and Ireland) communities. Himself a Protestant, he made a point of developing links with the Catholic community. In terms of labour relations, he believed in plant negotiations, not general industry agreements, and refused to take part in lockouts. Pirrie always negotiated with his workers to resolve grievances, and was generally a progressive employer. In 1898 he adopted a shorter working day with a three-shift system. He sometimes signed no-strike agreements in exchange for better working conditions. His wife Margaret was closely involved in worker welfare. Moss and Hume (1986: 45) note that: 'Unusually for a woman at that time, she was deeply interested in business. From the beginning of their marriage, she made it plain that she wished to share fully her husband's business life. He soon made no secret of his respect for her judgement and advice.'

In 1908 Pirrie took orders from White Star for two 46,000-ton liners capable of carrying 2,400 passengers, the *Olympic* and *Titanic*. Both were designed by Thomas Andrews, Harland & Wolff's chief designer and Pirrie's nephew. Andrews died when the *Titanic* sank on her maiden voyage; White Star's owner, J. Bruce Ismay, was among the survivors. Pirrie himself was deeply shocked by the tragedy and observers reported that he aged visibly; he never recovered his former vigour. Nevertheless, his response to the crisis was immediate. He ordered that Harland & Wolff should cooperate fully with the official inquiry into the sinking. Upon learning that much of the loss of life had been due to an inadequate number of lifeboats, he ordered that all new ships and older ships coming in for refit should have an adequate number of lifeboats installed, with immediate notice. He also ordered a review of the design of the *Titanic*, corrected the design flaw which had allowed her to sink, and ordered that all ships should have strengthened hulls capable of withstanding similar collisions. More Harland & Wolff built ships would collide with icebergs in the years to come, but no more would sink. These measures, and the speed with which they were taken, reassured worried customers that Harland & Wolff, despite making a tragic error, would continue to produce safe and reliable ships.

These new measures were expensive, however, and by 1914 the company was deeply in debt. However, the First World War brought a rush of new orders, and in the interwar years Harland & Wolff regained its position as the leading builder of passenger liners in the world. But Pirrie died in 1924, and his successors proved less able than he or Harland. The decline in maritime passenger traffic following the introduction of trans-Atlantic airliners hit the company hard, and in the 1960s and 1970s it seemed to have no answer to this new challenge. When other British shipyards were merged into the nationalised British Shipbuilders, Harland & Wolff was allowed to remain independent for political reasons, but it continued to dwindle. Today the shipyard still exists but it has shrunk greatly in size and employs just a few hundred people.

Pollard and Robinson (1979) cite shipbuilding as one of the great British success stories during the late nineteenth and early twentieth centuries. They see the industry as entrepreneurial, advanced in technological and labour practices and mastering good networks with its customers and suppliers. Harland & Wolff is one of the best exemplars of this success. Under Harland, the firm developed a culture on innovation, constantly seeking to employ the best new technologies. Pirrie added marketing expertise and, even more than Harland, deliberately aimed for a position of industry leadership with the aim of building ships better and faster than his rivals. Although shipbuilding was a crowded sectors with many competitors, Harland & Wolff always managed to stand out. For many years, it was not only the largest but the most technologically advanced shipyard in the world.

## Analysis

Some of the questions you might want to consider in connection with this case include:

- What are the key factors that led to Harland & Wolff's success from the 1860s to the First World War?
- How might the *Titanic* tragedy have damaged the firm? How important was it that Pirrie responded in the way he did?
- How would you classify Harland & Wolff's strategy using contemporary terms? Emergent strategy? Planned strategy? Some mixture of the two?

## Sources

Jefferson, H. (1947) *Viscount Pirrie of Belfast*, Belfast: Mullan.
Moss, M. and Hume, J.R. (1986) *Shipbuilders to the World: 125 Years of Harland and Wolff, Belfast, 1861–1986*, Belfast: The Blackstaff Press.
Pollard, Sidney and Robinson, P. (1979) *The British Shipbuilding Industry 1870–1914*, Cambridge, MA: Harvard University Press.

## Notes

1 Dates as early as the sixth century BC have been suggested, but these now seem unlikely. The American military historian Samuel B. Griffiths believes that the internal evidence of the book places it during the Warring States period in the fourth century BC.
2 Technically the honour of building the first weight-driven mechanical clock belongs to the Chinese engineer Su Sung in the eleventh century. However, his invention was later destroyed and the plans for its construction were lost; one of many cases of innovations not being fully exploited.
3 His exact date of birth is not certain, but 1335 is generally accepted.

# 4 Human resource management

---

**Learning objectives**

This chapter is intended to help readers do the following:

1 understand better how attitudes to labour and the management of people have changed and evolved;

2 analyse some of the common problems faced by managers of people over time;
3 think about some of the directions in which human resource management may continue to evolve in both theory and practice.

> The problems of internal equilibrium are chiefly concerned with the maintenance of a kind of social organisation in which individuals and groups, through working together, can satisfy their own desires.
> —Fritz Roethlisberger and W.J. Dickson, *Management and the Worker*

> The worker is selling time, just as the coal mine operators sells coal; but the purchaser is not buying time or coal; he buys output and heat units. The equivalency between operation and time (not wages) is of transcendent importance, exactly as equivalency between heat unit and fuel is of importance.
> —Harrington Emerson, *The Twelve Principles of Efficiency*

## 4.1 Introduction

Of all the disciplines of management, human resource management is one of those in which the greatest theoretical progress has been made over the past century. Only in financial management have our understanding of the key concepts and issues advanced more dramatically. Thanks in large part to developments in psychology, sociology, anthropology, linguistics and cultural studies, as well as advances in business research itself, we now know far more than we did a hundred years ago about the nature of work, human motivation in the workplace, how people act and react to stimuli both individually and in groups, and how human relationships both complicate and facilitate work processes. We are more aware too of the need to treat people fairly and honestly. The transition to a more democratic and egalitarian society in many parts of the world has had a strong impact on HR theory and practice.

In most of the developed world, the workplace of today is a far more pleasant place than it was a hundred years ago. Working conditions are better and safer, working hours are shorter, and workers are treated with more respect and decency by managers. This should not blind us to the fact that in many places in the developing world, and in some of the unregulated sweatshops inside developed countries, working conditions are still appalling; but in general, conditions have improved.

Yet, as this book goes to press in 2009, there has been another spate of 'bossnappings' in France, workers holding their senior managers hostage as a way of gaining publicity for their grievances. Strikes, if no longer the paralysing force they were a few decades ago, have not disappeared. Problems between labour and management continue. Workforces continue in many cases to be dysfunctional places torn by rivalries and where fear is the prevailing culture; in his book *Management and Machiavelli* (1967), Anthony Jay graphically describes life inside such organisations. And human resource managers have their own problems. In some organisations they are regarded as key members of the management team, and their advice and views are given equal weight to those of other managers. But in other organisations they are regarded with distrust by the workforce and lack status in comparison with other managers. Studies in both the USA and Britain in recent years have shown that human resource professionals earn less than finance or marketing professionals of similar experience, and it is still relatively rare for a human resources director to advance to become chief executive or chairman.

While we know a great deal more about the best and most effective ways of managing people, that knowledge has not always been translated into practice. Business schools often teach case studies of companies such as Semco, the Brazilian light industrial firm which, under the guidance of its owner and general manager Ricardo Semler, has evolved a radical business model based on decentralised authority, democracy and self-management. But only a few firms have copied the Semco model, just as only a few copied the model developed at Cadbury Brothers a hundred years ago. Cadbury introduced fairer working conditions, raised levels of workforce commitment to new heights, and harnessed the collective knowledge of its people to powerful effect; but although the company was widely admired, it was rarely imitated.

Is there something that stops organisations from adopting what is generally acknowledged to be best practice in human resource management? Stepping outside the confines of our own time and looking at the problems and challenges of managing people over a longer period may help to answer this question. It may also help to shed more light on those problems and challenges themselves. Finally, we should also begin to see how the historical legacy – good and bad – continues to have an impact on human resource management as practised today.

---

### The evil that men do lives long after them

History exposes both the good and the bad, and the history of management is no exception. In the past, some managers have employed slave labour, and some who held managerial posts have even been slaves themselves. Some readers may be uncomfortable with this, understandably so. But there are some good and cogent reasons why, instead of avoiding the subject, it might be useful to confront this particular demon.

Since the beginning of recorded history, some businesses and other organisations have employed slaves as workers. Today slavery is illegal, but the practice continues clandestinely. Many of those unfortunate people who are 'trafficked', or smuggled illegally from one country to another to work, are in effect slaves; their liberty may not have been taken away legally, but their freedom of movement and of choice is so circumscribed as to make them *de facto* slaves.

So vastly different are the conditions under which slaves have worked that it is almost impossible to generalise. In some cases, such as the work crews digging the Grand Canal in ancient China or the labour camps of the Third Reich, slaves were treated brutally and inhumanely, and tens of thousands died of overwork, illness and abuse. In other cases – such as that of Pasion, the Greek slave who became a trusted and reliable servant of his Athenian banker masters, was given a percentage of the profits and ultimately was freed and took over the ownership and management of the bank, or Leo Africanus, a slave at the papal court in the sixteenth century who became a confidential adviser to the papacy on Middle Eastern affairs – slaves were treated well and even won a degree of respect from the free people around them. There were, of course, far fewer of this latter group than the former.

In some societies, slaves were able to earn money, and could either purchase their freedom or receive it as a reward for good service. The bureaucracy of the government of Imperial Rome was largely run by slaves and ex-slaves, many of the latter reaching high rank and becoming wealthy men (Barrow 1928). Attaining freedom was sometimes possible in more repressive societies too. Many slaves in pre-Civil War America were harshly treated, but those with skills were sometimes able to find advancement. William Ellison, who was literate and had some knowledge of accountancy and was also a skilled mechanic, was able to purchase his freedom in 1816, along with that of his wife and daughter. Ellison then founded a business making and repairing cotton gins in the town of Stateburg, South Carolina, and became a respected member of the community, even winning a limited degree of tolerance from his white neighbours (Johnson and Roark 1984). Expanding his business and needing more labourers, Ellison then did what any white businessman in his position would have done: he bought slaves.

Despite these and other examples, the employment of slaves as workers was not a universal practice. In some cases, what were thought to be slave labourers turn out not to be. For example, recent research has shown that the Great Pyramids, once thought to have been built using slave labour, were in fact constructed by free labourers who received wages. Although there were exceptions, such as Imperial Rome and Ottoman Turkey in its early years, both of which employed large numbers of skilled workers as slaves, most societies would have struggled to find enough skilled slaves to undertake complicated tasks. Therefore, when slave labour was used at all, it was nearly always for very menial tasks: quarrying stone, picking cotton, digging canals and so on.

There was one major reason why many societies did not use slave labour, apart from the obvious ethical one: slave labour was inefficient. Slaves, even when they were physically healthy and well fed, were badly motivated. For every William Ellison who dreamed of freedom and worked towards it, there were thousands of others who simply suffered their fate. It is not that they lacked ambition or had no dreams of freedom. But slavery itself, as those who have experienced it have attested, is a horribly demotivating and debilitating condition. Slaves feel the shame of slavery and feel themselves to be the lowest of the low. The crushing of the spirit that accompanies the loss of liberty tends to drive out motivation and even the desire for life itself. Small wonder that such people do not make efficient workers.

The American economist Henry Carey (1853) estimated that one free worker would, under most conditions, be more productive than four slaves doing the same work. He attributed the relative economic under-development of the southern American states to their reliance on slave labour, which he said was holding back their economic advancement. In the northern states, where slavery had been abolished, economic growth was much more rapid. The economic stagnation that afflicted the later Roman Empire is also attributed in part to an over-reliance on slave labour.

So if slave labour was so inefficient, why was it used? Sometimes, enslaving people and putting them to work was a way of demonstrating one's own supposed racial or cultural superiority. Sometimes it was a short-term cost-cutting measure: slaves may be inefficient, but they also do not require wages. The same argument is applied today by the managers and owners of sweatshops (technically their employees are not slaves, but in many cases they might as well be): they may not work well, but they are cheap.

Today, of course, no manager with an ounce of ethical or moral feeling would dream of employing slaves in any capacity whatever. But the arguments for and against employing slave labour need to be remembered. In particular, the point that willing and motivated workers will always outperform unwilling and demotivated ones needs to be borne in mind. And the evils of slavery, as well as its inefficiencies, need to be remembered when we contemplate those businesses and managers who continue to treat their workers inhumanely – whatever the legal status of those workers might be. When contractors promise to supply goods or components at prices that seem too good to be true, it is always worth investigating how the contractor pays his or her workers and the conditions under which they live and work. Failure to do so can come back to haunt firms, as Nike and many others have discovered in the past twenty years.

## 4.2 Attitudes to work and workers

We can begin with a paradox, which can be observed all across the world and across every culture virtually since records began. There is on the one hand a belief that work itself is a good thing. Being a hard worker is a virtue, while sloth or laziness is a vice. As Donkin (2001) points out, in primitive societies there is a distinction between activities which are seen to be enjoyable, such as hunting, and those which are not, such as chores around the camp. Both are necessary, both are productive, but the former are seen to be 'fun' and the latter are seen to be 'work'.

However, as civilisation takes hold, societies are increasingly structured around work. By the sixteenth century in Europe, the need to work and be productive had taken on religious overtones. The 'Protestant work ethic' of Martin Luther and John Calvin reinforced the notion of the virtue of work, and continues to be active in European and American society today.

Yet, at the same time, in nearly every society it is held that those who do labour, especially manual labour, are at the lowest end of the social scale and occupy positions of inferiority. Indeed, the dirtier and harder the labour, the lower the labourer's position on the social scale. Logically, this makes no sense. Someone must dig ditches and clean out sewers and collect rubbish, or else there will be severe problems with public health. Yet for thousands of years we regarded the people who did these jobs as the lowest of the low, while at the same time looking up to and respecting those at the upper end of the social scale who did no manual labour at all. So, work is said to be virtuous and honourable, and yet workers are placed at the lowest end of the social scale, in the West, in India and in China and Japan alike.

We have to be careful here, of course, for 'work' does not just mean manual labour. Managerial work is still work. In *Das Kapital*, Karl Marx made it clear that 'mental work' was nonetheless work, implying that researchers, writers, librarians, musicians and even university lecturers might have some claim to be part of the proletariat. And non-proletarians work too. In Chapter 1 we noted that the knights of medieval England, far from frittering their days away attending tournaments and feasts and listening to minstrels, were extremely hard working; as well as their military service, they could be called upon to carry out a wide range of administrative duties, often at very little notice and usually without pay. So onerous were the duties that some who qualified for knighthood asked to be excused from being knighted on the grounds that the workload and costs would be too heavy. On at least one occasion in the fourteenth century, the English crown had to issue an edict ordering all those who were qualified for knighthood to come forward and accept the honour, or pay a large fine.

However, we have to recognise that for the past several thousand years, society has made a class distinction between those at the lowest scale, who do labour, and those on the upper levels who – theoretically – do not. Scholars and peasants, brahmans and dalits, equestrians and plebeians, knights and serfs, capitalists and labourers, white-collar and blue-collar, shopfloor and boardroom, them and us: the division has persisted throughout history, and is fundamental to many of the problems of human resource management today. We will return to this division later in the chapter. For the moment, however, for the particular purposes of this chapter, when we talk about 'work' and 'workers', we are talking about those lower down the organisation: labourers, shop floor workers, foremen and the lower grades of supervisors. Middle and upper management are for the moment excluded.

### 4.2.1 The ancient world and the Middle Ages

Most civilised societies since the dawn of civilisation itself have been structured vertically. A relatively small number of people have possessed power and authority over a relatively large number of people who have little of either. In ancient China the authority of the emperor was supreme over all; next came the keepers of wisdom, the scholars and sages, then the administrators and bureaucrats, then the merchants, and finally the peasants whose duty was to conduct public works and provide food and other necessities for the classes above them.

What the relationship between the classes should be was a matter for discussion. Confucius and his followers believed that the lower classes owed the upper classes a duty of obedience, in the same way that children owe obedience to adults; but at the same time there was a kind of social contract in which the upper classes owed the lower, the peasants in particular, a duty of care, as a father might care for his children. The Daoists argued for a loose arrangement in which the king and the sages provided guidance rather than control and people in the lower classes were left to manage their own affairs. Han Fei and the Legalist school, on the other hand, argued for very tight control. There was no room for a social contract in their thinking: the duty of the lower classes was to obey, and if they failed to do so then they should be punished harshly.

The Indian caste system put labourers at the bottom too, below priests, warriors and administrators. In the *Arthashastra* of Kautilya (see also Kumar 1990; Boesche 2002), the first major work of Indian political theory compiled around 300 BC, the relationship and roles of each are made clear. The lower castes are there to do the labour, while the others provide oversight, guidance, protection and administer to spiritual needs. Kautilya also sees the responsibilities as running in two directions; the lower castes are required to labour and to obey their masters, but the higher castes, the brahmans in particular, also have a duty to bring enlightenment to the people. The king, who is at the head of the hierarchy, has a duty to ensure peace, prosperity and enlightenment throughout his lands.

In ancient Egypt we find a similar hierarchy of priests and administrators overseeing the mass of labourers. Imperial Rome had a threefold strata below the emperor himself and his family, consisting of senators, equestrians and plebeians. The role of the plebeians was to labour, while the equestrians, the middle class, owned businesses and estates or managed them on behalf of others. Senators were legally forbidden to engage in business at all (we find this prohibition at times in other places too, notably at some times in imperial China and in early Japan), and were supposed to concentrate on their responsibilities relating to governing the state. This led to senators setting up shadow businesses run by other family members or trusted friends and servants; officially they had no connection with the business, in practice they provided most of the capital and took most of the profits.

Medieval Europe also had a threefold hierarchy, the so-called Three Estates of knights, priests and peasants.[1] Early medieval theologians spelled out the duties of each. The knights were to provide military service and protect society from physical harm; the priests were to minister to the spiritual needs of society and save souls. As these two classes had their own duties and were unable to labour in the fields, it was the duty of the peasants to provide food and other necessities, and to be obedient to the other two classes. This was a rather badly thought-out system, as it had no room for either business-people – craftsmen, traders, bankers and the like – or the professional classes such as lawyers, doctors and bureaucrats. Nonetheless, it persisted at least up until the time of the Protestant Reformation in the sixteenth century, and in some parts of Europe such as Russia, for longer still.

---

### Class tensions in the Middle Ages

Ah, World, why do you go astray? For this the poor lesser folk (who should stick to their work) demand to be better fed than the one who has hired them. Moreover, they clothe themselves in fine colours and handsome attire, whereas they were formerly clothed (without pride and without conspiracy) in sackcloth. Ah, World, I will not lie to you; if you cause these evils to come, I complain about your power. Ah, World! I know not what to say, but all the estates that I look at – from the first to the last – are getting worse, every one of them; the poor as well as the lordly are all full of vanity. The poor people are more haughty than their sovereign; everyone is pulling against the others.

–John Gower, *The Mirror of Mankind*

---

All three of these systems, Chinese, Indian and European, share common features. First, those that perform manual labour are subordinated to those that do not. Second, all three systems insist that people, especially those of the lower orders, should know their place and not seek to advance from it (the implicit fear being that if all the labourers decide to become knights or administrators or priests, there will be no one left to do the labouring). This meant that the poorest people were more or less condemned to stay poor, which was not always well received by the poor themselves. In medieval Europe the poor were offered a consolation prize: if they were meek and humble and performed their labours well, then whatever sufferings they might endure during life, they would receive their reward in the afterlife. And third, and most importantly for our purposes, all three systems demanded obedience and deference from the lower classes, who must respect their betters and carry out their orders unquestioningly.

---

**Reward in heaven**

It is fitting that we end our work with the class that God loves but the world hates – the poor, both men and women. We exhort them to patience because of the hope of the crown that is promised them, saying: O blessed poor by the judgement of God recorded in the gospels, waiting for the possession of Heaven by the merit of poverty patiently borne, rejoice in this great promise of joy which surpasses everything else and to which no other rich possession can be compared.

–Christine de Pisan, *Treasury of the City of Ladies*

---

This repeated emphasis on deference and obedience in contemporary texts might lead us to believe that people in earlier times were more deferential, knew their place and were more obedient to orders. But we must be careful. Imperial China was a highly authoritarian society, but the deference paid by peasants to bureaucrats and overlords was often a matter of form; China was also a society which placed a premium on correct behaviour. What people actually thought we can gather from folk literature and stories, which are full of rogues and tricksters who are elevated to heroic status (see for example some of the characters in classics of Chinese literature such as *Journey to the West* or *Outlaws of the Marsh*). China had its own Robin Hoods, bandit leaders who defied the empire and fought to defend the common people from injustice. In the seventeenth century the White Lotus Society, a semi-religious sect with overtones of both Buddhism and Daoism, actively encouraged people to rebel and fight injustice. India too has a long tradition of people taking matters into their own hands and fighting back against unjust overlords and administrators.

And there is little sign that the peasants and workers of Christian Europe took seriously the duty of obedience and deference laid on them by nobles. Poems and songs about corrupt clerics and incompetent nobles and kings were in widespread circulation. The student poets whose works were later collected as the *Carmina Burana* openly defied clerical authority, and the German poet Walther von der Vogelweide in the thirteenth century helped to begin a wave of

German anti-clericalism which built until, two centuries later, some German priests reported that they dared not enter their own parishes for fear of their lives. Nobles and kings were defied too, and the authority they represented was repeatedly questioned:

> When Adam delved and Eve span,
> Which then was the gentleman?

So went a protest song which was heard more than once in medieval England, the implication being that at the time of creation there were no class distinctions, everyone laboured equally, and God had intended that all should be equal. It was not just peasants in the countryside who refused to follow authority blindly; workers in towns took matters into their own hands too. Four times in the fourteenth century, in Rome, Florence, Genoa and the Flemish city of Ghent, striking textile workers not only forced employers to bow to their demands but toppled the existing government and brought in new, populist regimes sympathetic to their cause. Later that same century, peasant rebels invaded London and came close to overthrowing the English king Richard II.

While it is certainly true that in our time, deference and obedience are no longer demanded by right, to some extent that misses the point. This change has only taken place within the last hundred years, and 2,500 years of class antipathy cannot be wiped out at a stroke. Conflict between workers and owners or managers is deeply ingrained in our cultural memory, and still affects attitudes to labour and the management of people today.

### 4.2.2 The Industrial Revolution

In the period before the Industrial Revolution, the complaints of workers against managers can be divided into two categories. The first was that the workers were being unfairly deprived of the fruits of their own labours, and should have a share in the prosperity they were creating. The second was that the knights and priests and administrators who ruled their actions did so unjustly, and that the lower classes ought to be free to choose their own destiny and have more control over their own actions.

The Industrial Revolution brought these complaints into sharp focus. The factory system brought hundreds, and later thousands, of labourers together under a single roof, subject to the control of the owner and his superintendents. As Donkin (2001) points out, neither side really knew what to expect. The new factory owners, often former working men themselves, had no experience at running mills, and the workers had no experience of working machinery. The first factory owners like Arkwright used mostly male workers, but others hired entire families, putting the women and children to work in the mills and sending the men out to do other jobs such as construction or road building.

Finding separate work for men, often constructing or running properties on the mill owners' private estates, was another way in which these
entrepreneurs filled their mills with the wives and children of tradesmen. The whole family then could be conceived as an economic unit.
So many of the necessities of life – housing, groceries, coal – were
provided by these mill employers that employees often received no
more than a sixth of their wages in cash. It meant that families became
as tied to their place of work as their ancestors had been in the service
of the Lord of the Manor.

(Donkin 2001: 78)

The conditions under which people lived and worked in the factories of the
Industrial Revolution and the attempts to ameliorate their plight have been
widely discussed elsewhere (see Pollard 1965; Donnachie 2000 for good intro-
ductions). Socialists and Marxists argued then, and have argued since, that the
Industrial Revolution saw capitalists supplant the old ruling classes, nobles and
priests, and assert control over the working class. To the working class, exploitation was exploitation; the only difference seemed to be that the new generation of capitalists were rather more efficient at it. But this change in the balance
of power happened not just in factories, which even at the height of the
Industrial Revolution never employed more than about 10 per cent of the
working population in Europe or America, and even less elsewhere.

This was a time of a general squeeze on labour. Business owners thought
nothing of cutting wages once their own profits began to decline. In the early
1890s the Pullman Company, manufacturers of railway sleeping cars, cut wages
by 30 per cent during an economic downturn, and other firms cut wages by as
much as 50 per cent. The notion of a social contract, in which employers looked
after their employees and protected their interests, seemed to have flown out the
window. In London in the 1840s and 1850s, Henry Mayhew (1968) wrote of the
poverty and squalor in which workers lived in the slums of London, while
in New York around the same time Henry Carey wrote of women living in
unheated apartments in winter who had sold their clothes to buy food. In *The
Proud Tower*, Barbara Tuchman (1980) recounts the story of an unemployed
man in New York in the 1890s who was arrested for slashing a rich woman's
carriage horse with a knife. His reason was that the money spent on feeding and
grooming the horse for a week would have fed his wife and children for a year.
Once more, it seemed to some observers that those who did the labour were
being denied a fair share in the prosperity they had helped to create.

There were business leaders who urged their colleagues to take more
responsibility, and also argued the case that treating workers decently and
paying them well made good business sense. Robert Owen had made this
argument early in the nineteenth century, with limited success (see Case Study
1D). In America, the editors of *Freeman's Magazine*, a Christian-influenced
magazine aimed at business owners, launched similar pleas. But most of the
business community seemed incapable of learning this lesson. Why? The answer

is still not clear, but it is hard to disagree with the British economist Sidney Pollard (1965) who judged that management had failed the test. Rather than innovate and come up with new ways of managing workers, Pollard said, managers had simply slavishly imitated each other, and labour management practices in particular were justified on the grounds that 'that's the way things are done'.

This was not solely a Western phenomenon. As the factory system spread to Asia, similar problems arose. The maltreatment of factory workers in India – by Indian factory owners as well as British ones – threatened to turn into political violence which could have destabilised India. The young lawyer Mohandas K. Gandhi (afterwards Mahatma Gandhi) first came to prominence while working with striking textile workers in Ahmedabad (Bose 1956). In China, too, harsh labour practices in the new-style factories became commonplace. Emily Honig (1983) has described the activities of a group of recruiting agents known as the 'Green Gang' who supplied labour to the factories of Shanghai in the 1930s. The Green Gang travelled into the countryside around Shanghai and purchased – literally – girls aged between fourteen and eighteen from their families. Taken into the city, the girls were then offered as labourers to factory owners. They were housed in dormitories, into which they were locked once their shift on the shopfloor had ended. Their wages were handed over by the factory owners to the Green Gang recruiters, who kept the money in exchange for providing 'room and board' in the dormitories. Honig comments that none of the factory owners liked the system and constantly complained that the weak and undernourished young women were not capable of doing a full day's labour. Yet none seemed to be capable of summoning the initiative to change the system.

> Perhaps the most important conclusion to emerge is that 'management', in our sense, though not a barrier to progress, yet could not be shown to have been an initiator of change either. The pragmatic discovery of new methods was no doubt adequate, but management appears everywhere to have adapted itself merely to the needs of technology, discipline or financial control. Among the many competing explanations there can surely be nowhere a managerial theory of industrial revolutions.
>
> (Pollard 1965)

### 4.2.3 The politicisation of labour

Robert Owen had warned his fellow mill-owners that by failing to reform their methods they were sowing the seeds for conflict. In later years he himself helped to organise the trades union movement in Britain. During the nineteenth century various political movements – radicalism, socialism, communism, syndicalism, anarchism – emerged and championed the cause of the worker. As well as strikes, sabotage and direct action, all of these movements launched vigorous propaganda campaigns, aimed in part at mobilising the workers but in part too at waking the consciences of the middle and upper classes. Novels like Zola's *Germinal* about strikes in the French coalfields, or Upton Sinclair's *The Jungle* which depicted vividly working conditions in the Chicago slaughterhouses, were intended to tell people living comfortable lives in the suburbs of what was going on inside their own countries, and urge them to support the workers in their demand for greater rights and freedoms.

The newly created labour movement became, unsurprisingly, strongly associated with left-wing politics, while right-wing political parties supported the capitalists and the upper classes. This of course had the effect of polarising things still further and strengthening the perception of 'them and us'. By the end of the nineteenth century, relationships between workers and managers in the USA and Europe had reached an all-time low. In many cases, both sides actively sought confrontation. In Russia 1917, the government fell and was replaced by a left-wing government supported by the proletariat. In Italy, Germany and Spain there were right-wing backlashes, fascists took power and the labour movement was crushed. Elsewhere there were varying degrees of accommodation; governments sympathetic to workers came to power in France, Britain and the USA and passed legislation which gave workers better pay, shorter working hours and better working conditions, unemployment insurance and pensions. This defused the tensions a little, but as recently as the 1970s the trades unions launched a sustained challenge against the British government, and they remain a political force to be reckoned with in France.

## 4.3 The management of people

We have dwelt on this subject at length because, as noted earlier, the 'them and us' distinction between workers and those who oversee their work has a very long history. It poses, indeed, one of the most significant challenges faced by those who manage people. A business, or any other organisation, functions best and most efficiently when all its members share a sense of common interest and are prepared to work together. But how can this be done when, for two and a half thousand years at least, for all the reasons we have discussed above, there has persisted a division between managers and workers?

A variety of methods were used in the past by businesses and organisations to manage people. We can classify these methods into three broad categories. The first is through the use of *command and control*. The second is by adopting a management style based on *paternalism*. The third is by involving workers directly in the business through *cooperation and partnership*.

### 4.3.1 Command and control

The command and control approach does not attempt to overcome the division between managers and workers. Rather, it accepts that division and sometimes even reinforces it. Command and control organisations model themselves on the long-standing stratifications found in society, and create a hierarchy based on function, with shop floor or manual labourers at the bottom and the chairman and directors at the top. Authority flows downward. The chairman gives orders to senior managers, they pass them on to junior managers who in turn transmit them to foremen and so to the workers. It is the task of all those in the hierarchy to carry out the orders they receive to the best of their ability.

Of course there were many variations on this theme. On the one hand there were autocratic managers who drove their workers to ever greater efforts in the pursuit of ever-expanding profits, with little regard for the workers themselves or the effect it had on their lives. Money spent on worker welfare was money wasted, for it reduced profits. Nor did managers of this stamp believe the argument that shorter working days increased productivity, despite clear evidence being presented in its favour. By 1890 it was widely known that workers on a ten-hour day were something like 20 per cent more productive per day than those working fourteen hours, while those working eight-hour days were more productive still, but twelve- and fourteen-hour working days were still common in both Europe and America. The practice of 'driving' or 'sweating' workers to the extremes of endurance was condemned by authorities as varied as Frederick Winslow Taylor (1903) and Edward Cadbury (1908), but it continued nonetheless.

But there were also authoritarian and autocratic leaders who looked after their people. One such as John Patterson, chairman of National Cash Register. A strong-willed man who used ruthless means to drive his competitors out of business and fired directors who failed to obey his orders, Patterson was very protective of his workers. At his plant in Dayton, Ohio, learning that many workers and their families were inadequately nourished, he set up a canteen offering free meals. He was astonished at first to find that the workers refused to eat there, but then realised that it was not the meals themselves they objected to, but the idea of charity. A notional charge of five cents was then placed on every meal, and the canteen quickly filled with people. Patterson also decreed that the wives of all his staff – managers and directors included – must take cooking lessons (Crowther 1923). He went on to provide other benefits such as health care and a gymnasium. Accused by other business leaders of being excessively 'soft' in his treatment of employees, Patterson replied that the cost of employee benefits was repaid to the firm in terms of higher productivity and lower rates of sickness and absenteeism.

---

One of the most profitable investments that can be made in a manufacturing plant is to give the largest possible advantages in the way of conveniences and sanitary arrangements. Every kind of legitimate comfort and convenience that may be provided for operatives is a source of profit to the employer, although apart from the moral obligation to care for the health and comfort of the employee.

(John Patterson, quoted in Becker 1906: 552)

Patterson was not a paternalist or a philanthropist. When he did help arrange food aid and donate large sums of money for the relief of people made homeless by floods in Dayton some years later, he did so in exchange for a pardon from the governor of Ohio, having been indicted on anti-trust charges several years earlier. He provided benefits for his employees because he knew they would work harder and be more productive, and he would thus make a return on his investment.

Other autocratic leaders did not provide the range of services that Patterson did. Instead, they cultivated a reputation for fairness, for dealing honestly with workers and answering their complaints. Henry Ford, in the first stage of his career at least (see Case Study 9B), was one such. So was his chief production manager, Charles 'Cast-Iron Charlie' Sorenson, one of the hardest men in a hard industry, who managed to retain the respect of his workers. In the late 1920s on a visit to the Soviet Union, Sorenson was greeted with shouts of 'Hiya, Charlie!' by men working on a truck assembly line in a factory near Tula; they were former Ford men, who remembered their hard-nosed old boss with affection (Sorenson 1957).

Command and control relationships require, at a minimum, that management be respected and trusted by the workers. Richard Arkwright fell into dispute with his workers early in his career as a factory owner, and one of his mills at Chorley in Lancashire was burned to the ground by strikers. Arkwright did not make the same mistake twice; though hardly a model employer, he did treat his workers honestly and did not try to deceive them. His mills had little in the way of labour trouble thereafter.

### 4.3.2 Paternalism

A common alternative to command and control was paternalism. Paternalistic styles of management can be traced back to Imperial Rome and ancient China, and have remained highly popular. The paternalistic (or maternalistic) manager treats his (or her) organisation rather like the old Roman *familia*, or household: the head of the household is responsible for all persons in that household, including family members and servants. Although the members of the organisation are expected to obey the chairman or chief executive, the analogue to the head of the household, the latter is also expected to look after the other members of the organisation and to take responsibility for them.

The mill-owner Robert Owen, for all his later socialist principles, was by and large a paternalist leader. He provided benefits for his workers at the New Lanark textile mill, including housing, education and health care, but he did not admit them to the management of the firm, and he expected them to work hard and carry out his wishes. The German steel maker Alfred Krupp, the Yorkshire mill-owner Titus Salt and the consumer goods maker William Lever (see Case Study 3A) are other examples of paternalist leaders, combining authoritarianism with social responsibility.

Often, a paternalistic approach to management stemmed from the personal beliefs of the owner and/or senior manager. George and Edward Cadbury were Quakers, and this clearly influenced their attitudes to managing people (though there is an open question as to whether they were purely paternalistic; see Case Study 4A). Ma Ying-piao, founder of the Hong Kong department store Sincere, was a committed Christian, as was Ohara Magosaburo, chairman of Kurashiki Spinning Company, one of Japan's largest textile producers. Like his Western counterparts, Ohara provided free housing, health care and education for his workers, and also supplied them with food and other goods either free or at cost. Paternalism also appealed to the instincts of many managers who were devout Jews, Buddhists, Hindus, Jains or Muslims. Abol Hassan Ebtehaj, governor of Bank Melli in Iran, insisted on paying his staff good wages, provided health and education programmes, a subsidised restaurant and a gymnasium for his staff, all in the belief that providing these things was the duty of a good employer (Bostock and Jones 1989).

But religion was not the only factor; Robert Owen was a convinced atheist. Others were motivated by a concern for social justice. The point is that most of these people were paternalists for reasons of personal conscience, not for reasons that had anything to do with sound management. Again, as Sydney Pollard implies in his history of the Industrial Revolution (1965), management had failed the test.

---

### A Sincere approach to business

Ma Ying-piao's approach to management combined many of the features of both Chinese and Western-style management. As Chan (1997: 226) commented, 'Another important innovational aspect of the Sincere Company was that it combined both traditional Chinese moralistic and social concerns with the modern techniques of organization.' Classes providing religious and moral education for employees began in 1907, with Ma personally conducting lessons. These were followed by more formal classes teaching English, mathematics and accounting. The combination of Confucian paternalism, Christian values, Western organisation and accounting methods and a deep grounding in traditional Chinese culture was a potent one, and resulted in strong loyalty and commitment from staff. By 1925 Sincere had over 2,000 employees in its department stores and was capitalised at $7 million. The company remains highly prosperous with stores in several Chinese cities, under the direction of a descendant of the founder.

---

### 4.3.3 Cooperation and partnership

Or had it entirely failed? There were a few, just a few, firms whose managers regarded their employees as something more than a source of muscle power to be exploited, or a group of semi-helpless people who needed to be cared for. These firms and these managers saw that working with their employees, trying to close the gap between management and labour, could yield economic benefits.

Sometimes the benefits were simply labour peace, which in turn meant a stable business. Some managers met with their workers and offered concessions in terms of pay and working conditions in exchange for the workers signing agreements not to strike. Others went further. George Eastman, the founder of Kodak, and the German engineer Robert Bosch both introduced profit-sharing and worker welfare programmes as a means of keeping workers happy and making them less prone to become involved in strikes or sabotage. In both cases it worked; Bosch commented that so long as he kept his workers happy and did nothing to annoy them, the trades unions basically ran his labour force for him.

Others thought the process could go further. Walther Rathenau, the visionary Jewish business leader and statesman who became German Foreign Minister after the First World War (and who was the first person to be assassinated by the Nazis in 1923) thought that companies that employed manual workers ought to rotate them around jobs and allow them to spend part of their working week doing 'intelligence work', meaning some kind of creative work or research. This would allow them to develop as individuals, and in turn meant that they would have more to contribute to the firm in terms of ideas and knowledge. At Cadbury Brothers in Britain, workers were heavily involved in management and in innovation; as one observer said, 'at Cadbury's everybody thinks' (see Case Study 4A). This close cooperation and understanding between workers and managers was seen as key to Cadbury's competitive success.

Few firms went as far as Carl Zeiss Jena (Case Study 4D) where in a manner reminiscent of Semco, employees were given loose targets and then left to their own devices to meet those targets, or the John Lewis Group (Case Study 4C) where the chairman handed over ownership of the company to its employees and invited them to share in the profits and work to increase those profits in the future. But there were others like Tomas Bat'a of Bat'a Shoes (Case Study 4B) or Edward Filene of Boston-based Filene Stores who consulted their workers on important matters and listened closely to their views. While Filene handled day-to-day management himself, big strategic issues were often put to a vote of employees; and Filene abided by the results of these votes, even if he himself had voted in the minority group (Filene 1932).

The idea that management was something that could be done *with* people instead of *to* them, and that the separation between workers and managers was not inevitable, was understood in a very limited way by the early twentieth century. But it never really took root. Instead of moving towards a more cooperative model, the emerging science of management took a different turning. It chose instead to develop a sub-discipline, first called labour management, then personnel management, now generally referred to as human resources management. The development of this discipline led to many advances and improvements in the ways that people are managed at work. But it also led to some opportunities being lost.

## 4.4 The professionalisation of labour management

As discussed in Chapter 1, by the end of the nineteenth century the need for reform in management, and in particular the management of people, had become acute. Violent strikes were costing lives, reducing productivity, damaging businesses and communities. The initial aims of the pioneers of scientific management were to find a way of rewarding workers more fairly for their work and enabling them to share in the wealth they created. In his early works especially *Shop Management* (1903), the founding father of scientific management, Frederick Winslow Taylor, was explicit on this subject. Scientific management was the only fair way to reward people, and once workers realised they were being treated as fairly was possible, labour peace would result.

---

### Fairness at work

Perhaps the most prominent single element in modern scientific management is the task idea. The work of every workman is fully planned out by the management at least one day in advance, and each man receives in most cases complete written instructions, describing in detail the task which he is to accomplish, as well as the means to be used in doing the work. And the work planned in advance in this way constitutes a task which is to be solved, as explained above, not by the workman alone, but in almost all cases by the joint effort of the workman and the management. This task specifies not only what is to be done but how it is to be done and the exact time allowed for doing it. And whenever the workman succeeds in doing his task right, and within the time limit specified, he receives an addition of from 30 per cent to 100 per cent to his ordinary wages. These tasks are carefully planned, so that both good and careful work are called for in their performance, but it is distinctly to be understood that no workman is to be called upon to work at a pace which would be injurious to his health. The task is always so regulated that the man who is well suited to his job will thrive while working at this rate during a long term of years and will grow happier and more prosperous, instead of being overworked.

(Taylor 1911: 39)

### ... and its opposite

So, what we did was to ignore the regulations, and if we wanted to sharpen a tool, we simply cajoled the tool-room foreman to allow us to

---

touch it up ourselves. If the time-limit on a job was excessive, we went 'ca'canny' to hang the time out, and if the time was insufficient, we also adopted 'ca'canny', and lodged a complaint with the foreman. Should the 'feed and speed' man attempt to interfere, we either threatened him with, and sometimes applied (if we were big enough), physical violence, or we politely invited him to increase the speed himself, knowing full well (having provided for it) that as soon as he did so the job would be spoilt. When the bonus clerk came along to time the job with a watch, it was not difficult to persuade a clerk who knew nothing about such things that the metal was 'tough', by manipulating the tool so that it would not cut. The charts disappeared from the machines, despite the vigilance of the management. Harassed by the employers and bullied by the employees, the 'feed and speed' men had such a rotten time of it that no one could be persuaded to accept the position. One I knew personally became mentally deranged and another worried himself into an early grave. By such tactics – passive resistance and sabotage – the system was rendered almost unworkable.

(Watson 1931)

Again as noted in Chapter 1, this system did not always work. Some managers used the system to create not fairness and equity but their opposite, changing quotas and targets so that people had to work harder to earn the same amount of money. Taylor himself contributed to the problem to some extent; he had an obsession with workers who were lazy or deliberately worked more slowly than the norm – a practice he referred to as 'soldiering' – and urged employers to deal with these harshly. At the same time, many workers were suspicious of the motives of managers for introducing these methods, and as described by Watson (1931; see box) would deliberately sabotage the task-setting process. Hoxie (1915), in his detailed survey of the impact of scientific management on labour relations, concluded that among the unions, both their leaders and the rank and file, there was enthusiasm for scientific management itself; they saw its potential in terms of bettering the lot of the workers. But they distrusted many of the business leaders who were introducing scientific management and believed – correctly in some cases – that scientific management would be used to 'sweat' more labour out of the workers.

Instead of closing the gap between management and workers, then, in some cases scientific management actually increased it. The first generation of management scientists were adamant about the need for fairness – the engineer and consultant Harrington Emerson lists 'the fair deal for labour' among his twelve principles of efficiency in management – but it was not possible to force managers to be 'fair'. In sum, scientific management did not prove to be useful basis for solving the problems of managing people.

---

**The fair deal**

As to the man, the worker, without whom industry would collapse, all conditions ought to be standardized. Drinking water ought to be germ-free, life-destroying dust should be sucked away, safeguards should surround moving machinery, work illumination should be adequate, not ruinous to eyesight. Working hours should be reasonable and without overtime except in great emergencies, means should be provided for ascertaining directly his needs, his wishes, of listening to his recommendations. These general welfare considerations have their effect on the contentment of the worker and not one of them is recommended from any patronizing or altruistic motive. A locomotive or other machine is cleaned, housed, kept in repair, given good fuel and good water because its efficiency is thus increased; and in the interests of plant efficiency men should he treated at least as well as we treat machines. It is for mutual, not one-sided, benefit that the workers' counsel is considered.

(Emerson 1913: 188)

---

The other step, which some firms had begun to take by the 1880s with others gradually following suit, was the appointment of a manager whose sole purpose was to look after the workforce. These first 'labour managers' were often women. They had their origins in part in the welfare officers employed by more enlightened companies as far back as the 1840s, whose task was to look after the welfare not only of workers but of their families. Rather after the fashion of social workers today, they visited the homes of workers and checked to see if there were any problems such as issues of health or sanitation that needed dealing with; if there were, they made recommendations to the company, which would then provide doctors, engineers, plumbers or whatever service was needed. Welfare officers also provided pensions or handouts to retired or injured workers, ensured that the pregnant wives of workers received the attentions of doctors and midwives and so on. (All of this was of course in the days before state-provided pensions and medical care.)

There was a natural progression from looking after the welfare of workers and their families to looking after the workers themselves. In the 1880s and 1890s too, significant numbers of women were employed in factories and workshops (often because their labour was cheaper than that of men). Welfare officers gradually began taking on the role of labour management. They heard grievances, arbitrated disputes between workers and other managers, made recommendations on pay and workplace conditions and, crucially, provided oversight over hiring and firing, a subject which often gave rise to disputes. Until the 1880s (and longer in some companies), foremen had the sole right to hire and fire workers in their divisions. This gave foremen considerable power, which some abused (for example, taking bribes to hire untrained employees ahead of more qualified ones). The labour manager or labour officer could now be appealed to, and could override the foreman's decision.

Apart from accountants, these labour managers were some of the first 'specialist' managers to be appointed. In 1910, it was estimated that over 70 per cent of serving labour managers in the USA were women. That number declined steadily as the years went on, but it remains true to this day that women occupy more senior positions in HR than in any other branch of management.

Gradually the discipline began to professionalise. Training programmes for labour managers began to emerge in America, the most important at the Tuck School of Business Administration at Dartmouth College and at Bryn Mawr College, the latter for women managers. In 1920 two influential writers on labour management – or personnel management as it was now becoming known – Ordway Tead and Henry Metcalfe, urged that every company should have a fully staffed personnel department to deal with issues ranging from worker welfare to pay and working conditions to negotiations with unions. Now, finally, companies began to respond. Personnel departments became fashionable, and the fashion spread to Europe. By 1940, most companies of any size had a professional personnel department.

But did this result in closing the gap between workers and managers? In most cases it did not. These early personnel departments often found themselves in an invidious position. To the workers, they were the agents of top management: their purpose was to persuade the workers to do more work and accept less, particularly in terms of pay. But when the personnel department did take up workers' grievances and bring them before the chairman and the board, they were accused of being 'soft' on the workers. There were of course exceptions – Cadbury Brothers being one such – but in the majority of cases personnel departments struggled to establish trust and rapport either with workers *or* with their fellow managers. And, it is safe to say that this is still true in some cases today.

## 4.5 Themes and influences

Thus far we have been talking fairly generally about the conflict, or at least lack of understanding, between workers and managers. Industrial disputes, strikes, lockouts, sabotage and other forms of conflict, however, usually were sparked off by specific events or problems. What kinds of things could lead to problems, and what methods could be used for their resolution?

---

**Potential flashpoints**

Pay/working conditions
Hiring and firing/job security
Welfare
Discrimination
Desire for recognition
Social and political influences

---

The list of potential flashpoints probably contains few if any surprises for modern HR managers. The problems are perennial ones. They include pay and working conditions, hiring and firing and job security, the welfare of workers and their families, discrimination, the desire for recognition, and external social and political influences.

### 4.5.1 Pay

Pay is, unsurprisingly, the most common cause of problems. The world's first recorded strike, that of the royal tomb builders at Deir el-Medina in ancient Egypt in the twelfth century BC, was caused when the state failed to pay the workers the wages that were due to them. Pay was a perennial cause of strife in the cloth-manufacturing towns of the Middle Ages. Rates of pay were strictly regulated through a collective bargaining process that included the town authorities, representatives of the cloth manufactures and representatives of the journeymen cloth makers. The latter usually negotiated good rates of pay for themselves, but very low rates for their apprentices, who were excluded from the bargaining process. Strikes and riots over pay were usually led by these underpaid and overworked apprentices.

During the period of prolonged labour unrest in Europe and America from the 1870s to the outbreak of the First World War, pay was once again a frequent flashpoint. As noted, above, employers like Pullman would drastically cut pay as soon as economic downturn began. Even a hint that a pay cut was coming could often send workers out on strike. Yet if a pay cut was absolutely necessary and the reasons for it were explained to the workers openly and honestly, employers could sometimes count on their support, as happened at Bat'a Shoes in the 1920s (see Case Study 4B).

The simplest way of avoiding disputes over pay was to pay workers a living wage, or even slightly better, or to supplement the basic wage with bonuses or profit-sharing schemes. Employers like the German engineer Robert Bosch found that once they did so, many of their labour problems vanished overnight. Henry Ford went so far as to use pay as a means not only of satisfying his workers but of ensuring that he attracted the very best people. The standard rate of pay for workers in the Detroit automobile industry was then $1 a day.

At the Highland Park assembly plant, Ford offered wages of $5 a day. He received roughly a thousand applications for every available post, and by the end of the recruitment process the best engineers and shop floor workers in Detroit were working for Ford.

Ford was accused by his fellow car makers of betraying the interests of all car makers, and other German engineers christened Robert Bosch 'Red Bosch', alleging that he was a communist. In response, both could point to satisfied and committed workforces, and the cost of the higher wages was more than recouped by higher productivity. Not everyone understood the differential relationship between pay and productivity, but those that did and could make it work for them often went on to build very successful businesses.

---

**The more they pay, the harder they are to beat**

I have always felt that the last concern in the world with which I should want to compete would be that which paid high wages, which sold the best quality of goods, and which had such management as to lead its men upward all the time. I have never found any difficulty, as a salesman, in competing with a cheap shop.

–William C. Redfield, US Secretary of Commerce and
a former salesman (1916: 11)

---

### 4.5.2 Working conditions

The next most common cause for discontent concerns working conditions. Hours of work were a constant source of strife during the Industrial Revolution and right into the early twentieth century. Workers knew what many employers would not recognise, namely that if they worked fourteen or sixteen hours a day, they would be exhausted, more prone to fall ill and more likely to miss work, or to underperform while at work. Strikes for shorter working days were rarely effective, however, and in the end apart from a few enlightened companies like Carl Zeiss Jena, most employers only shortened their working day when forced to by legislation.

Again, from a purely objective standpoint, the attitude of employers is hard to understand. As noted earlier, the evidence in support of the view that workers who worked shorter days were more productive overall was overwhelming. And if that were not enough, there was the example of companies like Zeiss and Cadbury which, with shorter hours, turned into the world leaders in their sectors.

Not all disputes concerned shorter hours, however. In many towns in the Middle Ages, the authorities had established a number of religious holidays, known variously as 'fast days' or 'feast days', on which no work was allowed and all workshops had to shut. Le Goff (1980) notes how in some cities these could be more than a hundred days a year. When added to Sundays, on which work was also prohibited, this severely curtailed the number of days on which work could be done. For artisans who were paid on a piecework basis, this was a particularly heavy burden; if they could not work, then they could not earn. Occasionally, therefore, we find evidence of labour disputes in which workers demand to be allowed to work more, rather than less.

### 4.5.3 *Job security*

The primary issue here was often one of equity. In the days before employment regulation, workers could be and were made redundant with little or no notice. And with no unemployment insurance, this could spell financial disaster, especially for workers with families. Unfair dismissal was therefore a cause for real concern, and a cause around which workers tended to unite, in part out of loyalty to their fellows and in part out of a fear that they themselves might be next.

Yet as with pay cuts, there were plenty of examples where redundancies, if handled sensitively, could avoid creating unrest or even win the support of workers. When tasked with handling the merger of the Hudson's Bay and North West Companies, John Simpson knew he would have to make redundancies. He never disguised this fact from his people. In making the cuts, he was careful to make the reasons for them plain. Some workers were terminated on the grounds that they had not been performing well and deserved to go; others were junior and could find work more easily elsewhere. He also made sure that neither the Hudson's Bay nor North West Company men suffered job losses in undue proportion. In the end both sides agreed that the redundancies had been handled fairly.

Some companies also provided temporary support to workers who had been made redundant and could not find other jobs. If the cuts had been made because of an economic downturn, they might undertake to re-hire workers once the situation had improved.

In other cases, firms stuck by their workforces and made it clear that they would not make redundancies unless the situation became critical. In return they asked for things from their workers: temporary pay reductions, higher productivity, support for innovative working practices and the introduction of new technology and so on. Especially if an atmosphere of trust had already been created and workers were satisfied that the management was being fair and honest, such proposals usually received support. It was in this manner that Bat'a got through the European recession in the 1920s, and not a few European and American firms survived the Great Depression of the 1930s.

### 4.5.4 *Welfare*

In his novel *Germinal*, Émile Zola describes coal miners driven to strikes and violence out of a sense of desperation as they could not feed their families. In this case the mine-owners were not paying a living wage. But even in cases where workers were paid enough to buy food and clothes, they often could not afford costly medical care, or repairs to their homes should the roofs leak or the drains block up, or education for their children. With exceptions like the strike portrayed in *Germinal* (based on a composite picture of several real-life strikes), most of the time the welfare of workers and their families did not lead directly to conflict. But it was an important background figure. Workers who are desperate with worry over the health of their families are more likely to take extreme action; those whose families are comfortably fed and housed and in good health may feel they have more to lose. Thus not only paternalistic managers like Titus Salt and Ma Ying-piao, but autocrats like John Patterson made a point of seeing that their workers were looked after. The return on this investment was a workforce that was more likely to be loyal to management, keen to maintain peace in the workplace and ready to make concessions should hard times come.

### 4.5.5 Discrimination

We are used to cases of discrimination on the grounds of sex, race, disability, age and so on in the workplace today. In fact this is a relatively new phenomenon. If anything the position was reversed. The only time male workers at Sincere came close to striking was when Ma Ying-piao took a decision to recruit female staff, and during the First World War in Britain there were several brief strikes by workers at munitions plants when women were brought in to work alongside them.

Complaints about discrimination from the Middle Ages up to the twentieth century were mostly based on issues of qualification and seniority. If an experienced worker were suddenly laid off and his job given to a younger and less qualified man, who just happened to be the son of the foreman's or work's manager's sister, then complaints were sure to arise. Again, it was necessary that workers should perceive that they were being treated fairly and that hiring and firing decisions were based on merit. Most of the time these complaints amounted to little more than grumbling. But as with welfare issues, perceived discrimination affected workers' attitudes towards management and made people more suspicious and less trusting. On the other hand, if managers went out of their way to have an open and fair hiring and firing policy, then workers knew where they stood and were more inclined to trust managers.

### 4.5.6 Desire for recognition

Over and over again we see cases where workers demand not just more pay or a greater share of the profits, but some recognition that it is through their efforts that the firm has become prosperous. Often this demand is expressed rather inarticulately, and it takes different forms at different times. The peasant rebels of the Middle Ages and radical groups such as the Levellers during the English Civil War demanded an end to class distinctions and equal shares for all. During the Industrial Revolution, skilled workers in particular demanded recognition for their own efforts; it was galling for the men who had designed and built a bridge or a skyscraper to see the credit for it taken by the 'fat cats' who had put up the finance but rarely if ever visited the site and most certainly never got their hands dirty.

The same complaint could be found in some of the skilled crafts such as pottery and glassmaking where the designers, artists in their own right, asked to be allowed to sign their own works before they were sold. Some like Wedgwood agreed immediately, seeing in this the potential for additional branding. Others refused, and this led to a reaction. One of the tenets of William Morris, the artist and utopian socialist who helped set up a number of craft-based businesses in Britain in the later nineteenth century, was that those who made things with their hands should be recognised as artists or artisans in their own right and their names should be associated with their products.

Once again, as in the case of Wedgwood, we see that where managers were prepared to work with their people, a solution could be found which benefited both sides. But when for whatever reason – ideology, pride, stubbornness, cost-consciousness – managers refused to allow workers public recognition, then dissatisfaction and the sense of 'them and us' increased.

### 4.5.7 Social and political influences

Lastly, of course, we must not discount external social and political influences, which have often caused upset in workplaces which were otherwise peaceful with good relations between managers and workers. This happened most prominently in the late nineteenth century when Marxists and syndicalists, hoping for a world revolution and an end to capitalist control of labour, urged workers to strike en masse. In the early days of the French Revolution, too, there had been a series of strikes by weavers and other artisans in support of the republicans, and populist movements in medieval Italy seeking the overthrow of the established government nearly always began their attempted coups d'état by bringing some of the workers and apprentices out on strike.

The most effective managerial counter-measure seemed to be to give the workers as little temptation as possible to join in such movements. Once again we can cite the example of Robert Bosch, who provided pay and benefits on a scale that meant his workers had no reason to go on strike, while other employers in Germany struggled constantly with bellicose unions. Eliminating the causes of grievances means that grievances themselves have little chance of arising.

These are some of the problems that we have seen faced by managers in the past, and some of the solutions they have adopted. One common theme can be found running through all the successful cases. In each, management stepped over the line separating capital from labour, workers from management, and brought the two closer together to make common cause. The distinction was never eliminated entirely; even at the John Lewis Group, there was still a managerial cadre in control of the firm, even if the firm was owned by its employees en masse. Autocratic managers like John Patterson, and even many paternalists like Krupp, made it clear that the class distinction between owners/managers on the one hand and workers on the other still existed.

What they discovered, however, is that the class division need not inevitably lead to conflict. In every one of the cases of 'successful' management cited here – cases where at the very least labour peace was maintained and the firm worked efficiently, and at best the workers made a contribution to the firm over and above their labour – and in the case studies that follow this chapter, we find that management and the workers had realised that they were on the same side. It was in both their interests to make sure that the firm grew and was prosperous. Both would derive benefit from this: pay and profits and other benefits, yes, but in some cases a sense of job satisfaction too, even what psychologists would later term 'fulfilment'. In cases such as Cadbury and Carl Zeiss Jena, people began to enjoy their work for its own sake, not just for the benefits it brought them.

## 4.6 Questions and discussions: a new era, or forward into the past?

In the introduction to this chapter we asked the question: is there something that stops organisations from adopting what is generally acknowledged to be best practice in HR? If we look to the past, a number of possible answers present themselves. Marxist historians might argue that the greed of the capitalist owners and managers makes them unwilling to share prosperity with their workers, or that because the capitalists are fundamentally afraid of their workers they are reluctant to surrender even a small amount of control lest the workers demand more.

Conservative thinkers and writers have for centuries argued that it is wrong for workers to demand anything; their duty is to obey, and that managers who advocate cooperation and partnership with their workers, or even who pay them higher than the standard rate, are upsetting the social order and betraying their class. This is a habit of mind that is dying slowly and very hard. The author knows of one recent case where a shipbroker, who moved his office from London to a rural location in Britain, advertised for a secretary with an offer of pay at London rates, about double the going rate in his new location. Local business leaders wrote to him en masse to complain, telling him he was in danger of raising unrealistic expectations among their own staff and could even cause harm to the local economy.

These long-standing views and prejudices may have a role to play, but does not the examination of how we have handled, or mishandled, the problems of managing people in the past suggest that there are some deeper problems that have yet to be solved? Let us go back to the two quotes with which we opened the chapter. Let us take the Emerson quote first. In effect, Emerson is saying: employers are buying *output*, but workers are selling *time*.

Unless they are on profit-sharing schemes, it makes little difference to workers how much they produce in the course of a working day or a shift. What matters to them is how much of their time – which might otherwise be devoted to leisure activities, for example – they must give up, and how much pay and reward they will receive in exchange. Conversely – in theory at least – what matters most to the employer is not how many hours each employee spends in the workplace, but how much output they produce in the course of those hours.

There are of course many exceptions to this. Hotels require front desk staff to be on duty at all times, regardless of how many guests they check in or check out. Hospitals need to have staff standing by in accident and emergency departments regardless of how many patients they are currently treating. There are limits to Emerson's theory. Nonetheless, we need to consider whether the basic point he is making is correct. If so, then the whole history of labour-management relations has been hampered by the fact that the two sides are talking about something quite different. Perhaps Emerson's theory does not solve every problem in human resources management, but it might well help to solve some of them.

The other quote comes from Roethlisberger and Dickson's official report on the Hawthorne experiments, a large-scale study of behaviour in the workplace which concluded that motivated employees will outperform un-motivated ones, and suggested that the best way for employers to motivate workers was to take a personal interest in them and show them that they are more than just numbers on a payroll but valued members of a group. Roethlisberger and Dickson argued that business organisations are also social organisations. Let us consider this in the light of what we have seen in this chapter. Social organisations of course have their own hierarchies and stratifications. But they also have a sense of unity and of common purpose, something that binds all members and unites them.

We can hypothesise, then, that as long as a gap remains between managers and workers, them and us, and no attempt is made to bridge it or to see matters from the other perspective, there will be two consequences. First, it will be very hard to create a sense of common purpose. Second, there will be as Emerson said a fundamental mismatch between what each side is buying and selling; workers will try to maximise the income they receive for their time, employers will try to maximise the output that workers deliver. As long as this remains the case, does there not remain the risk that, for all its modern tools derived from psychology and sociology and business research, in practice human resources management will struggle to deliver what is asked of it? We have in the works of Mayo (1933), Lewin (1935), Maslow (1954), Trist *et al.* (1963) and many, many others of more recent origin that which tells us a great deal about how and why people behave in the workplace and how they are best motivated. But are we making best use of this knowledge?

This is not an easy question to answer. The picture is clouded by the fact that there are some excellent examples of best HR practice in the world today, many of which we are already familiar with through case studies and articles. There are also some unfortunate examples of bad practice. Our historical examination of human resources management concludes with the observation that while we need to study the examples of good practice and learn from them, we cannot ignore the persistence of bad practice. Understanding the root of the problem can hopefully mean that we are better able to avoid the mistakes of the past, and ensure that human resource management continues to evolve and improve in the future.

---

**Takeaway exercise**

Consider your own company or organisation, or one that you know well or have worked in during the past few years. What is the relationship between workers and managers at this organisation? Is it close and cordial, with a high degree of commitment and trust on both sides? Or is there a strong sense of 'them and us', with an atmosphere of suspicion and mistrust? Or is the real picture somewhere between the two?

If there are human resource problems, if there is unhappiness or discontent even among an element of the workforce, then consider what options are available. How could any existing grievances be overcome, in a way that would be advantageous to the firm? Remember, you are looking for a win-win situation here; the best solution is that which solves the problem *and* potentially adds value to the firm. How creative can you be?

---

## Case Study 4A

### *Cadbury Brothers*

The chocolate-making firm Cadbury Brothers (now Cadbury-Schweppes) was founded in the early nineteenth century. Like other English chocolate makers such as Rowntree and Fry, the Cadburys were Quakers who abstained from alcohol, tobacco, coffee and tea, believing that these contained harmful stimulants. Chocolate, however, was widely perceived as nourishing and possessed of health-giving qualities (this perception was not confined to Quakers; in the late nineteenth century the Swiss chocolate maker Henri Nestlé invented milk chocolate as a health food). The leading firms, particularly Cadbury and Rowntree, later branched out into confectionery and then food and drink production more generally.

In the 1860s, when George Cadbury and his brother Richard inherited the firm from their father, Cadbury Brothers was a small, struggling family business. By 1900 it was the largest British chocolate maker, with an annual turnover of £1 million. By 1920 it was the largest confectionery maker in the world, a global business with a turnover of more than £8 million. It continues to be one of the world's largest food and beverage makers.

The growth and also the culture of Cadbury Brothers owed much to the person of George Cadbury, who was both a talented business leader and a dedicated social reformer. He is most famous for building the model village of Bourneville. By the mid-1870s, Cadbury Brothers had outgrown its premises in central Birmingham. Seeking room to expand, George Cadbury built a new factory on a greenfield site at Bourneville, just outside Birmingham. Along with the factory Cadbury built large-scale housing and public amenities for workers, borrowing ideas from earlier schemes such as Robert Owen's New Lanark, in Scotland, and Titus Salt's Saltaire, near Bradford in Yorkshire. Bourneville became one of the most famous of the late Victorian 'social experiments' that combined industrial management with social reform: William Lever's Port Sunlight and the huge complex of housing and social amenities built by Alfred Krupp for his steelworkers in Essen, Germany, are other notable examples. Cadbury believed that he had a responsibility to the people who worked for him that went beyond the simple relationship of capital and labour: he was responsible also for their physical and spiritual health and well-being. Workers at Bourneville were provided with housing, education for themselves and their children, health care, exercise facilities, and shops selling subsidised food and clothing.

To observers in the twenty-first century this seems paternalistic, and doubtless it was; but it is important to remember the environment in which Cadbury operated. Victorian England was suffering all the familiar problems of rapid industrialisation, including poor quality housing, poor health (it was an epidemic of typhus in the slums of Bradford that finally propelled Titus Salt to move his workers out to the purpose-built village of Saltaire), little or no education and rising urban crime. Cadbury could not solve all of society's ills, but he could and did try to look after his workers.

But Bourneville was not just an exercise in pure philanthropy. In today's language, we would say that Cadbury believed he was investing in his workforce. A better fed, healthier, happier, better educated worker would be more productive and a greater asset to the firm. What was good for the community was good for the company, and vice versa. George Cadbury was happiest when he could introduce measures that helped employees and the company in equal measure. For example, he built swimming baths near the factory and encouraged employees to use these: the result was both improved employee health and fitness, and greater cleanliness in the factory. Cadbury's personnel management policies show a similar policy of enlightened self-interest. In the 1880s he cut working hours, not solely to benefit the employees, but also because research showed that workers on an eight-hour shift were more productive than those working ten hours.

However, it is in his experiments in industrial democracy that Cadbury showed himself at his most pioneering. In this area, George Cadbury and his son Edward worked closely together, and the results are described in detail by Edward Cadbury in his book *Experiments in Industrial Organization* (1912). The Cadbury system had three main elements: (1) the provision of employee welfare, as discussed above, with the aim of improving employees' physical and moral health; (2) a mixed wages policy which included piecework and productivity bonuses; and (3) a system for employee participation and involvement through a suggestion scheme and works committees.

The 1880s was a time of widespread discussion about the best means of remunerating employees in order to encourage productivity in both Britain and the USA. Basically, there were three schools of thought:

1. Pay high wages across the board in order to attract the best quality of worker. This was the system initially adopted by Henry Ford at Highland Park, to great effect.
2. Pay on a piece-rate basis, with workers earning more for greater effort, the system advocated by F.W. Taylor and many of the pioneers of scientific management.
3. Pay bonuses for overall productivity, encouraging workers to meet certain targets, seen as cheaper and easier to implement than piece rates.

All three systems were perceived to have problems. High wages across the board meant higher costs, and there was no guarantee that high levels of productivity could be maintained. Piece rates seemed attractive, but in practice employers tended to cut the rate once production targets had been reached, meaning employees ended up working harder for the same money. Productivity bonuses suffered from the same problem; further, American workers were resistant to these as it meant the hard-working employee earned the same bonus as one who did little or no work.

Cadbury solved the problem by adopting a mixed system with elements of all three. The company paid a good daily wage, enough to support a worker and his family. Piece rates were then paid on top of this for workers who managed to exceed their personal quotas. On top of this again, productivity bonuses were paid when the company as a whole hit its financial and quality targets. Though complex to implement, the system ensured workers could profit both by their own efforts *and* the general prosperity of the company.

The employee participation system was well ahead of its time. All employees were encouraged to make direct suggestions for improvements: for new products, for new production methods, for new administrative procedures, or in Edward Cadbury's words, 'any suggestion on any other subject, so long as it relates to the works at Bourneville in some way'. Prizes were given for the best suggestions, regardless of whether they were implemented. Edward Cadbury tracked the number of suggestions carried forward, and found that over time 20 per cent on average were accepted, and 5–10 per cent were actually put into practice.

As well as the suggestion scheme, employees also had a voice through the two works committees (there were separate committees for male and female workers). These committees were not just for show: they had a powerful voice in the running of the company, functioning at times almost as surrogate boards of directors. Each committee included a mix of people nominated by the directors, foremen and heads of sections, and workers nominated from the factory floor. Each was chaired by a director: Cadbury himself was chairman of the Women's Works Committee for many years (the only man serving on it), and had a lifelong interest in the problems and challenges faced by women in the workplace.

These two committees served as conduits for employees' views on virtually every aspect of the business. They had power of scrutiny over plans for new machinery, buildings and other facilities, health and safety, employee complaints, cases of employee distress and many other issues. Notably, the women's committee had virtually the same powers as the men's committee. Edward Cadbury's service on the Women's Committee sent a signal to the entire firm that female employees were just as important as male workers, and their opinions were considered equally valuable.

On one level, then, Cadbury's can be seen as a classic example of Victorian industrial paternalism, albeit carried to greater lengths than in most other companies of the day. On another level, though, the Cadbury system resulted in a very strong, highly flexible organisation which, thanks to the strong levels of employee commitment and participation, could draw on a large bank of experience and intelligence to solve problems and undertake what amounted to continuous improvement. The employee participation system in particular meant that Cadbury was constantly upgrading its processes and products. The management consultant Herbert Casson regarded Cadbury in the 1920s as one of the best-run companies in Britain, if not the world, and summed up the key to its success very succinctly: 'At Cadbury, everybody thinks.' That strength enabled Cadbury Brothers to successfully challenge Rowntree for market leadership, and to grow rapidly into a global company.

## Analysis

Some of the questions you might want to consider in connection with this case include:

- If the Cadbury system worked so well, why did not other companies adopt it? Why is it not widely used today?
- What are the factors that led the Cadburys to develop this particular approach to human resource management?
- What problems might be encountered using this approach?

- Are there any elements of the Cadbury approach that you think ought be used in modern management?

## Sources

Cadbury, Edward (1912) *Experiments in Industrial Organization*, London: Longmans, Green & Co.
Gardener, A.G. (1923) *Life of George Cadbury*, London: Cassell.
Wagner, G. (1987) *The Chocolate Conscience*, London: Chatto and Windus.
Williams, I.A. (1931) *The Firm of Cadbury, 1831–1931*, London: Constable.

## Case Study 4B

*Bat'a*

Born in 1876 in the town of Zlín in Moravia, then a province of the Austro-Hungarian empire (now part of the Czech Republic), Tomás Bat'a came from a family of shoemakers. He himself was apprenticed as a shoemaker but, breaking with tradition, left Zlín to go to Vienna and start a small business there. This failed, and Bat'a then returned to Zlín and founded another business in partnership with his brother and sister in 1894. This business also struggled at first, and it was not until 1900 that Bat'a was able to get the business onto a sound footing and pay off his debts. Up to this point the Bat'a business had made shoes by hand, with each worker responsible for making an entire pair of shoes. But Bat'a was interested in the new methods of volume production, and in 1900 he invested his entire capital in setting up a shoe-making factory in Zlín, with fifty employees.

This business was modestly successful, but growth was slow. Upon the outbreak of the First World War in 1914, Bat'a won an order for 50,000 pairs of boots for the Austrian army. This was far more than his own factory could produce, and Bat'a had to turn to the other shoemakers of Zlín for help. With all of them working together in cooperation, the order was filled on time.

By the end of the war the Bat'a company was employing 5,000 people. The year 1918 saw the collapse of the Austro-Hungarian empire and the establishment of the state of Czechoslovakia, but it also brought a severe post-war recession which hit the economy of the new state very hard. In 1922, facing financial troubles once more, Bat'a met with his employees and won their agreement to a pay cut which would enable the firm to lower its prices and win more orders, particularly in export markets. In exchange, Bat'a made up part of the pay cut by providing services such as subsidised food stores and housing. By 1923 the company was prospering again and Bat'a was able to restore wages to their former levels.

From the 1920s onward the company grew rapidly and expanded internationally. When exports to the USA were hurt by the introduction of import tariffs following the crash of 1929, Bat'a switched his attention to other markets. By 1930 Bat'a had ventures in China and India as well as in several European countries, and at the same time began opening its own retail outlets. Bat'a factories were now producing 100,000 pairs of shoes a day, and by 1932 there were over 650 retail outlets selling Bat'a shoes in thirty-seven countries.

Bat'a's success in building this large company in such a short period of time is usually attributed to his management methods, which he himself described as the 'Bat'a system of management'. His system was built first and foremost on an ability, by himself and by his firm, to analyse, understand and learn. Recognising that the USA was fast becoming a world leader in both technology and management methods, he visited the country three times: once in 1904, again in 1911 to study machine production methods and learn about mass production, and finally in 1919 to look at the methods used by American shoemakers. During this latter visit he also went to Detroit and was given a tour of the state-of-the art production plant at Highland Park where the Ford Model T was assembled, and had a personal meeting with Henry Ford.

Bat'a used the best and latest technology to achieve volume production of high-quality products. Zeleny (2001: 57) commented that Bat'a 'never hesitated to replace a good machine with a better one, even if the latter was not yet worn out'. If he could not find machinery on the market that would fit his purpose, then Bat'a designed and built his own. By 1926 the Zlín plant had been re-equipped using electric-powered production line machinery, devices which Bat'a referred to as 'electric robots'. He also sought maximum technical efficiency, insisting that all machines had to have standardised, interchangeable parts so as to speed up repairs. He abolished the belt transmission system, as used in most assembly lines (in belt transmission, all machines on a line were powered from the same source), and instead located each machine on an independent platform with its own electric motor. This allowed the plant to be reconfigured more quickly to make new products, and reduced costly set-up and configuration times. Zeleny comments that Bat'a never bothered to patent most of these devices, confident that his competitors could not catch up with him in any case. In fact, many of the technologies he developed in the 1920s did not come into standard use elsewhere in the world for three or four decades.

As well as technical efficiency, Bat'a also sought to create organisational efficiency. He decentralised the business, giving individual business units near-total autonomy. Each set its own targets, and was responsible for meeting them. Every shop and every department became an independent accounting unit. Relationships between them were handled by a series of contracts. In time this became an internal market, with shops 'selling' to each other during the various phases of production. Prices for these transfers were set centrally on a six-monthly basis in order to regulate the production flow, but it was up to the business units themselves to negotiate times of delivery, quantity and quality.

This heavily decentralised system was held together by several devices. First, there was the company's central analysis department, which played a number of critical roles. It monitored external market conditions, and made sure that all work units were regularly briefed. It also monitored the external contracts and handled inter-unit accounting, providing weekly digests and other statistics for top management. The analysis department reported directly to the chief executive, Bat'a himself.

Second, every senior employee at the Zlín plant carried a pager and his own signal in Morse code. When head office required to contact an employee or someone in his or her department, that employee's signal was transmitted over the pager system, and the latter would then telephone head office as soon as possible. This allowed for very rapid direct communication between all departments and head office. Finally, Bat'a himself believed in managing through direct contact with his workforce, and in leading by example. Famously, in 1931 he had a new office building built in Zlín and established his own office in a lift. When someone needed to see the chief executive, they did not need to come to his office; he brought his office to them.

Bat'a believed in efficient management, but it was an article of faith for him that the success of the company required the result of the efforts of all its employees, not just a few. In 1924, introducing the company's first profit-sharing scheme, he told his workers:

> We are granting you a share of the profits not because we feel the need to give money to people out of the goodness of our hearts. No, in taking this step we have other goals. By doing this, we want to achieve a further decrease of production costs. We want to reach the situation in which shoes are cheaper and workers earn even more. We think that our products are still expensive and workers' salaries too low.
>
> (Bat'a 1992: 181)

Profit-sharing schemes were becoming popular in Germany and Central Europe in the 1920s, so this in itself was not particularly an innovation. Some business owners and managers believed that profit sharing could help to combat the rising power of the trade unions and political left; others were genuine philanthropists who wanted to help their workers. Bat'a was neither. He made it clear to his employees that he was not *giving* them anything; he was holding out an opportunity for them to *take* profits if they chose to do so by working hard and advancing the company's goals. Bat'a believed that charity, or even the semblance of charity, would not motivate workers, whereas the belief that they were earning more through their own efforts usually would.

The components of the Bat'a system, then, were an emphasis on technology and on achieving a requisite organisation that would simultaneously create efficiency and innovation and motivate the workers. Allied to this was a strong sense of moral and social responsibility. Bat'a was elected mayor of Zlín in 1923, and helped to modernise the town and provide it with better health and education facilities. Although there is more than a whiff of paternalism about this, it seems clear that Bat'a did feel a strong sense of obligation to the community where he had grown up.

Bat'a anticipated many modern management movements such as workplace autonomy, decentralisation, flexible manufacturing and industrial democracy. His slogan, 'Every worker a capitalist!', which expressed his views on employee participation and the right to share in profits, earned him admiration in some quarters but antipathy in others. The political right hated him for upsetting the status quo, while the left believed that his progressive labour policies were distracting workers from the real goal of a socialist revolution.

In July 1932, en route to a business meeting in Switzerland, Bat'a was killed when his plane crashed shortly after take-off from Zlín airport. He was only 56 at the time, and it is interesting to speculate on what he might have achieved had he survived. However, the system that he had built proved robust enough to survive his loss. His half-brother, Jan Bat'a, took over as managing director and led the company through dramatic worldwide expansion during the mid-1930s. Despite the Great Depression, by 1937 the company was making nearly 60 million pairs of shoes a year, and had 65,000 employees in 63 countries.

In 1939, Czechoslovakia was annexed to Nazi Germany. Jan Bat'a tried, unsuccessfully, to prevent the company from being taken over by the German army, and then went into exile in the United States. As he had negotiated with the Nazis to try to save the company, he was then blacklisted by the Allied powers and in 1941 went into further exile in Brazil. Another member of the family, Tomik Bat'a, went to Canada in 1939 and re-established the company in Ontario, and it was this offshoot which grew into the modern Bata Corporation. Worse was in store for the company in Zlín; bombed and badly damaged by the US Army Air Force in 1941, it was taken over by the Soviet army in 1945 and nationalised by the communist Czech government in 1946. The Bat'a system of management was progressively dismantled by first the Nazis and then the communists, and Bat'a's legacy was all but forgotten. Since the fall of the Berlin Wall and the restoration of democracy in 1989, however, interest in Bat'a has revived both in the Czech Republic and abroad. In May 2001, the first ever academic conference on the Bat'a system was held in Zlín.

## Analysis

Some of the questions you might want to consider in connection with this case include:

- How did Bat'a motivate his workforce? How important was this motivation in the company's overall success?
- The success, at least in the short term, of the Bat'a company after his death suggests that the Bat'a system was not dependent on his leadership alone. Why do you think that other companies were not moved to imitate Bat'a's methods and adopt his system?
- Bat'a tried to overcome the divide between capitalists and workers in part by urging his workers to think entrepreneurially and behave like capitalists. How realistic was this? Why would some organisations find this difficult to put into practice?

## Sources

Bat'a,Tomás (1992) *Knowledge in Action: The Bata System of Management*, Amsterdam: IOS Press.

Cekota, A. (1968) *Entrepreneur Extraordinary: The Biography of Tomas Bata*, Rome: Edizioni Internazionali Soziali.

Zeleny, Milan (1988) 'Bat'a System of Management: Managerial Excellence Found', *Human Systems Management* 7(3): 213–19.

Zeleny, Milan (2001) "Bat'a, Tomás', in M. Witzel (ed.), *Biographical Dictionary of Management*, Bristol: Thoemmes Press, vol. 1, 56–63.

## Case Study 4C

### *John Lewis*

The John Lewis Group began as a small draper's shop on Oxford Street, London, in 1864. The owner was John Lewis, a draper's assistant who had saved money from his wages until he had accumulated enough to buy his own shop. From this modest beginning – sales on the first day of opening totalled sixteen shillings and four pence – Lewis built up his business and later expanded it into a department store. These large general retailers were then the latest fashion in retailing, and following on from the success of earlier establishments such as Au Bon Marché in Paris in the 1850s and Whiteley's in London in 1872, department stores were now springing up in London and the provincial cities of Great Britain. Lewis was a talented retailer and he had the additional advantage of an excellent location on Oxford Street, then in the process of becoming one of London's most important shopping streets for the affluent middle classes. The company's slogan, 'never knowingly undersold', promised consumers good value, and the company backed this up by providing high-quality goods at reasonable prices. By 1905 Lewis was able to purchase a second, already established department store, Peter Jones.

In 1906 Lewis transferred control of half the business to his two sons, John Spedan Lewis and Oswald Lewis (each received a quarter share of the business). John Spedan Lewis later recalled that in that year, the total annual profits shared by the three men amounted to £16,000. By coincidence the wage bill for the company's 300 employees amounted to exactly the same figure, £16,000, meaning an average annual salary of just over £53. John Lewis senior had at least worked his way up from nothing; John Spedan Lewis had done nothing except be born the son of a wealthy entrepreneur, and in his later writings he expressed his disquiet and sense of unfairness at this.

As the elder son of the owner and a major shareholder, John Spedan Lewis was expected to take a managerial role. He did so, but the relationship with his father was not a comfortable one. The two men often clashed. Both John Spedan and Oswald Lewis were interested in worker welfare, but John Lewis senior was of the old school of managers who felt that although workers should not be treated unfairly, they should know their place and not ask for more than their basic wages. For his part, John Spedan Lewis had little respect for his father's management methods. He later remarked that his father's business was 'no more than a second-rate success achieved in a first-rate opportunity' (Lewis 1948: 3).

In 1914 John Spedan Lewis was made chairman of the subsidiary store, Peter Jones, and ran it successfully. Peter Jones had been struggling, but he quickly made it into a highly profitable venture. Among other things he established a staff committee, which allowed his staff to air their views and raise matters of concern directly with himself. A good working partnership between management and staff was, in Lewis's own view at least, one of the key factors in the success of Peter Jones.

By 1919 John Spedan Lewis was taking a more important role in the management of the entire firm. He and his brother Oswald had already set up a staff magazine, the *Gazette*, and a sports club for employees. Lewis went on to replicate the experiment at Peter Jones and found a firm-wide staff committee. Gradually he began involving employees in key decisions and encouraging them to come forward with their views. But this was still not enough. Lewis remained acutely aware of a sense of unfairness, that the workers whose efforts had led to the prosperity of the firm were not being fairly rewarded. In the 1920s he suffered a serious accident while riding, and was forced to take more than a year off work to recuperate, and he used this time to reflect on the future of the firm. He was aware of profit-sharing schemes, which were used by many firms as a way of rewarding employees, but he did not feel these went far enough. In the end he hit upon a solution: instead of handing over profits to employees, why not hand over the entire firm to them?

In 1928 John Lewis senior died, and John Spedan Lewis inherited his shares. Oswald Lewis was no longer involved with the firm, and agreed to sell his shares as well. In 1929 Lewis created the John Lewis Partnership, one of the most radical experiments in worker ownership of all time. Every employee of the company was created a partner in the business. With the exception of a small tranche of shares that Lewis held back for himself, control of the shares was handed over to a trust: only the trustees could sell shares, individual workers could not. This measure prevented hostile rivals from buying up workers' shares and thus gaining control of the company. Each year, dividends were to be paid to each worker/partner, exactly as if they were active shareholders, while at the same time they continued to receive their standard salaries as employees.

According to the firm's new constitution, 'the partnership's supreme purpose is to secure the fairest possible sharing by all its members of the advantages of ownership – gain, knowledge and power; that is to say, their happiness in the broadest sense of the word so far as happiness depends on gainful occupation.' Lewis had made the connection between happiness, on the one hand, and a sense of purpose on the other. From now on, John Lewis employees knew that they were working for themselves and their colleagues, not for faceless shareholders or remote bosses. This had the dual advantage of increasing staff morale and encouraging people to work hard and grow the business.

This last they most certainly did. Despite the Great Depression of the 1930s, the company grew rapidly, buying up other department stores in other cities around the United Kingdom. In 1937 it bought Waitrose, a small chain of ten retail grocery shops. Several of its stores were badly damaged by bombs during the Second World War, but the post-war recovery was swift. In 1950 John Spedan Lewis re-negotiated the terms of the trust and handed over the last of his own shares for distribution to the partners, stepping back from active management soon thereafter; he retired as chairman in 1955 to devote the rest of his life to writing and charitable work. By 2009 the John Lewis Group included 27 department stores and more than 200 supermarkets in the Waitrose chain, and was one of the largest retail chains in Britain. It was also one of the most profitable, and during the economic downturn of 2008 it outperformed every other retail group in the country financially. Throughout this time it has remained an employee-owned partnership.

Lewis believed that 'an enterprise, a business, is a living thing with rights of its own' (Lewis 1948: 17). His advocacy of employee ownership was based partly on ethics and partly on a practical view that worker participation would lead to greater effectiveness and efficiency. In Lewis's view, happy, properly rewarded workers meant a prosperous company. In his book *Fairer Shares* (1954), Lewis spelled out his thinking most clearly, in particular his views on the relationship between profit, knowledge and power. An effective partnership scheme, he said, requires all three; simple profit-sharing schemes will be less acceptable because, in a democratic system, happiness requires that people have access to knowledge and have a degree of control over their own lives. Allowing worker participation in management increased that control, even if only to a limited degree. Lewis regarded the sharing of knowledge as most important of all: 'The sharing of managerial knowledge is indispensable not only if power is to be shared but also for happiness' (1954: 44). An entire chapter is devoted to the company's internal communications systems, revolving around the weekly house newspaper, the *Gazette*.

The creation of the partnership was in effect the putting of these ideas into practice. It should be added that Lewis's legacy to the company was twofold. The first was the partnership. The second was a corporate culture based on equity and fairness, a strong sense of values, and a belief among top management that they are in effect the servants of the partners, who own the business and pay their salaries. Under the chairmanship of Lewis's nephew Peter Lewis and his successor Sir Stewart Hampson, this latter point was taken very seriously indeed. Although as Donkin (2001) points out, the establishment of the partnership has not eliminated disputes between workers and managers, it has meant that these disputes are conducted and resolved in a very different way. In the end, the owner/employees of John Lewis tend to vote for what is best for the company, realising that its interests and their own are closely aligned.

Many people talked about employee ownership and co-partnership in the early twentieth century. John Spedan Lewis was one of the very few to put these principles into action. In doing so, he created an enduring organisation that continues to prosper today.

## Analysis

Some of the questions you might want to consider in connection with this case include:

- Lewis believed that 'the sharing of managerial knowledge is indispensable not only if power is to be shared but also for happiness'. What does he mean by this? Do you agree?
- As noted in the case, many business leaders talked about this kind of partnership, but few were willing to put their ideas into practice. What might have deterred them? What risks does this kind of arrangement create for management and for the firm as a whole?
- John Spedan Lewis was clearly motivated as much by idealism as by the desire to run an efficient business. Setting aside idealism, can a sound business case be made for employee ownership/partnership of this kind? Or might the John Lewis Group have done equally well – or better – without the partnership?

## Sources

Donkin, Richard (2001) *Blood, Sweat and Tears: The Evolution of Work*, London: Texere.

Lewis, John Spedan (1948) *Partnership for All*, London: Kerr-Cros Publishing/The John Lewis Partnership.

Lewis, John Spedan (1954) *Fairer Shares*, London: Staples Press.

Macpherson, H. (ed.) (1985) *John Spedan Lewis, 1885–1963*, London: The John Lewis Partnership.

# Case Study 4D

## *Carl Zeiss Jena*

The optical equipment maker Carl Zeiss Jena was founded in the south German city of Jena in 1846. Its founder was Carl Zeiss, who had been apprenticed as a maker of optical lenses in the city of Weimar before setting up his own small workshop in Jena. Zeiss had a particular interest in microscopes, which were still at this point fairly primitive in design. His speciality was making high-quality lenses that gave very sharp magnified images of the subject under the microscope. Jena was home to an important university with large departments in the physical and natural sciences, and Zeiss's microscopes were popular with biologists and chemists in particular. In the 1850s Zeiss began producing compound microscopes (microscopes with more than one lens, which increased their powers of magnification) and these too proved popular.

Zeiss's business prospered and he took on additional staff. A breakthrough came in 1861 when his compound microscopes were awarded a gold medal at a major industrial exhibition, which gave him a reputation throughout Germany. Orders now began to come in from other universities. By 1865 Zeiss was employing fourteen people and his business had an annual turnover of over 12,000 marks (around £2,500 in the money of the time).

However, by this point Zeiss had reached his technical limits. His compound microscopes could not be further improved: any attempts to increase the magnification beyond present limits resulted in distortion of the image through the lenses. Zeiss realised that the problem was a fundamental problem of physics, not just a matter of further improving the lens-making process. Although he had attended some lectures at the university, he lacked the necessary theoretical knowledge to tackle the problem. He therefore contacted Ernst Abbé, an up-and-coming young professor of physics at Jena, and asked for his help.

When Zeiss and Abbé first met the latter was twenty-six years old. The son of a manual labourer in a textiles factory, he had won scholarships that enabled him to attend university at Jena and later at Göttingen, where he took an undergraduate degree in physics and then received a doctorate in thermodynamics in 1861; he married Elise Snell, daughter of one of his doctoral supervisors, soon after graduation. He returned to Jena around 1864 to teach mathematics and physics, and was appointed a professor of physics in 1870. He was widely regarded as one of the most intellectually accomplished members of the faculty at Jena. In 1866 he accepted the unpaid post as Zeiss's director of research and set to work on the problem.

As Zeiss had suspected, the problem was not an easy one to solve, and it took Abbé six years to come up with a solution. In the end, Abbé fundamentally redesigned the mathematical basis for lens production, creating the formula known as the 'Abbé sine condition' on which much of subsequent lens production was based. This gave, in theory, a very high resolution image at powers of magnification much greater than previously possible. In 1873 Abbé published a paper detailing his findings. This paper was regarded as a major advance in the theoretical development of optical lenses.

However, a further problem then emerged; current methods of glass production were inadequate to the task and the glass used by Zeiss in his existing microscopes resulted in a fuzzy image. To solve the problem, in 1879 Zeiss and Abbé turned to another member of faculty at Jena, a young glass chemist named Friedrich Otto Schott who had just received his own doctorate. Schott began experimenting with new methods of glassmaking using lithium-based compounds, and by 1882 reported success. The three men then entered into a business arrangement. Abbé had already become a full partner in Zeiss's business in 1876, and now he, Zeiss and Schott together set up the Schott and Genossen Glass Works in Jena, which produced high-quality optical lenses exclusively for Carl Zeiss Jena. This firm later expanded into a number of other markets including decorative glass, and went on to achieve a worldwide reputation for quality in its own right.

From this point, Carl Zeiss Jena's growth was meteoric. The firm was in possession of a technology that was a generation ahead of that of any other lens makers in the world. Nor did it end there. Under Abbé's direction, a steady stream of innovations flowed out of Carl Zeiss Jena. He himself was responsible for a number of them, perhaps the most important of which was a sub-stage condenser system that introduced more light into the microscope and allowed for brighter and sharper images. By 1900 Carl Zeiss Jena had brought the microscope to the very limits of optical technology; not until the invention of the electron microscope were there any further advances.

At the same time, advanced lens technology was used to open up other markets. One such was for telescopes. Here again Abbé was at the forefront of design of new telescopes, going on to become director of the University of Jena's astronomical observatory. In 1896 another Zeiss scientist, Dr Paul Rudolph, developed the Planar photographic lens, which revolutionised the market and became the standard lens for many years, widely copied by other lens makers around the world. Other more specialist lenses, the Protar and Tessar, also were in advance of any other technology on the market and sold widely around the world.

Zeiss died of a heart attack in 1888, and his share of both Carl Zeiss Jena and Schott and Genossen passed to Abbé. When Schott too sold his shares and retired, Abbé was left as sole owner-manager of both concerns. In 1890 Abbé set up a trust in the name of the University of Jena and handed over all of his shares to this trust; thenceforth, all profits from both firms would be returned to the university where they would be used to fund research work. Thenceforth Abbé drew only his salary as chairman and took no further profits.

Abbé continued to grow Carl Zeiss Jena, and by 1905 the firm employed 1,400 people and had a turnover in excess of 5 million marks, or about £1 million pounds ($25 million) in the money of the time. He himself died in

1905, but the Carl Zeiss business continued to grow. In the 1920s and 1930s, Zeiss binoculars became a must-have accessory for travellers and scientists working in the outdoors, and Zeiss lenses were to be found in most of the world's cameras. The Zeiss name had become synonymous with high-quality optical products. During the Second World War several of the company's facilities were destroyed by Allied bombing raids. Jena was briefly occupied by the US Army in 1945, and some of the staff and equipment were taken away to the West to set up a new Zeiss firm in what was then West Germany, while the old Zeiss firm was revived in East Germany. Both firms continue to exist today, both claiming to be inheritors of the Zeiss tradition.

Although Zeiss was an intelligent and talented entrepreneur, the managerial genius that drove Zeiss's rapid growth in the 1880s and 1890s was Abbé. He had a genuine passion for innovation, and ensured that this same passion was diffused throughout the firm. According to Auerbach (1903), at least one new product was launched each year. Abbé head-hunted scientific talent not just from the University of Jena but from all over Germany and brought some of the best physicists and mathematicians in Germany, if not the world, together at Carl Zeiss. He gave his scientific and technical staff an entirely free hand. Their primary role was to do research and create knowledge. Once that was done, the results could be examined to see if they had commercial potential. If they did not, the researcher either proceeded to the next stage of the research or abandoned the project and picked up something new. What they did was entirely up to them, and Abbé backed his researchers even if it took them years to produce a viable product. (Paul Rudolph's work on the Planar photographic lens took four years to yield results, but Abbé remarked that he himself could hardly complain, having taken six years to come up with the Abbé sine condition.) Long before the term had been invented, Abbé had developed a knowledge-creating company.

Abbé was radical in other ways too. The son of a factory worker, he was a strong believer in industrial democracy. He believed that workers had the right to be heard and represented on major issues that affected the business. He paid high wages to all his staff. There was a profit-sharing plan, but this was considered an additional perquisite, not the main form of remuneration. He believed in guidance rather than control, and he tended to set loose targets and ask his workers to meet them while giving them considerable freedom in the execution of their tasks. This was considerably at variance with standard practice in Germany at that time.

Abbé also attracted much attention for his workplace and social reforms. A sick fund which paid benefits to workers who lost work due to illness was set up in 1875, and this was progressively extended to cover illnesses of up to one year's duration. A company pension scheme was established in 1888. Paid holidays and compensation in event of layoffs were introduced, and in 1900 the working day was cut back to eight hours; even the most progressive firms usually still had a ten-hour working day. These and other reforms at Zeiss attracted attention throughout Germany, and served as models for social legislation in several German states.

Today Abbé is remembered as a scientist rather than a manager. He has been commemorated in various ways: the home stadium of FC Carl Zeiss Jena football club and a crater on the moon have both been named after him. However, his policies with regard to managing people deserve closer attention. One the one hand, he treated his workers well and looked after them when they were ill or unable to work. On the other, he challenged them to be innovative and to succeed. While he established goals and made sure that everyone knew what these were, he allowed his staff freedom to be creative, to innovate and to take risks. Even today it is relatively uncommon to find firms that share all these qualities; in the autocratic Germany of the late nineteenth century, Carl Zeiss Jena was unique.

## Analysis

Some of the questions you might want to consider in connection with this case include:

- What are the key points of the human resources strategy (to use the phrase) of Carl Zeiss Jena? How did each point contribute to the firm's success?
- How much of this strategy is replicable? How much is unique to Carl Zeiss Jena?
- Does this example show that high-technology firms have different human resources needs? Or could low-technology firms have adopted at least some of Abbé's ideas?

## Sources

Auerbach, F. (1903) *The Zeiss Works and the Carl-Zeiss Stiftung in Jena*, trans. S.F. Paul and F.J. Cheshire, London: Marshall, Brookes and Chalkley, 1904.

Buenstorf, Guido and Murmann, Johan Peter (2005) 'Ernst Abbé's Scientific Management: Insights from a Nineteenth-Century Dynamic Capabilities Approach', *Industrial and Corporate Change* 14 (4): 543–74.

Sponsel, H. (1957) *Made in Germany: Die dramatische Geschicte des Hauses Zeiss*, Gutersloh: C. Bertelsmann Verlag.

## Note

1 This is a huge simplification of the medieval social system, which had many substrata and hierarchies within the Three Estates. These need not detain us here; the point is that in medieval Europe, as elsewhere, those who did manual labour were considered the inferior class.

# 5 Marketing

---

**Learning objectives**

This chapter is intended to help readers do the following:

1 compare and contrast marketing practices past and present and across different cultures;
2 understand how marketers in the past built relationships with customers and established reputations;
3 look at how the concept of value has developed and been used by marketers.

> There is only one valid definition of a business purpose: to create a customer.
>
> –Peter Drucker, *The Practice of Management*

> Marketing is a social process by which individuals and groups obtain what they need and want through creating and exchanging products and value with others
>
> – Philip Kotler, *Marketing Management*

## 5.1 Introduction

In marketing scholarship, the received wisdom is that marketing is an invention of the twentieth century. Before that time there was no need for marketing. Witzel (1999a) summarises the various reasons given: (1) before the present, or at least before the Industrial Revolution, there was an equilibrium of demand and supply and goods effectively sold themselves, (2) only when mass production brought about the possibility of overproduction did marketing become necessary, as firms then had to stimulate demand for their goods, (3) markets were small and highly localised and businesses and customers met face to face, meaning there was no need for marketing, and (4) only a limited range of products were available meaning that consumers had little or no choice in what they bought.

As we noted in Chapter 1, though, this rather contradicts the view of the early theorists on marketing. Paul Cherington, who founded the marketing department at Harvard Business School, devoted much of his work to gathering data on how businesses marketed to other businesses and to consumers. There was, said Cherington, a great deal of existing practice. His task as a researcher was to record this data and from it, to observe and report on those practices that were most common and most effective. He explicitly denied any credit for 'inventing'. Some of the other early pioneers of marketing including Walter Dill Scott of Northwestern University (Scott 1913) and Arch Shaw, the publisher and consultant who was the brains behind the Kellogg's Corn Flakes brand (Shaw 1912), agreed that marketing already existed; it just wasn't called 'marketing', at least not yet.

Scott, a psychologist, observed things that managers and firms did and the ways that customers responded, and used psychological theory to explain what he saw; the early Harvard marketers, Cherington and Melvin Copeland, were more inclined to seek for answers in economic theory. But either way, they were not inventing marketing. What they were inventing, as Usui (2008) says, is marketing *management*. Whereas before marketing had been done on an ad hoc basis by various people in the firm, including top management, now marketing, like personnel management, began to emerge as a discipline in its own right and, as a result, there developed specialist marketing departments in larger firms. But this was a slow process. Not until the 1950s did most large and mid-sized American firms have distinct marketing departments, and in Europe the practice did not take hold until the 1980s. Even in the early 1990s some British companies considered a marketing department to be something of a luxury.[1]

Marketing, then, had an existence before the modern discipline of marketing was developed by people like Cherington and Scott and Shaw in the early twentieth century. We begin by briefly examining the evolution of marketing practice, and then turn to the identification of some common practices and themes.

---

### Marketing as a competitive tool

The functions of the original market were fourfold. The first thing a producer had to know was where he could find a group of persons who would be willing to purchase his goods or services. Having discovered this market, he would transport his product to it. On arrival, he would display his wares to attract the attention of possible customers. Finally, having gained their interest, he would carry out the actual transaction of sale, centring round the question of price. All the complexities of our modern distributive system are merely new combinations and re-arrangements of these four basic processes. They constitute the four main activities carried on under the general heading of distribution.

Most of the modern methods of marketing, both here and in the United States, owe their origin to these pioneer traders of the seventeenth century. At that date, marketing problems appear to have been as pressing as those of production. The foundations of commercial supremacy were apparently laid then, because Englishmen knew how to sell better than their neighbours, rather than because of any extraordinary merit in English products.

(Urwick 1928: 156ff.)

---

## 5.2 The evolution of marketing

The most systematic and inclusive – in the sense that it looks back before the late nineteenth century – attempt to describe the evolution of marketing practice is probably that advanced by Philip Kotler in the introduction to his textbook *Marketing Management* (1997: 17–29). Professor Kotler is one of the most significant figures in the history of marketing thought in the twentieth century; his depiction of marketing as having a social as well as an economic function had a profound change on how marketing was studied and taught. His model of the evolution of marketing has five stages. Heavily summarised, these are as follows:

1 The *production concept*, where consumers favour goods that are widely available and at low cost, which usually means basic commodities. The key challenges for producers are production and distribution efficiency, making goods cheaply and getting them into the hands of consumers.
2 The *product concept*, where customers now look at quality, not just price. The emphasis here has switched from price to the bundle of benefits the consumer receives when making the purchase, or in other words, from price to value.
3 The *selling concept*, which comes about when firms find that customers are not buying enough of their products, whether because the firm is over-producing, customers are not familiar with the product, etc. Firms there-fore need to stimulate demand. There are various ways of doing so, ranging from the 'soft sell' which emphasises educating the customer about the product and allowing the latter to make a free decision, to the aggressive 'hard sell' which emphasises completion of the transaction.
4 The *marketing concept*, which in Kotler's words 'holds that the key to achieving organizational goals consists in determining the needs and wants of the target markets and delivering the desired satisfactions more effi-ciently and effectively than competitors' (1997: 22). Whereas selling is something that is done *to* customers, marketing emphasises a more coop-erative approach, working with customers to determine what they need and then supplying goods which meet those needs.
5 The *societal marketing concept*, Kotler's own contribution to marketing theory, 'holds that the organization's task is to determine the needs, wants, and interests of target markets and to deliver the desired satisfactions more effectively and efficiently than competitors in a way that preserves or enhances the consumer's or society's well-being' (1997: 29).

In Kotler's view there has been a linear progression from one stage to another. The product and production concepts were typical of earlier econo-mies; the selling concept came in with the Industrial Revolution when mass production of goods became possible, and thus led in time to mass marketing; the marketing concept arrived in the early twentieth century, and the intro-duction of the societal marketing concept is usually dated to a key article by Kotler himself at the end of the 1960s (Kotler and Levy 1969). This looks very neat, and is a good example of perfectibilism or what historians some-times call 'Whig history'; that is, progress is a constant and we are always advancing towards new and better ways of doing things, making the world itself better in the process.

However, a little bit of revision might be in order. Kotler's model is excel-lent in terms of describing the evolution of theory, but when we look at marketing in practice, the picture becomes rather more blurred. Kotler's own definition of *marketing* is that it is 'a social process by which individuals and groups obtain what they need and want through creating and exchanging products and value with others' (1997: 4). Earlier, Melvin Copeland (1917) had argued that in any transaction, the basic goal of both parties in an exchange is to complete the transaction in a way that is satisfactory to them; it falls to the marketer to learn the needs of the customer and then attempt to deliver a product that meets as many of those needs as possible. Only thus will the transaction be satisfactory to the customer.

If that is what marketing truly is, then we can see evidence for it going back far earlier than the twentieth century. Take for example the Tongrentang pharmacy (Case Study 5C), founded in China in the seventeenth century. The marketing logic here is very clear. People suffer from ailments; they need medicine to cure those ailments. Tongrentang identified this need and supplied high-quality medicines which would help make people well. In early nineteenth-century Britain elaborate black mourning garments became fashionable for families mourning the loss of a relative. One small London-based weaving firm, that of Courtauld, identified this need and began providing high-quality black crepe silk at a price affordable to the middle classes. This was the basis of Courtauld's fortune and later growth into a multinational textiles manufacturer. A carpenter named Thomas Cook learned that the middle classes were also developing an appetite for travel, and designed tours that would allow them to travel in comfort and safety (see Case Study 5E). The Chinese potters of the workshops at Jingdezhen in central China learned that Europeans liked and admired their work but wanted decorative motifs with which they were more familiar, European landscapes rather than Eastern ones. So the potters began developing new lines of cheaper pottery suitable for export and affordable by a larger audience, and decorated with designs suitable to European tastes. An English lady of fashion could even order a complete set of dinnerware decorated with her family crest or her own initials, and have it delivered from China a year or so later, and many did just that.

So, identifying customer needs and meeting them is nothing new, and we do not have to look far to find more examples than the ones given above. As for Kotler's definition of societal marketing, delivering goods 'in a way that preserves or enhances the consumer's or society's well-being', this was a familiar and well-discussed concept since antiquity. Confucius, sometimes depicted as disliking merchants, in fact believed that traders and craftsmen played a vital role in society, delivering goods that people needed and enhancing the quality of life for all (an argument which is made at length by Chen Huan-Chang (1911)). Following him, in the thirteenth century the Catholic scholar and theologian Aquinas saw the market as a place where buyer and seller met and conducted transactions for mutual benefit. He elaborated a theory of the 'just price', a price for goods that was fair to both sides and created benefit not just for the buyers and sellers but for all of society. He too maintained that the role of the merchant was to cater to society's needs (see de Roover 1955, 1958; Dempsey 1935). And much later, in

1923 W.D. Moriarty, professor of business administration at the University of Washington, argued that marketing was at its heart a matter of meeting social needs, not simply enriching the seller. Moriarty went on to argue that marketing, properly conducted, creates value for consumers.

---

### Cost and value

In marketing, as in other phases of human effort, the return to the individual increases not so much with the amount of actual effort, but rather in proportion as the producer furnishes what other people appreciate. Nor should it be overlooked that there are in the marketing field many who work hard for small returns, primarily because they are producing something very common, and perhaps something under-appreciated by the buyers. Thus the neighbourhood grocer may make his service so lacking in distinction that he will have an insufficient volume of trade to enable him to remain in business, and yet at the same time have the very customers who are being served at less than his actual cost feel that the grocer is a profiteer.

(Moriarty 1923: 23)

---

The societal aspect of marketing was also very much at the forefront of some of the debates over corporate responsibility in the mid to late nineteenth century. Unscrupulous sellers sometimes offered food products that were heavily adulterated, sometimes to the point of being injurious to health: salt could be mixed with white sand to bulk it out, or products sold as 'brandy' might turn out to be wood alcohol with caramel for colouring. The first regulations to protect the consumer, such as the Pure Food Act and Drug Act of 1906 in the USA were passed in order to force firms to recognise their social responsibilities. Canny marketers like Henry Heinz, who supported the Act, had already realised this and were making a virtue of their contributions to society (see Case Study 5A).

Marketing has evolved and changed in two important ways: in its *scale*, and in its use of *technology*. The first of these is in the first instance the result of increasing population. Thanks to wars, bio plagues and high levels of infant mortality, the world's population grew only slowly until the late nineteenth century. The population of China at the foundation of the Qing dynasty in 1644 is reckoned to be almost exactly the same as it had been at the end of the Han dynasty in 220 AD, i.e. about 60–70 million. The whole of Europe around 1200 might have had a population of 30 million; population levels rose steeply in the thirteenth century only to drop back by as much as 50 per cent as a result of the Great European Famine and the Black Death in the following century. At the height of the Roman Empire, Rome might have had a population of one million, but the largest cities of medieval Europe rarely surpassed 100,000.

---

**Medieval advertising**

Good, cool new wine from Auxerre and from Soissons; bread and meat, and wine and fish; within is a good place to spend your money; within is accommodation for all kinds of people; here is good lodging.

–advertisement for a French inn, thirteenth century
(quoted in Sampson 1874: 50)

---

In other words, markets were smaller, and production was accordingly smaller too. Even the largest enterprises, the big cloth-making workshops of Flanders and Italy, Bengal and eastern China, counted production in thousands of units per year, not millions. It was relatively easy for a producer to segment the local market, identify key customers and contact them (though of course the problem became very much more complex when firms began marketing over longer distances, thanks to the slow speed and risks associated with travel and transport).

But in the second half of the nineteenth century there was a radical change. First, advances in medical and sanitation technology increased longevity and, especially, reduced infant mortality. The population of Europe increased dramatically, and as the excess numbers emigrated, the populations of the Americas and Australia saw explosive growth. Similar improvements under the British Raj saw India's population also begin to rise, while a period of prolonged peace and stability under the Qing dynasty saw China's population increase to several hundred million. In other words, there were a lot more people wanting things. While much attention is paid to the growth in mass production created by the Industrial Revolution, without this growth in population and hence in demand, the new factories would have had no markets for their goods.

At the same time, there was an overall increase in affluence and the numbers of the middle class grew rapidly as well. Fitzgerald (2007: 399) notes that there was a 60 per cent rise in real incomes in Britain between 1860 and 1900, and there were similar if less dramatic increases in France, Germany and the USA. This increasing affluence opened up the possibility for entirely new products and services and also to new ways of marketing. The department store (see Case Study 5B) is an example of how new channels were opened to serve the aspirational and growing middle classes.

New technologies enabled marketers to reach people more effectively. The development of printing coupled with the availability of relatively cheap and high-quality paper revolutionised promotion; handbills could now be produced in their hundreds or even their thousands. The 'golden age' of newspapers in the eighteenth century, when London alone had at times as many as a hundred competing daily and weekly journals, was largely funded by advertising in those papers. More importantly, technology also made possible the development of new products; advances in gunpowder and metallurgy enabled the development of a market for sporting firearms in Europe as early as the seventeenth century, and in India perhaps even earlier. The railway was an essential technological precursor to the mass tourism industry (see Case Study 5E), and the telegraph to the wire service news agency (Case Study 7A).

It was the growing number of products coupled with the growing size of markets and the increasing number of large producers with extended geographical reach that caught the eye of the first theorists on marketing. That the first theoretical writings on marketing come from America is understandable. Between 1850 and 1880 America – or parts of it – experienced very rapid industrialisation, very rapid population growth, and an explosion in the number of medium-sized and large firms. Before 1850 only a handful of American companies – the group of trading and real estate firms owned by John Jacob Astor, for example – could match European companies for size. By 1880, American firms like Standard Oil and Carnegie Steel were among the largest in the world and there were many other rapidly growing companies. Many of these were vitally important to the economy and the country. For example, the large meat-packing firms such as Swift and Armour supplied the growing cities of eastern America with food; and if these firms did not operate efficiently and get meat from the slaughterhouses of Chicago to the dinner tables of New York and Boston, then people would quite literally starve. But many of these new large firms had been created by entrepreneurs who were self-made men. They had never worked for large firms before; they had never been 'gentleman apprentices' or had any opportunity to learn the arts of management. They had only common sense to guide them, and their approach to marketing was very much hit-and-miss.

Meat-packing was one of the industries most frequently studied by the early marketing theorists; others included textiles and clothing, shoes, soap and cosmetics, electricity and railway travel. They looked for patterns and developed tools which could be taught, things like Cherington's model of efficient distribution or Walter Dill Scott's attention-comprehension-understanding model of communication, the forerunner to the AIDA (awareness-interest-desire-action) model still sometimes used in advertising. The aim was to systematise and harmonise marketing, to identify best practice and teach it to future generations of managers. Men like Cherington, Scott, Shaw, Moriarty and others created the discipline of marketing. They did not, as they themselves frequently pointed out, create marketing itself.

Kotler's model is therefore a useful one to bear in mind as it shows the different attitudes to marketing that can be found in practice. But it should not be used as a linear model; there was no 'production era' (Fullerton 1988) or 'selling era' when one idea dominated. Looking back, we can find evidence of all five concepts co-existing side by side, pretty much as far back as records go. Indeed, if anything people in the ancient world were even more aware of the relational and social aspects of marketing than they were in the Industrial Revolution. One of the contributions of twentieth-century marketing literature has been to rediscover these and put them back at the heart of marketing.

---

**All stock must go**

The first loss is the best, especially in the Wine Trade, and upon that consideration Mr John Crooke will now sell his French claret for 4s. a gallon, to make an end of a troublesome and losing trade. Dated the 7th of January from his vault in Broad Street, 5 doors below the Angel and Crown Tavern, behind the Royal Exchange.

–advertisement in the *Daily Courant*, 1712
(quoted in Sampson 1874: 162)

---

## 5.3 Developments in marketing practice

In the previous section of this chapter we saw how at least some firms and managers had a fairly clear understanding of the fundamentals of what marketing was, although they did not of course call it marketing. (That title only came into common use by about 1920, after some debate; Paul Cherington of Harvard was one of those who did not like the term, preferring 'merchandizing' instead.) How they practised marketing and used the various elements of the marketing mix varied according to time and place. We turn now to the marketing mix. To save time, we shall use the simple Four Ps (product, price, promotion, place) model developed by Neil Borden and Jerome McCarthy (see McCarthy 1960), with some additional discussion of branding and customer relationships.

### 5.3.1 Product

In Chapter 2 we discussed how firms in earlier times either specialised in certain products or diversified into a broad range, in part as a reaction to environmental factors and a means of managing risk. There is certainly a great deal of difference between, say, the business of Francesco Datini and his fellow Italian merchants in the later Middle Ages and the Renaissance, who seemed to trade in everything under the sun, to the retailer of Chinese medicines Tongrentang, which stuck very much to one range of products and chose to expand geographically instead of through product diversification (though Tongrentang did expand its range of medical products as time passed). Nevertheless, this difference suggests that there were different approaches to product strategy and that managers were aware of these.

However, we can also observe firms and managers responding to market demand. This is most evident when we look at start-ups. Right back into the ancient world we can see examples of growing communities demanding certain goods, and firms emerging to provide these. In the ancient Middle East, the cities of Mesopotamia produced large quantities of grain but lacked metal goods; the people of the highlands of Anatolia and Persia produced metal goods but needed grain. By 2000 BC, if not earlier, trading firms had begun linking the two, acting as middlemen and providing each society with the things it lacked. We see the same thing right through the Middle Ages and up to the present day. When the demand for Eastern spices and silks increased, more trading companies emerged to supply them; and when the limits of price elasticity were reached, innovators found novel ways to expand the market at lower cost. Silk was formerly a Chinese monopoly, but by the fourteenth century that monopoly had been broken and there were weavers of silk cloth in several cities in Italy; accordingly, the price of silk fell, which further stimulated demand as more people could now afford it. When demand for saffron, a popular spice from North Africa and Iberia, exceeded supply, a group of entrepreneurs began its cultivation in England (the name of the town of Saffron Walden commemorates their efforts).

Many firms were founded with a view to supplying the demand for a particular product: Courtaulds for black crepe for mourning, Gibbs for the South American nitrates used in fertilisers and explosives, Armour and Swift for meat needed to feed the cities of eastern America, Krupp for steel used for rails and railway carriages. Alfred Nobel spotted a need for a safe explosive for use in quarrying and building railways, and invented dynamite and supplied the market accordingly.

Sometimes innovators spotted demand before customers were aware of it, as in the case of Henry Ford and cheap cars, or Thomas Cook and mass tourism (see Case Study 5E) or even used promotional techniques to create demand where none had existed before, as with Samuel Colt and revolvers (see Case Study 5D). In all these and many other cases, there is evidence that, at a rudimentary level, firms and managers were capable of taking a strategic view of what products to make, whether there was sufficient demand and who the likely customers would be. Sometimes they got the product decision wrong; Edwin Land believed that automobile makers would buy his polarising glass for use in car windscreens, but found the market he had imagined did not exist. Undeterred, Land looked around for other markets for his invention, and soon found them.

As well as the choice of which products to sell, there was also a great deal of attention paid to product quality. With prices heavily regulated (see below), much competition in individual markets took place on the basis of quality rather than price. Although some manufacturers and retailers aimed to cut quality and therefore costs so as to increase their margins, others sought to improve quality and use this as a basis for building a reputation. (The first tactic was actively discouraged in some cases, and many cities in medieval Europe had inspectors who examined the quality of goods offered for sale in markets and shops in order to ensure that customers were not being deceived. Those who were found to have fallen below acceptable standards were fined heavily.) In particular, Chinese brands such as Tongrentang put a great deal of emphasis on quality.

In conclusion, while earlier marketers lacked the sophisticated tools of their modern counterparts for analysing customer needs and tailoring products to meet those needs, they were certainly aware of the importance of product strategy, and the best of them designed products to meet specific needs and attempted to forecast trends in demand.

### 5.3.2 Price

In virtually the entire civilised world up until about 1600, price regulation was the norm. Depending on the culture, time and place, prices were either set by local authorities (mayors, city governors and the like), or determined by guilds and associations of merchants. The prevailing view was that without price fixing there would be ruinous competition, and was therefore to be avoided. Competition on price in individual markets was therefore limited.

However, each city and town fixed its own prices, and there was little or no harmonisation; thus cloth which sold for one price in Bruges might sell for another price in Ghent or Brussels or Courtrai. As a result, manufacturers looked for the markets where their goods could command the best price and where their margins would be highest. The gathering of information on prices was a major preoccupation with managers engaged in inter-city or international trade. The Italian *praticas*, or handbooks for merchants which appeared in increasing numbers from 1300 onward, also contained detailed information on foreign prices (see for example Pegolotti 1936). Walter of Henley, the fourteenth-century English author on agricultural management, stresses that familiarity with prices is among the primary tasks of managers of agricultural estates (Oschinsky 1971).

By around 1600 the system of price regulation was starting to break down in Europe, and by 1700 most products were traded on an unregulated basis, although some staples like grain remained under price regulations (in Britain this lasted until the early nineteenth century). Evidence now begins to appear of retailers and manufacturers using price as a way of attracting customers and sending signals about quality. John Crooke, the wine merchant whose advertisement was quoted earlier, was trying to establish a market in French claret at a time when port was very much the fashionable drink in London. His initial attempt to price claret as a high-priced luxury drink failed, and in a series of newspaper advertisements he informed customers that he was now pricing claret at the same price as port, in an attempt to woo some port drinkers away. Unfortunately we do not know if his attempt was successful, but the example certainly shows awareness of the importance of price in marketing.

### 5.3.3 Promotion and advertising

---

**Modern cave art**

The writer on media and culture Marshall McLuhan once described advertising as 'the cave art of the twentieth century'. In his book *The Mechanical Bride* he gave a strongly negative view of the subject:

Ours is the first age in which many thousands of the best-trained individual minds have made it a full-time business to get inside the collective public mind. To get inside in order to manipulate, exploit, control is the object now. And to generate heat not light is the intention. To keep everybody in the helpless state engendered by prolonged mental rutting is the effect of many ads and much entertainment alike.

(McLuhan 1951: v)

---

Promotion, like price, was at first heavily regulated. In Ancient Rome, the authorities made available a few sites near markets where merchants were allowed to post written notices of goods for sale. A similar system seems to have operated in China, and in medieval Europe there developed the famous practice of 'crying' goods for sale; each town and city had a crier, whose primary duty was to walk the streets calling out the names of merchants and what goods they had in stock. Often only the official crier could be used; businesses that used their own agents to cry goods could be punished with heavy fines. This restricted the number of firms that could use the crying service.

This system lasted without change for centuries; although Gutenberg had invented the moveable type printing press in the mid-fifteenth century, the use of printed advertising was rare. Sampson (1874) gives an example of one of the first printed advertisements in English, a handbill printed by William Caxton's firm in the early sixteenth century informing clergymen of a new set of regulations that had just been promulgated and advising them of where they could obtain copies. But it was not until the late seven- teenth century that printing and paper costs fell sufficiently to make mass advertising possible.

The Golden Age of advertising between 1700 and 1800 saw printed advertisements for every conceivable product appear in every conceivable venue, and what the early advertisers lacked in scientific application they more than made up for in enthusiasm. The nineteenth century saw developments including the use of pictures, either line drawings and paintings or, by the end of the century, photographs, and also the appearance of the first advertising agencies which specialised in producing high-quality poster and print advertisements (for more detailed histories of advertising, see Sampson 1874; Laird 1998; Nevett 1982; Sivulka 1998).

The next major advance in advertising was the introduction of ideas from the emerging science of psychology. The ideas of Freud and his contemporaries were studied with great interest by advertisers in Europe and America. At Northwestern University, under the direction of the psychologist Walter Dill Scott, there developed a centre for the study of the application of psychology to marketing and advertising. Herbert Casson (1911) and Lillian Gilbreth (1914) also discussed the importance of psychology, and advertising agencies began either hiring people with psychology backgrounds or putting psychologists on retainer as advisers. Formerly advertising had been a means of supplying customers with information. Increasingly, it became used to stimulate demand and build relationships with customers.[2] This in turn changed the nature of advertising and how and where it was employed.

---

### Some things never change

A gentleman of means, alone in this city, desires the acquaintance of a respectable, genteel young lady of refinement, who is, like himself, friendless and alone; the most honorable secrecy observed. Address with full particulars, Mercury office, 128 Fulton St., New York.

A French gentleman, newly arrived in this country and lonely, wishes to form the acquaintance of a lady who could prove as true a friend to him as he would be to her. Address, in confidence, as discretion will be absolute, Mercury office.

A gentleman of means wishes to make the acquaintance of a young lady of sixteen to eighteen years (blonde preferred); one who would appreciate a companion and friend may find one by addressing ____, Mercury office.

A lady would like to meet with a gentleman who would thoroughly appreciate her exclusive society. For particulars, address Box 2, No. 688 Broadway.

–personal advertisements from the New York *Sunday Mercury*, mid 19th century (quoted in Sampson 1874: 564–65)

---

A further result was the transformation of the importance of advertising relative to other forms of promotion. Hitherto, firms had relied on tactics such as giveaways and product samples (Heinz often handed out free samples of its preserved foods, and the Tongrentang pharmacy gave samples of its medicines to students coming to Beijing to sit the entrance exams for the Imperial civil service) and, above all, word-of-mouth recommendations. As a result, much work went into cultivating relationships with key groups of customers (we shall discuss this in more detail in a moment). Even the print advertising that began to emerge in the form of posters, handbills and newspaper advertisements in the seventeenth century was designed to do little more than create awareness. But the new, scientifically based advertisements of the twentieth century promised also to stimulate desire and motivate consumers to try the product. Fitzgerald (2007) suggests that modern advertising led to the invention of the concept of the consumer, as distinct from the customer; the purpose of advertising was to convert consumers into customers. By the middle of the twentieth century advertising had become the dominant form of promotion for many companies, and certainly the one requiring the highest level of expenditure.

## The marketing mix

When the Battle Creek Toasted Corn Flake Company was founded in 1906, it was one of forty-two competing cereal makers in the town of Battle Creek, Michigan. The town was also home of the Battle Creek Sanatorium, one of America's most fashionable health spas, owned by the physician and entrepreneur John Harvey Kellogg. Among other things the Sanatorium prescribed a strict low-fat diet for inmates, including breakfast cereals made from grain and nuts. A former patient, C.W. Post, set up a company selling cereals similar to those developed in the Sanatorium, and had an immediate success with the Post Grape Nuts brand. Other rivals quickly followed.

The Battle Creek Toasted Corn Flake Company came late to this competition. Its founder was Kellogg's brother, William K. Kellogg, who had been an employee of the Sanatorium – in a fairly junior capacity – for nearly twenty years. After he discovered the recipe for corn flakes more or less by accident, he applied to his brother for a licence to make and sell the product. This was granted for a fee of $175,000, though apparently without much enthusiasm; John Kellogg seems to have had little time for his less intellectually gifted brother. But William Kellogg was a tireless worker, and he had an important ally, the publisher and consultant Arch Shaw who had been working on the application of the new scientific methods of management to marketing.

Together, Kellogg and Shaw deployed the entire battery of promotional techniques. They ran door-to-door campaigns in major cities, handing out free samples of corn flakes. They gave away coupons promising a discount on the price of purchase of a package of corn flakes, and they handed out promotional leaflets in public venues. Using a new four-colour printing process which Shaw himself had developed, they designed visually appealing packages with appetising pictures of bowls of corn flakes. Kellogg's signature appeared on each package with the slogan, 'Beware of imitations, none original without this signature'.

Finally, there were advertising campaigns in major newspapers across the country. One advertisement in the *Ladies Home Journal* in 1906 begged customers to stop buying corn flakes for a while so as to let the company catch up on its backlog of orders. This advertisement alone resulted in a dramatic increase in sales.

Within a few years, the Battle Creek Toasted Corn Flake Company (later the Kellogg Company) had reached a position of dominance in the American breakfast cereals market. A few of its rivals such as Post survived; most went under.

(Butler *et al.* 1955; Greenwood 2001)

### 5.3.4 Distribution and place

Not surprisingly, given the comparatively low level of transportation infrastructure, distribution was one of the biggest marketing problems faced by early marketers. The physical act of getting goods to markets outside the immediate area where they were produced was arduous, expensive and risky. Indeed, some of the first books on marketing referred to the entire subject as 'distribution', and this remained true into the 1930s.

The basic model of distribution remained unchanged from the ancient world pretty much until the present day. Long-distance trade between regional centres was handled by trading firms who shipped goods in bulk. Once goods arrived at their destination they were sold either to other intermediaries, sometimes known as 'jobbers' who broke goods up into smaller consignments for sale to retailers, or directly to the retailers themselves. There were variations on how this was done. The Medici Bank and Francesco Datini owned the wholesale process and owned or part-owned the ships in which the goods were transported, but English and German firms in the Middle Ages preferred to subcontract transport to shipowners. Some firms did their own jobbing, while others dealt only in bulk. Vertical integration became more popular in Europe in the nineteenth century, and in America in the early twentieth century, as a means of controlling and regulating the supply chain (this became a controversial issue in America, see below). But on the whole, the distribution problems faced by the Medici, the salt shippers of the Hanseatic League, the pepper merchants of Venice and Alexandria and other large concerns were little different in kind from those described by Clarence Thompson (1914) and L.D.H. Weld (1921) in the early twentieth century.

Place also refers of course to the location where transactions take place, a particularly important issue for retailers. Once again, this aspect of marketing was heavily regulated in early societies. Retail businesses were often required by law to be near each other; thus butchers, bakers, drapers, jewellers, pharmacists, spice sellers and the like were required to congregate in the same street or district. Ordinances in Western Europe, India, China and Japan at various dates attest to this. One purpose may have been to keep retailers together so as to allow easier inspection and comparison and ensure that no one was breaking the regulations on price and quality. However, even after these regulations fell into abeyance in the West, shops of similar types still tended to congregate (and still do in many parts of the world; India in particular is notable for the large numbers of apparently very similar shops selling the same goods which congregate on certain city streets).

There were two revolutions in location strategy in the nineteenth century. The first was the department store, the brainchild of the husband-and-wife team Aristide and Marguerite Boucicaut in Paris in the 1850s (see Case Study 5B). Instead of rows of shops each selling a single range of products, the Boucicauts created a single shop where virtually every human necessity was catered for under one roof. The Boucicauts went still further, creating a luxurious environment that transformed the hitherto humble act of shopping from a chore to an experience. Department stores spread rapidly around the world, including to India and East Asia by the end of the century.

The second revolution was catalogue retailing, made possible when the railways and better roads had improved communications to the point where postal services were quick and reliable. The pioneers of catalogue retailing in the USA, Montgomery Ward (see box) and then Sears in effect created a 'virtual' shopping experience where customers could choose goods without ever leaving their homes. Catalogue retailing proved particularly popular in rural America, where people often had to travel long distances to find good quality shops (this was in the days before car ownership became commonplace). Recognising that there was a great deal of untapped demand in rural communities, Ward and Sears used innovative – for the time – methods of communications and distribution to reach customers, conduct transactions and deliver goods.

---

### Montgomery Ward

Aaron Montgomery Ward first hit on the idea of mail-order retailing while working as a travelling salesman in the American Midwest in the 1860s. He noticed that the quality of retail goods on offer in small towns was often poor, and prices were high. At the same time, the coming of the railways was putting these towns within easy reach of the large manufacturing centres of the East. He began by taking orders for goods as he travelled, buying directly from manufacturers, and selling on a cash, low-margin basis, delivering the goods himself as he made his rounds. As the business grew more sophisticated he began taking orders and despatching goods through the post.

Through family connections of his wife, Ward developed a relationship with a Midwest farmers' cooperative, the National Grange. This gave him access to the Grange's members, whom he used as a target market for mail-order advertising. The same formula was repeated with other groups across the country. Ward was at pains to build up a personal relationship with his clients, many of whom were farmers and their wives in isolated communities and who appreciated the perception of human contact; customers were always addressed by name, and letters responding to enquiries were often handwritten. Ward's famous catalogues became known as 'dream books'; beautifully illustrated, they placed attractive images of the manufactured consumer goods of the wealthy East before the eyes of the poor farmers of the West, and encouraging them to aspire to higher things. The marketing promise was backed up with sophisticated systems for managing stock and inventory, taking orders and despatching goods. Among Ward's innovations was a guarantee that customers could return their goods by post within ten days if not satisfied. Thanks to this efficiency, even though margins were often very thin, the company was extremely profitable.

Ward's success can be largely attributed to his balanced approach to marketing. Not only did he design a product mix and manage a promotion strategy which targeted consumers carefully, but he also established a highly effective distribution system. Ward's system was much admired, and as late as the 1930s marketing textbooks were still using Montgomery Ward as a case example for mail-order retailing.

(Latham 1972; Strasser 1989)

### 5.4.4 Branding

As noted above, firms in both the West and East were often restricted in their ability to compete on the basis of price, and there were restrictions on distribution and promotion as well. Reputation, for quality of goods and/or trustworthiness and honesty in dealing with customers, was one dimension that was largely unrestricted; even when there were set standards for the quality of the goods themselves, there was no restriction on the quality of the service that could be offered along with it, or the courtesy with which customers were treated. From a very early date, certainly as early as the medieval period in both Asia and the West, we see firms trying to establish their own identity and reputation and to distinguish themselves from competitors in the eyes of their customers. This became the foundation for later branding.

The corporatist nature of medieval society referred to above meant that few firms had the opportunity to create distinctive brands for themselves, although the Medici Bank certainly approached the status of a brand in financial services (as did a few other financial institutions, such as the Society of the Bardi (Florence), the Bank of St George (Genoa) and the Steelyard (the Hanseatic League's office in London)). Collectivities of producers, however, were very successful at establishing brands. The cloth manufacturers of Flanders, for example, chose niche product strategies, specialising in fabrics of a certain weave, weight and/or colour. Thus the fabrics became known as cloth of Arras, cloth of Douai, cloth of Tournai and so on, depending on where they were made, and they developed images and reputations for quality based on that name. The same process was repeated in a variety of industries: Bordeaux and Malmsey in wine, Cordoba in leather products, Telemark and Dalarna in steel and weapons, Bourgneuf in salt, and so on. Goods imported beyond Europe were subjected to the same process; by the seventeenth century the brand name 'china' was being applied to a range of goods of oriental origin including silk, tea and porcelain, in effect turning 'china' into a sort of prototype global brand (Witzel 1999b).

Symbols identifying the maker were often added to the finished product; this practice developed into the trade mark, which in turn, by the nineteenth century was on its way to acquiring the qualities of the brand mark. As Charles Babbage (1835) noted, trade marks served as indicators of quality in the mind of the customer, and conveyed an image to that customer. By the second half of the nineteenth century specialist agencies had evolved to help companies design and establish trade names and marks, and it was one of these that first suggested the name Sunlight to William Lever for his new brand of soap. These trade mark agents seem to have functioned, on a very basic level, as branding consultants.

Branding was also being developed in China at around the same time, and this was branding much more as we would recognise it today, with a brand mark serving as indication of quality and linked to a widely held customer image of a good. Brand-marked metal tools and implements began appearing in China as early as the Song dynasty in the tenth century, and corporate brands rapidly became popular in many sectors. Pharmaceuticals were heavily branded, and names such as Lei Yunshang from Shanghai and Tongrentang from Beijing became household names; the latter established multiple outlets and became known all over China. The Caizhi Zhai confectionery company in Suzhou also became known nationally for its distinctively shaped products. Qilu wine and Yipin Zhai calligraphy brushes are later examples of brands reaching national prominence, indicating how strong branding was in Chinese commercial thinking (Hamilton and Lai 1989).

### 5.4.5  Customer relationships

Before the development of mass marketing and mass advertising at the end of the nineteenth century, relationships between producer and customer were one of the salient features of marketing. Nowhere is this more evident than in the financial services sector. Cosimo dei Medici, Jakob Fugger of Augsburg, Thomas Coutts and the 'Banker to the World' Fateh Chand came from very different times and cultures, but all made close relationships with their key clients their first priority. In business-to-business marketing we see this importance too. William Pirrie of the Belfast shipbuilders Harland & Wolff, perhaps one of the best instinctive marketers of all time, is a particularly interesting example of this. Pirrie put customer relationships onto an institutional footing, creating a 'customer club' of shipowners who were given preferred access for both new orders and refits to existing ships, in exchange for a commitment to keep buying ships.

But retailers understood the importance of relationships too, especially in times and places where competition was restricted or controlled by regulation. Tongrentang, the Chinese pharmacy, leveraged its connections with the Chinese imperial court to build relationships with a key customer group, the Imperial civil service. In the training provided to their sales staff at the Paris department store Au Bon Marché, Aristide and Marguerite Boucicaut emphasised the importance of courtesy and good manners; customers, once they had entered the store for the first time, needed to be given every encouragement to come back. Catalogue retailer Montgomery Ward made a point of treating his customers as individuals, even – or especially – though they were physically remote and there was no face-to-face contact.

Relationship marketing became fashionable in the 1990s, but it was an equally hot topic eighty years earlier when the first generation of marketing writers and theorists, identifying the importance of relationship building, sought to explain it. Brown (1911), writing in the *Harmsworth Business Library*, describes the complex psychological forces at work around concepts such as branding, reputation and quality, echoing the earlier writing of Babbage on this same subject, and argues that the marketer can enhance all these things by developing close relationships with both customers and retailers. Writing for the same publication, Orange and McBain (1911) warn that the arrival of mass communication does not mean customers can be treated as a single mass. Discussing mail-order advertising, they argue for the personalising of mail-order advertisements, or 'shots'. They point out that mail-order customers, if treated well and if a relationship can be developed, have a high propensity to repeat business, which is where the real profitability lies:

> Usually it is possible to sell goods to people who are already customers at one-half to one-third the cost of effecting the sale in the case of a first transaction ... It is obvious, therefore, that a mail-order advertiser of this type makes his profit out of a particular customer, not on the first sale but on the sum total of the transactions that he has with that customer.
>
> (Orange and McBain 1911: 213)

This was another lesson that tended to be forgotten over the course of time, and in the 1980s articles in *Harvard Business Review* were still attempting to drive home the same point.

## 5.4 Themes and influences

Marketing before 1900 tended to be done in an ad hoc way. As Cherington and others rightly pointed out, it was not done systematically, and this led to repetition and errors. The good marketers, drawing on a combination of instinct, reason and the example of other successful marketers around them, were able to reach customers, building relationships and deliver value. Many others struggled to do so, and many failed.

There were several key issues that had been discussed and debated for some time; others emerged as the study of marketing practices began to accumulate more data. What exactly constituted value? Did marketers add value, or were they simply an additional cost? Should marketing be conducted by a separate department like accountancy and labour management, or should it continue to be the responsibility of top management? And finally, how should firms conduct their relationships with customers? What, in fact, were customers for?

### 5.4.1 Value and what it means

For centuries, it was commonly assumed that goods had an intrinsic value, and to further assume that – rather like modern perfect-market theory – the value of goods was represented by their price. Even sophisticated thinkers like the English philosopher John Locke in the seventeenth century believed that gold and silver had intrinsic value, though he accepted that the price of other goods fluctuated according to supply and demand.

Intrinsic value, said Locke, was not something that occurred naturally; rather, it was what people, or the great majority of people, agreed that an object was worth. In other words, if society felt that a bolt of cloth was worth a shilling, then that was indeed what a bolt of cloth was worth, and the fair price for that bolt of cloth was one shilling. This assumption that there is a universally agreed value for at least some goods was implicit in the systems of price regulation that we find throughout the world in earlier centuries. Businesses were required to set prices that reflected a product's intrinsic worth, no more – and no less. Anything else would be unfair, either to customers or to other businesses.

Long before Locke, the medieval scholar St Thomas Aquinas had poured scorn on the idea of intrinsic value. How do we define intrinsic value? he asked. Surely most people would agree that living things are intrinsically more valuable than inanimate things. But in that case, if we compare the value of a pearl with that of a mouse, because the mouse is alive it ought to be more intrinsically valuable. Clearly, that is absurd. In reality, pearls are scarce and expensive, whereas mice are plentiful and except in rare cases as pets, have no value at all (Dempsey 1935: 481).

Writing around 1270 in one of his most famous books, *Summa Contra Gentiles*, Aquinas identified what we now accept as orthodoxy: that value is assigned to a product in the mind of the customer, and that this value fluctuates according to the customer's own circumstances and needs. Relative scarcity, as in the case of the pearl, also influences value. Corn may sell in a city market for one price, but if the city is at war and corn becomes scarce, then the price will rise, despite the efforts of the city authorities to enforce price controls. From a purely economic standpoint, Aquinas says there is nothing wrong with this. The 'just price' is to be found in an equilibrium between buyer and seller and is the price that best suits each party. And that price will always vary, because the value that each party attaches to the product will vary. Aquinas added further that sellers can do things that will add value for customers – assuming some of the risks associated with purchase, for example – and this can increase the price the customer is willing to pay.

The opinions of Aquinas and his fellow scholars eventually prevailed, and over the course of several centuries price control systems in Europe gradually disappeared. They were replaced by a system of variable pricing, in which buyer and seller negotiated the price of each transaction. In theory this fits with the Aquinian principle of the 'just price', but in practice the system tended to work against poorer customers, who had less bargaining power, and in favour of the wealthy. Studies today have shown that in situations where variable pricing prevails, with the price fixed by bargaining or haggling, poorer customers nearly always pay more than richer ones. One of the insights of the Boucicauts at Au Bon Marché was that a fixed price, with everyone paying the same price for the same product regardless of status, would be perceived by customers as more fair – especially if the price could be kept relatively low.

Today, we see the inheritance of both systems. In department stores and supermarkets, we pay an egalitarian fixed price exactly the same as our fellow customers. With hotels and with airlines we pay a price that fluctuates by the day, sometimes by the hour as the seller tries to follow the fluctuating position of equilibrium. Often we can bargain and try to get the price down, and if we are the representatives of a large company we can usually negotiate a lower rate than ordinary guests or passengers. All this means that there is still no unanimity as to the best way of matching price to value – and probably never will be.

### 5.4.2 The marketing debate

As already noted, competition was restricted in many of the world's markets up until the end of the Middle Ages. The argument for free competition, or *laissez-faire*, was made forcefully by the French school of economists known as the physiocrats in the mid-seventeenth century, and later by Adam Smith in Britain. By the nineteenth century, a state of largely unfettered competition existed in both Europe and America. But there were doubts as to whether this was a good thing, and economists and business leaders on both sides of the Atlantic advanced views to the effect that competition was dangerous and wasteful. The large monopolies that emerged during this period, especially in America – Standard Oil, the copper monopoly ASARCO, United States Steel and so on – were attempts to eliminate the wastes that competition was said to engender.

---

**Let the laws rule**

The inspiration for the concept of *laissez-faire* comes not from France but from ancient China. The Daoist classic the *Daodejing* (or *Tao Teh Ching*) introduced the concept of *wu-wei*, meaning literally 'non-action'. The *Daodejing* suggests that society, and by implication markets, have a natural equilibrium; by interfering and adding regulations and controls, rulers upset that equilibrium and interfere with the natural order of things.

> The highest type of rule is one of whose existence the people are
>     barely aware.
> Next comes one whom they love and praise.
> Next comes one whom they fear.
> Next comes one whom they despise and defy.
> When you are lacking faith,
> Others will be unfaithful to you.
> The Sage is self-effacing and scanty of words.
> When his task is accomplished and things have been completed,
> All the people say, 'We ourselves have achieved it!'
>                                         –Daodejing 17 (Wu 1990)

By the early eighteenth century, Jesuit missionaries in China had translated many Chinese works of philosophy into French; the *Daodejing* was translated as *Le Livre de Ciel* (the Book of Heaven). The French economist François de Quesnay became a great admirer of Daoist ideas. He was particularly attracted to the idea of *wu-wei*. The perfect monarch, he argued in his *Le despotisme de Chine* (1764), 'should do nothing, but let the laws rule', an almost exact translation of another passage in the *Daodejing*. Famously, Quesnay translated *wu-wei* as *laissez-faire*, and the concept went on to become the foundation stone of free-market capitalism down to this day. The rest, as they say, is history.

(Hudson 1931; Witzel 2004)

---

One of the 'wastes' that competition was said to create was the cost incurred in marketing and selling. The impression in some minds, at least, was that the primary purpose of marketing was to win customers away from competitors, not to meet customer needs. Of particular concern was the impact of vertical integration, whereby manufacturers controlled distribution systems and in some cases set up their own retail outlets. Some economists such as Lewis Haney believed that this was wasteful and expensive and resulted in the consumer paying higher prices. Others believed that vertical integration was more efficient and meant lower prices. In the end the majority of opinion sided with Northwestern University's Professor Fred Clark (1924), who pointed out that, ultimately, the purpose of marketing was to gratify the wants of the consumer. Provided this was achieved, the marketing organisation could take any form necessary. W.D. Moriarty (1923) made the case that, properly managed, marketing and especially advertising are not only efficient and cost-effective, but – dimly echoing Thomas Aquinas – they can add value for the consumer, for example by making them aware of products that would improve their quality of life and their well-being.

Clark and Moriarty both referred to a study by Daniel Starch (1922) on the economic efficiency of advertising. He concluded that advertising was indeed cost-efficient when compared to personal selling, and gave examples such as the California Fruit Growers' 'Sunkist' campaign which had achieved significant results in terms of cost-effectiveness. But this was by no means the last time that the ethics and efficiency of modern marketing would be debated.

### 5.4.3 The relationship of marketing to the rest of the firm

Until the twentieth century there was no such thing as a marketing director or a marketing manager. That job was typically done by a member of the top management team. At shipbuilder Harland & Wolff, chairman Edward Harland deputed this task to William Pirrie, who continued to lead the firm's marketing effort after he became chairman in turn. At sewing machine manufacturer Singer, responsibility for marketing was taken over by Isaac Singer's partner Edward Clark. These and other executives in similar positions had a number of responsibilities, of which marketing was one. James Couzens initially had responsibility for marketing at Ford, while agricultural equipment maker Cyrus McCormick was effectively his own sales director, as was Ford's rival the car maker John North Willys.

There was also no such thing as a marketing department, although in some manufacturing firms there were such things as sales departments. In the eighteenth and early nineteenth centuries many manufacturing firms contracted out their sales to contract selling firms or independent sales agents, the famous 'travelling salesmen'. However, some firms – Singer, McCormick and Willys among them – realised that this was not the optimum solution. Contracted sales agents were paid on commission, and tended to put their own interests ahead of either the firm that paid them or, more importantly, the customer. An in-house sales force, properly trained and not solely reliant on commissions for sales, could be a much more powerful tool for building relationships with customers. This was discovered in the retail sector too, notably by the Boucicauts at Au Bon Marché, who trained their sales staff carefully and urged them to focus on building good rapport with customers rather then generating sales.

By the 1920s, separate sales and marketing departments were becoming increasingly common in larger firms, even if some executives continued to regard them as an unjustified expense. But now a new fear emerged. Handing over responsibility for these functions to separate departments might encourage the rest of the firm to think of marketing and sales as somehow 'separate' from their own activities, leading to what we now term the 'silo effect' where people look only at their own discipline rather than the needs of the whole firm. Writing in the *Journal of Political Economy*, Vanderblue warned of the shape of things to come:

> Unless care is taken to bring all factors together there is likely to develop the tendency to treat each function as in a distinct compartment, when, in point of fact, the performance of one function frequently governs the method of performing others. Sale is frequently dependent upon standardization; finance upon storing; risking upon selling and financing; and there is the close interrelationship of transporting, risking, storing, and financing, illustrated in the use of the order bill of lading and the warehouse receipt as collateral ... The functional approach, it must be remembered, is not an end itself, but a means to an end.
>
> (Vanderblue 1921: 678, 683)

The application of modern management methods to marketing and the development of marketing as a discipline had helped to professionalise marketing and make possible the diffusion of best practice. But it had also brought about the risk, at least in the eyes of some, that marketing would become a specialist activity which happened in one part of the firm, rather than something that involved the whole firm, or at least the whole of management.

### 5.4.4 The purpose and role of the customer

As we have seen, early marketers relied heavily on building customer relationships. However, there was always a risk that the influence of the 'selling concept', to use Kotler's term, would turn customers into mere numbers. Especially during the period when many firms used contract sales staff, this did happen. Early mass marketers counted the numbers of transactions and the revenue received from each, and often did not bother with concerns such as whether the customer returned for a repeat purchase. P.T. Barnum's catchphrase 'there's a sucker born every minute' summed up the prevailing attitude: parting people from their money was the primary objective of salesmen.

The best and most effective marketers, however, people like William Lever and Henry Heinz, knew instinctively what later twentieth-century research would prove: that the most profitable business of most companies is repeat business, and that customers who return time and time again are the backbone of most successful businesses. Lever and Heinz, and others we have mentioned above, John Willys, Cyrus McCormick, John Patterson of National Cash Register, drove home this point to their sales staff. The customer was not a cow to be milked, he or she was a valuable asset and should be treated as such. Individual transactions, John Willys told his sales staff, should be seen as a beginning, not an end.

In a sense, then, the 'marketing concept' was not so much something new, as a return to older marketing values. Kotler's argument that marketing should benefit the customer resonates with Thomas Aquinas's view of the equilibrium between buyer and seller and the need for both to benefit equally. The societal marketing concept and the just price have at heart quite a lot in common.

## 5.5 Questions and discussion: is there anything new under the sun?

It is tempting to see, in the rise of relationship marketing and the increasing emphasis on marketing systems such as customer relationship management (CRM) a return to marketing basics. On one level, perhaps, there is some truth to this. Ambler (2000) has argued consistently for more emphasis on customer relationships, and Barwise and Meehan (2004) suggest that marketing needs to get 'back to basics' and concentrate on customers. But marketing, as both these works also make clear, is an infinitely more complex field than it was a hundred years ago, or a thousand. There are now many communications and distribution channels, many more forms of transaction than there once were, and all these have their own nuances.

How far is it possible to learn from past marketing practices? Certainly, as the case studies accompanying this chapter indicate, there were some very successful marketers in the past. We can study their methods, but there is always the problem of replicability: are these methods suitable for companies today, or were they successful because of the conditions, the time and place and circumstances?

One point that does come through from the study of past practices is that the equilibrium between buyer and seller, the point at which maximal satisfaction is achieved for both sides, is very elusive. It changes according to economic circumstances and the nature of personal demand. Both these things have to be studied by marketers. The two most important influences on early marketing theory were psychology and economics, and today the marketer still has to be part economist and part psychologist in order to understand customers and the market.

And it would appear that no marketing method will ever be universally successful, at least not for long. There are certain things that successful marketers have always done, including scanning the environment and focusing attention on customers and meeting their needs. Marketers who do not do both these things tend not to last for very long. But once these basic things have been done, the recipe for success then tends to vary widely. Creative thinking is essential. As Barwise and Meehan point out, it is necessary to both stick to fundamentals *and* be innovative: that is, to think simultaneously both inside and outside the box. Past examples of best practice in marketing tend to confirm this.

On one level, marketing has changed very little. The basics remain the same as they always have. On another level, it has changed out of all recognition, with mass markets, new products and services, new channels and new communications media. But how much of what the marketer does is truly new, and how much is it a case of putting old wine into new bottles?

---

### Takeaway exercise

Consider your own organisation or one you have worked for in the past and know well. How well do you (or did you) know its customers? If you worked in marketing and sales, then the answer should be 'pretty well', but otherwise your answer may be less certain. Now ask yourself who your customers are. What are their needs and wants? Do you think your company is satisfying them?

Now, go out and gather the evidence to prove your theory. Ask your marketing and sales people by all means, but for preference talk to some customers themselves, even informally or at social functions. You don't need to duplicate the company's own market research, but you should try to satisfy yourself that you personally have some idea of how customers regard your company and its products. War, said the French president Clémenceau, is too important to be left to the generals. In the same way, marketing is too important to be left solely to the marketers. In the end, customer satisfaction is everyone's business, for without it, there is no business.

---

## Case Study 5A

### *H.J. Heinz*

The food processing company H.J. Heinz & Co. was founded in 1876 by Henry John Heinz, the son of a brick maker from a small community near Pittsburgh, Pennsylvania. He started his first business at the age of eight, selling surplus vegetables from the family garden. By age sixteen he had acquired several plots of land and was employing others to sell vegetables for him, and had contracts with several grocers in Pittsburgh. In 1859 he enrolled at Duff's Commercial College, a training school in Pittsburgh, where he learned bookkeeping and accounting and some basic management skills. He then decided to specialise in processed foods such as horseradish, pickles and sauerkraut. His first company, Heinz & Noble, was at first very successful, shipping goods by rail from Pittsburgh as far afield as Chicago and St Louis. But the company expanded too soon, and the financial crisis of 1875 caught Heinz without sufficient reserves; by the end of the year the company was bankrupt. Heinz later repaid his share of the debt in full.

Despite the bankruptcy, Heinz knew he had tapped into a potential market, and in 1876 he set up a new partnership with his brother and cousin. Initially the firm was known as F. and J. Heinz and later simply as H.J. Heinz. The new firm invested heavily in food preparation equipment, in particular in the newly invented processes of preserving food in tinned metal containers. Through the 1880s Heinz launched a constant series of new canned and bottled food products, including such modern staples as canned vegetables, canned spaghetti and canned baked beans. By 1890 his was one of the largest food-producing companies in the country; by 1900 it was one of the largest in the world, making over 200 products in nine factories and with branch offices around the globe.

The story of how the Heinz 57 Varieties brand was conceived is best told by Heinz himself, relayed by one of his close associates, E.D. McCafferty.

> Its origin was in 1896. Mr Heinz, while in an elevated railroad train in New York, saw among the car-advertising cards one about shoes with the expression: '21 Styles'. It set him to thinking, and as he told it: 'I said to myself, "we do not have styles of products, but we do have varieties of products." Counting up how many we had, I counted well beyond 57, but "57" kept coming back into my mind. "Five, seven" – there are so many illustrations of the psychological influence of that figure and of its alluring significance to people of all ages and races that "58 Varieties" or "59 Varieties" did not appeal at all to me as being equally strong. I got off the train immediately, went down to the lithographers, where I designed a street-car card and had it distributed throughout the United States. I myself did not realize how highly successful a slogan it was going to be.'

Branding by the 1890s was already fairly sophisticated, even by modern standards. Some industries, notably soap, had established strong brands and supporting advertising and publicity campaigns. However, the common practice of the day was to brand individual products or product lines separately. In Heinz's case, given the broad range of products, this would have been so expensive as to be impracticable. His solution was to create a single corporate brand that could be applied across all products.

Heinz had already shown himself to be an innovator in marketing. He had devoted much time in the 1880s to setting up a large and well-trained sales force, and had developed so-far untried methods such as product demonstrations and free samples given away at public events. These latter were a particular inspiration, as they allowed the public to taste the product and assure themselves of its quality before buying. At the Chicago World's Fair in 1893, Heinz hit on another give-away. Setting up a Heinz pavilion, he gave each visitor a free 'pickle pin', a small metal pin in the shape of a dill pickle, as a memento. This has been called 'one of the most famous give-aways in merchandising history'. So many people crowded into the pavilion that the floors began to sag and had to be reinforced.

In Pittsburgh in the late 1880s, Heinz built a new state-of-the-art factory in the grandiose 'Pittsburgh Romanesque' style, and then opened it to visitors, providing guided tours. At the height of the tourist season, the works saw as many as 20,000 visitors a year. His eye for promotional opportunities increased as time went on. In 1900 Heinz sponsored the first advertising billboard lit by electric light bulbs, in New York City. The sign included 1,200 light bulbs at a time when very few people had electric lighting at all, and was regarded as a technological marvel: the *New York Times* called it a 'work of advertising genius'. The billboard became an important tourist attraction in its own right until its demolition a few years later to make way for the construction of a new building.

Perhaps the most ambitious of all Heinz's promotional efforts was the Heinz Ocean Pier in Atlantic City, New Jersey, sometimes called the 'Crystal Palace by the Sea' and sometimes, less reverently, 'the Sea Shore Home of the 57 Varieties'. Nine hundred feet in length, the pier featured a glass pavilion with a sun room and reading room, and of course a kitchen giving out free samples of Heinz products. At the height of its popularity before the First World War, the pier, like the factory, was attracting over 20,000 people a year. Its popularity declined in the 1930s, however, and the pier was finally abandoned after being badly damaged by a hurricane in the autumn of 1944.

The showmanship of Heinz's marketing and promotion efforts was intended to do no more than attract the public's attention and make it think about Heinz and his products. Once consumers were aware of his products, Heinz's purpose was to make them into regular customers by providing high-quality goods cheaply. The entire purpose of the Heinz brand was to send a signal of quality: the message was that customers could trust the quality of what was inside the tin or the bottle. He insisted that all the goods his firm produced had to be of the best quality possible, and he made the company's name synonymous with quality in the public mind.

Quality was one of Heinz's watchwords, and had been almost from the beginning of his career as a market gardener. In order to maintain quality finished products, he also needed to have the best quality raw materials. Purchasing was one area where Heinz never skimped or cut corners. In the 1880s he began developing purchasing arrangements with farmers, especially growers of cucumbers and cabbage used in making pickles and sauerkraut. Heinz would agree to purchase the farmer's entire output of a given crop at a previously agreed price, usually well above the average market rate; for their part, the farmers had to allow inspection of crops by Heinz technicians and to plant and harvest specific crops at specific times to ensure best quality of output. Heinz got the quality he needed, the farmers were well paid, and the agricultural community of the Midwest learned more about scientific farming methods (Heinz's farming technicians were hired from the country's leading agricultural colleges). Other crops were grown under direct supervision on the 16,000 acres of land owned by the company, and Heinz also established his own plants for making bottles and tins and owned his own railway cars, all to ensure that the supply process worked effectively and that food arrived at the canning and bottling plants fresh and in prime condition.

As well as seeking the best quality in his own products, Heinz and his managers were constant advocates of higher standards in the food industry. Heinz supported the Pure Food Movement, which was founded in the 1890s. Food adulteration and the risk to public health this caused were major public issues at the time, and a number of pressure groups and crusading journalists began to attack food producers who adulterated their products – but not Heinz. One of the results of the movement was the Pure Food and Drug Act of 1906, legislation which Heinz again supported. In both cases he was strongly at odds with the other major food producers, but Heinz was never afraid to court professional unpopularity in order to protect his standards. His view was that his loyalty was to his customers, not his peers.

Promotional activity was costly, as too were the steps taken to protect quality. However, Heinz's first business training had been as a bookkeeper, and he never forgot the painful lessons of his bankruptcy. Accordingly, he maintained strong financial controls. In the early stages of the business, Heinz served as bookkeeper and accountant himself, and later continued to monitor closely the basic financial indicators. Yet Heinz was not a cost-cutting manager. He balanced financial requirements with the other needs of his business, and used accounting information to help determine where the most profitable opportunities lay. Heinz used accounting and financial data to explore opportunities for growth, rather than simply as a means of control.

As an employer, Heinz was strongly paternalistic in approach. He believed in hiring employees young, training them in his own business methods and promoting on merit. He believed that all employees ought to feel part of the Heinz family. His was one of the first companies in the USA to introduce free life insurance for employees. In part this may have been a means of warding off industrial unrest, but Heinz's entire life and career were characterised by firmly held social principles. He was deeply religious, although his faith had different varieties, and he seems at various times to have been a Lutheran, an Episcopalian, a Methodist Episcopalian and a Presbyterian (to the amusement of his wife, an Ulster Protestant). He was for twenty-five years a Sunday school superintendent, and later served on the executive council of both the International Sunday School Association and the World Sunday School Association. He took his Christian values into both civic life and business life. He served as vice-president of the Pittsburgh Chamber of Commerce and on a number of other civic bodies. He was also a noted art collector and philanthropist; among his many civic roles in later life was the presidency of the Pittsburgh branch of the Egyptian Exploration Fund.

One of Heinz's associates was later to argue that Heinz was always guided by attention to business fundamentals: 'He was not a dreamer or a visionary, who went into business and by chance made a success. He was a businessman by origin, by preference, and by training.' Yet attention to business fundamentals is not incompatible with being a visionary, and it seems most likely that Heinz was both at once; his particular genius lay in being able to translate his vision into reality. A later biographer, Robert Alberts, spells out what he calls the 'Eight Important Ideas' that guided Heinz's philosophy of business. These are:

1. Housewives are willing to pay someone else to take over a share of their more tedious kitchen work.
2. A pure article of superior quality will find a ready market through its own intrinsic merit – if it is properly packaged and promoted.
3. To improve the finished product that comes out of the bottle, can or crock, you must improve it in the ground, when and where it is grown.
4. Our market is the world.
5. Humanize the business system of today and you will have the remedy for the present discontent that characterizes the commercial world and fosters a spirit of enmity between capital and labour.
6. Let the public assist you in advertising your products and promoting your name.
7. Good foods, properly processed, will keep without the addition of preservatives.
8. If people could work together in religion, then lasting peace might be found.

Evidence of all these ideas can be seen in Heinz's approach to management, often co-mingled.

## Analysis

Some of the questions you might want to consider in connection with this case include:

- What were the key elements of the Heinz brand? Why was it successful?
- What was the relationship between advertising/promotion and product quality in the Heinz marketing programme?

- Do you think Heinz was aware of all the elements of what we would now call the marketing mix?
- From this account of Heinz's activities, what, if anything, would you do differently or better?

## Sources

Alberts, R.C. (1973) *The Good Provider: H.J. Heinz and His 57 Varieties*, London: Arthur Barker.
McCafferty, E.D. (1923) *Henry J. Heinz: A Biography*, New York: Bartlett Orr Press.

## Case Study 5B

### *Au Bon Marché*

At the beginning of the nineteenth century, the structure of the European retail sector had not changed greatly for many centuries. Small specialist shops sold small quantities of goods to highly localised markets. Goods were seldom displayed or available for inspection and were usually kept behind high counters and produced only when customers asked for them. The price controls of the Middle Ages had ended and prices were not fixed; what a customer paid for goods depended on their ability to bargain and negotiate. This tended to work to the advantage of wealthier customers, whose patronage was seen as more valuable and so could force prices down. Poorer people, with less bargaining power, paid higher prices. The fact that customers could not inspect the goods before they paid for them led inevitably to abuses. Charles Babbage (1835) complained that customers, when buying goods such as sugar or tea, had no idea of whether they had been sold the right goods in the right quantity; they could only trust that the retailer was honest.

During the nineteenth century, however, the retail sector underwent a revolution. One of the causes of this was the introduction of the department store, which dramatically changed the way the retail sector operated, and was perceived. In particular, it transformed the practices of retailing and the relationship between retailer and customer. Like most great innovations, the department store was based on a few very simple concepts. If retailers treated customers fairly and with respect, they would become repeat customers and the volume of sales would grow. If customers could see and judge the quality of the goods they bought and know they were being charged a fair price, this too would increase their loyalty. If consumers could buy most of the things they needed under one roof rather than having to visit many shops in turn, they would find this more convenient and a more pleasant experience. Finally, if they could shop in an atmosphere which was welcoming and which encouraged their own personal aspirations, they would spend more and would be encouraged to buy more and different products.

The first true department store, Au Bon Marché in Paris, was the creation of two remarkable people, Aristide Boucicaut and his wife Marguerite. Both came from humble backgrounds.

Aristide Boucicaut was born in Bellême, Normandy in 1810, the son of a hat-maker. After only a rudimentary education, he joined the family business and began selling hats in the market towns and fairs of Normandy. In 1835 he moved to Paris where he worked as a sales clerk in a clothing and drapery business. Soon after arriving in Paris he met Marguerite Guerin, who was born probably around the same time as Boucicaut, the illegitimate daughter of a peasant girl. She was working as a waitress in a restaurant when the two first met. They married at the end of 1835, and at first lived in conditions of considerable poverty.

But Boucicaut soon moved to another, larger drapery business, where his talents for business were recognised and he received promotion. By 1852, the couple had set aside enough capital to become part-owners of a new business, the drapery store Au Bon Marché. The Boucicauts took over the management of the shop, and made such a success of it that by 1863 they were able to buy out their partners and become sole owners.

It was at the original Au Bon Marché that the Boucicauts began to develop their ideas on retailing. One of the first innovations was in pricing: fixed prices were introduced so that every customer knew in advance what they would pay. The Boucicauts emphasised that their customers were getting a fair deal; the staff were there to help them, not to cheat them. Other innovations included doing away with the old-style high sales counters that kept customers away from the goods, and opening up the shop so that customers could browse among the goods and inspect them. They also brought in a more diverse range of goods so as to increase sales. By 1850, having expanded their original premises, they were now offering a wide range of goods which were sold in different 'departments'; thus drapery was sold in one unit, millinery in another, carpets and home furnishings in a third.

Other entrepreneurs began developing shops along similar lines. The Grand Magasins de Louvre, opened in 1855, had a new format. Rather than just selling textiles, it branched out into furniture and other household goods. Printemps, founded in 1865 by a former Au Bon Marché employee, followed the same pattern. All these establishments had realised that the future of retailing lay in offering a variety of goods to people at low prices, generating volume sales rather than high margins.

But the vision of the Boucicauts went further. Their plan was not for 'cheap and cheerful' retailing based on price alone. Instead, in a famous phrase, Aristide Boucicaut spoke of the 'democratisation of luxury', bringing the new products of the Industrial Revolution into the homes of the middle classes and prosperous tradesmen. Shopping could be more than just a means of satisfying needs; it could be an activity that people engaged in for social as well as personal reasons. The Boucicauts set out to design what we would today call a 'retail experience', a place where people would come not only to shop but to see and be seen.

In 1869 the cornerstone was laid for the new Au Bon Marché. Part designed by Gustave Eiffel, the new store used radical techniques in steel and glass construction, influenced in part by London's Crystal Palace. The grand opening of the new store was a major public event. The middle classes of Paris identified with the new store and saw it as part of their own aspirations; exactly as the Boucicauts had hoped they would.

Au Bon Marché dominated Parisian retailing for the remainder of the century. So popular was the store that new extensions were continually added; by 1887 it had 52,000 square metres of floor space, far more than any rival. In 1869 the original Au Bon Marché had a turnover of around 20 million francs; ten years later the figure was approaching 80 million. Aristide Boucicaut did not live to see the full flowering of Bon Marché's success; he died in 1877, and his son died two years later. Management of the business then fell into the hands of Marguerite Boucicaut, who ran Bon Marché for another ten years until her own death.

Marguerite had a 'hands off' management style, leaving day-to-day operations in the hands of capable subordinates and devoting her time to planning the store's continued expansion and setting in place a permanent ownership and management structure which would enable the business to carry on after her. So successful was she that by 1887, the year of her death, sales topped 120 million francs; in 1906 they reached 200 million. By now Au Bon Marché was not just a business, it was an institution in Paris. Concerts and cultural events were held in its halls. Émile Zola's novel *Au Bonheur des Dames* (1883) is partly set in Au Bon Marché and tells the story of the rags-to-riches rise of its founders, though under different names.

The success of Au Bon Marché was based on several things. First, as noted above, there was the principle of fair pricing, with prices fixed and margins kept low to make goods affordable. This sounds simple, but in fact it required a considerable change in thinking. Rather than concentrating on individual transactions, as had been the previous practice, the emphasis shifted to making sure the customer was satisfied. Satisfied customers, the Boucicauts reasoned, would come back, and repeat sales would more than compensate for low margins.

Display of goods was another important element. The Boucicauts had learned early on that their newly affluent middle-class customers wanted quality and were prepared to pay for it. They bought high-quality stock and paid careful attention to displaying it in the most attractive manner possible. The new Au Bon Marché building was designed as an impressive and spectacular piece of architecture in its own right; but it was also carefully designed to provide the best possible display space for a variety of goods.

Diversity of goods was also important. Before 1869 the Boucicauts and others had been experimenting with broad ranges of goods, and had seen the results in increased sales. By re-creating Au Bon Marché as a department store in the modern sense, they made it possible for consumers to satisfy a large variety of needs at a single location. This was particularly important for shoppers travelling in from the middle-class suburbs on the rapidly expanding railway network, who could now do their shopping in a leisurely fashion rather then rushing to and fro across the city.

Staffing was another area where the Boucicauts paid close attention to detail. The numbers of staff employed were huge by modern standards – 4,500 by 1900 – but one of the aims was to make sure that there were always enough sales assistants on hand to deal with every customer. Staff were meticulously trained in the methods of the new store, and were taught to be polite and deferential to customers, to dress cleanly and well, and to always seek to create a good impression. They were reminded constantly that they were not just sales clerks, but were representatives of the store; the impression they created on customers would be a lasting one. Finally, they were taught that their main function was to please customers, not to make profits. Attempting to haggle or bargain with customers on price was one of a number of offences for which sales staff could be summarily dismissed.

Above all, Au Bon Marché became a symbol for the bourgeoisie of Paris. This view was constantly reinforced by the Boucicauts themselves. Innovations such as regular programmes of musical concerts created an image not so much of a shop but of a palace of luxury, open to all. Retailing was no longer just a matter of making sales and counting up the cash at the end of the day; it had developed a culture all of its own. A later retailer and admirer of the Boucicauts, the American Gordon Selfridge, would go on to speak of the 'romance of commerce' and argue that 'few things in the modern world can stir the imagination or delight the senses so thoroughly as one of our great department stores' (Selfridge 1918).

The new industrial era of mass production meant that more goods of better quality could be produced more cheaply; while at the same time, rising prosperity meant that more people were willing to pay for goods which would improve their lives. Quality and luxury were the new bywords in retailing. Products which made homes more comfortable and people more healthy would find a ready market. Success in retailing was not just about selling products, it was also now about helping people to meet their own aspirations. The Boucicauts understood this change, and reflected it in their own approach to marketing.

The impact of Bon Marché and its radical new approach to retailing was felt around the world. Paris itself became the leader of the department store movement in part thanks to Au Bon Marché itself; other department store owners like Jules Jaluzot of Printemps and Louise Jay of Samaritaine learned their trade as managers at Bon Marché, and many others copied the methods of the Boucicauts. Across the Channel, the British entrepreneur William Whiteley had observed the new style of retailing and established his own department store in 1872, Whiteley's of Bayswater, nicknamed the 'Universal Provider'. Like Au Bon Marché, Whiteley's became a fashion icon as well as a store, and counted Queen Victoria among its patrons. When Whiteley was murdered in 1907 the business went into a decline, but not before other entrepreneurs such as Peter Jones, John Lewis and Gordon Selfridge had copied his example and built more lasting businesses.

And from London and Paris the department store movement circled the world. John Wanamaker, who greatly admired Marguerite Boucicaut, founded Wanamaker's Stores in Philadelphia, and Macy's in New York and Filene's in Boston were not far behind. By the end of the century the movement had reached the Far East, where Ma Ying-piao founded Sincere in Hong Kong in 1899, and the Mitsui family, owners of the ancient dry-goods emporium Echigo-ya (first founded in 1673), began restyling the business along the same lines as Au Bon Marché. Echigo-ya had already pioneered ideas such as fixed pricing and displaying goods to customers; now, as Japanese industrialisation and prosperity grew, the Mitsuis saw how the rest of the Au Bon Marché recipe could be employed. Other stores such as Mitsukoshi soon followed.

Aristide and Marguerite Boucicaut were poorly educated and with little to guide them other than practical experience and common sense. Yet they not only correctly read the future of retailing, they also developed a formula for success that has endured to this day. At the beginning of the twenty-first century, department stores face challenges from new retailing formats. Whether they can meet those challenges and survive may in part depend on how well they can interpret the original vision of Bon Marché.

## Analysis

Some of the questions you might want to consider in connection with this case include:

- What were the key elements of the Boucicauts' marketing strategy?
- How did they combine marketing with other aspects of management to achieve an overall recipe for success?
- What weaknesses might their marketing strategy have had? Can you think of ways that they might have been vulnerable to competition?
- Given that the Boucicauts had little education and no formal business training, and yet on their own managed to come up with an idea that revolutionised the world of retailing, is there any reason why we need formal research in marketing?

## Sources

Miller, Michael B. (1994) *The Bon Marché: Bourgeois Culture and the Department Store*, Princeton: Princeton University Press.
Ydewalle, Charles d' (1965) *Au Bon Marché: de la Boutique au Grand Magasin*, Paris: n.p.

## Case Study 5C

### *Tongrentang*

Founded in 1669 in Beijing, Tongrentang may be the world's oldest continuously operating retail business (Echigo-ya in Tokyo, which later became the Mitsui department store, was opened a few years later in 1663). The first shop, established by the Le family, was a fairly small business selling Chinese medicine. Details of the early years of the business are vague; China was still recovering from the aftermath of the Manchu invasion and conquest and establishment of the new Qing ruling dynasty in 1644, and it was not until the 1680s that the Chinese economy began to revive. However, under the rule of the Emperor Kangxi (1661–1722), his son Yungzheng (1723–35), and grandson Qianlong (1735–96), imperial China experienced her last great golden age. Trade flourished both internally and externally. With the country largely at peace, it was possible to travel throughout China with relative ease.

These conditions suited sellers of Chinese medicines, some of which require exotic ingredients only available in the tropical lands of south China and southeast Asia. Peace also meant rising affluence and more customers. After 1700 Tongrentang began to grow; in 1723 the incoming Emperor Yungzheng appointed the Le family and Tongrentang the official suppliers of medicine to the Imperial court.

Despite this patronage, the business fell on hard times. In 1754 the Le family were forced to sell, and the business was taken over by one of their former employees, Zhang Shiji. Zhang managed the business capably and restored its finances, and it may have been under him and his successors that Tongrentang opened its first retail outlets in other cities; there are indications that he sold shares or partnerships in the firm to merchants from other centres in north China.

In the early nineteenth century one of the descendants of the founding family, Le Pingquan, regained control of Tongrentang. Together with his wife, usually known only as Madame Xu, who co-managed the business with him, Le greatly expanded Tongrentang's markets and customer base. Imperial patronage had continued, but Le strengthened the relationship with the imperial court and began to promote Tongrentang as a brand based on the virtues of high product quality, reliability and trustworthiness.

Retail brands, or *hao* (as distinct from manufacturers' brands or *biaoji*), had been in existence in China for centuries. The oldest recorded brand in China is that of the Liu family firm of needle makers in the city of Jinan in Shandong province, which dates from some time during the Northern Sung dynasty (960–1126). Other early brands included the scissor maker Wang Mazi from Beijing, founded about the same time as Tongrentang, and the Zhang Dalong brand of scissors from the city of Hangzhou (Hamilton and Lai 1989). These were local brands, but by the late eighteenth and early nineteenth centuries there were brands that reached right across China, like the Suzhou-based confectionery firm Caizhi Zhai, or Jingdezhen pottery from the Yangtze valley, along with various brands of cotton and silk cloth; these latter included both manufacturers' brands and retail brands like the still existing Tongmenghui.

By the 1830s, Tongrentang had joined the ranks of these nationally recognised brands. Le's marketing strategy had several strands. First, he enlarged and refurbished the pharmacy's flagship shop in the Dazhalan district of Beijing (it remains one ,of the most imposing older buildings in the district). He invested in research and development, sending agents far afield to look for new ingredients and employing chemists to come up with new forumlae, aiming both to develop entirely new medicines and improve the formulation of existing ones. According to some accounts, many of the chemists employed were members of Le's own family; he was anxious to protect his formulae and safeguard them against imitation, and this meant that the formulae were quite literally kept in the family.

Le also engaged in promotions in other ways, improving the visibility of his brand by building schools and supporting other charitable activities. The nature of these ranged widely, from supporting a foundation that provided coffins for the very poorest people enabling them to have a decent burial, to part-funding a municipal fire brigade in Beijing. All of these things raised Tongrentang's profile and contributed to its image as a sincere and caring company.

Le's most important tactic, however, was the giving away of free samples of medicine to scholars coming to Beijing to sit the Imperial exams. For many centuries, entrance into the Imperial civil service had required the passing of an examination. Civil service posts offered good pay, prestige and the chance of advancement, and were highly coveted, and thousands of people came from all over China to sit them each year. By giving free medicine to the scholars, Le reckoned he would win the goodwill of those who passed the exams, thus creating an additional pool of high-ranking and wealthy customers. Not only did this tactic succeed, but even those who failed the exams returned to their homes with glowing reports of Tongrentang. Orders began coming in from all over the country, and before long Tongrentang began to expand its branch network. Although figures are not entirely clear, it appears that by 1911 Tongrentang had at least seventeen branches around China, and was exporting on a small scale to the Chinese community living overseas.

The Revolution of 1911 and the overthrow of the Qing dynasty hurt Tongrentang's business, as did the subsequent political turmoil in China and the shift of the political centre of power from Beijing to the south and west. A number of its branch stores are known to have closed during this period, though that in Shanghai remained open until the Japanese occupation during the Second World War. By the time of the 1948 Revolution and the establishment of the People's Republic of China, only the Beijing branch remained, and this was only just surviving. After 1948 Tongrentang was taken into national ownership.

Following the economic reforms that began in 1979, however, Tongrentang was partly returned to private ownership and the firm began to expand once more. With its long history and traditions it quickly grew to dominate the national market for traditional Chinese medicines, and then began to expand internationally. In 1993 Tongrentang opened its first shops in Hong Kong and London. Other overseas outlets have followed, notably in Sydney, Australia. By 2004 there were seventeen overseas branches in twelve countries and the export market was growing steeply. In 2006, total sales exceeded 2.5 billion yuan, and the company announced plans for an expansion of its domestic network to 200 stores. Ironically, one of the biggest problems facing Tongrentang today is the same as that it faced in the nineteenth century: the theft of its intellectual property and pirating of its brand by unscrupulous competitors both inside and outside China. Within the last ten years the company has refurbished and re-opened its old store in the Dazhalan district of Beijing, though it has also built a very modern showroom and warehouse on the edge of the city, where its headquarters is now located.

## Analysis

Some of the questions you might want to consider in connection with this case include:

- How would you describe Tongrentang's marketing strategy under the management of Le Pingquan and Madame Xu?
- How did the company link its marketing with other business activities?
- Today, Tongrentang's management makes a virtue of the company's age and the longevity of its brand. Why might having an 'old' brand as opposed to a 'new' one be an advantage in a market such as that for traditional Chinese medicine?

## Sources

Hamilton, Gary G. and Lai Chi-kong (1989) 'Consumption and Brand Names in Late Imperial China', in Henry J. Rutz and Benjamin S. Orlove (eds), *The Social Economy of Consumption*, Lanham, MD: University Press of America, pp. 253–79.
Tongrentang company website. www.tongrentang.com.

## Case Study 5D

*Colt*

The firearms manufacturer Colt, or at least the first version of it, was founded in Paterson, New Jersey in 1836. It was the creation of Samuel Colt, an entrepreneur from New England. Prior to founding the gun factory, Colt had had a somewhat chequered career. He was born in Hartford, Connecticut in

1814, the son of a textile maker who went bankrupt when Colt was still a small boy. It is hard to know details of his early life for certain as Colt himself later rewrote much of his own personal history. According to his own account, he went to work at age ten in a factory, where he developed an interest in firearms and explosives. He then attended Amherst Academy, presumably on a scholarship. In 1830 he designed a fireworks display for the Academy to celebrate American independence on the Fourth of July, but this misfired – literally as well as figuratively – and the school building was burned to the ground.

Threatened with expulsion, Colt left school and took a job as a merchant seaman. Again according to his own account, it was during a voyage to Calcutta that, watching the turning of the ship's paddle wheel, he thought of the idea for a revolver, a repeating firearm with a revolving cylinder that would rotate around a central pin rather as a paddlewheel did. In fact, it seems very unlikely that Colt was travelling on a steam-powered paddle wheel-propelled ship at this early date. Further, patents for revolvers had been issued in both Britain and the USA as early as 1813, and it is likely that with his interest in firearms, Colt knew something about these.

Returning home in 1831, he worked briefly in a textiles factory and then in 1832, aged eighteen, he took a job as a travelling salesman, touring New England and selling nitrous oxide, then widely used as an anaesthetic by doctors and dentists. He proved himself an adept salesman; he called himself 'Dr Colt' (although he had no medical qualifications and had never finished school), and quickly mastered the techniques of promotion. He used his earnings from this job to build prototypes of his revolver, and during 1835–36 took out US, British and French patents. In 1836, having found financial backing, he established his first factory in Paterson, New Jersey. There was at this point little civilian market for firearms, and Colt, like most gun makers, hoped to win contracts with the US Army. But despite Colt's repeated efforts, the army showed no interest in revolvers and his company failed in 1842.

Only a few hundred Colt Paterson revolvers (as they are now known to distinguish them from later models) were ever made, but by chance a small number had been purchased by the Texas Rangers, a paramilitary force responsible for policing the state of Texas, which had joined the USA a few years earlier. A patrol of Rangers led by Captain Samuel Walker, armed with Colt revolvers, was ambushed by a large force of bandits, but succeeded in driving off the enemy thanks to the superior firepower of their revolvers. Believing that the guns had saved the lives of him and his men, Captain Walker wrote an enthusiastic letter to Colt, describing what had happened and praising the new guns.

Colt at once realised that this could be a valuable source of publicity. He returned to Connecticut and set up a new business. The Connecticut River valley was already a centre of arms-making, on its way to becoming what Hosley (1996) calls America's first centre of machine-based manufacturing.

Initially, Colt did not make guns himself but instead outsourced the manufacturing to an existing firm, that of Eli Whitney, Jr. Whitney's firm made revolvers according to Colt's designs, while Colt himself promoted and sold the weapons. He exploited Walker's letter to the full and later invited the captain to come and give public speeches in New England and New York; Colt's publicity hailed Captain Walker as a hero, and then associated his revolvers with that heroic image.

From there, Colt began to develop his own image. In the 1850s he began calling himself 'Colonel Colt' (a title to which he had no more claim than the Dr Colt of his laughing-gas selling days) and embarked on an assiduous campaign of self-promotion. He deliberately cultivated myths about himself – or allowed others to do so for him – which added to the stature of his products. In some of the sensational popular novels of the time, known as 'dime novels', he appears as a heroic figure in his own right, travelling the Wild West and fighting off hordes of outlaws with his trusty revolver, while in fact Colt had never been west of the Mississippi river. He also moved into international markets, and showed himself to have few scruples as to whom he sold to. The British army were his primary target, but despite relentless lobbying the British preferred their own Adams revolvers. Elsewhere Colt had more success. One of his first major contracts was to the army of Ottoman Turkey, but during the Crimean War Colt also sold arms to Turkey's – and Britain's – enemy Russia. He also struck lucrative deals with various rebel and guerrilla movements including Garibaldi's Redshirts in Italy and the Fenians in Ireland – the latter despite the fact that they were engaged in a campaign of bombing and assassinations, what we might now call terrorism, in Ireland and Britain.

Colt was a very effective, if at times unscrupulous, marketer. But he also understood the fundamentals of business. Part of the reputation of his weapons was based on quality; they were billed as reliable guns that, in life-and-death situations, would not let their owners down. But he knew too that this image had to be backed up. Even a few stories of guns jamming in action and becoming useless would ruin the product's reputation. (He was absolutely right. Later, during the First World War, a rumour began to spread that the Ross rifle issued to Canadian soldiers was prone to jamming (i.e. the action freezing so the gun could not be fired or reloaded). Although not a single verifiable instance of jamming was ever found, the rumour was so potent that Canadian soldiers refused to use the weapon and the army had to switch to the British Lee-Enfield.)

Accordingly, after contracting production to Whitney for two years, Colt then decided to set up his own factory. Here he took a gamble, believing that the market for guns could be expanded and that investment in mass production would pay off. Skilled workers were recruited from all over New England and Europe to build and run the factory machinery, and the talented engineer Elihu Root was hired as factory superintendent. High-speed automated production was the centre of Colt's concept of the factory;

he later calculated that 80 per cent of his production costs were machine costs, while only 20 per cent were human labour costs, an astounding ratio for the time. Machine production ensured that quality could be engineered in, while maintaining a level of production high enough to meet forecast demand.

Mass production had been employed in America before, but to Colt goes part of the credit for popularising the idea and spreading it more broadly, first in the firearms sector and then more broadly in US industry. Colt's success inspired many emulators. Former Colt employee Christopher Spencer set up his own factory in 1860, making tube-fed magazine rifles of his own design, the famous Spencer rifle which was widely adopted by the Union Army in the American Civil War (according to one opponent, troops armed with the Spencer could 'load on Sunday and fire all week'). The rifle maker Oliver Winchester would later adopt many of Colt's methods in making and selling his rifles. Skilled artisans trained in the firearms factories helped spread factory techniques and methods into other industries as well. Colt is seen as an important anticipator of the systems of mass production based on division of labour.

Colt married for the first time at age 42, in 1856. He began to suffer from rheumatism in 1858, and a combination of disease and overwork brought about his death in 1862, shortly after the outbreak of the American Civil War. His wife Elizabeth Colt took over the firm and guided it through the war, when the factory made a variety of weapons for the Union Army. After the war, as population pressure and land hunger began pushing American settlers and migrants west towards the Pacific, Elizabeth Colt revived the image of the Colt as the preferred weapon of the rugged, individualistic frontiersman and cowboy, and marketed it with great success. Colt's greatest period of prosperity came under her management during the period 1870–90 when famous models such as the Colt .45 Peacemaker dominated the market, and when Colt finally also captured the contract for handguns sold to the US Army. She sold the firm and retired in 1901.

Hosley (1996) sums up Colt's contribution and abilities:

> Indeed, Colt's greatest invention was not repeating firearms – he had plenty of competition – but the system he built to manufacture these and the apparatus of sales, image management and marketing that made his guns ... the most popular, prolific and storied handgun in American history. Colt's ... name and personality became so widely associated with the product that ownership provided access to the celebrity, glamour and dreams of its namesake. What Colt *invented* was a system of myths, symbols, stagecraft and distribution that has been mimicked by generations of industrial mass marketers and has rarely been improved upon.
>
> (Hosley 1996: 73–74)

However, rugged and durable though Colt's guns were, they were inferior to other competing products, especially the British Adams revolver and the American Smith & Wesson, which were equally well made and equally durable. Both these latter were what were known as 'single-action' revolver, which meant that the user had only to squeeze the trigger to fire a shot. Colt revolvers were 'double-action' which meant that the user had to pull back the hammer which struck the firing pin and then squeeze the trigger. The rate of fire was thus much slower, which could be a huge disadvantage.

Colt was aware of this drawback, and it is probably for this reason that he chose to deliberately create an image of his revolvers. By positioning Colt revolvers as the weapon of choice of heroic figures like Texas Rangers, cowboys and US marshals in the Wild West, Colt managed to associate his guns with the 'romance' of the frontier. As a result, not only frontiersman and cowboys bought them; so did people in the settled east of the country, who had no particular need for a gun but wanted to be associated with that same heroic image and idea of individual freedom. Private gun ownership in America in the 1840s was relatively rare. By 1900 it had become commonplace and owning a gun, especially a Colt, was almost fashionable; the company even evolved a range of small pocket pistols which ladies could carry in their handbags. Just as Henry Ford helped to create America's 'car culture' in the early twentieth century, so in the mid-nineteenth century Colt helped to create its 'gun culture' (Hosley 1996: 72).

## Analysis

Some of the questions you might want to consider in connection with this case include:

- Why did Colt's guns succeed in dominating the market, even though they were arguably inferior in quality to competing brands?
- How would you describe the relationship between marketing and production at Colt? Which was dominant, and which followed the other?
- The final paragraph of the case study suggests that here is an example of the law of unintended consequences. Colt may not have set out to create a gun-owning culture in America, but it happened nonetheless. What kinds of things must marketers beware of when developing the market for a new product for the first time?

## Sources

Hosley, W. (1996) *Colt: The Making of an American Legend*, Amherst, MA: University of Massachusetts Press.
Rohan, J. (1935) *Yankee Arms Maker*, New York: Harper & Row.

# Case Study 5E

*Thomas Cook*

Thomas Cook, the company that pioneered the idea of mass tourism, actually had its origins in the temperance movement. Its founder, Thomas Cook, was born in Derbyshire in 1808. His father having died when he was young, he had only a basic education and was first apprenticed as a carpenter. In his late teens he moved to the town of Loughborough in Leicestershire. Like his parents before him, Cook was a devout Baptist, and in 1828 he was appointed bible reader and missionary for the county of Rutland. In 1832 he moved to the town of Market Harborough, where he set up in business as a carpenter and continued his missionary work, preaching and writing and handing out tracts. He married in 1832, and in the same year he 'took the pledge', remaining a teetotaller throughout his life. Much of his subsequent work with the Baptists involved preaching and writing tracts on the evils of alcohol. In 1840 he was appointed secretary of the Market Harborough branch of the South Midlands Temperance Association.

Thus far, there is not much evidence of an interest in mass tourism and little sign of entrepreneurship. But in 1841, Cook and members of his branch desired to attend a temperance meeting in Leicester. As a large number of people wished to go, ordinary carriages would have been expensive and impractical. Cook then had the idea of approaching the recently built South Midlands railway, which connected Market Harborough with Leicester. He asked to hire a special train to convey the party to and from the meeting, and found that this could be done fairly cheaply. The journey to and from the meeting duly took place on 5 July 1841.

This is sometimes claimed as the first railway excursion in Britain, but as Pudney (1953) points out, there had been other similar ventures organised before this. However, the experience did set Thomas Cook to thinking about the possibilities. In 1845 he organised an excursion purely for pleasure, selling tickets in Leicester, Nottingham, Derby and nearby towns for a railway day excursion to Liverpool and back. Cook struck a deal with the railway to arrange cheap fares, took a commission on the tickets sold, and organised the passengers at either end.

The excursion was both highly successful and profitable, and others followed. Cook realised that he had discovered an entirely new market. He abandoned his carpentry business and became a travel agent. He began organising longer tours, at first overnight and then later for a week or more, as far afield as Wales and Scotland. In what became the organisation's standard procedure in later years, Cook always travelled the route of each excursion in advance, inspected hotels and facilities and made prior arrangements, paid for all facilities to be used, and even wrote guidebooks for the use of his customers. Cook thus assumed the entire cost risk of the excursion, leaving the travellers to pay a fixed fee which covered all accommodation, travel and food.

Along with these longer tours, Cook continued to organise day excursions to beauty spots and country houses in the English Midlands; indeed, for a number of years these were his firm's most important source of income. One popular destination was Chatsworth in Derbyshire, home of the Dukes of Devonshire. Cook became friendly with Joseph Paxton, the head gardener at Chatsworth and designer of its glasshouse, one of the key attractions for visitors.

In 1851 the Great Exhibition opened in London, featuring the finest examples of manufactured goods, craftwork and artistic production from across the British empire and around Europe. The centrepiece of the Exhibition was the Crystal Palace, an amazing construction of glass and steel far in advance of its time, erected in Hyde Park. Its architect was Cook's friend Joseph Paxton, who helped Cook arrange exclusive tours for his customers. Cook organised tours to the Great Exhibition, with the now familiar inclusive package of travel costs, hotels and meals all covered by one fixed fee. These were wildly popular and were sold out weeks in advance, and this success in turn meant his firm became highly visible; newspapers carried articles about this new form of travel and more people began signing up for other tours as well.

In the early 1850s Cook ran into opposition from the railway companies, which up until then had been his willing partners. They now believed that they could cut out Cook as middleman and organise excursions and tours themselves. However, they lacked Cook's experience and organisational capabilities and most of these attempts failed; by the 1860s many railway companies in Britain were coming back to Cook and asking him to organise tours once again. Cook himself in the meantime had simply moved into Europe, where railway companies were more accommodating.

By now his business was growing at speed. In 1855 Cook organised excursions to the Paris Exhibition. By the early 1860s Switzerland and Italy had been added to the itinerary, with Greece following soon after. In 1869 Cook sent his first tour to Palestine, and that same year saw steamer excursions up the Nile taking 'tourists', as they were now called, to see the monuments of ancient Egypt. The first round-the-world tour came in 1872 and was very popular, and more round-the-world tours followed almost at once. Full internationalisation followed shortly; Cook began recruiting tourists in America, and in the 1880s his firm entered the Indian market, organising tours for wealthy Indians coming to Europe. It also got involved in the Mecca pilgrimage trade, carrying middle-class Muslims who wished to travel in comfort to and from Mecca. By 1890, 1,200 hotels in Europe alone were part of the Cook system, and tens of thousands of people annually were taking Cook's tours. The firm had added banking and currency exchange to the portfolio of services offered to customers.

Cook's system was simple, and relied on two fundamental assumptions about his market, both of which were proved true. The first assumption was that there were very many middle-class and prosperous working-class families who would enjoy the chance to travel abroad but were deterred from doing so by various risk factors. The two most important were (1) lack of familiarity with local customs, language and cultures, and (2) uncertainty about the costs of travel. Cook disposed of this risk by introducing 'conducted tours', whereby an agent familiar with the local area would accompany the party at all times and solve any travel-related problems as they arose (Cook himself worked as an agent until into the 1870s, and his son and grandson both worked as agents, particularly on newly established routes).

The second risk was dealt with by developing the all-inclusive holiday package, an elaboration of the excursions Cook had first developed in Britain. Every member of a particular tour paid a flat fee which included all travel, accommodation and food. The only thing tourists had to pay for themselves was alcoholic drinks; as teetotallers, Cook and his son could not be involved in the sale of alcohol (and indeed, they were later criticised for allowing the sale of wine and spirits on the Nile river steamers they owned). This custom was followed by other tour companies, and to this day it is commonplace for customers on package tours to have all their costs covered except for beer, wine and spirits, which they must pay for themselves.

Cook's second assumption was that railway companies, hotels and restaurants would be willing to reduce their fares provided he could guarantee them a sufficient volume of customers; in other words, they would put the emphasis on turnover rather than unit profit. In this he was correct. Each route covered by Cook's tours had to be worked out in advance, including a series of negotiations with many individual railway and steamship companies, hotels, restaurants and even cabdrivers and railway porters to ensure that a price was agreed in advance. For a new route in foreign countries, this could take months. At the end of this development process, though, the Cooks had a new package which could be offered to the travelling public at an affordable cost. Quality and price were both guaranteed. The mass tourism industry had been created, and continues to exist in much the same form today.

Cook's success can be measured in two ways: the vast increase in numbers of the travelling public, and the consequent outcry this provoked. In the year 1890, around the time Cook retired from the firm, more than 3.2 million tickets for Cook's tours were sold. By this time too, the organisation was employing more than 1,700 people worldwide. It owned a headquarters building on Ludgate Circus in London and had properties elsewhere in the capital. Its tours of the Swiss Alps, Palestine and the ruins along the Nile were particularly popular, and its round-the-world packages continued to be a draw.

However, the spread of mass tourism provoked outcry in some quarters. The English writer and art critic John Ruskin, appalled at the invasion by mass tourists of the mountains of Switzerland, complained to Cook: 'you have made race-courses of the cathedrals of the Earth. Your *one* conception of pleasure is to drive in railroad carriages around their aisles and eat off their altars' (Brendon 1991: 81). Charles Lever, an English diplomat in Italy, wrote anonymous newspaper articles claiming that the tourists in Cook's parties were convicts whom Australia had refused to accept, and were instead being deported to Italy in the guise of tourists. Writing in *Black-wood's Magazine* in 1865, he commented that 'these devil's dust tourists have spread over Europe, injuring our credit and damaging our character ... Take my word for it, if these excursionists go on, nothing short of another war ... will ever place us where we once were in the opinion of Europe' (quoted in Pudney 1953: 165).

Cook simply shrugged off these rants. In the mid-1890s the Duke of Kent, the future King George V, contacted Thomas Cook to arrange a private tour of the Christian holy places in Palestine. So efficiently was the visit managed that in 1898 Kaiser Wilhelm II of Germany contacted the company and asked for a similar tour, with a large party of courtiers and German nobles. The company used both these visits to generate a great deal of publicity for itself.

Cook, affected by blindness, retired from the business to his country house in Stonegate in Sussex, where he died in 1892. *The Times* in its obituary of Cook commented that:

> They [the Cooks] have organized travel as it was never organized before, and they have their reward in the enormous increase in the number of travellers ... They have applied the resources of civilization to a very general modern need, and for this they deserve and obtain full recognition.
>
> (quoted in Pudsey 1953: 19)

Cook was succeeded by his son John Mason Cook, described by Brendon (1991: 100) as 'a man of outstanding ability and ruthless determination', a great organiser who made his father's broader successes possible. He had begun working full-time for the firm in the 1860s, and was instrumental in organising the firm and putting it onto a solid commercial footing after the headlong expansion of the first two decades. He did much of the groundwork for routes in the Middle East, Egypt and India, and conducted personally many of the first tours there. Father and son seem to have had the perfect partnership; Thomas Cook's was the marketing genius and entrepreneurial spirit, while John Mason Cook provided the organisational and financial skills. In 1885 when war broke out in the Sudan, John Mason Cook chartered steamers to carry troops and supplies for the Gordon Relief Expedition travelling up the Nile to Khartoum. He died of the after-effects of a fever contracted while conducting Kaiser Wilhelm's tour to Jerusalem in 1898, and control of the company passed to his son in turn.

Thomas Cook continued to grow and retained its position as one of the world's leading mass travel providers. In 2008 Thomas Cook had revenues of £8.8 billion and in that year carried more than 22 million customers; it employed 31,000 people worldwide, and in addition to its tour, banking and currency businesses owned an airline with a fleet of more than 90 planes and a major travel publishing business.

## Analysis

Some of the questions you might want to consider in connection with this case include:

- What were the main ingredients in the Thomas Cook marketing mix? How did these change over time?
- Part of Cook's success seems to have rested on his ability to reduce risk for his customers. How important do you think this was? How important does this continue to be in the tourism industry?
- As the case notes, Cook made two fundamental assumptions (1) that there was a ready market among the rising middle classes of Victorian Britain, and (2) that railways, hotels and other service providers would be willing to go into partnership with him. Had either of these assumptions proved not to be true, what alternatives did he have? What alternative marketing strategies were open to him?

## Sources

Brendon, P. (1991) *Thomas Cook: 150 Years of Popular Tourism*, London: Secker & Warburg.

Pudney, J. (1953) *The Thomas Cook Story*, London: Michael Joseph.

## Notes

1 The author served as researcher on a project in 1989 in which British CEOs were asked what measures they would take to protect their firms in event of an economic downturn. At least half a dozen stated specifically that they would disband their marketing departments and make their marketing staff redundant, on the grounds that they were not really needed. Things have since changed – but that was only twenty years before this book was written!

2 Although there are a number of excellent histories of advertising, for a picture of life inside an advertising agency and how advertisers worked, it is hard to beat the portrait of a London agency in Dorothy L. Sayers's 1933 novel *Murder Must Advertise*. The author was an advertising copywriter for some twelve years, and was responsible for one of the most famous advertising straplines of the interwar years, 'Guinness is Good For You'.

# 6 Financial management

---

**Learning objectives**

This chapter is intended to help readers do the following:

1 learn more about the evolution of financial management and how it has changed over time;
2 understand the role played by financial managers in large organisations in the past;
3 gain new perpsectives on the relationship of financial management to other managerial disciplines.

The objects of a financier are, then, to secure an ample revenue; to impose it with judgement and equality; to employ it economically; and, when necessity to make use of credit, to secure its foundations in that instance, and for ever, by the clearness and candor of his proceedings, the exactness of his calculations, and the solidity of his funds.

—Edmund Burke

Money and values represented on paper are the passive forces; men who buy and sell or 'operate' are the active forces of trade. So we might inquire, what constitutes ... Wall Street? Not the granite pavements or the long piles of masonry covering stores of uncounted wealth, but the *men* who throng this thoroughfare and keep the machinery of commerce and speculation in motion.
– William W. Fowler, *Twenty Years of Inside Life in Wall Street*

## 6.1 Introduction

Since classical times, large businesses have been built around a solid financial core. The great international trading concerns of Tyre and Carthage were funded in part by the financial wealth of the temples of those cities. In Athens, successful bankers like Pasion invested their profits in trading and manufacturing businesses, as did his successors in Rome (Moore and Lewis 2000). Two thousand years later in the European Renaissance, we find the Medici family building up a large and diversified international business in textiles manufacturing, wholesaling and carrying trades centred on what was then Europe's largest bank. In the sixteenth century, Jakob Fugger of Augsburg used the profits of his silver mining concessions in the Tyrol to found first a bank and then a whole series of manufacturing and trading enterprises across Europe and into Asia, moving into businesses as diverse as horse-breeding and wine-making.

It is no coincidence that the rise of these two organisations, the largest privately-owned businesses the world had yet seen, came at a time and place when financial instruments and markets were undergoing rapid change and development. Max Weber, in his classic *The Protestant Ethic and the Spirit of Capitalism* (1905) dates the rise of the modern business organisation from the Protestant Reformation to the sixteenth century; but many of the changes Weber described date in fact to the later Middle Ages, and the impetus behind them was Catholic rather than Protestant. Theologians such as Thomas Aquinas, Antonio of Florence and Bernardino of Siena had concluded that money and trade were necessary for the welfare of the people. By the fourteenth century, trade and commerce had become socially acceptable; and in particular bankers and financiers, once treated almost as pariahs, were important and respectable figures in every country of Europe.

The rise of international trade went hand in hand too with the development of a range of financial instruments. Some of these, like bills of exchange, were designed simply to make transactions easier. Others allowed the extension of credit and gave businesses access to new source of finance. The late medieval period, especially in Italy, is sometimes referred to as 'the credit revolution', and there is little doubt that these new financial instruments both increased the quantity of money and made it easier to access. Italian innovations spread quickly to the rest of Europe. As early as 1340, we find the English government attempting to raise a new tax by creating a futures market in agricultural commodities and taxing the proceeds. In the sixteenth century the government of the same country sold bonds and bought money on the Antwerp money market to finance its foreign wars and internal debt. Sir Thomas Gresham, founder of the Royal Exchange, first came to prominence as the brilliant financial agent who manipulated the Antwerp money market so successfully that he was able to clear the English crown's overseas debts in under twenty years.

In India, too, the financial system grew more complex with bills of exchange being introduced by banking firms like the house of Jagat Seth (see Case Study 6C); but here, political instability led to the collapse of the banking system and then its replacement by one designed along British lines. China, which had pioneered the use of paper money, was much slower to adapt and innovate. The major institutions were guilds of bankers, and there were several of these in various parts in China; the most important was the Ningbo guild, a collection of around a hundred, mostly small banks, which between them supplied most of the financial needs of the merchant community of Shanghai (Morse 1932; McElderry 1976). The highly fragmented Chinese banking system was quite inadequate to the needs of the Chinese business community, and Western-style banks like the Hongkong and Shanghai were able to dominate the market, even loaning to the Chinese government (see Case Study 6D).

### End of a tradition

Following the 1911 revolution and the end of the empire, the Chinese banks in Shanghai developed rapidly, and became the most powerful non-Western economic force in the country. They learned quickly from Western methods and techniques, launched their own chartered banks and diversified into broking and share-dealing. The most important of these bankers, Yu Yajing, was one of the co-founders of the Shanghai Stock Exchange in 1921, and he also acted as agent or *comprador* for several large Japanese firms in Shanghai. He cultivated relationships with the Hongkong and Shanghai Bank, and became one of the more important middlemen between the Western and Chinese financial communities. As McElderry (1976: 1) notes, bankers such as Yu 'are an example of a traditional institution which was strengthened by contact with a modern outside influence rather than destroyed by it'.

Yu was a supporter of Sun Yat-sen, the leader of the 1911 revolution, and had once employed Sun's brother-in-law, Chiang Kai-shek, as a broker. When Chiang took power in China in the 1920s, Yu was initially a strong backer and served as an adviser to Chiang's government. The Western community also respected Yu, and in 1927 he became first Chinese to be elected to Shanghai Municipal Council, the governing body of the International Settlement.

However, in the late 1920s Chiang's prime minister, T.V. Soong, began pressing the bankers guild for loans. The government itself became increasingly corrupt and despotic. Yu distanced himself from Chiang, and grew closer to the Western bankers. But by 1935 the Chinese economy had collapsed; more than half the banks in Ningbo either failed or simply shut their doors, and those of Shanghai followed suit. Yu is last heard of in 1939 as part of a delegation from the Shanghai Municipal Council seeking a loan from the Hong Kong-Shanghai Bank. It is probable that he died sometime during the Japanese occupation of the city during the Second World War. Following the 1948 revolution in China, the Ningbo guild and other private banks were abolished.

Then as now, firms seeking to grow and expand had two options (Lescure 2007). They could finance themselves, using retained earnings, or they could seek finance from external sources. Up to the time of the credit revolution, the most common way of doing so was to bring in partners who would invest their own money. This continued to be popular. During the early years of the Industrial Revolution, Richard Arkwright became a kind of venture capitalist, taking stakes in other ventures and providing capital in exchange for a share of the profits. However, the growth in money and credit meant that bank financing had now become less expensive and was more widely available. Florence became the centre of the banking world in the fourteenth and fifteenth centuries, despite strong competition with Genoa. The political decline of both these centres saw a shift in gravity to northern Europe, particularly to Antwerp, which dominated in the sixteenth and seventeenth centuries. At the end of the seventeenth century London rose and challenged Antwerp for dominance. Occupation by France and the introduction of the Continental System by Napoleon broke most of the Antwerp banks, and London then became the capital of world finance until late in the nineteenth century when New York rose to prominence.

The rise of London also saw a transition in ownership structures. Partnerships began to decline in importance and joint-stock companies now became the preferred form of business venture, with shares bought and sold on exchanges. This development was not without its pains. Major financial scandals like the South Sea Bubble and the Mississippi Bubble threatened on occasion to bring down the entire European financial system. These scandals came about as a result of a credulous public seeking what appeared to be easy riches and the activities of dishonest promoters selling valueless or fraudulent securities (which, in 2009, has a familiar ring to it). In response, the British government moved to make the financial system more regulated, stable and secure; this in turn increased confidence in the London markets and made it more likely that people would want to do business there. Continental bankers like the Rothschilds began settling in London and opening branches there.

---

**The South Sea Bubble, 1720**

The most absurd and preposterous of all, and which shewed, more completely than any other, the utter madness of the people, was one started by an unknown adventurer, entitled, *'A company for carrying on an undertaking of great advantage, but nobody to know what it is.'* Were not the fact stated by credible witnesses, it would be impossible to believe that any person could be duped by such a project. The man of genius who essayed this bold and successful inroad upon public credibility, merely stated in his prospectus that the required capital was half a million [pounds sterling], in five thousand shares of £100 each, deposit £2 per share. Next morning, at nine o'clock, this great man opened an office in Cornhill. Crowds of people beset his door, and when he shut up at three o'clock, no less than one thousand shares had been subscribed for and the deposits paid. He was thus in five hours the winner of £2000. He was philosopher enough to be contented with his venture, and set off the same evening for the Continent. He was never heard of again.

–Charles Mackay, *Extraordinary Popular Delusions and the Madness of Crowds* (1841: 55–56)

---

Another important development in the nineteenth century was the rise of professional independent accountants to prominence. Accounting was a very ancient profession, and we know of accountants and bookkeepers as far back as the beginning of recorded history, in ancient Egypt and Babylon (Edwards 1989). Firms employed accountants of their own in order to monitor and control their finances. However, the growing complexity of new forms of joint-stock businesses, especially the railways, forced some companies to begin seeking outside help. One of the first prominent professional accountants was William Deloitte, whose auditing of the accounts of Great Western Railway in 1849 so impressed the railway's directors that they recommended to the British government that independent auditing of accounts should be made a legal requirement; a few years later it duly was. In the 1880s another London-based accountant, Edwin Waterhouse of Price Waterhouse, pioneered the use of forensic accounting to detect frauds, and also set up a consultancy system advising companies on how to improve their accounting and financial control systems.

If London had developed a reputation for security and probity, the situation was rather different across the Atlantic. The American financial system, up to at least the American Civil War (1861–65) and really for some years after was highly immature. A number of factors had contributed to this problem, not least of which was a stifling regulatory regime which prohibited large banks and discouraged the formation of large capital markets. This changed after the Civil War, and once again the railways were the catalyst for change. The long-distance railways that connected America's cities and then opened up the West were highly risky ventures but they also promised enormous profits; further, they demanded very high levels of capital investment for both construction and operation. In order both to share risk and to raise capital, many of the early railroad promoters set up joint-stock companies and sold shares. So strong was the influence of the management practices of the railroad corporations in other business sectors that it was only a matter of time before other sectors began to follow suit. Stock markets emerged in Chicago, Philadelphia, Boston and San Francisco, but the largest and most important was that which developed along Wall Street in lower Manhattan, New York.

Wall Street in 1880 was a village, in which not only the share dealers and brokers but also many of the major investors knew each other personally. W.W. Fowler, in his classic *Twenty Years of Life on Wall Street* (1880), describes this milieu and its operating practices in detail. With fewer than a hundred companies listed on the exchange and a total issued share capital of around $300 million, this was a relatively cosy financial community in which comparatively few Americans participated. Many quoted companies had a few score shareholders at most, shareholders who often represented larger communities of interest and who had a strong and active interest in the management of the companies they owned.

From 1880 this began to change, slowly at first and then more rapidly. The number of shareholders rose from a few hundred thousand to 7 million by 1900, and then doubled to 14 million in 1924. By the latter date, more than one thousand companies were listed with the New York Stock Exchange. Even more astonishing is the growth in share capital, from $300 million in 1880 to $70 trillion by 1925 (Ripley 1927).

Between 1880 and 1900 big business organisations increased greatly in power. This was a period of consolidation in American industry, and especially in financial markets. The prime mover in this trend was the banker J.P. Morgan, who with a coterie of like-minded bankers and financiers sought to amalgamate companies in key industries and consolidate shareholdings. Giant monopolies or near-monopolies such as United States Steel, Standard Oil, United States Shipbuilding, International Mercantile Marine, American Telephone & Telegraph (AT&T) and the mining and smelting giant ASARCO were created with Morgan's guidance and backing.

It was against this background that the modern discipline of corporate finance (originally known as corporation finance) emerged. There were a number of pressures, felt most acutely in America but present elsewhere too, that led to the development of a theory of financial management, as opposed to a collected body of practical knowledge:

- the urgent need for rapid growth, and the development of financial institutions as engines for these;
- a lax regulatory system which left companies, investors and markets open to fraud and deception and deprived shareholders of their rights;
- a lack of transparency due to the domination of the financial markets by a few large vested interests;
- a steady stream of criticism from government, the press and academia;
- the need for a balance between the financial power of the investors and the management abilities of the entrepreneurs.

In the American economy of the 1880s and 1890s, rapid growth was the order of the day. Often this growth was wild and uncontained, sometimes punctuated by short sharp depressions which in turn led to bank failures, misery and strikes. And growth required money. Debt instruments could not raise the capital required, and the only way forward was through the sale of equity; hence the amazing growth of Wall Street alluded to above. The rapid proliferation of companies requiring capital to be raised in this way meant a corresponding demand for managers who were familiar with the workings of financial markets and the techniques of financial management. With the disappearance of the Wall Street village and its replacement with a larger and more impersonal market, deals could no longer be done on the basis of relationships. The more complex economics of shareholder capitalism brought concepts like shareholder value into focus. How much dividend should companies pay, and when? How much equity should a company issue, and in what kinds of shares? These and other technical issues became the central focus of financial management.

From the late 1890s, textbooks intended for the instruction of managers began to proliferate and the first writers and theorists such as Jeremiah Jenks, Edward Meade and William Lough began to emerge (Witzel 2007a). The Wharton School at the University of Pennsylvania was the first university institution to offer degree courses in financial management, but Harvard and others soon followed. By 1914 it was recognised that financial management occupied a central place in the set of managerial skills. Modern corporate finance had been born.

---

### Managing money

By the early twentieth century it was apparent that without an understanding of the engines of finance, a manager could not be effective. The case of William C. Durant is instructive. The founder of General Motors, Durant was a talented engineer, designer and salesman, but he never mastered the arts of finance. His company was constantly in financial difficulties and his directors, who were usually also major shareholders, eventually deposed him. The same fate befell other car-makers, notably John Willys at Willys Overland. Understanding finance equated with understanding and maintaining control.

## 6.2 The nature of money

Financial management meant essentially the management of money. But many different things could constitute money. Over the course of human history, many objects have served as moneys of exchange: metals including gold, silver, copper, bronze, tin and electrum, gemstones, spices – the English term 'peppercorn rent' refers to property rents that were paid using pepper as the medium of exchange – paper notes, wooden chips or counters (succeeded by plastic ones in modern casinos), bills of exchange, bearer bonds and other exchangeable financial instruments, dried ears of corn and cowrie shells. In the Russian trading city of Novgorod during the Middle Ages, silver was scarce; market traders therefore used the dried heads of squirrels and martens as currency, keeping these on strings on their belts and using them as small change. In other words, pretty well anything could serve as a money of exchange provided that everyone agreed to accept it as money.

In most economies, however, precious metals were the primary money of exchange. Egypt is rare in having no money of exchange, continuing to use a barter system until the fourth century BC and only fully developing a money economy after Roman occupation in the first century BC. Gold and silver had certain advantages. They were acceptable internationally, and there was an established system for exchanging coins minted in one polity for those of another, based on weight and known purity. They also had a number of dis-advantages. First, they were heavy, transporting a large amount of gold or silver any distance was an expensive process. Second, they were easily lost, through theft or accident such as shipwreck, and could not be replaced like for like. Third and perhaps most important they could be easily counterfeited or adulterated. In the fourteenth century the French crown, desperately short of money, began mixing more base metal with silver in the coins it minted. News of this quickly spread and confidence in the French currency declined sharply. In England on the other hand, the famous 'long cross penny' retained its value and was very much in demand in the money markets of continental Europe. But this brought its own problems; like other later famous moneys of exchange like the Maria Theresa dollar or the American greenback, counterfeit versions became rife. If there was too much counterfeit money in circulation, then confidence in the original would decline also.

Some of these problems could be got around by using substitutes. Although the Chinese experimented with paper banknotes, there was little confidence in these and the experiment was gradually dropped. But one of the chief inventions of medieval Italy, the bill of exchange, was a different matter. A bill of exchange was effectively a promise to pay. It could be drawn for any amount of money, so long as the banker writing the bill had enough money to back it. A bill of exchange drawn on the Medici Bank in Florence could be redeemed for gold or silver at any other Medici Bank branch in Europe – or any other bank with which the Medici had a reciprocal arrangement. Other later banks such as Fugger of Augsburg and the Indian banking house Jagat Seth developed similar arrangements. Bills of exchange were easy to carry, hard to counterfeit and, if proven to be genuinely lost or destroyed, could sometimes be replaced. By the late Middle Ages bills of exchange themselves had begun to be traded on markets, and it was from these that modern banknotes emerged.

One of the key features of money from earliest times was that money was only acceptable if people had confidence in it. When the French currency collapsed, people resorted to the use of Italian currencies, Venetian ducats and Florentine florins, as these were believed to be secure. The same thing still happens. The American dollar remains a common currency in many parts of the world because people have faith in it. Other currencies are deemed to be worthless. During Lebanon's troubles in the 1980s when its currency lost much of its value, one householder in the city of Saida who desired to decorate his sitting room worked out that it would be cheaper to use banknotes than wallpaper, and accordingly papered his wall with Lebanese pounds. It can be safely said that he had no confidence in his own currency.

As well as moneys of exchange there are also moneys of account, and these too have existed since early times. The Chinese tael and the Indian lakh and crore are examples. During the Middle Ages English accounts operated on a system using pounds, shillings and pence, despite the fact that no coin of a value larger than one penny was minted until the fourteenth century. Similarly the mark was the standard money of account in Germany but no coin was ever minted with that value.

This is important because it demonstrates that people were used to working with purely notional sums of money. This meant that when the credit revolution happened, people were on the whole ready to accept it. Businessmen were already used to accounting for sums of money that had no physical existence. Credit was simply an extension of the supply of money. And that was vital for, as the economies of Europe grew, the supply of gold and silver began to be stretched thin. Existing gold and silver mines in Germany and Eastern Europe were worked out. Silver plundered by the Spanish conquistadors in Mexico and Peru helped bolster supplies for a time, but even this proved insufficient for demand. By about 1600 it was clear that without more widespread use of credit, the European economies would grind to a halt. This indeed happened in England, where scarcity of money through the seventeenth century put a serious brake on economic growth. Not until the foundation of the Bank of England in the early years of the following century, with its express remit of advancing credit and easing the money supply, did the English economy begin to expand once more.

---

**Credit and trust**

Credit duly imploy'd in trade, and duly encouraged, must effectually produce increase of money, enabling it to make it self good, at long run, to all who trust it.

–James Hodges, *The Present State of England*, 1697

---

### 6.2.1 The intrinsic value debate

For several hundred years there raged a debate as to the value of money and how it was determined. It was evident that money was a commodity; it was bought and sold along with other commodities, and its value fluctuated according to demand, scarcity and public confidence. In Chapter 5 we discussed briefly the ideas of the political philosopher John Locke. Like many others of his day, Locke (1692) believed that gold and silver had 'intrinsic value'. That is to say, they had a permanent fixed value that was inherent in themselves. An ounce of silver could be turned into coins, an ingot or a piece of jewellery, but its value would still be the same. While he accepted that the *price* of money might fluctuate in the short term, the *value* of money remained immutable.

Locke was immediately taken to task for this by several other economic thinkers, especially the MP Sir Richard Temple and the Scottish writer and pamphleteer James Hodges. The latter maintained bluntly that Locke did not know what he was talking about. The value of an ounce of silver is what it will buy in the marketplace:

Tho one ounce of silver will sometimes buy one bushel of wheat, and two ounces two bushels, and so in double quantity hath double value; yet at another time when there is dearth or scarcity ... then the two ounces of silver, which formerly could buy two bushels of wheat, will only buy one ... because the raising of the value of wheat to double doth lower the value of silver to the one half, tho in the same quantity.

(Hodges 1697: 143)

Money, said Hodges is a commodity. The only thing that makes money different from any other commodity is that its price and its value always fluctuate and always equal each other. Modern economists would regard this as simplistic, but Hodges's basic assertion that money itself is a tradable commodity that fluctuates in value continues to resonate today.

## 6.3 The tasks of financial management

Thus far we have seen that financial markets and financial management have both been around for a very long time, and their roots go far back in time. It is time to turn to more practical matters. What did managers of finance do? Broadly speaking, looking at a spectrum of businesses and other organisations across time and around the world, we can classify their tasks into three groups: (1) financial control, (2) raising capital, and (3) managing financial risk.

### 6.3.1 Financial control

Financial control tasks equate very roughly to the treasury function of modern corporate finance. The primary purpose was to safeguard the financial assets of the organisation. The first task was to keep an exact record of what those assets were. As noted earlier, we can identify people performing accounting and bookkeeping functions in businesses, temples and government bureaucracies for the past four thousand years, if not more. In classical times accounting methods were fairly simple; the first major advance came at the end of the thirteenth century with the appearance of double-entry bookkeeping in Italy. Edwards (1989: 46) believes it is no coincidence that double-entry bookkeeping emerged just as the 'credit revolution' was gathering strength in Italy, and that the appearance of this new system greatly facilitated the spread of credit. Certainly there is a close correlation between the increasing complexity of financial markets, the growing size of organisations and the development of new accounting methods down through the ages (see also Littleton and Yamey 1956; Chatfield 1977).

Financial control also included the direction of money flows: the payment of wages to staff and dividends to partners and/or shareholders, purchasing of stock, investment in new projects, setting aside money as savings, payment of pensions to former employees, donations to charity and so on. These tasks need little description: they differ from similar tasks today in degree, but not in kind.

### 6.3.2 Raising capital

Some companies funded growth out of retained earnings. Just how many did so and how widespread the practice was remains a matter for debate (Lescure 2007). We can observe that companies were more likely to be self-funding when banking systems were weak or inadequate. Thus Chinese firms were historically more likely to be self-funding not because of any innate cultural characteristic or propensity for thrift, but because there were few alternatives. As we saw earlier in this chapter, once the bankers of the Ningbo guild began to learn Western banking methods, they began to develop a client base among Chinese businesses in Shanghai. Earlier, the Hongkong and Shanghai

Bank had already proved that there was a ready market for bank finance in China. In India, where the banking system was more advanced, firms did use bank finance. European firms were the most likely to seek external funding as they had more ways of raising money.

Partnerships of course continued to be an important way to raise capital, though not all partnerships were for this purpose; in the case of Coutts bank (Case Study 6B) new partners were not required to contribute money and were brought in as a way of introducing new blood and maintaining continuity of top management. At other times partners were brought in to provide technical expertise. But for a firm needing to raise money, a partnership could sometimes be a useful option. Struggling sewing machine maker Isaac Singer found a way out of his difficulty selling part of his firm to Edward Clark and bringing him in as a partner; in this case, Clark also contributed very valuable management expertise. But partnerships had a cost; partners often wanted to be involved in the management of the firms they now part-owned, and often had very different ideas about how this should be done. The relationship between Clark and Singer, to take just one example, was full of conflict.

### 6.3.3 Risk management

We have noted frequently that businesses in the pre-modern era often operated under very high levels of political and environmental risk. Wars and other conflicts, bio plagues and extreme weather, coupled with very slow (by modern standards) communications all created huge levels of risk and uncertainty. Safeguarding financial assets and making provision against risk was an important managerial task. International merchants and traders assumed as a matter of routine that they would suffer losses on any venture. Fine calculations were made as to how much loss could be absorbed before the venture failed to make a profit. In one of the first Dutch expeditions to the East Indies in 1598–99, eight ships out of the twenty that left port were lost at sea and never returned. But this was a lower level of loss than the expedition's backers had expected, and they still turned a profit. And of course, there is the Venetian Marino Sanudo's famous calculation that if he sent out five ships and lost four, the cargo of the fifth should still sell for enough to cover his losses.

Risk management was an important part of strategic thinking (see Chapter 3), but it was a large part of financial management too. The top-level financiers of the Middle Ages and the Renaissance and after were adept at calculating risk levels and knew when to invest and when to steer clear. Thomas Martin at the London bank known as the Grasshopper (later renamed Martin's Bank), one of the few to steer clear of the wreckage of the South Sea Bubble was one such (see box). Some managers were of course more willing to accept risk than others; sometimes this was for personal reasons, but sometimes as in the case of Thomas Coutts (Case Study 6B) a low-risk investment policy was linked to the larger business strategy.

Just as firms often diversified into different product markets to reduce strategic risk, so they often diversified in terms of savings and investments so as to reduce financial risk. Financial assets might be distributed between savings – with reliable banks that were judged unlikely to fail – and investments in a range of other ventures, again after calculating how many of these could fail without seriously harming profits over the long term. When borrowing, too, we have plenty of evidence that well-managed firms knew how much it was safe to borrow, and how much would leave them exposed. While businesses knew how to do this, governments did not, and frequently overborrowed. Despite a huge influx of silver from the Americas to bolster his economy, the Spanish king Philip II went bankrupt twice in the late sixteenth century. In England in the fourteenth century, overborrowing by the crown forced its Italian bankers into bankruptcy on several occasions (Livingstone (2008), who draws a parallel between the reckless lending of these Italian banks and those of our own day).

---

### The rules of banking

In the aftermath of the South Sea Bubble, Thomas Martin of the Grasshopper wrote a list of 'proper considerations for persons concerned in the banking business' as rules for his staff. Some of these were specific to the time; others look rather familiar.

1 Some judgement ought to be made of what sum is proper to be out at constant interest.
2 A proportion of bonds, Land Tax tallies, and silver, to be ready on sudden demand.
3 A proportion of government securities, as Navy bills, etc.
4 Not to lend money without application from the borrower and upon alienable security that may be easily disposed of and a probability of punctual payment without being reckoned hard by the borrower.
5 All loans to be paid when due, and the rotation not exceeding six months.
6 Not to boast of a great surplus or plenty of money.
7 When loans do not offer, to lend on stocks or other securities, buy for ready money and sell for time.
8 When credit increased by accident upon an uncertain circulation, the money may be lent to goldsmiths, or discount bills of exchange.
9 'Tis prudence and advantage of a goldsmith that depend upon credit, to endeavour as near as possible upon the yearly settlement of accounts to have the investure of that money in effects that are easy to be converted into money.

10 To appear cautious and timorous contribute very much to give persons in credit an esteem among mankind.

11 Avoid unprofitable business, especially when attended with trouble and expense.

12 'Tis certainly better to employ a little money at a good advantage, if lent safely, in order to have a greater cash by you, tho' possibly you may extend your credit safely.

13 When it shall be thought proper to get in old loans, the demanding of them ought to be in the names of all the partners.

(quoted in Chandler 1964: 109–10)

## 6.4 Who was responsible for financial management?

Responsibility for financial management usually rested with the people at the very top of the business. In most cases they were also, if not sole owners, then at least partners or major shareholders, and thus had a vested interest to protect. But there was a sense too that financial management was so important that it could not be safely entrusted to others.

Of course there was a certain amount of delegation, especially in large businesses. This was particularly true after the credit revolution. Every bank or large business in Italy employed a team of accountants, trained at one of the *scuole d'abaco* or abacus schools whose main function was to train young accountants in the techniques of double-entry bookkeeping. Bookkeeping schools emerged later in northern Europe too, and by the 1870s they were proliferating in America, where they were sometimes known as commercial colleges. Henry Heinz and Frederick Winslow Taylor are among the more famous graduates of these institutions. Similar schools were set up in Japan at the instigation of the great Japanese education reformer Yukichi Fukuzawa. But while accountants and low-ranking managers performed certain tasks, even highly important ones, overall responsibility was concentrated at the top. Both Cosimo dei Medici and Jakob Fugger are known to have personally scrutinised all accounts coming from different parts of their businesses, and queried any items they did not understand or which looked suspicious.

Where the owner was not directly involved in the affairs of the business, responsibility passed to the most senior manager. The instructions for managers of landed estates written by Walter of Henley at the end of the thirteenth century required these managers to render faithful and accurate financial accounts to the landowners their employers (Oschinsky 1971) and Bernardino of Siena listed responsibility, including financial responsibility, as one of the key duties of the manager (de Roover 1967). Again, when the size of the business concern meant it was necessary to delegate financial responsibility, it was up to the senior managers to carefully scrutinise the work of the juniors, to prevent error and fraud. This same principle was followed in government; the English treasury, the Exchequer, one of the most efficient and honest government bureaucracies of its day, had a series of strict financial controls overseen by senior officials.

## A banking empire

The German banker Jakob Fugger was quite probably the most powerful businessman in the world during the sixteenth century. He came from a business family with interests in cloth manufacturing and mining in the mountains of the Tirol. In 1485 he became a partner in the family business and manager of its branch in Innsbruck, Austria, where he invested in more mines, especially copper and silver, right across central Europe. By 1500 he controlled most of the copper mines of Europe.

His interests led Fugger naturally into banking and minting, where he secured licences from the Holy Roman Empire to turn his mineral resources into circulating coinage; quite literally, he made money. From 1507 onwards Fugger lent increasingly large sums to the Emperor Maximilian. Many of these loans were mortgages on crown lands, and as many of these were never redeemed, Fugger also acquired extensive landholdings. The emperor relied on Fugger almost exclusively for financial assistance; records speak of some transactions as large as 300,000 guilders (over $50 million in today's money). In 1518, Fugger and his agents set up a massive loan syndicate, with investors in Spain, Italy, Germany and Eastern Europe, which raised around 550,000 guilders (around $90 million) to finance the election of Maximilian's grandson Charles V as Holy Roman Emperor.

The relationship with Maximilian and then with Charles was critical. Many of the loans he made to the emperors would never be recovered; some were secured on property, but few to the full value of the loan. However, so long as the loans to the emperors could be covered by profits gained in other fields, the cost was well worth it. The Imperial connection gave Fugger privileged access to other, more profitable customers. Even more importantly, in an age of political uncertainty and constant change, having a grateful emperor on his books as a client meant that Fugger could enjoy a measure of security and protection afforded to few of his rivals; put simply, if he was threatened either financially or physically, Fugger could call in powerful favours.

Known in Augsburg simply as 'Fugger the Rich', Jakob Fugger dominated the European financial world for two decades. The business, like most banks of its day, operated on a network basis with agents in all the major financial centres of Europe; sometimes these agents were directly employed, sometimes they were employed by partnerships established with other banks. As well as transacting business, these agents gathered information. At the headquarters in Augsburg, Jakob

Fugger himself kept the firm's master accounts and collated information received from agents abroad; both these things were done on a daily basis. Fugger once wrote that he could not go soundly to sleep at night without knowing that somewhere that day he had made a profit, however small it might be. This combination of tight monitoring of information and a flexible, far-flung network gave Fugger the ability to respond quickly to crises.

A contemporary wrote: 'The names of Jakob Fugger and his nephews are known in all kingdoms and lands; yea, and among the heathen also. All the merchants of the world have called him an enlightened man, and all the heathen have wondered at him. He is the glory of all Germany' (quoted in Ehrenberg 1928: 83). (The 'heathen' probably refers to Fugger's business contacts in Asia, where he had established a number of silk factories, adding to his manufacturing portfolio.) His nephew and successor Anton Fugger expanded the firm's operations to include cattle ranches in Hungary, the spice trade with the East Indies, and mining in Chile and Peru. By the time of his death in 1546 he had increased the company's capital to over 5 million guilders. But thereafter the bank's fortune began to decline. Anton's son and successor Marx Fugger was unable to prevent catastrophes like the Spanish state bankruptcy of 1575, which cost the bank heavily. Many of its manufacturing assets had to be sold to recoup the losses. By 1600 the firm was in irrecoverable decline. Jakob Fugger had made getting close to the centre of power a priority in ensuring the security of his business; his successors had failed to continue this policy, and paid the price.

(Ehrenburg 1928)

## 6.5 Themes and influences

Several important trends which affected financial management need to be noted. These include changing social attitudes to business and finance, the already-noted increase in the complexity of financial markets and financial instruments, and the trend in some countries towards the separation of ownership and control.

### 6.5.1 Changing social attitudes

People engaged in commerce are not always the most respected members of society, and of this class of people, those engaged in finance are often the most criticised and subjected to abuse. Several religions, Christianity and Islam included, banned usury, or the lending of money at interest; Islam still maintains this prohibition. As a result, those who lent money to others were sometimes considered to be undesirable members of society and might even be subject to physical attack.

By the thirteenth century this stigma was beginning to disappear in Europe, and bankers and other businesspeople became recognised as important members of society. There was a vigorous debate in both Catholic and Protestant churches about the rights and wrongs of usury, which dragged on into the nineteenth century, but the debate itself was academic; banking was big business, many businesses borrowed or lent money, and the popes themselves were some of the most prominent borrowers and banking customers of all. Still, there remained in European society the belief that people engaged in 'trade' were not the equals of the landed nobility.

The Industrial Revolution broke down many of these barriers, though not all. The new generation of capitalists were too rich to be ignored. Richard Arkwright was knighted, and other knights of commerce followed. Soon they were being granted peerages; William Lever and William Pirrie of Harland & Wolff were both made viscounts. Angela Burdett-Coutts, grand-daughter of the banker Thomas Coutts, became the first woman to be ennobled in her own right and enter the British House of Lords. The new social mobility extended to various parts of the British empire – knighthoods were granted to prominent local businesspeople in India and Hongkong for example – and to continental Europe. In Japan after the Meiji Restoration of 1867, financiers and other businesspeople enjoyed a similar leap forward in status.

Nowhere was the change more rapid or profound than in America. In the 1820s and 1830s, Americans were profoundly suspicious of banks in particular and big business in general. After the American Civil War of 1861–65, however, attitudes quickly changed. In the 1880s and 1890s a class divide opened up. On the one hand there were those members of the working classes, members of labour unions and others who supported them, who feared and even resented the power of business leaders and bankers like J.P. Morgan. On the other hand, there were many who admired them and hoped to emulate them. Fowler (1880) comments on the multitude of speculators who came to Wall Street hoping to make a fortune as they had seen others – Daniel Drew, Jay Gould, the Vanderbilts – do before them.

---

## What is Wall Street?

What is Wall Street? A thoroughfare in name, but something more. To the banker and stock broker it is a financial center, collecting and distributing money, regulating the exchanges of a continent and striking balances with London and Frankfurt. To the outside observer and novice it is a kind of work-shop thronged by cunning artisans who work in precious metals, where vessels of gold and vessels of silver are wrought or made to shine with fresh lustre, and where old china is fire-gilt as good as new. The moralist and philosopher look upon it as a gambling-den – a cage of unclean birds, an abomination where men drive a horrible trade, fattening and battening on the substance of their friends and neighbours – or perhaps as a kind of modern coliseum, where gladiatorial combats are joined, and bulls, bears and other ferocious beasts gore and tear each other for public amusement. The brokers regard it as a place of business where, in mercantile parlance, they may ply a legitimate trade, buying and selling for others on commission. To the speculators it is a caravanserai where they may load or unload their camels and drive them away betimes to some pleasant oasis. To the financial commanders it is an arsenal in which their arms and chariots are stored, the stronghold to be defended or besieged, the field for strategy, battles and plunder. All these ideas and a multitude of others, more or less true, rise up at the mention of Wall Street.

–William W. Fowler, *Twenty Years of Inside Life in Wall Street* (1880: 19–20)

American society, and to a lesser extent European and Asian societies, went on to develop a kind of love-hate relationship with finance. Generally speaking, it is possible to correlate the prevailing social mood with economic performance. In boom times, like the 1920s, the 1950s and the 1990s, financiers are hailed as heroes, leading their countries into a new age of prosperity. In downturns, the 1930s, the 1970s and the end of the first decade of the twenty-first century, they are regarded as villains who have wrecked their economies and plunged people into poverty and misery. Both points of view, it can be argued, are exaggerated and not realistic, but they exist in the popular imagination nonetheless.

How do these changing moods impact on financial management? First, they change popular expectations – and by this we mean the expectations of shareholders, regulators and governments, not just the general public. In times past, when those in charge of the wealth of banks and companies were identified as 'bad' people, they had to make certain changes in behaviour. For example, they made a point of dressing modestly in public so as not to flaunt their wealth, or they gave away large amounts of money to charity. But when they are hailed as heroes, they are expected to behave as heroes. Then the most important thing is that they should generate large profits for their shareholders, and any who fail to do so tend to be jettisoned by their companies. As time passes, the fluctuations in public mood and social pressures have become more rapid. Holt (2006) detailed that in America senior financial managers reported suffering from stress and disillusionment with their jobs and that as many as a third were considering exiting the profession altogether; and this was at a time when the economy was performing well. Societal pressures and attitudes can complicate the lives and work of managers in finance, and sometimes force them to retire altogether.

### 6.5.2 *Increasing complexity of instruments and markets*

There has been a steady increase in the complexity of financial instruments and markets. This is not to say that markets were not somewhat complex before; any study of the bewildering variety of circulating currencies in the Middle Ages, or the complex range of bonds issued by the British government in the eighteenth century, quickly reveals this. But there were a limited number of financial markets, and a limited number of players in them, and it was possible, as Fowler suggests in his portrait of Wall Street in the years before 1880, to master the markets in a relatively short space of time.

Since 1880, though, markets have grown much larger and there are now many more of them, particularly since the rise of Asia began in the mid twentieth century. It is now much harder to know the markets well, much harder to predict their behaviour, and much harder to understand the full implications of all the various derivatives and other instruments now available. A few years of apprenticeship or a spell at a bookkeeping college is now no longer enough to equip a financial manager. Holt (2006) has argued for the tasks of financial management to be simplified, but there are as yet few signs of this happening.

### 6.5.3 *The separation of ownership and control*

We have alluded earlier to the change from partnerships to joint-stock corporations which began in the sixteenth century. Until the end of the nineteenth century, it was still common (though by no means universal) for major stockholders to be actively involved in management. But in the decades that followed, ownership and control began to separate in America. The reasons for this are not entirely clear, but one factor was that the younger generations of America's large share-owning families were no longer willing to become actively involved in the management of the businesses they owned.

Opinion was divided as to whether this was a good thing. The term 'separation of ownership and control' had originally been coined in Germany by the financier and statesman Walther Rathenau (1921), who advanced the theory that the owners of capital should step back and hand over control to professional salaried managers. These would run the business impartially, and in the best interests of the business itself. Owner-managers, Rathenau felt, were likely to have their judgement clouded by personal interests, for example, taking profits from the business rather than investing.

Many agreed with him. Others did not. William Ripley, an outspoken professor from Harvard University, accused shareholders of 'selling their birthright for a mess of pottage', or handing over control of what they rightfully owned in exchange for money (Ripley 1927). He considered that shareholders had a duty to manage what they owned. Another critic, the political philosopher James Burnham (1941) warned that control would turn into *de facto* ownership and that in time managers would start behaving like owners, regardless of where legal ownership lay. The most judicious treatment of the subject, that of Berle and Means (1932), saw both risks and advantages in the system.

---

**Selling their birthright**

What an amazing tangle this all makes of the theory that ownership of property and responsibility for its efficient, far-sighted and public-spirited management shall be linked the one to the other. Even the whole theory of business profits, so painstakingly evolved through years of academic ratocination, goes by the board. All the managers, that is to say the operating men, are working on salary, their returns, except on the side, being largely independent of the net result of company operation year by year. The motive of self-interest may even have been thrown into reverse, occasionally, so far as long-time up-building in contradistinction to quick turnover in corporate affairs is concerned. And what has become of the relation between labor and capital? What guaranty may possibly be given by the *real owners* to the working class that there shall not be taken from it an opportunity for future welfare and development as a result of these changes? Veritably the institution of private property, underlying our whole civilization, is threatened at the root unless we take heed.

(Ripley 1927: 86)

---

The separation of ownership and control went on to become orthodoxy in American management thinking, and it is considered to be the best form of corporate governance. When Bill Ford, a descendant of Henry Ford and a major shareholder in Ford Motors, took over as head of the car maker from professional manager Jac Nasser, he was criticised by some sections of the press; shareholders should not manage, they should step back and pay others to do this for them. Yet the separation of ownership and control has never really become accepted elsewhere. Cheffins (2008) demonstrates that despite much discussion of the subject, the separation of ownership and control in Britain only became widespread in the late 1960s and the 1970s, and then for reasons that had more to do with the British economy rather than for any drive for management effectiveness. He notes further that outside the Anglo-Saxon world the separation of ownership and control is not widely practised, and is indeed regarded with puzzlement in some Asian countries.

The separation of ownership and control can put financial managers under different constraints. As noted by Burnham and by Berle and Means, it can lead to a tension between shareholders and managers, each of whom have different ideas about how the company should be managed and, especially, how its profits should be allocated. This tension was largely absent when companies were managed by their owners, or a small group of partners. For financial managers, it is an additional complicating factor.

## 6.6 Questions and discussion: money talks, but does anyone listen?

We have seen that financial management has become far more complex than in the past. Given this, is there any point in studying how finance was managed in the past? Curiously, of all managerial disciplines, this is the one which has had the most attention paid to its history. Books on the history of marketing can be numbered on the fingers of two hands.[1] But there are many books on the history of financial institutions and financial markets, and the history of accounting has developed an extensive literature and is regarded as a fit subject for academic study and analysis. Edwards (1989), introducing the subject, stated what many believe, that 'the examination of past events ... enables us to appreciate the complexity and persistence of the problems presently facing accountants'.

Financial markets, financial instruments, financial institutions and above all financial management have evolved and grown. Many of the instruments are new, and the markets and institutions no longer look much like their old selves. But there are a few things that the history of financial management throws up, which are worthy of consideration and discussion.

First, there is the nature of money itself. At its heart, financial management is about managing money. But money is an elusive thing, whose value and nature change often. We sometimes talk disparagingly about people 'not understanding the value of money'. But in reality, how many of us actually do? And it is critically important that we do so. Money, like knowledge, is to the business what blood is to the human body; if it fails to circulate, the body dies. The credit crisis of 2008 suggests that we don't know as much as we ought, or as we once thought we did, about what money is and how it behaves.

Second, when we look at successful financial managers of the past, we find that the actual skills of financial management are only part of the picture. Financial managers would appear to be relationship managers, just as marketing managers and HR managers are. The value of a company is to some extent dependent on others' perceptions of it. In that case, should not financial managers spend more time managing those perceptions, as Cosimo dei Medici and Jakob Fugger did so ably? True, shareholder relations are considered part of the task of the corporate finance manager today, and many managers take that responsibility seriously. But others do not, and consider shareholders to be at best a nuisance (although they are careful not to say so publicly).

More than any other managerial discipline, financial management is prone to the silo effect, with financial managers distinct and apart from the rest of the management team. Holt (2006) called for an end to this and for financial managers to be more closely integrated with the rest of the organisation.

In the examples from the past that we have considered here, there were no silos; financial management was at the heart of the organisation. Perhaps we need to consider how to get back to something resembling that state of affairs. But this will be no easy task, given the evolution of financial management in the years since. It may be that as Edwards (1989) says, there are some long-standing problems that simply do not have solutions.

---

### Takeaway exercise

Consider your own company or organisation, or one that you know well or have worked in during the past few years. How well do you understand its financial management? You have undoubtedly seen the financial statements and read the annual report, but unless you work in the finance department itself, there is a good chance you don't really know that much about how the finance department works. What are the key priorities of its managers? How do you view them and their work, and how do you think they view you and your work? What are their goals and how do they achieve them?

The answers to these questions are not always easy, and in the past some have described the process of asking them as 'disquieting'. But there is also learning to be found here. Good financial management lies at the heart of any successful organisation. That being so, it is too important to simply delegate to someone else and then wait for the annual report to find out what has been happening. Sound financial management is everyone's business.

---

### Case Study 6A

#### *United States Steel*

At the time of its incorporation on 1 April 1901, United States Steel was the world's largest business entity.[2] Formed through the merger of the Carnegie Company with a number of other steel producers, United States Steel was intended to consolidate the steel industry and, by reducing competition, improve profits and corporate performance within the industry.

The American steel industry had grown very rapidly in the decades after the Civil War (1861–65), in part thanks to the demand from the railways for heavy steel rails and rolling stock components. There was a large number of new entrants into the industry in the 1880s, so that by the end of the decade there were several hundred steel mills, most of them small independent operations, scattered across the eastern and mid-western USA. By 1890 supply had begun to outstrip demand, and in 1893 the added pressures of a general financial depression created a crisis. Dozens of small steel makers went bankrupt, their assets bought up by the few surviving firms. This led naturally to a process of consolidation, such that by 1898 when the depression ended, the entire steel industry including the making of bar iron, rolled iron, steel rails, sheet steel, wire and other, more finished products was in the hands of a small number of fairly efficient and well-managed companies (they had to be efficient and well managed in order to survive the depression). By 1900 the industry was dominated by five companies:

- Federal Steel, formed in 1898 through the merger of two other bankrupt firms in Illinois, with a capitalisation of $200 million.
- American Steel & Wire, formed also in 1898 through the merger of a number of wire makers and having a near monopoly on wire making in the USA, controlling well over 90 per cent of production, and capitalised at $90 million.
- National Tube Company, formed in 1899 through the merger of more than a dozen companies, most of them on the edge of bankruptcy, and also now having a near monopoly on steel tube production in the USA. Capitalised at $300 million, it was the world's third largest steel producer of any kind, following behind the Carnegie Company and the German firm of Krupp.
- The American Tin Plate Company, capitalised at $60 million and formed out of forty bankrupt companies in 1899 by a group of lawyers known as the 'Rock Island Crowd'. This group also controlled several smaller firms, including the National Steel Company and the American Sheet Steel Company, which were likewise consolidations of bankrupt firms. The concentration here was on finished goods.
- The Carnegie Company, which unlike the others was a – comparatively – old and established firm which had expanded through internal growth rather than acquisition. It had been founded in 1866 by Andrew Carnegie, a Scottish immigrant and former telegraph operator who had made a fortune in oil during the Civil War and then saw opportunities in the steel industry during the early stages of the railway boom. It had grown to the point where by 1900 it was the world's largest steel producer. Its annual production of 10 million tons represented about 35 per cent of total world steel production. Carnegie was sole owner so no capitalisation figures are available, but the company was valued at somewhere between $400 million and $500 million.

Although a number of smaller companies remained, it was estimated that these five firms between them controlled just under 90 per cent of American steel production, with the percentage even higher in some forms of specialist production such as steel wire and steel tubes.

During the economic recovery that followed 1898, all five of these companies prospered. However, the industry remained in what one observer, the economist Edward Meade (1910), called a state of 'unstable equilibrium'. One of the problems of the steel industry, as Andrew Carnegie had pointed out during the recent depression, was that steel production required large amounts of fixed capital and it was difficult to adjust the volume of production suddenly to meet changes in demand. Further, demand in the steel industry tended to extreme fluctuations, meaning that the industry could lurch from overproduction to underproduction and back again very quickly.

Aware that the good times it was enjoying would not last, the industry's leaders began to search for ways of making their firms more secure. The first step was a series of backward integrations, with three of the newcomers – American Steel & Wire, National Tube and American Tin Plate – acquiring coal mines, iron ore deposits and railways in order to ensure at least a fixed supply of raw materials. However, Carnegie and Federal Steel, which already controlled their own mines and transport operations to a large extent, saw this move as a threat. Particularly provocative was the announcement of plans by American Steel & Wire to build two large plants, one in Milwaukee, Wisconsin, the centre of operations of Federal Steel, and one in Pittsburgh near Carnegie's largest plant, the Edgar Thomson Steel Works. Federal Steel now threatened to start large-scale steel wire production, breaking American Steel & Wire's effective monopoly, while Carnegie prepared to retaliate by increasing his own production of finished goods and starting a price war with both American Steel & Wire and National Tube. It was well known that Carnegie had the drive and the resources to compete effectively against both the latter, and would be prepared to suffer short-term losses in order to drive his rivals out of the market.

The situation was full of dangers, especially for the first four of the 'Big Five'. Carnegie could survive a war between the producers because, in the words of one observer, its managers 'felt confident of the ability of their organisation to finance and make highly profitable in the end whatever new construction might be necessary', but the other four were relatively new and unstable companies. All four were capitalised up to the limit of their earning power, and their stock had been sold initially on the promise of large and regular dividends. Moreover, large amounts of the stock were still owned by the original promoters and underwriters who had set up these firms, who had retained holdings in hopes of making a profit themselves. The management and stockholders of these companies were not, therefore, keen to enter into a period of prolonged and vigorous competition, especially when the only likely winner would be Carnegie.

The solution resolved upon was the effective merger of all five large corporations under the umbrella of a holding company, to be named United States Steel. The driving force behind this was the banker J.P. Morgan, who controlled the world's largest bank and was generally believed to be the world's richest individual human being. Morgan's participation in this scheme was absolutely essential, as he dominated Wall Street and his participation would make other shareholders much more likely to subscribe to the new venture. Morgan's participation in effect validated the venture in the eyes of other shareholders. The four new companies were quick to see the advantages of the plan and agreed at once. Andrew Carnegie took longer to come around, but ultimately J.P. Morgan was able to persuade Carnegie that while he could compete with his four rivals individually, he could not do so if they were combined together; they would have resources and economies of scale which even he could not match. Carnegie finally agreed to sell all his bonds and stocks in his own company to the new corporation; Morgan initially offered $400 million, and finally agreed to pay $498 million in gold bonds. Carnegie, whose plans for spending his money were focused on a wide range of charitable institutions, took care to extract as much money as he could from Morgan and his fellow bankers.

The merger of the Big Five, as well as several smaller companies belonging to the Rock Island Crowd, was agreed in late 1900, and incorporation took place in April 1901, with the new corporation capitalised at $1.1 billion. Morgan's syndicate, which included the corporation chairman, Judge Elbert Gary, owned $200 million of this total. Stockholders in the old companies exchanged their stocks for those in United States Steel, at an attractive premium; preferred stock holders in National Tube and American Tin Plate received $125 of United States Steel stock for every $100 they had owned in the old companies, while those in American Steel & Wire and Federal Steel received slightly less, $117 and $110 respectively. Common stockholders received an average of $107 of United States Steel stock per $100 of old stock. A substantial new issue, just under $200 million, was then sold through the Wall Street market, and 98 per cent was sold within a few weeks of issue.

United States Steel looked to be in an unassailable position, dominating the American market and able to compete on even terms with Krupp and the leading French and British steel makers overseas. However, doubts began to emerge almost at once. First, it was revealed that the promoters of the scheme, J.P. Morgan and his associates, had made colossal profits out of the deal, around $46 million according to best estimates (there were no financial disclosure rules, so no one was sure of the precise figure). Morgan had used $200 million of his own cash to buy out Carnegie quickly and get the venture moving, and was believed to have taken a profit of around $25 million, with the rest going to other bankers and underwriters.

Second, the corporation then embarked on an aggressive acquisitions policy, buying up other small independent companies and funding each acquisition through further stock issues. By the end of 1901 two more companies, American Bridge and Lake Superior Consolidated Iron Mines, had been purchased, and total capitalisation had risen to nearly $1.4 billion. Seven more companies were acquired in the next five years, and further expansion of the facilities of the existing corporation was undertaken, notably the building of a $75 million steel rolling mill at Gary, Indiana. Yet more stock and bond issues were required. By 1907, stockholders had begun to complain about dilution, and although dividends were paid regularly, the price of the stock was more or less stagnant. Critics wondered why, when United States Steel already dominated the market, it was bothering to spend shareholders' money on acquiring small companies which did not present a threat.

Still more serious concerns emerged about whether the company was over-capitalised. These concerns became more cogent still when the steel industry slumped once again in 1903. Many, including important stockholders in the company itself, argued that its capitalisation was in excess of its earning capacity. The benchmark for capitalisation was then believed to be a company's ability to earn over a given period of time, perhaps ten or twenty years. When steel prices fell, United States Steel's earning capacity fell with it, at a time when its capitalisation was still increasing. Some observers now believed that, using this benchmark, the company was overcapitalised by as much as 20 per cent. John Gates, former head of American Steel & Wire, who owned $80 million in United States Steel shares, testified before the Federal Industrial Commission in 1910 that 25–30 per cent of his holdings were 'water', that is, constituted shares issued over and above proper capitalisation. United States Steel argued that its capitalisation should be based on its assets, not its earning capacity, and produced figures showing its assets to be valued at just under $1.5 billion, not counting goodwill, only slightly less than its capitalisation. The company claimed the gap would be filled by increasing and expanding assets, particularly as in 1907 the price of steel had started to rise again and demand was increasing.

In 1910, observers were very much divided over United States Steel. Some felt it was an overcapitalised behemoth, which was bent on unnecessary acquisition and expansion when it should be adopting a safety-first policy, especially given the harsh fluctuations in the industry. Others believed that the short-term fluctuations could be ridden out thanks to United States Steel's size and economies of scale, and that being big was the only way to survive in the steel industry. All were agreed that much would depend on the quality of management, especially financial management, at the corporation, and this would probably be the deciding factor in whether it succeeded or failed.

### Analysis

Some of the questions you might want to consider in connection with this case include:

- Is this kind of consolidation the only way to survive in an industry subject to fluctuations?
- Thinking strategically, what would you have done if you were Andrew Carnegie? Sell, or stay in and compete to win?
- Was United States Steel overcapitalised?
- After the events described in this case, United States Steel was charged under the provisions of anti-trust laws aimed at preventing monopoly and threatened with being broken up (it ultimately escaped this fate but lost its dominant position in the steel industry). Was this the right thing to do?

## Sources

Berglund, Abraham (1907) *The United States Steel Corporation: A Study of the Growth and Influence of Combination in the Iron and Steel Industry*, New York: Columbia University.

Cotter, Arundel (1921) *United States Steel: A Corporation With a Soul*, Garden City, NY: Doubleday, Page & Co.

Lough, William H. (1910) *Corporation Finance*, New York: Alexander Hamilton Institute.

Misa, Thomas (1998) *Nation of Steel: The Making of Modern America, 1865–1925*, Baltimore: Johns Hopkins University Press.

Warren, Kenneth (2001) *Big Steel: The First Century of the United States Steel Corporation, 1901–2001*, Pittsburgh: University of Pittsburgh Press.

## Case Study 6B

### *Thomas Coutts & Co.*

The bank known today as Coutts & Co. was founded in London in 1692 by the Scottish goldsmith John Campbell. It was originally known as the Three Crowns, after the badge displayed on the sign over his shop door in the Strand, the street in London where many bankers and goldsmiths were to be found. Goldsmiths in the late seventeenth and early eighteenth centuries often doubled as bankers; gold and silver were still the primary currencies of everyday commerce, and there were vaults in which valuables could be kept. Goldsmiths like Campbell functioned as the retail bankers of their day, while the nearest equivalent to merchant banks were firms like the Grasshopper, founded by Sir Thomas Gresham in the sixteenth century and later to become Martin's Bank, which specialised in lending to businesses, marine insurance and the like.

In 1708 Campbell granted a partnership to his son-in-law George Middleton, who took over as manager. Middleton seems to have had little knowledge or understanding of banking, and he made a number of risky loans; he also invested capital in various get-rich-quick schemes which were promoted as part of the South Sea Bubble. When the bubble burst and the British stock market crashed in 1720, Campbell's bank like many others incurred heavy losses. It survived but only as a very minor player in the London banking scene. Middleton died in 1747 and control passed to John Campbell's son, George Campbell, who likewise was unable to do much more than keep the business afloat.

The bank's fortunes changed when in 1755 Campbell recruited an ambitious young Scottish banker, James Coutts, and made him a partner (James Coutts also married Campbell's daughter Polly to seal the bargain). Coutts, the son of a well-known Edinburgh banker, was anxious to make his mark in London, and also had political ambitions. He proved to be a superb networker, and not only fulfilled his desire to enter politics – he became an MP in 1762, but he also pulled off a remarkable coup. In 1760 he persuaded King George III to name Coutts as his private bankers. That same year George Campbell died, and James brought his younger brother Thomas south from Edinburgh to become a partner, renaming the bank James and Thomas Coutts (after James Coutts's retirement in 1775 it became simply Thomas Coutts and Co.).

When James Coutts entered the House of Commons, management of the bank fell to Thomas Coutts, then twenty-five years old. He had a limited amount of banking experience, having worked with his father in Edinburgh, but he did not know London society well. Nevertheless, he at once followed his brother's lead. Acting as bankers to the king gave Coutts access to the highest levels of the court and government. Over the next four decades he built up an impressive list of clients that included not only the king and the Prince of Wales but also prominent politicians such as William Pitt and Charles James Fox (who were bitter rivals, the one a Tory and the other a Whig) and others including the Duke of Wellington and Lady Hester Stanhope, Pitt's niece, who had considerable influence over female society in London. Absolutely impartial in his business dealings, he lent money not only to the Hanoverian king George III and also his successors, but also to Clementina Walkinshaw, former mistress of the Catholic pretender Prince Charles Stewart. Coutts became the bank of the Establishment, without taking sides or getting involved in politics.

The American Revolution (1775–81) caused a financial crisis in London and nearly a hundred banks failed over a ten-year period, but thanks to its long list of blue-chip clients Coutts was able to weather the storm. Amsterdam, hitherto the centre of European finance, was even more badly damaged, and by 1790 the major Dutch banks had either gone under or relocated to the safer environment of London. The French Revolution further damaged the European centres of finance, and by 1800 London was the acknowledged capital of European banking, with established firms like Coutts now competing with newer bankers like Baring, Goldsmid and Rothschild. Coutts, forecasting the trends correctly, began opening up international links in the 1780s and by 1800 had developed ties with several Swiss banks; through these, he was able to offer private banking services to clients in the Mediterranean and the Levant. With a chain of correspondent banks stretching from Lisbon to Bombay, Coutts became the bank of choice for international travellers. British officers serving in Spain during the Napoleonic Wars were even able to negotiate Coutts drafts with banks in cities within the war zone.

Although Rothschild and Baring moved aggressively into merchant banking, funding businesses, backing share issues and funding overseas trade ventures and many of the rapidly growing businesses of the Industrial Revolution – and made fortunes in doing so – Coutts stuck to what he knew best. Personal banking at this time was becoming much more complex, thanks largely to the rapidly growing range of government bonds issued to finance the national debt. Investing in these could yield handsome profits, but the investor had to know what he or she was doing. Coutts effectively became a 'wealth management' firm, looking after the investments of the rich and famous, moving their money around between stocks and bonds depending on the fluctuations of the market. Because he was close to the government (no matter whether Whigs or Tories were in power), Coutts was bound to have at least a few clients in the cabinet, including often the prime minister himself. Through his contacts, he could provide his own clients with a level of information available nowhere else, and advise them on the investment packages that would suit their needs. (He was also ideally placed to receive maximal government support and protection in event of a downturn or threat to his bank.)

Coutts built a reputation for reliability, quality of service and probity. Rarely, when following his advice, did clients lose money on investments, and they almost always recouped their losses swiftly. In order to achieve this, he adopted a policy of very low risk. He favoured government bonds over shares, and only invested in the latter if the companies in question were believed to be rock-solid. The slightest hint of a scandal or dishonesty would cause Coutts to withdraw his investment immediately. He also managed a very conservative lending policy, and maintained large cash reserves to cover himself in case clients defaulted on loans (a doubly important precaution given that one of his clients was the perpetually indebted Prince of Wales, the future King George IV).

Several decades before Coutts came to London, in the aftermath of the South Sea Bubble, Thomas Martin of the Grasshopper had advised that for a banker, 'to appear cautious and timorous contribute very much to give persons in credit an esteem among mankind'; in other words, that the best way to win a reputation was to play it safe. Coutts carried out this advice to the letter. His reputation for caution meant that other investors and bankers tended to watch and follow his moves; it was reasoned that if Coutts thought an investment was safe enough to place his own money in, then that investment was probably as safe as it could be.

On one level, Coutts was not an innovator. He brought in no radical new methods of management, and he made no great contributions to the management of finance. He did help to bring the management of private wealth in Britain into a new dimension, expanding into international markets and offering an investment and advisory service that many came to rely upon. Above all, Coutts understood the fundamentals of sound financial management, and understood how to make the best investments, maximising profits and minimising risks. His profile was high in royal and political circles, but he did not seek to create a popular image for himself or his bank – unlike his brash young competitor N.M. Rothschild, for example. His image was founded on discretion, probity and reliability. As a result, while many other banks failed or were dissolved during the turbulent years of the French Revolution and Napoleonic Wars, his endured. He managed his clients with a skill that allowed him to take on loss-making accounts (like those of Fox and the Prince of Wales) in the knowledge that they would give him access to contacts that would allow him to turn a profit elsewhere. He understood too the importance of London's emergence as a financial capital, and of the need to build an international network. Above all, he set a standard of service which became part of the Coutts corporate culture and which endures largely to this day.

Coutts died in 1822 and left both control of the bank and his own personal fortune, estimated at £900,000, to his widow Harriot. An former actress forty years her husband's junior, Harriot Coutts proved to be a perfectly capable bank owner and hired a number of talented junior managers. Coutts & Co. continued to grow, and when Harriot Coutts died in 1837 her granddaughter Angela Burdett-Coutts inherited a fortune of at least £3 million along with the bank. The latter took no part in management, devoting herself instead to a series of charitable causes, and the managers of the bank were given a free hand. Growth continued into the twentieth century, with Coutts continuing to follow the model introduced by Thomas Coutts, concentrating on offering private banking services to the wealthy. In 1969 Coutts was acquired by National Westminster Bank, which in turn was taken over by Royal Bank of Scotland in 2000. It remains Britain's largest and most prominent private bank.

## Analysis

Some of the questions you might want to consider in connection with this case include:

- Unlike Rothschild in particular, Coutts was very risk-averse. Was this the right thing to do? Should he have engaged in more risky investments in order to make more money for his clients?
- Coutts also stuck to private banking, the sector he knew best. Should he have expanded into merchant banking? What risks would he have run in doing so?
- Coutts combined shrewd financial management skills with a sound knowledge of marketing. Does this suggest that financial managers might benefit from knowing more about marketing, and vice versa?

## Sources

Healey, E. (1992) *Coutts & Co: The Portrait of a Private Bank*, London: Hodder & Stoughton.

Witzel, M. (1992) 'Thomas Coutts and the Rise of Modern Banking', *The Strand*, January: 7–9.

## Case Study 6C

*Jagat Seth*

The Indian banking house known as Jagat Seth (Bankers to the World) has its origins in a small trading house set up by a trader named Hiranand Shah in the 1650s in Bengal province. His family came originally from Jodhpur in Rajasthan, but had settled in Bengal in the early part of the century. Other details are obscure: according to some accounts Hiranand was a jeweller, while others say he was a trader in saltpetre. This product, one of the key ingredients in gunpowder, was much sought after by traders from the English and Dutch East India Companies and also by French merchants who had set up trading posts in southern India, and there was a thriving saltpetre export business. As well as trading on his own account, Hiranand lent money to other traders, and it seems that at times he also lent money to some of the foreign merchants, handling bills of exchange as well as cash.

About the only other thing known about Hiranand and his family is that they were Jains, a small sect which had broken away from the Hindu faith and had communities all over India. Many Jains were involved in banking and commerce, notably the famous Vitji Vora from Surat, who dominated banking in Western India in the seventeenth century and played a key role as a middleman working between European and local traders in Bombay and other western ports.

In 1680, Hiranand's son Manik Chand had taken over the business and established himself in Dacca (in modern Bangladesh). Dacca was then a centre of fine cloth production, and again there was a growing export trade. Manik Chand bankrolled both sides of the trade, financing the cloth producers and issuing loans to the foreign trading companies, especially the English. The latter, operating thousands of miles from home, badly needed banking services, and Manik Chand, perhaps foreseeing that the English traders would become a growing force, cultivated close links with them. Agents of the East India Company, as well as buying and selling for their employer, were also allowed to conduct a limited amount of private trade on their own account, and Manik Chand offered a personal banking service for these men as well as for the company.

As well as building relationships with the East India Company and other foreign traders, Manik Chand also forged ties with the local ruler, the Nawab of Bengal. According to some sources he was given control of the mint in Bengal, giving him the sole right to mint coins, but it is not clear if this happened under Manik Chand's direction or later under that of his nephew and successor Fateh Chand. But certainly Manik Chand was acting as banker to the government of Bengal, and when the capital of the province was relocated to Murshidabad, Manik Chand moved his office there too, leaving Fateh Chand in charge in Dacca. By 1710, if not before, the bank had established a network of branches all over Bengal and was deeply involved in trade. In 1712, Manik Chand also backed the future emporer Farroukshah in his successful bid for the imperial throne of India and was given further rewards for the loans he had made to finance Farroukshah's campaign.

Manik Chand died in 1714 and control of the bank passed to Fateh Chand. He went on to become the most powerful financier in India, and very possibly in the world at the time. He continued the policy of support for Emperor Farroukshah, and became in effect the imperial banker. In 1723 the emperor gave Fateh Chand an emerald seal and the title Jagat Seth, or Banker to the World. The title was intended to be passed on to Fateh Chand's heirs, but it also became widely used as the name of the bank itself; in effect, Jagat Seth became a kind of brand name.

In Bengal, the house of Jagat Seth grew still more powerful and influential. The bank was given control of the two royal mints in Dacca and Patna, and thus had control of the money supply for the entire province. The East India Company had originally been allowed to mint a limited amount of coinage for its own use, but now that privilege was rescinded; the Company had to send all its gold and silver to Dacca to be reminted. At its height Jagat Seth was minting 5 million rupees a year, taking a profit of 350,000 rupees for itself in the process. Jagat Seth also controlled the foreign exchange market, negotiated virtually all bills of exchange between merchants, became the effective setter of interest rates given its control of the loan market, and gradually was given management of most of the royal finances of the Nawab of Bengal; it is estimated that by 1750 they were responsible for two-thirds of all revenue collection in this, one of India's richest provinces.

Fateh Chand also extended the influence of the house of Jagat Seth far beyond Bengal. The network of bank branches, or *kothis*, set up by his uncle was extended right across northern India to Delhi, the imperial capital. He also built relationships with big banking houses in other parts of India, such as the Chellabys of Surat and the Chettys of Coromandel, helping to establish a financial structure which covered all of India. In Delhi, Fateh Chand was regarded as at least as important and powerful as the Nawab of Bengal himself. Foreigners also admired him; Edmund Burke later compared the house of Fateh Chand to the Bank of England, while the East India Company's Robert Clive said it was far richer than any business in London at the time.

One of the great banking innovations of the period, in which Fateh Chand played a major role, was the development of the bill of exchange (*hundi*). This was made possible by the development of banking networks referred to above. In the seventeenth century, the revenues of Bengal were sent to Delhi in the form of cartloads of specie (gold and silver coin or bars). Jagat Seth reformed the system so that a single bill of exchange could be sent from Murshidabad to Delhi and drawn on his agents in the capital, who would provide the necessary coinage to the imperial treasury. He also seems to have encouraged the rapid development of trade in bills of exchange; in Bengal, where Jagat Seth had a virtual monopoly on this trade, this became a major source of profits.

From the 1720s onward, aware of his power, the East India Company took pains to cultivate Fateh Chand. He in turn seems to have regarded them as useful commercial partners but nothing more. After his death, however, his successors grew closer to the British. The Mogul Empire was breaking up under the pressures of civil war and foreign invasion from Afghanistan, and Bengal was one of many provinces that shook off imperial control. In these circumstances, the East India Company may have looked like a stabilising force. Following the death of Fateh Chand in 1744, his successors increased the bank's exposure, loaning increasing amounts to the declining Mogul empire – and suffering heavy losses when Afghan invaders sacked Delhi – and also loaning increasingly large amounts to the Nawabs of Bengal and various foreign traders, especially the East India Company.

In 1757 the young and aggressive Nawab of Bengal, Siraj-ad-daula, having declared his independence from the Mogul empire, declared war on the East India Company with a view to driving them out of their post at Calcutta. A number of British prisoners were taken and later died of suffocation in an overcrowded jail known to posterity as the 'Black Hole of Calcutta'. In revenge, the East India Company mustered an army led by Captain Robert Clive and invaded Bengal. Fateh Chand's grandson Mahatab Chand, the new head of Jagat Seth, sided with the Company against Siraj-ad-daula, and provided financial support for Clive, who went on to defeat the Nawab and overthrow him. But this led to a power vacuum and the economy of Bengal collapsed. In the ensuing political and economic chaos, Jagat Seth's business suffered badly; the more so as some Bengalis denounced the bankers as traitors for having sided with the British. Although the East India Company honoured its loans from Jagat Seth, the government of Bengal and many local traders did not.

In 1763, the anti-British leader Mir Kasim Ali seized Bengal and declared himself Nawab. Mahatab Chand and his cousin Swarup Chand were both murdered by Kasim's troops. Khoshal Chand, the third Jagat Seth, tried to rebuild the business, but by now he was facing increasing competition from both British interests and new rising local houses such as that of Bolakida. Despite good relationships with the British, who had finally taken control of Bengal themselves, the business declined steeply. In 1844, his business in ruins, the head of Jagat Seth, Gobind Chand, was reduced to asking the East India Company for a pension in order to feed himself and his family. He and his descendants were awarded a monthly pension of 1,200 rupees. The last Jagat Seth died in 1912 and the family became extinct, the bank itself having long since disappeared.

## Analysis

Some of the questions you might want to consider in connection with this case include:

- In the 1740s and early 1750s, the house of Jagat Seth was immensely wealthy and powerful. Its decline in subsequent years was very rapid. What brought on the decline? What could the bank have done to prevent this?

- Might the bank have fared better if it had stayed out of politics? Was this a feasible option? What were the risks of becoming involved with both local government and the foreign traders?
- Might the bank also have fared better if it had backed the Bengal government more fully and reduced its ties with the British and other foreign traders early on? Is there a sense that, with hindsight, the British were the wrong people to do business with? Or was Jagat Seth right to try to finance both sides of the trade?

## Sources

Bhattacharya, S. (1969) *The East India Company and the Economy of Bengal from 1704 to 1740*, Calcutta: K.L. Mukhopadhyay.

Jain, L.C. (1929) *Indigenous Banking in India*, London: Macmillan.

Little, J.H. (1967) *The House of Jagat Seth*, Calcutta: n.p.

Long, J. (1869) *Selections from the Unpublished Records of Government for the Years 1748 to 1767 Inclusive*, Calcutta: Office of the Superintendent of Government Printing, vol. 1.

## Case Study 6D

### *Hongkong and Shanghai Banking Corporation*

The Hongkong and Shanghai Banking Corporation was established in 1865 for the purpose of providing a banking service for merchants in Hong Kong. The majority of its early clients were the *hongs*, the trading houses that acted as middlemen in the trade between China and Europe, but the new bank soon began providing services also to other local firms, both British and Chinese. A branch was opened in Shanghai, the other major centre of British commerce in China, later in 1865, and a branch in Japan followed in 1866. The bank's head office was in London, where the board of directors sat, but most of its operations in the early days were in the Far East.

The first ten years of operation saw rather uneven performance. Markets in China in particular were likely to fluctuate rapidly, in part because of the extremely delicate political situation. Following China's military defeat by Britain and France in 1860, the Chinese empire had become very fragile. A large-scale revolt against central authority, the Taiping Rebellion, threatened to break China apart; this was eventually suppressed, but at immense cost in lives and economic damage. The emperor was a child, and power rested in the hands of the regent, his mother the formidable Empress Cixi. A political conservative, Cixi resented foreign influence in China and accepted the presence of foreign traders and bankers only reluctantly.

In 1874–75 the new bank nearly failed, thanks to a combination of bad investments and bad loans. Several of its senior staff were fired for incompetence, including the chief manager, the most senior manager in the Far East and reporting directly to the managing director in London. One of the few managers to escape blame for the crisis was the manager of the Japanese branch in Yokohama, Thomas Jackson. With few other options available, the bank's directors invited him to take up the post of chief manager. In 1876, the thirty-five-year-old Jackson took over the management of the troubled bank.

Born the son of a farmer in Northern Ireland, Jackson had been apprenticed with a clerk with the Bank of Ireland in Belfast. Seeking a life of adventure, he went to India and joined the Agra Bank, and soon after was sent to be its agent in Hong Kong. The Agra Bank collapsed in 1866 and Jackson, out of a job, was then hired by the new Hongkong and Shanghai Bank. Here he rose rapidly, partly through his own abilities and partly, as King (1987) says, because there was a shortage of qualified staff in the region. Jackson became in quick succession chief accountant in Shanghai, agent in Hangzhou and manager in Yokohama. In 1872 he was invited to take over the important post of manager in Shanghai but declined, preferring to concentrate on growing the bank's business in Japan. But in 1876 he answered the call to come and rescue the bank, and returned to Hong Kong.

As chief manager, Jackson's energy and skills at once made an impact. He reorganised the moribund Shanghai office, instituted new controls to prevent further bad loans, and began developing new relationships and agencies. Largely at his urging the bank opened offices in New York and Hamburg, establishing links with foreign competitors operating in China and in the process becoming a truly international bank. He also expanded in the Far East, most notably into Thailand. This independent kingdom was the only country in South-east Asia to escape being colonised. Thailand had no banking system of its own; Hongkong and Shanghai Bank helped to set up the country's financial system including the mint, oversaw the production of the first banknotes, and set up the first retail bank in the capital, Bangkok.

In 1888 Jackson returned to the UK, where he was knighted for his services (he was later made a baronet) and made managing director of the bank. However, in 1892 his successor in the Far East ran into difficulties, and the directors asked Jackson to return to Shanghai. From then until 1902 the head office of the bank was *de facto* in Shanghai; Jackson ran the bank almost independently of the directors and was the dominant leader and managerial force. In 1902 he returned to England and retired, but continued to serve as a director until his death in 1915. Under his leadership, Hongkong and Shanghai Bank had become the largest bank in the Far East, and it continued to grow. Today HSBC, as it is usually known, is both one of the world's largest and one of its longest established banks, with a global reach and operations on every continent. It was also one of the few large banks to escape serious damage during the financial crisis of 2007–8. Much of its subsequent growth and success was due to the foundations laid by Jackson. His statue in a public square in Hong Kong remains a tourist attraction in its own right.

Jackson's greatest impact lay in his development of relationships with the Chinese government. In the 1870s and 1880s China's leaders, or at least some officials such as Li Hongzhang, were taking tentative steps towards modernisation. Under Jackson's management, the Hongkong and Shanghai Bank became the leading lender to the Chinese government, pushing aside not only other foreign competitors but domestic Chinese banks. The bank also financed several of Li's commercial ventures, notably the China Merchants' Navigation Company in 1872, an inland and coastal shipping company set up to combat the increasing domination of Chinese shipping by foreign firms such as Jardine Matheson and Butterfield & Swire. With support from Hongkong and Shanghai Bank, the CMNC was able for a time to take over the bulk of the local shipping trade from these rivals. There were complaints in Hong Kong that Jackson was funding the Chinese to compete against other British firms, but his response was that this was a good business opportunity and it was up to the foreign merchants to work out how best to compete against the Chinese.

This was in many ways typical of Jackson's attitude. Despite its political problems, China was still a rich country and the banking opportunities were many, and Jackson knew how to spot the most lucrative. Much of the bank's business was in foreign exchange, and Jackson also had a talent for spotting market trends and knowing where to shift his money; foreign exchange profits were a mainstay of the bank under his management. Many other foreign banks, lacking his skills, went bankrupt or were forced to close, giving Jackson a still greater share of the market.

Jackson's achievements are all the more impressive given the volatile and highly risky environment in which he worked. The sense of insecurity in the region increased with the passage of time. Politically, the Chinese empire was struggling to survive; Empress Cixi and her allies such as Li Hongzhang were holding the empire together almost by force of will. But Li died in 1901 and Cixi a few years later, and then the writing was on the wall. No one knew what would happen when the empire fell, or what would replace it. Britain, France, Germany and Russia had all occupied cities on the Chinese coast and Japan, after a short war, had seized Taiwan and occupied China's ally Korea. Friction between Japan and Russia in Manchuria exploded into another war in 1904–5. Even when there was no actual conflict, the rumours and threats of conflict kept markets in a perpetual state of anxious suspense.

But Jackson was adept at managing in an environment of change and flux. He regarded the rapid market fluctuations of the Far East as opportunities, not as threats. He was not a gambler; he managed his finances prudently and to strict controls, and the risks he ran were always calculated ones. His contemporaries regarded him as lucky ('Lucky Jackson' was his nickname from early in his career), but King (1987) concluded that much of his 'luck' was in fact the result of his own talents and skills. To this should also be added his knowledge and his high-level contacts in every country in the region, especially at the Chinese court. When rumours began to circulate, Jackson was among the first to hear of them. His experience and knowledge of local markets then helped him evaluate the truth of these rumours and what the likely reaction of the markets would be. Jackson succeeded because he knew more, thought faster and moved faster than most of his rivals. Hongkong and Shanghai Bank could find profit in situations where other banks failed and went under. As a result, the bank was strong enough to get through the chaos that followed the collapse of the empire in 1911 and then of Sun Yat-sen's republic a few years later. The company did suffer heavy losses during the Second World War – two of its chief managers and many other staff died during the Japanese occupation of China – but the bank rebuilt its position quickly after the war and expanded across Asia.

Jackson was an adept financier, and was fully familiar with all the various financial instruments and markets in which his firm dealt. These were of course far simpler than today, but Jackson also had fewer resources. His chief assets, those which allowed him and his bank to succeed, were his ability to read markets and to understand how other players in the markets would behave, and his skill at cultivating relationships with business and political leaders, British, Chinese, Japanese and Thai. The culture he created at HSBC combined financial prudence with entrepreneurship, and the bank became known for its ability to spot business opportunities and take advantage of them while avoiding ventures that were excessively risky. Its reputation for prudence made the bank attractive to savers, and many Chinese also banked with Hongkong and Shanghai Bank, and continue to do so to this day. Although vastly larger and with greater global reach, culturally HSBC is still in many ways the bank that 'Lucky' Jackson built.

## Analysis

Some of the questions you might want to consider in connection with this case include:

- Jackson was an entrepreneur whose business was built on establishing key relationships rather than financial models. Is there still a place for managers like him in the world today? Could he survive as a financial manager in modern times?
- Do you agree with King's assessment that Jackson's success was based on skill rather than luck? Or must an element of chance have been present and in part responsible for his success?
- Under Jackson, Hongkong and Shanghai Bank balanced prudence with risk. How in the current market would you go about doing this? Is it even possible?

## Sources

Collis, Maurice (1965) *Wayfoong: The Hongkong and Shanghai Banking Corporation*, London: Faber & Faber.

Hao, Y. (1986) *The Commercial Revolution in Nineteenth-Century China*, Berkeley, CA: University of California Press.

King, F.H.H. (1987) *The History of the Hongkong and Shanghai Banking Corporation*, vol. 1, *The Hongkong Bank in Late Imperial China, 1864–1902*, Cambridge: Cambridge University Press.

Morse, H.B. (1921) *The Trade and Administration of China*, 3rd edn, London: Longmans, Green.

## Notes

1 Although there is a larger literature on the history of advertising.
2 25 February is also sometimes given as the date of incorporation.

# 7 Technology, innovation and knowledge

---

**Learning objectives**

This chapter is intended to help readers do the following:

1 understand better the ways that knowledge has been used by companies and managers in the past;
2 understand better the different approaches to innovation that have been used in the past;
3 gain new perspectives on the interrelationship between technology, innovation and knowledge.

If it will go ten miles without stopping, I can make it go around the globe.
– Samuel Morse, inventor of the telegraph

I have found that knowledge is infinite. The longer I live, the more I realize that what I know is only a very small thing. On every road I have travelled, I have found there is no end to it. Every man who wishes to live a worth-while life must keep on learning as long as he has breath. I dare say that when my doctor tells me I have only three more days to live, I shall begin to study coffins.

– Herbert N. Casson, *The Story of My Life*

## 7.1 Introduction

This chapter brings together three related themes: *technology*, the tools we use in order to do business; *innovation*, the process of improving business by making the business itself more efficient, offering new products and services to customers and so on; and *knowledge*, which as we shall see is an important prerequisite for both the use of technology and innovation.

Today, technology management, innovation and knowledge management all have their own literature and their own disciplines of study; many business schools offer separate courses on each. Each subject is complex and deserves to be studied intensively. But, as we have noted elsewhere in this book, this division into different disciplines can run the risk of developing the silo effect, in which each is studied and practised in isolation. The strong linkages between these three subjects need to be borne in mind.

Managers in the past were well aware of the importance of all three. Though the pace of technological change increased steadily from the late eighteenth century onward, technological advances had been occurring slowly but steadily for centuries. The progression from stone to bronze and then to iron tools, for instance, was a technological revolution in its own right, as was the efficient harnessing of water power in the Middle Ages. Each advance in technology saw innovations in terms of new products, new production processes, sometimes new industries and markets. And beyond these revolutions, progressive businesses were constantly engaged in the search for ways to improve, to go beyond what already existed, to put distance between themselves and their competitors. Similarly the importance of knowledge has long been recognised, even if its role was not clearly understood.

The pace of change in all three fields picked up greatly during the Industrial and Scientific Revolutions that began in the late eighteenth century, and even more so in the late twentieth century with the advent of the computer age. Our technologies are far more complex than those of earlier times, and we have much more knowledge at our disposal – although it is not yet clear if this has made us any more innovative! In some respects we are now glutted with both knowledge and technology, and many of us strive to make sense of and use effectively the resources we have. Perhaps it is fairer to say that the face of innovation has changed. In former times, innovators made do with a limited amount of knowledge and technology: the contest was to see who could use these most effectively. Today the process has become more oriented towards pattern recognition: innovators look around at our complex world and search for things that they can use to create new products or new value.

## 7.2  Technological advances

We begin with a look at technology itself, how it has advanced and changed, and in particular how those changes have impacted on management. It should be emphasised that what follows is not a history of technology itself.

### 7.2.1  Production technologies

Advances in production technologies – technologies used in order to make goods – can be divided for practical purposes into two groups: (1) power generation and (2) tools.

The earliest power sources were animals, including human beings. At the beginnings of civilisation, agricultural land was tilled by hand, corn was ground by hand and so on. The gigantic stone blocks that were used to build the pyramids of Giza four and a half thousand years ago were quarried by hand using stone tools and dragged physically from the quarry to the building site using teams of paid labourers. As human beings are not comparatively very strong, large projects tended to be very labour intensive and only powerful and wealthy state governments could afford them; such projects were far beyond the means of private enterprise.

The domestication of the horse, ox, donkey and other animals meant that human muscle-power in some fields could be superseded. The first major advances, however, came in the harnessing of wind and water power. Both of these were known in ancient times; water-powered mills were known in both China and the Roman Empire from about the first century BC. In both cases they were rather primitive in design, as were the windmills that began appearing in the Middle East around the same time. None of these were used for any purpose beyond grinding corn; as Gimpel (1976) notes, there was no policy of mechanisation during the Roman Empire, the state and private sector alike preferring to rely on muscle power.

During the Middle Ages in Western Europe, however, water power especially took an immense leap forward. There were more than five thousand watermills in England alone at the time of the Domesday Book survey in 1086, and the number increased steadily all over Europe. The development of gears and cams meant that power could be used more efficiently. The introduction of the cam led in turn to the development of the triphammer. Mills for fulling cloth and forging iron became widespread. The Cistercian monastic order led the way in much of this mechanisation; virtually every Cistercian monastery had at least one watermill, and there was a steady process of innovation and improvement in technology that led to increased power generation.

---

**The first machine age**

The Middle Ages introduced machinery into Europe on a scale no civilization had previously known. This was to be one of the main factors that led to the dominance of the Western hemisphere over the rest of the world. Machines were known in the classical world, of course, but their use in industry was limited. Cogs and gears were employed only for creating toys or automata. In medieval society, however, machinery was made to do what previously had been done only by manual, and often hard, labour.

(Gimpel 1976: 1)

---

The increase in power enabled increases in production, especially in textiles. Investing in the technology to take advantage of this required capital, but the growth of banks and development of new credit instruments around the same time supplied this need at least in parts of Europe, such as northern Italy and Flanders. As a result, we begin from the twelfth and thirteenth centuries onward to see the growth of larger multi-site cloth-making businesses. Individual workshops expanded in size, and successful entrepreneurs invested in other businesses as well, enabling an expansion in scale and scope.

Water power was favoured over wind power as being more reliable and capable of generating more power at a single site. But even so there were limits to the amount of what could be generated, and over the course of several centuries production capacity expanded and then reached its limits. By the time of the establishment of the first cloth-making factories of the Industrial Revolution such as Richard Arkwright's mill at Cromford (see Case Study 7B), the technology for generating power from water was being stretched to its limits. This provided a push factor which led to the development of the next stage in power technology, steam.

Steam engines had been discussed in theory by Hero of Alexandria in classical times, and by Leonardo da Vinci in the early sixteenth century. In the seventeenth and eighteenth centuries, experiments by Thomas Savery and Thomas Newcomen produced working steam engines, but these were very large, expensive and rather inefficient. But at the end of the eighteenth century James Watt produced a smaller and more efficient engine, and by 1800 some factory owners were experimenting with using these for power generation. By the 1830s water mills had largely been phased out, and steam engines were powering most factories in Europe and America.

The steam turbine, patented by Charles Parsons in 1884, could produce up to 7.5 kilowatts of power, meaning a single generator could now power an entire factory (Clark 1985). Parsons turbines also became standard in ships. Most importantly, though, they were used in power stations generating electricity. Following Thomas Edison's breakthroughs in the 1870s and 1880s (Clark 1997; Millard 1990), electric power became increasingly important in both domestic and business use. Steam continued to power ships and factories for many years, with oil-fired engines gradually taking over from coal once petroleum production began. Taken together, these new engines represented a huge leap forward in power generation. This in turn enabled businesses of all kinds to expand and take advantage of economies of scale. However, with businesses now reaching unprecedented sizes, the new power generation technology also required much adaptation in methods and systems of management. The advance of technology also created its problems.

---

### The quiet innovator

Charles Parsons never achieved the heroic status of Edison or Westinghouse, but his work in power generation was easily as important. The younger son of the Earl of Rosse, he was born in 1854 and educated at St John's College, Cambridge where he was graduated in mathematics. Fascinated by machinery since childhood, he was apprenticed with the engineer Sir William Armstrong (whose house at Cragside was the first in Britain to use electric lighting throughout). In 1884 he became junior partner in Clark, Chapman & Co. in Gateshead, where he was put in charge of the electrical engineering department. Here he developed the invention that would make him famous, the turbine generator. In 1889 Parsons went on to set up his own business, C.A. Parsons & Co., in Heaton, near Newcastle. In 1890 he built the Forth Banks power station near Newcastle, the world's first turbo-dynamo electrical power station.

As cities all over the developed world moved to develop their own electricity grids, and as Parsons's generators were vastly more efficient than any constructed so far, orders rushed in. Parsons's patents (he took out over 300 in all) protected his initial idea, but he was shrewd enough to license production to several other companies in the same field, notably Westinghouse in the USA. At the same time, he developed the steam turbine as a method of propulsion for ships, and by 1900 had successfully convinced the Royal Navy to begin adopting steam turbines for new ships. Private shipbuilders and owners soon followed suit, and from 1910 for at least another two decades, virtually every large steamship built used Parsons turbines.

Parsons had a high regard for his workers and their technical skills; Clark (1986) notes that he referred to them as artisans rather than workmen. He paid very high wages for the time, hoping to attract the most skilled and most creative engineers. A number of engineers who rose to later prominence in other fields worked at Parsons early in their careers. In 1919 Parsons, who had long been concerned that the country lacked sufficient numbers of engineers for its needs, set up an apprentice school at Heaton. He also introduced profit-sharing and other employee benefits.

Parsons succeeded in creating a culture of innovation at Heaton, where highly paid and highly motivated staff maintained a technological edge over the competition for four decades. During that period, Parsons's firm had probably the largest skills base of any engineering firm in the world; it was also one of the most profitable.

(Clark 1986; Parsons 1934)

Advances in production tools clearly had limits imposed by the amount of power available, but this did not prevent a great deal of innovation within those limits. We have already mentioned how water power and the introduction of the cam and triphammer enabled mechanical production of cloth and iron, among other things. These in turn enabled expansion of production and business growth. Other important advances in the cloth industry included the spinning jenny, Arkwright's water frame and, significantly, development of the Jacquard loom in 1801 with its system of punch cards for automatic control. The punch card system was later adopted for use with computers, and served as the primary means of programming computers into the early 1980s.

The punch card system highlights another feature of the development of production technologies, namely that developments in one field often spin off into others. Medieval churches had bells, which tolled the hours and summoned the congregation to services. Bells were expensive, and therefore needed to last for a long time without cracking or bending under stress. Over time, medieval metallurgists came up with techniques for both making bronze and casting the bells themselves which made the metal very hard and able to stand up to stress. This expertise was transferred to the armaments industry, where the methods used by bell founders were adopted by the makers of cannon (bronze being the primary metal from which cannons were made until the nineteenth century). In turn, cannons required very straight and perfectly round bores in order to fire round shot accurately over distance. Metal boring methods were developed, and these in turn were adopted by the makers of steam engines, who in turn required very straight and precise cylinders in order for the machines to operate efficiently.

**Jacquard punch cards**

The Jacquard punch card is an example of a device invented to perform one function, but whose true impact was felt in another field entirely. It was designed by the French silk weaver Joseph Jacquard in Lyon as part of a means of automatically weaving patterns in silk cloth. The idea was not his alone; as far back as 1725 another silk weaver, Basile Bouchon, had experimented with a system for automated pattern weaving. Bouchon developed a moving tape perforated at intervals, the holes corresponding to the pattern desired. The needles of the loom pressed against the tape, and when an individual needle encountered a hole it passed through and then retracted, weaving on one element of the design.

Jacquard's system used cards rather than tape. The cards were thicker and heavier than later computer punch cards, as they had to withstand the pressure of the needles, but they used the same rectangular holes. The needles were held stationary against the card until they encountered a hole, at which point they passed through and inserted a thread. The card was then moved mechanically and other needles performed the same function, repeating the process until the design was complete.

Jacquard's system had several advantages over Bouchon's. The cards were more durable than tape, but most importantly the system could be entirely operated. While Bouchon's system still required an operator to move the tape, Jacquard automated the process so that the cards were moved mechanically into the desired position to create the required pattern. This meant that the process could be speeded up and production increased.

Jacquard's invention received mixed reactions. The French government of Napoleon I honoured him and gave him a pension. On the other hand, master weavers, fearing the loss of their jobs if weaving were to be automated, destroyed Jacquard's looms and threatened him with personal violence. This campaign had little effect; by 1810 there were more than ten thousand Jacquard looms operating in France, and the system was also being used in Britain and America.

(Essinger 2004)

Similarly, the systems of gears developed in medieval water mills were studied by the pioneers of mechanical clocks, which began appearing in the fourteenth century. Over time, the gears of these clocks became very precise, enabling accurate timekeeping. Clockmakers were in effect master engineers. When the first factories were built in northern England and Scotland at the end of the eighteenth century, clockmakers were hired to fashion the gears and assemblies needed to transmit power to the machines. At one point, fashionable London residents complained that it was impossible to get anyone to build a clock; all the clockmakers had gone north to build factories.

Apart from the constraints imposed by lack of power, the development of production tools and machinery went on at a steadily increasing rate, at least from the Middle Ages up until the end of the nineteenth century. Each advance not only improved efficiency, product quality or both, but it also opened the door to further advances. The wave of innovations in the nineteenth century in turn paved the way for even more advances in the twentieth (Landes 1969).

### 7.2.2 *Product technologies*

Improved production methods and tools in turn changed the nature of what could be made. Again, changes fall into two categories; improvements to existing products, and the development of entirely new products. An example of the first can be taken once again from the textiles industry. Thanks to new production methods, this became one of the most important industries of the European Middle Ages. That rise was accompanied by nearly continuous innovations and improvements in product quality. New fabrics were introduced, with silk, hitherto an expensive import, established in production in several centres in Italy and France. New dyes were imported from the Far East and later from Africa and the Americas, giving a greater range of colours. New methods of fixing dyes into cloth to ensure durability were invented. Nor did the innovation stop with the Middle Ages. More new fabrics were invented; Indian cotton was in part superseded by domestically made cotton fabrics. In Yorkshire, Titus Salt developed a process for making alpaca wool (see Case Study 8C). Then in the nineteenth century artificial fabrics like viscose, nylon and rayon were invented. More new dyes were developed, this time from chemical processes, creating the bright and gaudy (to the modern eye) colours that were very popular in Victorian times. Product innovation in fabrics has been going on for hundreds of years, and seldom has there been a generation without some new advance.

New technologies also led to new products. Here as an example we can take the bicycle. Eighteenth- and early nineteenth-century advances in metallurgy meant that more lightweight metals were available for making frames and wheels (early bicycles were made of wood, but they tended to be very unreliable). The first bicycles, such as the 'penny-farthing' model, tended to require a great deal of physical strength to propel them, but the safety bicycle, patented in 1879, used a bush roller chain to drive power from the pedals to the rear wheels and could be ridden easily by women and children. Within a few years the market for bicycles had soared, offering opportunities for both the makers of bicycles and those who made components for them, like Hans Renold (see Case Study 7C).

But the dominance of the bicycle did not last for long. Experiments with automobiles led to the first production model, the Mercedes, in the 1880s. At first these were high-luxury items. The first car makers had often started life as carriage makers, and this continued to be betrayed in their designs; some early American car makers continued to provide a whip complete with holder next to the driver's seat, on the grounds that drivers used to horse-drawn carriages would expect to find a whip close to hand. Eventually car designers such as Ford, Renault and Morris began developing more efficient cars and such anachronisms disappeared. But the car too began a long period of evolution in terms of production methods, product quality and features, a process which has not ended today (see for example Womack *et al.* (1990) on the series of innovations at Toyota).

New product technologies in the past have been enabled by two things. The first is the availability of tools or machinery, which as we saw is in turn partly dependent on power. The lack of tools or machinery is not necessarily a handicap; Richard Arkwright is one of many who, finding a particular machine was lacking, designed his own to fill the gap. Sometimes, indeed, product innovation starts with a product and then works backward to develop the technology needed to make it, as in the case of McCormick's development of a mass production system for mechanical reapers (see Case Study 7D) or Henry Ford's production plant at Highland Park. The second enabling factor is raw materials, be these naturally occurring, like silk and cotton, or man-made, such as chemical dyes or the chemicals required to make photographic film and turn it into photographs (see Carlson 1991).

In order to learn more about and take advantage of the latter, clever managers have spent much of their time looking around at the world and studying new advances in science in other areas. As we have noted elsewhere in this book, the Industrial Revolution and Scientific Revolution went almost hand in hand, feeding off each other. The eighteenth-century Enlightenment in Europe produced, among other things, an upsurge in popular interest in all forms of science. Societies like the Manchester Philosophical Society, dedicated to the study of science, included businessmen among their members; as a young mill manager, Robert Owen was a member of the Manchester Philosophical Society and read a paper before it. There were also informal groups like the 'Lunar Men', a group of businessmen and scientists from the Birmingham area including Erasmus Darwin (grandfather of the naturalist Charles Darwin), the potter Josiah Wedgwood and the engineers Matthew Boulton and James Watt (Uglow 2002). The latter three were all very successful businessmen, and it is known that Wedgwood in particular used ideas gleaned from discussions at meetings of the Lunar Men to inform his own management, in particular the development of new glazes and new designs (see Blasczyk (2000) for other examples of influences on both design and process innovation). We shall discuss the 'social context' of innovation again later in this chapter.

### 7.2.3 Communications technologies

The first – and still in some ways one of the more important – advances in communications and distribution technologies was the wheel, still in use in the same basic design for millennia, even if changed radically in terms of technology and construction. The building of efficient ships to enable transport and communication by water has also had a very powerful influence and played a major role in expanding businesses outside their home markets, first along rivers and then by sea. As noted in Chapter 3, geographical expansion and diversification has been a major strategic priority for centuries, and boats and ships enabled this to happen in the first instance.

Advances in shipbuilding technology and navigation allowed European sailors to venture outside of home waters in increasing numbers from the Middle Ages onward. Long before the first 'official' explorers such as Columbus and Cabot and Cartier sailed to North America, Portuguese and French fishermen were crossing the Atlantic to fish off the Grand Banks of Newfoundland. Nevertheless, it took a steady campaign of funding and innovation led by Prince Henry of Portugal, later nicknamed 'Henry the Navigator', before the first ships pushed down the coast of West Africa. Once this initial exploration stage was complete, advance was rapid, and within a few decades the Portuguese had pushed on to Brazil, the Cape of Good Hope and India, going on to reach Indonesia, China and Japan. Throughout this period there was a constant push for better ships, better navigational instruments and better maps. There began in Europe a steady process of innovation in what we might call 'marine technology' which led to such famous inventions as the marine chronometer (to indicate longitude), the astrolabe and the sextant, improved hulls and rudders, and eventually iron and steel hulled ships and turbines and propellers driven by steam engines. All of these increased both the speed at which ships could travel and the likelihood that they would reach their destination without sinking, and improved the carriage of both goods and information.

But the most important advance before our own day was the telegraph. Again, there were push factors: the need for faster transmission of information had long been recognised, and from the eighteenth century there had been experiments with mechanical semaphore systems. These were chains of towers arranged in line of sight, transmitting messages using flags or (at night) lanterns, each tower relaying the message until it reached its destination. Richard Edgeworth, one of the Lunar Men, had developed such a system in Britain but could not find backers, while in France a government-funded semaphore system linked Paris with several Atlantic ports by 1800.

However, semaphore was crude and slow compared to the telegraph. From the early 1840s, at first slowly and then with gathering speed, telegraph lines began to spread across Europe and America; the first submarine cable linking Britain and America was completed in 1858 and trans-Pacific cables followed. This first 'wiring of the world' was complete by the end of the nineteenth century by which time it was quite literally possible to send a telegraph message around the world. The telegraph not only enabled the rapid transmitting and receiving of information, cutting transmission times from days or weeks to minutes. It also enabled the efficient management of companies with very dispersed operations. It is hard to see how the railways could have been controlled and managed as they were without the telegraph; and railways in turn enabled a great leap forward in distribution, giving firms the ability to send goods hundreds or even thousands of miles across continents in just a few days.

Even after the invention of the telephone a few decades later, the telegraph continued to be the main means of long-distance communication; the first integrated trans-continental telephone network in America was not completed until 1915, and international telephony remained unreliable until the development of satellite networks much later in the twentieth century. Another important communications technology was wireless radio, developed by Marconi in – yet again – the late nineteenth century and slowly coming into use over the course of the twentieth.

All of these were used by businesses, and all had an impact on how businesses were managed (Vail 1918; Israel 1992). More and better information enabled better coordination of businesses over distance. It had been possible to run businesses over distance before: the Medici Bank, for example, had proved it could be done in the Middle Ages, and the Hudson's Bay Company and East India Company had done likewise in later centuries. But better communications and better information flows decreased risk and improved efficiency, and managers could see the bottom line impact of this. The rush to internationalisation and globalisation that began in the twentieth century might have happened still without the advances in communications technology of the nineteenth, but we can hypothesise that it would have happened on a much reduced scale.

---

### The birth of the computer

The computer, which has enabled the latest advances in information and communications technology, has had a somewhat troubled history. Both at the time of its invention and for long after, few believed it had much practical value. Until that perception changed, the computer was treated as a specialist device used mainly for scientific research.

Although mechanical calculating machines had been in existence, and commercially available, since the sixteenth century – the mathematician Blaise Pascal had made part of his living by making and selling such machines – it was Charles Babbage in the early nineteenth century who designed the first computer in the modern sense. A brilliant mathematician and scientist, Babbage began working in 1820 on a prototype that he called a 'difference engine' (the name stems from the fundamental principle of calculation involved, the method of finite differences). The difference engine was basically an advance, albeit a major one, on previous calculating machines, and was intended to provide rapid, accurate calculations for a variety of purposes. The prototype was completed in 1822 and was a success, leading Babbage to press on with the construction of a far larger and more complex model. However, the second engine was never completed; Babbage quarrelled with his business partner, the engineer Joseph Clements, who in retaliation destroyed all the designs and withdrew from the venture.

By this time Babbage himself was already considering a far more radical invention, which he called the 'analytical engine'. Unlike the difference engine, the primary purpose of which was to make calculations and lay them out in tables, the analytical engine was in effect a programmable calculator which could take instructions and perform a variety of different functions. Instructions and data were fed in using series of punched cards, originally developed for Jacquard power looms (see above). Calculations were then printed out, in a variety of forms. The machine was also designed to be capable of storing data in memory.

When Babbage first proposed the idea and began soliciting funds, he was astonished to find himself the object of widespread criticism and ridicule. Fellow scientists, especially his rivals, claimed the project was impossible. The government refused support. A few private individuals did provide money, but funds were never enough to see the project through. Babbage also lacked technical expertise, though he did have invaluable assistance from Ada, Countess of Lovelace, daughter of Lord Byron and a mathematician whose genius exceeded even Babbage's own. The Countess corrected a number of his calculations, and together they succeeded by 1840 in getting a part of the analytical engine built, but then funds ran out. Babbage and the Countess then devised a scheme for winning large sums of money by gambling on racehorses, using mathematical calculations of bets and odds. Inevitably, this scheme failed and this cost yet more money. Babbage died in 1871, bitter and alone.

In 1872, a committee from the Royal Astronomical Society examined his designs for the analytical engine and concluded that if the design had been carried out, the result might have been the beginning of a new epoch in mathematics, astronomy and science at large, so great were the possibilities. Nevertheless, no one could be found to provide the money to take the designs forward. In the end, it took a war for Babbage's dream to be finally realised. In the 1940s, the British scientist Alan Turing and his colleagues, engaged in developing computers for breaking German codes, realised that Babbage had already effectively invented the programmable computer and consulted his notes and designs. Colossus, the first modern programmable computer built at the code-breaking station at Bletchley

Park, relied on Babbage's principles. So did the Lyons Electronic Office (LEO), the world's first computer designed for business use and introduced by British firm J. Lyons & Co. in 1951. Yet still the age of the computer had not yet dawned. Even Thomas Watson Jr., head of IBM, famously remarked that he thought the world market for computers was probably no more than five units. It took the advent of microcomputers to truly change perceptions.

This highlights an important point about technology. The value of a computer, as Paul Strassman (1990) remarked, is precisely what it will fetch at auction. Technology is inert unless human beings engage with it and use it productively; and human beings will not do so unless they understand the technology and believe that value – to themselves and other people – will result. This is as true today as it has been for the last several thousand years.

(Kyman 1985; Urwick and Brech 1947; Strassman 1990; Simmons 1962; Caminer *et al.* 1996)

## 7.3 The role of knowledge

Thus far we have talked mainly about technology, which is important but not the whole story. Managers in the past used technology to leverage knowledge, but they also used knowledge not just to create new technology but to manage organizations more efficiently and effectively.

Managers have always been aware of the importance of knowledge. Thirty-five hundred years ago at Deir el-Medina in ancient Egypt, workers on the royal tombs in the Valley of the Kings were selected in part for their skills and mastery of their craft, be they quarrymen, plasterers or artists (see Case Study 1B). In the late twelfth century the English writer on estate management, Walter of Henley, maintained that knowledge of local market conditions was essential to good management (Oschinsky 1971); in the eighteenth century the Japanese writer Ishida Baigan believed that inner knowledge and introspection were key qualities in a merchant (Takemura 1997), and in the early nineteenth century Senior (1830) noted the importance of knowledge in directing and organising others.

But, like so much else in early management, the management of knowledge was done on an ad hoc basis. The term 'knowledge management' was not used (in fact, it did not come into common currency until the 1980s). Once again, with no body of supporting literature, we need to turn to examination of what companies did in practice to acquire and use knowledge.

### 7.3.1 First steps in knowledge management

The first and most obvious area where we find evidence of knowledge management is in skills and training. This can be found in most cultures and economic systems, which each had their own variety of 'on-the-job' training. In Japanese and Chinese firms, there is a centuries-old tradition of younger employees learning skills and knowledge from older ones. More senior employees, be they on the shop floor or in management, are seen as custodians of tradition and corporate culture, and pass these thing on to their younger counterparts.

Medieval Europe had a well-regulated system of learning through apprenticeships. Originally these were organised by craft and trade guilds, but as these declined in influence, individual companies set up their own apprenticeship programmes. The great majority of successful managers and business leaders from the thirteenth to the early twentieth centuries passed through apprenticeship programmes, where they learned not only specific skills but general knowledge about the industry and market. Nor did they always stay on with the firms where they had been apprenticed, and interestingly in England, even the sons of successful family business owners were sent out to do their apprenticeships elsewhere. Titus Salt, son of the Yorkshire cloth merchant Daniel Salt, was apprenticed with a cloth maker and then another cloth seller before returning home to become a partner in his father's firm. There were other variations on the theme, such as the schemes for 'gentleman apprentices' who were destined for careers in senior management, and who were given programmes of experience that would enable them to learn about a wide variety of subjects from technical work to accounting and top management.

Supplements to the apprentice system were not uncommon. Law students at Oxford University in the late thirteenth century, many of whom were destined for careers in estate management, also studied rudimentary management methods. Also in England, the diocese of Winchester provided training for its estate managers, and doubtless there were similar systems elsewhere in Europe. The *scuole d'abaco*, or abacus schools of late medieval Italy provided training in bookkeeping and accountancy, but also as time went by in basic management methods as well; in the nineteenth century, bookkeeping schools and commercial colleges in Britain and America offered similar programmes. In 1805, realising that a higher level of training and understanding of both administration and local culture was needed by its administrators in India, the East India Company set up a college at Hayleybury in Bedfordshire which provided training in a number of different disciplines. Hayleybury is sometimes described as the first modern business school, or school of administration.

Perhaps the most famous training programme of all was the entrance programme for the Imperial Chinese civil service. This was not a unified programme as such, as candidates for entrance could pick their own tutors. However, they knew in advance the structure of the examination, and studied along pretty much the same lines. The examination required students to be fully familiar with the works of the classical masters of Chinese philosophy and literature, especially Confucius but many others as well. This is not quite as irrelevant as it seems, for these classical philosophers had devoted much effort to ideas of political and social philosophy, ethics, interpersonal relations and other things which would have been very useful to a junior bureaucrat. The examinations were also notoriously hard, and most who took them failed. In theory, though not always in practice, this ensured that the civil service was staffed by the most intelligent and knowledgeable people.

There were also written works that could guide the manager seeking knowledge. The work of Walter of Henley on estate management has already been alluded to. In Italy there was a series of *praticas* or handbooks for merchants that provided details about overseas markets, trading conditions, exchange rates and so on. Judging from the numbers of these still in existence, they were widely read and frequently updated. From the seventeenth century onwards, hundreds of books were published in English on management in various trades and industries including agriculture, forestry, fishing, ship-building, textiles manufacturing and others. These were mostly filled with technical knowledge rather than general knowledge of management; but knowledge nonetheless, and important. But from the time of Charles Babbage's *The Economy of Machinery and Manufactures* (1835), we find increasing numbers of books on general management principles too. Even before this there had been attempts to provide compendia or collections of business knowledge, such as Jacques Savary's *Le parfait négociant* of 1675.

### 7.3.2 Knowledge-creating companies

Finally, managers and companies could create knowledge themselves, usually with the purpose of turning that knowledge into useful products and services. But some companies had an ethos of knowledge creation that went beyond commercialisation; they were willing to create knowledge for its own sake. Chain maker Hans Renold (see Case Study 7C) often published his firm's innovations in scientific papers which he made available to all, as did the turbine maker and engineer Charles Parsons. Scientific instrument maker Horace Darwin believed in sharing knowledge with competing firms (see box).

Few firms went quite as far in this respect as Carl Zeiss Jena, the German optical equipment maker (see Case Study 4D). Under its second leader, the physicist Ernst Abbé, Carl Zeiss Jena developed a culture of knowledge creation. Its scientists were given leave to create and generate knowledge on any subject they believed in. Many also held teaching posts at the University of Jena and were part of the spectacular outpouring of research from Jena in the years before the First World War. Along the way, they also developed some phenomenally successful commercial products, but it is hard to escape the impression that Carl Zeiss Jena was primarily a knowledge-creating firm with its physical products emerging out of that knowledge-creation process.

A slightly different case is Thomas Edison, who commercialised many of his one thousand-plus patents, not always with particular success. But Edison kept his business and scientific interests separate. The companies he set up to exploit inventions such as the electric light bulb did not by and large do research; they were purely commercial ventures. Instead, the 'Wizard of Menlo Park', as Edison was known to the American press, used the profits derived from earlier inventions to fund further research which he carried out in his private laboratories.

---

### Horace Darwin

Horace Darwin was the son of naturalist Charles Darwin and great-grandson of Erasmus Darwin, one of the Lunar Men. After taking a degree from Trinity College, Cambridge he served an apprenticeship with an engineering firm. In 1881 he helped found the Cambridge Scientific Instrument Company, becoming its chairman in 1885. Darwin was the firm's principal designer. The most important factor in the firm's success was the excellence of its design. By the mid-1880s the firm was building instruments for laboratories and organisations all over the UK and beginning to take orders from abroad. '"Go and talk to Horace Darwin" was the advice given to anyone who needed some delicate new scientific instrument' (Chancellor 1973: 209).

But Darwin also employed a highly sophisticated form of relational marketing, using his own and his family's scientific contacts to attract the attention of likely buyers. This was a time and a place when direct advertising was not possible; instead, Darwin made sure his firm's name was known in the market through personal contact and word of mouth. The combination of awareness and reputation for quality meant that Cambridge Scientific Instrument Company was both the best and most recognised competitor in a crowded field.

Darwin was also the founder of the Cambridge 'cluster' of science-related industries. He believed in collaboration rather than competition, and saw the growth of rival firms as being important in both growing the market and generating new knowledge. Many of his foremen and assistants such as W.T. Pye, Robert Whipple and Henry Tinsley went to other established firms or to establish their own businesses but continued to work with Darwin on collaborative projects.

(Chancellor 1973; Gee 1986)

---

Knowledge could also become a product in its own right, as was discovered by Julius Reuter, founder of the eponymous news agency (see Case Study 7A). But, long before any of the examples noted above, another entrepreneur had discovered how to use knowledge to innovate in terms of both product and process, creating both a successful business and making certain of his own place in history.

William Caxton was born in Kent some time in the 1420s. At age sixteen he began an apprenticeship with a cloth merchant in London, and in 1446 he moved to Bruges in Flanders (modern Belgium), one of the leading centres of woollen cloth manufacturing in Europe. Here he established a business dealing in wool and cloth, and became very successful, eventually rising to become leader of the English merchant community in Bruges. He also became friendly with Duchess Marguerite of Burgundy, herself an Englishwoman, who encouraged Caxton's literary interests and invited him to translate a number of French, Dutch and Latin works into English. By the 1460s, as well as a successful merchant, Caxton was also an accomplished editor and translator.

However, it was a new technology, the printing press, that first sparked his imagination. Sometime in the early 1470s he travelled to the German city of Köln, one of the centres of printing (Gutenberg in the 1450s had worked in the city of Mainz, and other printers had since established businesses all through the Rhineland). Returning to Bruges, he set up a partnership with the Flemish artist Colard Mansion and together they produced the first book printed in English, *The Recuyell of the Histories of Troye*, a romance which he himself had earlier translated into English from French.

In about 1478 Caxton returned to England and established the country's first printing press at Westminster, near London. It is believed that the first book he published was Chaucer's *Canterbury Tales*, followed by other popular works such as Thomas Malory's *Morte d'Arthur*. But Caxton also published works of theology and philosophy, in the process making these works more accessible to a wider audience who perhaps could not have afforded the scarce hand-copied editions which were the only alternative before the printing press arrived. Some thought Caxton was vulgarising culture and ideas by putting them in the hands of the masses, but Caxton was not deterred. He printed more than a hundred books before his death in 1492, and others carried on the work of his firm after him. Still others, former employees, were encouraged to set up their own presses and by early in the following century printing was a major industry in and around London (Deacon 1976; Painter 1976).

Caxton had seen not only that knowledge could lead to the creation of entire businesses, but also that knowledge itself was a commodity that, in the right package, could be bought and sold. His was, in every sense, a knowledge-creating company, five hundred years before the term was conceived and popularised by Nonaka and Takeuchi (1995). Examples like this show that at least some managers were aware of the value and importance of knowledge, even if as yet there was no systematic approach to the subject.

## 7.4 Innovation

By now we have seen a number of examples of innovation at various times and places. The case studies accompanying this chapter show more examples, in process (Richard Arkwright), product (Hans Renold) or both (Cyrus

McCormick, Julius Reuter). Yet another example that is worth studying is that of the Cistercian monastic order (Case Study 2B), which innovated both in technology and in organisation. We know that innovation, and innovative organisations, have been around for a long time.

The sources of innovation are varied. Personal inspiration and imagination were of course important. Some organisations went out of their way to acquire knowledge and to get close to sources of further knowledge. But we have also seen how at some times and places innovation has come about as a result of push factors from outside. The need for an innovation sometime results in the innovation itself, as innovative people identify the need and take steps to meet it.

### 7.4.1 Forces for innovation

Dobbin (2004) has discussed the way that social pressures act to create pressure for innovation. Nowhere is this more evident than in late nineteenth-century Japan. Following the establishment of the Tokugawa Shogunate in the late sixteenth century, Japan had isolated itself from the outside world and some technologies, particularly those of foreign introduction such as firearms, were deliberately abandoned. That does not mean that Japan abandoned technological process entirely, but in certain areas the country definitely lagged behind the West (Morris-Suzuki 1994).

Increasing pressure from the outside world and the fear that Japan might be occupied or colonised by Western powers led Japan to a radical shift in views. Following the end of the shogunate in 1867, the Meiji Emperor and his advisers encouraged innovation in every field, from science and technology to education, business and military organisation. The education pioneer Yukichi Fukuzawa founded the first universities in Japan, while old Japanese firms like Mitsui and Sumitomo undertook radical modernisation and reorganisation programmes and new firms like Mitsubishi emerged on the scene, modelled on the West. But, despite prevailing views in the West, there was not the mere slavish copying of Western models. The Japanese leaders and their advisers deliberately chose those elements of Western practice that would work and grafted them onto Japanese culture.

In neighbouring China there was a similar movement, but this failed. Its leaders, including the mandarin Li Hongzhang (Case Study 9E), did not have the support and backing of the rest of the establishment, including the Empress Cixi. In Japan, the modernisation movement succeeded because the establishment encouraged and supported innovation in all forms.

What this tells us about innovation is that it will only succeed if it has support. We have seen how Charles Babbage failed to develop his analytical engine because no one believed that it was either possible or had any practical value. Caxton's printing press succeeded, however, because there was enough popular demand for his products to overcome resistance from conservatives worried about the harm it might do to the social order.

As Dobbin (2004) says, successful innovation often depends on power: not the power of muscles or water mills or steam engines, but political and social power to drive it forward and make certain it takes root. In a fascinating article, Schroeder and Borgerson (2002) compare the relative role played by patronage in the artistic world of the Italian Renaissance and the modern development of information technology. Their primary point is that the control of information and communications technology allows people to control their own image in the same way that patrons of Renaissance artists were able to dictate how they themselves were portrayed and the image they presented to the outside world. But what also emerges is the importance of patronage itself for the artist/innovator. Those who attract the attentions of powerful patrons get commissions. In just the same way, in many software companies development teams vie for attention and compete to get approval for their project to be taken forward to the market.

As well as individual patronage, society also exerts its own pressure for innovation. The fifteenth- and sixteenth-century expansion by the European powers overseas was driven by a mixture of desires that were widespread among the ruling elites, if not all of society: the conversion of people of other faiths to Christianity, the extension of national interests and the desire for wealth. The Spanish conquistador Bernal Diaz summed it up efficiently when he describes the Spanish invasion of Mexico: 'We came to serve God and Spain, and to grow rich.' In order to do this, better ships and better navigational instruments were needed, and industries developed around innovators who could meet these needs.

That these innovations served a deplorable purpose, the conquest and subjugation of large parts of the globe and the beginnings of the colonial period, should not be forgotten. Nor should it be forgotten that there have been other innovations, such as the development of Zyklon-B and the pioneering genetic experiments of Dr Joseph Mengele, that have been undertaken for terrible reasons. Not all innovation is morally good, and even those innovations which are intended as a force for good can have terrible consequences.

### 7.4.2 Barriers to innovation

That conclusion too is nothing new. There have always been those who, like those English who opposed the printing press or the master weavers who smashed Jacquard looms, see innovation as a threat to life, liberty or society, and sometimes they are right.

Social attitudes to innovation tend to fluctuate, usually depending on what else is going on in society. Max Weber's *The Protestant Ethic and the Spirit of Capitalism* (1905) depicted the Catholic Middle Ages as a time of intellectual stagnation and equated the coming of Protestantism with the dawn of a new period of intellectual inquiry. In fact, it is hard to make this equation work. The Catholic Middle Ages saw a great leap forward in technology, and Catholic countries, especially France, continued to see innovations in both business and society, even if these were sometimes hotly opposed by conservatives. At the same time some Protestant societies, especially in Germany, remained intensely conservative and backward.

Indeed, there is no real pattern, in Europe or elsewhere. In Japan, after a lengthy period of technological progress, the Tokugawa shoguns began a policy of discouraging progress, if not actually forbidding it. The Ming dynasty, one of the most cultured dynasties to rule China, turned its back on many forms of technology, particularly its famous navy (see Case Study 7E), while their successors the Qing, Manchu 'barbarians' from outside, encouraged innovation in some areas even if they did not rebuild the navy (for more on Chinese technology generally see Needham (1954–95 *passim*)).

Sometimes innovation is deliberately opposed for the harm it will do. Sometimes it is simply not recognised for what it is. Smith and Alexander (1988) describe the development of a prototype personal computer at Xerox which, thanks largely to managerial incompetence, never saw the light of day. Railways almost never happened thanks to widespread ignorance and belief that they were dangerous; one eminent physician announced that anyone riding in a railway carriage travelling at thirty miles an hour would surely be killed, the air sucked from their lungs by the velocity of their travel. At the first demonstration of George Stephenson's prototype locomotive the *Rocket*, the British MP William Huskisson slipped and fell under the wheels, losing a leg and dying soon after. It took some intensive public relations work to assure the public that railway travel was not likely to prove fatal in every instance.

The conclusion must be that not all innovations are accepted at once, and many are not accepted at all. Those which have the best chance of seeing the light of day are those with an immediate and demonstrable social function over and beyond making money for the innovator, and those that are believed in and supported rather than treated with suspicion. Having powerful backers and supporters, either within the organisation or outside it, is certainly valuable. But also, there are certain times and places where innovations will be more socially acceptable than others. We have only to look at varying attitudes around the world to stem cell research to see this in our own time.

---

### The megatechnic wasteland

Typical of how views on innovation and technology could change is the American sociologist Lewis Mumford, who went from being an active supporter of technological progress to a strong opponent. In the 1920s and 1930s Mumford's views were strongly influenced by his socialist beliefs and displayed a strong leaning towards utopianism. The book that made his international reputation, *Technics and Civilization* (1934) classifies the history of technology into three periods, the eotechnic, the paleotechnic and the neotechnic. The eotechnic age was the period before the Industrial Revolution – most of human history, in fact – when technology was based on 'natural' and renewable power sources such as wind, water and muscle. Then came the paleotechnic phase of industrialisation founded on the exploitation of fossil fuels and, says Mumford, a consequent exploitation of the working classes by those who had control of technology and so could concentrate power into their own hands. The third phase, the neotechnic, was that which he felt civilisation was about to enter into; new scientific developments and above all common access to electrical power would democratise power and allow the masses to participate in its use and distribution.

In *The Myth of the Machine* (1967), Mumford describes instead a dystopian nightmare, a 'megatechnic wasteland' in which society is dominated by bureaucracy and control of technology remains centred in the hands of a few. At the centre of the wasteland, he says, is 'Organization Man – he who stands at once as the creator and creature, the originator and the ultimate victim, of the megamachine' (Mumford 1967, vol 1: 276). The ideal 'organization man', by which Mumford means administrators and managers, is in fact a machine, a robot creature whose only function is to achieve efficiency and productivity; all human feeling, all sensibilities, all love of art and of one's fellow creatures, have been stamped out. Organisation man, says Mumford, gave us the gas chamber and atrocities in Vietnam; he cites Adolf Eichmann as an exemplar of the type.

This sort of society, says Mumford, has only two possible ends. On the one hand, organisation man may triumph and the world may indeed become a terrible dystopia. But organisation man faces a threat, one of his own creation: the rapid rise of mass communications, allowing the instantaneous transmission of large volumes of information and knowledge from one place to another. Mumford does not believe that the iron hierarchies built by organisation man will be able to cope with this onslaught of information; he believes they will lapse into a kind of 'electronic entropy' and will crumble and fall, leaving society with little or no structure of any kind. The end of the information revolution will be not utopia, but the annihilation of culture.

Mumford's brutal choice, between iron bureaucracy on the one hand and information overload followed by cultural obliteration on the other, has serious implications. The social and, indeed, political dangers in an age of globalisation are well recognised; less so, it seems, are the implications of the free flow of information brought about by the Internet and wireless communication. Finding a balance between these two alternatives, between excessive rationalism and information-based chaos, may be one of the great management challenges of the coming century.

## 7.5 Themes and influences

From this discussion, several important themes present themselves. Readers will doubtless think of others, but three that appear to have particular resonance for our own time are the appearance of new sources of knowledge, the increasing pace of innovation, which develops over time a kind of snowball effect, and the problem of forgetting the past and then re-inventing the wheel.

### 7.5.1 New sources of knowledge

Throughout the history of civilisation there has been a steady growth in the amount of knowledge we have available, and an increase too in the sources of that knowledge. In classical times, the bulk of learning was experiential. There were books, but their numbers were comparatively small. A large library, in China or India or Imperial Rome or Europe in the Middle Ages, was one with several thousand volumes or scrolls; a few hundred or a few dozen was nearer the mark. That meant that a scholar setting out to make himself or herself master of all available knowledge on a given subject could usually do so quite easily. After that, it was up to them to create new knowledge themselves, through thought or action.

The advent of printing produced, after an interval in which the process was improved and the costs of both printing and paper were brought down to acceptable levels, an increase in the amount of knowledge in circulation. More people wrote more books and pamphlets, while older works often continued to stay in circulation. New communications media, the telegraph, telephone, radio, television and Internet, have added still further. Meanwhile we have developed tools, especially the computer, which can process and digest large quantities of information, especially numerical data, and present it to us in summary form.

Science has also opened up new realms of knowledge. The natural sciences have come a long way from the crude observations of Aristotle and the only slightly more sophisticated musings on the natural world by Mencius and Xunzi. We now know much more about how things work, including our own bodies and brains, and including the workings of organisations, the behaviour of consumers, the nature of financial markets and all those things that make up the art or science – call it what you will – of management.

All of this has both eased and complicated the task of management. In days when stocks of knowledge were limited and new discoveries were comparatively infrequent, it was relatively easy to keep up with new developments. Even in the late eighteenth century the Lunar Men and others like them could keep in touch with new developments through meetings, discussions and journals. Today, that is pretty much impossible. Ironically, the flood of new knowledge has created a degree of uncertainty that once was lacking. In our attempts to distinguish signals from noise, and to focus on the most important things we need to know, we run the constant risk of overlooking something vital; something that our competitors may find and use against us. Instead of a level playing field, the new realm of knowledge has become a complex place with many shadows and dark corners.

### 7.5.2  *The pace of innovation: the snowball effect*

The growth in the quantity of knowledge has had a corollary effect on the growth of the pace of innovation. Society, and business, produce innovations at a far greater rate than they used to, and this adds yet another complication for the manager.

We have a tendency to become dazzled by the pace of innovation around us today. We should not forget that the innovations of the nineteenth century were equally dazzling to those who lived at the time. And also, consider how many of the technologies and devices we rely on today were actually invented then: the computer, the automobile, the airplane, the internal combustion engine, electricity, the light bulb, the telephone, radio and wireless communication. Very few of these were in common use by the end of the nineteenth century, and many were not fully developed until well into the twentieth century. This should remind us that it is one thing to invent something new: it is another to see that innovation fully established. Many successful innovations take years to work through and become widely accepted.

### 7.5.3  *Forgetting the past*

A complaint sometimes heard from business historians is that it is on the whole easier to learn more about a company and its management in the eighteenth and nineteenth centuries than about one in the early twenty-first century. The reason is that in the former cases, records and correspondence were kept on paper, and have often been preserved. In the latter case, records and correspondence use electronic media, and are usually wiped – often as a matter of deliberate policy – after a very short period of time.

It is in fact no harder to preserve records on electronic media than on paper. Instead, a culture has grown up which disregards the value of records and correspondence because they are so easily created, and easily disposed of. People were more likely to keep records which it had taken them hours to create, whereas a note dashed off by e-mail will be deleted without thought.

One of the results is that the tendency to forget the past, always a problem for managers, has been exacerbated. But the problem itself is not new, merely the scale of it. Because businesses and managers spend so much time trying to figure out what is going to happen in the future, there is a natural tendency for the past to slip out of sight. One of the noticeable differences between successful managers and those who lag behind – and this trend again can be identified as far back as the Middle Ages – is that the former group remember what has happened. They learn from past successes, and they learn from mistakes. In the twentieth century, Japanese and Indian businesses in particular have continued to have a tradition of learning from the past, but Western businesses – in part perhaps because of the problem of information overload – have lost some of the art of doing so. As a result, there has been a tendency to re-invent the wheel.

The Internet retailers of the late 1990s faced many of the same problems of marketing reach and distribution as the early catalogue retailers, Montgomery Ward and Sears. It seems reasonable to assume that had the Internet retailers studied the example of the latter, they would have noticed the absolute importance of solving distribution problems and ensuring that the marketing promise was fulfilled. In fact, this is precisely the area where many fell down; the handing over of products to customers after purchase, which was supposed to be easy and convenient, turned out to be the opposite. A good many companies failed in part because of this, and it took other Internet retailers several years to figure out how to solve the problem. Ironically, it was traditional retailers like Tesco, which already had their own distribution systems and knew how to manage distribution networks, who solved the problem first.

## 7.6 Questions and discussion: creating opportunities, creating value

In his book *The Innovator's Dilemma*, Christensen (1997) distinguished between 'sustaining technologies', which improve the performance of existing products, and 'disruptive technologies', which transform markets and can render existing products obsolete. Disruptive technologies actually appear to offer lower product performance: for example, small cheap motorcycles, when first introduced, had worse performance than high-powered large ones. Yet they nonetheless found a market which rapidly ate into the share of the more conventional producers. Disruptive technologies transform markets in ways that are hard to understand and harder to predict.

Companies which begin as innovators, says Christensen, are tempted to pursue the path of their original innovation rather than looking ahead towards the next revolutionary or disruptive technology. In doing so, they remain innovative; but they do so along the wrong lines. Christensen's solution is that managers should learn to harness the forces of disruptive technology.

We have seen a number of disruptive technologies in the past, including gunpowder, printing, the factory system, the telegraph and the automobile. Each has offered immense business opportunities for the companies prepared to take advantage of them. But what is not at all clear is whether the companies that did not do so necessarily prospered as a result. It took a very long time for some of these technologies to become established. Nor did they necessarily render existing technologies obsolete. True, firearms did replace the longbow and crossbow over a period of about a hundred and fifty years, and printing did eventually render hand-copying obsolete. But not all production in the nineteenth century was factory production: craft production retained a position. The telegraph did not displace the postal system, it became instead a complementary medium of communication. The most disruptive of all, the automobile, did threaten the bicycle with extinction; but manufacturers shrewdly repositioned bicycles as a cheap leisure product, and their popularity continued, and continues, around the world.

Disruptive technologies are more exciting, more sexy: they grab the headlines, and win prizes and rewards for their inventors. But the evidence of the past suggests that 'sustaining technologies' may continue to have a place.

What makes the difference between success and failure in each case? Here we probably need to turn away from technology and look at the role of knowledge. Here, it would seem, is the true battleground. The company that can best manage knowledge is the one that, as Arie de Geus (1988) said, is the one with the best chance of achieving competitive advantage over the long run. Knowledge alone can help us distinguish between a disruptive strategy and a sustaining one, and knowledge alone can help us decide which course to adopt in response to the appearance of the former.

Companies that have succeeded in the past are usually those that have put a premium on knowledge, on its acquisition and dissemination within the organisation, and its use. The Medici Bank was not more than ordinarily innovative; it invented no new business models or new products. But it rose to dominate the European banking and trading system in part thanks to a formidable bank of accumulated knowledge on the part of its owners and managers. The same can be said of the private banker Thomas Coutts & Co., which tended to steer clear of radical innovation but was very much committed to knowledge of its markets and its customers.

Is being knowledgeable more important than being innovative? The reverse of the coin of course is that knowledge on its own, like technology on its own, has little value. It is only when knowledge is put to use that it becomes valuable, and helps to create value. One of the tasks of the manager, then, would appear to be to make this happen, to make certain that neither knowledge nor technology sit inert, but are both put to work in order to yield value. That, in the end, may be more important than chasing disruptive technologies.

---

### Takeaway exercise

Consider your own organisation or one you have worked for in the past and know well. It will be difficult to define what and how much you know about that organisation, so instead try asking yourself this question: what *don't* you know about it? And when you have made a list of things you don't know, ask a further question: *why* don't you know these things? What is it that has created these gaps in your knowledge? Is it possible that you can now learn them and close the gaps? And if so, what benefit will this bring you, and the business? Then try learning some of them, and see what happens.

The point here is not just to increase your learning. It is to identify the problems and barriers that may be preventing you from learning. Of course, not everyone can know everything, and in some cases there are sound commercial and regulatory reasons for keeping things confidential. But beyond those constraints, it should always be possible to know more.

## Case Study 7A

### *Reuter's*

Reuter's News Agency was founded by Julius Reuter on 10 October 1851, in a small office in London's Royal Exchange. Reuter transformed the concept of the news agency by taking advantage of a new communications technology, the telegraph. The first telegraph patents were taken out in Britain and the USA in 1837, and Morse patented his famous telegraph code for sending messages in 1840. But governments in both countries failed to see the importance of the telegraph: the US government finally agreed to construct the first line in 1843, and the first British line followed in 1844. Even these experiments failed to convince the respective governments, and it was left to the private sector to appreciate and adopt the new technology.

Initial progress was very slow. In 1846 there were still only sixty kilometres of telegraph line in America and perhaps half as much in Britain. But by 1850, as investment money came in and new telegraph companies were founded, there were 20,000 kilometres in the USA and Europe, and by 1852 there were nearly 50,000 kilometres. The first telegraph across the English Channel was laid in 1851; the first trans-Atlantic cable was laid in 1858.

The telegraph revolutionised communications. Right from the beginning, the telegraph's inventors recognised its potential to link nations and cultures by common channels of communication and transmission of information. As Samuel Morse said during trials of an early prototype, 'If it will go ten miles without stopping, I can make it go around the globe.'[1]

The importance of information and knowledge was well understood in the nineteenth century. Big companies maintained their own intelligence-gathering systems that collected information on prices in various markets and on the activities of competitors. In the early nineteenth century the London banker N.M. Rothschild set up a system for transmitting information by carrier pigeon from the Continent to London. It was this system which allowed him advance news of the British victory at Waterloo in 1815, before the rest of the market. Fearing a British defeat, the London stock market had begun to slide; Rothschild kept the information to himself and bought shares at the bottom of the market, making a substantial profit.

However, information systems of this type were expensive, and only big firms with deep pockets could afford to set them up. For smaller firms, the only option was to buy information from news agencies. Most major cities in Europe had at least one of these agencies, who digested information from local newspapers and news sheets and sold it on a subscription basis to clients in other cities. The information had to be transmitted in writing using the post, and was often days out of date by the time it arrived. Apart from the Rothschild carrier pigeons, it had taken four days for the news of Waterloo to reach London. The information asymmetries were huge, and large firms enjoyed great advantages. The telegraph, which could transmit information quickly and cheaply, threatened to end that advantage, or at least greatly reduce it.

One of the first to glimpse the potential of the new medium was the French journalist Charles Havas, who owned a small news agency in Paris. In the late 1840s Havas tried selling news over the telegraph on an experimental basis. The results were very mixed. The telegraph network was still incomplete, and Havas also faced hostility from the telegraph operating companies, who had ambitions to move into news-gathering themselves. However, Havas's experiments were then taken up by one of his employees, Julius Reuter.

Born in 1816 in the German city of Cassel, Reuter had had a somewhat chequered career. Most recently he had been a bookseller in Berlin, but in 1848 his activities as a political pamphleteer led to his exile from Prussia. He settled in Paris, where he first worked as a translator for Havas. He then founded a small newspaper of his own, which quickly failed. But like Havas, he understood the potential of the telegraph, and in 1849 he moved to Aachen where he founded a news agency and also offered contract courier services to fill in the gaps in the telegraph network. Initially he worked in partnership with several telegraph companies, who themselves fed him the information he asked for; Reuter merely packaged and transmitted the information to his clients. But in 1850 the companies informed Reuter they had no further need for his agency's services: they intended to go into the news-gathering and distribution system themselves.

The telegraph companies were, in effect, technology companies and they had no experience of gathering or managing news. Reuter knew he could do the job better and more efficiently. In 1851 he moved to London, the financial capital of Europe, and set up an agency selling financial information and data. Now, instead of relying on the telegraph companies for information, he developed his own network of correspondents in other European centres. The telegraph companies might not be willing to supply information themselves, but they could not prevent others from using the network to transmit information to London. Prices from the Paris Bourse and other European stock exchanges were sent by telegraph to London and sold to client subscribers, while at the same time information from London was transmitted back to the Continent and sold to clients there. The information, if not quite real time, was at least available within 24 hours, and was also comparatively cheap.

Something like a level playing field was now emerging in financial information. More people had access to more information at the same time, and decisions could be made on a more equitable basis. A further consequence was that more investors could be made aware of opportunities in other countries, and more companies could seek investment from overseas. Cross-border investment had of course been happening for a long time, through the auspices of big international bankers like the Rothschilds, but in these cases the banks perforce acted as gatekeepers, supplying information and recommending and making investments that often suited them rather better than their clients. Now, with more information available, investors could make their own decisions and transmit instructions directly to agents in other cities. One unexpected consequence of the activities of Reuter's and other agencies like it was that international capital flows and cross-border investment began to increase sharply.

Powerful though the impact of Reuter's agency was on financial markets, it was his general news-gathering that perhaps had the greatest financial, political and social consequences. Reuter had been right in guessing that the telegraph companies could not handle news-gathering, and the information they offered for sale to newspapers was often late or incorrect. Nevertheless, he had a difficult time persuading newspaper editors that he could offer a better product. *The Times* in particular, which had its own network of correspondents, refused to buy from Reuter and most other newspapers followed its example. Finally in 1858 he struck deals with a couple of small newspapers, including the *Manchester Guardian* and the *Morning Advertiser*.

Within a few months, Reuter had shown what he could do. On 7 February 1859 he achieved a combination of journalistic scoop and technological coup by transmitting from Paris the text of a vitally important speech by Emperor Napoleon III of France, while the speech itself was actually being delivered. Reuter's agents had first persuaded the Imperial Secretariat to let them have a copy of the speech under embargo, and had then booked the Paris–London telegraph line in advance for the hour the speech was to be given. The speech, made at noon in Paris, was printed in the London evening papers.

When war broke out between France and Austria later that year, Reuter's correspondents were on the battlefield. Five years earlier, news from the front during the Crimean War had taken days or even weeks to reach London. Now, readers of the London papers – and by now even *The Times* was buying from Reuter – could read details of the battles of Magenta and Solferino within twenty-four hours of their happening. The effect was electrifying: as CNN was to do during the Gulf War of 1990–91 with its images from the battlefields of Iraq, Reuter was bringing the news into people's homes as it was actually happening. The laying of the submarine cable connecting Europe with North America enabled further scoops; Reuter's reported the events of the American Civil War (1861–65) to European audiences, and it was through Reuter's that Europeans first learned of the assassination of US President Abraham Lincoln in 1865.

Again as with CNN, it was not only the news itself that made an impact. There was also a fascination with how it was transmitted. Reuter himself capitalised on this, referring to his product as 'Electric News' and offering discounts to newspapers if they would print credit lines establishing that articles had come from his agencies. In this way Reuter managed to brand the news he sold, and made his company's name synonymous with news-gathering. Rivals, especially the American Associated Press (AP) and United Press International (UPI), would later displace Reuters as the largest news agency in the world, but by then the recipe had been tried and proven.

There are obvious comparisons to be made between Reuters and modern Internet-based businesses. Reuter showed that technology needs both vision and competence to make it work effectively and profitably. The telegraph companies, who lacked both, failed to make an impact in news-gathering and ultimately surrendered the European market to Reuter. But probably more important in the long term are the implications for organisations. Flying in the face of the trends of his own time, Reuter showed that it was possible to create and manage a highly dispersed and very diverse organisation by using technology links to maintain communications. Particularly when knowledge is a company's principal product, there is no advantage to concentration; instead, staff need to be located where they can work most effectively. His correspondents in the field worked on their own, linked to the rest of the organisation by communications technology in a fashion very similar to modern virtual organisations.

Reuter was neither a journalist nor a technologist. Instead, he was what one historian has described as a 'news entrepreneur', in the same tradition as modern media groups like Pearson and News International (although the interests of these latter now go far beyond news). He knew enough about both information and technology to see how the link between them could be made and exploited, and he succeeded because he knew how to manage the interface between, on the one hand, the intangible but highly valuable commodity he was gathering and selling, and on the other hand, the technology he relied upon to make his system work. One contemporary newspaper described him as 'not only the man of the time, but the master of Time'.

## Analysis

Some of the questions you might want to consider in connection with this case include:

- What is the relationship between knowledge and technology?
- Why did the telegraph companies, despite their control over the communications channels, fail in their attempt to monopolise news distribution?
- Is it valid to draw parallels between the telegraph age and the Internet age? Can other parallels beyond those mentioned in the case also be drawn?
- What are the main qualities that allowed Reuter to succeed as an entrepreneur?

## Sources

Read, Donald (1992) *The Power of News: The History of Reuters, 1849–1989*, Oxford: Oxford University Press.

Read, Donald (1994) 'Reuters: News Agency of the British Empire', *Contemporary British History* 8 (2): 195–214.

## Case Study 7B

### *Richard Arkwright*

The Industrial Revolution has its origins in northern England and southern Scotland during the final decades of the eighteenth century. One of the most important early developments was the factory system, which is generally credited to Richard Arkwright. The first factory in the modern sense was his cotton mill at Cromford in Derbyshire, developed over the course of several years from 1771–75. By the end of the century the factory system was in use in dozens of locations in Britain and had spread to the United States and continental Europe. The factory system played a key role in the rapid industrialisation of the Western world in the century that followed.

Arkwright was born in the town of Preston in Lancashire in 1732, the thirteenth and youngest child of a tailor. He received a rudimentary education at home, and was then apprenticed to a barber. In 1750 he opened his own barbershop and also branched out into wig-making, and by 1762 had acquired a tavern. It is difficult to know when or how he first became interested in cotton-spinning machinery, but he was certainly in the right place at the right time. The spinning of cotton yarn by hand was slow, and the limited production capacity of hand-spinning enterprises meant that cotton cloth was scarce and therefore expensive. The eighteenth century in Britain was a time of great popular interest in science and mechanics, and there had been experiments with cotton-spinning machines from the 1740s onward.

In 1767 Arkwright teamed up with John Kay, a clockmaker who already had several patents to his name. According to the standard accounts, Arkwright had an idea for a spinning frame, a powered machine which would spin cotton using a system of rollers. Lacking the technical expertise to put the idea into execution, he called on Kay's skills to build the first working models. However, Kay had also worked with the inventor Thomas Highs, who later claimed that Kay and Arkwright had stolen his own idea for a spinning frame. Accusations of theft of intellectual property dogged Arkwright for the rest of his career.

Regardless of whether the original idea was Arkwright's, there can be no doubt that he exploited it with great ability. In 1768 he moved to Nottingham, then a centre of cotton manufacturing, and with two partners, David Thornley and John Smalley, set up a horse-powered mill for spinning cotton yarn. The experiment worked, but more capital and a better source of power were needed for full commercial exploitation. With two new partners, Samuel Need and Jedediah Strutt, Arkwright built a second mill at Cromford in Derbyshire, using water power (his spinning frame is thus more usually known as the 'water frame'). The streams around Cromford were warmed by geothermal activity and thus did not freeze in winter, assuring a supply of power the year round.

The new mill was a success, and Need and Strutt began buying the yarn it produced for their own hosiery manufacturing businesses. The next obstacle to full commercial exploitation was regulatory. Arkwright's raw material, Indian cotton, was subject to a high import tariff, a protectionist measure which had been enacted for the benefit of the Lancashire woollen industry. In 1774, lobbying by Arkwright and his partners succeeded in gaining an exemption from the tariff for raw cotton to be used for manufacturing in England. Cotton imports then rose dramatically, from 4.7 million pounds (in weight) in 1771 to 56 million pounds by 1800.

Over the course of the period 1771–75 Arkwright continuously improved and expanded his mill at Cromford. His aim was to develop a single system which would not only spin cotton yarn but also handle all the preparatory processes including carding, drawing and roving, making raw cotton ready for spinning. No contemporary accounts survive which tell exactly how Arkwright developed these processes, but it seems clear that, although he used individual pieces of technology invented by others along with ones he invented himself, the concept of the continuous process was his alone. The actual work of building and testing the new machines was difficult; capital was not in short supply, but skilled workmen were. Only clockmakers had the necessary skills and tools to create the fine precision machinery Arkwright needed, and these were recruited wherever they could be found (some years later, during the great boom in factory construction, Londoners found that there were almost no clockmakers left in the capital; all had gone north to build factories). Direct supervision of the designs and building process was undertaken by Arkwright himself, who seems to have carried most of the designs in his head.

In 1775 Arkwright patented his new manufacturing process. At Cromford, he now had a true factory in the modern sense of the term;[2] a single machine, capable of continuous production through multiple stages, driven by a permanent supply of power and capable of being worked in shifts. Its commercial potential was enormous, far beyond the capabilities of one man, or even a small group, to exploit. Arkwright recognised this, and as well as building new factories of his own, he sold licences to other groups of capitalists who wished to build factories using his design. Often he also invested sums of his own in these licensed factories, or mills. By 1780, as many as fifteen Arkwright-patent mills were operating, either directly owned or under licence; Arkwright himself reckoned they employed as many as five thousand people.

In fact, the Arkwright patent on the spinning process was indefensible in both theory and practice. Although the design for the overall process was

Arkwright's own, many of its components were not; he had borrowed freely from other engineers and inventors during the design process. Further, although some entrepreneurs bought licences from him, others simply pirated the design and set up mills without licenses. In 1781 Arkwright took nine of these pirate mill-owners to court, but lost the case on the grounds of lack of specificity in the patent, which was declared null and void.

Arkwright seems to have been unperturbed by this development. Nor did the Chorley riots of 1779, when rioting workers sacked and burned one of his newly built mills in Lancashire, cause him more than a momentary setback. He was already a very rich man, with plenty of capital to enable further expansion. He was also ahead of his rivals in terms of technological development. The six years from 1775–81 had allowed him to build up a priceless competitive advantage.

Now, rather than selling licences, he sold water frames and other machinery to those who did not wish to build their own; by 1794 his sales of original equipment alone had amounted to £60,000 (Fitton 1989: 91). Of his original partners, Samuel Need died in 1781 and the partnership with Strutt came to an end, but Arkwright created many further partnerships. His son had by now joined the business and was involved in many new ventures. Sometimes Arkwright simply invested in ventures without requiring control, as when he financed Samuel Oldknow's first mill, or advised David Dale on the establishment of the mills at New Lanark (later controlled by Robert Owen). More often, though, he took a large share of equity and control. His partnerships in these instances were carefully chosen. For instance, for a new mill in Manchester in 1786 he took into partnership two local cotton merchants, William Brocklehurst and John Whittenbury. These men were also involved in a variety of further partnerships with other merchants and businessmen. By bringing them into the business, Arkwright not only secured their capital but tapped into their business networks in Manchester.

As well as partnerships with other merchants, Arkwright developed a core of highly skilled senior managerial and technical staff. These were often moved around from one Arkwright concern to another, especially when new mills were planned. They were also in great demand elsewhere. The most famous example of an ex-Arkwright man going onto greater things is Thomas Marshall, a former mill superintendent who introduced Arkwright's methods to New England in 1791 and founded the American cotton spinning industry.

Technological experimentation and advancement was a constant preoccupation with Arkwright. In particular he was interested in power generation. Water power had the drawback of limiting location; plants had to be sited where streams generated sufficient force to turn the water wheels, and also in areas where there was no risk of the water freezing over in winter. In the 1780s Arkwright began experimenting with steam engines, using Thomas Newcomen's original designs, but found them unsatisfactory. His interest in steam, however, brought him to the notice of Matthew Boulton and James Watt, then in the process of improving Newcomen's engine. Much correspondence ensued, and steam was experimented with on several occasions; however, widespread adoption of steam power did not begin until after Arkwright's death.

Many commentators (Fitton 1989; Chapman 1992; Langlois 1999) credit Arkwright with the founding of the factory system, and it seems correct to assume that his combination of organisational genius and ability to use and exploit new technologies not only enriched him personally but contributed to the broader revolution in business and the economy. The impacts of that system were, of course, enormous, but exactly what those impacts were continues to be the subject of debate. Marxist economists and historians have argued that the main impact of the factory system was that it concentrated capital and allowed for greater exploitation of labour. On the other hand, transactions costs theorists have argued that the factory system allowed for greater efficiency, as it reduced transactions costs and lowered the costs of coordination and monitoring quality. Langlois (1999) believes that the real revolution lay not in the concentration of capital or of labour, but in the switch of emphasis from *product* to *process*. In contracting or putting-out systems, the main methods of producing goods prior to the factory system, the business owner could only monitor the end product; he or she had no control over the process. By bringing the process under direct managerial control, Arkwright could concentrate on engineering that process to produce high-quality output at lower cost. In Langlois's view: 'The factory system arose because growth in the extent of the market ... opened up entrepreneurial possibilities for high-volume throughput. This meant not only an extended division of labour but also investment in new capabilities ... that, by making production more routine, permitted lower unit costs' (1999: 47).

There was of course a darker side to the Industrial Revolution. Arkwright, as the founder of the factory system, is often criticised for many of its abuses. Like most mill owners of his day he used child labour; children as young as eight could be found working his mills, though Arkwright's son later put a stop to this practice. In terms of health and safety, his mills seem to have been better than some but worse than others. He was by no means as enlightened as Robert Owen, but visitors to his factories reported them to be clean, sanitary and well ventilated (by no means the usual case among his competitors). Workers put in long hours – Arkwright factories were on continuous production, and twelve-hour shifts were the norm – but were paid better than in other concerns, and Arkwright not only paid bonuses but spent considerable sums on housing and occasional entertainments for his workers. Although conditions were harsh, Arkwright employees had a better standard of living – and life expectancy – than in some other mills.

A compulsive worker who was poor at delegation, Arkwright was at his desk from 5 am to 9 pm every day, continuing to do so even after he was made a knight in 1786. He died of heart disease in 1792. Fitton, author of the most important modern biography of Arkwright, describes him as 'a business genius of the first order. The founder of the modern factory system, he was the creator of a new industrial society that transformed England ... into the workshop of the world' (1989: 1).

## Analysis

Some of the questions you might want to consider in connection with this case include:

- What are the key features of Arkwright's 'technology strategy'?
- In what ways did he leverage technology in order to achieve competitive advantage more generally?
- Having acquired a technological advantage, should Arkwright have tried harder to protect that advantage, and perhaps even sought a monopoly?
- Arkwright's use of other people's ideas has been described as unscrupulous. Were his methods justified?

## Sources

Berg, M. (1985) *The Age of Manufactures: Industry, Innovation and Work in Britain, 1700–1820*, Oxford: Blackwell.

Chapman, Sidney (1992) *Merchant Enterprise in Britain*, Cambridge: Cambridge University Press.

Fitton, Richard S. (1989) *The Arkwrights: Spinners of Fortune*, Manchester: Manchester University Press.

Fitton, R.S. and Wadsworth, A.K. (1958) *The Strutts and the Arkwrights 1758–1830: A Study of the Early Factory System*, Manchester: Manchester University Press.

Guest, R. (1823) *A Compendious History of the Cotton Manufacture; With a Disproval of the Claim of Sir Richard Arkwright to the Invention of its Ingenious Machinery*, Manchester: Joseph Pratt.

Langlois, R.N. (1999) 'The Coevolution of Technology and Organisation in the Transition to the Factory System' in P.L. Robertson (ed.), *Authority and Control in Modern Industry*, London: Routledge.

Pollard, Sidney (1965) *The Genesis of Modern Management*, London: Edward Arnold.

## Case Study 7C

### *Hans Renold Ltd*

One of the most important but least regarded engineering inventions of the Industrial Revolution was the drive chain. A comparatively simple device in its own right, it became the standard method of power transmission not only in many factories, but also in bicycles, automobiles and airplanes. Without drive chains, as one observer at the time commented, the Earth would have stood still.

Renold Chains was for many years one of the world's leading makers of drive chains. It was founded by the entrepreneur Hans Renold, who was born in Switzerland in 1852, the son of a baker. His family were moderately well off, and Renold was able to study engineering at the polytechnic in Zurich. In late 1871 he moved to Paris, where he found a job with the engineering firm of Claparède and helped to rebuild French industry after the Franco-Prussian War (1870–71). In 1873 he moved to London and then soon after to Manchester; like many other foreign entrepreneurs, including Friedrich Engels, he saw Manchester as a place of opportunity. He spent several years working with a machinery exporting firm, which gave him the opportunity to learn about the local engineering market.

In 1879 Renold bought Slater's, a small chain-making business in Salford, near Manchester, changing the name to Hans Renold Ltd. This firm's primary market was drive chains for textile mills. Most mills at this date were steam-powered, and drive chains transmitted power from the steam engines to the spinning machines, power looms and other items of powered machinery. However, there was already quite a lot of competition among drive chain makers supplying factories, and Renold had a brand new market in mind.

In 1879, J.K. Starley had patented the safety bicycle. One of its features was that the pedals were not directly attached to a wheel, as with the older 'penny-farthing' types. The safety bicycle needed a drive chain to transmit the rider's energy from the pedals to the rear wheel. To meet this need, in 1880 Renold patented the bush roller chain, which proved to be simple, safe and effective. During the 1880s and 1890s the bicycle was the dominant mode of personal transport in Britain in particular; this period, before the advent of mass motoring, is sometimes known as the 'age of the bicycle' (H.G. Wells's novel *The Wheels of Chance* offers insights into the influence of the bicycle and how it revolutionised personal transport). Renold's chains powered tens of thousands of bicycles sold not just in Britain but in many parts of the world.

However, the bicycle market was only the beginning. The internal combustion engine was becoming more efficient and entering greater use. By the early twentieth century it had become the standard means of propulsion for two new forms of transport, automobiles and aircraft. These again needed drive chains, and the bush roller chain was the most efficient and effective chain on the market. Renold, holding the patent and with the greatest manufacturing expertise in the field, had a considerable head-start on his competition. Only a few other chain-makers were able to seriously challenge his dominance, which lasted for over four decades. Meanwhile Renold had begun developing other chain types such as the inverted tooth or silent chain – he did not patent the original, but made a number of improvements to it – and developed markets for drive chains in diverse manufacturing industries and also wood-cutting and coal-cutting. During the First World War Renold helped test and build tracks for tanks, then in the process of being introduced into warfare.

As well as his chain designs, Renold was responsible for a number of innovations in machine tool technology which were then diffused throughout industry. He was not possessive about intellectual property; astonishingly, not only did he never patent the bush roller chain in the USA, he even encouraged and provided technical support to the American firms which made and sold it there. The UK and European market was more than large enough to suit his own goals; he seems not to have been interested in developing a global business, and indeed, was only passingly interested in money. Nor did he need to fear competition in his main markets; Renold was always ahead of his rivals in terms of technology.

Urwick and Brech (1949) cite the firm of Hans Renold Ltd as the epitome of scientific management in the UK, a scientific management that had developed a unique national flavour. One of the characteristics of the British brand of scientific management, they comment, was its enlightened attitude to labour. Renold introduced the forty-eight-hour working week in 1896, believing that shorter hours would lead to greater efficiency and productivity. In 1910 the firm was one of the first in the UK to establish a personnel department, which it called the 'employment department'. A shop stewards' committee was formed in 1917, and the policy of joint consultation with management and workers on decisions of importance also dates from this time. Profit-sharing was introduced in 1922.

Much emphasis was placed on employee and management development. Renold once remarked: 'Our job is not to make chains; it is to make men and women – they will make the chains for us' (Tripp 1956: 25). The firm recruited young workers as apprentices and gave them a thorough technical training which lasted for a number of years. Those who showed promise were also educated in the techniques of management and quickly promoted through the ranks.

In 1913, Renold read a paper entitled 'Engineering Workshop Organisation' before the Manchester Association of Engineers. The paper, summarised by Urwick and Brech (1949), provides an excellent example of best practice in engineering firms in the early twentieth century. Renold describes in detail how he structured his organisation, and also how he had adopted many of the techniques of scientific management. He understood that the heart of scientific management was the gathering, use and transmission of knowledge. Every department of the firm, on both the commercial and manufacturing sides, prepared a monthly balance sheet giving statistics which, taken together, summarised the position of the firm at a glance. Adopting a version of the line and staff model of organisation, Renold developed a 'general services' group of departments which served as the coordinating body for the entire firm. This group included the employment department, mentioned above, which was responsible for recruitment and training; the statistical department, which prepared all the balance sheets and checked their accuracy; the instructions department, which drafted and recorded all instructions necessary to carry out decisions reached at directors' and management meetings;

and a publishing department which issued all sheets of prices and instructions as well as monthly bulletins to agents.

Renold also placed great emphasis on the importance of leadership. The most efficient system imaginable, he said, would not work unless there were 'men of tact and power to lead' (Urwick and Brech 1949: 169). Renold himself exemplified this style of leadership; he was a motivator rather than a driver of his workforce, and tended to carry them with him through a combination of mutual respect and a joint desire to do well. He had a strong sense of social responsibility: he played a role in the foundation of the establishment of the Manchester Mechanics' Institute and the Manchester College of Technology. The Hans Renold Social Union, established in 1909 partly at the instigation of his son, coordinated and supported many of the workers' social and sporting activities. According to his son Charles Renold, 'the keynote of his whole life was a passion for good work. He enjoyed money when it came, but commercial success was of quite secondary interest. What drove him on was the joy of creation – of doing something just as well as he knew how. "Good enough" was a sentiment that was quite unknown to him' (Tripp 1956: 32). His obituary sums up his contribution:

> Few realise how extensive is the influence of Renold's inventiveness on both civil and industrial life through the world. Virtually every form of modern transport, by road, sea, or air, employs or depends on chain … the automobile has at all stages of its development been one of the major industries utilising chain as an essential feature of design; in fact, there is hardly a phase of any industry or public works in which the chain is not to be found making an obscure but vital contribution to our welfare.
>
> (Tripp 1956: 31–32)

## Analysis

Some of the questions you might want to consider in connection with this case include:

- What does this case tell us about the commercial exploitation of innovations? What factors help to ensure that innovations become commercially viable?
- Renold was described as having 'an enlightened attitude to labour'. How important is such an attitude in high-technology industries?
- Renold is also described as having a passion for excellence; the making of money was of secondary importance. Might his business have achieved more if he had been more strongly motivated by financial gain?
- How important was knowledge in the success of Hans Renold Ltd?

## Sources

Tripp, B.H. (1956) *Renold Chains: A History of the Company and the Rise of the Precision Chain Industry, 1879–1955*, London: George Allen & Unwin.

Urwick, L.F. and Brech, E.F.L. (1949) *The Making of Scientific Management*, vol. 2, *Management in British Industry*, London: Management Publications Trust.

## Case Study 7D

### *Cyrus McCormick*

Cyrus Hall McCormick was an innovator on three dimensions. First, he designed and patented the first mechanical reaper, ancestor of the modern combine harvester, which became a standard piece of technology used in agriculture in many parts of the world. Second, he pioneered methods of mass production which enabled him to take advantage of a very large potential market. Third, his marketing methods were well in advance of their time and were later widely studied and held up as an example of best practice.

McCormick was born in Virginia in 1809, the son of a prosperous farmer who was also a mechanic and inventor. Robert McCormick tried for many years to develop a successful design for a mechanical reaper. In the early nineteenth century, crops such as wheat, oats, barley and rye were still being harvested as they had been for thousands of years, by hand using scythes and sickles. This was slow and fatiguing work, and the slow speed of harvesting meant that farmers were sometimes unable to harvest their crops in time to avoid the onset of bad weather. A mechanical reaper which could speed up the process would both save labour and reduce risk.

As a boy, Cyrus McCormick worked in his father's workshop and received his training there. He has been described, with the benefit of hindsight, as 'a natural mechanical genius' (Casson 1909: 27). Whether this is true or not, he solved the design problems of the mechanical reaper and completed his first successful prototype in 1831. He filed for patents in 1834. Thereafter development languished while McCormick tried his hand as an entrepreneur in an iron-mining venture. This failed, and McCormick now decided to try making and selling horse-drawn mechanical reapers on a commercial basis. He established this business in 1837, but by 1844 he had sold only fifty reapers.

In 1847 McCormick moved from Virginia to Chicago. This proved to be a wise move, as the American Midwest was beginning to attract many immigrants and many new farms were being established. Chicago had good transport links and was close to these new farming districts. It became clear that there was much interest in mechanical reapers and a strong potential market. However, in 1848 McCormick's patent expired. He attempted to protect his intellectual property, but other companies challenged him and there were a series of legal battles (Abraham Lincoln first made his name as a lawyer while representing McCormick's opponents). McCormick lost, which meant that he now faced intense competition. By 1860 there were more than 100 companies making reaping machines.

Having lost one advantage, McCormick turned to developing others. Having designed the original mechanical reaper and with more experience of producing them, he knew more about quality than did his competitors (many of whom also tried to cut corners on quality so as to underprice him). As well as maintaining quality standards, McCormick also hit on the idea of using interchangeable parts so that reaping machines could be assembled more quickly. From here he went on to develop a prototype mass production system, one of the earliest in America; only the firearms maker Colt can claim to have developed a mass production system before McCormick. His factory system was widely imitated in the later nineteenth century, and may have been one of the models studied by Henry Ford. Mass production meant that McCormick could also keep pace with demand when it began to rise.

The ability to stimulate demand was McCormick's other great advantage. Although farmers were always likely to be interested in a device that saved them labour and time, the mechanical reaper was a complex device whose uses were not fully understood. The machinery also had to be explained to customers so that they could maintain and repair the reapers, as many were located far from workshops. His marketing methods were far in advance of their time. Creative advertising and demonstrations of his machines were backed up by methods such as warranties and extension of credit to customers (this later became a standard feature in the automobile industry).

McCormick also rejected the old method of contracting out the selling of reapers to independent salesmen, on the grounds that these would know little more about the product than his customers. He established an in-house sales force and trained these thoroughly, teaching them how to demonstrate the reapers and how to explain their features to customers. Having educated his sales force, McCormick then sent out his salesmen to educate his customers. His salesmen made a point of working with customers and building relationships with them, answering questions and giving advice, rather than simply completing sales. According to one later observer, McCormick did not just invent the mechanical reaper: 'he invented the business of making reapers and selling them to the farmers of America and foreign countries' (Casson 1909: 47).

These methods helped McCormick draw steadily away from his rivals. By 1860 he was selling 5,000 reapers a year in the USA and had begun to penetrate the European and other overseas markets. Continuous improvements to the basic design, including features that made the machines more durable and more reliable, helped him keep his technological and marketing advantage. And this was only the beginning. In the 1870s and 1880s the population of the USA grew rapidly and millions of acres of land, especially in the Midwest and West, were put under cultivation. In 1871 McCormick's factory in

Chicago was destroyed by fire, but this proved to be a blessing in disguise. McCormick built a new and far larger plant which used improved mass production methods and greatly increased output. By 1885 the plant was producing 50,000 machines a year and selling around the world.

A successful inventor, McCormick's claim to fame lies also in his pioneering business methods. These methods continued to be used by his son and successor Cyrus McCormick Jr, who took over the firm after McCormick's death in 1884. He went on to create the world's largest manufacturer of agricultural machinery, International Harvester, in 1906. By 1935 when he retired, International Harvester had annual sales of $350 million around the world.

## Analysis

Some of the questions you might want to consider in connection with this case include:

- How did McCormick combine the use of product technology, production technology and marketing methods? What was the relative importance of each?
- McCormick was serving a new and rapidly growing market. What risks did he face in trying to meet the demands of this market?
- What does this case tell us about the management of innovation more generally?

## Sources

Casson, Herbert N. (1909) *Cyrus Hall McCormick*, Chicago: A.C. McClurg.
Hutchinson, W.T. (1930–35) *Cyrus Hall McCormick*, 2 vols, New York: Century.

## Case Study 7E

### *The Ming dynasty's navy*

In the early centuries of Imperial China, shipbuilding was developed to a fine art. As well as a variety of river vessels, the big ocean-going Chinese vessels known as 'junks' sailed to ports in Japan, South-east Asia, the Philippines and Indonesia, trading in a wide variety of goods ranging from staple foodstuffs to luxury goods such as medicines and spices. As Needham (1954–95: vol. 4) describes, Chinese shipbuilders and scientists were in advance of their European counterparts, not just in shipbuilding but in matters such as preserving food and water aboard ships during long voyages so as to maintain the health of the crews. They had also begun using the compass (interestingly, Chinese compasses were oriented towards the south, not the north) several centuries before European navigators did so.

Somewhat surprisingly, given their desert origins, the Mongols also proved to be keen sailors. When they conquered China in 1264 they at once set out building a large and efficient navy for the purpose of expanding their conquests overseas. A Mongol fleet attacked Indonesia in 1292 and forced local rulers to acknowledge the Mongol leader Kubilai Khan as their overlord. Two attempts to invade Japan, in 1274 and 1281, were less successful. The second invasion force was said to include over 4,000 ships, and would surely have overwhelmed Japan had it not encountered a severe typhoon which sank many ships and destroyed others. The grateful Japanese referred to this typhoon as the *kamikaze*, the divine wind that had saved their country.

The Ming dynasty, which drove out the Mongols in 1368, had learned much from the former conquerors about naval operations, and were efficient sailors themselves. The naval battle of Lake Poyang in 1263 was one of the decisive battles which led to the Ming dynasty's ultimate victory. Upon assuming power, the Ming dynasty continued the tradition of a strong navy, building some of the largest ships the world had yet seen. Chief among these were the so-called 'treasure ships' with nine masts and ranging up to four-hundred feet in length. There is debate as to the purpose of these ships, and it is now generally agreed that their size meant they were unsuitable for ocean sailing; they were more likely intended for ceremonial use by the emperor and his court, and were probably restricted to China's rivers and the Grand Canal that linked the Yangtze and Yellow rivers. Ocean-going warships had four or six masts and were about two hundred feet long, and there were also specialist ships for carrying supplies and water. All of these ships were substantially larger than anything built in Europe at the time. During the first few decades of the Ming dynasty these warships often sailed to escort convoys of merchant ships travelling to South-east Asia, Indonesia and west into the Indian Ocean.

Some time after 1402 command of the Chinese navy was given to Zheng He, a eunuch and former slave who had been captured by a Ming army engaged in suppressing a revolt by the Hui (Muslim) people of Yunnan province. Zheng He seems to have remained a Muslim, but he also became friendly with Prince Zhu Di, uncle of the reigning emperor, Jianwen. In 1402 Zheng He helped his friend overthrow Jianwen. The latter took the throne under the name Yongle and appointed Zheng He, still only in his early thirties, as his admiral.

Between 1405 and Emperor Yongle's death in 1424, the Chinese fleet under Zheng He made six voyages to the south and west. These were not small squadrons of ships like the later expeditions of Columbus, Magellan or Vasco da Gama, but grand processions with large fleets of ships. According to some accounts the first expedition of 1405 included more than three hundred ships. Even allowing for exaggeration, this must still have been an impressive fleet.

The motive behind these expeditions is not altogether clear. The first three expeditions called at several ports in the South-east Asian peninsula and then Indonesia, before moving on to Sri Lanka and then up the west coast of India to places like Cochin and Calicut, important intermediary ports on the trade routes that linked East Asia with the Middle East and Europe. Some of the countries of South-east Asia paid tribute to China, and it is likely that the appearance of large fleets of ships was meant to impress local rulers and encourage them to continue to acknowledge Chinese authority. In reality the purpose may have been to establish Chinese control over seaborne trade. Further west, it is not clear whether the Chinese were actively considering competing with the Arab merchants who controlled the trade, or were simply exploring and gathering more information about the world around them. Their visits to India were entirely peaceful, and Zheng He and his officers received a friendly reception from the Indian authorities.

The next three voyages, from 1413–15, 1416–19 and 1421–22, were more adventurous still. After reaching India, Zheng He and his ships crossed the Arabian Sea and called at Muscat and Hormuz, both major trading centres that controlled the entrance to the Persian Gulf, and then Aden, which similarly controlled the entrance to the Red Sea. Some of the ships explored the Red Sea and called at Jiddah, the port of Mecca, although whether the devout Muslim Zheng He ever made the pilgrimage to Mecca is not known. Leaving Aden, the fleet called at Mogadishu in Somalia and several other points down the East African coast. The sixth voyage, that of 1421–22, was devoted to a lengthy exploration of the coasts of Africa and Asia, and it is possible that Zheng He ventured as far as the Cape of Good Hope where the Indian Ocean meets the Atlantic (the theory that he crossed the Atlantic to South America is not generally accepted).

Emperor Yongle died in 1424 and his successors, Hongxi and Xuande, were less interested in exploration to the west. The Chinese empire was not secure; the Mongols were menacing the northern border once more, and resources were required for the army, not the navy. Also, there were doubts as to whether these voyages were achieving any purpose; as early as 1407, despite the overwhelming superiority of the Chinese fleet, the Vietnamese kingdom of Annam declared independence and refused to pay tribute to China. Zheng He's own position was undermined by jealous court bureaucrats who resented the favour Yongle had shown him. In 1431 he obtained permission to make another voyage and led his fleet west for the seventh time, calling in Sri Lanka, the west Indian port of Calicut, and Hormuz. He died in 1433 on the voyage back to China.

When the fleet returned from its seventh voyage, the commanders were ordered to moor their ships and pay off their men. The ships themselves rotted away and sank or otherwise disappeared; not one of them has survived and even the plans and details of their construction appear to have been deliberately destroyed. The Ming dynasty turned its back on the sea, and although Chinese trading ships continued to sail to Indonesia until the nineteenth century, there were no more explorations outside of China. In general China retained its relatively high level of technology, but in terms of maritime technology, many of the advances of previous centuries were lost.

Imperial China under the Ming dynasty and its successor the Qing became increasingly insular, concentrating on affairs inside and immediately outside its borders. Succeeding emperors showed little interest in anything that was not Chinese. As a result, the Chinese came to understand less and less of what was going on in the outside world. A later emperor, Qianlong in the late eighteenth century, told a British ambassador that China already produced everything it needed, and had no interest in foreign goods. During the First Opium War of 1839–42, another emperor told his army that the British could never land in China because, as they lived their entire lives on ships, they had no knees and were unable to walk on dry land. By cutting itself off from the world, China made itself very vulnerable.

Examples of technological regression – that is, a society or an institution deliberately abandoning an advanced technology to retreat to an older one – are rare, but they do happen. In neighbouring Japan in the sixteenth century, Portuguese and Dutch traders passed on knowledge about the making of muskets and gunpowder. During the long series of civil wars that afflicted the country that century, the armies of the rival warlords were often armed with large numbers of muskets. But when the Tokugawa shoguns took control and united the country, ending the war, they decreed an end to the use of firearms; factories for making muskets and gunpowder were closed down and the knowledge of how to make them was lost. Here, as with the Ming dynasty's navy, the choice to abandon an advanced technology was a deliberate one.

## Analysis

Some of the questions you might want to consider in connection with this case include:

- What might prompt a society, or any institution, to engage in technological regression?
- Can you think of any examples of this happening in modern times?
- What other kinds of regression are there? Think of examples of the loss of knowledge or skills, either deliberately or by neglect, and consider how these have impacted on business and on society.

## Sources

Dreyer, Edward L. (2006) *Zheng He: China and the Oceans in the Early Ming Dynasty, 1405–1433*, London: Longman.

Levathes, Louise (1997) *When China Ruled the Seas: The Treasure Fleet of the Dragon Throne, 1405–1433*, Oxford: Oxford University Press.

Mills, J.V. (1970) *Ma Huan Ying Yai Sheng Lan: The Overall Survey of the Ocean Shores*, Cambridge: Cambridge University Press.

Wang Gungwu (2002) *The Chinese Overseas*, Cambridge, MA: Harvard University Press.

## Notes

1 It is worth pausing to remember that at the same time as Morse, Charles Babbage was working on the prototype of the modern computer. Like Morse, he met with resistance and obstruction from government, and was not able to raise enough private capital to carry on. Had he done so, and had the first computer been married to the first Internet in the 1850s, the information revolution might have happened a century earlier than it did.

2 The term 'factory' in earlier times had referred to an outpost or trading station separate from the main business enterprise; see Chapter 1. In Arkwright's day, factories were often known as 'mills'.

# 8 Business and society

---

**Learning objectives**

This chapter is intended to help readers do the following:

1 understand how and why society's attitudes to business, and the demands it makes on business, change over time;
2 better understand the relationship between business and society;
3 gain further insights into the problems and challenges of ethical business.

There is something alarming to those who believe that commerce should be a peaceful pursuit, and who believe that moral law holds good throughout the entire range of human relations, in knowing that so large a body of young men in this country are consciously or unconsciously growing up with the idea that business is war and that morals have nothing to do with its practice.

–Ida M. Tarbell, *The History of the Standard Oil Company*

Corporate forms and functions and the environment by which they are influenced are all products of time. They are all meaningless except as they register past experience or predict future social growth, stagnation or decay. They must therefore be subjected to historical treatment.

–John P. Davis, *Corporations*

## 8.1 Introduction

The financial crisis of 2008 has led to a new round of debate about ethics in business, the need for more regulation to prevent unscrupulous and dishonest behaviour, and the responsibility of business to society. Beyond high-profile cases like that of Bernard Madoff, or of Enron earlier in the decade, there has emerged a more general concern that a few people in high places in business have the ability, through their actions, to affect the lives of millions of others. Should they have that power, and if they do, should they be required to use that power in a more responsible manner?

This is in fact just the latest chapter in an ongoing debate which has stretched back quite literally to the dawn of recorded history. There has been first of all the recognition that some people – in any walk of life, not just business – will behave selfishly and dishonestly, and these must be dealt with. But prevention is better than cure, and philosophers and others have spent a great deal of time puzzling over the problem of how to make people more ethical.

But there is also a much larger issue. Is business itself ethical? Are practices such as the trading of goods or the lending of money for profit harmful to society, or good for it? On the whole, opinion has come down on the side of the latter, but with a caveat: the purpose of business is not *solely* to make a profit. Views like those of the economist Milton Friedman in the twentieth century, who said that the sole purpose of a business was to make money and return profits to shareholders, are in a distinct minority. The general view, including that of many businesspeople, is that businesses are part of society and have a responsibility to society.

Of course, there is a divergence between theory and practice, and it is quite possible to find examples such as Henry Ford who preached the doctrine of responsible business while treating his own workers in an autocratic and overbearing manner. Or there is John D. Rockefeller who made a large fortune in business using unethical, illegal and even violent methods, and then gave away much of that fortune to charities. One response to this is that business leaders are merely being cynical, and donations to charity are merely a way of distracting attention from earlier offences. But that is too simple. For every Ford or Rockefeller, there are others like the American department store owners Edward Filene and John Wanamaker, or the British entrepreneur-philanthropists George Cadbury and Titus Salt who put into practice the views they espoused.

We know that businesses can be socially responsible, and we know that the majority view over time is that they should be. But a stronger argument still comes from John Davis, the American lawyer and historian who, at the turn of the nineteenth and twentieth centuries, produced a major book on the role of corporations in society (Davis 1905). We quoted from him at the head of the chapter. Business corporations, argued Davis, are products of an evolution that has occurred in society. As countries and economies grew, their needs became more complex and diverse. America had also begun to expand geographically. The small and largely localised businesses which had comprised most of the American business community before the Civil War (1861–65) were no longer capable of meeting society's needs. America therefore had to imitate the European model and evolve its own large corporations which had sufficient scale and geographical scope to serve society. Davis had earlier written a history of the Union Pacific Railway, and had studied the practical effects this evolution. The railway system enabled the transfer of goods quickly over long distances. It provided a means of transporting food from the farms and cattle ranches of the Midwest and West to the populous cities of the East. It was therefore not just a means of making profits; it was also vitally important to American society.

Davis's argument was that forms of business are created by society. That is, they do not simply come out of nowhere: they are responses to social needs. When a society feels a need for education, it creates schools and universities. When it feels a need for better health care, it creates hospitals and sanatoriums. And when it feels a need for more material goods and services to feed people and enhance the quality of life, it creates business corporations. But, says Davis, the reverse is also true. When society feels those corporations are *not* meeting its needs, it turns against them. Society destroys businesses as well as creates them.

Davis was anticipating events in Russia, and later China, where revolutionary governments abolished virtually all private businesses and took them under state control. But he might also have been anticipating modern examples such as the tobacco industry. Fifty years ago, despite concerns from doctors and a growing weight of medical evidence suggesting that smoking was harmful, society as a whole was supportive of the tobacco industry. Cigarettes were given out with rations to soldiers in the Second World War, and one Canadian political leader described them as 'one of the working man's few affordable luxuries'. Today the situation has changed, and governments in many countries, with broad popular support, are turning against the tobacco industry. Society no longer wants it.

## 8.2 Changing social attitudes to business

Before getting into specifics, it is worth surveying general social attitudes to business and how they have changed. We need to remind ourselves that business is a universal activity that can be found in any civilised society. Moore and Lewis (2000) have shown the extent of business activity in ancient Mesopotamia and classical Greece and Rome. The world's first known law code, that of Hammurabi of Babylon who reigned from 1795–1750 BC (Luckenbill and Chiera 1931), devotes much space to the regulation of trade and business, and the problem of dishonest businesspeople is clearly shown. Those who commit fraudulent transactions must make restitution and pay fines; if a builder builds a house that then collapses and kills its occupants, he too is to be put to death, and so on. Likewise we have plenty of evidence of business activity in ancient India and China (Guetzlaff 1834; Liu 1998; McLaughlan 2009).

All of this activity might be said to support the assertion of the American businessman Henry Dennison (1932) that the desire to earn money and accumulate is a basic human need and cannot be denied. It also supports the notion of a link between business and society. Business, trade and commerce emerged along with civilisation, as society and its needs became more complex. Businesses that met society's needs were encouraged; those that did not were punished.

### 8.2.1 Asia

The tension between the need for businesses to create wealth and generate prosperity on the one hand, and the need to curb the actions of the selfish and the greedy on the other, is strongly evident in Asian cultures. The first Asian philosopher of note, the Chinese sage Confucius, reflects this debate. For a long time it was thought that Confucius was opposed to business and trade and profit. However, Chen Huan-Chang (1911) argues that this is due to a misunderstanding of Confucian thinking that arose in later centuries. In the key Confucian texts, the *Analects*, the *Great Learning* and the *Doctrine of the Mean*, Confucius presents himself as a supporter of business activity so long as it is carried out justly and fairly and enriches all. Although he believes that scholars, bureaucrats and kings themselves should abstain from economic activity, he not only believes that the other orders of society should be allowed to make a profit, he actively encourages them to do so (Chen 1911: vol. 1, 95–96).

In the *Analects*, Confucius argues that society's leaders have two duties to the poor: first to enrich them, then to educate them. A not dissimilar argument is found in India in the political philosophy of Kautilya (1997), who believes that the duty of the state is to bring both prosperity and enlightenment to the people. Both Kautilya and Confucius believe the two go hand in hand; people who are poor are too busy trying to feed themselves to be educated or enlightened. Only when their bellies are full and they have the comforts of life around them will they have leisure time to contemplate higher things.

---

**Virtue and wealth**

The superior man will first take pains about his own virtue. Virtue is the root, and wealth only the result. If he make the root his secondary object, and the result his primary, then he will only wrangle with his people, and teach them rapine. Hence, the concentration of wealth is the cause of driving the people away, and the diffusion of it among them is the way to collect the people. And hence the wealth, got by improper ways, will depart by the same. The virtuous man, by means of his wealth, makes his personality more distinguished. The vicious man accumulates wealth at the expense of his life.

–Confucius, *Great Learning* (quoted in Chen 1911: vol. 1, 98)

---

One of the other main Chinese systems of thought, Daoism, took a slightly different view. Daoist writers like Laozi (Lao Tzu) suggested that people would, if left to their own devices, conduct trade amongst themselves and create prosperity and would regulate their own affairs. (This philosophy formed the basis of the later Western concept of *laissez-faire*; see Chapter 5.) But Daoism and Confucianism had in common the view that business was necessary for society. The dominant role, however, was played by society; the businessperson was the servant of society, not its master.

Very similar ideas are found elsewhere in Asia. One of the earliest expressions of Japanese political philosophy, the Shotoku Constitution of AD 604 (Kachi 1998) does not pronounce directly on the role of business, but does emphasise that prosperity is an important goal, and inveighs against corruption and bribery as being harmful to this goal. Despite the prohibition of usury (lending money at interest), early Islamic scholars praised merchants as people who helped to create prosperity and alleviate the lot of the poor, so long as they obeyed the laws of God. Many charitable foundations, orphanages, schools and the like were established with endowments from wealthy merchants, and these were seen as being a meritorious act. It should be remembered that the Prophet Muhammad was a trader, and his wife Khadija was a prosperous merchant in her own right at the time of their marriage.

This is the positive side of the Asian attitude to commerce. The negative side can often be seen during times of economic hardship, when merchants take the blame for society's problems and the poverty of the people is blamed on their 'greed'. The Ming dynasty in China (1368–1644), for all its military strength and cultural brilliance, became increasingly embroiled in economic troubles. The introduction of paper money was a disaster; people had no confidence in it, and the currency's actual exchange value shrank to about 2 per cent of its face value. Merchants and traders were blamed, and suffered high taxes and restrictions. The Qing dynasty which took power in 1644 had a much more enlightened attitude and encouraged manufacturing and trade as a way of rebuilding national prosperity.

Similarly in Japan the Tokugawa Shogunate, coming to power at the end of the sixteenth century, suppressed trade, especially foreign trade, and demoted merchants and other businesspeople to an inferior social status. As a result, trade and the economy languished. In the mid-eighteenth century the scholar Ishida Baigan argued that this policy was wrong. Merchants, he said, were the source of national prosperity and their activities helped to dispel poverty. Merchants should be honest and humble people and should not be ostentatious in their display of wealth, and should remember that they are the servants of society, but society in turn should support merchants for the good they do (Takemura 1997). Ishida Baigan's work helped to change perceptions of merchants in Japan, and by the nineteenth century mercantile activity was encouraged, with even nobles and *samurai* sometimes becoming involved.

### 8.2.2 Europe

We see a similar dichotomy of views in Europe. Classical scholars such as Plato and Aristotle had, like their Eastern counterparts, recognised the role played by businesspeople in creating prosperity and thought they were an important part of society. But the status of businesspeople had waxed and waned under the Roman Empire, depending on the character of the emperor. Some like Marcus Aurelius (AD 161–80) had supported and encouraged traders, while others such as Septimus Severus (193–211) treated them with contempt and taxed them brutally.

Medieval Christianity started from a position which we can describe as vague antipathy to trade and merchants. Businesspeople were not included in the medieval social order of three estates, nobles, priests and peasants; they did not fit in, and were in some cases regarded with contempt by all three estates. The early medieval church also prohibited usury, and regarded the acquisition of wealth as being at best suspicious, at worst downright sinful. 'It is easier for a camel to pass through the eye of a needle than for a rich man to enter the kingdom of heaven' was a proverb widely repeated.

But over time this position began to erode. As trading centres developed in Italy and north-western Europe, and as the benefits of trade began to be seen, not just in general increased prosperity but in donations to and support for the church, the theological position began to change. Another important influence was the development of scholastic learning following the 'renaissance' of the twelfth century (Haskins 1927), when there was an awakening of interest in the social, political and ethical idea of the ancient world. Under the influence of the ideas of Plato and Aristotle, Christian philosophers re-assessed the role of business.

The most important figure here is the writer St Thomas Aquinas, who died in 1274 and was widely regarded as the greatest scholar and theologian of his day. In passages in his two principle works, *Summa theologiae* and *Summa contra gentiles*, Aquinas set out again the arguments in favour of trade and supported merchants as valuable members of society. But he also went much further. In Aquinas too we can find an exposition on the laws of supply and demand, of the equilibrium they create between buyer and seller, and the concept of a 'just price' which is fair to both parties and which creates value to both (Dempsey 1935; de Roover 1955, 1958). Aquinas was adamant that businesspeople should take profits; these were a fair reward for the risks they ran (which in the Middle Ages were numerous).

Other Catholic theologians, notably Bernardino of Siena and Antonio of Florence followed this lead, and the status of merchants and traders improved greatly. Governments recognised their importance and rewarded them for their services. In the fourteenth century the English wool merchants John Pulteney and William de la Pole were both knighted for their services in lending money to the crown, setting a precedent which would be followed hundreds of times. In Scotland in the fifteenth century the Flemish-Genoese merchant Anselm Adorne was made a baron. Distinctions between the nobility and the upper levels of the mercantile classes began to break down.

The view that business was an activity whose purpose was to enrich society, not individuals, persisted very strongly. Typical is John Dunning, Lord Ashburton, an eighteenth-century lawyer and politician who in the 1760s defended the East India Company, which some thought was becoming overly powerful and its directors overly rich. It could not be denied that the directors were rich, said Dunning, but they had created a great deal of wealth also in Britain and in India,[1] and the rewards they received were just and fair considering the risks they ran (Dunning 1762). But to Dunning, wealth had to be gained honestly. When an East India Company officer, Robert Clive, accepted a large gift of money from a group of Indian princes following the Company's conquest of Bengal, Dunning denounced Clive in Parliament and insisted he should return the money.

The breakdown of this view that business should be responsible to society coincides almost exactly with the start of the Industrial Revolution. We need to be careful with our terms of reference here. We are talking now about the generally accepted relationship between business and society: *not* actual practice. There had been greedy and corrupt businesspeople before this, and there were times when it appeared for a while that they would come to dominate (for example during the South Sea Bubble in the early eighteenth century). But always a more socially responsible, more ethical model seemed to come back and dominate thinking, if not always practice. But during the early years of the Industrial Revolution, the old social contract between business and society somehow got lost.

The Industrial Revolution, and the introduction of the factory system in particular, resulted in several trends in Europe. One was a general worsening of working conditions, and of social conditions generally as workers squeezed into cramped and dirty housing (see Pollard 1965 and also Chapter 4 of this work for working conditions; see Case Study 8C for living conditions in the English city of Bradford). Second, there was a sharp increase in the disparity of wealth. The gap between rich and poor widened considerably, first in Britain and then across Europe. The newly wealthy included not just factory owners but traders, ship-owners and bankers who had profited from the increase in trade. The word 'millionaire' came into popular use in English in the 1820s, indicating that there were now people with fortunes of more than one million pounds. By the middle of the century there were so many of these that the word had lost much of its significance.

Again, we must be careful not to take too narrow a view. It was not only the very wealthy who benefitted. Although the working classes suffered, the middle classes prospered too; their incomes rose steadily in the nineteenth century, and their numbers were greatly expanded. We can see the change in literature, from the genteel landowning middle classes of Jane Austen at the beginning of the century to the business-owning and managerial professionals and their families depicted by Elizabeth Gaskell and Marcel Proust – and Émile Zola – in later decades. The expansion of the middle classes of middle-class prosperity made possible the development of entire new industries, such as mass tourism and the department store.

So, the big business owners and bankers of the Industrial Revolution *could* have argued that they were doing their part in increasing prosperity and therefore benefitting society. But they did not. The closest thing to an apologist for big capital that we find during this period is Alfred Krupp, the so-called 'Cannon King' who was most famous for making artillery for the German army but who actually made most of his fortune out of steel rails and components for rolling stock for the growing railway industry (many of the early railways in America used Krupp steel rails). In his *General Regulations*, a handbook for managers at his steel firm written while recuperating from a nervous breakdown in 1871, Krupp argued that businesses like his own had helped to enrich society and make it a better place, pointing as he did so to the extensive housing and other benefits he had provided for his own workers at Essen in Germany.

---

### The spirit of business

The spirit which inspires all, from the top to the very bottom, must be permeated throughout, in particular, by respect for morality and the law. A sound ethical outlook, closely allied to discipline and loyalty, makes for prosperity and contentment. Without it, frustration, disorder, vice, perfidy and corruption ensue.

–Alfred Krupp, *General Regulations* (quoted in Klass 1954: 91)

More typical is the anonymous English mill owner in 1830 who, when told that his workers were complaining about the long hours and lack of pay, retorted that they should be grateful to have work at all. Profit had become a motive in itself; putting the result before the root, as Confucius would have said.

Of course there were many exceptions. George Cadbury, Titus Salt and later, William Lever in Britain, Krupp and Ernst Abbé in Germany, the Boucicauts and many others in France all treated their workers well, and all believed implicitly or explicitly in the social contract, the notion that business was there to serve the needs of society. There were very many others who took similar positions. But from about 1780 to at least the middle of the following century, theirs were not the dominant voices. The dominant voices were those who demanded the right to make profits, and opposed anything that interfered with this. The bitter opposition faced by William Wilberforce and his allies in their long struggle to abolish slavery in the British Empire is an example of this. The opposition to slavery did not come from those who believed it was right in and of itself, but from those who feared the end of slavery would harm their profits.

Some, including some businesspeople themselves, were baffled by this. Robert Owen, a self-made man like many of the entrepreneurs of the Industrial Revolution, believed that the purpose of ventures like his own was to create prosperity, to bring about wealth which would support Britain's increasing population, and to alleviate poverty. Instead, he saw the opposite happening. He tried to talk to his fellow entrepreneurs, explaining what he had found at New Lanark, namely that by ensuring employees were healthy and restricting their working hours, they became more productive and his business was more profitable. They refused to listen. Later, in Germany, the engineer Robert Bosch, who paid good wages and offered benefits to employees, was accused by his fellow employers of being sympathetic to communism. The capitalist class, as Marx and Engels acutely observed, seemed to close ranks and be prepared to defend its position. And although enlightened employers like Owen, Cadbury, Salt, Abbé and the like showed what was possible, they were not widely imitated.

---

### The acquisition of wealth

The acquisition of wealth, and the desire which it naturally creates for a continued increase, have introduced a fondness for essentially injurious luxuries among a numerous class of individuals, who formerly never thought of them, and they have also generated a disposition which strongly impels its possessors to sacrifice the best feelings of human nature to this love of accumulation. To succeed in this career, the industry of the lower orders, from whose labour this wealth is now drawn, has been carried by new competitors striving against those of longer standing, to a point of real oppression, reducing them by

> successive changes, as the spirit of competition increased, and the ease
> of acquiring wealth diminished, to a state more wretched than can be
> imagined by those who have not attentively observed the changes as
> they have gradually occurred. In consequence, they are at present in a
> situation infinitely more degraded and miserable than they were before
> the introduction of these manufactories, on which the success of their
> bare subsistence now depends.
>
> –Robert Owen, *Observations on the Effect of the*
> *Manufacturing System* (1815: 5)

Why was this so? The psychology of the managerial classes during the
Industrial Revolution has not been fully investigated, but we can make a
couple of hypotheses. First, there may have been a kind of 'gold rush' mentality. Many of these new businesses and new industries made immense profits
very quickly. Did the lure of making still more profits blind people to their
former responsibilities, or convince them that these no longer matter? The
second, as Marxist historians and sociologists like Michel Foucault (1966)
remind us, is that the factory system concentrated labour in one place and
gave the employer an immense amount of power and control. William Lever,
an enlightened employer by many standards, built his factory at Port Sunlight
as a panopticon, so that from the windows of his office he could see the entire
factory and know what everyone was doing. Did this access of power, to men
who had often been workers themselves a few years before and had no
experience or understanding of their new roles, simply go to their heads?

### 8.2.3 North America

The problem in North America sometimes appears more acute, but only
because it came on more quickly and on an even larger scale. The United
States, with its tradition of individual liberty and freedoms, was at first suspicious of any organisation which threatened to encroach on those freedoms,
and this included big businesses. Many followed the example of the third
president of the USA, Thomas Jefferson, and rejected the use of banks
(Hammond 1957). This included some businesspeople: in his portrait of
Peter Chardon Brooks, a Boston merchant in the post-Revolutionary period,
Freeman Hunt (1858) notes that Brooks seldom lent money and never
borrowed it, adding his own view:

> It is highly probable that, in the aggregate, as much property is lost
> and sacrificed in the United States by the abuse of credit, as is gained
> by its legitimate use. With respect to the moral mischiefs resulting
> from some of the prevailing habits of our business community, the
> racking cares and the corroding uncertainties, the mean deceptions,

and the measureless frauds to which they sometimes lead, language is inadequate to do justice to the notorious and appalling truth.

(Hunt 1858: vol. 1, 151)

Brooks was an exemplary man of business, said Hunt, because he sought always to do good for society while taking only a modest profit himself, deliberately restricting the size of his own business and refusing to lead an opulent lifestyle.

Evidence of a change can be found in the years before the American Civil War (1861–65), for example in Henry Carey's exposure of the poverty in which many workers in New York City lived and in the corruption and fraudulent activities of some manufacturers and retailers who were not only cheating their customers but selling them dangerous goods (Carey 1853). But it was not until after the war that the change in public sentiment becomes more noticeable. As in Europe, the rapid growth in large industries and the fortunes created by entrepreneurs such as Andrew Carnegie, Daniel Guggenheim, John D. Rockefeller, Cornelius Vanderbilt and others was also accompanied by an equally rapid growth in middle-class wealth and prosperity, even as the incomes and working conditions of the lower classes either remained steady or in some cases declined.

---

### The moderate entrepreneur: Peter Chardon Brooks

Moderation was perhaps the most conspicuous single trait in his character. Possessing the amplest facilities for acquisition, he was moderate in the pursuit of wealth. This moderation was founded on a principle that carried him much further than mere abstinence from the licensed gambling of the stock exchange. He valued property because it gives independence. For that reason, he would be neither enslaved to profit, nor harassed by putting it at risk. At the most active period of his life, he never stepped beyond the line of a legitimate business. He often, with playful humility, said that 'he preferred to keep in shoal water', not because the water was shallow but because he knew exactly how deep it was.

(Hunt 1858: vol. 1, 163)

---

The change is one of attitude and acceptance. Apart from the working classes themselves, who remained relatively voiceless, society as a whole approved of these powerful new entrepreneurs. Books like Herbert Casson's *The Romance of Steel* (1907) held up the steel barons – Carnegie, Henry Clay Frick, Charles M. Schwab and others – as heroes of the modern age, titanic figures who had helped to build an economy, even a civilisation. Casson had only recently abandoned socialism for capitalism and was writing with the zeal of a convert; later, he would become altogether more cynical. But his attitude was typical of many, in high places and on the street. These men were heroes, and could do no wrong. And incidents like the attempted assassination of Frick by an anarchist, when Frick himself, wounded and bleeding, had still managed to overpower his assailant, added to that stature.

With this came a growing acceptance that the ends justified the means. Fraud and cheating, on the stock exchange and in other business dealings, now seemed fair ways to compete, so long as one emerged the winner. Daniel Drew, one of the most corrupt speculators of the day, was affectionately known as 'Uncle Daniel' and always had a coterie of admirers who sought to emulate his methods, and his profits (Fowler 1880). One observer, the liberal journalist Ida Tarbell, referred to the onset of what she called 'commercial Machiavellianism' and, as the quote at the head of this chapter suggests, believed that the new generation of managers and business leaders believed that business was like war, when it was permissible to use any means in order to achieve victory (Tarbell 1906). Again, as in Europe, there were business-people who opposed this view, but as yet they lacked a voice.

It was Tarbell herself who helped set the change in motion. Her series of articles on Standard Oil, followed by a book (Tarbell 1904), helped expose corrupt practice at the heart of one of the country's most admired businesses and ultimately led to the company being broken up by court order (see Case Study 8A). Her articles were part of a larger movement known as the 'Muck-Rakers', journalists and writers who uncovered corruption in business and government. Their efforts changed the public mood, and a new atmosphere emerged in which big business and its leaders were treated with suspicion and even contempt. This attitude lasted until at least the end of the First World War, when a new generation of entrepreneurs emerged and captured the public's attention; only for many to fall from grace in their turn with the Wall Street crash of 1929. Ever since, American public opinion has swung back and forth between admiration of big business, and suspicion and hatred of it.

### The iniquities of big business

The goose that lays golden eggs has been considered a most valuable possession. But even more profitable is the privilege of taking the golden eggs laid by somebody else's goose. The investment bankers and their associates now enjoy that privilege. They control the people through the people's own money. If the bankers' power were commensurate only with their wealth, they would have relatively little influence on American business. Vast fortunes like those of the Astors are no doubt regrettable. They are inconsistent with democracy. They are unsocial. And they seem peculiarly unjust when they represent largely unearned increment. But the wealth of the Astors does not endanger political or industrial liberty. It is insignificant in amount as compared with the aggregate wealth of America, or even of New York City. It lacks significance largely because its owners have only the income from their own wealth. The Astor wealth is static.

The wealth of the Morgan associates is dynamic. The power and the growth of power of our financial oligarchs comes from wielding the savings and quick capital of others. In two of the three great life insurance companies the influence of J. P. Morgan & Co. and their associates is exerted without any individual investment by them whatsoever. Even in the Equitable, where Mr. Morgan bought an actual majority of all the outstanding stock, his investment amounts to little more than one-half of one per cent. of the assets of the company. The fetters which bind the people are forged from the people's own gold.

–Louis M. Brandeis, *Other People's Money, and What the Bankers Do With It* (1914: 5)

---

For always builders want to build, bakers want to bake, manufacturers want to produce, railroads want to carry, workingmen want to work, merchants want to sell, and housewives want to buy. And why is it that sometimes all these operations seem to stop? Just because when things are going well some men will say: 'This is the time to make a big haul. People begin to want what we have to sell; therefore it is a good time to boost the price; they're in the mood to buy and they will pay more.'

This is criminal, just as criminal as cashing in on a war. But it springs from ignorance. A part of industry understands so little of the essential laws of prosperity, that times of business revival appear like grab-bag periods in which the highest business wisdom is to get while the getting is good.

–Henry Ford, *Today and Tomorrow* (1926: 34)

---

In both Europe and America, this change in mood was reflected by a change in attitude on the part of many – though not all – business leaders. For example, European firms began looking more seriously at profit-sharing, and hundreds of firms adopted profit-sharing schemes, partly out of self-interest so as to achieve labour peace but in at least some cases out of conviction.

To summarise, we have seen changes of mood, changes in the acceptance of business and businesspeople and their rights to make profits in exchange for providing goods and services to society. For centuries, the prevailing view was that businesspeople played a role in society by supplying wants and ensuring prosperity; in return, they were entitled to a 'fair' profit. That arrangement broke down at the beginning of the Industrial Revolution in Europe and then America, but the result in the early twentieth century was a backlash in which business leaders and managers came in for heavy criticism. It is not yet clear whether at present, we are going to return to the old equilibrium or evolve towards some new arrangement. At the moment, as public reaction to the financial crisis of 2008 continues to reverberate, things remain in a state of flux.

## 8.3 The meaning of ethics

When we look up 'ethics' and 'morals' in the *Oxford English Dictionary*, we find these terms defined by the use of other terms such as 'rightness', 'correctness' 'behaving honourably', 'virtuous in general conduct' or 'concerned with the distinction between right and wrong'. This leaves us some latitude for interpretation. Some ethicists argue that there are things which are *always* right and others which are *always* wrong, but others see the issue as being somewhat more fuzzy. Most would agree with St Thomas Aquinas, who said that ethical standards – i.e., things that are right and things that are wrong – are mutually agreed by society, which then expects its members to conform to its rules. That of course leaves the door wide open for moral relativism; things which might be right in one place or one set of circumstances are wrong in another.

Looking back over the past, we can see that some things are universally agreed to be unethical. These include:

- defrauding customers, either by selling them short measure or lying about the quality of goods sold;
- taking money under false pretences from customers by promising to deliver goods or a service and then not doing so;
- selling goods and services which are likely to result in death or injury to customers;
- theft of money or goods which properly belong to the owners/shareholders of the business;
- causing physical harm to employees, whether deliberately or by negligence;
- failing to pay employees the wages that are owed to them without due cause;
- failing to pay taxes or acknowledge other responsibilities to government and state.

These things were often done, but they were not done with the general approbation of society, and when they were done there was an excellent chance of the transgressors being punished; if they were under the jurisdiction of the law code of Hammurabi, then the penalty might well be death. Medieval merchants who sold short measure were paraded through the streets and pelted with dung and rotting vegetables. Today's punishments are altogether more genteel.

The only item which might arouse controversy is the third, where there is discussion over what actually constitutes a harmful product or service. We will come on to this in a moment.

More interesting is the list of things on which there have been divergences of opinion:

- using armed force to defend one's own business interests or attack competitors;
- trading in slaves or using slave labour;
- trading in harmful substances which are not prohibited by law;
- supplanting local governments or taking over the role of government entirely from local rulers;
- using deception or trickery in competitive situations;
- deliberately forcing rival firms out of the market;
- paying and receiving bribes.

All of these things have been done by business managers in the past, and all have been justified; but equally, all have been criticised. In the early sixteenth century the Dutch and English East India Companies fought an outright war for control of trade routes and spices in Indonesia, which resulted in several hundred deaths (see Case Study 3C). The Dutch East India Company's manager, Jan Pieterszoon Coen, argued that this was justifiable in order to protect the interests of his own company. His directors disagreed, and were clearly uneasy with the level of violence that Coen was prepared to employ, but eventually they gave in and let him have his way (the fact that he was winning the war may have swayed their decision). Other companies which have used force to defend their property and assets, or to take over those of others, have similarly justified their actions on the grounds of expediency, but have continued to face criticism. When the East India Company assumed political power in Bengal in the aftermath of its victory over local forces at the Battle of Plassey in 1757, there were fears in England that this would lead to the Company establishing dominion over the whole of India, and calls for it to surrender its conquests. This did not happen, and the Company did indeed go on to rule much of India for the next hundred years.

Even the highly ethical Robert Owen used American cotton harvested by slave labour, and many other European, American and Asian businesses have been directly or indirectly involved in the trade in slavery or have used slave labour. Not everyone in society agreed that this was justifiable at the time, and there were furious debates over both the morality of using slaves and the economic efficiency of slavery. The American economist Henry Carey (1853) condemned slavery on both grounds.

The selling of harmful products is an issue which has generated much heat. In general this is perceived as unethical, but what if there is dispute as to whether the products are harmful? For decades, the tobacco industry denied that its products were harmful and argued that there was a popular demand which should be satisfied. In the early nineteenth century, physicians and missionaries pleaded with the British government to halt the sale of opium into China, arguing that this was harmful to both the physical and mental health of the Chinese people. The opium traders disagreed, pointing out that opium was not universally harmful and was used in many medicines (Queen Victoria used laudanum, an opium-based product, to treat headaches). It took decades before the trade was finally halted.

The use of deception and trickery and the deliberate forcing of clients out of the market are two issues that have not gone away. On the one hand, it is argued, firms are engaged in a competitive struggle, and losing that struggle means they might not survive. Therefore, any means which help them to survive should be allowed. On the other hand, a free and fair market depends on free and fair competition, and violation of the spirit of that competition distorts the market, injuring the interests not just of competitors but of customers. The same arguments are deployed on both sides when it comes to bribery. While agreeing that bribery is wrong in principle, some managers argue, there are times – when dealing with corrupt government officials, for example – when it is expedient to pay bribes. Not doing so might harm the business.

---

### A case of survival?

During the Great Depression of the 1930s, a small shipyard in the north-east of England found itself struggling to survive. With its last orders completed and no more orders on the books, the young shipyard manager knew that he would have to lay off his workers in a matter of weeks. The yard was also the main employer in the local town, and the effect not just on the workers but on the town itself would be devastating.

By chance, the manager heard that the state-owned oil company of Romania was planning to commission the building of two tankers. In a desperate hope of keeping his yard alive, the manager flew to Bucharest and met with officials of the oil company and of the Romanian government, who had to approve the deal. To his delight, negotiations proceeded quickly and a deal was put together in a few days. Then the Romanian government officials informed him privately that he would need to pay them a large bribe. Without this, there would be no contract.

The manager now faced a dilemma: pay the bribe, which he knew to be morally and legally wrong, perhaps risk going to prison and ruining his career, but at the same time win the orders and keep his shipyard and the town alive? Or do the honourable thing, refuse to pay the bribe, and then go home and close his shipyard and lay off his workers and see the town sink into poverty?

Which would you do? To find out what happened, read on to the end of this chapter.

---

### 8.3.1  *Behaving ethically – or not*

While it was generally agreed, including by most business people, that businesses and managers should behave ethically, there was no universal agreement on what that meant. Nor would everyone have agreed with the American businessman Henry Dennison (1932) when he said that he would prefer to fail honourably than to triumph using underhanded means. There was, and is still, an argument which says that the interests of the business must be protected because, after all, the interests of the business are those of society, and if the business goes bankrupt when it could have saved itself by using underhanded means, then there will be damage not just to the owners of the business but to employees and their families, customers, suppliers and others who derived an income or value as a result of the company's activities.

All this has led some to suggest that what is ethical in business is not necessarily the same as what is ethical in the rest of society, and that there ought to be two different ethical standards. This was rejected emphatically by Tarbell (1906), who stated categorically that businesses and managers had to abide by the same moral standards as the rest of the population. Anything else would promote businesses and managers into a special position where they were able to do things forbidden to other people, which would merely increase their power. This, said Tarbell – never a woman to mince her words – was a threat to democracy. It should be added that Tarbell was not a mere anti-capitalist ranter. Many in the business world thought highly of her, and she wrote a number of articles on management issues for the magazine *System* which was closely associated with the scientific management movement. She also wrote a favourable biography of Owen Young, the chairman of GE and one of the founders of RCA, describing his own attitudes to ethics and the relationship between business and society and holding him up as a role model for younger managers.

In the end, we come back to two problems. The first is that some managers will always behave unethically, no matter what the societal or other pressures are for them to behave honestly. Either their own experience and education has not prepared them to act morally, or, and perhaps more often, they convince themselves that things they know to be wrong are in fact right. In a much more recent study, Norberg (2005) commented that 'brokers feel confident in doing right, and do not feel urged to take much moral responsibility. They experience little of moral stress, no matter the existence of moral support structures.' There are plenty of examples of this in other branches of management throughout history. The second problem is that of the grey areas: either values have changed and what is moral in one time and place is immoral in another, or else we have a paradox where *all* choices seem to involve a degree of immorality. In the case of the latter, as Henry Dennison said, all one can do is use one's judgement and try to be honest.

---

**Unfool yourself**

In any complex social situation, and especially in one as complex as business, whatever standard [the manager] may adopt he will seldom find any sharp line between right and wrong; not all the sheep are sheep, nor the goats goats; and a flock of half-breeds and quarter-breeds offer difficult problems of classification.

For the solution of these infinitely varied border-line cases of business conduct no one can give him any specific rules. There is, however, one important warning to be given. In choosing his course in the middle ground of doubtful action, where there are no sharp contrasts, he must realize that he has a deeply inherited ability to 'kid' himself into believing that whatever he finally decides to do is right. When his desires are deeply involved, or his old traditions concerned, man's unfortunate gift of fooling himself as to the real facts and the real principles involved in an actual case before him for action, sometimes amounts to genius. The first and great commandment, then, for all who care to make sincere efforts to live up to whatever codes of ethics they may adopt should be, 'don't fool yourself', or rather, since unconsciously and often inevitably you will fool yourself, 'unfool yourself, systematically, persistently, mercilessly.'

(Dennison 1932: 7-8)

---

## 8.4 Themes and influences

In his satirical novel of 1932, *Brave New World*, the author Aldous Huxley portrays a world in which business culture has come to dominate popular culture. Henry Ford has been elevated to the status of a deity, and people offer prayers to 'Our Ford' instead of 'Our Lord'. The benevolent dictator who rules the world is Mustapha Mond, a deliberate swipe at Alfred Mond, chairman of ICI in Britain, who in the 1920s had embarked on a series of more than a hundred acquisitions of companies in many different industries (the British press had already nicknamed him 'the Great Conglomerator'). The alphanumeric system of marketing segmentation, ABC1, C2 and so on, had now become a system of social classification; who you were and your rank in society was determined by what you consumed.

Instead of portraying the future, as is sometimes assumed, Huxley was in fact reflecting the tensions of the present. In *Brave New World* one can find all the contradictions of contemporary society's attitude to the world of business: on the one hand, wanting the goods and services it produces, and on the other, fearing and sometimes hating its apparent dominance and the threat it seems to pose to personal liberty. That dual attitude still exists today, and we can find evidence for it stretching far back into the past.

### 8.4.1 The morality of profit

Whether it was 'right' or 'fair' for people to profit from business is a subject that has been discussed since the time of Confucius, and does not seem ready to go away. That, in theory, people should be allowed to take profit in exchange for the risks they run in supplying society and meeting its needs, was agreed by Confucius, St Thomas Aquinas, the early Muslim jurists, and later commentators including Ida Tarbell, Henry Dennison and Freeman Hunt. The problem has traditionally lain not in the principle, but in the amount of profit taken. Confucius believed that profits should be restricted, for he was not in favour of excessive wealth, and a host of commentators from all the major faiths and beyond have agreed with him. Too much wealth in the hands of a few, it is said, harms the interests of the many.

But how are profits to be restricted? How much wealth is enough? How is the amassing of vast fortunes to be prevented, and is it even wise to attempt to do so? Seeing the fortunes of others is one of the spurs to ambition which makes men and women desire to acquire fortunes of own. Andrew Carnegie was one such, and in the end he amassed a fortune of nearly half a billion dollars. His disposal of that fortune unquestionably brought good to the world. One project alone, the building and endowing of public libraries in hundreds of towns in North America and Britain, contributed immeasurably to the spread of literacy and knowledge in the Western world. Was Carnegie ethical or unethical? Did he fulfil his responsibility to society, or did he unfairly withhold wealth from others? To argue either case seems illogical; is it possible to argue both at once?

Freeman Hunt's portrayal of the early American merchant Peter Brooks portrays a man who preferred not to amass a great fortune. He did indeed give most of it to charitable causes; but who has had the greatest impact on the world, Brooks or Andrew Carnegie? The argument that by amassing more wealth one can do more good is a powerful one.

The argument of the morality of profit, then, seems to be in many cases a cover for arguments about the merits and actions of individual people. Some people amass great wealth and behave responsibly and ethically; others do not. Perhaps we should be focusing more on individual cases than on principles?

### 8.4.2 Business and society: giving something back

Following on from this there is the notion that it is alright to take profits and amass wealth so long as something is given back to society. This is a twist on the corporate social responsibility argument which suggests that businesses have a duty to the societies in which they operate. The idea of reciprocity, which stretches back at least to Aquinas, is more complex. His notion of equilibrium suggests that there is a balance between the needs of business and the needs of society, and both sides need to seek to find that balance. An atmosphere of mutual respect and tolerance is necessary if this is to work, a point made powerfully by the Boston department store owner Edward Filene (1932; see also Case Study 8B).

There has been an argument that by providing goods and services, companies are already 'giving' something to society. Carnegie sold steel which was used to build railways which in turn enabled the feeding of America's cities. Rockefeller sold oil which was refined as kerosene and used as a lubricant for machinery in the factories which made America's finished goods. Richard Arkwright furnished Britain with cheap, high-quality cotton garments. For this they took a profit. Was this not enough?

In general the answer to this question has been 'no', although during the Industrial Revolution it did become socially acceptable to amass large profits and keep them for oneself. Sometimes people thought of clever solutions which benefitted themselves and society. In Renaissance Florence, Cosimo dei Medici patronised some of the world's greatest artists and gave Florence some spectacular works of art; but in doing so, he also enhanced his own reputation and that of his business. His altruism was in fact a cleverly disguised bid for further advantage. Generally, though, it is expected that large corporations and those investors and shareholders who have made large profits from owning them *should* be altruistic; and many over the centuries have been happy to use their wealth for the betterment of society.

There is no managerial or economic logic to this. Indeed, if we were to follow logic we would adopt the position of Milton Friedman, referred to earlier: the purpose of a business is to make money, and all wealth not required for re-investment in the business should be returned to shareholders. A business which gives money to charity is in effect committing an act of theft; that money belongs to the shareholders and is not the business's money to give. If the shareholders want to give *their* money to charity, of course, that is their business and they are free to do so.

Looking back over time, however, we can see two reasons why this does not work. The first concerns the management of perceptions. If a company is seen to be amassing a fortune and making its owners rich, then no matter what benefits it is providing to society through its goods and services, then the public will begin to see that company as being greedy and taking excessive profits. If the company is managed by its owners and it is hard to distinguish between corporate profits and those of the owners, then the problem is compounded. Supporting charitable causes, helping the less fortunate or sponsoring projects in developing countries, taking on social responsibilities all help to assuage public fears. Sometimes these are simply public relations exercises, designed to distract the public – that accusation was made against John D. Rockefeller when he announced that he was setting up a charitable trust just as the US government began legal proceedings to break up his company. But sometimes these are cases of genuine commitment and belief on the behalf of the individuals involved, that having earned a fortune they have a duty to use it for the benefit of others.

This brings us to the second point which is that, against all economic logic, human beings seem to have the wish to be altruistic. We know we are part of society and we know we depend on society for our own needs and wants. And, we should not forget that many of the most successful and wealthiest managers and leaders from the past, like Carnegie and Ernst Abbé and Sarah Breedlove Walker (Case Study 9C), came from humble backgrounds and sometimes conditions of real poverty. The desire to do something to help other families like one's own is powerful and not easily denied. So perhaps Henry Dennison was not completely right; we have a desire to accumulate, but we also have a desire to help those around us, and both are deeply ingrained in the psyches of most – though not all – of us.

---

### Standards in public morality

For the present, it is not to any machinery that we must look for the solution of these difficulties. It is to a wider sense of responsibility on the part of directors and general officers. The man who selects his sub-ordinates solely for their fitness in making the results of the year's accounts look best, and instructs them to work for these results at the sacrifice of all other interests, encourages the employees to work for themselves in defiance of the needs either of the corporation or of the public, and does more than almost any professional agitator to foster the spirit which makes labor organizations unreasonable in their demands and defiant in their attitude. For the laborers, like some of the rest of us, are a good deal more affected by feeling than by reason; a good deal more influenced by examples than by syllogisms.

(Hadley 1907: 84)

---

### Power and responsibility

Society cannot afford to have individuals wield the power of thousands without personal responsibility. It cannot afford to let its strongest men be the only men who are inaccessible to the law. Modern democratic society, in particular, cannot afford to constitute its economic under-takings upon the monarchial or aristocratic principles and adopt the fiction that the kings and great men thus set up can do no wrong which will make them personally amenable to the law which restrains smaller men; that their kingdoms, not themselves, must suffer for their blind-ness, their follies, and their transgressions of right.

It does not redeem the situation that these kings and chiefs of indus-try are not chosen on the hereditary principle (sometimes, alas! they are) but are men who have risen by their own capacity, sometimes from utter obscurity, with the freedom of self-assertion which should characterize a free society. Their power is none the less arbitrary and irresponsible when obtained. That a peasant may become a king does not render the kingdom democratic.

–future US President Woodrow Wilson speaking in
1910 (quoted in Ripley 1927: 6)

### 8.4.3  *The purpose of business*

But philanthropy, whether corporate or private, does not discharge the duties of the business to society. Early in this chapter we discussed the ideas of John Davis, who argued that society creates businesses in order to fulfil its own needs, and when businesses no longer fulfil those needs, it destroys them. The trades in slavery and opium are two examples of this. In the case of the latter some of the businesses involved, such as the Hong Kong-based trading house Jardine Matheson, diversified into other, acceptable activities and survived. Other smaller trading concerns either closed down or continued to trade illegally. Illegal slave dealing survived for some years too, thanks to a continued (legal) demand for slaves in the southern states of the USA, but the complete abolition of slavery there in 1865 destroyed the market and ended the West African trade. Today, as noted, the tobacco industry faces similar sanctions, and the many millions that firms have given to charitable causes, including cancer research, have not so far distracted society from its aim of abolishing this industry.

It is of course a matter of simple marketing logic that if a firm provides goods and services that people want and need then it will survive, whereas if it fails to do so then it will fail. The added dimension of social responsibility – implicit too in the 'societal marketing concept' developed by Kotler (1997; see also Kotler and Levy 1969) – is that the goods and services provided must also enhance the well-being of the consumer and of society as a whole. If not, then society will take notice and may begin imposing sanctions, even attempting to outlaw the company or the industry altogether.

Just such a thing happened in America in the first part of the twentieth-century. The majority of public opinion, bolstered by business leaders and some respected economists, had accepted with some reservations the view that large monopolies like Standard Oil and United States Steel and the Beef Trust were good things, beneficial to society. But by 1900 doubts were setting in, and Ida Tarbell's articles in *McClure's* beginning in 1902 magnified those doubts. Within a few years, public opinion had swung against the trusts, and the government of President Theodore Roosevelt bowed to pressure and commenced legal action against Standard Oil. Other trusts were broken up by court order too, while still others like the Tobacco Trust saw the writing on the wall and dissolved themselves. The trusts were no longer serving society; or more important, society *believed* they no longer were, and they had to go.

The long-held view, from Confucius and Aquinas to Robert Owen, Ida Tarbell and John Davis, has been that businesses exist to serve social needs. Society creates them, and can destroy them. Experience suggests that businesses which ignore this concept substantially increase their own risks.

---

### The social aspect of business

All human activity has its social as well as its individual aspect. Man is so essentially a 'social animal' that his every act, however insignificant, has its effect, directly or indirectly, on his fellows. All men sustain social relations to all other men. The effect of the social relations – growth, stagnation or decay – is a product of two factors, the content (function) of the human activity and the organization (form) within which it is exerted. The existence of each factor implies the existence of the other. Social functions are exercised only through the machinery of social forms; yet the forms are continually suffering modification to meet the demands of new or altered functions. In general, function and form depend on and react upon each other; growth, stagnation and decay in each are reflected in some degree in the condition of the other. The corporation is a group of natural persons embodied in one of the many forms of organization within or through which certain classes of social functions are exercised.

(Davis 1897: 278)

---

#### 8.4.4 Towards a stakeholder theory

It is only relatively recently that we have seen the emergence of a coherent and all-inclusive stakeholder theory that encompasses all interest groups, considering customers, employees and society at large to be stakeholders along with shareholders. Yet the elements have been present in rudimentary form for a long time. From the Middle Ages, if not longer, it has been accepted that businesses have a relationship with their customers, and that the latter in turn exercise influence over the business. That businesses have a duty of care and responsibility to their employees has also been discussed for centuries. Whether for paternalistic reasons or for reasons of self-interest, managers have established relationships with employees, and managers in some top-performing firms like Cadbury, Carl Zeiss Jena, Filene's Sons and John Lewis encouraged employees to play a greater role in the business.

The responsibility of business to society has been one of the focal points of this chapter. We have seen how society's expectations and needs have changed and fluctuated, just as do those of customers and employees – and for that matter, those of shareholders. What has happened up until now is that the needs of each group have been managed individually. Sometimes, as in the case of Cadbury, the needs have been aligned. In other cases such as that of National Cash Register, whose senior managers had a good and sympathetic relationship with employees but were indicted for criminal offences relating to their competitive tactics, the alignment has not been there.

We are still probably some distance from a working stakeholder model that encompasses the whole firm and all its stakeholders. But those who are working towards such a theory might be heartened to know that all the individual elements have been discussed in detail for hundreds of years, and put into practice in many cases. There remains the not inconsiderable task of coordinating them all and aligning them with each other.

## 8.5 Questions and discussion: what is a business for?

This is a seldom-asked question. It is not the same as the much more frequent question, what is our purpose? Identifying purpose usually means defining aims and goals, or it is sometimes couched in general terms such as, 'our purpose is to create satisfied customers' or 'our purpose is to achieve excellence in all areas of activity'.

But these responses don't answer our first question. To identify what a business is for, if we follow the logic of commentators such as John Davis, we first of all have to identify what people want from it. That means customers, primarily but not solely; the wants and needs and demands of other interest groups must be taken into account too. Customers are not the only people whose needs must be taken into account; were that so, then the tobacco industry would be flourishing as never before.

The relationship between a business and society is a much more complex one than is indicated by the terms 'corporate social responsibility'. To state that businesses are responsible to society is like stating that children are responsible to their parents; it is true, but the relationship goes much deeper than that. In many of the theories we have seen in the past, and in the actions of at least some managers and business leaders, 'responsibility' is only one element. Truly successful businesses are not just ones that feel responsible. They understand, very often implicitly, the nature of the bond that connects them with society. They understand that they and society cannot do without each other; that society *needs* the goods and services they provide and that they themselves have a duty to provide it. But even duty is too weak a word in some cases. In the case studies that have accompanied this book, we have seen people like William Lever (Case Study 3A), Father José Maria the founder of Mondragón (Case Study 2D), Tomas Bat'a (Case Study 4B) and Hans Renold (Case Study 7C) who had about them a sense of passion. Many were only secondarily interested in money; profit was a by-product of their real work, and their true calling lay in the conduct of business itself. Their purpose was not just to serve society but to be part of it, engage with it and, if at all possible, improve it.

Looking at these examples, however, we have to ask the question as to whether this is realistic in every case. These were extraordinary people leading extraordinary organisations. Can every manager, every business realistically expect to make this kind of impact?

And if not, then what should be their aims? What is the modest best we should hope for? Or should we not aim so low? Dream no little dreams, said the German philosopher Goethe; should we take him at his word, and all of us as managers aim to do something that will change society around us for the better? It is by answering these questions that we will truly discover our own purposes, and those of the businesses we run.

---

### A case of survival? cont'd

After much soul-searching, the shipyard manager arranged to pay the bribe to the Romanian government authorities and the contract was signed the following day. He returned home to a hero's welcome in the town, and the shipyard at once began work on the two tankers. The income from this project kept the yard going over a year, by which time the economic situation had eased and new orders began coming in; the yard soon returned to prosperity.

The young manager was not there to see it. Six months after the events described above, he was arrested by British police and charged with corruption. He cooperated fully with the police investigation and pleaded guilty to the charges, having determined earlier that he would face the consequences of his actions. He served a two-year prison term and was barred from ever serving as company director or holding a senior managerial post again. His career wrecked, he spent much of the rest of his life working as a clerk.

A fictional account of this story, romantic but capturing the dilemma, can be found in Nevil Shute's novel *The Ruined City*.

---

### Takeaway exercise

This exercise comes from my colleague Marianne Jennings of Arizona State University. She asks her students the following question: what is the minimum standard of ethical behaviour that you set for yourself? In other words, where do you draw the line between things you might be prepared to do, even though distasteful, and those you would not do under any circumstances? Ask yourself this question, and if you feel brave, ask your colleagues too and compare the answers. Once again, this is an exercise that could do with repeating at intervals.

## Case Study 8A

### Standard Oil

The Standard Oil Company was largely the creation of a single remarkable entrepreneur, John Davison Rockefeller. The son of a travelling salesman, he founded the company and built it up to become the world's largest oil company. He was widely admired for his managerial and financial skills, his determination to succeed, his religious faith (he was a devout Baptist) and not least for his charitable giving; in later years he spent millions of dollars a year from his private fortune on a wide variety of charitable causes. Ironically, it was his skill and determination that also made him widely hated and feared. At the height of his power he was regarded by many, including some in high places, as a danger to the American state.

Rockefeller began his working life as a clerk at a shipping company. In 1859, using his savings, he started a small shipping business of his own, managing a small fleet of boats carrying goods on the rivers of Pennsylvania. The discovery of oil in Pennsylvania offered an opportunity, especially during the American Civil War when northern factories required large amounts of kerosene (which was used as a machine lubricant). Rockefeller's shipping company made substantial profits, and was well placed to take advantage of the post-war economic boom.

Standard Oil itself was founded in New York state in 1866, initially as a kerosene-refining business. The oil industry, like many infant industries, had a large number of players, and competition among refiners grew increasingly severe. Rockefeller, like J.P. Morgan and many other business leaders of his age, grew alarmed at the extent and nature of competition, which he saw as potentially ruinous not only to the industry but to society at large. In 1870 he began a sustained campaign to corner the market in refining petroleum.

Ironically, the tactics he used were even more ruthless than those of his competitors. Standard Oil and another Rockefeller company, the Southern Improvement Company, undercut their competitors in every way they could. They struck deals with the railways to arrange lower freight rates for themselves, then used these lower margins to underprice their rivals until the latter were driven out of business. Standard Oil then bought up these bankrupt rival companies, often for far less than their assets were worth, and added them to Rockefeller's growing empire. Other rivals were pressured into selling their companies to Rockefeller, at first by means of fair offers, and then later by intimidation; there were frequent accusations of sabotage and violence done to the employees of rival firms whose owners refused to sell.

In 1877 the Pennsylvania Railroad, formerly a Rockefeller ally, announced that it wished to diversify into refining. Rockefeller's response was to shift all his oil tank cars to the rival New York Central and Erie lines, and even to shut down his refineries in Pittsburgh, which could only be serviced by the Pennsylvania. After a stand-off of a year, and a strike on the Pennsylvania allegedly encouraged by Rockefeller, the Pennsylvania board called off the planned diversification.

In 1882, Rockefeller organised the Standard Oil trust. He took the legal concept whereby a parent could hold property in trust for a minor, and applied it to oil companies. All of the shares held by the stockholders of the forty Standard Oil companies in several states were transferred to a new group of nine trustees, led by Rockefeller himself. The Standard Oil trust was now created as a new umbrella organisation based in the state of Ohio. Stockholders were issued trust certificates, which were effectively shares in the new umbrella corporation, in exchange for handing over their original shares. The nine trustees owned two-thirds of Standard Oil and thus together controlled the corporation and all its subsidiaries. Legally, the forty subsidiary firms were independent, but in practice they were a $70 million monopoly, all profits of which went to the Ohio-based trust. Restructured, Standard Oil now began taking over oilfields, investing in exploration of new fields and beginning operations in Europe, Asia and Latin America, becoming in the process a multinational corporation.

Standard Oil was investigated for unfair trading practices by the US Congress in 1888, and its trust was dissolved in 1892 by the Ohio Supreme Court. Undeterred, Rockefeller founded a new trust in New Jersey in 1899. Standard Oil of New Jersey was a holding company permitted by that state's law to hold stock in other companies. It was run by Rockefeller and fourteen other directors, who controlled an empire of $205 million in 1900, and $360 million by 1906. It was the most powerful company in the nation, rivalled only by United States Steel, although the rise of Royal Dutch/Shell and new independent Texas oilmen would cut its worldwide share of petroleum production to around 60 per cent.

Two things in particular aroused opposition to Standard Oil. The first was the vindictiveness of its competitive methods. Rockefeller offered rival refiners the chance to sell up and join Standard Oil and some, like Henry Rogers, did so; Rogers sold his company to Rockefeller in exchange for a top management position, and went on to become a powerful and very wealthy figure within Standard Oil. But those who refused were driven out of business and ruined. Many were never able to work in the oil industry again, or did so only as manual labourers to support themselves and their families.

The second was the company's obsessive secrecy. Few figures are available about Standard Oil's financial performance because records were never disclosed and were routinely destroyed. When called to account before Congressional committees, Rockefeller executives proved masters of 'stone-walling'. The following extracts from the minutes of committee hearings, published in Henry Lloyd's book *Wealth Against Commonwealth*, is typical:

'What is your business and where do you reside?' another of the trustees was asked by the State of New York.
'I decline to answer any question until I can consult counsel.'

'What is the capital stock?' was asked of another.

'I do not know.'

'How much has the capital increased since?'

'I don't know.'

'Where are the meetings of the Standard Oil Company held?'

'I don't know.'

'How many directors are there?'

'I don't know.'

'Do they own any pipelines?'

'I don't know.' ...

'What quantity of oil was exported by the different concerns with which you were connected from the port of New York in 1881?' the president [of Standard Oil] was asked.

'I do not know.'

'How many millions of barrels of oil were refined by such concerns in the vicinity of New York in 1881?'

'I don't know how much was refined.'

'Did not the concern with which you were so connected purchase over 8,000,000 barrels of crude petroleum in 1881?'

'I am unable to state.'

He was asked to give the name of one refinery in this country, running at the time (1883), not owned or substantially controlled by his concern. 'I decline to answer.'

He was asked if he would say the total profits of his trust's companies for the last year (1887) were not as much as $20,000,000.

'I haven't the least knowledge on that subject.'

(Lloyd 1894: 467)

*Wealth Against Commonwealth* was an early attempt to expose the abuses of Standard Oil. However, its author was a crusading socialist journalist and newspaper editor, and his anti-capitalist agenda made it easy for Standard Oil and its supporters to discredit the book. A far more formidable challenge appeared in 1903 with the appearance of a series of articles in the popular magazine *McClure's* by another journalist, Ida Tarbell. Although her father had been one of the Pennsylvania oilmen driven out of business by Rockefeller, this was not her primary motive for writing the book. She was a liberal in favour of open competition and free trade, and felt that monopolies such as Standard Oil were dangerous. She was a best-selling author already, and her work commanded immediate attention. Her articles, later collected in book form as *The History of the Standard Oil Company* (1904), were careful to give credit to the skill and enterprise of Rockefeller and his managers. Indeed, she said, this was what made Standard Oil so particularly dangerous:

While there can be no doubt that the determining factor in the success of the Standard Oil Company in securing a practical monopoly of the oil industry has been the special privileges it has enjoyed since the beginning of its career, it is equally true that those privileges alone will not account for its success. Something besides illegal advantages has gone into the making of the Standard Oil Trust. Had it possessed only those qualities which the general public has always attributed to it, its overthrow would have come before this. But this huge bulk, blackened with commercial sin, has always been strong in all great business qualities – in energy, in intelligence, in dauntlessness. It has always been rich in youth as well as greed, in brains as well as unscrupulousness. If it has played its great game with contemptuous indifference to fair play, and to nice legal points of view, it has played it with consummate ability, daring and address. The silent, patient, all-seeing man who has led it on its transportation raids has led it no less successfully in what may be called its legitimate work. Nobody has appreciated more fully than he those qualities which alone make for permanent stability and growth in commercial ventures. He has insisted on these qualities, and it is because of that insistence that the Standard Oil Trust has always been something besides a fine piece of brigandage, with the fate of brigandage before it, that it has been a thing with a life and future.

(Tarbell 1904: vol. 2, 231–32)

Her exposure of the practices of Standard Oil, ranging from the securing of illegal rebates from railway companies in order to keep prices down, to violence and intimidation against the employees of other companies – and on occasion, its own employees – was deeply shocking. Nor could much of her evidence be discredited, for she revealed early on that she had a source at the highest level inside the companies. This was Henry Rogers, a director and trustee, who was engaged in his own battles with some of his senior colleagues and saw a chance to discredit them; he met with Tarbell on a number of occasions, supplied her with confidential papers, and even read and commented on drafts of her articles before publication. Tarbell's conclusion was that public action was needed to break the power of the big monopolies like Standard Oil, for moral as well as economic reasons, and that further, a wholesale change in the mentality of businesspeople was required.

There is something alarming to those who believe that commerce should be a peaceful pursuit, and who believe that moral law holds good throughout the entire range of human relations, in knowing that so large a body of young men in this country are consciously or unconsciously growing up with the idea that business is war and that morals have nothing to do with its practice.

And what are we going to do about it? For it is *our* business. We, the people of the United States, and nobody else, must cure whatever is wrong in the industrial situation, typified by this narrative of the growth of the Standard Oil Company.

(Tarbell 1904: vol. 2, 291–92)

Tarbell's attack on Standard Oil became the centrepiece of a liberal crusading movement known as the Muck-Rakers, who attacked monopoly and protectionism and argued in favour of free trade (although some of its members were socialists who carried the attack out against all big capitalists). Political leaders, notably President Theodore Roosevelt, listened to this change in public opinion and instituted legal action in 1906 to have Standard Oil broken up; this action finally succeeded in 1911, resulting in the creation of more than thirty separate companies out of the old trust. However, Standard Oil New Jersey quickly gained control of many of its former subsidiaries, and in the decades following the First World War under a new leader, Walter Teagle, Standard Oil rose to become once again one of the world's largest oil companies. In 1937 Teagle and his two chief rivals, John Cadman of Anglo-Persian (later British Petroleum) and Henri Deterding of Royal Dutch/Shell, met in Scotland and signed the so-called Achnacarry Agreement to fix the worldwide price of oil, setting a precedent for the modern OPEC cartel.

As well as detractors like Lloyd and Tarbell, Rockefeller has also had his defenders. He himself believed strongly that God had given him his fortune, estimated at about $1 billion, in order that he should use it for right ends. After 1911 he put much of this money into the Rockefeller Foundation, and during his own lifetime gave an estimated $500 million to charities of many kinds. His supporters argue that only through the creation of his business empire could he have accumulated the wealth which he later used to create much good.

## Analysis

Some of the questions you might want to consider in connection with this case include:

- Can Rockefeller's attitudes and actions be defended, and if so, how?
- Standard Oil may have restricted the free market and attempted to create a monopoly; but it grew out of a very free market in which there were few regulations. What does this tell us about the nature and role of regulation?
- Is it right that government and the media should intervene in the markets in the manner shown in this case? What role should public scrutiny play?
- What parallels with Standard Oil, if any, exist in the world today?

## Sources

Chernow, R. (1999) *Titan: The Life of John D. Rockefeller, Sr.*, New York: Random House.

Lloyd, Henry D. (1894) *Wealth Against Commonwealth*, New York: Harper & Bros.
Tarbell, I.M. (1904) *The History of the Standard Oil Company*, New York: McClure's.

## Case Study 8B

### *Filene's Sons*

Some businesspeople believe that the primary purpose of a business is to make money; others believe that its primary purpose is to serve society. The Boston department store owner Edward Filene took a different view. While he agreed emphatically that business had a social role, he also believed that business was an integral part of society, and further, that society needed to get behind the business community and support it. Writing in the early years of the Great Depression, he urged an end to the anti-business attitudes that he saw prevalent in some parts of America, on the grounds that these were damaging to both business and society itself.

Filene was born in Salem, Massachusetts in 1860, the son of a Jewish immigrant from Poznań (then in Prussia, now in Poland). Filene's father had worked as a travelling salesman before making enough money to found a dry goods store in Boston, but was forced to retire due to ill health in 1879. At age nineteen, Filene found himself in charge of the business, in partnership with his fourteen-year-old brother Lincoln Filene.[2]

Young though they were, the brothers at once made their mark. At a time when there was virtually no legal protection for customers and deception and outright fraud on the part of retailers – adulteration of food and soap products, selling bolts of cloth at shorter measure than advertised, mixing sand with salt and so on – were rife, the Filenes built a reputation for honesty. They treated customers fairly and made sure that they received the full quantity of goods paid for. The feature which first got the public's attention was a guarantee of a full refund if the customer was not satisfied with the goods purchased. Such guarantees were known in Europe but were still comparatively rare in America, and the store, now renamed William Filene's Sons, attracted a loyal customer base.

Filene's next step was to convert the original dry goods retail outlet into a department store. Again despite his youth, he was aware of advances in retailing elsewhere. The concept of the department store, pioneered in Paris in the 1850s, had spread rapidly to England and then to America, where stores such as Wanamaker's in Philadelphia and Macy's and Gimbel's in New York had proved popular. By 1891 Filene's Sons had expanded both the range of goods it carried and its premises and re-opened as a department store. This continued to trade using the same principles of the original shop. Filene's guiding principle, according to Urwick (1956) was that 'the customer is always right'. Customer service and customer care became important virtues.

From 1891 until his retirement in 1928 Filene served as president of William Filene's Sons, building the business into one of the largest retail operations in the USA. More locations were opened and in 1906 Filene developed a second brand, Filene's Basement, which operated on the 'bargain basement' principle and sold reliable goods very cheaply. This enabled the firm to capture a share of the working-class market which did not usually shop at the more upmarket department stores.

Filene also became a noted philanthropist and respected social commentator. Along with Henry Ford he supported the peace movement during the First World War, and after the war was a prominent supporter of the League of Nations, roundly criticising the US government for refusing to join it. He was a major funder of the Geneva-based International Management Institute, described by Urwick (1956: 86) as 'an international clearing-house for the exchange of information on better methods of management', in 1927, and he was also one of the major sponsors of the Twentieth Century Fund in America. During a visit to India he became acquainted with the local cooperative banks, and on returning home pressed the US government to follow this example; the result was the establishment of the credit union movement in America. Strangely, despite his philanthropy and sense of responsibility to customers and society, he was a difficult man who made few close friends. Johnson (1948) described him as a paradox, capable of both great generosity and great meanness, and Urwick (1956) suggests that his abrasive temper may have alienated some of his natural allies and prevented his ideas from becoming more widely disseminated.

Filene's principles of marketing for retail operations were publicised in several books, notably *More Profits from Merchandizing* (1925) and *The Model Stock Plan* (1930), and were of considerable influence in the development of retailing in the USA; Urwick (1956) described the latter work as one of the most influential works on marketing of all time. Filene believed that the primary purpose of marketing is not to make a profit, but to satisfy customer needs; if this is done successfully, then profits will follow. He competed successfully with his rivals on cost, aiming for low margins and rapid turnover of stock, the ancestor of the 'pile it high and sell it cheap' philosophy used by later retailers such as Sam Walton of Wal-Mart and German supermarket chains such as Aldi and Lidl. This philosophy was backed up with detailed accounting and inventory control systems. Filene is generally credited with being the first person to apply the principles of scientific management to retailing.

Filene was also a strong proponent of industrial democracy. Major decisions affecting the running of the business were often put to a vote among staff. Filene would always make his own position clear, but urged his staff to vote as they saw fit. When they voted down his ideas, he respected the decision of the majority and accepted defeat. He paid well and also reduced working hours; he was one of the first American employers to introduce the now standard five-day, forty-hour working week.

In 1932, five years before his death, Filene published his final book, *Successful Living in This Machine Age*. Here he spells out his own view of the relationship between business and society. In particular, he discussed the social changes that mass production and the rise of large corporations had wrought on America. He linked the rise of mass production to the rise of what the economist Thorstein Veblen (1924) had called 'the leisure classes', pointing out that many of the goods being produced and sold *en masse* were being purchased by those who had time and money to spare; thus mass production both led to greater consumer demand and was itself a product of greater consumer affluence. He believed that business owners and managers had a twofold responsibility to society: firstly, to provide employment which made affluence possible, and secondly to provide goods which satisfied the needs of the newly affluent.

But Filene's views went far beyond the conventional attitudes to socially responsible business. 'Even if I were in possession of an accurate formula by which everyone might become a great business leader', he wrote, 'I should hesitate to give it out. Business leadership is the crying need of the moment; but a world made up only of business leaders would be a horrible world to live in. On the other hand, a world in which business is not carried on successfully is always a horrible world' (Filene 1932: 5).

Filene argues that there is a balance that must be struck between the needs of business and the needs of society. On the one hand, 'business success, concededly, is not everything. If it were everything, in fact, it would be nothing. It might keep the race alive, but what would be the use of keeping a race alive if it had nothing more to do than keep alive?' (Filene 1932: 5). But at the same time, it is the world of business, and especially the new techniques of mass production, that were making it possible for more and more people to turn their minds to higher things. The new techniques in business were providing more goods more cheaply to consumers and improving both standards of living and the quality of life. The new generation of businesses were also paying better wages and helping to lift people out of poverty.[3] This last to Filene was particularly important:

> It is poverty which standardizes, and mass production cannot endure mass poverty. Poverty standardizes because it necessitates the spending of all one's time and energy upon the problem of keeping alive. If one's income is limited to fifteen cents a day, he must live in much the same way as does anyone else whose income is limited to fifteen cents a day, for there simply are not many ways of keeping alive on fifteen cents a day. Raise the general income to fifteen dollars a day, and there is at least some choice.
>
> (Filene 1932: 15)

In making these arguments, Filene was striking back at left-wing theorists such as Veblen who believed that the capitalist system was impoverishing people, and also at those who believed that big business was a threat to democracy. On the contrary, said Filene, business was *enabling* democracy:

Whether for good or ill, mass production is surely liberating man. It is giving him power, but it is as yet a most confusing power, for it is power which cannot be employed successfully in the domination of his fellow man. All man's experiences, all his traditions, have caused him to associate the possession of power with such domination: but mass production substitutes facts for tradition, even in the matter of achieving a successful life.

(Filene 1932: 15)

We may choose to disagree with Filene's view that mass production, by increasing personal wealth, created a more egalitarian society, but it was certainly his strongly held view. Business had a duty to help increase personal wealth, and society in turn had a responsibility to support business in this great endeavour to improve the lot of all people, everywhere. 'Business success is very definitely related to human success', he wrote, adding that even the family is basically an economic institution (Filene himself was not married and had no children). But business success was not an end in itself, but rather the means to an end. Filene concludes:

Mass production, then, is good for employers and workers and the consuming public. That means all of us. But it does not mean *all* of all of us. We are all employers or workers or consumers, to be sure, but most of us are something vastly more. Most of us are human beings, and because we are human beings, we long to rise above the mere job of staying alive.

(Filene 1932: 11)

## Analysis

Some of the questions you might want to consider in connection with this case include:

- Filene believed that business and society were mutually dependent and have responsibilities to each other. How far do you feel this is true?
- Urwick believed that Filene's own personality prevented his ideas from becoming more widely known and accepted. This may be true, but what other factors might have prevented Filene's ideas – and his own style of management – from being widely recognised? What arguments can be advanced against him?
- Have attitudes to social responsibility changed since Filene's day? If so, for better? Or for worse?

## Sources

Filene, Edward A. (1925) *More Profits from Merchandizing*, Chicago: A.W. Shaw.
Filene, Edward A. (1930) *The Model Stock Plan*, New York: McGraw Hill.

Filene, Edward A. (1932) *Successful Living in This Machine Age*, London: Jonathan Cape.

Johnson, Gerald (1948) *Liberal's Progress*, New York: Coward-McCann.

Stillman, Yanki (2004) 'Edward Filene: Pioneer of Social Responsibility', *Jewish Currents*.

Urwick, Lyndall (1956) 'Edward Albert Filene', in *The Golden Book of Management: A Historical Record of the Life and Work of Seventy Pioneers*, London: Newman Neame.

## Case Study 8C

### *Titus Salt*

Along with George Cadbury and Robert Owen, Titus Salt is one of the primary examples of a nineteenth-century British entrepreneur-philanthropist, a man who attempted to combine the management of a successful business with responsibility to society. Of the three, it was probably Salt who did most to put his beliefs into practice, becoming actively involved in his community and dividing his time between his business and his obligations to society.

Salt was born in 1803, the son of Daniel Salt, a moderately prosperous cloth merchant in Yorkshire. He received a good education at a grammar school and then served as an apprentice to a cloth manufacturer in the city of Bradford, learning about cloth-making and the fundamentals of business; like nearly every business leader of his day, Salt received his training 'on the job'. In 1822 he became a partner in his father's firm, and Daniel Salt & Son became a very prosperous business.

In the late 1820s Salt bought cheaply a large quantity of high-quality Russian wool known as Donskoi wool, and tried to sell this on to the cloth manufacturers of the cities of Leeds and Bradford. The fibres of Donskoi wool were longer than those of English wool and would require technical adjustments to spinning frames in order to be spun into yarn; accordingly, local manufacturers were not interested. Undeterred, Salt designed the requisite machinery and set up his own factory in Bradford to make what was known as 'worsted' cloth. This was a very successful venture, and provided capital for further expansion.

In 1833 Daniel Salt retired and Titus Salt became sole proprietor. His next step was to investigate methods for making high-grade cloth using alpaca wool from South America.

Previous experiments with alpaca had not been successful, and Salt's friends and family refused to invest in the new venture. However, Salt assembled a small group of weavers and engineers and began experimenting in secret. By 1836 they had designed the necessary technology to produce fine alpaca cloth, and another factory was established. Alpaca cloth at once became very fashionable, in London and across Europe, owing to its softness and fine appearance. Salt within a short time had developed the technology to produce alpaca cloth of very high quality. By 1850 Salt owned six cloth factories in Bradford and was a very wealthy man.

Despite his wealth, Salt and his workers lived in one of the most polluted cities in the world. Bradford was sometimes described as the 'dirtiest city in Britain'. The city's factories were powered by steam, the boilers heated by coal, and smoke and soot poured constantly from hundreds of chimneys in and around the city. The river which flowed through the city was both the source of drinking water and the drain for its untreated sewage. Rates of infant mortality, even by the standards of the time, were very high and other diseases flourished. Average life expectancy was the lowest in the country.

In the early 1840s Salt had launched a campaign for cleaner air in the city, without success. It may have been this failure to persuade his fellow mill-owners to do anything about the city's terrible environmental and health problems that persuaded him to stand for election as mayor of Bradford (he had been an alderman, a member of the city council, since 1837). He served only a brief term as mayor, in 1848–49. During his term he conducted an enquiry into the state of the city's working-class housing and was shocked at the conditions he found. In 1849 Bradford suffered a severe epidemic of cholera caused by the polluted waters, and much of Salt's efforts as mayor were devoted to dealing with this crisis.

In 1850, despairing of ever reforming conditions in Bradford, Salt resolved to move his own operations out of the city. He did this partly in order to protect his own workers, and partly in hopes of persuading others to follow his example. His choice was a greenfield site three miles north of the city, where he intended to concentrate all his business operations on a single site. Work began on a state-of-the-art factory which employed some of the most modern cloth-production technology in Europe. Further, the factory was designed to provide a safe and clean working environment. Ventilation was introduced to keep dust levels down, and the shafts and chains that drove the machinery were placed under the floors of the workshops in order to reduce noise. The new factory, which opened in 1853 with a production capacity of 30,000 yards of cloth per day, was not only efficient but clean and safe.

Salt's next step was to follow the example of Robert Owen and build housing for his workers. The town of Saltaire eventually included housing for 4,500 workers and their families. It included schools, a hospital, a Congrega-tional church and a Methodist chapel, shops, a community centre and ale-houses for recreation. Clean water was provided from a purpose-built reservoir, and there were also a number of public bath houses. Saltaire pro-vided a standard of accommodation far higher than that available to ordinary millworkers in the UK, and the settlement was studied by both industrialists and sociologists from home and abroad. The success of Saltaire influenced both George Cadbury and William Lever in their later developments at Bourneville and Port Sunlight.

As Reynolds (1986) points out, Saltaire was not unique, and there were other examples of model worker communities. But the combination of high-quality housing and state-of-the-art manufacturing technology was very suc-cessful. Salt enjoyed generally good relations with his workers, and despite two brief strikes in the 1860s, which were settled peacefully, labour relations at Saltaire were far better than in most of the industry. Although he opposed the Factory Act of 1833 which banned child labour, he supported attempts to reduce working hours, and was the first employer in Bradford to introduce the ten-hour working day.

Salt continued to be a very successful and innovative manufacturer, but he also continued to be involved in public life. He served as MP for Bradford for several years until forced to resign on grounds of ill health. He served as President of the Bradford Chamber of Commerce and continued to campaign for better public health and public education, and did finally persuade the Bradford city authorities to take steps to provide better sanitation and clean drinking water. He was also an advocate of greater personal freedom and campaigned to extend the right to vote beyond its present narrow limits (women and men under the age of thirty were still denied the right to vote in England). He was also, quietly, a philanthropist and benefactor who gave away most of his personal fortune – according to some estimates, £500,000 – before his death. He was knighted, and in 1869 made a baronet, largely because of his devotion to charitable causes. When he died in 1876 as many as 100,000 people – virtually the entire population of Bradford – turned out to watch the funeral procession.

## Analysis

Some of the questions you might want to consider in connection with this case include:

- Salt tried to be a business manager and a social reformer, and had a measure of success as both. Might he have achieved more if he had concentrated on one or the other?
- Current writers on Salt stress his qualities as a 'virtuous' and 'enlightened' entrepreneur. What do these terms mean in a practical sense? Does being 'virtuous' or 'enlightened' make a more successful entrepreneur? If so, how do these qualities contribute to success? Or do you think Salt's business management and social responsibility activities were two quite separate interests?
- Are there business advantages to some of Salt's activities, especially the building of Saltaire? Can you think of situations today where similar policies might also be advantageous for firms?

## Sources

Balgarnie, R. (1878) *Sir Titus Salt Baronet: His Life and Letters*, London: Hodder & Stoughton.
Bradley, Ian Campbell (1987) 'Titus Salt: Enlightened Entrepreneur', *History Today* 37 (5): 30–36.

Holroyd, Abraham (1873) *A Life of Sir Titus Salt*, Bradford: T. Brear and
  F. Hammond.
Styles, John (1990) *Titus Salt and Saltaire: Industry and Virtue*, Saltaire: Salts Estates.

## Case Study 8D

### *Sir Basil Zaharoff*

Basil Zaharoff, known variously as the 'Mystery Man of Europe' and the
'Merchant of Death' was an arms dealer in the late nineteenth and early
twentieth century who rose to be chairman of one Europe's largest arms
makers and was partly responsible for the 'arms race' that led to the First
World War. He was extremely able, very talented and, judging by the evidence
of his actions, had little in the way of moral inhibitions or scruples.

Zaharoff was born in 1849 in the Ottoman empire, the son of a Russian
father and Greek mother. His name at birth was Basileios Zachariadis. He
grew up in Constantinople, where as a boy he worked as a guide and translator for tourists visiting the Ottoman capital, and apparently also worked for
a time as fireman. His family were reasonably well off, and some time around
1871 he went to England, apparently for the purpose of attending university.
Instead he became involved in a rather murky business deal involving the
import of Turkish goods of uncertain origin into Britain. He also married a
young Englishwoman, Emily Ann Burrows, using a false name.

Late in 1872 Zachariadis was arrested by the British police on charges of
fraud. He promised to make restitution to the victims of the fraud and to
remain in Britain until the matter was finally settled, but upon being released
from Britain promptly skipped bail and fled to Cyprus. There he remained
until 1880, becoming a prosperous trader and dealer in firearms. As he accumulated capital he diversified into various ventures, including becoming part-
owner of a ship. In 1880 he moved briefly to America, where he bought a
cattle ranch and also contracted a second marriage to an American woman,
Jeannie Billings, in New York. The cattle ranch did not prosper and in 1882
Zachariadis and his second wife returned to Greece, where they were confronted by his first wife in Athens. Zachariadis was arrested on charges of
bigamy, but managed to evade these on the grounds that as his first marriage
had been contracted using a false name, the marriage itself was invalid. His
second wife divorced him, the newspapers took a great interest in the subject,
and in 1884 Zachariadis changed his name to Basil Zaharoff in an attempt to
evade unwelcome publicity. He seems to have learned something from this,
for he became adept thereafter at keeping his private life out of the newspapers and away from public scrutiny.

During his days as a firearms dealer, Zaharoff had developed useful contacts with governments in the Eastern Mediterreanean. In the mid-1880s he
became interested in submarines, a very new and as yet untried weapon. He
persuaded Nordenfeldt, the first firm to make and sell submarines on a

commercial basis, to appoint him as their commission agent, and used his contacts to sell a submarine to the Greek navy. Here was the basis of what later became known as the Zaharoff system. Having sold a potentially potent weapon to Greece, he at once went to the government of Turkey, Greece's enemy, and warned of the danger this new weapon posed. The Turks, anxious to counter the Greek threat, contracted to buy two more submarines. Zaharoff then moved onto Russia, also an enemy of Turkey, and repeated the process; the Russians agreed to buy four more submarines. By 1889 Zaharoff had sold seven submarines and made himself rich on commissions.

In 1890 he settled in Paris. When Nordenfeldt was taken over by the machine-gun maker Maxim, Zaharoff negotiated a contract giving him a 1 per cent commission on orders for machine guns all over the world. He plunged into this new venture with his usual energy, and is reputed to have bribed senior army and navy officers in a number of countries, including Japan, to buy machine guns from him. Zaharoff also used part of his profits to quietly buy up shares in Maxim, eventually achieving parity of ownership with the company's founder and chairman, Hiram Maxim. In 1897 the shipbuilder and cannon maker Vickers offered to buy Maxim; Zaharoff helped negotiate the deal, which included a large tranche of Vickers's shares, a seat on the board of directors, and a similar commission deal for all of Vickers's range of armaments. Zaharoff could now profit from sales in two ways, from commissions on the sales themselves and from dividends as Vickers's shares rose on the back of his salesmanship.

In the years before the First World War, Zaharoff continued his old methods of stimulating sales. In 1907, for example, he caused a false press release to be circulated in France, to the effect that the French government was thinking of increasing military spending. He then submitted a copy of this to the German government, warning of the danger this posed. Within a few days the German government announced its own increase in military spending – and of course a large portion of this money went on machine guns and other arms purchased from Vickers. Zaharoff also sold warships indiscriminately around Europe, and helped the Russian navy rebuild after the losses suffered in its war with Japan in 1904–5. During the period 1905–14 especially, all the major powers and many of the minor ones greatly expanded their armies and fleets and modernised their weapons systems in preparation for a possible war. Vickers and Zaharoff made huge profits from this expansion.

Zaharoff himself was now one of the richest men in Europe. On one occasion he loaned money to his employers Vickers when they encountered temporary financial problems. He also began moving into arms production and research, funding a chair in aviation at the University of Paris in 1909 and establishing a company to manufacture torpedoes in 1913; he also funded experiments in military aviation. Still resident in Paris, he bought a bank which he used to help fund his own arms deals, and a newspaper which published a series of articles supporting military expansion and greater expenditure on armaments. Shortly before the outbreak of the First World

War in 1914, Zaharoff received the Legion of Honour from the president of France.

During the First World War Zaharoff, with his wide network of high-level political contacts, became much sought after as a political intermediary. His greatest coup was the setting up of negotiations with the Turkish leader Enver Pasha which led to Turkey's exit from the war in 1918. For this, Zaharoff was knighted in 1919 (as he was not a British citizen the knighthood was only an honorary one, but he insisted on being referred to as Sir Basil Zaharoff). He became involved in a variety of political plots. He was very right-wing in his political views and hated and feared communism, and became involved in several ultimately fruitless plots to destabilise the communist regime of Lenin after it came to power in Russia in 1917.

When the war ended in 1918 the government of Germany collapsed and a communist-inspired revolt began. Opposition was led by volunteer units of German army and navy officers known as Freikorps. Zaharoff went to Berlin to help restore order and donated money and weapons to the anti-communist forces. When in early 1919 a Freikorps unit captured two of the most prominent communist leaders, Karl Liebknecht and Rosa Luxemburg, Zaharoff urged that they be executed immediately without trial, to prevent their escaping and also to avoid any displays of sympathy that might accompany a public trial. According to some accounts, he joined personally the group of officers who shot Liebknecht and Luxemburg to death soon after.

Although his role in this affair was kept quiet for many years, Zaharoff's wider responsibility for the war itself was beginning to come out into the open. The 'arms race' that had preceded the war was held by many to have been one of its causes, and Zaharoff was held by the British public in particular to be one of the instigators of the war, which had killed 20 million people around the world. The British popular press nicknamed him the 'Merchant of Death'. Quite unaffected by this, Zaharoff moved to Monte Carlo. Here he married his long-time mistress, Maria, Duchess of Marchena, and devoted himself to running Monte Carlo's famous casino, which he had purchased outright from its previous owners. He died in Monte Carlo in 1936.

## Analysis

Some of the questions you might want to consider in connection with this case include:

- Zaharoff was a fraudster, a bigamist, a giver and taker of bribes, a seller of weapons of mass destruction and possibly a murderer, or at least an accessory. He became one of the world's wealthiest men, was made a knight, married a duchess and died peacefully at the age of 87. Given all this, is there any point in even *trying* to be ethical?

- Assuming the answer to the above question is 'yes', how can society best protect itself against unscrupulous businessmen like Zaharoff?

## Sources

Allfrey, Anthony (1989) *Man of Arms: The Life and Legend of Sir Basil Zaharoff*, London: Weidenfeld & Nicolson.

Neumann, Robert (1935) *Zaharoff the Armaments King*, London: George Allen & Unwin.

## Notes

1 Whether this was true in India is of course a highly debateable point.
2 Stillman (2004) puts this date ten years later, but his account is not always reliable. The date 1879 is given by Urwick (1956) who knew Filene personally and heard at least part of his story from his own lips.
3 Remember that Filene is writing this in 1932, in the darkest years of the Great Depression. Unemployment was rife, but for many of those still in work, real wages had never been higher, for even if many firms reduced wages, the prices of goods were also falling. In Britain, real wages among the middle classes in particular rose steadily through the 1930s.

# 9   Leadership

---

**Learning objectives**

This chapter is intended to help readers do the following:

1 observe how the nature of leadership and what is expected of leaders has evolved over time;
2 consider some different approaches to leadership and the circumstances under which they are effective;
3 learn more about the factors that make leadership successful in different times and different situations.

Often a person with eyes misses the track while a blind person finds the correct path. Whoever takes the world to be safe, it will be betray him. Whoever regards the world as great, it will humiliate him. Every one who shoots does not hit. When authority changes, the time changes too.

– 'Ali ibn Abi Talib, fourth Caliph of Islam, *Peak of Eloquence*

At its heart, the traditional view of leadership is based on assumptions of people's powerlessness, their lack of personal vision and inability to master the forces of change, deficits which can only be remedied by a few great leaders.

– Peter M. Senge, *The Fifth Discipline*

There is no substitute for leadership.

– Peter Drucker, *The Practice of Management*

## 9.1 Introduction

The first two quotes at the head of this chapter come from the somewhat unlikely pairing of the Caliph 'Ali, leader of Islam and son-in-law of the Prophet Muhammad, and Professor Peter Senge of Massachusetts Institute of Technology, author of one of the most popular books on knowledge management. They give us, from different times and different parts of the world, two contrasting images of leadership. For Caliph 'Ali, writing to his son and teaching him the lessons he would need to know in later life, leadership was a difficult task. Leaders need to remember that they are fallible, that they do not always get things right, and they do not always reach their goals. And further, what is required of a leader changes according to time and circumstance, meaning that leaders must always be adaptable.

Professor Senge, on the other hand, describes the tradition of leadership which had grown up in Europe and America. Here the leader is perceived as a heroic figure, someone out of the ordinary with special talents and powers. Elsewhere he likens the traditional view of business leadership to that found in films, where heroes lead cavalry charges and save the situation in the nick of time. It should be added that Professor Senge disagrees with that style of leadership and thinks its day is done; in his view, the organisation of the future requires leadership that is more democratic and more attuned to the wish of the organisation.

Although few people in history would have disagreed with Peter Drucker's assertion that there is no substitute for leadership, that is about the extent of the consensus. Today there remain debates as to what exactly leadership is and whether it is the same thing as management or an entirely different phenomenon (see for example Kotter 1990; Bennis 1989; Adair 2002; Gosling *et al.* 2007, among many others). In past times this debate was less important than now, although in China a distinction was definitely made between the leader, the emperor, and the managers, the bureaucrats of the Imperial civil service. Much more important issues, which we see reflected in both theory and practice, included the nature of leadership itself, what people expected of their leaders and how leadership was exercised. What were the responsibilities of the leader? How did one lead? What was the best way to lead people so as to achieve the best results? These were the questions that early leaders considered and tried to answer.

## 9.2 The nature of leadership

Many societies have been concerned with the nature of leadership and there is a rich literature from around the world which gives different views on the subject. Perhaps unsurprisingly, there is also a rich diversity of views. The Sioux medicine man Black Elk believed that his role was to provide wisdom for the people of his tribe, to give them guidance and help them make decisions rather than to provide for them (Black Elk and Neihardt 1979). The classical Chinese philosopher Han Feizi thought that the role of the leader was to take all decisions and then order his people to implement them without question (Watson 1964). The twentieth-century political scientist Mary Parker Follett believed that leaders did not control anything, and that control itself was an illusion; the true task of the leader was to coordinate the parts of an organisation and keep them focused on their goal (Follett 1924).

We begin our discussion of leadership with an examination of some of the various views on leadership and ways in which it has been practised around the world.

### 9.2.1 Leaders in Asia

#### 9.2.1.1 China

The most important influence on the theory and practice of leadership in Asia is the philosophy of Confucius. Today, Confucian leadership is thought of primarily as a paternalistic system. The family, the most basic social unit, plays a major role in Confucian thought, and Confucius and his followers assigned a primary social role to the parents, especially the father. Other family members were expected to obey their parents and elders and show them respect. But this was not a purely authoritarian concept. The act of honouring others and acknowledging them as one's superiors is, said the Confucians, an essential element of human society. It confers dignity not only on those being honoured, but on those who submit themselves and acknowledge authority.

The relationship also goes two ways. In exchange for obedience, leaders have a duty of care to those who follow them. This is true of relations between people and the state, or workers and their employers. It has often been observed that the employer in Chinese businesses plays the role of a surrogate parent; employers are frequently expected to help solve their employees' domestic personal problems, often outside of office hours. In return, employees show much more respect and deference than is common in Western businesses. There is of course a danger that with their subordinates required to be openly deferential and respectful, leaders themselves might become overly proud and 'big-headed'. Confucius recognises this danger, and frequently advises those in positions of authority to remember who they are, be true to themselves and cultivate a mild and quiet manner.

Confucian leaders lead by a mixture of precept and example. They are expected to really lead, to give direction and show the way forward. Even today, Western managers in Chinese businesses who ask their employees what should be done next receive blank looks: that, the manager is told, is your job to determine. That is not to say that Confucian leaders do not sound out their people's views before making decisions. But often this is done through a longer process of familiarisation with employees and their views, rather than asking the question directly. And decision-making itself is the province of the leader; his or her decision, once made, is final.

---

### Confucian precepts

Lord Chi K'ang asked how he could persuade the people to be reverent and loyal. The Master said: 'Preside over them with solemn dignity, then the people will be reverent. Honour your parents and cherish your children, then the people will be loyal. Promote the worthy and instruct the feckless, then the people will be persuaded.'

–Confucius, *Analects*

---

One of the key elements of Confucian philosophy is the search for self-enlightenment, which is perceived as the ultimate form of knowledge. Leaders accordingly spend a good deal of time searching for knowledge, for it is through knowledge we understand what is right and what our true goals should be, and this understanding guides our actions in work and in life. But once knowledge is achieved, it is important also to communicate it. Confucius was a strong supporter of mass education, which he believed to be an important vehicle for spreading knowledge of virtue among those without the capacity to become sages in their own right, as this proverb suggests:

> When a person is capable of understanding your words, and you refuse to speak, you are wasting a person. When a person is not capable of understanding your words, and you speak anyway, you are wasting words. The wise waste neither words nor people.

In a business context, this is often manifested in the way that Confucian leaders spend a great deal of time scanning their environment and looking at events and things around them, rather than getting involved in detailed planning and budgeting. These things are done by subordinates (when they are done at all).

Confucianism had a strong influence not only in China but also in Korea, Japan and those parts of South-east Asia where Chinese influence was strongest. The second important school of thought on leadership was Legalism, whose influence was largely confined to China itself. The first exponent of Legalism was the philosopher and statesman Shang Yang, prime minister of the north Chinese state of Qin in the fourth century BC. The most important figure in the movement, however, was Han Feizi, who died in 233 BC. Han Feizi developed Shang Yang's original ideas into a systematic philosophy of government and statecraft, and attracted a considerable following, including most notably Zheng, the king of Qin. Ten years after Han Feizi's death, and using the principles of Legalism as his main basis of government, Zheng unified all the warring states of China and proclaimed himself emperor under the title Qin Shi Huangdi. Arguably China's greatest emperor, responsible for the building of the Great Wall and the Grand Canal, Qin Shi Huangdi was also a terrifying tyrant who ruled through fear.

Han Feizi rejected the Confucian notion that most men tend towards the good and can be relied upon to behave ethically through a social system which exerts pressure on people to conform. To Han Feizi, the only way to achieve conformity was through the rule of law. His system of thought was based on three important principles. The first of these was *fa*, meaning roughly 'prescriptive standards', but also with connotations of law and punishment. People should comply with *fa* so that their behaviour conforms with the public good, or else be punished as a result. The second was *shi*, meaning 'authority' or 'power'. The exercise of *shi* is necessary to ensure compliance with *fa*; but conversely, *shi* should also be governed by the dictates of *fa* to prevent abuses of power. The third was *shu*, the technique of controlling the bureaucracy by comparing 'word' with 'deed' (or more generally, potential performance with the actuality).

---

### The way of the ruler

This is the way of the enlightened ruler: he causes the wise to bring forth all their schemes, and he decides his affairs accordingly; hence his own wisdom is never exhausted. He causes the worthy to display their talents, and he employs them accordingly; hence his own worth never comes to an end. Where there are accomplishments, the ruler takes credit for their worth; where there are errors, the ministers are held responsible for the blame; hence the ruler's name never suffers. Thus, though the ruler is not worthy himself, he is the leader of the worthy; though he is not wise himself, he is the corrector of the wise. The ministers have the labour; the ruler enjoys the success. This is called the maxim of the worthy ruler.

–Han Feizi

The ruler does not try to work side by side with his people, and they accordingly respect the dignity of his position. He does not try to tell others what to do, but leaves them to do things by themselves. Tightly he bars his inner door, and from his room looks out into the courtyard; he has provided the rules and yardsticks, so that all things know their place. Those who merit reward are rewarded; those who deserve punishment are punished. Reward and punishment follow the deed; each man brings them upon himself. Therefore, whether the result is pleasant or hateful, who dares to question it?

–Han Feizi

Repeatedly, Han Feizi urges leaders to judge their subordinates by how well they have performed their duties and deliver on the promises they have made. Judgement is made by matching people's words to their actions, according to *shu*. Did people achieve what they said they would? Did they carry out the functions of their offices as required? If so, reward them; if not, punish them. This philosophy, as noted, was the guiding philosophy of the Qin dynasty. Succeeding dynasties moderate the harshness of Legalism, but this 'iron hand' approach continued to influence Chinese leadership down to the twentieth century, and, as has often been remarked, has its modern counterpart in the leadership style of Mao Zedong.

The third philosophy to come out of ancient China was Daoism (Taoism), which emerged around the same time as Confucianism. Daoism was particularly fond of paradox, liking to contrast things with and then relate them to their opposites. Unsurprisingly, then, the Daoists argued that the best form of leadership was to lead as little as possible. They believed that order and efficiency were natural constants in the universe. To lead effectively, it is necessary only to create the conditions in which order and efficiency can flourish. Intervention by leaders disrupts the natural order of things. The leader should therefore cultivate the principle of *wu-wei*, non-action, and do as little as possible while letting his subordinates get on with their lives and work. The Daoist leader sets the goals and determines the path, but then leaves people to accomplish their work without interference. Active leadership, especially the kind that drives people through fear of punishment, is to be avoided:

The highest type of ruler is one of whose existence the people are barely aware.
Next comes one whom they love and praise.
Next comes one whom they fear.

Next comes one whom they despise and defy.
When you are lacking in faith,
Others will be unfaithful to you.
The Sage is self-effacing and scanty of words.
When his task is accomplished and things have been completed,
All the people say: 'We ourselves have achieved it!'

*–Daodejing* 17

Much wisdom is required of the leader as he follows the Daoist Way, in particular, the wisdom to understand that stillness is superior to action. Whereas the Confucians believed that good government consisted in making wise and ethical decisions, the Daoists argued that the greatest good came from making no decisions at all.

---

### Leading by non-action

You govern a kingdom by normal rules;
You fight a war by exceptional moves;
But you win the world by letting alone.
The more taboos and inhibitions there are in the world,
The poorer the people become.
The sharper the weapons the people possess,
The greater confusion reigns in the realm.
The more clever and crafty the men,
The oftener strange things happen.
The more articulate the laws and ordinances,
The more robbers and thieves arise.
Therefore the Sage says:
I do not make any fuss, and the people transform themselves.
I love quietude, and the people settle down in their regular grooves.
I do not engage myself in anything, and the people grow rich.
I have no desires, and the people return to simplicity.

*–Daodejing*

---

It has to be said that while there are plenty of examples of Confucian and Legalist principles of leadership being put into practice, purely Daoist examples are more rare. But we can see Daoism – and Buddhism, imported into China from India and sharing a number of key concepts with the former – at work in the way in which some Chinese managers strive to achieve harmony, both internally within their businesses and externally with stakeholders and the world at large.

In general, apart from Daoism, China has taken an authoritarian view of leadership. The leader is expected to lead, and not to shy away from decisions or delegate them to others. There is a high degree of personal responsibility (although Han Feizi's advice that when things went well the leader took the credit but when things went badly the subordinates took the blame can be observed in practice) and a strong tendency on the part of the rest of the organisation to identify with the leader. Leaders in turn are expected, certainly in Confucian thinking, to be responsible for the people they lead and to care for them and their welfare.

### 9.2.1.2 *Japan*

Japan was heavily influenced by both Confucian and Buddhist ideas, and to a large extent shares the same philosophy of leadership, although Japanese businesses have been and continue to be even more hierarchical than the Chinese. Yet at the same time they also take the idea of the leader's responsibilities just as seriously if not more so. The concept of *genba-shugi* or 'honourable shop floor' by which Japanese managers spent periods of time working on the shop floor or behind the cash desk of a retail outlet in order to experience the life of the ordinary worker dates back to at least the 1880s, and probably before that. Japanese leaders are expected to watch over the subordinates and to understand their thinking and what motivates them, and the best and most effective leaders in Japan have been those that do this well.

Another aspect of Japanese leadership worth remarking on is the idea of 'self-leadership' or 'personal mastery'. The idea here is that one is not fit to be master over others until one is master over oneself. Self-mastery can involve intensive physical, mental and spiritual training, in which the would-be leader tries to purge himself or herself of vices and faults. When this is done, what remains behind is a pure vessel, a person who is solely focused on a goal and is dedicated to reaching it. Self-mastery was much discussed by writers on swordfighting such Musashi Miyamoto in his *Book of Five Rings*, and also by the samurai philosopher Tsunetomo Yamamoto in the *Hagakure* (Hidden Leaves) in the early eighteenth century. The latter also shows some influence of Confucianism, with its lists of precepts for success and its insistence that the leader should always be ready to learn, and indeed should never cease to learn.

---

### This is not enough

It is not good to settle into a set of opinions. It is a mistake to put forth effort and obtain some understanding, and then stop at that. At first putting forth great effort to be sure that you have grasped the basics, then practising so that they may come to fruition, is something that will never stop for your whole lifetime. Do not rely on following the degree of understanding that you have discovered, but simply think, 'This is not enough.'

> One should search throughout his whole life how best to follow the Way.
> And he should study, setting his mind to work without putting things
> off. Within this is the Way.
>
> (Yamamoto 1979: 31)

What little we know about Japanese businesses in the period before the Meiji
Restoration in 1867, from firms like the copper mining concern Sumitomo and
the Tokyo dry goods store Echigo-ya, suggests that their leaders were influ-
enced by Confucianism and took this idea of learning to heart. Their leaders
were authoritarian yet at the same time responsible to their workers, and at
Echigo-ya, responsibility to customers was taken seriously too. After the
Restoration there was a great emphasis on knowledge and training for leaders,
and the educational reforms led by the great teacher and translator Yukichi
Fukuzawa, founder of Keio University, were motivated in part by the view that
Japan itself could not aspire to leadership unless it increased its knowledge.
This becomes blended with the notion of personal mastery, which is less concerned with fitness and spiritual purity and more with the need to understand
and learn about oneself as well as the world around one. Later Japanese business leaders such as Ibuka and Matsushita would comment on the search for
inner fulfilment going hand in hand with the search for business success.

### 9.2.1.3 India

The first Indian work which discusses leadership in India is the *Arthashastra*
of Kautilya, written around 300 BC. Much of this book is taken up with a
listing of specific duties and responsibilities, but Kautilya also comments on
leadership itself. The task of the leader is to maintain peace, order, law and
justice, to protect his citizens, and 'to encourage moral, religious and material
progress' (Kumar 1990: 3). The leader is only one element in the administrative system. It is up to the leader to provide leadership, but most of all he is
required to be the embodiment of the *dharma*, the rules and customs which
hold society together and make life possible. In ancient Hindu thought, the
*dharma* were not rules made by men, but were believed to be part of the fabric
of the universe itself (not unlike the later Western concept of natural law).
Upholding the *dharma* was both a duty and a necessity, not only for leaders
but for all lesser managers and administrators. In a passage which is similar
to Confucius, Kautilya also comments that it is the duty of leaders to bring
not only prosperity but also enlightenment to the people.

Much more complex, and betraying many influences, are the ideas on
leadership set out by Mahatma Gandhi in the first half of the twentieth century. Gandhi was much interested in the notion of leadership and wrote on it
frequently. In a fashion typical of much of his philosophy, he drew together
ideas from classical Indian philosophy and literature on the one hand, and the

world around him, including Western influences, on the other. Gandhi agreed with Kautilya on the notion of the leader being the embodiment of the *dharma*, and also agreed that the leader was not alone but was part of an organisation and depended on others to exercise leadership effectively. He was also much interested in the idea of self-mastery, and urged would-be leaders to cultivate the mind and spirit and shun the senses: 'if a man is not master of his senses, he is always musing on the objects of sense and conceives an attachment for them, so that he can hardly think of anything else' (quoted in Narayan 1968: vol. 6, 12).

But Gandhi was also very much interested in heroism and courage. Early in his career he seems to have been drawn to the idea that leaders should be heroes, but later rejected this. Leaders should have the *attributes* of courage – courage, endurance, fearlessness, self-sacrifice – but not seek the status of heroes. Gandhi also cautions other people not to worship leaders as heroes while nonetheless admiring heroic deeds and attitudes: 'we must worship heroism, not heroes. The hero may later on disgrace himself and in any case must cease to exist, but heroism is everlasting' (quoted in Iyer 1973: ch. 6).

Of all the virtues of the leader, self-sacrifice is the one on which Gandhi places the most stress. Writing as he was in the midst of the struggle for Indian independence, this is understandable; today, perhaps, this virtue would take a slightly different form. It is noticeable that while not all Indian business leaders admired Gandhi, they nonetheless espoused many of the virtues that he described. This is likely to be due less to the influence of Gandhi himself and more to the fact that he was describing generally admired virtues in Indian society. Business leaders like J.R.D. Tata (see Case Study 9D) are noted for their willingness to speak out on issues that concern them, their idealism and their belief in doing good for society, and their desire for consensus, but in particular for the way in which they regard themselves less as leaders than as servants or stewards of their organisations. This in turn means a much less autocratic approach to leadership; many Indian leaders have a very hands-off approach. (The author recalls a conversation with the chairman of one of India's leading companies in 2008, discussing the history of the company then being prepared for him by a team of scholars. When would this be completed? he was asked. 'I have no idea', came the answer, 'and I would not dream of even asking.' A Chinese chairman would have felt no hesitation in demanding an answer.) As a final note, if we wish to find examples of courage, endurance and self-sacrifice in Indian business, we need look no further than the conduct of staff and management at the Taj Mahal Palace Hotel during the terrorist attacks in Mumbai in late 2008.

## The qualities of the leader

Gandhi's plea for heroism in society involved him in the recognition of the need for inspired leadership in political and social activity and the role of small groups as pioneers and pathfinders, but also in a stout refusal to distinguish sharply between the elect and the masses. 'All cannot be leaders, but all can be bearers,' he declared in 1921. Courage, endurance, fearlessness and above all self-sacrifice are the qualities required of our leaders. 'A person belonging to the suppressed classes exhibiting these qualities in their fullness would certainly be able to lead the nation; whereas the most finished orator, if he has not got these qualities, must fail.' In well-ordered organisations, leaders are elected, he said, for convenience of work, not for extraordinary merit. A leader is only first among equals. Someone may be put first, but he is no stronger than the weakest link in the chain. And yet the true leader shows his capacity to assume heavy burdens of responsibility by taking upon himself the errors and failings of those weaker than he is, and if necessary atoning for them and using them as the basis of his own self-examination.

(Iyer 1973: ch. 6)

### 9.2.1.4 The Islamic world

Leadership has been a subject of intense discussion within the Islamic world ever since the foundation of the faith in the seventh century AD. Islamic writings on leadership and leaders throughout the period often reflect different priorities from their Western counterparts. Islamic writers have tended to focus on the relationship between the leader and his followers, the duties of the leader, and the need for the leader to have integrity and be trustworthy.

Unsurprisingly, 'Islamic leadership' is grounded in religious ideals. For devout Muslims, the first and original leader is God, and all pious men and women are bound by their faith to obey God's law. All Muslims, then, are followers of God. In turn, God had made his will known through certain individuals, the most important of whom is the Prophet Muhammad (the next most important being Jesus and Moses).

Thus any leader of any organisation – business, political or religious – is also *ipso facto* a follower, of God. This very fact imposes limits on Islamic leaders, and recalls to them very forcibly their duties to the people they lead. In Islamic thought, the ideal leader was at the same time both exalted and humble, capable of vision and inspiration, yet at the same time dedicated to the service of his people. Notably, while some Islamic leaders claim to be inspired by God, they do not claim to lead by 'divine right' as did medieval kings and emperors in Western Europe.

The Prophet offered some ideas on the duties of leaders, but the first writer to attempt to analyse the tasks of leadership was his son-in-law the Caliph 'Ali, quoted at the head of this chapter. In an essay known as the 'Document of Instruction' written for Malik al-Nashtar, the newly appointed governor of Egypt, Ali sets out his duties and tasks in detail. As well as obeying the will of God, 'Ali urges Malik to rule on behalf of all the people, not just the upper classes, and to interest himself in their welfare and listen to their complaints. What we would now call transparency and honesty are enjoined on the leader. He too urges the leader not to exalt himself or seek heroic status: 'You should avoid self-admiration, having reliance in what appears good in yourself and love of exaggerated praise because this is one of the most reliable opportunities for Satan to obliterate the good deeds of the virtuous.' He also makes it plain that the leader has an equal duty to all subjects, regardless of rank: 'The way most coveted by you should be that which is the most equi-table for the right, the most universal by way of justice, and the most com-prehensive with regard to the agreement among those under you.' Repeatedly, he stresses the need for justice, equity and even-handedness: 'If the subjects suspect you of high-handedness, explain to them your position openly and remove their suspicion with your explanation, because this would mean exer-cise for your soul and consideration to the subjects while this explanation will secure your aim of keeping them firm in truth.'

---

### A leader is a human being

Habituate your heart to mercy for the subjects and to affection and kindness for them. They will commit slips and encounter mistakes. They may act wrongly, willfully or by neglect. So, extend to them your for-giveness and pardon, in the same way as you would like God to extend His forgiveness and pardon to you, because you are over them, while God is over him who has appointed you. He (God) has sought you to manage their affairs and has tried you through them.

Then, do not keep yourself secluded from the people for a long time, because the seclusion of those in authority from the subjects is a kind of narrow-sightedness and causes ignorance about their affairs. Seclusion from them also prevents them from the knowledge of those things which they do not know and as a result they begin to regard big matters as small and small matters as big, good matters as bad and bad matters as good, while the truth becomes confused with falsehood. After all, a governor is a human being and cannot have knowledge of things which people keep hidden from him.

–Caliph 'Ali ibn Abi Talib, 'Document of Instruction', in
*Nahjul Balagha* (1978)

---

The sense that leaders are responsible to and part of the community they inhabit is also a feature of the works of the Egyptian theologian Muhammad 'Abduh, writing at the end of the nineteenth century. 'Abduh believed that human beings need communities, but they are not always very good at making them work: 'Man has a natural propensity for community. But unlike bees and ants, for example, he has not been granted the instinctive faculty for what community requires.' Individual desires and needs pull us in different directions, threatening the unity of the community. The role of the leader, then, is akin to that of guide or shepherd, who recalls people to their sense of communal purpose and reminds them of the needs of the community. It follows that the need for leadership is inherent in any community or organisation.

The most powerful tool at the leader's disposal for helping to create this sense of solidarity, says 'Abduh, is love. 'God has bestowed on man a gift which in truth takes up the role of love, re-establishing it in men's souls in their loveless waste land.' Love, in his view, requires humility and submission to others; to truly love someone means the willingness to follow them, or at least, work with them. Here once again we see the notion of the leader as servant emerging. For leaders must love their followers in order to serve them, and a leader's first duty is to serve the community. And in turn, the example of the leader inspires others: 'So the pretentious learn to submit and the refractory are humbled. The intelligent find their reason brought up sharp and so back into a true course, while the ignorant are overwhelmed and turn away from their deceits' (quotes from 'Abduh 1966 *passim*).

When we come to look at leadership in practice in the Islamic world, we find many of these ideas – the sense of the leader as servant of the community, the emphasis on fairness and equity, the strong bonds between the leader and the led – are traits of the best and most admired leaders. Even those who are autocrats, like the twelfth-century military leader Salah ad-Din Yusuf, better known in the West as Saladin, saw themselves as servants to some degree; Saladin believe that he was obeying God's will, and also established strong bonds with his officers and soldiers; he was rewarded with their intense loyalty. In the modern business world we can think of examples such as Rafiq Hariri, a successful businessman who donated much of his fortune to the rebuilding of his native country, Lebanon, later giving up his business altogether to serve as prime minister until his assassination; or Muhammad Younis, the former university professor who founded the Grameen group of companies for the purpose of bringing prosperity to the poor rural inhabitants of Bangladesh.

### 9.2.2 Leaders in the West

Apart from semi-mythical figures such as Abraham and Gilgamesh, the earliest leaders about whom we know very much are the kings of ancient Assyria and the pharaohs of Egypt. The one striking factor about these early rulers is their association with divine status. Although Chinese and Japanese emperors later claimed to be at least semi-divine – the Chinese emperors were known as the 'Sons of Heaven' – this tendency was far more marked in the West. Early kings and princes were also often priests, or were crowned by priests, thus giving the seal of divine approval. This led to several things. First, the leader had to obeyed; refusal to obey was an act of impiety and would be severely punished. Second, there was also a 'trickle-down' effect. The vizier of Upper Egypt, who reported to the pharaoh, gave orders according to the will of the divine ruler; thus, his orders too had to be obeyed, and those of his chief scribes and other officials and so on down the line, for all drew their authority from the pharaoh or king, whose authority came from the heavens.

The Greeks of ancient Athens rejected this and insisted on electing – and deposing – their leaders by using a form of democracy. Rome at first followed this example, but beginning with Augustus Caesar (27 BC–AD 14), emperors claimed divine status, at first upon death, then later upon ascending the imperial throne. When the empire converted to Christianity this practice was abolished, but it was still conceded that the emperors enjoyed special heavenly protection or 'divine grace' and that they ruled by 'divine right' meaning that their orders still had to be obeyed much as before. This divine right passed to the Byzantine Emperors, then the Holy Roman Emperors and on to other sovereigns. As late as the seventeenth century we find Kings Louis XIV of France and Charles I of England – the latter unsuccessfully – claiming that they ruled by divine right.

Business leaders did not draw their authority from the crown (save in very special cases where they might also be appointed to serve as royal officials) but they nevertheless benefitted from this trend. There had developed by the time of the Roman Empire, and probably long before, the notion that those who were in positions of authority, be they in government, business or the religious hierarchy, were there because they deserved to be. The fact of authority was enough to require obedience. And although writers on politics and society such as the medieval scholar John of Salisbury urged those in positions of authority to remember they had a duty of care over those below them, the fact remains that authority demanded deference and obedience.

---

**The health of the commonwealth**

Then and then only will the health of the commonwealth be sound and flourishing, when the higher members shield the lower and the lower respond faithfully and fully in like measure to the just demands of their superiors, so that each and all are as it were members of one another by a kind of reciprocity, and each regards his own interest as best served by that which he knows to be most advantageous for others.

–John of Salisbury, *Policraticus* (1979: 92)

---

Business leaders, like political leaders, also came to believe that leadership was hereditary, and tended to pass leadership on to their sons – and very rarely, their daughters – just as kings handed on their crowns. There came to develop the notion in Europe that leaders, including business leaders, were 'born and not made'. In other words, leadership was an inherent quality; you either had it or you did not, and it could not be trained or learned. As late as 1949, the director-general of the principal body of British business leaders, the Federation of British Industry, resigned in protest when members passed a motion suggesting that leadership was not inherent and could be learned. And of course, it was believed that you had a far better chance of being a successful leader if your father had been one – despite the example of dozens of successful business leaders who had risen from nothing.

The 'born and not made' idea never took firm root in America, almost certainly because of traits in American culture itself. From the early nineteenth century America was seen as a place where people could better themselves and rise up the social ladder. Self-made men and women were no more common in America than in Europe, but the heroic myths of American leadership concentrated on these, not on those leaders who had inherited their position. And certainly some American leaders did emerge from very obscure and humble backgrounds, as the case of Sarah Breedlove Walker (Case Study 9C) indicates. But Walker herself might not have risen in the way that she did without the encouragement and inspiration of Booker T. Washington, the author and educator who made it his mission to encourage African-Americans to become entrepreneurs and leaders.

A second feature of Western leadership is the association of leadership with heroic status. Whereas in India and the Islamic world conscious attempts had been made to disconnect the two, in the West the connection was made early and reinforced constantly. The ancient Greeks studied Homer's heroes of the war against Troy as examples of leaders, and later such figures as Alexander the Great, Julius Caesar, Charlemagne, Richard the Lion-Hearted and so on became examples of leader-heroes. James Wolfe, the young British general who led the campaign against the French in Quebec in 1759, read lives of Alexander, Caesar and the Dutch hero of the wars of independence, Stadtholder Maurice of Nassau, for inspiration and tried consciously to emulate them. Frederick the Great and Napoleon similarly were accorded the status of heroic leaders.

Curiously, what little we know about the reading habits of business leaders suggests that for a long time they too tended to turn to military and political hero-leaders for inspiration. Biographies of Richard Arkwright and Robert Owen and the like were produced, but read only in limited quantity. The first major work of business biography came in 1858 when the journalist Freeman Hunt wrote his *Lives of American Merchants*. His subjects were quiet heroes, who behaved modestly, gave to the poor and lived according to Christian principles. By the end of the century business heroes of a more traditional type were beginning to emerge. Casson's *The Romance of Steel: The Story of a Thousand Millionaires* (1907) cast subjects such as Andrew Carnegie, Henry Clay Frick and Charles Schwab as Napoleonic heroes, marshalling their armies of workers, building their factories and going on to triumph over great odds. Business leaders had finally become identifiable heroes in their own right.

This need for leaders to be heroes is a curious one. Not all heroes are conquerors, of course. There are saintly heroes too, like Florence Nightingale whose attempts – not entirely successful – to introduce professionalism and discipline into the British volunteer nursing corps during the Crimean War of 1854–55 were transformed out of all recognition by later myth-makers. From a tough disciplinarian and manager who believed in tight control of her organisation, she became the 'Lady of the Lamp' who healed the sick almost by touch. Saintly heroes became a kind of counterweight to those who disliked or distrusted the boldness and brashness of the conquering type of hero.

This has been a very quick summary of Western attitudes to leaders, but it is hopefully lengthy enough to allow a contrast with the approaches to leadership that we find in other cultures. There were, however, important changes in attitudes to leadership, and it is to these that we now turn our attention.

### 9.2.3 Changing expectations of leaders

Not every Western culture treated its rulers as gods. The Athenians and inhabitants of other Greek cities had rejected the notion of divine right and instead chose their rulers, who then ruled according to the will of the people. In pagan Scandinavia, too, there was a tradition of electing kings, a tradition which eroded after Scandinavia converted to Christianity in the ninth and tenth centuries. England, possibly because of Scandinavian influences, also resisted the notion of divine right, and there was a series of intermittent conflicts between sovereigns claiming divine right to rule and a populace determined not to allow this, lasting from 1215 and the signing of Magna Carta to the English Civil War (1642–51). By the end of the seventeenth century it had become accepted in England that the leader ruled by the consent of the governed, not through divine will.

This was important because it challenged the whole notion of absolute authority. It became recognised, not just in England but as time passed across Europe – especially in the aftermath of the French Revolution in 1789 – that no matter what the political system, be it democracy or monarchy, the relationship between the leaders and the led had changed. The Tennis Court Oath (see box), sworn by members of the French National Assembly when the royal authorities attempted to close the Assembly down, was a significant moment. In effect, the Assembly members were saying that power resided with them, not the crown, and that henceforth the king would govern only with their consent. John of Salisbury's notion that the lower orders submitted to the leadership of the upper classes and obeyed orders in exchange for protection was now compromised. Once it was accepted that leaders governed by the will or consent of the people, then other implications emerged: first, that the people might demand more say in choosing their leaders, and second, that they might demand more say in running their own affairs. The first trades

unions to emerge in Britain in the early nineteenth century, followed quickly
by others elsewhere, did not demand a voice in choosing their leaders, but
they did demand the right to be heard when it came to determining policies
that affected themselves, such as pay and working conditions.

---

### The Tennis Court Oath

We swear never to separate ourselves from the National Assembly, and
to reassemble whenever circumstances require, until the constitution of
this realm is fixed upon solid foundations.

>               –members of the French National Assembly, 1789

---

Leaders were now expected to be responsive. Instead of merely protecting
those they led in a paternalistic fashion, they were increasingly being asked to
treat those who followed them as partners – not equal partners, but people
who had a right to be heard. Some leaders resisted this bitterly, fearing an
erosion of their authority. Others saw an opportunity. Leaders like George
Cadbury of Cadbury Brothers and Ernst Abbé of Carl Zeiss Jena realised that
worker democracy could bring many benefits: labour peace, at the very least,
but if managed well, greater worker participation and the unlocking of the
ideas and knowledge that lay dormant in the minds of the workforce. In both
examples given above, worker democracy and sharing of authority translated
into real and lasting competitive advantage.

We must be careful not to overstate the case. Intelligent leaders had been
consulting with their followers for a long time (see Witzel 2007b). The Greek
general Xenophon noted in his memoirs that he and his colleagues sometimes called meetings of their army and asked for ideas and took votes on
difficult decisions during their march across Persia. In England during the
Middle Ages, landlords and their estate managers used local manor courts
not just as a means of resolving disputes but also as a vehicle for consulting
with tenants and agreeing key decisions for the coming year's agricultural
work. The Florentine writer and statesman Niccolò Machiavelli believed that
a city that was governed with the consent and participation of the governed
would always be stronger than one governed by a despot. Wise leaders
have always known that they lead with the consent of the led (Goffee and
Jones 2006).

In the mid-nineteenth century in Europe and America, the idea of participation and democracy began to be urged as the best way of leading. The
writings of Mary Parker Follett (1924) gave the concept of democratic leadership in business an important boost; her works were read and admired on
both sides of the Atlantic. The concept gradually took hold, and from the
1970s and 1980s the concept of democratic leadership in business has become
the orthodox approach, at least in academia (see for example Adair 2002,

referring to his own earlier work; Bennis 1989; Kotter 1990). But, it needs to be remembered that this concept is still relatively new, and is not in universal use. India, China, Japan and the Islamic world still have their own models of leadership and are very much influenced by them. At the time of writing, there has still not been developed a standard, universally accepted worldwide model of leadership.

### 9.2.4 How leaders learned leadership

Until very recently, the primary means of learning about leadership was through example and emulation. This could happen in one of two ways. First, if one was in the right place at the right time, one could observe leaders in person, see how they acted and learn why they were successful. Many leaders were aware of this and took care to act as mentors to people around them and pass on the lessons they themselves had learned. This was one reason the hereditary principle was favoured: men in positions of power often invested much time in carefully preparing their sons – or rarely, their daughters – to follow in their footsteps. This did not always work: the sons of Richard Arkwright and Robert Owen both showed little interest in business, and turned to other interests after their fathers' deaths. But succession was not always hereditary. William Pirrie, a young gentleman apprentice at Belfast shipbuilders Harland & Wolff, was identified early on as a potential leader, and managing partner Edward Harland made it his personal responsibility to see that Pirrie gained the necessary experience and knowledge to make him ready to take over the firm when Harland retired.

The other way of learning about leadership was, as mentioned above, to study the lives and careers of 'great' leaders and glean lessons from these. What traits had made them successful? How had they reacted to adversity? How had they motivated those around them? Why had they in particular been successful when their opponents, perhaps equally talented in many ways, had not? These lessons were also passed on in schools: until the second half of the twentieth century, the study of history in both Europe and America consisted largely of the study of 'great men' and their lives. In India and Japan, and especially China, people also studied the lessons of the past. Figures such as Cao Cao and Zhuge Liang, the two famous generals and statesmen from the third century, were still being studied in Chinese schools up to the early twentieth century and offered as examples of leaders to be emulated.

Although writers as diverse as Confucius and Machiavelli discussed the secrets of successful leadership and offered precepts and advice, there was no systematic analysis of what leaders actually *do* until the second half of the twentieth century. Models of leadership such as John Adair's 'three circles' model (which divided leadership into three elements, the task, the individual and the team) or Warren Bennis's characteristics of the successful leader – guiding vision, passion, integrity, curiosity, daring – are now widely recognised.

Leadership is now taught in business schools, schools of public administration and military academies, and there are centres for research in leadership.

Again, the idea that leadership can be analysed, dissected into its component parts and taught is, in historical terms, very new. It remains to be seen what impact this will have on leadership styles in the future. It is worth considering what this impact might be, however. Learning about leadership by studying past leaders has, over the centuries, tended to produce a certain 'sameness'; leaders tended to react as they had observed other leaders to react in similar circumstances. Sometimes this worked, sometimes it did not. Every so often there came a 'leader of genius' who broke the mould and invented some new way of doing things, which in turn sparked a new round of emulation. It will be interesting to see if the new approach to leadership training produces a more analytical style of leadership.

## 9.3 Themes and influences

Despite all the differences in attitudes to leadership described above, and the changes that have taken place in the last 150 years, there are some common themes that can be pulled out. There are several different conceptions of the role of the leader. There is also the question of the relationship between leaders and followers, and there is finally the debate, still ongoing today, as to whether and how leadership differs from management.

### 9.3.1 The leader as hero

We saw that the idea of the leader as a heroic figure has been especially strong in the West, although Gandhi discussed the idea too. Islamic and some classical Chinese writers strongly urged leaders to steer clear of the idea of heroism, and emphasised the need for leaders to be humble servants (see below).

Yet the qualities of heroism that Gandhi described – courage, endurance, fearlessness, self-sacrifice – are still very much admired in leaders. In his book *On Leadership*, Allan Leighton (2007) observes many of these qualities in other business leaders and suggests that they are still valuable. Courage in particular is a virtue that continues to be in demand. At a very basic level, people want to know that the leaders they follow will not desert them in their hour of need. In one of his first battles as commander, Frederick the Great allowed himself to be persuaded by his staff officers that his life was in danger and that he should leave the battlefield. On learning of this, the rest of his army decided that there was no point in fighting, and retreated. Frederick learned his lesson, and from thenceforward always stayed with his army to the end, even on one occasion when he himself had been wounded.

Personal courage is just as important in business, even without the risk to life and limb. In 1911, morale at the failing Minnesota Mining and

Manufacturing Company was at rock bottom; many senior managers had quit and the company seemed to have no future. Newly appointed sales manager William McKnight took the lead, faced the future and inspired others to follow him in the search for ways to turn the company around. He went on to become president of the company and 3M became a world-class corporation. This was in part thanks to McKnight's vision and skill, but part of the turnaround was due also to his calmness and courage at a time when all seemed to be lost. His attitude influenced those around him and persuaded them that there was still hope.

Yet McKnight was not a 'heroic' character. He was not a 'flag-waving' leader; he preferred to remain behind the scenes, and one of the main elements of his leadership style was the inspiring of others to work to their full potential (Huck 1955). Perhaps Gandhi was right, and it is 'heroism' that matters, not 'heroes'. We need our leaders to behave in a heroic manner, but without seeking heroic stature.

### 9.3.2   The leader as servant

Alternatively there is the view found in Islamic and Indian writings, and to an extent in Chinese works too, that the leader is in some sense also a servant. This idea has become popular in recent years (see Gosling *et al.* 2007), but it has a long history, as we have seen above. The idea has particular resonance in the Islamic milieu because of the notion that all people are servants of God. In Kautilya's concept of leadership, the leader is the servant of the *dharma*, while Daoists and Confucians believe that the leader has a duty to help people find enlightenment and the Way.

The idea that leaders are servants of society is not entirely absent in the West, and John of Salisbury notes that kings are in effect stewards of their kingdom, responsible to a higher authority (i.e. God). But the concept remained less explicit until the nineteenth century when, partly as a result of social changes, some leaders began taking the idea of service more seriously. In Britain, Quaker business leaders such as Joseph Rowntree and George Cadbury espoused the idea. It was an article of faith with Rowntree that his products had to make a contribution to the community; producing and selling second-best goods would be tantamount to a dereliction of duty (he also refused to advertise his products on the grounds that advertising might unfairly influence people into buying when they had no need to do so). His attitude to his workers was much the same: he made it clear that he was there to help them serve their own best interests, not his. As a result, says one writer, 'his ability to inspire loyalty with his meticulous, quiet and approachable manner was widely acknowledged' (Fitzgerald 1995: 54).

The idea of the leader as servant was taken to its logical extreme by John Spedan Lewis, who handed over ownership of his department store to his employees. The notion that the leaders of the organisation are stewards, whose prime responsibility is to others, continues to be an important part of the John Lewis Group's corporate culture (Donkin 2001). One question which arises is, if leaders are servants, can they also be heroes, or at least behave in a heroic manner as suggested by Gandhi? The examples of John Spedan Lewis and William McKnight suggest that this is possible, but the exact mix of service and heroism is likely to vary from case to case.

### 9.3.3 The leader as coordinator

Follett (1924) argued that control is an illusion; no leader actually 'controls' anything, but instead coordinates the actions of others. Instead of giving orders and expecting them to be obeyed, leaders motivate others so as to work for the common interest. This was not the first time this view had been expressed. Machiavelli in the sixteenth century had argued that the power of despotic leaders to influence events is limited, and the most successful leaders are those whose own interests are identical with those of the people who follow them. The Chinese Daoists believed that coordination was a naturally occurring function, and that if left free of interference from above, people would naturally coordinate their own actions to achieve the best possible result. At the other end of the scale, even one of the most highly centralised command-and-control organisations the world has ever seen, the Prussian army, recognised the importance of coordination and motivation. In the preface to his *Remarks on Cavalry*, the Prussian general Karl Emmanuel von Warnery wrote that 'if a soldier, whether on foot or horseback, is not animated with ambition, if he has not that patriotic spirit ... he cannot be depended upon on any occasion where it is not sufficient to act mechanically' (Warnery 1798: xix).

The principle of the leader as coordinator can be seen very clearly in the large Florentine businesses of the later Middle Ages and the Renaissance, such as the Medici Bank (Case Study 1A) and the business concerns of the merchant of Prato, Francesco di Marco Datini (Case Study 3B). These businesses were structured as a series of interlocking partnerships, the identities and numbers of the partners varying, and with each partnership renegotiated every two or three years. Although there were dominant partners – Cosimo dei Medici in the case of the Medici Bank, Datini in the case of his various business ventures – those dominant partners could not merely give orders. They had to coordinate the activities of the other partners and those lower down the hierarchy. Attempts to give direct orders often failed, as Datini discovered when he tried to prevent one of his Spanish partners from engaging in illegal currency trading. These businesses were managed through a series of negotiations and discussions that went on through the life of the partnership. Datini's voluminous correspondence, with around 130,000 letters still surviving, shows how he managed this process and demonstrates that the correspondence itself was a vehicle for coordination, not control.

> **Leadership is fun**
>
> Leadership is, above all, great fun. Leaders need to have a great sense of humour and the ability to laugh at themselves and not take themselves too seriously. If it weren't fun, there would be no point in pushing yourself to the limits. Fun enables you to get things done that you otherwise couldn't do.
>
> (Leighton 2007: 5)

### 9.3.4 Leaders and followers

Goffee and Jones (2006) suggested that one of the key factors in leadership is the nature of the interaction between leaders and followers, and Witzel (2007b) argued that this interaction and its importance can be traced back through both theories of leadership and leadership in practice to the classical world. In other words, whether leaders see themselves as heroes or as servants, they have always relied on coordination as well as – or instead of – control to achieve their goals.

The idea of 'followers' makes some people uncomfortable today, as it is seen as being incompatible with the democratic approach which puts everyone on an equal level. The idea that there are 'leaders' and 'followers' is one that has very deep roots, and has its origins in the broader social classifications that every society develops, such as the 'three estates' of medieval Europe or the caste system of India. In these and other cases, it is assumed that there are those whose duty it is to lead, and those whose duty it is to obey orders. In the early twentieth century, in part influenced by theories of evolution and eugenics, Emerson (1909) and Casson (1928) argued that this was a natural state of affairs. Some people are better equipped, by reason of nature, temperament and/or superior intelligence to lead, and others are better equipped to follow the lead given by others.

The response to this is to point to examples of companies such as Semco (Semler 1993), where, in effect, everyone is expected to share the responsibility for leadership. However, companies that follow this model are rare. The question must be asked: is this rarity because the proposition is true and not everyone is capable of leading? Or is it because still-prevailing ideas of hierarchy and class distinction mean that leaders – and for that matter, followers – expect that the division between the two should be preserved? Or, indeed, is it possible that both are partly true?

A further complicating factor is that we know that the people we identify as 'followers' are also capable of acting as leaders, and sometimes combine the two roles at once. A junior army officer is a leader to his platoon, but a follower to his company and battalion commanders. A general manager of a business unit is a leader to the rest of the business unit, but follows the directions given by head office. Distinctions between leaders and followers are often very fuzzy.

### 9.3.5 Leadership and management

As noted earlier in this chapter, there remains a debate as to whether leadership and management are two quite different things, or whether they in fact overlap. Without getting directly involved in that debate, we can observe here that the debate itself had much less significance in the past. When the managers of businesses were also wholly or partly the owners, then the roles of leader and senior manager tended to overlap. We can see this overlap in other cases too, such as Robert Owen, who served as general manager of Peter Drinkwater's textile mill in Manchester. During Owen's tenure as manager, the owner only visited the mill once, and left Owen a completely free hand. Again, Owen filled the role of both leader and manager.

There were of course people in junior managerial roles: estate managers, factors in charge of overseas trading posts, managers of mills and factories and so on. These took their orders from headquarters, but were they also leaders? In the sense that others looked to them for leadership and guidance, then they undoubtedly were. The factor in charge of the Hudson's Bay Company's trading post at York Factory in Canada, thousands of miles from head office in London, needed to be a leader; it was impossible for head office to provide more than general oversight, given the distance and the slow speed of communications at the time. Even relatively junior managers like workshop foremen or forewomen were regarded as leaders, and had responsibilities for issues such as discipline, hiring and firing, and morale. Alice Kelly, the forewoman and production supervisor at the C.J. Walker manufacturing plant in Indianapolis, was undoubtedly regarded as a leader by the plant's staff, even though she in turn reported to Sarah Breedlove Walker, the plant's owner and the company's senior executive.

The idea that leadership and management need to be treated separately may have two origins. The first is the identification of leadership itself as a separate discipline for study, which has led people to begin to draw comparisons between the tasks and requirements of leadership and those of management. The second may be that faster and broader communications networks have improved the ability of senior managers to control/coordinate actions over long distances and large areas. This might in turn mean that the leadership responsibilities of junior managers have been diminished. (On the other hand, it could be argued, the increasing trend towards democratic leadership and leadership by coordination means that those responsibilities might actually be increasing.)

We can conclude by observing that while leadership and management may be two different things, in the past and until very recently, they were carried out by the same people. This is true across the world, as well as back through time.

## 9.4 Questions and discussion: what makes an effective leader?

Discussions of how leadership was perceived, conceptualised and practised tend to generate more questions than answers. The question of what makes an effective leader is as much open to debate now as it was two and a half thousand years ago when Confucius and Laozi first considered the issue.

We have seen that a variety of leadership styles have evolved in different cultures and at different times. This might tend to support modern theories of 'situational' or 'contingent' leadership, which suggest that styles of leadership that are effective in one situation may be ineffective in another. The example of Winston Churchill, a highly effective wartime leader as prime minister of Britain who failed when asked to lead the country in a time of peace, is often cited. But the issue goes beyond individual leaders. Analysis of the past suggests that there are broader trends in leadership styles, and that the nature of leadership will always to some extent reflect the dominant values and philosophies of the societies in which they lead.

And if *that* is the case, then it might also be that in order to find the most effective way of leading people, we need to look outside our own organisations and at society as a whole. What do people value? What do they expect from leaders (assuming that the distinction between leaders and followers still holds good)? And can we adapt our leadership styles to match?

Questions about the role of leaders and whether leadership and management are different are important, and need to be answered. But the one common factor that seems to link successful leaders is that they have responded to the needs of those who followed them. Whether they behaved as heroes or servants, whether they exercised control or preferred quiet coordination, they provided something that their followers needed. Those leaders who failed, did so in many cases because they disappointed their followers and lost their confidence. Of course there are examples of brave generals who went down fighting or business leaders whose ventures failed through no fault of their own. But were those failures, failures of *leadership*, or of something else?

And finally, from what we can observe although there is indeed no substitute for leadership, it is also the case that leadership is not everything. Organisations need leaders, but having a strong, gifted, intelligent, courageous leader does not guarantee success. The German army during the Second World War had an extraordinary number of extremely gifted and talented leaders: Rommel, Manstein, Kleist, Bock, Guderian and many others. The Allied armies, by contrast, produced some generals who were good organisers but very few who had a real genius for leadership (a point made by Hart 1948). Yet, thankfully, the German leaders could not prevail and the Allies won the war. Leadership is not everything. Organisation, technology and, perhaps most of all, the beliefs and ideals of the ordinary members of the organisation and the support the organisation receives from the rest of society, all play critical roles. Leadership is necessary for success: but leadership alone is not sufficient.

**Takeaway exercise**

Are you now or have you ever been in a position of leadership? Anything will do: coach of a sports team, leader of a choir, head of a team at work, or even as parent. Now ask yourself what those who 'followed' you wanted from you. What were you required to do for them or give them? Write down a list of things, and group them into categories if it helps. Now – and this is the hard part – ask yourself whether you did indeed give them what they asked for. How well did you do as a leader? Honest answers will help you to identify gaps between their expectations and your performance, and this in turn may help you to improve your own ability to lead.

## Case Study 9A

*Four leaders (George Eastman, Edwin Gay, Edwin Land, John Patterson)*

### 1 'My work is done': George Eastman[1]

Born in New York State in 1854, George Eastman founded the Eastman Kodak Company and dominated the photographic industry for almost half a century. He was an innovative and progressive employer whose investments in research were widely emulated and employee welfare programmes widely praised. He was also an important philanthropist, donating almost his entire fortune to educational and health institutions.

After beginning work as a clerk in an insurance office at the age of thirteen, Eastman became a bank clerk. In his late teens he began experimenting with photography, and from this grew the idea of commercially manufacturing photographic plates. He was attracted to the possibility of developing a 'dry-plate' emulsion as an alternative to the cumbersome and difficult coating and developing of wet plates. He hoped his dry-plate emulsion would drastically reduce the size and weight of photographic equipment. By 1879 he was ready to patent his dry plate process, and in 1880 he entered into a partnership with Henry A. Strong, quit his bank job, and devoted himself full-time to his small photographic business.

In 1884 Eastman began searching for a transparent and flexible film and achieved his first breakthrough, preparing a paper-backed film. By 1888 he had expanded from dry plates and film to cameras, marketing the first Kodak. The Kodak (the name was invented by Eastman and chosen for its unique nature) was priced at twenty-five dollars and held film containing 100 exposures. The camera had to be mailed back to the factory, where the exposures were developed and the camera reloaded and returned to the customer. Despite this cumbersome process, it was a huge success. By 1889, Eastman had patented a transparent film. This film proved crucial in the development of motion pictures.

By the end of the 1880s Eastman had emerged as a major figure in the plate, film, camera and motion picture industries. By the end of the 1890s, he dominated all of these fields. The company increased rapidly in size and capitalisation and continued to offer important innovations and improvements in its products. In short order Eastman introduced daylight loading film, a pocket Kodak, a five-dollar camera and stronger and more reliable motion picture film. To manage the necessary production and expansion Eastman adhered to four key principles, all relatively new to American business: mass production, low unit cost, extensive advertising, and international distribution. In 1891 Eastman opened his Kodak Park plant, with over 7,000 employees. Here, Eastman perfected the techniques of mass production long before Henry Ford brought them to the automobile industry. The resulting low costs were a necessary step in reaching Eastman's goal of making photography affordable to most Americans.

With production increasing, Eastman's early and innovative use of advertising played an important role in helping to stimulate demand. The name Kodak joined the small list of brand names which came to be identified with their product: 'Kodak' and 'camera' became synonymous. Kodak's early slogan, 'You press the button. We do the rest', was so successful Gilbert and Sullivan wrote it into the lyrics for their 1893 operetta *Utopia, Limited*. Kodak's targeted advertising especially sought to reach women, moving the camera from a predominantly male hobby to a family necessity. Finally, Kodak's early expansion overseas allowed it to rapidly consolidate control of the international market for film.

In addition, Eastman recognised the importance of scientific research and pioneered in the creation of corporate research and development facilities. He actively recruited scientists of international reputation and devoted a substantial sum to building research laboratories in Rochester. Control of between 75 and 80 per cent of the American film market combined with massive profits, however, brought the attention of the Justice Department. Anti-trust investigations were begun in 1911. The case was ultimately dismissed on appeal after Eastman signed a consent decree agreeing to sell some subsidiaries and change certain business practices. Thereafter, Eastman continued to fear government involvement in his business. This fear led him to cooperate with the government whenever possible to forestall scrutiny. During the First World War Kodak produced photographic materials for the Army and Navy, trained the US Signal Corps in photography, and manufactured numerous synthetic chemicals in an attempt to make the USA more economically independent. After the war Eastman made a point of cancelling government bills and refusing what he decided were excessive profits on war work.

Eastman shared with many progressive era industrialists the belief that corporations had a responsibility to serve the public good. He designed a number of employee welfare programmes, most of which were economic in nature. As Eastman said, 'You can talk about cooperation and good feeling and friendliness from morn to midnight, but the thing the worker appreciates is the same thing the man at the helm appreciates – dollars and cents.' Kodak offered a share in the profits for executives, accident and sickness insurance for all employees, a building and loan association, a pension system and a stock purchase programme, along with the more common and less substantial corporate culture building events like company picnics, dances, sports leagues and amateur theatricals. On three occasions Eastman distributed substantial amounts of his personal wealth to employees, either directly or by endowing various welfare programmes. Perhaps most unusual among the list of Kodak benefits was the wage-dividend, instituted in 1912.

These programmes also originated in less idealistic and more practical concerns. Prominent among these was the desire to prevent the spread of unionisation, something the deeply conservative and staunchly Republican Eastman adamantly opposed. Eastman was also continually concerned with the public reputation of his company, fearing more anti-monopoly proceedings and greater government regulation. All of Eastman's large stock gifts to his employees were bestowed during periods when he perceived unionisation as a threat, and his announcement of the wage-dividend came just as the government's anti-trust case was beginning. A related motivation for corporate welfare work was Eastman's recognition that employee loyalty was a crucial component of his company's success. Eastman recognised that his plants were unusually dependent on the disposition of its labour force; sabotage was easy in a work environment where direct supervision was almost impossible and the high concentration of Kodak plants in a few locations meant a strike could prove disastrous.

By the 1920s, with his company's dominant position consolidated and his edifice of welfare programmes constructed, Eastman decreased his involvement in Eastman Kodak and began to expand his philanthropic activities. His charitable giving had begun with a gift of $200,000 to the Rochester Mechanics Institute in 1899 and a later smaller gift to the University of Rochester. Eastman had a lifelong dislike for publicity and attention, and his early gifts to a favourite institution, the Massachusetts Institute of Technology (MIT), were presented on the behalf of 'Mr. Smith'. It was not until 1920, when Eastman, seeking to break up his large holdings of Kodak stock, gave MIT a large gift of shares that his identity was revealed. By then he had donated $20,000,000 to the university. All told, he also donated more than $35,000,000 to the University of Rochester and millions more to other education institutions.

Eastman had no wife or children. By the early 1930s he was no longer directly involved either at the plant or at the office and rarely visited either. His health was deteriorating. On 14 March 1932, immediately after the signing of his last will, Eastman shot himself in the heart, leaving the note 'To my friends; my work is done. Why wait?'

## Sources

Ackerman, C.W. (1930) *George Eastman*, Boston and New York: Houghton Mifflin.
Brayer, E. (1996) *George Eastman: A Biography*, Baltimore and London: Johns Hopkins University Press.

## 2 'One of my serious regrets': Edwin Gay

Born in Detroit in 1867 into a prosperous family, Gay was educated at schools in Michigan and in Europe and then took a degree in philosophy and history from the University of Michigan in 1890. He then went to the University of Berlin for graduate study in medieval history. Becoming attracted to the scholar's life, he remained in Europe for the next twelve years, studying at various universities including Leipzig, Zurich and Florence, and finally completing his PhD at Berlin in 1902. He had married his university classmate Louise Randolph in 1892; a notable scholar herself, she accompanied Gay to Europe and worked with him. Both the Gays would later recall this as an idyllic time in which they were able to completely immerse themselves in their passion for study.

In 1902 Gay returned to the USA and took up a post as instructor in economics at Harvard University. Both his intellectual power and hitherto undiscovered administrative talents marked him out as a rising star, and he was made professor and chairman of the department of economics in 1906. When Harvard's president, Charles Eliot, began developing his plan for a business school, Gay was one of his key advisers in the run-up to the school's establishment in 1908. When Eliot's first choice as dean, the Canadian politician William Lyon Mackenzie King, turned the post down, Gay was invited to take over the new school.

He accepted with reluctance, fearing it would take him away from his research, already hampered by his administrative duties in the department of economics – he had still yet to publish a book. However, he worked hard to make the new school a success. After his initial reluctance was overcome, Gay came to see the school as a chance to combine scholarship and action:

> To fashion, build, and manage a school which would train men for business as a profession; to bring his wide range of knowledge to bear on planning and guiding that training; to inculcate an awareness of the social obligations and consequences of business enterprise; and to do this for a country that was travelling fast toward economic maturity and pre-eminence – here indeed was a call to active service that could not be declined.
>
> (Heaton 1952: 69)

His commitment to Harvard Business School was total; as Charles Eliot later said, 'he transferred himself body and soul to the new School, put all his time and strength into it' (Heaton 1952: 74).

Gay was working with no models to guide him; only the University of Pennsylvania and Dartmouth College had previously established graduate schools of business (the Wharton and Tuck schools, respectively). No matter how much managerial and academic talent he was able to recruit to the school, the blueprint for it had to be his own. It was Gay who determined the guiding philosophy of the school, which he saw as resting on two key ideas. First, he defined the task of the business manager as 'making things to sell at a profit (decently)'. Second, he defined the school's own task as 'to experiment and to learn what the *content* and *form* should be for the training of mature students primarily for "making" or "selling"' (Heaton 1952: 76). The key qualities necessary in a successful manager were courage, judgement and sympathy, and it was the school's role to inculcate and strengthen these in students through education.

It was Gay who determined that the degree offered by the school would be called 'Master of Business Administration', a title which became adopted around the world. It was Gay too who adapted the case system pioneered by Harvard Law School to the study of management. This proved to be a difficult task, as there was no pre-existing body of case material, and he commissioned a number of writers and publishers to help develop material. Most important of all, Gay sought to move away from the traditional format of classroom lectures, towards teaching methods that would involve and challenge students and stimulate their imaginations. Melvin Copeland, who was recruited by Gay in 1909 and asked to begin teaching a marketing course at thirty-six hours' notice, later recalled encountering Gay a couple of weeks after teaching had begun. When the dean asked how the course was going, Copeland replied, 'I have found enough to talk about so far.' 'That is not the question', replied Gay. 'Have you found enough to keep the students talking?' Copeland, taking the broad hint, abandoned his lecturing style for one of classroom discussion, and followed this through the rest of his career. Much later, he realised that Gay had selected him as a 'guinea pig' for introduction of classroom discussion and the case method in marketing (Copeland 1958: 59–60).

By 1917 the school was beginning to prosper and Gay, exhausted, resigned as dean. He served as adviser to the United States Shipping Board during the First World War. In 1919, deciding not to return to Harvard, he accepted an offer from Lamont to take over the editorship of the New York *Evening Post*, which the latter owned. This move was not a success, and in 1924 the newspaper went bankrupt. Gay then returned to Harvard as a professor of economic history, where he remained until he retired in 1936; moving to California, he served on the research staff of the Huntingdon Library until stricken with pneumonia in January 1946. He died at Pasadena, California on 8 February 1946.

Gay's achievements at Harvard Business School were considerable. The pedagogic methods he developed there were widely imitated: the case method remains standard at most business schools today. Gay's philosophy of business education likewise remains at the heart of most thinking on the subject. His personal managerial accomplishment in getting the school off the ground should not be overrated: the progenitor of the case study could himself be regarded as a useful case example of developing and carrying through a highly successful innovation.

Yet Gay himself, in his later years, regarded his own career as a failure. In 1908 he had departed from the historical and economic research that he loved, and was never able to recapture the passion for his work that he had felt in his youth. He wrote to a friend in 1935: 'It is one my serious regrets that I ever undertook the deanship of the Business School' (Heaton 1952: 6).

### Sources

Copeland, M. (1958) *And Mark the Era: The Story of Harvard Business School*, Boston: Little, Brown.
Heaton, H.K. (1952) *A Scholar in Action: Edwin F. Gay*, Cambridge, MA: Harvard University Press.

### 3  Science and knowledge: Edwin Land

Land was born in Bridgeport, Connecticut in 1909, the son of Russian immigrants; the Land family name was originally Solomonovich; the name 'Land' stems from the arrival of the family at Ellis Island in 1880, who misunderstood the immigration officer who asked them their names and told him they had just 'landed'. Land grew up in Connecticut where his father ran a thriving scrap metal business. As a small boy he became fascinated with optics, particularly after reading one of the leading books on the subject, Robert W. Wood's *Physical Optics*, which had been published in 1905. Land went to Harvard University in 1926 to study physics, already experimenting with stereoscopes and the polarisation of light. At Harvard, Land also read Oswald Spengler's *The Decline of the West* and was inspired by the latter's vision of a future dominated by technology and engineers.

In 1928, while still an undergraduate, Land borrowed money from his father to set up a laboratory, and in 1929 filed a patent application for a polariser. In 1932 he set up a business to manufacture polarisers for two applications: to be applied to car windscreens so as to diffuse the dazzling beams of oncoming headlights during night driving, and for the making and viewing of three-dimensional cinema films. The former market never took off, the car manufacturers of the day deciding that the resulting safety benefits would not be worth the cost of installing polarised windscreens; 3D films, despite a brief period of popularity, never really caught on. However, many other applications were developed from the original technology. By the end of the 1930s there was a burgeoning market for polarising sunglasses, and Land also developed devices such as the vectograph, for viewing three-dimensional photos, which was widely adopted by the US Army during the Second World War.

Following the war, Land's Polaroid Corporation led the way in the development of colour photography, but a chance conversation with his daughter led him on to his next major innovation, instant photography. By 1947 Land had a working model, but picture quality was far too poor to be marketable. Some years were to pass before first black-and-white and then colour instant cameras were perfected. It was not until 1972 that the famous Polaroid SX-70 camera came on the market.

Land was also involved in national scientific and defence work, and in the 1950s played a major role in the development of the high-altitude reconnaissance aircraft, the U-2. His work in such high-profile fields as 3D cinema and instant cameras made him something of a celebrity figure; tall and darkly handsome, with a distinct facial resemblance to Cary Grant, he became an apostle of science to the American public, who hailed him as a hero. Within Polaroid, however, dissatisfaction with Land's management style was rising; there were product quality and cost problems with the SX-70 which Land did not appear to be addressing. In 1980 a boardroom coup forced Land to step down as chief executive officer and president. By 1985 he had sold his last remaining shares in Polaroid and severed all connections with the company, devoting himself to research for the remaining years of his life.

Land had a number of well-documented failings as a manager, including lack of attention to costs and a reluctance to abandon a project even when it had little or no chance of success. He did, however, have a strong vision of the role of science, technology and knowledge in making business enterprises successful, and it was this vision that carried him and Polaroid through the years of growth from the 1930s to the 1960s. Land conceived of the ideal business of the future being what he called a 'science-based corporation', in which the core of the corporation was a team of researchers whose sole function was to generate knowledge and potential new products. The exploitation of these products would then be carried out by management teams centred around each product line. Polaroid itself was structured along these lines, and it is possible that this model was the partial inspiration for the matrix organisation. But the model only worked as long as rapid growth and high profits were being generated; in times of slow growth, the costs of maintaining the scientific core, rather than the benefits to be expected from research, were what tended to obsess directors.

But although the specific model may have had its functional problems, the core concept of science generating knowledge which could be turned into commercial advantage has been and remains a very powerful one, and has played a major part in the development of new high-technology industries and sectors around the world in the 1990s and up to the time of writing.

## Source

McElheny, V.K. (1998) *Insisting on the Impossible*, New York: Perseus.

## 4 'Every kind of legitimate comfort': John Patterson

Patterson was born in Dayton, Ohio in 1844. His family were well-to-do Ohio landowners, and Patterson received a good education and went on to attend Dartmouth College, taking a degree in 1867. He served in the Union Army during the American Civil War, but to his disappointment his regiment never saw action. After completing his degree he returned to Ohio and went into business with his brother, Frank Patterson, dealing in coal and mining equipment. The business struggled, and eventually failed in 1883. However, the experience had one important impact on Patterson: struggling to manage cashflow, he chanced across a recent invention, the cash register, which had been patented by James Ritty.

Cash registers were being made on a small scale by the National Manu-facturing Company in Dayton, and Patterson purchased two machines. So impressed was he by their potential that he purchased the company, even though it was then making a loss, changing the name to National Cash Reg-ister (NCR) and throwing himself into this new business. The company's first factory was established in 1888, and growth was rapid thereafter; although he continued to manufacture his cash registers from a single factory in Dayton, by 1900 he was selling across the country and around the world.

Patterson encountered the problem faced by many high-tech businesses, namely, that of creating a market for innovative technologies. Few people outside of Dayton had ever heard of cash registers, and even fewer recognised their potential in terms of controlling costs and revenue and cutting down on theft and loss. Yet Patterson knew the market was there; the problem was how to stimulate demand. His response was what he called 'constructive selling', or proactive marketing of his products through a campaign that was at least as much about providing information to customers as it was about urging them to buy the product.

At the core of his sales programme was the creation of a dedicated sales force which worked as a coordinated team according to a centrally deter-mined strategy. Rather than being simply turned loose to sell according to their own methods, each salesman was set a defined territory and was issued with a precise set of instructions on selling techniques. This latter included a period of staff training for each salesman before they were sent into the field. Patterson told his salesmen not to emphasise the product's technical cap-abilities – most customers would have little interest in knowing how a cash register actually worked – but instead to analyse the customer's business, work out how a cash register could help that business, and impart this infor-mation to the customer. Relationship building and information were thus at the heart of Patterson's sales strategy.

Patterson was also an innovator in labour management. NCR was one of the first firms in the USA to set up a labour department to focus specifically on human resource issues. According to one story, while touring the Dayton factory Patterson observed a female employee heating her lunch on a radiator. Appalled at the lack of facilities, he set up a canteen and offered workers free lunches; when the workers refused to accept what they saw as charity, Patterson priced the lunches at five cents. Honour was satisfied on both sides, and workers flocked to use the canteen. Following on from this, Patterson began offering other benefits such as health care, gymnasiums and exercise facilities, and later paid vacation excursions to resorts and attractions such as the St Louis World's Fair. His attitude to labour management was strongly paternalistic, and occasionally cranky – the wives of all male employees were required to attend compulsory cooking classes, organised and paid for by the company – but were always well intentioned. Accused by other business leaders of being excessively 'soft' in his treatment of employees, Patterson replied that the cost of employee benefits was repaid to the firm in terms of higher productivity and lower rates of sickness and absenteeism:

> One of the most profitable investments that can he made in a manufacturing plant is to give the largest possible advantages in the way of conveniences and sanitary arrangements. Every kind of legitimate comfort and convenience that may be provided for operatives is a source of profit to the employer, although apart from the moral obligation to care for the health and comfort of the employee.
>
> (Becker 1906: 552)

Patterson's technological advantage in his field could not be long maintained, and by 1900 rival cash register makers were springing up across the country. His response was energetic and, some said, unprincipled; he bought out as many competitors as he could, and drove most of the rest out of the market. In this Patterson was aided by the hard-nosed manager of the Rochester branch office, Thomas J. Watson (the later founder of IBM), whom Patterson brought to head office and eventually promoted to be his deputy. In 1912, however, the US government stepped in and charged thirty NCR managers, Patterson and Watson included, with violations of anti-trust legislation. Convicted, Patterson and Watson were fined $5,000 and sentenced to a year in prison.

Shortly thereafter, Dayton was badly affected by tornados and flooding and thousands of people were made homeless. Patterson stopped all work at the factory, sent his employees into the affected areas to distribute food and relief supplies; his medical department provided doctors and nurses to tend the sick, and Watson went to New York to organise the despatch of further supplies by train. In the aftermath of the disaster, thousands petitioned President Wilson to grant Patterson a pardon (in fact, the conviction was overturned by an appeal court in 1915 before the pardon became necessary).

Patterson was badly affected by the death of his wife in 1894, and became more eccentric as he grew older; a hypochondriac, he affected a variety of unusual diets, and insisted that his long-suffering senior executives should share these with him. He grew solitary and increasingly difficult to deal with, leading to a quarrel with and the departure of Watson, his most talented executive. On the credit side, he became a strong proponent of world peace; although during the First World War his company made munitions for the US Army, he took the lead in returning to do business in Germany after the war and was a strong supporter of the League of Nations. He died on board a train in 1922 while going to seek a health cure in Atlantic City.

## Sources

Becker, Oswald M. (1906) 'The Square Deal in Works Management', *Engineering Magazine*, January: 536–54.
Crowther, Samuel (1923) *John H. Patterson: Pioneer in Industrial Welfare*, London: William Heinemann.

## Analysis

Some of the questions you might want to consider in connection with this case include:

- Could any of these four be legitimately called a 'great' leader? What does it really mean to be a 'great' leader?
- What were the strengths of each? What were the weaknesses?
- Does the comparison of the four take us any closer to an idea of an ideal 'type' of leader? Is such a thing even possible?
- Do you think any of them were truly happy?

## Case Study 9B

*Henry Ford, 1910 and 1927*

### 1 1910: Highland Park

In 1910, Ford Motor Company opened its state-of-the-art automobile assembly plant at Highland Park, Michigan. It was like nothing the world had ever seen. Designed by architect Albert Kahn and purpose-built for the production of the Ford's new Model T, launched on the market two years earlier, the Highland Park plant covered sixty-two acres. It featured the largest assembly line ever built, and had been carefully engineered to increase car production to speeds beyond anything yet attempted. Instead of 12–14 hours to assemble a finished car, the previous norm, Model Ts could now be assembled from stocks of finished parts in an hour and a half. Others had developed systems of mass production before, but Ford had taken the concept into a new dimension.

The opening of Highland Park sent a shock through the US business world. Visitors from other companies and even other countries flocked to see it. Ford won plaudits not only for his mechanical engineering but for his attention to detail and carefully engineered production system. To the shock and outrage of other car makers he later offered his workers $5 a day, at a time when many workers in the industry were making $1 a day and no one was paying more than $3. For every job advertised at the factory, Ford claimed to have had a thousand applications. The best and most skilled automotive workers in the country came to work at Ford's plant. Ford later went on to establish what he called a 'sociological department' staffed with scientists who studied the workers and their actions and motivations and then reported back to Ford with new ideas on how to keep workers motivated, productive and happy.

When Highland Park opened, Ford himself was forty-seven years old. He had indeed worked hard for his success. One of eight children of a poor farmer, he had been badly educated and was barely literate when he finished school. He began work as an apprentice in a Detroit machine shop at sixteen, and also developed an interest in watches, taking on part-time work as a watch repairman. His skill with cogs and gears would later become very valuable. After marrying in 1888 he took a series of jobs, first with the Westinghouse company travelling and servicing steam engines, then with the Edison Illuminating Company, suppliers of electricity in Chicago. By 1893 he was chief engineer for the Chicago area and might easily have spent the rest of his career as a successful middle manager for a large corporation.

In the 1890s, however, he became interested in automobiles and set out to design his own. His early experience with watches and gears helped him solve one of the major problems faced by early designers, that of how to convert the motive power provided by a steam or internal combustion engine into drive through the wheels. His simple design for a transmission led to his development of a working automobile in 1896. The car, which he called a quadricycle, ran on bicycle wheels and weighed just five hundred pounds in total. Ford promptly sold it to raise capital for further experiments, and continued to make and sell experimental prototypes in this fashion for some years. In 1899 with capital provided by a Detroit lumber dealer, William Murphy, Ford established the Detroit Automobile Company and resigned from Edison to become the new firm's superintendent in charge of production. This company failed almost at once, largely because Ford knew nothing about production, and managed to make only a handful of cars. Undeterred, Ford and his backers tried again, setting up the Henry Ford Company in 1900. Again, few cars were actually built, but one of these proved to be a successful racing car. Ford became suddenly enthusiastic about motor racing and neglected his business, and accordingly was fired from the Henry Ford Company in 1902 (the company went on to become the Cadillac Motor Car Company and eventually became part of General Motors). Ford then joined the former racing car driver Tom Cooper in a partnership which built the 999, a car which set a world land speed record.

But racing cars were no more than a passing fancy. Ford had by now developed his vision: he wanted to build cheap, efficient cars which could be widely sold on an affordable basis. With fresh backing, this time from the Detroit coal dealer Alexander Malcolmson, and with more engineering talent in the person of Childe Harold Willis, Ford established the Ford Motor Company in Detroit in June 1903. Partners included John and Horace Dodge, who supplied Ford's original engines, and James Couzens, a Malcolmson employee who acted as treasurer. Ford provided the engineering and production knowledge, and was appointed vice-president and general manager. There were more problems: Ford's strategy of building small, cheap cars did not find favour with Malcolmson, who wanted to build luxury cars for the high end of the market. Ford bought out Malcolmson in 1906 and went ahead with the development of the Model N, a cheap runabout that went on sale later that year for $600.

Another significant development was the purchase of the John R. Keim steel works in Buffalo, New York, one of Ford's major suppliers. From Keim, Ford acquired the services of yet another talented manager, William 'Big Bill' Knudsen. Ford now had the nucleus of one of the most talented teams in managerial history. In Knudsen he had found a genius, a man who could solve any production problem and who, with his deputy Charles Sorenson, designed the mass production system on which Ford relied. James Couzens was in charge of both financial controls and marketing, and handled the latter with particular ability. And Ford himself was at the height of his powers as engineer and designer.

In 1908, Ford launched the Model T. Designed by himself and Childe Harold Willis, the Model T, or 'Tin Lizzie' as it was nicknamed by affectionate drivers, first went on sale for $825, but Ford constantly sought to drag the price down, trading volume of sales for unit profits; in the mid-1920s prices fell as low as $275 for a new Model T. With a 22-horsepower engine and advanced chassis and steering design, the car was technologically advanced when first launched, yet its design was so simple that interchangeable parts could be easily mass produced and then assembled. Between 1908 and 1927, 17 million Model Ts were sold, more than all other models of car put together at the time. The Model T was not just a product; it was an icon. And it did what Ford had intended; it brought motoring to the masses in America. Even clerks and manual workers could now afford a car. Ford had democratised transport, and changed the face of America in the process; the country's long love affair with the automobile had begun.

The Model T and Highland Park between them propelled Ford into a position of utter dominance in the industry, far outstripping rivals like the fledgling General Motors of William C. Durant. During the next decade, only John Willys at Overland ever seriously threatened Ford's dominance, and that not for long; a talented marketer, Willys was poor at managing finances and frequently ran into problems as a result. Ford simply went from strength to strength. Ford himself was hailed as a hero in the USA, one of a new kind of entrepreneur who would revolutionise the way business was done, an enlightened capitalist who was an example and an inspiration to others. Moreover, he was a self-made man, with little education but a talent for engineering which he had made the most of. Hundreds, even thousands of young men dreamed of following in his footsteps.

'Fordism' became a philosophy of mass production, a model of enlightened and efficient capitalism. It was studied in business schools and universities, in Europe as well as the USA. After the communists took power in Russia in 1917, articles on Fordism appeared in *Pravda* (Ford's books were later serialised in the newspaper), and delegations of Soviet officials and factory managers came to Detroit to study 'Fordism' in action. Ford was admired for his vision, which had created a new market and had changed life in America, for his creative genius, and for his skill at managing people. He was, quite literally, the most respected business leader in the world.

## 2 1927: River Rouge

In 1927, with great fanfare and publicity in newspapers around the world, Ford Motor Company opened its new production facility at River Rouge, Michigan. One of the largest industrial plants in the world, it was far larger and more technologically complex than Highland Park. More complex too was the new car, the Model A, which was more comfortable and mechanically reliable than the Model T. Ford had clearly made great advances in technology in the last seventeen years.

But other things had changed too. The Model T itself had been discontinued, driven off the market by its competitor the Chevrolet, marketed aggressively by Ford's rival General Motors. Management had changed too. Ford's great team had been broken up. James Couzens had departed during the First World War after a dispute with Ford, and had gone on to a career in politics. The production genius William Knudsen had gone too; again, there had been a personal dispute with Ford, but this time the damage was more serious, for Knudsen was at once hired by Pierre du Pont, chairman of General Motors, to take over production of the Chevrolet. Knudsen's production skills had played a key role in pushing the brand to the top position and driving the Model T out of the market.

But most of all there had been a change in Ford himself. He was no longer the man of the people that he had been in 1910. He had become, in the words of the British writer John Buchan in his novel *The Courts of the Morning*, 'a law unto himself, an object to admire, but not to emulate'. A few years later Aldous Huxley promoted him to the status of deity in his satirical novel *Brave New World*, where people prayed to 'Our Ford' rather than 'Our Lord'. And Ford himself seemed to have come to believe his own publicity. If not exactly above the law, he certainly felt himself to be above the common people. Various touches, such as the building of a lavish mansion near Detroit, and the taking of a teenage dancer as his mistress and having an illegitimate son with her, suggest a man in the grip of hubris. His books, written by himself or ghost-written by the journalist Samuel Crowther, had earlier been full of homespun philosophy. By the end of the 1920s they suggest a man out of touch with reality: he put forward grand schemes for world peace and pondered on the future of civilisation, almost as if he believed he had the power to influence these things.

Certainly by the mid-1920s he had lost touch with his market. Convinced that his original recipe for success was the correct one, he continued to produce the same cars in the same way, failed to see that times had moved on. The novelty of car travel was wearing off; now people wanted more features from their cars and were developing different sets of needs and motivations for buying cars. General Motors was willing to cater to these different needs; Ford was not. The famous remark, 'a customer can have a car of any colour he wants, so long as it is black', is apocryphal but is indicative of a mindset. When Chevrolet began cutting into Ford's market, Ford's only method of fighting back was to cut prices still further, which meant that Charles Sorenson, now in sole charge of production, had to find new ways of cutting costs. The atmosphere in Ford factories changed, too. Wages were cut by nearly half, and worker education and many other benefits were done away with. Ford's famous sociological department which had studied worker motivation was closed down. Strict discipline was enforced which prevented workers from whistling or even talking during shifts.

It had taken the combined efforts of Sorenson and Ford's son (by his wife Clara), Edsel Ford, to convince Ford that the Model T's days were numbered and that a new model had to be introduced which could compete with the Chevrolet. The Model A was indeed a success – 400,000 advance orders were received before the first car was ever produced – but it was not as revolutionary as the Model T. It sold in large numbers, but nothing like so large as the Model T had done, and by 1930 it was clear that Ford was now lagging third in numbers of cars sold in America, behind General Motors and Chrysler. Sorenson and Edsel Ford also attempted to diversify, developing an aircraft production division. Again the product, the Ford Trimotor, was a success, but Ford himself was not interested and production was shut down in the 1930s. The acquisition of Lincoln Motor Company was more successful, and under the direct guidance of Edsel Ford, Lincoln became the maker of USA's most luxurious cars, competing successfully with the Cadillac. But Ford himself had nothing to do with this venture and showed little interest.

The 1930s saw continued decline. Edsel Ford, bullied by his father and increasingly ill, had lost all influence. Even Sorenson could do little to reason with Ford, now in his late sixties. Ford's new confidante was Harry Bennett, a former prizefighter who was connected to the Mafia in Chicago, who now ran the Ford Service Department, a group of informers and thugs who enforced discipline among the workforce with an iron hand. The workers, tried beyond any reasonable limits of loyalty, finally rebelled and tried to unionise. When Bennett's men beat up several union organisers, the workers struck in 1941 and compelled recognition of the United Auto Workers. Ford suffered a stroke in 1938, and from then on was both physically and mentally ill, paranoid and, in the words of the normally loyal Sorenson, suffering from hallucinations.

In 1940 Ford refused to participate in the government's aircraft manufacturing programme largely because of a paranoid delusion that President Franklin D. Roosevelt was out to destroy him (the fact that William Knudsen was in charge of the programme probably did not help allay Ford's suspicions). Edsel Ford and Sorenson finally persuaded him to take part, and the Willow Run production plant was established near Ypsilanti, Michigan to make heavy bombers. Even so, Ford would never go near the plant, convinced he would be assassinated by government spies. Harry Bennett was now virtually in control of both the company and Ford himself; Charlie Sorenson recalls the sight of Clara Ford in tears at the thought of what 'that monster' was doing to her husband.

Edsel Ford's death in 1943 brought about a crisis, as Ford insisted on resuming the presidency of the firm. Clara Ford and her widowed daughter-in-law now staged a rebellion of their own, threatening to sell their shares to outsiders unless the octogenarian leader stood down. He finally gave way; intervention at the top levels of government secured the release of Edsel's son, Henry Ford II, from military service and he returned home to take up the presidency. Despite no management training or background whatever, Ford proved adept at his job, and the recovery of the company began.

## Analysis

Some of the questions you might want to consider in connection with this case include:

- Henry Ford's leadership style changed dramatically between 1910 and the late 1920s and early 1930s. What aspects changed most?
- What were the key factors that led to this change?
- What does this case tell us about the role of individual leaders and the impact they can have on organisations?
- Henry Ford is often described as a 'great leader' and even today polls taken among businesspeople suggest he is one of the world's most admired business leaders. Are there things about him that other leaders could learn from? Or should we follow John Buchan's view and admire him but not emulate him?

## Sources

Burlinghame, R. (1949) *Backgrounds of Power: The Human Story of Mass Production*, New York: Charles Scribner's Sons.

Ford, Henry (1926) *Today and Tomorrow*, New York: Garden City.

Ford, Henry (1929) *My Philosophy of Industry*, London: Harrap.

Ford, Henry and Crowther, Samuel (1922) *My Life and Work*, New York: Doubleday.

Nevins, A.N. and Hill, F.E. (1954) *Ford: The Times, the Man, the Company*, New York: Charles Scribner's Sons.

Nevins, A.N. and Hill, F.E. (1957) *Ford: Expansion and Challenge, 1915–1933*, New York: Charles Scribner's Sons.

Nevins, A.N. and Hill, F.E. (1962) *Ford: Decline and Rebirth*, New York: Charles Scribner's Sons.

Sorenson, Charles (1957) *Forty Years with Ford*, London: Jonathan Cape.

Watts, Steven (2005) *The People's Tycoon: Henry Ford and the American Century*, New York: Alfred A. Knopf.

## Case Study 9C

### Sarah Breedlove Walker

Few business leaders have come so far from such humble beginnings as Sarah Breedlove Walker, better known to a generation of African-Americans as 'Madam C.J. Walker'. She was born Sarah Breedlove in Louisiana in 1867, just two years after the end of the Civil War and the emancipation of American slaves. Her parents were now free, but continued to work in the cotton fields and were nearly as poor as when they had been slaves. Both parents died when Breedlove was seven, and she and her sister moved to Vicksburg, Mississippi where they found work as laundresses. Breedlove married another ex-slave at age fourteen and had a daughter, but her husband died in an accident when she was twenty.

Soon after being widowed, Breedlove and her daughter moved north to St Louis, Missouri, a rapidly growing city where work was said to be plentiful. She continued to work as a laundress until 1904, earning just enough money to keep herself and her daughter alive.

At the age of thirty-seven, Breedlove was afflicted with a painful scalp disease that also caused her hair to begin falling out, and began searching for a remedy. According to her own family's history, she had a dream in which a man appeared and gave her the formula for a successful remedy and then urged her to go out and start a business selling it to other afflicted women like herself. While the dream story is undoubtedly true, it is not the whole story. At the St Louis World's Fair of 1904, Breedlove visited a stand run by Annie Turnbo-Malone, another child of former slaves who had been living in St Louis since 1900 and had developed a small range of hair care products for black women. At the Fair, she gave out free samples and encouraged women to try the products. This gave her an immense amount of publicity, and soon after Turnbo-Malone's business began to expand spectacularly, and by 1906 her Poro brand was being sold across America.

Breedlove not only tried the products but was offered a job by Turnbo-Malone as a sales agent. She accepted at once, seeing an opportunity to build a better future for herself and her daughter. She was further motivated by reading some of the works of Booker T. Washington, who in 1900 (with funding from steel tycoon Andrew Carnegie) had established the National Negro Business League and was actively encouraging young black entrepreneurs to start businesses (Harlan 1983). In 1905, Breedlove moved to Denver as Turnbo-Malone's chief commission agent in the west. However, personal differences arose between the two women and Breedlove resolved to strike out on her own, developing a small range of hair care products specifically aimed at the black female market.

Soon after Breedlove married again, this time to an advertising executive named Clarence J. Walker. Walker played an important role in the early growth of the business, designing eye-catching advertisements and teaching Breedlove how to use publicity to good effect. He suggest that she rebrand the business, and herself, as 'Madam C.J. Walker', an imposing name which would give status to her products. This was at once successful, and even after the marriage dissolved six years later, she continued to call herself Madam C.J. Walker.

The Poro and Madam C.J. Walker brands were now competing head to head, and there seems to have been little love lost between Walker and Turnbo-Malone. Perhaps it was this personal rivalry that drove both to greater efforts. But the black middle classes were increasing steadily in numbers and buying power, and there was in fact room for both products. In 1910 Walker relocated to Indianapolis, which had a flourishing African-American business community and was also a major transportation hub, meaning that products could be distributed around the country. Here the C.J. Walker Manufacturing Company, the main production centre, was established. Walker delegated most of the management of the factory to her general manager, F.B. Ransom, and to Alice Kelly, the principal forewoman and production supervisor, and concentrated on what she knew best, marketing and selling.

After 1910 the company diversified rapidly, from simple hair care products into hair straighteners, cosmetics and beauty aids. Walker personally hired and trained the sales force, which eventually numbered 3,000 people, teaching them about the product but also instructing them in how to provide customer service. Working for Walker transformed the lives of the young women she hired. Not only did they earn as much in a week as they had formerly been earning in a month, but they were inspired by her to advance themselves still further; many of her agents saved their money and went on to higher education, or founded businesses of their own.

As well as direct sales she also started a mail order business, run by her daughter A'lelia, who took over its management when she was just twenty-one. The Walkers also targeted hairdressing salons, and set up schools in Pittsburgh and New York where hairdressers could come and be trained in how to use their products. By 1917 the C.J. Walker business was the largest African-American business in the United States. There continues to be debate as to which was the first African-American female millionaire, Walker or her rival Turnbo-Malone; there can be no doubt that they both reached that status. Walker herself died in 1919 of complications brought on by hypertension, itself almost certainly a result of overwork.

Madam C.J. Walker lived her own brand. She cultivated an image as a successful, stylish middle-class black woman, someone whom other women could look up to and aspire to emulate. She owned several properties, and in 1917 built a three-storey mansion on the outskirts of New York, which her obituary in the *New York Times* later described as 'one of the show places of the city'. A committed Christian, she used her associations with the church to further bolster her own image for respectability. She was also a philanthropist who gave many thousands of dollars to causes ranging from support for African-American educational institutes (she was a major donor to Tuskegee College, where Booker T. Washington had been principal) to other more urgent causes such as a publicity campaign to alert people to the horrors of lynching – the organised murder of black people by gangs in the southern United States, often carried out with support from the local police and authorities – organised by the National Association for the Advancement of Colored People (NAACP). She was a passionate believer in the rights of black people and many of her donations were motivated by personal belief; yet even those passionate personal convictions helped to bolster her image.

Walker believed in leading by example. To her employees and to her community, she stressed that she had achieved her status by hard work and self-belief, implying that they could do likewise. She was a superb motivator, and both her factory staff and her salespeople were dedicated to her and shared some of her passion for her product. Walker believed that she was helping people to better themselves, by becoming healthier and by boosting their self-confidence and image of themselves, and this too was part of her marketing pitch; it was implied that women who used her products would feel more self-confident and proud of themselves, and thus be enabled to go out and change their own lives. Another obituarist said of her: 'It is given to few persons to transform a people in a generation. Yet this was done by the late Madam C.J. Walker. She made and deserved a fortune, and gave much of it away generously' (Bundles 1991: 105).

## Analysis

Some of the questions you might want to consider in connection with this case include:

- How would you describe Walker's leadership style? What factors led to her success?
- Can you think of other examples of successful leaders who have 'lived the brand'? What did they have in common with Walker?
- Walker is not the only leader to have died relatively young (51, in her case) of overwork. Is this an occupational hazard for leaders? What if anything can be done about it?

# Sources

Bundles, A'lelia Perry (1991) *Madame C.J. Walker: Entrepreneur*, New York: Chelsea House.

Ingham, J.N. and Feldman, L.B. (1994) *African-American Business Leaders: A Biographical Dictionary*, Westport, CT: Greenwood Press.

Smith, Jessie Carney, Jackson, Millicent Lownes and Wynn, Linda T. (1994) *Encyclopedia of African American Business*, Westport, CT: Greenwood Press.

Witzel, Morgen (2001) 'Annie Turnbo-Malone', in Morgen Witzel (ed.) *Biographical Dictionary of Management*, Bristol: Thoemmes Press, vol. 2, 1001–2.

# Case Study 9D

## *J.R.D. Tata*

India has produced many talented business leaders, but one name stands out: that of Jehangir Ratan Dadabhoy Tata, widely known simply by his initials, J.R.D. Taking over the chairmanship of Tata Sons in 1938, he built it into India's largest industrial group and a corporation with an increasing presence on the world stage, India's first true multinational. When he took over as chairman, Tata Sons had fourteen subsidiaries and turnover of under 3 million rupees. When he stepped down as chairman in 1990 there were 95 subsidiary companies, and turnover was close to 3 billion rupees.

Tata was not a typical Indian businessman. His father, R.D. Tata, was a director of the Tata company that had been founded in 1859 and had interests in steel, power generation and shipping as well as owning one of India's landmark buildings, the Taj Mahal Hotel in Bombay (now Mumbai). Under the chairmanship of Jamsetji N. Tata, who died in 1904, Tata became one of India's most powerful companies. R.D. Tata spent part of his working life based in Paris, where he married a Frenchwoman, Suzanne Brière. Their son, J.R.D., grew up speaking French as his mother tongue, and was educated in part in Paris, India and Japan. As the holder of a French passport he was liable for French military conscription and served for a French cavalry regiment. He had planned to attend university at Cambridge, but the death of his father in 1926 meant that instead he returned to India, becoming at age twenty-two a director of Tata Sons.

His first years as a director were remarkable mostly for his exploits as an aviator. As a small boy in France, he had become fascinated by flying when he had watched Blériot's first flight across the English Channel in 1909. In the 1920s he took flying lessons, and joined the Bombay Flying Club in 1929. In 1930 he competed for the Aga Khan trophy, to be awarded to the first person to fly solo between England and India. According to Lala (1996), he diverted en route to the assistance of another pilot who was stranded in Alexandria owing to defective spark plugs. Tata provided his rival with the parts he needed and the two men took off together. The rival pilot went on to beat Tata to the trophy by just a few hours. Tata's interest in aviation grew steadily, however, and a couple of years later he founded Tata Airlines, himself piloting the airline's first flight between Karachi and Bombay. He served as chairman of Tata Airlines and its descendant, Air India, until 1978.

In 1938, Tata was elected chairman of Tata Sons. Apart from the airline industry and a spell spent with the subsidiary Tata Steel in the late 1920s, he had little experience of management and no technical qualifications. Freely admitting this, he adopted a policy of hiring the best professionals he could find and putting them into positions of responsibility, and then trusting them to do their best. A few years before his death, he explained his own role to his biographer, R.M. Lala, as follows:

> Every man has his own way of doing things. To get the best out of them is to let them exploit their own instincts and only intervene when you think they are going wrong. Therefore all my management contributions were on the human aspect through inducing, convincing and encouraging the human being ... As I had no technical training, I always liked to consult the experts ... When I have to make a decision I feel I must first make sure that the superior knowledge of my advisors confirms the soundness of my decision; secondly, that they would execute my decision not reluctantly but being convinced about it; thirdly, I see myself in Tatas as the leader of a team, who has to weigh the impact of any decision on other Tata companies, on the unity of the group.
>
> (Lala 1992: 225)

Tata's ability to spot talent is frequently mentioned as one of his greatest strengths. Eminent scientists and economists as well as engineers and technicians were hired and given licence to create. Some of these went on to high positions in business, government or academia; others remained with Tata throughout their working careers. Although himself a member of the owning family, Tata created a meritocracy where anyone who had talent and was willing to work hard could be recognised and promoted. This attitude ran all through the group. Tata Steel was the first Indian business to have a dedicated human resources department, and J.R.D. Tata himself was strongly interested in the well-being of his workers. He consulted the unions and worked closely with them, so much so that the head of one union at Tata Steel commented in the 1970s that he felt the union was an important part of the business.

His attitude to unions is typical of Tata's belief in leadership by consensus. In his various dealings with his own senior managers and the managing directors of Tata subsidiaries, he made a point of never forcing his own views on them. Instead, he listened to their views and then expressed his own opinions, disagreeing with his colleagues where necessary, but always seeking to find a consensus solution. Politeness and respect were important, and Tata took care to preserve good personal relations even during disagreements. 'To be a leader, you have got to lead human beings with affection', he once said, adding that his own main responsibility as chairman was 'to inspire respect'. Mutual trust, respect and regard were important parts of Tata's style of leadership.

Not a scientist or an engineer himself, Tata fostered the efforts of those who were. He believed in innovation and quality, and believed too that Tata had a responsibility to help the Indian economy and society grow. One way of doing this was to provide high-quality goods and services to the people. Tata had a strong sense of service, not just to his customers and employees, but to India itself. This sense of idealism led him to stand up and speak his mind when he felt that things were going wrong. He was sometimes at odds with the Indian government, which for decades held tight control over the economy, often nationalising key industries and forcing others to comply with the government's economic plans. So respected was Tata, however, that the government would usually listen to his views, even if the course it chose was usually the opposite of what he had suggested.

Tata's ideals were also expressed through support for a variety of charitable causes, both personally and through Tata Sons. He founded and supported a range of bodies from research institutes and educational institutions to performing arts bodies. His most important contribution, however, was the handing over of majority ownership of Tata Sons to a series of charitable trusts, founded by earlier generations of the family. As a result, each year tens of millions of rupees in profits are handed over to these trusts which in turn disburse them as grants for a variety of programmes in health, education, sports and many other fields.

Tata saw himself as the steward or servant of the organisation he led. He had inherited the post of leader, and knew also that in time he would pass it on. One of his primary goals was to turn the Tata group into a structure which would have permanence and stand the test of time. Contemporaries spoke of him as being a humble man – as witness his emphasis on consensus – yet one with a very strong will and strongly held beliefs. He died in 1993, but remains India's most admired and respected business leader.

## Analysis

Some of the questions you might want to consider in connection with this case include:

- How would you describe Tata's leadership style? What are the key features of that style?
- What were his greatest strengths as a leader?
- Tata believed himself to be a kind of steward or servant of the organisation he led. What do you think this means? How far is this true – or should be true – of other leaders?
- How do you think Tata motivated people?

## Sources

Lala, R.M. (1992) *Beyond the Last Blue Mountain: The Life of J.R.D. Tata*, New Delhi: Viking.

Lala, R.M. (1996) 'Tata, Jehangir Ratan Dadabhoy', in Malcolm Warner (ed.), *International Encyclopaedia of Business and Management*, London: International Thomson Business Press.

Piramal, Gita (1997) *Business Maharajahs*, New Delhi: Viking.

Piramal, Gita (2001) 'Jehangir Ratan Dadabhoy Tata', in Morgen Witzel (ed.) *Biographical Dictionary of Management*, Bristol: Thoemmes Press, vol. 2, 964–68.

Sampson, Anthony (1984) *Empires of the Sky: The Politics, Contents and Cartels of World Airlines*, New York: Random House.

## Case Study 9E

### Li Hongzhang

Li Hongzhang (known in older transliterations as Li Hung-chang) was born 15 February 1823 in Luzhou, Anhui Province, China, the son of a middle-ranking bureaucrat. He followed his father into the civil service, passing his entrance examinations in 1844 and going to Beijing to study; he graduated in 1847.

In 1853, a major rebellion broke out in southern China, quickly spreading to many provinces. The rebels were led by Hong Xiuquan, a Chinese Christian convert who, after failing the civil service entrance examinations, suffered from a severe nervous breakdown and imagined that he was the younger brother of Jesus Christ, sent to Earth to establish a 'Kingdom of Heavenly Peace' in China. The revolt, known as the Taiping Rebellion, threatened the very stability of the Chinese empire, and Li was one of a number of young men called upon to help organise resistance. Returning to his home province of Anhui, he raised a regiment of militia and fought against the Taiping movement with great distinction, being promoted several times.

By 1860 Li was in command of Imperial forces in Shanghai and led the defence of the city against the Taiping rebels, and then in 1863 organised a counter-attack on the Taiping forces based at Nanjing. Among the troops under his command were the Western mercenaries known as the Ever-Victorious Army led by a British army officer, Colonel Charles Gordon. This was Li's first experience of dealing with Westerners, and although relations were not always cordial – Gordon threatened to shoot Li on one occasion, when the latter ordered the execution of some rebel warlords whom Gordon's men had captured – it seems Li learned a great deal about Western society and trade, and military capabilities. Li went on to defeat the Taiping rebels and drive them out of Nanjing, effectively crushing the rebellion.

Following the defeat of the rebellion Li was hailed as a hero in China and promoted to the rank of provincial governor of Hunan and Hebei provinces in central China in 1869. He became governor of Zhili province in 1870, governor-general of the important coastal city of Tianjin in 1872, Grand Secretary in 1872 and tutor to the heir apparent in 1879. He became a supporter and friend of the powerful Empress Cixi, and in 1875 after the death of Emperor Tongzhi, Li played a key role in the *coup d'état* which installed Cixi as regent for her infant son Kangxi. He may have later regretted this, for Cixi was intensely conservative and Li believed that China needed to modernise, but he remained Cixi's loyal supporter until his death.

As one of the few senior Chinese officials with experience of dealing with Westerners, Li was commonly called upon to lead negotiations with foreign powers, and from the 1870s until his death he played a major role in the long and ultimately futile struggle against Western and Japanese encroachments on China (details of his diplomatic career are given in Hummel (1943)). Li became convinced that only by using Western methods and technology could China hold its own against the West. He took note of the success of the Meiji Emperor in Japan in forcing through rapid modernisation and, in so doing, confirming Japan's status as an independent power. However, his attempts to promote similar reforms in China were blocked by conservatives led by the Empress Cixi, who often blocked his desire to introduce Western technology and social reforms. She criticised him harshly on several occasions, but whereas she punished others who opposed her will with brutal methods – her own son Kangxi, who sided with the liberals, was arrested and imprisoned, others were killed or fled into exile – Cixi recognised that Li was both loyal and intensely valuable. Honest and honourable, he was one of the few men she could trust, and her reliance on him grew even as their disagreements increased. For his part, Li's own sense of loyalty meant that he would never disobey a direct instruction from the Empress. He was in turn criticised by the growing liberal movement for not pushing reforms further.

Li believed that the Chinese economy had to become modern and adopt Western technology, but without compromising the integrity of the Chinese state and culture. Rather than adopting an open-door policy, when allowed to do so, he encouraged Chinese entrepreneurship and technological know-how. He encouraged particularly the development of infrastructure, such as a national postal system, and of financial systems such as modern banks and stock exchanges. Early in his career, in 1863, he rejected a petition from US and British merchants to build a railway from Shanghai to Suzhou, not because he was opposed to railways – far from it – but because 'railways would only be beneficial to the Chinese when undertaken by the Chinese themselves and under their own management' (Morse 1921: 431).

Li's most direct involvement in business came with the formation of the China Merchants' Steam Navigation Company in 1872, an inland and coastal shipping company set up to combat the increasing domination of Chinese shipping by foreign firms such as Jardine Matheson and Butterfield & Swire. Though Li did not directly manage the firm, delegating that responsibility to two experienced shipowners from Guangzhou (Canton), he acted as chief stockholder and chairman of the board, and also worked to win concessions for the new company from the Chinese government. He also was involved in negotiations with the Hongkong and Shanghai Bank, which partly financed the company. The company expanded rapidly from 1872–83, even buying a rival line, Shanghai Steam Navigation Co., from its American owners in 1876. So effective was their operation – admittedly, aided by concessions such as exemption from tax and duties on inland trade – that the China Merchants' Steam Navigation Company eventually forced its major Western competitors to the negotiating table, to set a system of fixed rates and divide up the trade so as to avoid ruinous competition for all parties.

In the early 1880s, however, Li was increasingly preoccupied with diplomatic affairs, war with France and a further threatened war with Japan. Failure to modernise meant that the Chinese army and navy were now very weak, and could be easily defeated by the modern armies and fleets of the West and Japan. Li tried to forestall war, and when this failed, to bring the wars to a conclusion as soon as possible. China was forced to sign a number of humiliating treaties with foreign powers, giving up control of much of the southern coast, Taiwan and Manchuria, and losing its influence over Korea. Some conservatives called Li a traitor for signing these treaties, although Empress Cixi defended him. Meanwhile at China Merchants' Steam Navigation Company the original managers were replaced by bureaucrats and the company's fortunes declined.

A prophet without honour, Li was one of the first Chinese to realise that Western business and management methods could and must be adapted to the needs of China if the country was to combat Western encroachment. Had his efforts commanded the support of his colleagues and of the Empress, and had China been able to stage a Meiji-type economic reform in the 1880s and 1890s, much of the history of twentieth-century Asia might have been rather different.

### Analysis

Some of the questions you might want to consider in connection with this case include:

- Li was a talented and energetic man, respected by Chinese and Westerners alike. He was a good negotiator and diplomat and had a clear vision and goals. Yet as a leader, he may be said to have failed, for he did not reach those goals. Is that a fair judgement?
- What were the chief obstacles faced by Li? What does this example tell us about the limits to what leadership can achieve?
- Can you think of anything Li could have done to improve his chances of success and reach his goals?

# Sources

Giles, H.A. (1898) *A Chinese Biographical Dictionary*, Shanghai: Kelly & Walsh.

Hao, Y. (1986) *The Commercial Revolution in Nineteenth-Century China*, Berkeley, CA: University of California Press.

Hummel, A.W. (ed.) (1943) *Eminent Chinese of the Ch'ing Period*, Washington, DC: United States Government Printing Office, vol. 1, 464–71.

Morse, H.B. (1921) *The Trade and Administration of China*, 3rd edn, London: Longmans, Green.

Spence, Jonathan (1996) *God's Chinese Son: The Taiping Heavenly Kingdom of Hong Xiuquan*, London: HarperCollins.

# Note

1 This portion of the case is taken from Robert Vanderlan (2001), 'George Eastman', in Morgen Witzel (ed.), *Biographical Dictionary of Management*, Bristol: Thoemmes Press.

# 10  Conclusion: how history impacts on management

The function which distinguishes the manager above all others is his educational one. The one contribution he is uniquely expected to make is to give others vision and the ability to perform. It is vision and moral responsibility that, in the last analysis, define the manager.

– Peter Drucker, *The Practice of Management*

Worthiness in the industrial sphere can have reference to one thing only, namely the contribution of industry to the sum total of human welfare. On this basis only must industry and all its works finally be judged … The lessons of history teach us that no efficiency of procedure will save from ultimate extinction those organizations that pursue a false objective; on the other hand, without such efficient procedure, all human group effort becomes relatively futile.

– James D. Mooney, 'The Principles of Organization'

Kings are the slaves of history.

– Leo Tolstoy, *War and Peace*

## 10.1 Introduction

As stated in the Preface, one of the purposes of this book is to use the past experience and past practices of management to help people think in new ways about management as it is done in the present, and even perhaps as it might be done in the future. We have not tried to cover the whole history of management practice; indeed, we have barely scratched the surface of this huge and complex subject. Instead, the purpose has been to use past experience and practice as a mirror or a lens with which to view the present from a different angle. That means that, out of necessity, we have been selective in our choice of examples. We have tried to indicate the breadth and variety of views and practices and show how some of the most important have evolved over time, until we have reached the present day.

What can we learn from this picture, however incomplete, of the past? Another purpose of this book was to create a forum for discussion and to encourage people to draw their own lessons from the material. In keeping with that spirit, we will not set out any hard conclusions here. Instead, let us concentrate on some of the key themes that have run through this book.

One theme that emerges is that, for all that managers spend much of their time concentrating on and thinking about the future, the past still exercises a powerful influence over what they do. Some of the management practices and theories that we think of as 'new' actually have deep roots in the past. Others, while genuinely new in themselves, are nonetheless the product of social and environmental forces that in some cases go right back to the birth of civilisation. Memory, even sub-conscious memory, still plays a part in our decisions and actions. Tradition and innovation often go hand in hand. Perhaps the most important theme of all is the way that past actions and decisions can constrain those that we take in the present, narrowing our options and reducing our scope for action.

Yet the past can also enable greater freedom of action in the present, if we use it in the right way. The past is just one of many sources of inspiration and knowledge that managers have available to them. Further, examination of the past helps us to understand *why* we do things the way we do them now. This enables self-examination, and if necessary self-criticism, and these in turn can be first steps to improvement.

## 10.2 The force of the past

There is evidence, sometimes patchy and indistinct but evidence nonetheless, of people doing things we would now describe as managerial tasks as far back as the beginning of recorded history. Some of them ran businesses, small by comparison with today's global giants but large by the standards of the time, serving not just local markets but sometimes establishing locations hundreds of miles apart. Some of these managers were in government bureaucracies, some were priests in temples; some were all three of these things at once.

Awareness of the importance of management is to be found in the *Duties of the Vizier*, written three and a half thousand years ago, and in many other writings of antiquity, from China, India, the Middle East and Europe. By the Middle Ages there is evidence of rudimentary forms of management training in some places, and more complex forms of financial management were emerging. In the nineteenth century the Industrial Revolution led to further advances, and at the very end of the nineteenth century, in response to both the changing needs of businesses and changing social trends, a coherent body of management theory began to emerge.

Over these centuries and millennia there has been a great deal of innovation and change. Management methods and practices have come and gone, discarded when they no longer fit the needs of the time. Yet at the same time, there has been a great deal of continuity.

For example, two of the oldest forms of organisation are the family and the bureaucracy. Both have been adapted and re-adapted and used as the basis of new forms, time and time again. We saw in Chapter 2 how du Pont produced a flexible version of the bureaucratic form of organisation which enabled first his family firm Du Pont and later General Motors to expand rapidly. But most business organisations today are still, at heart, either familial-type organisations or use some version of bureaucracy – or both. Something about these forms of organisation is clearly deeply satisfying to us as human beings. Do they fulfil some latent need for organisation and structure? It is fashionable today to castigate both family organisations and bureaucracies as being old fashioned and out of date. But it may be that, at least as basic models, they still have a purpose. It would appear that both are usable as bases, from which firms can adapt, innovate and find the best organisational model that fits their purpose.

Talk of purpose brings us to strategy, the means by which purposes are achieved. Strategy in the past was a matter of principle rather than rule. There were certain things that strategists had to do if they desired success, such as gathering sufficient resources to achieve their aim, gathering knowledge of the competition and the environment, and understanding the capabilities of their own organisation. Those things are as true as when Sunzi and Vegetius first wrote about them more than two thousand years ago. Yet, as Machiavelli identified, strategists also have to be flexible and adaptable, able to respond to whatever problems emerge; and problems, as Clausewitz noted, always will emerge, this is inevitable. So strategists have to be able to innovate, respond, think and react quickly while at the same time planning for the future. Strategists, in other words, have to be very good at managing paradox. We discussed some examples of successful strategists who were both proactive and reactive, and looked at some of the options strategists have used in the past. Some of these options looked very similar to the strategic options companies use today; some did not. Strategy, it turns out, is a matter of adaptation and innovation, but often harks back to the same basic principles.

Organisations are made up of people, and strategies are carried out by people. We know far more today than our ancestors ever did about how to manage people, but for all that, human resource management continues to face many problems. Not the least of these is the continued distinction between 'managers' and 'workers', 'them' and 'us', and the tensions this creates. Is there a solution to this problem? The distinction has its roots in social hierarchies and class distinctions, which are universal and which go back to the beginnings of civilisation, if not further. Is it realistic to expect people in an organisation to put aside all thought of them and us, and to become completely egalitarian overnight? Some managers try to behave as if it were, and although this might be laudable from the point of view of those who believe in egalitarianism and democracy, this attitude creates problems of its own. At a fundamental level, the problems and tensions involved in human resource management have not changed much for thousands of years. Society has moved on, the class distinctions have become less pronounced, but the problem of 'them' and 'us' remains.

Marketing is another of those fundamental business activities for which there is evidence of practice for a very long time. Marketing practice has, unsurprisingly, evolved and changed in response to the environment and changing needs of consumers. Marketers – or what we would now call marketers – have on the whole proved fairly adept at reading both sets of changes and responding. Impressive too is the way in which marketers in earlier times, prohibited or at least restricted from competing on price and forced to use the same distribution methods, evolved other ways of distinguishing themselves from competitors, using branding and quality, for instance. Quality was an extremely important issue during the Middle Ages when there were stiff price restrictions. During the Industrial Revolution, when prices were free, the emphasis on quality sometimes declined. Early marketers were aware of all the elements of the marketing mix, but not all of them understood how those elements fitted together and interacted with each other. One of the achievements of early marketing scholarship and research was to make that relationship more clear.

Today, financial markets and financial instruments are far more complex than they were even two hundred years ago, and financial management has accordingly become much more complex. Yet it is still fundamentally a matter of managing money. The basic tasks of safeguarding the organisation's assets, raising new capital when required, directing cash inflows and outflows and managing risk, remain at the heart of financial management. It is also interesting to look at the factors that have driven innovation and development in this field. In the Middle Ages, the technological advances of the twelfth and thirteenth centuries enabled new kinds of businesses, and expansion of existing ones, but taking advantage of this technology required capital investment. As a result, there was an expansion of the financial system and developments in lending in credit which enabled the required capital to be found. The costs of overseas exploration and the increasing complexity and expense of war drove further changes in the early eighteenth century. Mirroring almost exactly the situation in the Middle Ages, technological advances and the growth of new, capital-intensive industries such as the railways in the nineteenth century resulted in still more expansion, and so on. Innovations in financial management have had their costs, and have helped to contribute at times to market instability; but while the need for innovation persists, innovation is likely to go on.

We see the same trend when we come to look at technology. Technological innovations more than not have been driven by societal needs; the need for more food or better health, the need for faster and better communications, the demand for a greater variety of goods, and so on. Looking back to the past we can see frequent examples of both entrepreneurs and existing firms identifying a need and innovating new products to fill that need. Along the way there have also been innovations in process and communications technologies that have made businesses more efficient and more effective. If innovation itself is nothing new, then neither is the importance of knowledge, the importance of which has always been recognised by a well-managed firm. What is particularly noticeable is how knowledge begets knowledge; the more knowledge we have, the easier we find it to learn and to innovate. Thus the speed at which knowledge generation and innovation happen is constantly increasing.

For centuries, the idea that businesses existed as part of society and that there were strong relationships between the two was not even a subject for discussion. It was an accepted fact. Around the time of the Industrial Revolution, for reasons we can only hypothesise, that understanding broke down and some business owners and managers began to behave as if no relationship existed. This in turn generated a great deal of tension, between managers and workers and between business owners and society. Today, we are struggling to come to a new understanding of that relationship. Again, though, it needs to be noted that the relationship changes over time. Businesses evolve and grow in response to social needs, and how well the business can satisfy those needs. Marketing logic says that businesses that cannot meet the needs of customers will fail. The logic of business and society says that businesses that do not meet the needs of society will fail too; in some cases, society will deliberately drive them out of business. This has implications for how we think about the relationship between managers and stakeholders.

The nature of leadership has changed too, and has emerged in varied forms in different cultures. Is it possible that leadership, like organisation, adopts the profile it does in response to deeper demands? Do people ask for a certain kind of leadership: authoritarian or democratic, responsive or autocratic, heroic or submissive to the needs of the people? Do people always get the leadership they want, or need? What we can see of the changing ways in which leadership is exercised and understood suggests that there is support for situational leadership theory, but there do also seem to be constants. Although the nature of leadership changes, there are similarities in the things that people have always demanded of their leaders: courage being one example.

### 10.2.1 The persistence of memory

When we look at the continuities in management, things that have remained basically the same even though their outward form may have changed, we are at once confronted by the question of why. What makes these things – the persistence of certain organisational forms, similar ways of thinking about leadership and strategy, the problem of class division when managing people – endure?

It is tempting to think that these are eternal verities, core concepts of management which have endured unchanging from the beginning, and will endure to the end. That is one possibility, but there are others. Consciously or sub-consciously, we inherit a great deal from the past. Our concepts of society and relationships, our own basic needs – for food, shelter, pleasure, love, self-fulfilment and so on – our concepts of value, our morals and ideas of right and wrong are all part of the basic fabric of our lives, and those of our parents and ancestors. We inherit these things for the most part without questioning them. These things are not part of management theory; but they do have an immense impact on how we do management in practice. So it may be that the features we see coming up over and over again in management are a result of memory or inheritance, rather than having some fundamental truth-value of their own.

The reinforcing of past practice may also be a feature of the way managers have traditionally been trained and educated. The apprenticeship system undoubtedly contributed to the reinforcing of existing practice. In some cases apprentices would train with more than one firm, which broadened their horizons, and in some cases people were able to train at external institutions such as the Italian abacus schools or the nineteenth-century commercial colleges, but we do not know enough about the curricula of these to know if they encouraged innovation. The advent of business schools did not necessarily solve the problem; most business schools still use the case study method pioneered at Harvard Business School which teaches managers how to face the present and future by looking at how problems have been solved in the past (a practice of which this book, of course, is fundamentally guilty as well). Of course it is possible to learn from the past, but when this becomes a matter of mere rote learning – see what they did in the past, then repeat it – there is a danger that the practices of the past will become enshrined as the dominant logic, whether they are good or bad.

And finally, there is the possibility that we imitate the past because we see this as fundamentally less risky than trying to innovate. We tend to fall back on the things we know, rather than venture into the unknown. Doing what has always been done might be imperfect, but at least we know it works most of the time; trying something new could result in things going disastrously wrong. There is also a tendency, as we noted in Chapter 8, to forget what has gone on before and re-invent the wheel. In their excellent book on management innovation, *Giant Steps in Management*, Mol and Birkinshaw (2008: 2) comment that 'rather like the propensity of Hollywood directors for remaking classic movies in contemporary settings, management thinkers are very good at reconceptualizing old ideas, giving them a new twist and packaging them for an audience that wasn't exposed to the original idea'.

### 10.2.2 Tradition and innovation

Mol and Birkinshaw go on to comment that

> today's management practices are all built on prior practices. A useful analogy is the process of sedimentation in a lake or river estuary: new layers of sediment get laid down on top of old ones, but the old layers still influence the contours of the river bed, and they occasionally poke their way through to the surface. It's the same with management practices. Despite all the rhetoric about hierarchies disappearing in the workplace, we still litter our conversations with military-style terminology.
>
> (Mol and Birkinshaw 2008: 3)

The twelfth-century philosopher Bernard of Chartres had another metaphor: 'We are like pygmies seated on the shoulders of giants. We can see further than our ancestors could, and to that extent our knowledge is greater than theirs; yet without their accumulated knowledge to guide us, we would know nothing.'

The argument is often made that organisations should try to break with the past: tradition is a hindering force which inhibits creativity. Tradition, it is said, gives us reasons *not* to do things, rather than reasons to do things. But this all depends on tradition itself, and how it is managed. If tradition gives way to slavish imitation, of the sort that says, 'we do things this way because that is how we have always done them', then yes, the danger exists. But recourse to tradition should not be used to answer 'how' questions; its purpose is to answer 'why' questions. If we want to understand the purpose behind a particular way of doing business, and understand why it was adopted in the first place, we must go back to the past. Reference to the past may show that there is valid reason why this practice was adopted and it must remain, or equally that the reasons why it was adopted are no longer valid and the practice should be discarded; either way, the question cannot be answered without historical inquiry.

When firms cut themselves off from tradition in the belief that by discarding the past they are enabling themselves to better concentrate on the future, they are actually doing quite the opposite. They are cutting off an important source of knowledge about themselves. Again as we saw in Chapter 8, knowledge breeds knowledge. Without prior knowledge of what *has* happened, the task of understanding what *will* happen becomes much harder and more complex.

Without its foundations, the river bed will erode and the course of the river itself may change. Without the shoulders of giants to lift us up and give us a view of the far horizon, we can only see what little is immediately around us. Tradition does not necessarily hamper innovation; it can be an important source of knowledge which enables innovation, if used wisely.

### 10.2.3  The past constrains the present – and enables it

When Tolstoy wrote in *War and Peace* that 'kings are the slaves of history', he meant that no leader ever has quite the freedom of action that they imagine they have. Tolstoy believed in the inevitability of history. He thought that events piled on top of other events created an unstoppable momentum of their own, and that human beings are simply carried along by events as if being swept out to sea by a tide.

Although Tolstoy presents a picture which many might think is exaggerated, it does seem that past events can constrain and limit action in the present. Decisions made in the past have consequences, often unintended ones, that can hamper present actions (see Teece 1987; Pavitt 1990 for discussions of how past decisions constrain future strategy).[1] Take for example a company at the moment of its foundation. It might have a choice of three or four different product markets it could move into, but having limited resources it chooses just one. It invests in capacity, marketing and so on to support that market. That decision is now made, and made irrevocably. If at some point in the future the company wishes to abandon that market and move into another, then it can do so; but that decision will have costs and consequences of its own.

For a practical example, we can look at the early years of the car industry in America. Cars were seen as high-priced luxury items, and the early car makers concentrated on designs for that market, using essentially craft-based methods of production. Their choice meant that they did not seek out the mass market or invest in mass production. Ford decided to do both of these things. By the time Ford began to dominate the market, it was too late for many of the original firms to change their minds. Some were unwilling to do so, believing that they had made the right decision in the first place and/or being unwilling to abandon their original investment (and of course in some cases they were right to do so, some of these luxury brands went on to be successful). Some, like Durant's original General Motors, were unable to do so. Durant's attempts to compete with Ford met with failure, for thanks to decisions taken earlier, he had the wrong structure and the wrong products to match Ford's recipe for success.

But when Pierre du Pont and Alfred Sloan took charge of General Motors, things changed. General Motors moved onto a new competitive footing. Now it was Ford's turn to be caught in the trap of its own past decisions. Ford had concentrated on just one brand and one segment, the mass market for cheap cars. General Motors offered a range of brands that appealed to different segments. Ford could have chosen to differentiate sooner than it did, but again its top managers were unwilling to do so. Abandoning the original Model T and developing new lines would be costly, but it would have also meant sacrificing a brand that, emotionally, meant a great deal to Ford himself in particular. So the original path was adhered to, until eventually General Motors overtook Ford in terms of market share and change was forced.

Economists refer to this as 'path dependency'. A commonly cited example is the QWERTY keyboards that nearly all of us use on computers today. This keyboard was originally invented for typewriters, and became the standard design around the world. Despite experiments which have shown that this is by no means the most efficient layout for a keyboard, its use continues. The costs of replacing every keyboard with a more efficient design and retraining millions of people who have learned to touch-type using it would be far higher than the inefficiencies the present keyboard creates. So, a decision taken long ago about keyboard layout continues to affect the way we type and input information, and we are unable to break out of this trap without great cost in time and money.

But – as the example of General Motors shows – path dependency is not inevitable. The past itself shows this. Companies do reinvent themselves, like the Finnish forestry products company Nokia turning itself into a global mobile phone maker, or they can enter completely new markets, like Japanese soap maker Kao suddenly turning into the world leader in the computer floppy disks market. How do they do this? One thing we can observe from past practice is that companies that leave their options open are less prone to path dependency, while those that focus tightly are more likely to be caught out. In other words, the narrower the path, the greater degree of dependency. Ford was – at first – a well-managed company but with just one core market. General Motors was an organisational shambles but with a variety of brands and markets. Theoretically, it had a greater range of choices open to it, and was fortunate to have in du Pont and Sloan leaders who were able to assess those choices, make the right ones and then drive the firm forward accordingly.

The diversified firms we found in Italy in the Middle Ages, which were highly flexible and traded in many different markets, were certainly less prone to path dependency than the chartered trading companies that followed them a couple of centuries later. The Hudson's Bay Company, which chose to concentrate on just one product, fur, became moribund and nearly succumbed to competition; only the energy and drive of its new governor, John Simpson, turned things around (see Case Study 1C). The East India Company descended into being a bureaucratic manager of land and revenue, losing all its dynamism, and without support from the British government would have collapsed long before it did, in 1858.

The other factor required to break out of path dependency is will; not just on the part of leaders, but on the part of the whole organisation. (Leaders who urge change when the rest of the organisation does not wish to change have a very hard task in front of them.) The will to change is not enough to make change happen successfully; in late Imperial China the powerful mandarin Li Hongzhang certainly desired change, but was prevented from making it happen (see Case Study 9E). It is not just the investment and time required that create barriers to change; change also takes people out of their comfort zone and creates the impression of risk. Strong leadership and strong commitment from below are both required, as we saw in the example of William McKnight and 3M quoted in Chapter 9, or the radical change in direction at Oneida (see Case Study 2C).

## 10.3 Using the past for competitive advantage

Firms which fall into the trap of strategic path dependency often do not see it coming until it is too late. For all their earlier successes, both General Motors and Ford fell into this trap in the opening years of the twenty-first century by committing themselves to certain markets and brands and backing these with heavy investments. When market conditions changed as a result of high energy prices and the economic downturn a few years later, they were unable to respond quickly.

One of the key lessons of the past, therefore, is that this trap exists. The second is that there are ways it can be avoided, or at least ways to lessen its impacts. We know that flexibility and keeping options open help to lessen the danger. But this is not just a matter of strategic planning; it is also a matter of strategic *thinking*, of understanding and knowing and recognising the signs (and here again, examples taken from the past can help us to recognise those signs). And the response has to go beyond strategy. A new form of organisation may be required, as Pierre du Pont discovered when he took over at General Motors. A new approach to managing people may be required so as to secure workforce commitment. Not only new markets but new methods of marketing may be needed. New sources of finance and a new approach to financial management may be in order. Innovation and new knowledge become crucial, and the firm's links to society may make the difference between success or failure. And last of all, the firm needs leaders to provide vision and guidance and ensure everyone works towards the required goals.

Some managers are good at some of these things. But as we have seen in the past, some – Cosimo dei Medici, Pierre du Pont, William Lever, William Pirrie, Henry Heinz, the Boucicauts, Thomas Jackson, Hans Renold, Sarah Breedlove Walker, J.R.D. Tata, just to name some from the case studies in this book – were good at all of them.

Here is one lesson from the past that would seem to be incontrovertible. The firm that does a few things well will be beaten by the firm that does everything well. Genuine all-round competence at everything will succeed; genius in one area but lack of competence in others might succeed, but the odds become higher with each weak area identified. Of course it is hard to find individuals who are good at everything, which is why all the people mentioned above concentrated on their own strengths and spent a great deal of time and energy finding, training and mentoring people whose strengths were complementary to their own.

We cannot simply reach into the past and pull out ideas that will give us competitive advantage. What we can do is look at the past and understand why things are done as they are done, and then use that knowledge to either reinforce and strengthen existing ways of doing things, or innovate and create new ones.

## 10.4 Summing up: why we manage as we do

In some ways, the structure of this book is artificial. It follows now standard divisions into managerial functions: organisation, strategy, HRM, marketing, finance and so on. This is how management is studied and taught, and especially in large firms, increasingly this is how it is practised.

There are real advantages to specialisation. Arguably, the need for specialist knowledge in areas like finance in particular has never been greater. But we need to remember that until a little over a hundred years ago – with the partial exception of finance, which in large firms was managed by specialists – these divisions did not exist. Most managers were in effect general managers. And the model was not ineffective. Some very large and powerful businesses, by the standards of the day, were built using this method. Some of them spanned continents. Some operated and traded right around the world.

There is a tendency to believe that the management methods we use now are the best that there are. The best practices we use in marketing and HRM, for example, are exactly that: the best ways of doing things, tried and proven through both theoretical analysis and practical observation. It may be that they are. Or it may be that they are relics, even if cleverly disguised ones, old wine poured into new bottles, old methods recycled and given new names. Why do we manage as we do? Why do we use the methods that we do, and not other ones? The question needs to be asked, and asked repeatedly, as to whether the ways we manage are indeed the ways best suited to the time and place. Sometimes we will find that the answer is yes, and that is comforting for we know we are on the right track. Sometimes the honest answer will be no, and then the real test comes, for we must challenge ourselves and organisations to find another way. This is hard. But the final lesson of the past is this: that unless these questions are asked, the company risks falling into the path-dependency trap. Escaping that trap will be even harder and more painful. There is more than one way to do management, more than one way to go forward. Remember the past, as you think of the future.

## 10.5 Research projects

The second half of this chapter consists of notes for research projects. The MBA module on which this book was based featured team research projects in which students used some of the learning they gained from the module to examine management practices in particular industries, how practice evolved over time, and how methods developed in certain industries impacted on management more generally. These can be used as formal research projects or simply as research exercises by teams or individuals.

The notes for each are intended as starting points for research; they suggest questions for analysis and give a brief list of possible sources. They are not complete discussions of each topic, nor are they meant to be. Their purpose is to illustrate some of the ideas in this book, and serve as the basis for yet further discussion and analysis.

Once again, there are no right or wrong answers. Readers are encouraged to use the projects as means of enhancing their own knowledge and understanding of what management is. Provided that end is achieved, the actual projects and their outputs can take any form that is desired. At the University of Exeter Business School, we asked teams to produce a 10–15-minute presentation in class, followed by a short 2,000–3,000-word report. But it should be possible to configure the outputs in any way that is desired. Again, I very much welcome comments on the utility of these projects, how well they work and what people are able to learn from them.

### 10.5.1 The steel industry

Steel has been manufactured on a small-scale basis since ancient times, but only became an industry of importance during the Industrial Revolution. The advent of new blast furnace technology and new methods such as the Bessemer process in the early nineteenth century meant it was now possible to mass produce steel and steel products. Simultaneously, the invention of the steam locomotive and the railway building boom greatly increased the demand for steel in the nineteenth century; the development of modern artillery also had an impact, though a little later. One of the first modern steel makers, Krupp, grew to prominence through making steel rails and steel cannon. Later, the car industry and shipbuilders became major markets for steel producers.

American steel making got off to a late start, and the first American railways were built using rails made by Krupp or by British firms. However, the gap was quickly filled by Andrew Carnegie and then other producers such as Charles Schwab at Bethlehem. By 1900, American steel makers were the largest in the world, with most production concentrated in the conglomerate United States Steel, headed by Judge Elbert Gary and backed by the money of J.P. Morgan.

Steel making on a large scale required a large amount of technology and manpower. Early steel plants were vast places employing tens of thousands of people. It became quickly apparent that these big enterprises were not being run efficiently. Some sort of managerial system was needed to make them more efficient and profitable. It is no accident that the first attempts at systematising management – scientific management – came in engineering, and that steel plants were among the first companies to employ the methods of scientific management. Elsewhere in the world, attempts at developing management systems often appeared first in the iron and steel industries.

### Approaches to the project

The steel industry was an incubator for many modern management methods, including quite a few still in use today. One starting point could be to look at the industry itself, the technological changes and the growth in demand in steel. How far did demand drive the evolution of the industry?

Second, how did that evolution require a management response? Why and how did management change? What were the key drivers of change? What forms did the change take? Here you may well find you need to get into a discussion of scientific management and similar systems, in terms of organisation and technical/people management.

Third, consider an evaluation of that system (or indeed, systems). How well did it/they work? What were the strengths? What were the weaknesses?

Fourth, what if any lasting effects have there been? What influences can you still see in modern management methods and theory, either in steel and engineering or more generally? Again, feel free to criticise these influences and developments.

### Sources

Biographies of figures like Carnegie, Krupp, Schwab, Frick and other major players in the industry are a good place to start, and if you choose to explore scientific management in detail there are both the original works of Taylor, Gantt, the Gilbreths and others to choose from, and a rich secondary literature. Be sceptical about some of this; Taylor is blamed for a good many things which were properly the responsibility of the people who put his system into practice.

Other works that might be useful include:

Ashton, T.S., *Iron and Steel in the Industrial Revolution*.
Birch, Alan, *The Economic History of the British Iron and Steel Industry, 1784–1879*.
Temin, Peter, *Iron and Steel in Nineteenth-Century America*.
You should find plenty of other sources as you go along, but these and the biographies noted above will help you get started.

### 10.5.2  The railway industry

The railways revolutionised transport, in a way that earlier systems such as canals had not managed to do. For their time, the railways were very technologically sophisticated, relying on a range of new technologies, notably the steam engine (improved by Boulton and Watt in the late eighteenth century), new steel processes that allowed for stronger rails able to bear the weight of locomotives and rolling stock, and most critically of all, the telegraph, which enabled operations to be coordinated over long distances.

The first railways appeared in the 1830s and 1840s, and were mostly short-haul lines dedicated to particular cargoes, shipping goods from a factory or group of factories to a seaport, for example. Gradually in Europe the lines became linked, and passenger travel became more common. Thomas Cook started organising railway excursion parties in the 1840s, and by the 1860s was introducing the beginnings of mass tourism based on railway transport.

In North America, railways had been developing along the Eastern Sea-board before the Civil War, but the big boom in long-distance railway build-ing came after the war with the drive to the west in both the USA and Canada. Long-distance routes like the Union Pacific and Canadian Pacific were built rapidly, although at a terrible cost in lives.

The advent of the railways meant it was possible to transport goods quickly over long distances, much more quickly than by water. (Consider the relative speeds of a nineteenth-century train versus those of a sailing ship or canal barge.) This meant it was possible to integrate businesses over large geo-graphical spaces, and the railways played a major role in pulling together the emerging large corporations of America such as Carnegie Steel, Standard Oil and the meat packers such as Armour and Swift.

However, the real importance of the railways for our purposes may well be in the management methods they were forced to develop. Instead of con-centrating thousands of workers at one point, as in a steel mill, the railways spread their workers over large areas, often across countries or continents. How could their operations be coordinated? Even time itself had to be re-organised; the builders of the Great Western found that time in Bristol was eight minutes behind time in London, which could have cata-strophic results for scheduling. Alfred Chandler in his book *The Visible Hand* credits the railways with inventing many of the coordination and commu-nications methods we still use today.

But the early railways were costly in terms of money and lives to build – and to run. Many companies went bankrupt. Many lives were lost in building the railways, and as late as 1888, over 1,000 people a year were being killed in railway accidents in Britain, and many more in America. Were the railways really as efficient as Chandler suggests?

*Approaches to the project*

Initially, you will need to look at the history of the industry. Think about the advances in technology and the needs of growing economies. Did the railways drive economic growth, or were they driven by it?

Second, why and how did management and organisation change? What were the key drivers of that change? What forms did the change take? How were railways different from other forms of organisation? Who were the 'managers'?

Third, consider an evaluation of railway management. How well did it work? What were the strengths? What were the weaknesses?

Fourth, what if any lasting effects have there been? What influences can you still see in modern management methods and theory, either in transport management or more generally? Again, feel free to criticise these influences and developments.

Other elements are up to you. You might consider criticising or evaluating Chandler's approach, or you might want to look at special features such as coordination and communication. This is a big subject with lots of scope, so be sure to target your investigations closely.

## Sources

Company histories of the big railways will be useful, and Chapters 3–6 of Alfred Chandler's *The Visible Hand* will probably be essential reading. Be aware that Chandler has been criticised, however. You might also look at changes in railway travel, in which case you might want to have a look at works on Pullman and Nagelmackers/Orient Express.

There are plenty of histories of the railways. Some are for 'train spotters' rather than serious students, so be careful not to get bogged down. Look for works which talk about the economics and organisation of railways, and then sift through these looking for details of how the railways were managed.

Other works that might be useful include:

Chandler, Alfred D., *The Railroads: The Nation's First Big Business.*
Cochran, Thomas C., *Railroad Leaders, 1845–1890.*
Grodinsky, Julius, *Transcontinental Railway Strategy.*
Reed, Malcolm C., *Railways in the Victorian Economy.*

### 10.5.3 The textiles industry

Textiles were big business in Europe since the Middle Ages, and were, after agriculture, the largest sector by proportion of GDP until the nineteenth century. With the exception of a few big cloth-making centres, most production was craft production, with various steps in the process farmed out to local spinners, weavers and so on, most of whom worked at home, or in small independent workshops. Each stage of cloth production, and there were many, was handled by a different person or group of people working in effect as subcontractors.

In the second half of the eighteenth century, however, there were a number of rapid technological advances, including the spinning jenny, the water frame and the mule, to name just a few of the most famous. These enabled mechanised production, and some of the first true factories began to appear, notably Arkwright's mill at Cromford in Derbyshire. Originally driven by animal power, they were then powered by water, and by the end of the century the advances in the steam engine pioneered by Boulton and Watt saw the introduction of steam power. Steam remained the main motive power in factories for many decades thereafter.

The first factories were primarily for spinning cotton into yarn, but later inventions allowed mechanised weaving and fulling as well. By the mid-nineteenth century, most of the important stages of cloth manufacturing could be done by machine. Although the putting-out or contract system did not disappear overnight, it began to decline. Meanwhile, other technological innovations allowed the new system to be applied to woollen cloth, muslin and other fabrics, and eventually the development of new synthetics such as rayon. More importantly, the utility of the factory system was appreciated by businesses in other sectors.

The factory system was widely adopted but heavily criticised. Working conditions were often very poor and unsanitary, and campaigners in Britain and elsewhere tried repeatedly to make factories safer and healthier places. Marxists saw the factory system as an effort by capital to concentrate and therefore to control labour. Others saw it as a response to rising demand levels, given growing populations and increasing prosperity in much of Europe. More recently, transaction costs theorists have seen the factory system as reducing transaction costs and therefore making production cheaper, more efficient, and even of better quality.

## Approaches to the project

A natural focus for this project would be the development of the factory system and associated methods of management, a system for which the textile industry was the primary incubator. Other focuses may occur to you, of course.

Initially, you will need to look at the history of the industry and how it evolved. Second, how did that evolution require a management response? Why and how did management change? What were the key drivers of change? What forms did the change take? What were the defining features of the new organisation? Who were the 'managers' as such?

Third, consider an evaluation of that system (or indeed, systems). How well did it/they work? What were the strengths? What were the weaknesses? In this context, I suspect you will have to look at the social impacts and the problems of health, safety and so on that were so widely criticised at the time, and since.

Fourth, what if any lasting effects have there been? What influences can you still see in modern management methods and theory, either in textiles or more generally? Again, feel free to criticise these influences and developments.

Other elements are up to you. You might consider looking at some of the different interpretations of the factory system alluded to above, or you might feel that a closer examination of some of the key entrepreneurs is in order to look at changing patterns of entrepreneurship. This is a big subject with lots of scope, so be sure to target your investigations closely.

## Sources

It may be hard to find, but Andrew Ure's *The Philosophy of Machinery and Manufactures* or his *History of the Cotton Industry* may be quite helpful. Richard Fitton's biography of Arkwright may also be valuable, as might Ian Donnachie's biography of Robert Owen. Richard Donkin's book *Blood, Sweat and Tears* has at least one chapter on working under the factory system. Generally, the textile industry has been well studied, so you should not lack sources.

Other works that might be useful include:

Baines, Edward, *History of the Cotton Manufacture in Great Britain*.
Copeland, Melvin T., *The Cotton Manufacturing Industry of the United States*.
Edwards, M.M., *The Growth of the British Cotton Trade*.
Jenkins, D.T. and Ponting, K.G., *The British Wool Textile Industry, 1770–1914*.
Kerridge, Eric, *Textile Manufactures in Early Modern England*.
Wadsworth, A.P. and de Mann, Julia de L., *The Cotton Trade and Industrial Lancashire, 1600–1780*.

### 10.5.4 The automotive industry

It is not uncommon for particular industries to be described as having 'transformed' society, but in the case of the automobile industry in the first half of the twentieth century, the term can be fairly used. Cars went from being expensive luxuries to mass market goods within a few decades, and in doing so changed the way many people lived their lives, how companies did business, and how war was waged, among other things.

Even simple early cars were complicated pieces of machinery, and the early automotive entrepreneurs faced a constant challenge: how to build a reliable car at an affordable price. The initial reaction was to build for the luxury market and adopt a price-skimming strategy, but following the appearance of Ford and, to a much lesser extent, Louis Renault and William Morris, this became increasingly difficult as prices were forced down and the techniques of mass production applied.

Ford introduced not just one but a whole series of revolutions. The first was a design for a cheap, mass-produced car that could be afforded by the middle classes, thus opening up a huge new market sector. The second was a mass production system, based around the purpose-built assembly plant at Highland Park, that actually worked and was able to deliver the marketing promise. The third was that promise, the idea that owning a car could change your life and give you mobility and freedom, hooking into the American Dream. All these combined into an ideology known as Fordism.

Attention has focused on the struggle between Ford and his rivals, first Willys Overland and then, much more seriously, General Motors, which ultimately dethroned Ford as king of the auto makers. Quite a lot can be done just by comparing their approaches and seeing how each firm approached management, their marketing and their strategy, their organisations and their leadership.

*Approaches to the project*

First, get to grips with the history of the industry itself. Material on this should be plentiful, possibly even too plentiful. Nevins and Hill needed three volumes for their history of Ford alone. The main thing you will need to understand is the nature of the technical challenges and the nature of the market.

Second, think about how and why management within the industry changed as the car industry developed. The first car makers worked on a craft production basis, or something close to it, rather like specialist sports car makers such as Morgan do today. What had to change? What were the production, operational, marketing and other requirements? How would you describe the system that evolved to meet these requirements?

Third, consider an evaluation of that system (or indeed, systems). How well did it/they work? What were the strengths? What were the weaknesses?

Fourth, what if any lasting effects have there been? What influences can you still see in modern management methods and theory, either in the car industry or more generally? Again, feel free to criticise these influences and developments.

## Sources

Biographies of the people mentioned above, and on other early car makers too, are a good start. Again, there is plenty of material on Ford, although much of it is either too admiring or too harshly critical. But be sure to go beyond Ford.

Other works that might be useful include:

Bardou, J.-P *et al.*, *The Automobile Revolution*.
Cusumano, Michael A., *The Japanese Automobile Industry*.
Epstein, Ralph C., *The Automobile Industry*.
Richardson, Kenneth, *The British Motor Industry, 1896–1939*.
Whipp, Richard and Clark, Peter, *Innovation and the Auto Industry*.
Wood, Jonathan, *Wheels of Misfortune: The Rise and Fall of the British Motor Industry*.

### 10.5.5 The financial services sector

In 1800, banks in the West, at least, were small affairs, usually family owned and run, although there were a few joint-stock institutions like the Bank of England and the Bank of Scotland which fulfilled an important role in state finance (though still in the private sector). Gold and silver were still the primary circulating medium, and although there were a bewildering variety of credit instruments for financing state and private debt, capital markets were still comparatively small. The world financial market was dominated by London until around 1900 when New York began to overtake it.

Capital markets grew rapidly. There were both push and pull factors here. First, rising prosperity meant that there was more liquidity and thus more push for investment. Second, the Industrial Revolution and subsequent capital-intensive projects like the railways required huge – for the time – injections of finance. Although the London markets grew rapidly, those of New York grew more rapidly still. Wall Street was little more than a genteel row of trading houses in 1860; by 1900 it was an economic powerhouse, if an occasionally shaky one. Increasing globalisation, especially around and after the First World War, led to further changes, with international banking and finance increasingly expanding, and the first steps being taken towards the foundation of true international capital markets.

At the same time, the problems of financial control grew more acute. Accountants, formerly merely clerks who added up figures in ledgers, became more important. Not only did they devise new methods of cost control and cashflow management, but they were also important in preventing abuses and fraud. Two of the great forensic accountants in history, William Deloitte and Edwin Waterhouse, helped to put in place some of the financial control measures we still use today.

This is a very big subject indeed, and you will want to narrow it down. You could look at the growth of capital markets and the impact this had on management; you might want to focus on either London or New York, but you should be able to do a brief survey of both. Or you could forget about the markets and look at financial management, corporate finance in our terms, and how the treasury function developed and how accounting became increasingly essential. Or, you could look at banking specifically and developments within that industry, at how banks were managed and how banks affected management. Other options may occur to you.

*Approaches to the project*

Initially, you will need to look at the history of the subject. Think about the changes that took place. What drove those changes, and why? What was the broader impact on economies, companies, managers?

Second, how did that evolution require a management response? Why and how did management change? What were the key drivers of change? What forms did the change take?

Third, consider an evaluation of that change. What opportunities were created, what threats were posed? How well did companies respond, and how and why did they fail?

Fourth, what if any lasting effects have there been? What influences can you still see in modern management methods and theory? Feel free to criticise these influences and developments and state what you think should have happened.

Other elements are up to you, and will depend on your ultimate focus. This is a big subject with lots of scope, so be sure to target your investigations closely.

## Sources

If you are going down the capital markets route, there is a wealth of material on the City of London, including David Kynaston's multi-volume work, and on Wall Street. Look for institutional histories too, of key organisations: Salomon Brothers, Goldman Sachs, J.P. Morgan, Chase, Lloyds, Barings, Warburgs, Gibbs, the Stock Exchange, the Bank of England and so on. There are also plenty of histories of New York capital markets, though you might have to resort to inter-library loans.

If you are looking at banks, much the same applies. If you want to look at accountancy and financial controls, you might find it harder; there are several journals of accounting history which should also be available online.

Other works that might be useful include:

Born, Karl Erich, *International Finance in the Nineteenth and Twentieth Centuries.*
Carosso, Vincent P., *Investment Banking in America: A History.*
Jones, Geoffrey, *Banks as Multinationals.*
Kindleberger, Charles Poor, *A Financial History of Western Europe.*
Redlich, Fritz, *The Molding of American Banking: Men and Ideas.*

### *10.5.6 Retailing*

Retailing developed from a business of largely family-owned single-outlet enterprises in the early nineteenth century into many of the forms we see today; department stores, chain stores, remote ordering and so on. There were both push and pull factors involved in this change. Growing populations and rising affluence meant that more people could afford more, and better, goods. The Boucicauts' famous phrase 'the democratisation of luxury' was intended to convey the notion that the benefits of the Industrial Revolution were now available not just to the wealthy but also the middle classes and even the more affluent working classes. At the same time, new technologies such as the telegraph and telephone enabled better transport and communications, meaning more goods could be offered, and at more outlets. Finally, of course, these same technologies enabled the development of catalogue retailing, or mail order.

Taking advantage of such technologies, however, involved changing the mindset of the retail manager. The early department store retailers, especially the Boucicauts in Paris, the developers of Au Bon Marché, created not only a new kind of business but also developed a new approach to the customer. The mail order pioneers, Sears and Montgomery Ward, similarly were able to think outside the box; if the customer cannot come to the store, we will send the store to the customer. The chain store developers like Woolworth and J.C. Penney also looked for new ways of satisfying customers.

We are often accustomed to thinking of the development of marketing in terms of formal theory, the 4Ps and the like. However, the retail industry shows that managers have been capable of working out for themselves the best way to do business without necessarily having any formal guidelines or theories to work to. Three important new forms of retail outlet, all three still thriving, were developed before the term 'marketing' had really been invented, or at least before it was in widespread use.

*Approaches to the project*

Initially, you will need to look at the history of the industry. Oddly enough, general histories of the retail industry are quite hard to come by, but there are biographies of individuals and firms. Try to build up a composite picture of the changes. You might also want to focus on just one aspect: department stores, mail order, etc. rather than trying to cover them all, but that is up to you.

Second, why and how did management and organisation change? What were the key drivers of that change? What forms did the change take? How were retail business different from other forms of organisation? Who were the 'managers'?

Third, consider an evaluation of retail management as it changed. How well did management systems work? What were the strengths? What were the weaknesses?

Fourth, what if any lasting effects have there been? What influences can you still see in modern management methods and theory, either in retail management or more generally? Again, feel free to criticise these influences and developments.

Other elements are up to you. You might want to compare the practice you observe with the formal marketing theory you have learned, noting similarities and discrepancies. Or you could think about whether any of the practices you observed should be given more prominence in modern retail management, or any other kind of management. These are some possibilities; you may think of others.

## Sources

As mentioned, there are not that many general histories, but search for material on firms that interest you; you should be able to put your composite picture together from these specific sources. Beware of claims to have 'invented' concepts; almost everyone claims to have 'invented' the department store, for example. Be sure to check dates.

Other works that might be useful include:

Benson, J. and Shaw, G., *The Evolution of Retail Systems, c. 1800–1914.*
Mahoney, Tom and Sloane, Leonard, *The Great Merchants: America's Foremost Retail Institutions and the People Who Made Them Great.*

Strasser, Susan, *Satisfaction Guaranteed: The Making of the American Mass Market.*
Tedlow, Richard S., *New and Improved: The Story of Mass Marketing in America.*

If you are looking specifically at department stores there is a small body of literature on these, plus most major store chains have produced a history at some point.

### 10.5.7 Computers and electronics

The development of the computer and its ancestor, the electric calculating machine, is arguably one of the most significant technological advances of the twentieth century. In this project, you will be looking at the development of the industry that made the exploitation and diffusion of that advance possible. You could begin with the pioneers, Charles Babbage and Hermann Hollerith, and then look at some of the early firms like IBM before turning to the post-war period.

The early period under consideration begins with the relatively crude electric calculating machines, which became increasingly important to business as time went on. During the Second World War, there were great advances in computer technology, and after the war it was only a matter of time before those were exploited. The first steps forward came in the 1950s, when the technological advances made by the likes of Wang An and Jay Wright Forrester began to be exploited. The two giants of the industry, IBM and Hewlett-Packard, began to grow and were challenged by the likes of Ken Olsen's DEC. Other entrepreneurs like Robert Noyce served as incubators for new businesses, in his case first Fairchild and then Intel.

There are two facets to this subject, and you may wish to choose one or the other, or combine the two. First, the nature of this industry meant that traditional command-and-control style organisations were often not appropriate. People began experimenting with new forms and new philosophies of management, and often those spilled over into management in other sectors. Second, the computer of course changed the working practices of virtually every other type of business. You might want to explore the course of that change and development and the relations between these high-tech industries and their target markets. How has this relationship affected how we use computers at work today?

### Approaches to the project

Initially, you will need to look at the history of the industry. Think about the advances in technology itself, but particularly about the management of technology. Did computers drive economic growth, or was their rapid development driven by the more general need for growth?

Second, why and how did management and organisation change? What were the key drivers of that change? What forms did the change take? You could even indulge in some counterfactual speculation if you like, and think about what management might be like if the computer had not been invented. You might want in that case to take a closer look at Babbage and the importance of knowledge.

Third, consider an evaluation of management within the industry. How well did it work? What were the strengths? What were the weaknesses? If you are going down the 'impact of the computer' route, look instead at what good and bad points have emerged in current managerial and working practice.

Fourth, related to the above, what have the lasting effects been? Did computers utterly revolutionise management, or did they just create paper blizzards and information overload? Have a look at some current theory on the subject and then decide what you think.

Other elements are up to you. One issue that you may decide is worth a look is communications. The computer industry by and large – or at least, best practice within the industry – sets great emphasis on internal communications within firms; why is this, and is that idea transferrable? This is a big subject with lots of scope, so be sure to target your investigations closely.

## Sources

Generic histories of the industry are thin on the ground, but a few are given below. You may have better luck with histories of firms and individuals; there is a lot of literature on IBM, and Apple, DEC and others have been studied. The journal literature is fairly rich in works on the impact of IT going back some years. Your main problem should be to work out the scope of your project fairly early on and then target your search for materials.

Other works that might be useful include:

Anchordoguy, Marie, *Computers Inc: Japan's Challenge to IBM*.
Cortada, James W., *The Computer in the United States: From Laboratory to Market, 1930–1960*.
Flamm, Kenneth, *Creating the Computer*.
Morris, P.R., *A History of the World Semiconductor Industry*.

## Note

1 My thanks to Professor Steve Brown of the University of Exeter Business School for drawing Keith Pavitt's article to my attention.

# Select bibliography

'Abduh, M. (1966) *The Theology of Unity* (*Risalat al-tawhid*), trans. I. Masaad and K. Cragg, London: Allen & Unwin.

Ackerman, C.W. (1930) *George Eastman*, Boston and New York: Houghton Mifflin.

Ackoff, Russell L. (1994) *The Democratic Organization*, New York: Oxford University Press.

Ackoff, Russell L. and Emery, Fred E. (1972) *On Purposeful Systems*, London: Tavistock Institute.

Adair, John (2002) *Effective Strategic Leadership*, London: Macmillan.

Adler, Nancy J. (1997) *International Dimensions of Organizational Behavior*, 3rd edn, London: International Thomson Publishing.

Alberts, R.C. (1973) *The Good Provider: H.J. Heinz and His 57 Varieties*, London: Arthur Barker.

Ali ibn Abi Talib (1978) *Nahjul Balagha* (Peak of Eloquence), trans. S.A. Reza, Elmhurst, NY: Tahrike Tarsile Qu'ran.

Allfrey, Anthony (1989) *Man of Arms: The Life and Legend of Sir Basil Zaharoff*, London: Weidenfeld & Nicolson.

Ambler, Tim (2000) *Marketing and the Bottom Line: The New Metrics of Corporate Wealth*, London: FT-Prentice Hall.

Ambler, Tim, Witzel, Morgen and Xi, Chao (2008) *Doing Business in China*, 3rd edn, London: Routledge.

Andrews, Kenneth (1987) *The Concept of Corporate Strategy*, New York: McGraw-Hill.

Ansoff, H. Igor (1965) *Corporate Strategy*. New York: John Wiley and Sons.

——(1979) *Strategic Management*, New York: John Wiley and Sons.

——(1988) *The New Corporate Strategy*, New York: John Wiley and Sons.

Ansoff, H.I., Declerck, R.P. and Hayes, R.L. (1976) *From Strategic Planning to Strategic Management*, New York: John Wiley and Sons.

Argyris, Chris (1964) *Integrating the Individual and the Organization*, New York: Wiley.

——(2000) *Flawed Advice and the Management Trap: How Managers Can Know When They're Getting Good Advice and When They're Not*, Oxford: Oxford University Press.

Argyris, Chris and Schön, Donald (1974) *Theory in Practice*, San Francisco, CA: Jossey-Bass.

Auerbach, F. (1903) *The Zeiss Works and the Carl-Zeiss Stiftung in Jena*, trans. S.F. Paul and F.J. Cheshire, London: Marshall, Brookes and Chalkley, 1904.

Babbage, Charles (1835) *The Economy of Machinery and Manufactures*, London: Charles Knight.

Balgarnie, R. (1878) *Sir Titus Salt Baronet: His Life and Letters*, London: Hodder & Stoughton.

Barrow, R.H. (1928) *Slavery in the Roman Empire*, London: Methuen.

Bartels, Robert (1976) *The History of Marketing Thought*, Columbus, OH: Grid.

Barwise, Patrick and Meehan, Seàn (2004) *Simply the Best: Winning and Keeping Customers by Delivering What Matters Most*, Boston: Harvard Business School Press.

Bat'a,Tomás (1992) *Knowledge in Action: The Bata System of Management*, Amsterdam: IOS Press.

Becker, Oswald M. (1906) 'The Square Deal in Works Management', *Engineering Magazine*, January: 536–54.

Bennis, Warren G. (1989) *On Becoming a Leader*, Reading, MA: Addison-Wesley.

Bensa, E. (1928) *Francesco di Marco da Prato*, Milan: n.p.

Benson, J. and Shaw, G. (1992) *The Evolution of Retail Systems, c.1800–1914*, Leicester: Leicester University Press.

Berg, M. (1985) *The Age of Manufactures: Industry, Innovation and Work in Britain, 1700–1820*, Oxford: Blackwell.

Berglund, Abraham (1907) *The United States Steel Corporation: A Study of the Growth and Influence of Combination in the Iron and Steel Industry*, New York: Columbia University.

Berle, Adolph A., Jr., and Means, Gardiner C. (1932) *The Modern Corporation and Private Property*, New York: Macmillan; all citations are to the revised edition, New York: Harcourt, Brace and World, 1967.

Bhattacharya, S. (1969) *The East India Company and the Economy of Bengal from 1704 to 1740*, Calcutta: K.L. Mukhopadhyay.

Bierbrier, M. (1982) *The Tomb-Builders of the Pharaohs*, London: British Museum.

Black, Jeremy (2007) 'War and Business', *European Business Forum*, September.

Black Elk and Neihardt, John G. (1979) *Black Elk Speaks*, Lincoln: University of Nebraska Press.

Blaszczyk, Regina (ed.) (2000) *Imagining Consumers: Design and Process Innovation from Wedgwood to Corning*, Baltimore: Johns Hopkins University Press.

Boesche, Roger (2002) *The First Great Political Realist: Kautilya and his Arthashastra*, Lanham, MD: Lexington.

Boisot, Max (1987) *Information and Organizations*, London: Fontana/Collins.

Bose, R.N. (1956) *Gandhian Technique and Tradition in Industrial Relations*, Calcutta: All-India Institute of Social Welfare and Business Management.

Bostock, F. and Jones, G. (1989) *Planning and Power in Iran: Eftehaj and Economic Development Under the Shah*, London: Frank Cass.

Bradley, Ian Campbell (1987) 'Titus Salt: Enlightened Entrepreneur', *History Today* 37 (5): 30–36.

Bradley, Keith and Gelb, A. (1983) *Co-operation at Work: The Mondragón Experience*, London: Heinemann.

Brandeis, Louis M. (1914) *Other People's Money, and How the Bankers Use It*, New York: Frederick A Stokes.

Brayer, E. (1996) *George Eastman: A Biography*, Baltimore and London: Johns Hopkins University Press.

Brech, E.F.L. (2002) *The Evolution of Modern Management*, Bristol: Thoemmes Press, 5 vols.

Brendon, P. (1991) *Thomas Cook: 150 Years of Popular Tourism*, London: Secker & Warburg.

Brody, David (1980) *Workers in Industrial America: Essays on the Twentieth Century Struggle*, Oxford: Oxford University Press.

Brown, R. Arnold (1911) 'The Manufacturer as Advertiser', in T. Russell (ed.), *Harmsworth Business Library*, London: Educational Book Co., vol. 5, 170–79.

Brun, R. (1930) 'A Fourteenth-Century Merchant of Italy: Francesco Datini of Prato', *Journal of Economic and Business History*.

Buenstorf, Guido and Murmann, Johan Peter (2005) 'Ernst Abbé's Scientific Management: Insights from a Nineteenth-Century Dynamic Capabilities Approach', *Industrial and Corporate Change* 14 (4): 543–74.

Bundles, A'lelia Perry (1991) *Madame C.J. Walker: Entrepreneur*, New York: Chelsea House.

Burlinghame, R. (1949) *Backgrounds of Power: The Human Story of Mass Production*, New York: Charles Scribner's Sons.

Burnham, James (1941) *The Managerial Revolution: Or, What is Happening in the World Now*, London: Putnam.

Butler, M., Thornton, F. and Ashley, M. (1955) *The Best to You Each Morning: W. K. Kellogg and the Kellogg Company*, Battle Creek, MI: Heritage Publications.

Cadbury, Edward (1908) *Sweating*, London: Headley Brothers.

——(1912) *Experiments in Industrial Organization*, London: Longmans, Green & Co.

Cadbury, Edward and Shann, George (1908) *Women's Work and Wages*, London: Headley Brothers.

Campbell, Bruce M.S. (2000) *English Seignorial Agriculture 1250–1400*, Cambridge: Cambridge University Press.

Cameron, R. and Bovykin, V.I. (eds) *International Banking, 1870–1914*, Oxford: Oxford University Press.

Caminer, D.L., Aris, J.B.B., Hermon, P.M.R. and Laird, F.F. (1996) *User-Driven Innovation: The World's First Business Computer*, London: McGraw-Hill.

Carey, Henry (1853) *The Slave Trade, Domestic and Foreign: Why it Exists and How it May be Extinguished*, Philadelphia: A. Hart, late Carey & Hart.

Carlson, Bernard (1991) *Innovation as a Social Process: Elihu Thomson and the Rise of General Electric, 1879–1900*, Cambridge: Cambridge University Press.

Carus-Wilson, E.M. (1967) *Medieval Merchant Venturers*, London: Methuen.

Cary-Elwes, C. (1988) *St Benedict and His Rule*, London: Catholic Truth Society.

Cassis, Y. (1997) *Big Business: The European Experience in the Twentieth Century*, Oxford: Oxford University Press.

Casson, Herbert N. (1907) *The Romance of Steel: The Story of a Thousand Millionaires*, New York: A.S. Barnes.

——(1909) *Cyrus Hall McCormick*, Chicago: A.C. McClurg.

——(1911) *Advertisements and Sales: A Study of Advertising and Selling from the Standpoint of the New Principles of Scientific Management*, London: Pitman.

——(1928) *Creative Thinkers: The Efficient Few Who Cause Progress and Prosperity*, London: Efficiency Magazine.

——(1931) *The Story of My Life*, London: Efficiency Magazine.

Cekota, A. (1968) *Entrepreneur Extraordinary: The Biography of Tomas Bata*, Rome: Edizioni Internazionali Soziali.

Chakravarthy, Bala and Lorange, Peter (1991) *Managing the Strategy Process: A Framework for a Multibusiness Firm*, Upper Saddle River, NJ: Pearson Education.

Chan, Anthony B. (1997) *Li Ka-shing: Hong Kong's Elusive Billionaire*, Hong Kong: Oxford University Press.

Chan, Wellington K.K. (1982) 'The Organizational Structure of the Traditional Chinese Firm and its Modern Reform', *Business History Review* 56 (2): 218–35; repr. in R. Ampalavanar Brown (ed.), *Chinese Business Enterprise: Critical Perspectives on Business and Management*, London: Routledge, vol. 1.

Chancellor, J. (1973) *Charles Darwin*, London: Weidenfeld and Nicolson.

Chandler, Alfred D., Jr (1962) *Strategy and Structure: Chapters in the History of the American Industrial Enterprise*, Cambridge, MA: MIT Press.

——(1977) *The Visible Hand: The Dynamics of Industrial Capitalism*, Cambridge, MA: Harvard University Press.

——(1990) *Scale and Scope: The Dynamics of Industrial Capitalism*, Cambridge, MA: Harvard University Press.

Chandler, Alfred D., Jr and Salsbury, Stephen (1971) *Pierre S. du Pont and the Making of the Modern Corporation*, New York: Harper & Row.

Chandler, G. (1964) *Four Centuries of Banking*, London: B.T. Batsford.

Chapman, Sidney (1992) *Merchant Enterprise in Britain*, Cambridge: Cambridge University Press.

Chatfield, Michael (1977) *A History of Accounting Thought*, New York: Robert E. Krieger.

Cheffins, Brian R. (2008) *Corporate Ownership and Control: British Business Transformed*, Oxford: Oxford University Press.

Chen Huan-Chang (1911) *Economic Principles of Confucius and His School*, New York: Columbia University Press, 1911, 2 vols; repr. with an introduction by Morgen Witzel, Bristol: Thoemmes Press, 2002.

Chen, Min (1995) *Asian Management Systems*, London: Routledge.

Cherington, Paul T. (1920) *The Elements of Marketing*, New York: Macmillan.

Chernow, R. (1999) *Titan: The Life of John D. Rockefeller, Sr.*, New York: Random House.

Child, John (1969) *British Management Thought*, London: George Allen & Unwin.

——(1981) 'Culture, Contingency and Capitalism in the Cross-National Study of Organisations', *Research in Organizational Behavior* 3: 303–56.

Christensen, Clayton (1997) *The Innovator's Dilemma*, New York: HarperCollins.

Clanchy, Michael T. (1993) *From Memory to Written Record, England 1066–1307*, 2nd edn, Oxford: Blackwell.

Clark, Fred (1924) *Principles of Marketing*, New York: Macmillan.

Clark, J.F. (1985) 'Parsons, The Honourable Sir Charles Algernon', in David J. Jeremy (ed.), *Dictionary of Business Biography*, London: Butterworths, vol. 4, 539–48.

Clark, R.W. (1997) *Edison: The Man Who Made the Future*, London: Macdonald and Jane's.

Clarke, J.J. (2000) *The Tao of the West: Western Transformations of Taoist Thought*, London: Routledge.

Clausewitz, Karl von (1984) *Vom Kriege*, ed. and trans. Michael Howard and Peter Paret, *On War*, Princeton, NJ: Princeton University Press.

Clegg, Hugh (1985) *A History of British Trades Unions Since 1985*, Oxford: Clarendon.

Cole, G.D.H. (1930) *The Life of Robert Owen*, London: Macmillan.

Colenbrander, H.T. (1934) *Jan Pieterszoon Coen*, s'Gravenhage: Martinus Nijhoff.

Colli, Andrea and Rose, Mary (2007) 'Family Business' in Geoffrey Jones and Jonathan Zeitlin (eds) *The Oxford Handbook of Business History*, Oxford: Oxford University Press, 194–218.

Collins, James C. and Porras, Jerry I. (1994) *Built to Last: Successful Habits of Visionary Companies*, New York: HarperCollins.

Collis, Maurice (1965) *Wayfoong: The Hongkong and Shanghai Banking Corporation*, London: Faber & Faber.

Confucius (1938) *The Analects of Confucius*, trans. A. Waley, New York: Vintage Books.

Copeland, Melvin T. (1917) *Problems in Marketing*, Chicago: A.W. Shaw.

——(1958) *And Mark the Era: The Story of Harvard Business School*, Boston: Little, Brown.

Cotter, Arundel (1921) *United States Steel: A Corporation With a Soul*, Garden City, NY: Doubleday, Page & Co.

Crowther, Samuel (1923) *John H. Patterson: Pioneer in Industrial Welfare*, London: William Heinemann.

Cummings, Stephen (1993) 'Brief Case: The First Strategists', *Long Range Planning* 26 (3): 133–35.

Cuff, R.D. (1996) 'Edwin F. Gay, Arch W. Shaw, and the Uses of History in Graduate Education for Managers', *Journal of Management History* 2 (3): 9–25.

Davis, John P. (1894) *The Union Pacific Railway: A Study of Political and Economic History*, Chicago: S. Griggs & Co.

——(1897) 'The Nature of Corporations', *Political Science Quarterly* 12: 273–94.

——(1905) *Corporations*, New York: G.P. Putnam's Sons, 2 vols.

Davis, W. (1987) *The Innovators: The Essential Guide to Business Thinkers*, London: Ebury Press.

Day, Clive (1904) *The Policy and Administration of the Dutch in Java*, New York: Macmillan.

de Geus, Arie (1988) 'Planning as Learning', *Harvard Business Review*, March–April: 70–74.

de Roover, Raymond (1955) 'Scholastic Economics: Survival and Lasting Influence from the Sixteenth Century to Adam Smith', *Quarterly Journal of Economics* 69 (2): 161–90; repr. in Mark Blaug (ed.), *St Thomas Aquinas*, Aldershot: Edward Elgar, 1991, 67–96.

——(1958) 'The Concept of Just Price Theory and Economic Policy', *Journal of Economic History* 18: 418–34; repr. in Mark Blaug (ed.), *St Thomas Aquinas*, Aldershot: Edward Elgar, 1991, 97–113.

——(1962) *The Rise and Decline of the Medici Bank*, Cambridge, MA: Harvard University Press.

——(1967) *San Bernardino of Siena and Sant'Antonio of Florence: The Two Great Economic Thinkers of the Middle Ages*, Boston: Baker Library, Harvard Graduate School of Business Administration.

Deacon, Richard (1976) *A Biography of William Caxton*, London: Muller.

Dempsey, B.W. (1935) 'Just Price in a Functional Economy', *American Economic Review* 25: 471–86; repr. in M. Blaug (ed.), *St Thomas Aquinas*, Aldershot: Edward Elgar, 1991, 1–16.

Dennison, Henry S. (1932) *Ethics and Modern Business*, Boston: Houghton Mifflin.

Dickson, W.J. and Roethlisberger, F.J. (1966) *Counseling in an Organization: A Sequel to the Hawthorne Researches*, Boston, MA: Harvard Business School Press.

Dixon, Norman (1976) *On the Psychology of Military Incompetence*, London: Pimlico.

Dobbin, Frank (2004) *The New Industrial Sociology*, Princeton, NJ: Princeton University Press.

Donkin, Richard (2001), *Blood, Sweat and Tears: The Evolution of Work*, London: Texere.

Donnachie, Ian (2000) *Robert Owen*, East Linton: Tuckwell Press.

Doz, Yves and Kosonen, Mikko (2008) *Fast Strategy: How Strategic Agility Will Help You Stay Ahead of the Game*, Engelwood Cliffs, NJ: Wharton School Publishing.

Dreyer, Edward L. (2006) *Zheng He: China and the Oceans in the Early Ming Dynasty, 1405–1433*, London: Longman.

Drucker, Peter F. (1946) *Concept of the Corporation*, New York: The John Day Company.

——(1954) *The Practice of Management*, London: Heron Books.

——(1989) *The New Realities*, London: Heinemann.

Drury, Horace B. (1915) *Scientific Management: A History and Criticism*, New York: Longmans Green.

Dunlop, John (1958) *Industrial Relations Systems*, New York: Henry Holt.

Dunning, John (1762) *A Defence of the United Company of Merchants of England Trading to the East-Indies and their Servants*, London: n.p.

Dyer, Davis, Dazell, Frederick and Olegario, Roweno (2004) *Rising Tide*, Boston: Harvard Business School Press.

Edmonds, W.D. (1948) *The First Hundred Years, 1848–1948*, Oneida, NY: Oneida Ltd.

Edwards, John Richard (1989) *A History of Financial Accounting*, London: Routledge.

Egmond, W. Van (1976) *The Commercial Revolution and the Beginnings of Western Mathematics in Renaissance Florence, 1300–1500*, Ann Arbor: University of Michigan.

Ehrenberg, R. (1928) *Capital and Finance in the Age of the Renaissance: A Study of the Fuggers and Their Connections*, trans. H.M. Lucas, London: Jonathan Cape.

Elbourne, Edward Tregaskis (1914) *Factory Administration and Accounts*, London: Longmans, Green & Co.

Elletson, D.H. (1966) *The Chamberlains*, London: John Murray.

Emerson, Harrington (1909) *Efficiency as a Basis for Operations and Wages*, New York: John R. Dunlap.

——(1913) *The Twelve Principles of Efficiency*, New York: The Engineering Magazine Co.

Essinger, James (2004) *Jacquard's Web: How a Hand-Loom Led to the Birth of the Information Age*, Oxford: Oxford University Press.

Evans, G.R. (2000) *Bernard of Clairvaux*, Oxford: Oxford University Press.

Fayol, Henri (1917) *Administration industrielle et generale* (General and Industrial Management), Paris: Dunod et Pinat; trans. I. Gray, New York: David S. Lake, 1984.

Fear, Jeffrey R. (2005) *Organizing Control: August Thyssen and the Construction of German Corporate Management*, Cambridge, MA: Harvard University Press.

——(2008) 'Cartels', in Geoffrey Jones and Jonathan Zeitlin (eds), *The Oxford Handbook of Business History*, Oxford: Oxford University Press, 268–92.

Filene, Edward A. (1925) *More Profits from Merchandizing*, Chicago: A.W. Shaw.

——(1930) *The Model Stock Plan*, New York: McGraw Hill.

——(1932) *Successful Living in This Machine Age*, London: Jonathan Cape.

Fitch, L.C. (1997) *Make Democracy Work: The Life and Letters of Luther Halsey Gulick, 1892–1993*, Berkeley, CA: Institute of Government Studies.

Fitton, Richard S. (1989) *The Arkwrights: Spinners of Fortune*, Manchester: Manchester University Press.

Fitton, R.S. and Wadsworth, A.K. (1958) *The Strutts and the Arkwrights 1758–1830: A Study of the Early Factory System*, Manchester: Manchester University Press.

Fitzgerald, Robert (1988) *British Labour Management and Industrial Welfare 1846–1939*, London: Croom Helm.

——(1995) *Rowntree and the Marketing Revolution*, Cambridge: Cambridge University Press.

——(2005) 'Products, Firms and Consumption: Cadbury and the Development of Marketing, 1900–39', *Business History* 47: 511–13.

——(2007) 'Marketing and Distribution', in Jonathan Zeitlin and Geoffrey Jones (eds), *The Oxford Handbook of Business History*, Oxford: Oxford University Press, 396–419.

Fleming, Quentin (2000) *Keeping the Family Baggage out of the Family Business*, New York: Fireside.

Flint, Charles R., Hill, James J., Bridge, James H., Dodd, S.C.T. and Thurber, Francis R. (1902) *The Trust, Being a Presentation of the Several Aspects of the Latest Form of Industrial Revolution*, New York: Doubleday.

Follett, Mary Parker (1924) *Creative Experience*, New York: Longmans Green.

——(1937) 'The Process of Control', in Luther Gulick and Lyndall Fownes Urwick (eds), *Papers on the Science of Administration*, New York: Institute of Public Administration, 159–69.

Ford, Henry (1926) *Today and Tomorrow*, New York: Garden City.

——(1929) *My Philosophy of Industry*, London: Harrap.

Ford, Henry and Crowther, Samuel (1922) *My Life and Work*, New York: Doubleday.

Foucault, Michel (1966) *The Order of Things*, trans. A. Sheridan, New York: Vintage, 1970.

——(1975) *Discipline and Punish*, trans. A. Sheridan, New York: Pantheon, 1977.

Fowler, William W. (1880) *Twenty Years of Inside Life in Wall Street, or the Revelations of the Personal Experience of a Speculator*, New York: Orange Judd.

Frontinus, Sextus Julius (1925) *Stratagemata*, trans. Charles E. Bennett, New York: Loeb.

Fullerton, R. (1988) 'How Modern is Modern Marketing? Marketing's Evolution and the Myth of the Production Era', *Journal of Marketing* 52: 108–25.

Freyer, Tony (1992) *Regulating Big Business: Antitrust in Great Britain and America, 1880–1990*, Cambridge: Cambridge University Press.

Gabor, Andrea (1999) *The Capitalist Philosophers*, New York: Times Business.

Gardener, A.G. (1923) *Life of George Cadbury*, London: Cassell.

Gee, D. (1986) 'Darwin, Sir Horace', in D.J. Jeremy (ed.), *Dictionary of Business Biography*, London: Butterworths, vol. 2, 14–17.

Geneen, Harold (1997) *The Synergy Myth, and Other Ailments of Business Today*, New York: St. Martin's Press.

George, Claude S. (1972) *The History of Management Thought*, Englewood Cliffs, NJ: Prentice-Hall, 2nd edn.

Gersick, Kelin E., Davis, John A., Hampton, Marion McCollum and Landsberg, Ivan (1997) *Generation to Generation: Life Cycles of the Family Business*, Boston: Harvard Business Press.

Gilbert, Felix (1986) 'Machiavelli: The Renaissance of the Art of War', in Peter Paret (ed.), *Makers of Modern Strategy*, Princeton, NJ: Princeton University Press, 11–31.

Gilbreth, Lillian (1914) *The Psychology of Management*, New York: Sturgis & Wilton.

Giles, H.A. (1898) *A Chinese Biographical Dictionary*, Shanghai: Kelly & Walsh.

Gimpel, Jean (1976) *The Medieval Machine: The Industrial Revolution in the Middle Ages*, London: Penguin.

Goffee, Rob and Jones, Gareth (2006) *Why Should Anyone Be Led By You? What It Takes to Be an Authentic Leader*, Boston: Harvard Business School Press.

Gosling, Jonathan, Case, Peter and Witzel, Morgen (eds) (2007) *John Adair: Fundamentals of Leadership*, Basingstoke: Palgrave Macmillan.

Gower, John (1992) *The Mirror of Mankind*, trans. William Burton Wilson, East Lansing, MI: Colleagues Press.

Greenwood, Regina (2001) 'Kellogg, William Keith', in Morgen Witzel (ed.) *Biographical Dictionary of Management*, Bristol: Thoemmes Press, vol. 2, 525–31.

Grove, Andrew (1996) *Only the Paranoid Survive: How to Exploit the Crisis Points that Challenge Every Company and Career*, New York: HarperCollins,

Guest, R. (1823) *A Compendious History of the Cotton Manufacture; With a Disproval of the Claim of Sir Richard Arkwright to the Invention of its Ingenious Machinery*, Manchester: Joseph Pratt.

Guetzlaff, Carl (1834) *A Sketch of China's History, Ancient and Modern: Comprising a Retrospect of the Foreign Intercourse, and Trade with China, etc.*, London: n.p., 2 vols.

Guilmartin, John (1976) *Gunpowder and Galleys*, Cambridge: Cambridge University Press.

Gulick, Luther H. (1948) *Administrative Reflections from World War II*, Birmingham, AL: University of Alabama Press.

Gulick, Luther H. and Urwick, Lyndall Fownes (eds) (1937) *Papers on the Science of Administration*, New York: Institute of Public Administration.

Hadley, Arthur Twining (1907) *Standards in Public Morality*, New York: Macmillan.

Hale, J.R. (1977) *Florence and the Medici*, London: Thames and Hudson.

Hally, M. (2005) *Electronic Brains*, Washington, DC: Joseph Henry Press.

Hamel, Gary (2001) *Leading the Revolution*, New York: McGraw-Hill.

Hamel, Gary and Prahalad, C.K. (1989) *Competing for the Future: Breakthrough Strategies*, Boston, MA: Harvard Business School Press.

Hamel, Gary, Doz, Yves and Prahalad, C.K. (1989) 'Collaborate With Your Competitors – And Win', *Harvard Business Review*, January–February.

Hamilton, Gary G. and Lai Chi-kong (1989), 'Consumption and Brand Names in Late Imperial China', in Henry J. Rutz and Benjamin S. Orlove (eds), *The Social Economy of Consumption*, Lanham, MD: University Press of America, pp. 253–79; repr. in R. Ampalavanar Brown, *Chinese Business Enterprise*, London: Routledge, 1996, vol. 3.

Hammond, Bray (1957) *Banks and Politics in America from the Revolution to the Civil War*, Princeton: Princeton University Press.

Hampden-Turner, Charles and Trompenaars, Fons (1993) *The Seven Cultures of Capitalism*, Garden City, NY: Doubleday.

Handy, Charles (1976) *Understanding Organizations*, London: Penguin.

——(1994) *The Empty Raincoat*, London: Hutchinson.

Hao, Y. (1986) *The Commercial Revolution in Nineteenth-Century China*, Berkeley, CA: University of California Press.

Harlan, L.R. (1983) *Booker T. Washington: The Wizard of Tuskegee*, New York: Oxford University Press.

Hart, Basil Liddell (1948) *The Other Side of the Hill*, London: Cassell.

Haskins, Charles Homer (1927) *The Renaissance of the Twelfth Century*, Cambridge, MA: Harvard University Press.

Healey, Edna (1992) *Coutts & Co: The Portrait of a Private Bank*, London: Hodder & Stoughton.

Heaton, H.K. (1952) *A Scholar in Action: Edwin F. Gay*, Cambridge, MA: Harvard University Press.

Herrigel, Gary (1990) *Industrial Constructions: The Foundations of German Industrial Power*, Cambridge: Cambridge University Press.

Hibbert, Christopher (1979) *The Rise and Fall of the House of Medici*, London: Penguin.

Hodges, James (1697) *The Present State of England, as to the Coin and Publick Charges*, London.

Hofstede, Geert (1980) *Culture's Consequences: International Differences in Work-Related Values*, Beverly Hills, CA: Sage.

——(1991) *Cultures and Organizations: Software of the Mind*, London: McGraw-Hill.

Holroyd, Abraham (1873) *A Life of Sir Titus Salt*, Bradford: T. Brear and F. Hammond.

Holt, Jeremy (2006) *Reinventing the CFO*, Boston: Harvard Business School Press.

Honig, Emily (1983) 'Pre-Liberation Cotton Mills of Shanghai', *Modern China* 9 (4): 421–54; repr. in R. Ampalavanar Brown, *Chinese Business Enterprise*, London: Routledge, 1996, vol. 3.

Hosley, W. (1996) *Colt: The Making of an American Legend*, Amherst, MA: University of Massachusetts Press.

Howard, Michael (1961) *The Franco-Prussian War: The German Invasion of France, 1870–71*, London: Rupert Hart-Davis.

Hoxie, Robert F. (1915) *Scientific Management and Labour*, New York: D. Appleton.

——(1916) *Scientific Management and Social Welfare*, New York: Survey Books.

Huang Quanyu, Joseph Leonard and Chen Tong (1997) *Business Decision Making in China*, London: Haworth Press.

Huck, V. (1955) *Brand of the Tartan: The 3M Story*, New York: Appleton-Century-Crofts.

Hudson, G.F. (1931) *Europe and China*, London: Edward Arnold.

Hummel, A.W. (ed.) (1943) *Eminent Chinese of the Ch'ing Period*, Washington, DC: United States Government Printing Office, vol. 1, 464–71.

Hunt, Freeman (1858) *Lives of American Merchants*, New York: Derby & Jackson.

Hutchinson, W.T. (1930–35) *Cyrus Hall McCormick*, 2 vols, New York: Century.

Hyma, A. (1942) *The Dutch in the Far East: A History of the Dutch Commercial and Colonial Empire*, Ann Arbor, MI: George Wahr.

Ingham, J.N. and Feldman, L.B. (1994) *African-American Business Leaders: A Biographical Dictionary*, Westport, CT: Greenwood Press.

Innes, Harold A. (1930) *The Fur Trade in Canada*, Toronto: University of Toronto Press.

Israel, Paul (1992) *From Machine Shop to Industrial Laboratory: Telegraphy and the Changing Context of American Innovation, 1830–1920*, Baltimore: Johns Hopkins University Press.

Iyer, Raghavan N. (1973) *The Political and Moral Thought of Mahatma Gandhi*, Oxford: Oxford University Press.

Jain, L.C. (1929) *Indigenous Banking in India*, London: Macmillan.

Jarrett, Michael (2009) *Changeability: Why Some Companies Are Ready For Change – And Others Aren't*, London: FT-Prentice Hall.

Jay, Anthony (1967) *Management and Machiavelli*, London: Hodder & Stoughton.

Jefferson, H. (1947) *Viscount Pirrie of Belfast*, Belfast: Mullan.

Jeffreys, J.B. (1954) *Retail Trading in Britain, 1850–1950*, Cambridge: Cambridge University Press.

Jenkins, Reese V. (1975) *Images and Enterprise: Technology and the American Photographic Industry, 1875–1925*, Baltimore: Johns Hopkins University Press.

Jeremy, David J. (ed.) (1984–86) *Dictionary of Business Biography*, London: Butterworths, 5 vols.

John of Salisbury (1979) *Policraticus*, ed. and trans. Murray F. Markland, New York: Frederick Ungar.

Johnson, Gerald (1948) *Liberal's Progress*, New York: Coward-McCann.

Johnson, M.P. and Roark, J.L. (1984) *Black Masters: A Free Family of Color in the Old South*, New York: W.W. Norton.

Jolly, H.P. (1976) *Lord Leverhulme: A Biography*, London: Constable.

Jones, Edward D. (1912) 'Military History and the Science of Administration', *Engineering Magazine*, vol. 44.

Jones, G. (1993) *British Multinational Banking, 1830–1990*, Oxford: Oxford University Press.

Jones, Geoffrey (2005) *Renewing Unilever: Transformation and Tradition*, Oxford: Oxford University Press.

Jones, Geoffrey and Zeitlin, Jonathan (eds) (2007) *The Oxford Handbook of Business History*, Oxford: Oxford University Press.

Joyce, Patrick (1980) *The Culture of the Factory in Later Victorian England*, London: Methuen.

Kachi, Yukio (1998) 'Shotoku Constitution', in Edward Craig (ed.), *Routledge Encyclopedia of Philosophy*, London: Routledge, vol. 8, 752–54.

Kaplan, Robert and Norton, David (1996) *The Balanced Scorecard*, Boston: Harvard Business School Press.

Kautilya (1997) *Arthashastra*, trans. R.P. Kangle, New Delhi: Motilal.

Kelley, R.E. (1992) *The Art of Followership*, New York: Knopf.

Kennedy, Michael H. (1999) 'Fayol's Principles and the Rule of St Benedict: Is There Anything New Under the Sun?', *Journal of Management History* 5 (5).

Kets de Vries, Manfred F.R., Carlock, Randel S. and Florent-Treacy, Elizabeth (2007) *Family Business on the Couch: A Psychological Perspective*, New York: Wiley.

Keynes, John Maynard (1933) *Essays in Biography*, London: Macmillan

King, F.H.H. (1987) *The History of the Hongkong and Shanghai Banking Corporation*, vol. 1, *The Hongkong Bank in Late Imperial China, 1864–1902*, Cambridge: Cambridge University Press.

Klass, Georg von (1954) *Krupps: The Story of an Industrial Empire*, trans J. Cleugh, London: Sidgwick and Jackson.

Klaw, Spencer (1993) *Without Sin: The Life and Death of the Oneida Community*, London: Penguin.

Kluckhohn, F.R. and Strodtbeck, F.L. (1961) *Variations in Value Orientations*, Evanston, IL: Row, Peterson & Company.

Kotler, Philip (1997) *Marketing Management*, Englewood Cliffs, NJ: Prentice-Hall.

Kotler, Philip and Levy, Sidney J. (1969) 'Broadening the Concept of Marketing', *Journal of Marketing*, January: 10–15.

Kotter, John P. (1990) *A Force for Change: How Leadership Differs from Management*, New York: The Free Press.

Kumar, U. (1990) *Kautilya's Thought on Public Administration*, New Delhi: National Book Organization.

Kyman, A. (1985) *Charles Babbage: Pioneer of the Computer*, Oxford: Oxford University Press.

Laird, P. (1998) *Advertising Progress: American Business and the Rise of Consumer Society*, Baltimore: Johns Hopkins University Press.

Lala, R.M. (1992) *Beyond the Last Blue Mountain: The Life of J.R.D. Tata*, New Delhi: Viking.

——(1996) 'Tata, Jehangir Ratan Dadabhoy', in Malcolm Warner (ed.), *International Encyclopedia of Business and Management*, London: International Thomson Business Press.

Landes, David (1969) *Unbound Prometheus: Technological Change and Industrial Development in Western Europe from 1750 to the Present*, Cambridge: Cambridge University Press.

Langlois, R.N. (1999) 'The Coevolution of Technology and Organisation in the Transition to the Factory System' in P.L. Robertson (ed.), *Authority and Control in Modern Industry*, London: Routledge.

Langworth, R.M. and Norbye, J.P. (1986) *The Complete History of General Motors, 1908–1986*, New York: Beekman House.

Larreche, Jean-Claude (2008) *The Momentum Effect*, London: FT-Prentice Hall.

Latham, Frank (1972) *1872–1972, A Century of Serving Consumers:The Story of Montgomery Ward*, Chicago: Montgomery Ward & Co.

Lazonick, William (1990) *Competitive Advantage on the Shopfloor*, Cambridge, MA: Harvard University Press.

Le Goff, Jacques (1980) *Time, Work and Culture in the Middle Ages*, trans. Arthur Goldhammer, Chicago: University of Chicago Press.

Leighton, Allan (2007) *On Leadership: Practical Wisdom from the People Who Know*, London: Random House.

Lescure, Michel (2007) 'Banking and Finance', in Jonathan Zeitlin and Geoffrey Jones (eds), *The Oxford Handbook of Business History*, Oxford: Oxford University Press, 319–46.

Lesko, Leonard H. (ed.) (1994) *Pharaoh's Workers: The Villagers of Deir el Medina*, Ithaca, NY: Cornell University Press.

Levathes, Louise (1997) *When China Ruled the Seas: The Treasure Fleet of the Dragon Throne, 1405–1433*, Oxford: Oxford University Press.

Lewin, Kurt (1935) *A Dynamic Theory of Personality*, New York: MacGraw Hill.

Lewis, David Charles (2001) 'Alpinus, A. Decius', in Morgen Witzel (ed.) *Biographical Dictionary of Management*, Bristol: Thoemmes Press.

Lewis, John Spedan (1948) *Partnership for All*, London: Kerr-Cros Publishing/The John Lewis Partnership.

——(1954) *Fairer Shares*, London: Staples Press.

Lewis, Joseph Slater (1896) *The Commercial Organization of Factories*, London and New York: Spon.

Little, J.H. (1967) *The House of Jagat Seth*, Calcutta: n.p.

Littleton, A.C. and Yamey, Basil S. (1956) *Studies in the History of Accounting*, London: Sweet & Maxwell.

Liu Xinru (1998) *Ancient India and Ancient China: Trade and Religious Exchanges, 1–600 AD*, Oxford: Oxford University Press.

Livingstone, Marilyn (2001) 'Fitz Neal, Richard', in Morgen Witzel (ed.) *Biographical Dictionary of Management*, Bristol: Thoemmes Press.

——(2008) 'Plus ça Change: Why Banks in Trouble Are Nothing New', *Corporate Finance Review*, March–April.

438    *Select bibliography*

Lloyd, Henry D. (1894) *Wealth Against Commonwealth*, New York: Harper & Bros.

Locke, John (1692) *Some Considerations of the Consequences of the Lowering of Interest, and Raising the Value of Money*, London; repr. in P.H. Kelly (ed.), *Locke on Money*, Oxford, 1991, vol. 1, 203–342.

Long, J. (1869) *Selections from the Unpublished Records of Government for the Years 1748 to 1767 Inclusive*, Calcutta: Office of the Superintendent of Government Printing, vol. 1.

Lopez, Raymond (1933) *Benedetto Zaccaria: Genova Marinara nel Duecento*, Milan: Messina.

Lough, William H. (1910) *Corporation Finance*, New York: Alexander Hamilton Institute.

Lowenthal, E. (1927) 'The Labor Policy of the Oneida Community Ltd.', *Journal of Political Economy* 35 (February): 114–26.

Luckenbill, D.D. and Chiera, E. (1931) 'The Code of Hammurabi', in J.M.P. Smith (ed.), *The Origins of the Laws of the Hebrews*, Chicago: Chicago University Press.

Luo Guanzhong (1991) *The Three Kingdoms*, trans. Moss Roberts, Beijing: Foreign Languages Press.

Machiavelli, Niccolò (1970) *Discorsi sopra la prima deca di Tito Livio* (Discourses on the First Decade of Livy), ed. B. Crick, trans. L.J. Walker as *The Discourses*, Harmondsworth: Penguin.

——(1961) *Il principe* (The Prince), trans. G. Bull, Harmondsworth: Penguin.

Mackay, Charles (1841) *Extraordinary Popular Delusions and the Madness of Crowds*, London: Richard Bentley.

MacKay, Douglas (1936) *The Honourable Company; A History of the Hudson's Bay Company*, Indianapolis: Bobbs-Merrill.

Macpherson, H. (ed.) (1985) *John Spedan Lewis, 1885–1963*, London: The John Lewis Partnership.

Marshall, Alfred (1890) *Principles of Economics*, London: Macmillan.

Marx, Karl (1933) *Das Kapital*, London: J.M. Dent.

Maslow, Abraham (1954) *Motivation and Personality*, New York: Harper & Bros.

Mathew, W.M. (1981) *The House of Gibbs and the Peruvian Guano Monopoly*, London: Royal Historical Society.

Mayhew, Henry (1968), *London Labour and the London Poor*, London: Constable.

Mayo, Elton (1933) *The Human Problems of an Industrial Civilisation*, New York: Macmillan.

McCafferty, E.D. (1923) *Henry J. Heinz: A Biography*, New York: Bartlett Orr Press.

McCann, J. (1937) *Saint Benedict*, London: Sheed & Ward.

McCarthy, Jerome (1960) *Basic Marketing*, Homewood, IL: Irwin.

McElderry, A.L. (1976) *Shanghai Old-Style Banks (Ch'ien-chuang) 1800–1935*, Ann Arbor, MI: Centre for Chinese Studies, University of Michigan.

McElheny, V.K. (1998) *Insisting on the Impossible*, New York: Perseus.

McGraw, Roger (1992) *A History of the French Working Class*, Oxford: Blackwell, 2 vols.

McGraw, T.K. (1988) *The Essential Alfred Chandler: Essays Towards a Historical Theory of Big Business*, Boston, MA: Harvard Business School Press.

McLaughlan, Raoul (2009) *Rome and the Distant East: Trade Routes to the Ancient Lands of Arabia, India and China*, London: Continuum.

McLuhan, Marshall (1951) *The Mechanical Bride*, New York: Vanguard.

Meade, Edward S. (1910) *Corporation Finance*, New York: D. Appleton.

Meyer, Stephen (1981) *The Five-Dollar Day: Labor Management and Social Control in the Ford Motor Company, 1908–1921*, New York: Charles Scribner.

Michie, R.C. (1999) *The London Stock Exchange: A History*, Oxford: Oxford University Press.

Miles, Raymond E. and Snow, Charles C. (1978) *Organizational Strategy, Structure and Process*, New York: McGraw-Hill.

Millard, André (1990) *Edison and the Business of Innovation*, Baltimore: Johns Hopkins University Press.

Miller, Michael B. (1994) *The Bon Marché: Bourgeois Culture and the Department Store*, Princeton: Princeton University Press.

Mills, J.V. (1970) *Ma Huan Ying Yai Sheng Lan: The Overall Survey of the Ocean Shores*, Cambridge: Cambridge University Press.

Milton, Giles (1999) *Nathaniel's Nutmeg*, London: Sceptre.

Mintzberg, Henry (1973)*The Nature of Managerial Work*, New York, Harper & Row.

——(1989) *Mintzberg on Management*, New York: Free Press.

Misa, Thomas (1998) *Nation of Steel: The Making of Modern America, 1865–1925*, Baltimore: Johns Hopkins University Press.

Mol, Michael and Birkinshaw, Julian (2007) 'Why Management Innovation Matters', *European Business Forum*.

Mol, Michael and Birkinshaw, Julian (2008) *Giant Steps in Management: Innovations That Change the Way We Work*, London: FT-Prentice Hall.

Moltke, H. von (1992) *The Franco-German War of 1870–71*, intro. by M. Howard, London: Greenhill.

Mooney, James D. (1937) 'The Principles of Organization', in L.H. Gulick and L.F. Urwick (eds), *Papers on the Science of Administration*, New York: Institute of Public Administration, 91–98.

Mooney, James D. and Reilley, Alan C. (1931) *Onward Industry! The Principles of Organization and Their Significance to Modern Industry*, New York: Harper & Bros.

Moore, Karl and Lewis, David (2000) *Foundations of Corporate Empire*, London: FT-Prentice Hall.

Moore, Karl and Lewis, David (2009) *The Origins of Globalization*, London: Routledge.

Morgan, Gareth (1986) *Images of Organization*, Newbury Park, CA: Sage.

Moriarty, W.D. (1923) *The Economics of Marketing and Advertising*, New York: Harper & Bros; repr. Bristol: Thoemmes Press, 2000.

Morris-Suzuki, Tessa (1994) *The Technological Transformation of Japan*, Cambridge: Cambridge University Press.

Morse, H.B. (1921) *The Trade and Administration of China*, 3rd edn, London: Longmans, Green.

——(1932) *The Guilds of China*, London: Longmans, Green.

Moss, M. and Hume, J.R. (1986) *Shipbuilders to the World: 125 Years of Harland and Wolff, Belfast, 1861–1986*, Belfast: The Blackstaff Press.

Mumford, Lewis (1934) *Technics and Civilization*, London: George Routledge & Sons.

——(1967) *The Myth of the Machine*, London: Secker & Warburg, 2 vols.

Murphy, Sean Eisen (1998) 'Bernard of Clairvaux', in E. Craig (ed.), *Routledge Encyclopedia of Philosophy*, London: Routledge, vol. 1, 753–54.

Narayan, Shriman (ed.) (1968) *The Selected Works of Mahatma Gandhi* Volume 6, *The Voice of Truth*, Ahmedabad: Navajivan Publishing House.

Needham, Joseph (1954–95) *Science and Civilization in China*, Cambridge: Cambridge University Press, 7 vols.

Neumann, Robert (1935) *Zaharoff the Armaments King*, London: George Allen & Unwin.

Nevett, T.R. (1982) *Advertising in Britain: A History*, London: Heinemann.

Nevins, A.N. and Hill, F.E. (1954) *Ford: The Times, the Man, the Company*, New York: Charles Scribner's Sons.

——(1957) *Ford: Expansion and Challenge, 1915–1933*, New York: Charles Scribner's Sons.

——(1962) *Ford: Decline and Rebirth*, New York: Charles Scribner's Sons.

Newman, Peter C. (1987) *Company of Adventurers*, Markham, Ont.: Viking.

Noiriel, Gérard (1989) *Workers in French Society in the Nineteenth and Twentieth Century*, London: Berg.

Nonaka, Ikujiro and Takeuchi, Hirotaka (1995) *The Knowledge-Creating Company*, Oxford: Oxford University Press.

Norberg, Peter (2005) 'Financial Markets: Beyond Good and Evil', working paper, Center for Ethics and Economics, Stockholm School of Economics.

Northcott, Clarence H. *et al.* (1928) *Factory Organization*, London: Pitman.

Noyes, Pierrepont (1937) *My Father's House: An Oneida Boyhood*, London: John Murray.

Ohmae, Kenichi (1982) *The Mind of the Strategist*, New York: McGraw-Hill.

Orange, George J. and McBain, J. (1911) 'Mail Order Advertising', in T. Russell (ed.), *Harmsworth Business Library*, London: Educational Book Co., vol. 5, 209–24.

Origo, Iris (1957) *The Merchant of Prato*, London: Jonathan Cape.

——(1962) *The World of San Bernardino*, London: Jonathan Cape.

Ormachea, J.M. (1993) *The Mondragón Cooperative Experience*, Mondragón: Mondragón Cooperative Corporation.

Oschinsky, Dorothy (1971) *Walter of Henley and The Treatises on Estate Management and Accountancy*, Oxford: Clarendon Press.

Owen, Robert (1812) *A Statement Regarding the New Lanark Establishment*, Edinburgh: n.p.

——(1815) *Observations on the Effect of the Manufacturing System*, London: n.p.

Painter, George (1976) *William Caxton*, London: Chatto & Windus.

Pakenham, Thomas (1991) *The Scramble for Africa*, New York: Random House.

Palmer, R.R. (1986) 'Frederick the Great, Guibert, Bülow: From Dynastic to National War', in Peter Paret (ed.), *Makers of Modern Strategy*, Princeton, NJ: Princeton University Press, 91–119.

Parkinson, C. Northcote (1937) *Trade in the Eastern Seas, 1793–1813*, Cambridge: Cambridge University Press.

——(1958) *Parkinson's Law*, London: John Murray.

Parks, Tim (2005) *Medici Money: Banking, Metaphysics and Art in Fifteenth-Century Florence*, New York: W.W. Norton.

Parsons, G.L. (ed.) (1934) *Scientific Papers and Addresses of the Honourable Sir Charles A. Parsons*, Cambridge: Cambridge University Press.

Pavitt, Keith (1990) 'What We Know About the Strategic Management of Technology', *California Management Review* (Spring), 17–26.

Pegolotti, Francesco di Balduccio (1936) *La pratica della mercatura*, ed. A. Evans, Cambridge, MA: The Medieval Academy of America.

Peters, Thomas J. and Waterman, Robert H. (1982) *In Search of Excellence: Lessons from America's Best-Run Companies*, New York: Harper & Row.

Pincas, Stepháne (2008) *A History of Advertising*, London: Taschen.

Piramal, Gita (1997) *Business Maharajahs*, New Delhi: Viking.

——(2001) 'Jehangir Ratan Dadabhoy Tata', in Morgen Witzel (ed.) *Biographical Dictionary of Management*, Bristol: Thoemmes Press, vol. 2, 964–68.

Pisan, Christine de (1985) *Treasury of the City of Ladies*, trans. Sarah Lawson, London: Harmondsworth.

Pollard, Sidney (1965) *The Genesis of Modern Management: A Study of the Industrial Revolution in Britain*, London: Edward Arnold.

Pollard, Sidney and Robinson, P. (1979) *The British Shipbuilding Industry 1870–1914*, Cambridge, MA: Harvard University Press.

Pope, D. (1983) *The Making of Modern Advertising*, New York: Basic Books.

Porter, Michael E. (1980) *Competitive Strategy: Techniques for Analyzing Industries and Competitors*, New York: The Free Press.

——(1985) *Competitive Advantage: Creating and Sustaining Superior Performance*, New York: Simon & Schuster.

Pound, R. (1960) *Selfridge: A Biography*, London: Heinemann.

Prahalad, C.K. and Hamel, Gary (1990) 'The Core Competence of the Corporation', *Harvard Business Review,* May–June.

Puckey, W. (1945) *What Is This Management?* London: Chapman and Hall.

Pudney, J. (1953) *The Thomas Cook Story*, London: Michael Joseph.

Rathenau, Walther (1921) *In Days to Come*, London: Allen & Unwin.

Ratner, Gerald (2007) *Gerald Ratner: The Rise and Fall ... and Rise Again*, Oxford: Capstone.

Read, Donald (1992) *The Power of News: The History of Reuters, 1849–1989*, Oxford: Oxford University Press.

——(1994) 'Reuters: News Agency of the British Empire', *Contemporary British History* 8 (2): 195–212.

Reader, W.J. (1985) 'Lever, William Hesketh', in D.J. Jeremy (ed.), *Dictionary of Business Biography*, London: Butterworth, vol. 3, pp. 745–51.

Redding, S. Gordon (1990) *The Spirit of Chinese Capitalism*, New York: Walter de Gruyter.

Redfield, William C. (1916) 'The Employment Problem in Industry', *Annals of the American Academy of Political and Social Science*, May.

Refuge, Eustache de (2008) *Treatise on the Court*, trans. J. Chris Cooper, Boca Raton, FL: Orgpax Publications.

Reynolds, J. (1986) 'Salt, Sir Titus', in D.J. Jeremy (ed.) *Dictionary of Business Biography*, London: Butterworths, vol. 5, 29-35.

Richards, G.R.B. (1932) *Florentine Merchants in the Age of the Medici*, Oxford: Oxford University Press.

Richardson, H.G. and Sayles, G.O. (1963) *The Governance of Mediaeval England from the Conquest to the Magna Carta*, Edinburgh: Edinburgh University Press.

Richardson, Kurt A. (2008) 'Managing Complex Organizations: Complexity Thinking and the Science and Art of Management', *Corporate Finance Review*, July–August.

Ripley, William Zebina (1927) *Main Street and Wall Street*, London: Brentano.

Roethlisberger, Fritz and Dickson, W.J. (1939) *Management and the Worker*, Cambridge, MA: Harvard University Press.

Rohan, J. (1935) *Yankee Arms Maker*, New York: Harper & Row.

Roy, William G. (1997) *Socializing Capital: The Rise of the Large Industrial Corporations in America*, Princeton, NJ: Princeton University Press.

Sampson, Anthony (1984) *Empires of the Sky: The Politics, Contents and Cartels of World Airlines*, New York: Random House.

——(1991) *The Seven Sisters: The Great Oil Companies and the World They Shaped*, New York: Random House.

Sampson, Henry (1874) *History of Advertising*, London: Chatto & Windus.

Schein, Edgar H. (1985) *Organisational Culture and Leadership*, San Francisco, CA: Jossey-Bass, 1985; 2nd edn, 1992.

——(1999) *The Corporation Culture Survival Guide: Sense and Nonsense about Corporate Culture*, San Francisco, CA: Jossey-Bass.

Schevill, Ferdinand (1961) *Medieval and Renaissance Florence*, vol. 2, *The Coming of Humanism and the Age of the Medici*, New York: Harper & Row.

Schroeder, Jonathan E. and Borgerson, Janet L. (2002) 'Innovations in Information Technology: Insights from Italian Renaissance Art', *Consumption, Markets and Culture* 5 (2): 153–69.

Scott, Walter Dill (1913) *The Psychology of Advertising*, Chicago: Dodd, Mead & Co; revised edn published 1921.

Selfridge, Harry Gordon (1918) *The Romance of Commerce*, London: Bodley Head.

Semler, Ricardo (1993) *Maverick! The Success Story Behind the World's Most Unusual Workplace*, London: Arrow.

Senge, Peter M. (1990) *The Fifth Discipline*, New York: Doubleday.

Senior, Nassau (1830) *Political Economy*, London: n.p.

Shaw, Arch W. (1912) *Some Problems in Market Distribution*, Cambridge, MA: Harvard University Press.

Sheldon, Oliver (1923) *The Philosophy of Management*, London: Pitman.

Silver, Morris (1995) *Economic Structures of Antiquity*, Westport, CT: Greenwood Press.

Simmons, J.R.M. (1962) *LEO and the Managers*, London: Macdonald.

Sivulka, J. (1998) *Soap, Sex and Cigarettes: A Cultural History of American Advertising*, Belmont, CA: Wadsworth.

Sloan, Alfred P. (1964) *My Years With General Motors*, New York: Doubleday.

Smith, Adam (1776) *An Inquiry into the Nature and Causes of the Wealth of Nations*, ed. Edward Canaan, New York: Random House, 1937.

Smith, Douglas K. and Alexander, Robert C. (1988) *Fumbling the Future: How Xerox Invented, Then Ignored, the First Personal Computer*, New York: Morrow.

Smith, Jessie Carney, Jackson, Millicent Lownes and Wynn, Linda T. (1994) *Encyclopedia of African American Business*, Westport, CT: Greenwood Press.

Sorenson, Charles E. (1957) *Forty Years with Ford*, London: Jonathan Cape.

Spence, Jonathan (1996) *God's Chinese Son: The Taiping Heavenly Kingdom of Hong Xiuquan*, London: HarperCollins.

Sponsel, H. (1957) *Made in Germany: Die dramatische Geschicte des Hauses Zeiss*, Gutersloh: C. Bertelsmann Verlag.

Stacey, Ralph (1993) 'Strategy as Order Emerging from Chaos', *Long Range Planning* 26 (1).

Starch, Daniel (1922) *The Principles of Advertising*, Chicago: A.W. Shaw.

Stillman, Yanki (2004) 'Edward Filene: Pioneer of Social Responsibility', *Jewish Currents*.

Strasser, Susan (1989) *Satisfaction Guaranteed: The Making of the American Mass Market*, New York: Pantheon.

Strassman, Paul (1968) *Technological Change and Economic Development*, Ithaca, NY: Cornell University Press.

——(1990) *The Business Value of Computers*, New Canaan, CT: Information Economics Press.

Styles, John (1990) *Titus Salt and Saltaire: Industry and Virtue*, Saltaire: Salts Estates.

*Sunzu Bingfa* (The Military Methods of Master Sun), ed. and trans. L. Giles, *Sun Tzu on the Art of War*, London, 1910.

Swift, L.F. and Van Vlissingen, A. (1970) *The Yankee of the Yards*, New York: AMS Press.

Takemura, E. (1997) *The Perception of Work in Tokugawa Japan: A Study of Ishida Baigan and Ninomiya Sontoku*, Lanham, MD: University Press of America.

Tamagna, F.M. (1942) *Banking and Finance in China*, New York: Institute of Pacific Relations.

Tang, Jie and Ward, Anthony (2002) *The Changing Face of Chinese Management*, London: Routledge.

Tarbell, Ida M. (1904) *The History of The Standard Oil Company*, New York: McClure's, 2 vols.

——(1906) 'Commercial Machiavellianism', *McClure's* 23: 453–63.

Taylor, Frederick Winslow (1895) *A Piece Rate System*, New York: American Society of Mechancial Engineers; repr. Bristol: Thoemmes Press, 2000.

——(1903) *Shop Management*, New York: Harper and Row.

——(1911) *The Principles of Scientific Management*, New York: Harper and Row; repr. Norwalk, CT: The Easton Press, 1993.

Tead, Ordway and Metcalfe, Henry (1920) *Personnel Administration: Its Principles and Practice*, New York: McGraw-Hill.

Teece, David J. (1987) *The Competitive Challenge*, New York: Harper & Row.

Thompson, Clarence B. (1914) 'Scientific Management in Retailing', in Clarence B. Thompson (ed.), *Scientific Management*, Cambridge, MA: Harvard University Press, 544–59.

Tolliday, Stephen (ed.) (1998) *The Rise and Fall of Mass Production*, Cheltenham: Edward Elgar, 2 vols.

Tripp, B.H. (1956) *Renold Chains: A History of the Company and the Rise of the Precision Chain Industry, 1879–1955*, London: George Allen & Unwin.

Trist, Eric L., Higgin, G., Murray, H. and Pollock, A. (1963) *Organizational Choice: Capabilities of Groups at the Coal Face under Changing Technologies: The Loss, Rediscovery and Transformation of a Work Tradition*, London: Tavistock Publications.

Tsutsui, William M. (1998) *Manufacturing Ideology: Scientific Management in Twentieth-Century Japan*, Princeton, NJ: Princeton University Press.

Tuchman, Barbara W. (1980) *The Proud Tower: A Portrait of the World Before the War, 1890–1914*, London: Macmillan.

Uglow, Jenny (2002) *The Lunar Men*, London: Faber & Faber.

Ure, Andrew (1835) *Philosophy of Manufactures*, London: H.G. Bohn.

Urwick, Lyndall Fownes (1928) 'Marketing and Advertising', in Clarence H. Northcott *et al.*, *Factory Organization*, London: Pitman, 154–88.

——(1933) *Management of Tomorrow*, London: Nisbet.

——(1956) *The Golden Book of Management: A Historical Record of the Life and Work of Seventy Pioneers*, London: Newman Neame.

Urwick, Lyndall Fownes and Brech, E.F.L. (1947–49) *The Making of Scientific Management*, 3 vols, London: Management Publications Trust.

Usui, Kazuo (2008) *The Development of Marketing Management: The Case of the USA, c.1910–1940*, Aldershot: Ashgate Publishing Ltd.

Vail, Theodore N. (1918) *Wire Systems: Discussion of Electrical Intelligence*, Washington, DC.

Vanderblue, Homer B. (1921) 'The Functional Approach to the Study of Marketing', *Journal of Political Economy* 29: 676–83.

Vanderlan Robert (2001) 'George Eastman', in Morgen Witzel (ed.), *Biogaphical Dictionary of Management*, Bristol: Thoemmes Press, vol. 1: 265–68.

van den Boorn, G.P.F. (1988) *The Duties of the Vizier*, London: Kegan Paul International.

Vasconellos e Sá, Jorge A. (2005) *Strategy Moves: Fourteen Complete Attack and Defense Strategies for Competitive Advantage*, Engelwood Cliffs, NJ: FT-Prentice Hall.

Veblen, Thorstein (1924) *A Theory of the Leisure Class*, London: George Allen & Unwin.

Vegetius (1993) *Epitoma Rei Militaris*, ed. and trans. N.P. Milner, Liverpool: Liverpool University Press.

Vronskaya, J. and Chuguev, V. (1992) *The Biographical Dictionary of the Former Soviet Union*, London: Bowker-Saur.

Wagner, G. (1987) *The Chocolate Conscience*, London: Chatto and Windus.

Wang Gungwu (2002) *The Chinese Overseas*, Cambridge, MA: Harvard University Press.

Wang Xuanming (1995) *Sixteen Strategies of Zhuge Liang*, trans. Alan Chong, Singapore: Asiapac.

Ward, John (2004) *Perpetuating the Family Business*, Basingstoke: Palgrave Macmillan.

Warner, Malcom (ed.) (1998) *IEBM Handbook of Management Thinking*, London: International Thomson Business Press.

Warner, Malcolm and Witzel, Morgen (2004) *Managing in Virtual Organizations*, London: International Thomson Business Press.

Warnery, Karl Emmanuel von (1798) *Remarks on Cavalry*, London; repr. London: Constable, 1997.

Warren, Kenneth (2001) *Big Steel: The First Century of the United States Steel Corporation, 1901–2001*, Pittsburgh: University of Pittsburgh Press.

Watson, Burton (1964) *Han Fei Tzu: Basic Writings*, New York: Columbia University Press.

Watson, W.F. (1931) 'Scientific Management and Industrial Psychology', *English Review* 52: 444–55.

Watts, Steven (2005) *The People's Tycoon: Henry Ford and the American Century*, New York: Alfred A. Knopf.

Weber, Max (1905) *The Protestant Ethic and the Spirit of Capitalism*, trans. T. Parsons, New York: Charles Scribner's Sons, 1958.

Wedgwood, C.V. (1938) *The Thirty Years War*, London: Jonathan Cape.

Wee, C.H, Lee, K.S. and Hidajat, B.W. (1991) *Sun Tzu: War and Management*, Singapore: Addison-Wesley.

Weld, L.D.H. (1921) 'Integration in Marketing: A Reply to L.H. Haney', *American Economic Review* 11: 93–97.

Wendt, L. and Kogan, H. (1952) *Give the Lady What She Wants*, Indianapolis, NY: Bobbs-Merrill.

Whyte, William Foote (1996) 'Mondragón' in Malcolm Warner (ed.) *International Encyclopedia of Business and Management*, London: Routledge, vol. 4, 3518–22.

Whyte, W.F. and Whyte, K.K. (1989) *Making Mondragón: The Growth and Dynamics of the Worker Cooperative*, Ithaca, NY: ILR Press.

Whitehead, Thomas North (1936) *Leadership in a Free Society: A Study in Human Relations Based on an Analysis of Present-Day Industrial Civilization*, London: Oxford University Press.

Williams, I.A. (1931) *The Firm of Cadbury, 1831–1931*, London: Constable.

Wilson, Charles, (1954) *The History of Unilever: A Study in Economic Growth and Social Change*, London: Cassell, 2 vols.

Wilson, John F. and Thomson, Andrew W. (2006) *The Making of Modern Management: British Management in Historical Perspective*, Oxford: Oxford University Press.

Witzel, Morgen (1992) 'Thomas Coutts and the Rise of Modern Banking', *The Strand*, January: 7–9.

——(1998) 'God's Entrepreneurs', *Financial Times Mastering Management Review* 18: 16–19.

——(1999a) 'Introduction', *Key Texts in Marketing*, Bristol: Thoemmes Press, 8 vols.

——(1999b) 'China: The First Global Brand', *Financial Times Mastering Management Review*.

——(ed.) (2001) *Biographical Dictionary of Management*, Bristol: Thoemmes Press, 2 vols.

——(2002) *Builders and Dreamers: The Making and Meaning of Management*, London: FT-Prentice Hall.

——(2004) 'Wealth and Virtue: The Persistence of Chinese Classical Economics', *European Business Forum*.

——(2007a) 'Early Contributors to Financial Management: Jeremiah Jenks, Edward Meade and William Ripley', in Geoffrey Poitras (ed.), *Pioneers of Financial Economics*, vol. 2, 31–44.

——(2007b) 'The Leaders and the Led: Dyadic Approaches to Leadership', in Jonathan Gosling, Peter Case and Morgen Witzel (eds), *John Adair: Fundamentals of Leadership*, Basingstoke: Palgrave Macmillan.

Womack, James P., Jones, Daniel T. and Roos, D. (1990) *The Machine that Changed the World*, New York: Macmillan.

Woodcock, George (1970) *The Hudson's Bay Company*, Toronto: Collier.

Wren, Daniel A. (2005) *The Evolution of Management Thought*, Hoboken, NJ: Wiley, 5th edn.

Wren, Daniel A. and Greenwood, Ron G. (1998) *Management Innovators*, New York: Oxford University Press.

Wu, John C.H. (trans.) (1990) *Tao Teh Ching (Daodejing)*, Boston and London: Shambhala.

Yamamoto, Tsunetomo (1979) *Hagakure*, trans. William Scott Wilson, Tokyo: Kodansha International.

Ydewalle, Charles d' (1965) *Au Bon Marché: de la Boutique au Grand Magasin*, Paris: n.p.

Yonekawa, S. and Yoshiharo, H. (eds) (1987) *Business History of General Trading Companies*, Tokyo: University of Tokyo Press.

Yurko, Frank J. (1999) 'Deir el-Medina' in Kathryn A. Bard (ed.), *Encyclopedia of the Archaeology of Ancient Egypt*, London: Routledge, 247–50.

Zeleny, Milan (1988) 'Bat'a System of Management: Managerial Excellence Found', *Human Systems Management* 7 (3): 213–19.

——(2001) 'Bat'a, Tomás', in M. Witzel (ed.), *Biographical Dictionary of Management*, Bristol: Thoemmes Press, vol. 1, 56–63.

# Index